CONTEMPORARY SOCIOLOGICAL THEORIES

CONTEMPORARY SOCIOLOGICAL THEORIES

Edited by
Alan Wells
Tulane University

Goodyear Publishing Company, Inc.
Santa Monica, California 90401

Library of Congress Cataloging in Publication Data

Main entry under title:

Contemporary sociological theories.

    Includes bibliographies.
1. Sociology. I. Wells, Alan, 1940-
HM24.C655   301   77-16597
ISBN 0-87620-138-9

Y-1389-9

Current Printing (last digit):
10 9 8 7 6 5 4 3 2 1

Printed in the United States of America

Cover and Text Design: John Odam

PREFACE

The aim of this book is to survey the diversity of contemporary sociological theory; specifically, work done during the last twenty to thirty years. It is aimed primarily at undergraduate students of sociology. Traditionally, "theory" courses in American universities have too often turned out to be just the history of social thought from Comte to the death of Max Weber more than fifty years ago. My objective is to fill the gap between the work of sociology's founders and the contemporary disputes and ongoing developments of current sociological theory. Material for this book was selected to do as much justice as possible to existing sociological theories. Although, like most other sociologists, I have my own personal preferences about the correctness and fruitfulness of these different approaches, my primary aim is to present what I believe to be the main thrusts in contemporary sociology for the students' own evaluation and analysis.

Chapter introductions are intended as brief orienting summaries of each theoretical school, not as comprehensive treatments of modern theories. The reader should refer to more lengthy texts for added depth. Suggested reading lists are provided for each chapter and may be consulted by those advanced undergraduate and graduate students who use this reader as a brief introduction to their studies in contemporary theory.

I would here like to acknowledge the contribution of my former teachers who have influenced my thinking and who no doubt also sometimes led me astray. These include Irving L. Horowitz, Nicholas J. Demerath, Wolf Heydebrand, Bennett Berger, and Robert Hamblin. Several of my students in contemporary sociological theory seminars have sharpened my thinking on this topic. Among them are Ed Lampman, Noel Cazenave, Don Strickland, and George Thompson. Some of my colleagues have critically reviewed parts of the book and, as consulting editor, Jonathan Turner has improved the entire volume. Robert Becker provided research assistance and Karen McLafferty cheerfully typed in all of my errors, along with some of her own. Finally, Mary C. McCarthy patiently endured my verbal versions of this volume.

Alan Wells

CONTRIBUTORS

Becker, Howard S.
Blalock, Hubert M.
Blum, Alan
Blumer, Herbert
Buckley, Walter
Collins, Randall
Denzin, Norman K.
Flacks, Richard
Friedrichs, Robert W.
Garfinkel, Harold
Glass, John F.
Gouldner, Alvin W.
Heap, James L.
Homans, George C.
Horowitz, Irving Louis
Huber, Joan
Lehmann, Timothy
Lynch, Frederick R.
Manning, Peter K.
McHugh, Peter
Merton, Robert K.
Mullins, Nicholas C.
Parsons, Talcott
Reynolds, Paul D.
Roth, Phillip A.
Sacks, Harvey
Schroyer, Trent
Stinchcombe, Arthur L.
Turner, Jonathan H.
Van den Berghe, Pierre L.
White, Harrison C.
Young, T. R.

CONTENTS

INTRODUCTION CONTEMPORARY SCHOOLS IN SOCIOLOGICAL THEORY

Sociology is not a uniform discipline. Beneath the surface of professional association membership are numerous disagreements, tensions, and disputes that threaten to break up even the formal unity of sociologists. Even the parentage of the discipline, although not a serious issue in itself, produces several champions not acknowledged by many sociologists. Some would claim that sociology has its roots in ancient Greece, others point to the medieval world of Thomas Aquinas or Machiavelli, while others would claim Montesquieu, Comte, or Spencer as founders of sociology. While Marx, Durkheim, and Weber have emerged as the consensus founders of sociology in the modern period, their work, despite attempts to synthesize it, leads to differing conceptions of what sociology is and should be. And of course the selection of these three leaves out such figures as George Herbert Mead and Alfredo Pareto, whom many in the discipline see as their immediate precursors. Such disputes reveal that sociologists are as yet unsure of the foundations of their discipline, and to some, the foundations have yet to be laid. For this latter group, sociology proper has not yet begun—or has done so only very recently.

There are other areas of disagreement that are far from resolved and that must be taken seriously because of their vital importance in shaping the perspective of the sociologist. Although sociology is usually considered a social science, this category is seldom clarified. There are a few proponents of sociology as an art form, and there are numerous interpretations of what the "science" in the term social science actually conveys. For some it merely means empiricism and an awareness of the existence of social behavior, while for others it is a cry for increasing quantification and mathematical model building. The subject matter for the discipline is equally undetermined. It may include anything that can be considered social or human, or it may include merely the remnants of more specialized social sciences. The approach to the subject matter may be one of general theoretical interest, of understanding a specific subject matter for its own sake, or may merely treat "data" as the raw material for developing precise scientific methods. The task of sociology is seen alter-

natively as building a general and abstract theory of society, as interpreting social life and events for the benefit of potentially political publics,
or as the humanistic goal of liberation of others and self-realization.

From these underlying differences stem numerous conflicts at a practical level. Can or should sociologists be value free, or—in lay language
—"objective"? What roles should sociologists serve in society? Should
they be ivory tower theorists, applied sociologists, Mandarinlike bureau-
crats, or professional gadflies? These and other differences make for a
disorganized but exciting discipline. Given this existing turmoil in sociology, it should come as no surprise that dividing contemporary sociological work into separate theory groups will not lead to unanimity.

One way of dividing sociology is on the basis of political criteria:
between conservative and radical or bourgeois and Marxist categories.
But as Bottomore (1974:11–16) notes, this is by no means a simple division. As Bottomore describes it:

The "new sociology" was proclaimed some years ago. Growing mainly out of the
work of C. Wright Mills, it was connected through him, with the doctrines and
movements of the New Left in the later 1950's and early 1960's. But just as the
New Left grew old quite quickly and was supplanted by still newer movements
so also the "new sociology," without ever having established itself properly as
a distinct style of social thought, has been pushed aside by yet more recent
attempts to give the discipline a fresh orientation. In less than a decade, we have
had "critical sociology," "radical sociology," and such innovations, less closely
tied to political commitments, as ethnomethodology and structuralism—not to
speak of the sociology liberation movement, which is perhaps more a mode of
feeling than thinking. Now Alvin Gouldner offers us yet another diversion in the
shape of "reflexive sociology," or the sociologist contemplating his own navel.
(1974:44)

Gouldner (1970) has probed the clash between functionalism and Marxism, but, as Bottomore (1974:46) notes, without giving much attention
to anything outside the work of Talcott Parsons, who was probably never
as commanding in sociology as Gouldner portrays him. Although political issues have given rise to different sociologies, then, they do not provide very satisfactory criteria for describing current sociological theories.

Robert Friedrichs (1970) has attempted to apply Kuhn's (1962) notion
of paradigms to social theories; that is, he investigates the basic assumptions underlying a theory and its "universally recognized scientific
achievements" that provide models for further work. Like Gouldner,
Friedrichs claims that the systems and functionalist paradigms became
dominant in the 1940s and 1950s. Social events in the 1960s broke up
this hegemony, and theory moved from the priestly (or normative, accommodative, establishment) to the prophetic (or activist, revolutionary)
modes of doing sociology. According to Friedrichs, this type of change
has also been recurrent in the history of sociology. The breakup did not
lead to a new paradigm establishing hegemony but rather to multiple
contending paradigms, each with it own historical roots. Among these
new paradigms Friedrichs lists conflict theory, whose history runs from
Heraclitus, Hobbes, Smith, Marx, Mills, and Dahrendorf to "new" sociology; Etzioni's development of evolutionary action theory; the Freudian

imagery of Dennis Wrong; Homans' behaviorism; Catton's positivism; the work of Berger and Luchmann on subjective reality; and the dialectical work of Gurvich. He leaves out what I would call neopositivism, and, more surprisingly, he also omits symbolic interactionism. To Friedrichs, systems and conflict paradigms are the main ones today, with several minor competing ones.

Rather than trying to abstract underlying general paradigms, Mullins (1973) has attempted to identify theoretical schools on the basis of the social interaction of sociologists. Thus he says, "Theories are productions (in any form, but usually written) that attempt to *analyze* and to *generalize* about the interaction of human beings, using a set of concepts and/or variables whose relations are governed by specific rules for theory building. One further element is needed in this basic definition: a theory is a statement that is an acceptable general principle to some group" (1973:5). Any work that meets these criteria is treated as a sociological theory.

Like the other writers I have mentioned, Mullins notes the recent decay of established sociology and the challenge of new competitors: "The theories that dominated sociology from 1951 to 1968 were based on a combination of pre-1920 European and American social theory, survey research, and cross-tabulation methodology" (p. 143). Now, however, this "Standard American sociology and its alternatives are still alive, but no longer dominant. New groups are developing in the elbow room of the much larger discipline. This is a period of recognized revolutions in sociological theory" (p. 143), which caught many sociologists by surprise (p. 146). Mullins believes that the position of new groups and the development of additional ones is tenuous.

The two groups in the Standard American sociology were the "self-conscious empiricists" and the "rather defensive theorists" (p. 216)—the structural functionalists and the survey researchers. They were paralleled by symbolic interactionism, which Mullins terms the "loyal opposition," and by small-groups theory, which he claims has failed as a sociological group. (In social psychology, of course, it has clearly had a continuing and thriving existence.) The new theory groups discerned by Mullins are the social forecasters, ethnomethodology, new causal theory, the structuralists, and radical-critical theory. My classification includes the work of the new causal theory and structuralists under the heading "neo-positivism," which is seen as a continuation of the survey-positivism of the 1950s. I would add exchange theory as another emerging theory—one which Mullins overlooks, seeing it as a minor development within standard American sociology. "Exchange theory and other systems of thought that meet the basic definitions stated earlier, have been omitted because they have never generated sufficient enthusiasm to gather a coherent group" (p. 13). "In short, one can still understand exchange theory if one first understands structural functionalism" (p. 15). Many sociologists, I think, would contest this argument.

Worsley (1974) holds that Kuhn's theory doesn't really apply to sociology—that the major conflicts are *within* theoretical schools (for example, Marxism). He complains of the irrelevance of sociological theories to substantive understanding and criticizes grand theory, other formal types of sociology, and the assumptions of positivism:

The demise of the positivist notion of theory as a linear accumulation of knowledge has carried with it the implication that theory is not unitary. The thought of even the most systematic of thinkers, moreover, displays internal inconsistencies, and changes over time: thus Parsons, notably, moved away from sociology of social action towards a model of society as a "social system." Evidently, it is not just that there is no paradigm articulate in the social sciences, not even that we are in a pre-paradigmatic era in which several candidates are contending for eventual supremacy. The social sciences, rather, do not follow the Kuhnian model. (1974:2)

Wagner (1963) also notes the lack of a cumulative and unified body of knowledge, then attempts his own classification. He utilizes three main categories: positive, interpretative, and nonscientific (or evaluative) social theories. The first includes neopositivism, structural-functionalism, and behaviorism, among others. "Interpretative" includes symbolic interactionism and phenomenology, while conflict theory and neo-Marxism are labeled "nonscientific." Again, it is doubtful that this gross tripartite division will be widely accepted by sociologists.

Two sociologists have recently attempted to discern the underlying modes of sociological theorizing. Boskoff (1971) identifies what he calls correlational theory, sequence theory, grand theory, and—the type that he finds most fruitful for sociology—process theory. Ritzer (1975 a and b), by contrast, sees three main theoretical divisions in sociology: the social-facts, social-definition, and social-behavior paradigms. He examines Kuhn's notion of paradigm and argues the case for the most general usage of the term. He ends up defining it as "a fundamental image of the subject matter within a science. It serves to define what should be studied, what questions should be asked, how they should be asked, and what rules should be followed in interpreting the answers ascertained. The paradigm is the broadest unit of consensus within a science and serves to differentiate one scientific community (or sub-community) from another. It subsumes, defines, and interrelates the exemplars, theories, and methods and instruments that exist within it" (Ritzer, 1975a:7). He argues persuasively that sociology is a multiple-paradigm science that is currently experiencing considerable internal conflict (1975a:9). He argues that Friedrichs mistakenly equated theories with paradigms. To Ritzer (p. 20) paradigms are much broader. Ritzer considers the confusions of dealing with several paradigms, but the three underlying paradigms that he develops would not be readily recognizable by most sociologists. His social-facts paradigm is based on the work of Durkheim (1975a: 25–26), but it encompasses structural functionalsim, conflict theory, and what I would call neopositivism. The social-definitions paradigm is based on the work of Weber. The subject matter is "not social facts, but the way in which people define those social facts" (1975a:27). Under this rubric are the work of Parsons, symbolic interactionism, and also phenomenological sociology. Ritzer's social-behavior paradigm stems from the work of B. F. Skinner (1975a: 29–30) and is limited to what is known as exchange theory or behaviorism in psychology. This is somewhat peculiar in that a minor theory is given the status of a "big three" paradigm.

Ritzer's conclusion (pp. 31–32) is that the main conflicts occur between his three paradigms, a claim that verges on the absurd. After all, ethnomethodologists are waging war with symbolic interactionists, conflict theorists with functionalists, and so on.

My own division is largely a pragmatic one, although it is based on the conclusion that sociology cannot be simply arranged into three or four categories. The "multiple paradigms," if that's what they are, or better, the multiple styles of doing sociology, comprise a complex reality that defies simplification. The categories that I have chosen, I believe, convey everyday common referents for most sociologists. As the chapter introductions indicate, however, there is no unanimity *within* these categories, much less among them. Chapter titles are common labels used in sociology, but they only roughly convey group affiliation or coherent subsets of knowledge, research, and methodological orthodoxy. These groupings do, however, correspond fairly closely to those employed by two recent texts on contemporary theory (Mullins, 1973; Turner, 1974).

The first four groupings I see as "respectable" sociologies: functionalism, neopositivism, symbòlic interactionism, and exchange theory. By "respectable" I mean that most sociologists would not be perturbed by one's confession as a devotee. Of course, most of the variants of these four can be used aggressively or passively, radically or conservatively. The second group—conflict, radical-critical-neo-Marxist (obviously not a tightly organized category), and ethnomethodology—are theories less legitimate to many professional sociologists, and practitioners of these styles are not found in many academic sociology departments. The concluding chapter examines some new directions that may bloom into new sociologies. They indicate that the previous seven groupings are by no means exhaustive.

It should be remembered throughout this book that all styles of sociological theorizing exhibit good and bad work. My aim in selecting readings has been to choose the good, so that the student may take what is valuable from each style. Perhaps too often, we reject work in one style because of shallow reading or selection of poor work in that style.

References and Suggested Readings

Bates, Alan P. *The Sociological Experience*. Boston: Houghton Mifflin, 1967.

Blackburn, Robin, ed. *Ideology in Social Science*. New York: Vintage, 1973.

Block, Fred. "Alternative Sociological Perspectives," *Catalyst*, 7 (Winter), 29–41.

Boskoff, Alvin. "Process-Orientation in Sociological Theory and Research: Untasted Old Wine in Slightly Used Bottles," *Social Forces*, 50 (1971), 1.

Bottomore, Thomas B. *Sociology as Social Criticism*. New York: Pantheon, 1974.

Catton, William. *From Animistic to Naturalistic Sociology*. New York: McGraw-Hill, 1966.

Curtis, James E., and John W. Petras. "The Sociology of Sociology: Some Lines of Inquiry in the Study of the Discipline," *Sociological Quarterly*, 13 (1972), 197–209.

Friedrichs, Robert W. *A Sociology of Sociology*. New York: Free Press, 1970.

Gouldner, Alvin. *The Coming Crisis of Western Sociology*. New York: Basic Books, 1970.

Hollander, Paul. "Sociology, Selective Determinism, and the Rise of Expectations," *American Sociologist*, 8 (November 1973), 147–153.

Horowitz, Irving L. *Professing Sociology*. Chicago: Aldine, 1968.

Horowitz, Irving L., ed. "Sociological Self Images: A Collective Portrait," *American Behavioral Scientist*, 12 (September–October 1969).

Katz, Fred E., ed. *Contemporary Sociological Theory*. New York: Random House, 1971.

Kuhn, Thomas S. *The Structure of Scientific Revolutions*. Chicago: University of Chicago Press, 1962.

Kuklick, Henrika. "A 'Scientific Revolution': Sociological Theory in the United States, 1930–1945," *Sociological Inquiry*, 43 (1973), 3–22.

Masterman, Margaret. "The Nature of a Paradigm," in Imre Lakatos and Alan Musgrave, eds., *Criticism and the Growth of Knowledge*. Cambridge: Cambridge University Press, 1970, pp. 59–89.

Merton, Robert K. "Insiders and Outsiders: A Chapter in the Sociology of Knowledge," *American Journal of Sociology*, 78 (July 1972), 9–47.

Merton, Robert K., Leonard Broom, and Leonard S. Cottrell Jr. *Sociology Today: Problems and Prospects*. New York: Basic Books, 1959.

Mills, C. Wright. *The Sociological Imagination*. New York: Oxford, 1971.

Mullins, Nicholas C. *Theories and Theory Groups in Contemporary America*. New York: Harper & Row, 1973.

Parsons, Talcott, ed. *American Sociology*. New York: Basic Books, 1968.

Phillips, Derek L. "Paradigms and Incommensurability," *Theory and Society: Renewal and Critique in Social Theory*, (Spring 1975), 37–61.

Ritzer, George. *Sociology: A Multiple Paradigm Science*. Boston: Allyn and Bacon, 1975. (a)

———. "Sociology: A Multiple Paradigm Science," *The American Sociologist*, 10 (August 1975), 156–167. (b)

Tiryakian, E. A., ed. *The Phenomenon of Science*. New York: Appleton-Century-Crofts, 1971.

Turner, Jonathan H. *The Structure of Sociological Theory*. Homewood, Ill.: Dorsey, 1974.

Urry, John. "Thomas S. Kuhn as Sociologist of Knowledge," *British Journal of Sociology*, 24 (1973), 462–473.

Wagner, Helmut R. The Types of Sociological Theory, *American Sociological Review*, 28 (October 1963), 735–42.

Worsley, P. M. "The State of Theory and the Status of Theory," *Sociology: The Journal of the British Sociological Association*, 8 (1974), 1–17.

CHAPTER 1

FUNCTIONALISM AND SYSTEMS THEORY

Introduction

Functionalism has been widely recognized as the dominant theoretical perspective of sociology; it has, however, come under increasing attack in the last decade. The central focus of this perspective is *culture*—the organized values, norms, and beliefs that pattern all of social life. For any society, culture is seen as stable and relatively permanent. It gives society its order. Traditionally, then, functionalism has investigated how the parts of culture (for example, norms regulating kinship) function for the total culture—that is, what their purpose (function) is in the overall culture (child socialization, regulation of fertility, and so on).

In a very broad sense, most sociologists are concerned with the relational task of functionalism. Kingsley Davis (1959), for example, argued that functionalism is not a special method in sociology, that we are all functionalists now. More recently, Fallding (1972) has repeated the claim. To him, functionalism is "a view of society (association, interaction) as a contrived structure that's tested by its capacity to function in producing need satisfaction" (1972:93). So long as they are dealing with social rather than psychological factors, sociologists who stress conflict, exchange, symbolic interaction, or evolution—purportedly rival perspectives—are in fact functionalists (p. 94). Fallding goes on to claim that Marx was a functionalist, one who stressed the dysfunctional aspects of society (for a similar claim, see Sztompka, 1974).

The main rival to functionalism, conflict theory, is rather briefly dismissed by Fallding. Dahrendorf, he claims, becomes too extreme in his conflict position, for, according to Fallding, "there is . . . no point in two opponents shouting that 'conflict' or 'equilibrium' is a natural state of society. Which is the more *prevalent* can be decided empirically and that each occurs a certainty" (1972:95). Actually Fallding is probably wrong on this point. Empirically it isn't too difficult to prove that equilibrium never exists. It is merely a model that is only approximated, even in relatively stable societies. While it is true that cooperation is an empirical fact, its presence in social life does not mean that a *society* is in equilibrium. Fallding concludes with a view of functionalism that is probably too general for either opponents or proponents of this perspective: "I do not think 'functionalism' is anything more than an orientation to inquiry, or what I would call an 'analytical theory.' It is not a comprehensive explanatory theory of society and, as yet, sociology has none to speak of" (1972:99–100). Most sociologists, I believe, would disagree, although they are tolerant of the vague, rather innocuous functionalism used to organize most introductory texts in the field.

The origins of functionalism go back to early thinkers who posited organic models of society. That is, they believed society was like (or indeed was) an organism whose parts were biologically interrelated. This tradition runs from the thought of Plato (whose *Republic*, although more utopian than descriptive, outlines how a well "integrated" society would work) to some of the recognized founders of modern sociology: Comte, Spencer, and Durkheim. Elaboration of this organicist tradition can be found in most standard texts on the history of social theory.

The organic variety of functionalism has strongly influenced cultural anthropology, most notably through the work of Radcliffe-Brown and Malinowski. According to Turner (1974) the former preferred the label "structuralist," and "he felt that no universal human or societal needs would be postulated; rather, the question of which conditions were necessary for survival would be an empirical one, an issue that would have to be discovered for each given social system" (p. 22). Structural analysis was possible if one assumed that "1) one necessary condition for survival of a society is minimal integration of its parts; 2) the term *function* refers to those processes that maintain this necessary integration or solidarity; 3) thus, in each society structural features can be shown to contribute to the maintenance of necessary solidarity" (p. 22). But Radcliffe-Brown was often guilty of wholistic distortion and teleology, what Turner (p. 3) calls "circular reasoning." Malinowski, according to Turner, was even more organismic: "The functional view of culture insists therefore upon the principle that in every type of civilization, every custom, material object, idea, and belief fulfills some vital function, has some task to accomplish, represents an indispensable part within a working whole" (Malinowski, cited in Turner, 1974:24). Malinowski, claims Turner, based his functionalism on individual needs and therein exhibits "reductionistic tendencies." This, however, has made Malinowski's work far more useful as a *method* for social analysis. Later functionalists, says Turner (p. 25), avoided this style of reductionism and teleological reasoning.

Before examining the work of sociology's two most prominent functionalists, Robert K. Merton and Talcott Parsons, we will briefly consider the general state of functionalism and its critics. The Polish sociologist Piotr Sztompka (1974) has written perhaps the most detailed examination of functionalism yet produced. He clearly shows that there are many different types of functionalism, and he claims that their strongest features offer sociology its best basis for building a comprehensive theory of society.

Sztompka believes that sociology is now ripe for a general theory that will explain both how society persists and how it changes. The best tool for this, he thinks, would be a reconstructed "systemic-functional" model derived from the functionalist theorists from Malinowski to Parsons. It is a model, he claims (1974:168–78), that in its early form was applied by Karl Marx, contrary to the beliefs of muddled, idealistic, neo-Marxists (p. xiii). The "functional orientation" is not itself a theory in the full sense of the term, but it provides a viable conceptual scheme for analysis and theory construction. Generalized systemic models, he concluded, "are *free from the static and ahistoric biases* usually found in older versions of functionalism. They are equally able to handle both the static and dynamic, historic and ahistoric, features of social reality" (pp. 180–181). They can handle problems of order and change, and, since they are readily available as analytical models, he sees no crisis in contemporary theory (p. 182).

The general criticisms of functionalism have been summarized by Cohen (1968) as teleology, wholism that neglects social diversity, and political conservatism. Interesting critiques include Homans (1964), Dore (1961), and anthologies by Gross (1959, 1967) and Demerath and Peterson (1967).

Robert Merton is the leading proponent of an "open" functionalism, one that is more a *method* than an all-encompassing theory or conceptual scheme. (The best single evaluation of Merton's work is Coser, 1975). Merton is concerned with utilizing empirical research findings to generate what he calls "theories of the middle range," rather than leaping prematurely to general, abstract theories of society. He assumes that "the search for a total system of sociological theory, in which all manner of observations promptly find their preordained place, has the same large challenge and the same small promise as those all-encompassing philosophical systems which have fallen into deserved disuse" (Merton, 1957:6). He is by no means uncritical of other functionalists (see Merton, 1957: 19–50). The first selection reprinted in this book sets forth the principles that he would like sociological analysis to follow. Here there is no simple assumption that if a thing exists it is useful for society. Some functions actually harm society (dysfunctions) and some are hard to perceive and unintended (latent functions). (For further discussion, see Merton, 1957: 60–82.) There can be functions for individuals, groups, or society as a whole, and these can be in conflict.

In a recent article, Herbert Gans (1972) has used Merton's method to analyze the poverty in the United States. Gans demonstrates that functionalism need not be conservative in orientation and that as a methodological tool it can be used as a critical weapon. He points out that although poverty is certainly dysfunctional to the poor, it has a series of positive functions for the affluent in America. Thus, what is dysfunctional to one group may be functional to another. The existence of poverty ensures that the dirty work of society is done at low cost, which permits upper class accumulation of capital. Poverty creates a series of respectable jobs for the managers of welfare bureaucracies and supports a wide range of lucrative illegal activities. The poor provide necessary recruits for the armed services, and they live off the inferior products and services that would not be used at all if the poor no longer existed. Their example reinforces the legitimacy of middle-class norms and allows all of the nonpoor to feel some satisfaction in their relative affluence. The poor are a source of upward mobility for their middle-class managers, and they provide churches and philanthropists with something useful to do.

Finally, there are political uses. Although the poor are usually recruits for the left and enemies of the political right, they remain powerless and, hence, easily manipulated. Gans argues that poverty does not
have to persist, that it has dysfunctions for the affluent as well as for the
poor. But some of its functions cannot be easily replaced, and the most
affluent will face many dysfunctions before they willingly consent to a
redistribution of their wealth.

The work of Talcott Parsons has been so prolific and important for
contemporary theory that he is perhaps best seen as a "school" of functionalism by himself. His central model, derived in part from Pareto, is
mechanical rather than organic and emphasizes equilibrium and tension
management. (Parsons' evaluation of contemporary functionalism and
his relationship to Merton may be found in Coser, 1975:67–83). He has,
however, been an active participant in anthropological debates on the
nature of culture (see Parsons, 1972).

Parsons' main task has been in developing an abstract conceptual
scheme, which he holds to be essential before theory construction proper
can be undertaken (see Turner, 1974:30). The selection reprinted here
outlines his conceptions of society, which is one of four *action* systems.
The scheme presented here is a highly complex one that is intended to
apply to *all* societies and their evolution.

As the preeminent social theorist in the United States, Parsons has
been criticized as strongly as he has been lauded. Mills (1959) satirized
his ponderous style, his neglect of power, and the ideological implications of his work. Bottomore claims that Parsons' conception of a unity
of thought stemming from the work of Marshall, Pareto, Durkheim, and
Weber is "sadly deficient, because it ignores almost completely the work
of two thinkers—Marx and Freud—who were above all responsible for
a revolution in men's conception of their individual and social life"
(1974:29–43). He finds Parsons' social systems idea basically conservative: "In this way, Parsons' conceptual scheme conveys a view of society
as a stable and enduring structure, while paying little attention to the
factors of strain, conflict, and change which appear in it" (p. 33). Parsons,
he adds, separates theory both from substantive concerns and methodological considerations (pp. 37–38). Bottomore concludes:

Nowhere is this remoteness from the real world of action more evident than in
Sociological Theory and Modern Society. One of the oddest characteristics of the
book is that it does not seem to be about modern society at all, in any serious
way. Science, industry, population growth, starvation, revolution, race prejudice,
and conflict, nuclear war, are either not mentioned at all, or get only the most
fleeting attention . . . How is it possible to discover a vital interest and concern,
a clear direction in thought which is so willfully irrelevant? (1974:43)

Other critics have been less heated in their objections (the best source
of these is probably still Black, 1961) but have consistently questioned
the legitimacy of Parsons' concept building. (The most thorough single
critique is Gouldner, 1970.)

Walter Buckley has rejected both mechanical and organic functionalism (see Buckley, 1967:Chapter 2) as a prelude to his own development

of modern systems theory, a view of social systems that takes cybernetics and information theory into account. His more open scheme, outlined in the selection reprinted here, has attracted a fairly wide following among empirical researchers. It is perhaps a more flexible and applicable model than those developed by earlier functionalists.

References and Suggested Readings

Black, Max, ed. *The Social Theories of Talcott Parsons*. Englewood Cliffs, N. J.: Prentice-Hall, 1961.

Bottomore, Thomas B. "Out of This World: The Sociological Theory of Talcott Parsons," in *Sociology as Social Criticism*. New York: Pantheon, 1974, pp. 29–43.

Buckley, Walter. *Sociology and Modern Systems Theory*. Englewood Cliffs, N.J.: Prentice-Hall, 1967.

———. *Modern Systems Research for the Behavioral Sciences: A Sourcebook*. Chicago: Aldine, 1968.

Cohen, Percy S. *Modern Social Theory*. New York: Basic Books, 1968.

Coser, Lewis A., ed. *The Idea of Social Structure* (papers in honor of Robert K. Merton). New York: Harcourt Brace Jovanovich, 1975.

Davis, Kingsley. "The Myth of Functional Analysis as a Special Method in Sociology and Anthropology," *American Sociological Review*, 24 (1959), 757–772.

Demerath, N. J., III and Richard A. Peterson, eds. *System, Change and Conflict*. New York: Free Press, 1967.

Dore, Ronald Philip. "Function and Cause," *American Sociological Review*, 26 (Dec. 1961), 843–53.

Fallding, Harold. "Only One Sociology," *The British Journal of Sociology*, 23 (March 1972), 93–101.

Gans, Herbert J. "The Positive Functions of Poverty," *American Journal of Sociology*, 78 (September 1972), 275–89.

Gouldner, A. W. *Coming Crisis in Western Sociology*. New York: Basic Books, 1970.

Gross, Llewellyn. *Sociological Theory: Inquiries and Paradigms*. New York: Harper & Row, 1967.

Gross, Llewellyn, ed. *Symposium on Sociological Theory*. New York: Harper & Row, 1959.

Homans, George C. "Bringing Men Back In," *American Sociological Review*, 29 (December 1964), 809–18.

Katz, Fred E., ed. *Contemporary Sociological Theory*. New York: Random House, 1971.

Kuhn, Alfred. *The Logic of Social Systems*. San Francisco: Jossey-Bass, 1974.

McKinney, John C., and Ed A. Tiryakian, eds. *Theoretical Sociology: Perspectives and Development*. New York: Appleton-Century-Crofts, 1970.

Merton, Robert K. *Social Theory and Social Structure*. New York: Free Press, 1957.

Mills, C. W. *The Sociological Imagination*. New York: Oxford, 1959.

Parsons, Talcott. *The Structure of Social Action*. New York: McGraw-Hill, 1937.

———. *Essays in Sociological Theory*. Glencoe, Ill.: Free Press, 1949.

———. *The Social System*. Glencoe, Ill.: Free Press, 1951.

———. *Toward a General Theory of Action*. Cambridge, Mass: Harvard University Press, 1951.

———. *Working Papers in the Theory of Action*. Glencoe, Ill: Free Press, 1953.

———. *Essays in Sociological Theory*. Glencoe, Ill.: Free Press, 1954.

———. *Family, Socialization and Interaction Process*. Glencoe, Ill.: Free Press, 1955.

———. *Societies: Comparative and Evolutionary Perspectives*. Englewood Cliffs, N.J.: Prentice-Hall, 1966.

———. "On Building Social Systems Theory: A Personal History," *Daedalus: The Making of Modern Science: Biographical Studies*, 99 (Fall 1970), 826–881.

———. *The System of Modern Societies*. Englewood Cliffs, N.J.: Prentice-Hall, 1971.

———. "Culture and Social System Revisited," *Social Science Quarterly*, 53 (September 1972), 251–266.

Pope, Whitney. "Durkheim as a Functionalist," *The Sociological Quarterly*, 16 (Summer 1975), 361–379.

Sztompka, Piotr. *System and Function: Toward a Theory of Society*. New York: Academic Press, 1974.

Turner, Jonathan H., and Leonard Beeghley. "Current Folklore in the Criticisms of Parsonian Action Theory," in R. Serge Denisoff, Orel Callahan, and Mark H. Levine, eds., *Theories and Paradigms in Contemporary Sociology*. Itasca, Ill.: Peacock, 1974, pp. 392–405.

Turner, Jonathan H. *The Structure of Sociological Theory*. Homewood, Ill.: Dorsey Press, 1974.

A PARADIGM FOR FUNCTIONAL ANALYSIS

ROBERT K. MERTON

Robert K. Merton is professor of sociology at Columbia University. He is past president of the American Sociological Association.

As an initial and admittedly tentative step in the direction of codifying functional analysis in sociology, we set forth a paradigm of the concepts and problems central to this approach. . . . The paradigm presents the hard core of concept, procedure and inference in functional analysis.

Above all, it should be noted that the paradigm does not represent a set of categories introduced *de novo*, but rather a *codification* of those concepts and problems which have been forced upon our attention by critical scrutiny of current research and theory in functional analysis. . . .

1. *The item(s) to which functions are imputed*
The entire range of sociological data can be, and much of it has been, subjected to functional analysis. The basic requirement is that the object of analysis represent a *standardized* (i.e., patterned and repetitive) item, such as social roles, institutional patterns, social processes, cultural pattern, culturally patterned emotions, social norms, group organization, social structure, devices for social control, etc.

Basic Query: What must enter into the protocol of observation of the given item if it is to be amenable to systematic functional analysis?

2. *Concepts of subjective dispositions (motives, purposes)*
At some point, functional analysis invariably assumes or explicitly operates with some conception of the motivation of individuals involved in a social system. . . . [These] concepts of subjective disposition are often and erroneously merged with the related, but different, concepts of objective consequences of attitude, belief and behavior.

Basic Query: In which types of analysis is it sufficient to take observed motivations as *data*, as given, and in which are they properly considered as *problematical*, as derivable from other data?

3. *Concepts of objective consequences (functions, dysfunctions)*
We have observed two prevailing types of confusion enveloping the several current conceptions of "function":

(i)   The tendency to confine sociological observations to the *positive* contributions of a sociological item to the social or cultural system in which it is implicated; and

(ii) The tendency to confuse the subjective category of *motive* with the objective category of *function*.

Appropriate conceptual distinctions are required to eliminate these confusions.

The first problem calls for a concept of *multiple consequences* and *a net balance of an aggregate of consequences*.

Functions are those observed consequences which make for the adaptation or adjustment of a given system; and *dysfunctions*, those observed consequences which lessen the adaptation or adjustment of the system. There is also the empirical possibility of *nonfunctional* consequences, which are simply irrelevant to the system under consideration.

In any given instance, an item may have both functional and dysfunctional consequences, giving rise to the difficult and important problem of evolving canons for assessing the net balance of the aggregate of consequences. (This is, of course, most important in the use of functional analysis for guiding the formation and enactment of policy.)

The second problem (arising from the easy confusion of motives and functions) requires us to introduce a conceptual distinction between the cases in which the subjective aim-in-view coincides with the objective consequence, and the cases in which they diverge.

Manifest functions are those objective consequences contributing to the adjustment or adaptation of the system which are intended and recognized by participants in the system; *latent functions*, correlatively, being those which are neither intended nor recognized.

The relations between the "unanticipated consequences" of action and "latent functions" can be clearly defined, since they are implicit in the foregoing section of the paradigm. The unintended consequences of action are of three types:

(i)   those which are functional for a designated system, and these comprise the latent functions;

(ii)   those which are dysfunctional for a designated system, and these comprise the latent dysfunctions; and

(iii) those which are irrelevant to the system which they affect neither functionally nor dysfunctionally, i.e., the pragmatically unimportant class of non-functional consequences.

Basic Query: What are the effects of the transformation of a previously latent function into a manifest function (involving the problem of the role of knowledge in human behavior and the problems of "manipulation" of human behavior)?

4. Concepts of the unit subserved by the function

We have observed the difficulties entailed in *confining* analysis to functions fulfilled for "the society," since items may be functional for some individuals and subgroups and dysfunctional for others. It is necessary, therefore, to consider a *range* of units for which the item has designated consequences: individuals in diverse statuses, subgroups, the larger social system and culture systems. (Terminologically, this implies the concepts of psychological function, group function, societal function, cultural function, etc.)

5. Concepts of functional requirements (needs, prerequisites)

Embedded in every functional analysis is some conception, tacit or expressed, of the functional requirements of the system under observation. As noted elsewhere,[1] this remains one of the cloudiest and empirically most debatable concepts in functional theory. As utilized by sociologists, the concept of functional requirement tends to be tautological or *ex post facto*; it tends to be confined to the conditions of "survival" of a given system; it tends, as in the work of Malinowski, to include biological as well as social "needs."

This involves the difficult problem of establishing *types* of functional requirements (universal vs. specific); procedures for validating the assumption of these requirements; etc.

Basic Query: What is required to establish the validity of such a variable as "functional requirement" in situations where rigorous experimentation is impracticable?

6. Concepts of the mechanisms through which functions are fulfilled

Functional analysis in sociology, as in other disciplines like physiology and psychology, calls for a "concrete and detailed" account of the mechanisms which operate to perform a designated function. This refers, not to psychological, but to social, mechanisms (e.g., role-segmentation, insulation of institutional demands, hierarchic ordering of values, social division of labor, ritual and ceremonial enactments, etc.).

Basic Query: What is the presently available inventory of social mechanisms corresponding, say, to the large inventory of psychological mechanisms? What methodological problems are entailed in discerning the operation of these social mechanisms?

7. Concepts of functional alternatives (functional equivalents or substitutes)

As we have seen, once we abandon the gratuitous assumption of the functional indispensability of particular social structures, we immediately require some concept of functional alternatives, equivalents, or substitutes. This focuses attention on the *range of possible variation* in the items which can, in the case under examination, subserve a functional requirement. It unfreezes the identity of the existent and the inevitable.

Basic Query: Since scientific proof of the equivalence of an alleged functional alternative ideally requires rigorous experimentation, and since this is not often practicable in large-scale sociological situations, which practicable procedures of inquiry most nearly approximate the logic of experiment?

8. Concepts of structural context (or structural constraint)

The range of variation in the items which *can* fulfill designated functions in a social structure is not unlimited (and this has been repeatedly noted in our foregoing discussion). The interdependence of the elements of a social structure limits the effective possibilities of change or functional alternatives. The concept of structural constraint corresponds, in the area of social structure, to Goldenweiser's "principle of limited possibilities" in a broader sphere. Failure to recognize the relevance of interdependence and attendant structural restraints leads to utopian thought in which it is tacitly assumed that certain elements of a social system can be eliminated without affecting the rest of that system. This consideration is recognized by both Marxist social scientists (e.g., Karl Marx) and by non-Marxists (e.g., Malinowski).[2]

Basic Query: How narrowly does a given structural context limit the range of variation in the items which can effectively satisfy functional requirements? Do we find, under conditions yet to be determined, an area of indifference, in which any one of a wide range of alternatives may fulfill the function?

9. Concepts of dynamics and change

We have noted that functional analysts *tend* to focus on the statics of social structure and to neglect the study of structural change.

This emphasis upon statics is not, however, *inherent* in the theory of functional analysis. It is, rather, an adventitious emphasis stemming from the concern of early anthropological functionalists to counteract preceding tendencies to write conjectural histories of non-literate societies. This practice, useful at the time it was first introduced into anthropology, has disadvantageously persisted in the work of some functional sociologists.

The concept of dysfunction, which implies the concept of strain, stress and tension on the structural level, provides an analytical approach to the study of dynamics and change. How are observed dysfunctions contained within a particular structure, so that they do not produce instability? Does the accumulation of stresses and strains produce pressure for change in such directions as are likely to lead to their reduction?

Basic Query: Does the prevailing concern among functional analysts with the concept of *social equilibrium* divert attention from the phenomena of *social disequilibrium?* Which available procedures will permit the sociologist most adequately to gauge the accumulation of stresses and strains in a social system? To what extent does knowledge of the structural context permit the sociologist to anticipate the most probable directions of social change?

10. Problems of validation of functional analysis

Throughout the paradigm, attention has been called repeatedly to the *specific* points at which assumptions, imputations and observations must be validated.[3] This requires, above all, a rigorous statement of the sociological procedures of analysis which most nearly approximate the *logic* of experimentation. It requires a systematic review of the possibilities and limitations of *comparative* (cross-cultural and cross-group) *analysis.*

Basic Query: To what extent is functional analysis limited by the difficulty of locating adequate *samples of social systems* which can be subjected to comparative (quasi-experimental) study?[4]

11. Problems of the ideological implications of functional analysis

. . . Functional analysis has no intrinsic commitment to an ideological position. This does not gainsay the fact that *particular* functional analyses and *particular* hypotheses advanced by functionalists may have an identifiable ideological role. This, then, becomes a specific problem for the sociology of knowledge: to what extent does the social position of the functional sociologist (e.g., *vis-a-vis* a particular "client" who has authorized a given research) evoke one rather than another formulation of a problem, affect his assumptions and concepts, and limit the range of inferences drawn from his data?

Basic Query: How does one detect the ideological tinge of a functional analysis and to what degree does a particular ideology stem from the basic assumptions adopted by the sociologist? Is the incidence of these assumptions related to the status and research role of the sociologist? . . .

PURPOSES OF THE PARADIGM

The first and foremost purpose is to supply a provisional codified guide for adequate and fruitful functional analyses. This objective evidently implies that the paradigm contains the minimum set of concepts with which the sociologist must operate in order to carry through an adequate functional analysis and, as a corollary, that it can be used here and now as a guide for the critical study of existing analyses. It is thus intended as an all-too-compact and elliptical guide to the formulation of researches in functional analysis and as an aid in locating the distinctive contributions and deficiencies of earlier researches. . . .

Secondly, the paradigm is intended to lead directly to the postulates and (often tacit) assumptions underlying functional analysis. . . . Some of these assumptions are of central importance, others insignificant and dispensable, and still others, dubious and even misleading.

In the third place, the paradigm seeks to sensitize the sociologist not only to the narrowly scientific implications of various types of functional analysis, but also to their political and sometimes ideological implications. The points at which a functional analysis presupposes an implicit political outlook and the points at which it has bearing on "social engineering" are concerns which find an integral place in the paradigm.

NOTES

1. R. K. Merton, "Discussion of Parsons' 'Position of Sociological Theory,' " *American Sociological Review*, 13 (1949), 164–168.

2. In *A Contribution to the Critique of Political Economy* (appearing in 1859 and re-published in Karl Marx, *Selected Works*, Moscow: Cooperative Publishing Society, 1935, pp. 354–371). [Marx] observes for example: "No social order ever disappears before all the productive forces for which there is room in it have been developed; and new higher re-lations of production never appear before the material conditions of their existence have matured in the womb of the old society itself. Therefore, mankind always sets itself only such tasks as it can solve; since, looking at the matter more closely, we will always find that the task itself arises only when the material conditions necessary for its solution al-ready exist or are at least in the process of formation" (p. 357). Perhaps the most famous of his many references to the constraining influence of a given social structure is found in the second paragraph of *The Eighteenth Brumaire of Louis Napoleon:* "Man makes his own history, but he does not make it out of whole cloth: he does not make it out of conditions chosen by himself, but out of such conditions as he finds close at hand." (From the para-phrase of the original as published in Marx, *Selected Works*, II, 315.) . . .

And for other language with quite different ideological import and essentially similar theoretic implications, see B. Malinowski, "Given a definite cultural need, the means of its satisfaction are small in number, and therefore the cultural arrangement which comes into being in response to the need is determined within narrow limits" ("Culture," *Ency-clopedia of the Social Sciences*, p. 626).

3. By this point, it is evident that we are considering functional analysis as a method for the *interpretation* of sociological data. This is not to gainsay the important role of the functional orientation in sensitizing sociologists to the *collection* of types of data which might otherwise be neglected. It is perhaps unnecessary to reiterate the axiom that one's concepts *do* determine the inclusion or exclusion of data, that, despite the etymology of the term, *data* are not "given" but are "contrived" with the inevitable help of concepts. In the process of evolving a functional interpretation, the sociological analyst invariably finds it necessary to obtain data other than those initially contemplated. Interpretation and the collection of data are thus inextricably bound up in the array of concepts and propositions relating these concepts.

4. George P. Murdock's *Social Structure* (New York: Macmillan, 1949) is enough to show that procedures such as those involved in the cross-cultural survey hold large promise for dealing with certain methodological problems of functional analysis. See also the pro-cedures of functional analysis in George C. Homans and David M. Schneider, *Marriage, Authority, and Final Causes* (Glencoe: Free Press, 1955).

THE CONCEPT OF SOCIETY: THE COMPONENTS AND THEIR INTERRELATIONS

TALCOTT PARSONS

From Talcott Parsons, *Societies: Evolutionary and Comparative Perspectives*, © 1966, pp. 5–20, 28–29. Reprinted by permission of Prentice-Hall, Inc., Englewood Cliffs, New Jersey.

Talcott Parsons recently retired from a long career at Harvard University. The preeminent theorist for several decades, he is past president of the American Sociological Association.

The society is a special kind of social system. We treat the social system as one of the primary subsystems of the human action system, the others being the behavioral organism, the personality of the individual, and the cultural system. (The reader may find it helpful in following this discussion to refer to Tables 1 and 2 for graphic representation of the interrelations between these systems.)

THE GENERAL CONCEPTUAL SCHEME OF ACTION

Action consists of the structures and processes by which human beings form meaningful intentions and, more or less successfully, implement them in concrete situations. The word "meaningful" implies the symbolic or cultural level of representation and reference. Intentions and implementation taken together imply a disposition of the action system—individual or collective—to modify its relation to its situation or environment in an intended direction.

We prefer the term "action" to "behavior" because we are interested not in the physical events of behavior for their own sake but in their patterning, their patterned meaningful products (physical, cultural, and other), ranging from implements to works of art, and the mechanisms and processes that control such patterning.

Human action is "cultural" in that meanings and intentions concerning acts are formed in terms of *symbolic* systems (including the codes through which they operate in patterns) that focus most generally about the universal of human societies, language.

There is a sense in which all action is the action of individuals. However, both the organism and the cultural system involve essential elements which cannot be investigated at the individual level.

For the organism, the primary structural reference is not the anatomy of the particular organism, but the *species-type*.[1] To be sure, this type does not actualize itself, but works through the genetic constitutions of unique individual organisms, which involve both varying combinations of the genetic materials characteristic of the species and the effects of different environmental conditions. But however important individual variations may be in determining concrete action, it is the common patterns of large human groups—including their differentiation into two sexes—which constitute the massive organic sub-stratum of action.

It would not be correct to say that the genetic constitution of an organism is modified by environmental influence. Rather, the genetic constitution comprises a general "orientation" which develops into specific anatomical structures, physiological mechanisms, and behavioral patternings as it interacts with environmental factors during the life of the organism. The environmental factors can be analyzed into two categories: first, those responsible for the non-hereditary elements of the physical organism; second, those responsible for the *learned* elements of behavioral systems, which is the category upon which we must focus. Although an organism may certainly be capable of learning in immediate environments devoid of other behaving organisms, the theory of action is primarily concerned with learning in which other organisms of the same species constitute the most important feature of the general environment.

Symbolically *organized* cultural patterns, like all other components of living systems, have certainly emerged through evolution. Yet, the human linguistic *level* of their development is a phenomenon entirely unique to man. The capacity to learn and use language clearly depends on man's special genetic constitution, as the failure of attempts to teach it to other species (especially the primates and "talking" birds) has shown.[2] But only this general capacity is genetically determined, *not* the specific symbolic systems which are actually learned, used, and developed by specific human groups.

Furthermore, despite the great capacity of human organisms for learning and, indeed, for creating cultural elements, no individual can create a cultural system. The *main* patternings of cultural systems change only over periods of many generations and are *always* shared by relatively large groups; they are never special to one or a few individuals. Therefore, they are always learned by the individual, who can make only rather marginal creative (or destructive) contributions to their change. Thus the more general cultural patterns provide action systems with a highly stable structural anchorage quite analogous to that provided by the genetic materials of the species-type, focusing on the learned elements of action just as the genes focus upon the inheritable elements.[3]

Within the limits imposed by the genetic species-type on the one hand, and the patterning of the culture on the other, lies the opportunity for given individuals and groups to develop independently structured behavioral systems. Because an actor is genetically human, and because his learning occurs in the context of a particular cultural system, his learned behavioral system (which I shall call his personality) shares certain broad features with other personalities—e.g., the language he habitually speaks. At the same time, his organism and its environment —physical, social, and cultural—are always in certain respects unique. Hence, his own behavioral system will be a *unique variant* of the culture and its particular patterns of action. It is therefore essential to consider the personality system as not reducible to either the organism or the culture—*what* is learned is part of neither the "structure" of the organism in the usual sense nor a feature of the cultural system. It comprises an *analytically independent system.*[4]

Though intimately intertwined with the personalities of the interacting individuals and the patterns of the cultural system, the process of social interaction forms a fourth system that is analytically independent of both personal and cultural systems, as well as of the organism.[5] This independence becomes most evident in regard to the requirements for integration that impinge upon systems of social relationships because of their inherent potential for conflict and disorganization. This is sometimes known as the *problem of order* in society, posed in classic form by Thomas Hobbes.[6] The system of interaction constitutes the social system, the sub-system of action with which this book is primarily concerned.

The above classification of four highly general sub-systems of human action —the organism, personality, social system, and cultural system—is an application of a general paradigm which can be used throughout the field of action, and which I shall use below to analyze social systems. This paradigm analyzes *any* action *system* in terms of the following four functional categories: 1) that concerned with the maintenance of the highest "governing" or controlling patterns of the system; 2) the internal integration of the system; 3) its orientation to the attainment of goals in relation to its environment; 4) its more generalized adaptation to the broad conditions of the environment—e.g., the non-action, physical environment. Within action systems, cultural systems are specialized around the function of pattern-maintenance, social systems around the integration of acting units (human individuals or, more precisely, personalities engaged in roles), personality systems around goal-attainment, and the behavioral organism around adaptation (see Table 1).

Table 1. Sub-systems of Action

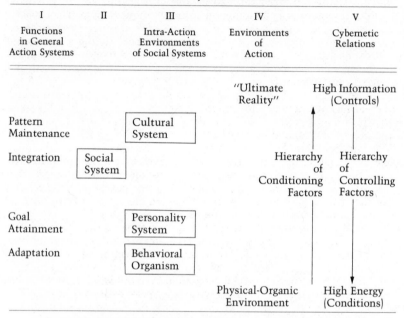

I	II	III	IV	V
Functions in General Action Systems		Intra-Action Environments of Social Systems	Environments of Action	Cybernetic Relations
			"Ultimate Reality"	High Information (Controls)
Pattern Maintenance		Cultural System		
Integration	Social System		Hierarchy of Conditioning Factors	Hierarchy of Controlling Factors
Goal Attainment		Personality System		
Adaptation		Behavioral Organism		
			Physical-Organic Environment	High Energy (Conditions)

Table 1 presents the main relations between the social system and its total system of environments in terms of the functional scheme we have used. Column I lists the functional categories, interpreted here at the general action level. Column II singles out the social system from the others according to its integrative functions within the action system. Column III, corresponding to Column IV of Table 2, lists the other three primary sub-systems of action as immediate (i.e., as intra-action) environments of the social system. Column IV presents the two environments within which action systems function—at least so far as they are distinguished here— namely, the physical-organic environment, relations with which are mediated in the first instance through the behavioral organism, and the environment we have called "ultimate reality," relations with which are mediated through the constitutive symbol systems (i.e., religious components) of the cultural system. Finally, Column V indicates the two directions in which factors exert their effect on these systems. The upward-pointed arrow indicates the hierarchy of conditions, which at any given cumulative level in the upward series is, in the common formula, "necessary but not sufficient." The downward-pointed arrow designates the hierarchy of controlling factors, in the cybernetic sense. As we move downward, control of more and more necessary conditions makes the implementation of patterns, plans, or programs possible. Systems higher in the order are relatively high in information while those lower down are relatively high in energy.

THE CONCEPT OF THE SOCIAL SYSTEM

Since the social system is made up of the interaction of human individuals, each member is *both actor* (having goals, ideas, attitudes, etc.) *and object* of orientation for *both* other actors and himself. The interaction system, then, is an *analytical aspect abstractable* from the total action processes of its participants. At the same time, these "individuals" are also organisms, personalities, and participants in cultural systems.

Because of such interpenetration, each of the other three action systems (Culture, Personality, Behavioral Organism) constitutes a part of the environment —or, we may say *an* environment—of a social system. Beyond these systems are the environments of action itself, standing above and below the general hierarchy of factors that control action in the world of life. These relationships are depicted in Table 1.

Below action in the hierarchy stands the physical-organic environment, including the sub-human species of organisms and the "nonbehavioral" components of human organisms. This is a particularly important boundary of action because, as humans, we know the physical world *only* through the organism. Our minds have no direct experience of an external physical object unless we perceive it through physical processes and the brain "processes" information about it. In their psychologically known sense, however, physical objects are aspects of action.

In principle, similar considerations apply to the environment above action —the "ultimate reality" with which we are ultimately concerned in grappling with what Weber called the "problems of meaning"—e.g., evil and suffering, the temporal limitations of human life, and the like. "Ideas" in this area, as cultural objects, are in some sense symbolic "representations" (e.g., conceptions of gods, totems, the supernatural) of the ultimate realities, but are not themselves such realities.

A fundamental principle about the organization of living systems is that their structures are differentiated in regard to the various exigencies imposed upon them by their environments. Thus the biological functions of respiration, nutrition-elimination, locomotion, and information-processing are bases of differentiated organ-systems, each of which is specialized about the exigencies of certain relations between the organism and its environment. We will use this principle to organize our analysis of social systems.

We will consider social systems in their relations to their most important environments. I will contend that the functional differentiations among the three sub-systems of action other than the social—the cultural system, the personality system, and the behavioral organism—and the articulation of two of them with the two environments of the entire action system, constitute very major references for analyzing the differences among social systems. That is, my analysis will be developed on the basis of the fundamental system-and-environment relations of Table 1.

In the functional terms of our paradigm, the social system is the *integrative* sub-system of action in general. The other three sub-systems of action constitute principal environments in relation to it. In the analysis of societies or other social systems, then, the above principle can be applied. We will see that three of the primary sub-systems of the society (Table 2, column III) are functionally specialized around their interrelations with the three principal environments of a social system (Table 2, column IV), each relating most directly to one of these environments. Each of these three societal sub-systems may also be considered a distinct environment of the sub-system which is the society's integrative core (Table 2, column II). We will employ this *dual* application of the functional paradigm throughout the exposition of our general theoretical scheme . . . [7]

Table 2. The Societal Community and Its Environments

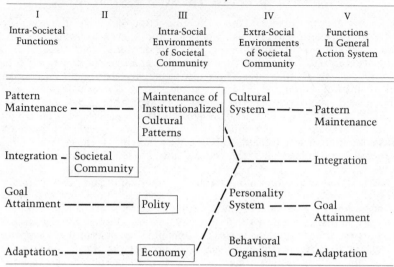

I	II	III	IV	V
Intra-Societal Functions		Intra-Social Environments of Societal Community	Extra-Social Environments of Societal Community	Functions In General Action System

Pattern Maintenance ————— Maintenance of Institutionalized Cultural Patterns | Cultural System ———— Pattern Maintenance

Integration — Societal Community | ————— Integration

Goal Attainment ————— Polity | Personality System ——— Goal Attainment

Adaptation ·————— Economy | Behavioral Organism——— Adaptation

Table 2 presents schematically the set of relationships which have been outlined in the text concerning the primary structure of the society as a system, centering on the place of the societal community. Column I lists the four primary functional categories according to their place in the cybernetic hierarchy of control. In relation to column I, column II identifies the societal community as the integrative sub-system of the society—i.e., that *analytically* defined sub-system characterized by the primacy of integrative function in the larger system. Column III designates the other three primary analytical sub-systems (the functions of which are also given in relation to column I) as constituting environments of the societal community which are *internal* to the society as a social system. It both carries on processes of input-output interchange and shares certain zones of interpenetration with them. Column IV details in the cognate order the pimary sub-systems of action other than the social system itself, showing them as in turn constituting environments for the social system, presuming the same order of interchange and interpenetration, but with different specific content. The slanting dashed lines indicate that the *entire* societal system, not each of its sub-systems, is involved in these interchanges with the action environments. Finally, Column V lists the functional categories in terms of which action systems are differentiated, this time in the context of the general action system rather than, as in Column I, of the social system.

THE CONCEPT OF SOCIETY

In defining a society, we may use a criterion which goes back at least to Aristotle. A society is a type of social system, in any universe of social systems, which attains the highest level of self-sufficiency as a system in relation to its environments.

This definition refers to an abstracted system, of which the other, similarly abstracted sub-systems of action are the primary environments. This view contrasts sharply with our common-sense notion of society as being composed of concrete human individuals. Organisms and the personalities of members of the society would then be internal to the society, not part of its environment. We cannot argue the merits of these two views of societies here. But the reader must be clear about the usage . . .

With this understanding, the criterion of self-sufficiency can be divided into five sub-criteria, each relating to one of the five environments of social systems —Ultimate Reality, Cultural Systems, Personality Systems, Behavioral Organisms, the Physical-Organic Environment. The self-sufficiency of a society is a function of the balanced *combination* of its controls over its relations with these five environments and of its own state of internal integration.

We have referred to a hierarchy of control which organizes the interrelations of the analytically distinguished systems. This includes the *cybernetic* aspect of control by which systems high in information but low in energy regulate other systems higher in energy but lower in information (Table 1, column V).[8] Thus, a programed sequence of mechanical operations (e.g., in a washing machine) can be controlled by a timing switch using very little energy compared with the energy actually operating the machine's moving parts or heating its water. Another example is the gene and its control over protein synthesis and other aspects of cell metabolism.

The cultural system structures commitments vis-à-vis ultimate reality into meaningful orientations toward the rest of the environment and the system of action, the physical world, organisms, personalities, and social systems. In the cybernetic sense, it is highest within the action system, the social system ranking next, and personality and organism falling respectively below that. The physical environment is ultimate in the *conditional,* as distinguished from the organizational, sense. Insofar as physical factors are not controllable by the cybernetically higher-order systems, we must adapt to them or human life will disappear. Human dependence on oxygen, food, tolerable temperatures, and so on, are very familiar examples.

Because of our wide evolutionary perspective, our major concern among the non-social sub-systems of action will be with the cultural system. Because they develop over long periods and under widely varying circumstances, forms of social organization emerge which have increasingly broad adaptive capacities. In their broad characteristics, they tend to become decreasingly subject to major change from narrow, particularized, conditional causes operating through specific physical circumstances or individual organic or personality differences. In the more advanced societies, the range of individual personalities may even broaden whereas the structure and processes of the society become less dependent on individual idiosyncrasies. Thus we must focus on the cybernetically higher-order structures—the cultural system among the environments of the society—in order to examine the major sources of large-scale change.

THE SOCIETAL COMMUNITY AND ITS ENVIRONMENTS[9]

The core of a society, as a system, is the patterned normative order through which the life of a population is collectively organized. As an order, it contains values and differentiated and particularized norms and rules, all of which require cultural references in order to be meaningful and legitimate. As a collectivity, it displays a patterned conception of membership which distinguishes between those individuals who do and do not belong. Problems involving the "jurisdiction" of the normative system may make impossible an exact coincidence between the status of "coming under" normative obligations and the status of membership, because the enforcement of a normative system seems inherently linked to the control (e.g., through the "police function") of sanctions exercised by and against the people actually residing within a territory.[10] Unless these problems become critical, the societal collectivity can act effectively as a unit when required, and so can various of its sub-collectivities.

We will call this one entity of the society, in its collective aspect, the societal community. As such, it is constituted both by a normative system of order *and* by statuses, rights, and obligations pertaining to membership which may vary for different sub-groups within the community. To survive and develop, the social community must maintain the integrity of a common cultural orientation, broadly (though not necessarily uniformly or unanimously) shared by its membership, as the basis of its societal identity. This problem concerns its connection with the superordinate cultural system. However, it must also meet systematically the conditional exigencies regarding the integration of members' organisms (and their relations to the physical environment) and personalities. All these factors are complexly interdependent, yet each is a focus for the crystallization of a distinctive type of social mechanism.

The Cultural System as Environment to Society[11]

The central functional exigency of the interrelations between a society and a cultural system is the *legitimation* of the society's normative order. Legitimation systems define the reasons for members' rights and for the prohibitions incumbent upon them. Above all, but not exclusively, the use of power requires legitimation. The present concept of legitimation need not imply the adjective "moral" in a modern sense. But it does imply that it is in some sense "right" that things be done in accord with the institutionalized order.

The function of legitimation is independent of the *operative* functions of a social system. No normative order is ever *self*-legitimating in the sense that the approved or prohibited way of life simply *is* right or wrong and admits of no questions. Nor is it ever adequately legitimized by necessities imposed at lower levels of the hierarchy of control—e.g., that things *must* be done in a *specific* way because the stability or even survival of the system is at stake.

However, the *extent* of the culturally-grounded independence between the bases of legitimation and specific lower-order operative mechanisms (e.g., bureaucratic organization and economic markets) is highly variable among societies. By and large, an increase in this independence is a main trend of the evolutionary process, involving differentiation between cultural and societal structures and processes. Whatever its position on this line of development, however, a legitimation system is always related to, and meaningfully dependent on, a grounding in ordered relations to ultimate reality. That is, its grounding is always in some sense religious. In quite primitive societies, there actually is little differentiation between the general structures of a society and its religious organization. In more advanced societies, the interrelation of social and cultural systems in the religious and legitimation contexts involves highly specialized and complicated structures.

Cultural value patterns provide the most direct link between the social and cultural systems in legitimizing the normative order of the society. The mode of legitimation in turn is grounded in religious orientations. As cultural systems become more differentiated, however, other cultural structures assume increasing independent importance, particularly the arts, which have special relations to the autonomy of personalities and empirical cognitive knowledge, which at an advanced level becomes science.

Personality as Environment to Society

A society's relation to the personality system differs radically from its relation to the cultural system, because the personality (like the behavioral organism and the physical-organic environment) stands *below* the social system in the cybernetic hierarchy. The society as a system, and *each* of its constituent units, is subject to constraining conditions—which are also opportunities to be utilized —in each of these three contexts. Behavior, of which social systems comprise one analytical aspect, is always in another aspect the behavior *of* living human organisms. Every such organism has at any given moment a given location in physical space which can be changed only through physical motion. Hence, the ecological aspect of the relations among individuals and their actions is never safely neglected. Similar considerations apply to organic processes and to personality functioning and development, both of which are also constantly present as factors of concrete action. Exigencies relating to personalities, behavioral organisms, and the physical-organic environment account for many of the complex, cross-cutting dimensions of the actual organization and functioning of social systems, which require careful analysis and which constantly raise difficulties for social scientists.

The major functional problem concerning the social system's relation to the personality system involves learning, developing, and maintaining through the life cycle adequate motivation for participating in socially valued and controlled patterns of action. Reciprocally, a society must also adequately satisfy or reward its members through such patterns of action, if it is continually to draw upon their performances for its functioning as a system. This relationship constitutes "socialization," the whole complex of processes by which persons become members of the societal community and maintain that status.

Since personality is the *learned organization* of the behaving individual, the socialization process is always critical to its formation and functioning. Successful socialization requires that social and cultural learning be strongly motivated through the engagement of the pleasure mechanisms of the organism. Hence, it depends on relatively stable intimate relations between young children and adults, whose own erotic motives and relations tend to be deeply engaged too. This complex of exigencies, which we have come to understand much more fully since Freud, is an essential aspect of the functioning of kinship systems in all human societies. Kinship always involves an ordering of the erotic relations of adults, of their statuses in relation to presumptive parenthood, of the statuses of the new generation, and of the socialization process itself.[12] It is an evolutionary universal found in *all* societies, though its forms and relations to other structural complexes vary enormously.

A kinship system requires some stable arrangements for day-to-day living which involve organic and psychological as well as social factors. Hence it is a zone of interpenetration among behavioral, personality, and social systems and the physical environment. The latter reference involves the institutionalization of *residence* with respect to location and the constitution of the social unit we call the *household*. The household members are the people who live together as a unit. They share a definite location with physical arrangements, such as a hut or house, or in temporary settlements, a "camp." In most societies, people normally sleep, prepare and eat most of their food, and carry on at least most formally approved sexual activity in that physical and social setting. The household unit is, with all its variations, perhaps the primordial unit of solidarity in social systems.

Although its forms vary greatly, adult status involves the assumption of a certain amount of autonomous responsibility in all societies. The individual performs *services* in some context of collective organization. As a product of a long evolutionary process, these performances become institutionalized in modern societies primarily around the occupational role in a specific-function collectivity, or bureaucratic organization. In any case, the *primary* functional relation between adult individuals and their societies concerns the contributions adults make through performing services and the satisfactions or rewards they derive from them. In sufficiently differentiated societies, capacity for service becomes a mobile resource of the society, mobilizable through the market. When this stage is reached, we can speak of services as an output of the economic process, available for "consumption" in non-economic connections.

For most people in most societies, the places of residence and work are not differentiated. Where this differentiation does occur (mainly in advanced urban communities), these *two* locations constitute the locational axis of the individual's more routine life. Furthermore, the two places must be mutually accessible, a functional requirement about which the major ecological structure of modern cities is generally formed.

A variety of functional relations between personalities and their environments must be treated in other contexts relative to the social system. An individual's value-commitments and their maintenance link primarily with the cultural system, especially as it interrelates with the society through religion. The maintenance of adequate levels of motivation involves mainly the social structures concerned with socialization, particularly kinship. Although physical health is another matter, it shades complexly into the important but vague areas of mental health and the will of the sick to regain health. It seems that *no* society is without motivation-maintenance mechanisms that operate through some kind of "therapeutic" procedures.[13] In many societies these procedures are predominantly religious or magical, but in modern societies they have been emerging into an applied science. Yet, in no case are they radically dissociated from kinship on a society-wide basis—rather, therapy generally supplements kinship, which is the focal support for the security of personalities.

Surprising as it may seem, the relation between personality and social system, socially structured through what we have called *service*, provides the basic unit for the *political* aspect of societies.[14] Political structures are concerned with organizing collective action for the attainment of collectively significant goals, whether on a society-wide basis or on more narrow bases, either territorially or functionally defined. Advanced political development requires status-differentiation within the adult population on some combination of two bases. The first involves levels of responsibility for coordinated collective action and grounds the institutions of leadership and authority. The second concerns levels of competence, based on knowledge, skill, and the like, and assigns greater influence in collective deliberations to the more competent. A political system's differentiation from the matrix of the societal community involves institutionalizing higher-order statuses in both these contexts, often in very complex combinations. The relation of such statuses to religious leadership, particularly the degree of differentiation between leadership in religious and in political contexts, may also present major complications. The imperative of legitimation, not only of the societal order, but also of political authority in particular, indicates a main context of such complications.

Lower in the cybernetic hierarchy is another basis of complication. As we mentioned earlier, the maintenance of a normative order requires that it be implemented in a variety of respects; there must be very considerable—even if often quite incomplete—compliance with the behavioral expectations established by the values and norms. The most basic condition of such compliance is the internalization of a society's values and norms by its members, for such socialization underlies the consensus basis of a societal community. In turn, socialization to the grounds of consensus is reinforced at various points by interlocking interests, notably economic and political. However, no society can maintain stability in the face of varying exigencies and strains unless the interest constellations of its members are grounded in solidarity and internalized loyalties and obligations.

Beyond consensus and the intermeshing of interests, there is still need for some machinery of *enforcement*. This need links in turn with the necessity for an authoritative interpretation of the institutionalized normative obligations. Hence, all societies have some type of "legal" procedures by which rights and wrongs can be decided without recourse to violence, and by which parties deemed in the wrong can be constrained from acting upon their interpretations, interests, or sentiments at the expense of others.

Because of the indicated territorial involvements of residence, work, religious activities, political organization, and various other factors, the maintenance of a normative order cannot be dissociated from control over activities within territorial areas. The function of government must include responsibility for preserving the *territorial integrity* of the society's normative order. This imperative has both an internal and an external reference. The first concerns the conditions of enforcing general norms and facilitating the performance of essential functions by the various units of the society. The second concerns the prevention of disruptive interference by non-members of the community. By virtue of the organic-locational exigencies we have discussed, the two references have one thing in common: The *ultimate preventive* of disruptive action is the use of physical force.[15] The use of force takes many forms, notably defense vis-à-vis outside territory and deprivation of liberty (imprisonment) within. The control or neutralization of the organized use of force is one functional necessity of maintaining a societal community. In more highly differentiated societies, this always involves some degree of governmental monopolization of socially organized force.

Thus a society's *primary* exigency vis-à-vis the personalities of its members is the motivation of their participation, including their compliance with the demands of its normative order. This exigency may be divided into three levels. First is the highly generalized commitment to the central value patterns that relate directly to the religious orientations. Second is the "sub-stratum" of the personality which, stemming from early socialization, links with the erotic complex and the motivational significance of kinship and other intimate relations. Third is the level more directly involved with services and the instrumental activities which vary with particular goals and situations. These levels of the personality correspond roughly to the superego, id, and ego in Freud's classification.

Secondarily, the linkage of the personality with the organism and the organism's involvement with the physical world operates in two relevant contexts which we have noted here. The first concerns the generalized organic processes that condition adequate personality functioning, especially in relation to the complexes of kinship, residence, and health. Second is the relation between coercion by physical force and the problem of maintaining the integrity of a societal normative order throughout a varied territory.

Organism and Physical Setting as Environment to Society

Consideration of the social system's relation to its organic base and, through that, to the physical world must begin with the physical requirements of organic life. Here the primordial problems concern the provision of food and shelter, but many other factors are also problematic in all known societies. Ramifying from the relatively simple tools and skills of primitive peoples to the very complex systems of modernity, technology is the socially organized capacity for actively controlling and altering objects of the physical environment in the interest of some human want or need. In limiting cases, the social organization may involve simply teaching skills to individual craftsmen who produce by themselves. But even in such cases, if the technology is important, the craftsman is unlikely to remain totally insulated from practitioners of his craft other than the master who taught him. Furthermore, if his work is specialized, he *must* have some organized relations with consumers of his product and, very likely, with sources of his materials and equipment. Truly, there can be no craft wholly divorced from social organization.

Technological processes obviously serve to meet human needs and wants. They depend on the cultural system for their *techniques* [16]—one person's addition to the total technical lore of his society is always an increment rather than an entirely "new system." Furthermore, technological tasks in this sense are always performed in a socially defined *role*. Products are very generally, though by no means always, the outcome of *collectively* organized processes, not the work of one individual. Thus some executive or coordinating functions must be performed in a broad variety of social relations with consumers, suppliers, workers, researchers, and the like.

Technology, then, is the primarily physical reference of the complex which includes the *economy* as its primary social system reference. The economy is the aspect of the societal system which functions not just to order technological procedures socially, but more importantly to fit them into the social system and control them in the interests of social units, whether individual or collective.[17] The institutional complexes of property, contract, and the regulation of terms of employment are important integrating elements here. The more strictly economic aspects of the complex are, in primitive and archaic societies, embedded in diffuse structures where kinship, religion, or political interests are paramount. Under certain circumstances, however, markets develop, along with money as a medium of exchange.

Technological organization, then, should be regarded as a boundary-structure between the society as a system and the organic-physical environment. On the societal side of the boundary, the economy is the focal structure, providing linkage with the societal community. Here, as the traditions of economic theory strongly emphasize, the function of *allocation* is central. Resources must be allocated toward the satisfaction of the vast variety of wants present in *any* society, and opportunities for satisfying wants must be allocated among different categories of the population. As socially organized, technological considerations also apply to the utilization of services. As the services of individuals become a truly mobile and *allocable* resource, they comprise an economic category, as their bracketing with physical goods in the economists' formula "goods and services" makes clear. Once involved (through employment) in an operating organization, however, they become engaged in what is in analytical terms political functioning—organizational processes oriented toward attaining the specific goals of the society or a relevant sub-collectivity.

These considerations imply that technology involves a complex of territorial references parallel to residence. In fact, it differentiates from the residence complex only late in social evolution.[18] Its major concern is the location of "industry." Insofar as personnel perform differentiated occupational or service roles, they must work *where* their services are needed, though this location must be coordinated with residential factors. However, location must also depend on access to materials and equipment and on distribution of output. Industry in the strict sense represents the case in which such economic considerations take primacy. But the location problems of governmental administration or of specialized religious personnel can be analyzed in somewhat similar terms.

THE SOCIETAL COMMUNITY AND SELF-SUFFICIENCY

Certain priorities of control are inherent in the linkages between the societal subsystems that relate the society to its environments and the societal community itself. The societal community is dependent on a super-ordinate *cultural* orientation system which is, above all, the primary source of legitimation for its normative order. This order then constitutes the most essential higher-order reference for the political and economic sub-systems, which connect most directly with the personality and organic-physical environments, respectively. In the political sphere, the priority of the societal normative order is highlighted most sharply in the function of enforcement[19] and in the need for agencies of the society to have some final control over sanctioning by physical force—not because physical force is the cybernetic controller, but because it must *be* controlled in order for the higher-order controls to operate. In the economic sphere, the parallel is that economic processes in the society (e.g., of allocation) must be institutionally controlled. Both cases also indicate the functional importance of *normative control* over the organism and the physical environment. When used as sanctions, force and other physical-organic factors contribute much more to the security of collective processes than they can as mere "conditional exigencies." Similarly, the priority of economic over technological considerations—questions of *what* is to be produced (and *for whom*) take precedence over questions of *how* things are to be produced—is a basic requirement for making technology actually useful.[20]

We may now sum up the ramifications of the self-sufficiency criterion we used in defining the concept of a society. A society must constitute a societal *community* that has an adequate level of integration or solidarity and a distinctive membership status. This does not preclude relations of control or symbiosis with population elements only partially integrated into the societal community, such as the Jews in the Diaspora, but there must be a core of more fully integrated members.

This community must be the "bearer" of a cultural system sufficiently generalized and integrated to legitimize a normative order. Such legitimation requires a system of constitutive symbolism which grounds the identity and solidarity of the community, as well as beliefs, rituals, and other cultural components which embody such symbolism. Cultural systems are usually broader than any one society and its community organization, although in areas containing many societies distinct cultural systems may indeed shade into one another. A society's self-sufficiency in this context, then, involves its institutionalizing a sufficient range of cultural components to meet its *societal* exigencies tolerably well. Of course, the relations among societies having the same or closely related cultural systems present special problems, some of which will be discussed later.

The element of collective organization imposes additional criteria of self-sufficiency. Self-sufficiency by no means requires that *all* the role-involvements of all members be carried on within the society. However, a society does have to provide a repertoire of role-opportunities sufficient for individuals to meet their fundamental personal exigencies at all stages of the life cycle without going outside the society, and for the society itself to meet its own exigencies. A celibate monastic order does not meet this criterion, because it cannot recruit new members by birth without violating its fundamental norms.

We have shown that the implementation of a normative order in a collectively organized population entails control over a territorial area. This is a very fundamental imperative regarding the integrity of governmental institutions. Furthermore, it is a major reason why no functionally specific collectivity such as a church or a business firm can be called a society. In relation to members as individuals, then, societal self-sufficiency requires—perhaps this is most fundamental—adequate control of motivational commitments. With exceptions which are inherently limiting (such as the establishment of new colonies), this requires that membership be recruited by birth and socialization, initially and primarily through a kinship system, however much it may be supplemented by formal education and other mechanisms. The recruitment complex may be considered a mechanism of social control over the personality structures of the membership.

Finally, self-sufficiency implies adequate control over the economic-technological complex so that the physical environment can be utilized as a resource base in a purposeful and balanced way. This control is intertwined with political control of territory and with control of membership in relation to the residence-kinship complex.

No one of these sub-criteria of self-sufficiency is paramount, except in regard to their generalized relations in the cybernetic and conditional hierarchies. Severe deficiency in any one or any combination of the criteria may be sufficient to destroy a society, or to create chronic instability or rigidity that prevents its further evolution. Hence this scheme will prove particularly useful in explaining breakdowns in the process of social evolution.

THE STRUCTURAL COMPONENTS OF SOCIETIES

The foregoing exposition of the relations between a society and its environment has employed a relatively systematic classification of structural components. . . . Our initial definition of the societal community focused on the interrelatedness of two factors—namely, a *normative order* and a *collectively* organized population. For most general purposes in analyzing societies, we need not extend our classification of components beyond a single distinction within each of these factors. We will distinguish between the aspects of each factor which are primarily internal to the societal community and those which primarily connect it with environing systems.

On the normative side, we can distinguish between *norms* and *values*. Values —in the pattern sense[21]—we regard as the primary connecting element between the social and cultural systems. Norms, however, are primarily social. They have regulatory significance for social processes and relationships but do not embody "principles" which are applicable beyond *social* organization, or often even a particular social system. In more advanced societies, the structural focus of norms is the legal system.

On the side of organized population, the *collectivity* is the category of intrasocial structure and the *role* is the category of boundary-structure. The relevant boundary relation is with the personality of the individual member of the social system of reference. The boundary with the organic-physical complex is of an order that does not require distinct conceptualization in this context, although outputs from both personalities and the cultural system converge upon the organism in socialization processes, in the operation of skills, and in various other ways.

These four structural categories—values, norms, collectivities, roles—may be related to our general functional paradigm.[22] Values take primacy in the pattern maintenance functioning of a social system. Norms are primarily integrative; they regulate the great variety of processes that contribute to the implementation of patterned value commitments. The primary functioning of the collectivity concerns actual goal attainment on behalf of the social system. Where individuals perform *societally* important functions, it is in their capacity as collectivity members. Finally, the primary function of the role in the social system is adaptive. This is particularly clear for the category of service, as the capacity to fulfill valued role-performances is the most basic generalized adaptive resource of any society, though it must be coordinated with cultural, organic, and physical resources.

Any concrete structural unit of a social system is always a combination of all four components—the present classification involves *components, not types*. We often speak of a role or collectivity as if it were a concrete entity, but this is, strictly speaking, elliptical. There is no collectivity without member roles and, vice-versa, no role which is not part of a collectivity. Nor is there a role or collectivity which is not "regulated" by norms and characterized by a commitment to value patterns. For analytical purposes we can, for example, abstract the value components from a structure and describe them as *cultural* objects, but when they are employed technically as categories of social structure they *always* refer to components of social systems which *also* contain all three of the other types of components.

Nevertheless, the four categories of components are, in the nature of the case, independently variable. Knowing the value pattern of a collectivity does not, for example, make it possible to deduce its role-composition. Cases in which the contents of two or more types of components vary together so that the content of one can be deduced directly from another are special and limiting, not general, cases.

Thus, the *same* value patterns generally form structural parts of a wide variety of different units or sub-systems in a society and are frequently found at many levels in structural hierarchies. Furthermore, the *same* norms are often essential to the functioning of a variety of kinds of operative units. Thus, the legal rights of property entail common normative elements whether the holder of such rights is a family, a religious body, or a commercial firm. Of course, norms are differentiated by situation and function, but the bases of their differentiation are never the same as those of collectivities and roles. Within limits, then, it appears that *any* collectivity involved in a certain situation or performing a certain function will be regulated by a certain norm *regardless* of its other features. Finally, such independent variation is also characteristic of roles. For example, executive or managerial roles and certain types of professional roles are common to many types of collectivity, not just one.

The same basic principle of independent variation applies to the relations between the social system and its environing systems. It is the person in role, not the total concrete individual, who is the member of a collectivity, even the societal community. For example, I am a member of certain international collectivities which are not parts of the American societal community. The plural character of the roles assumed by one personality is a major foundation of sociological theory and must be kept in mind continually. As society evolves, role pluralism becomes more rather than less important, but it characterizes *any* society.

NOTES

1. Good modern reviews of evolutionary biology are George Gaylord Simpson, *The Meaning of Evolution* (New Haven: Yale University Press, 1950); and Ernst Mayr, *Animal Species and Evolution* (Cambridge: Harvard University Press, 1963).

2. See Chap. V in Roger Brown, *Words and Things* (Glencoe, Ill.: Free Press, 1958).

3. This point has been clearly stated by Alfred Emerson in "Homeostasis and Comparison of Systems," in Roy Grinker, ed., *Toward a Unified Theory of Human Behavior* (New York: Basic Books, 1956), pp. 147–162, especially p. 152.

4. A more detailed discussion of the relations of the personality to the other sub-systems of action is contained in Jesse R. Pitts, "Introduction " to Part Three of Talcott Parsons, Edward A. Shils, Kasper D. Naegele, and Jesse R. Pitts, eds., *Theories of Society* (New York: Free Press, 1961).

5. "Some Fundamental Categories of the Theory of Action," the general collaborative essay, and "Values, Motives and Systems of Action," the contribution of Talcott Parsons and Edward A. Shils in *Toward a General Theory of Action* (Cambridge: Harvard University Press, 1951). Also see Talcott Parsons, "Interaction," in the forthcoming *International Encyclopedia of the Social Sciences.*

6. I used Hobbes' statement as a major point of departure for my own treatment of the theory of the social system in *Structure of Social Action* (New York: McGraw-Hill, 1937).

7. Cf. Talcott Parsons, "Social Systems and Subsystems," in the forthcoming *International Encyclopedia of the Social Sciences.*

8 The theory of cybernetics was first developed by Norbert Wiener in *Cybernetics* (Cambridge: M.I.T. Press, 1948, second edition, 1961) and was applied to social problems in his *The Human Use of Human Beings* (Garden City, N.Y.: Anchor Books, 1954). A good introductory statement for the social scientist will be found in Karl W. Deutsch, *The Nerves of Government* (New York: Free Press, 1963).

9. This section concerns the relations between column II and columns III and IV in Table 2.

10. Talcott Parsons, "Some Reflections on the Place of Force in Social Process," in Harry Eckstein, ed., *Internal War: Basic Problems and Approaches* (New York: Free Press, 1964).

11. The following three sections concern relations obtaining between columns III and IV in Table 2.

12. Cf. Talcott Parsons and Robert F. Bales, *Family, Socialization, and Interaction Process* (Glencoe, Ill.: Free Press, 1955).

13. Cf. Benjamin Nelson, "Self-Images and Systems of Spiritual Direction in the History of European Civilization," in S. Z. Klausner, ed., *The Quest for Self-Control* (New York: Free Press, 1965).

14. Talcott Parsons, "The Political Aspect of Social Structure and Process," in David Easton, ed., *Varieties of Political Theory* (Englewood Cliffs, N.J.: Prentice-Hall, 1966).

15. Parsons, "Some Reflections on the Place of Force in Social Process."

16. *Skill* is essentially the internalization of certain elements of culture in the *organism*.

17. Talcott Parsons and Neil J. Smelser, *Economy and Society* (Glencoe, Ill.: Free Press, 1956).

18. Neil J. Smelser, *Social Change in the Industrial Revolution* (Chicago: University of Chicago Press, 1957).

19. The emphasis on enforcement here is concerned with the conditions of security of a normative order. Where collective goal-attainment, as discussed above, is at issue, the corresponding emphasis will be on the effective mobilization of services and non-human resources. They are linked by the fact that adequate normative order in the political system is a condition of effective mobilization for goal-attainment.

20. Clearly, such priorities do not preclude two-way relations between the levels involved. Certainly a technological innovation leading to a new product can "stimulate" a demand for that product. But such a change always raises a new problem of allocation at the economic level: Is it justified in terms of alternative ways the relevant resources may be used?

21. It is important not to confuse this usage with the one referring to *valued objects*, which has been maintained by such theorists as Thomas and Znaniecki, Lasswell, Easton, and Homans.

22. Cf. Talcott Parsons, "General Theory in Sociology," in Robert K. Merton, Leonard Broom, and Leonard S. Cottrell, Jr., eds., *Sociology Today* (New York: Basic Books, 1959, and Harper Torchbooks, 1965).

SYSTEMS

WALTER BUCKLEY

From Walter Buckley, *Sociology and Modern Systems Theory*, © 1967. Reprinted by permission of Prentice-Hall, Inc., Englewood Cliffs, New Jersey.

Walter Buckley is professor of sociology at the University of New Hampshire. He previously worked with the RAND Corporation and taught at the University of California, Santa Barbara.

We shall not . . . indulge to any great extent in the sport of defining the general concept of "system" in formal terms. Our main emphasis will be on the differences among the major types of systems specified in terms of their structural arrangements and dynamics, and on the methodological problems of analysis they raise.

The kind of system we are interested in may be described generally as a complex of elements or components directly or indirectly related in a causal network, such that each component is related to at least some others in a more or less stable way within any particular period of time.[1] The components may be relatively simple and stable, or complex and changing; they may vary in only one or two properties or take on many different states. The interrelations between them may be mutual or unidirectional, linear, non-linear or intermittent, and varying in degrees of causal efficacy or priority. The particular kinds of more or less stable interrelationships of components that become established at any time constitute the particular structure of the system at that time, thus achieving a kind of "whole" with some degree of continuity and boundary. Also, we are mainly interested in systems within which some process is continually going on, including an interchange with an environment across the boundary. It is generally agreed that when we deal with the more open system with a highly flexible structure, the distinction between the boundaries and the environment becomes a more and more arbitrary matter, dependent on the purpose of the observer.

SYSTEMS AND ENTITIES

In fact, it is becoming clear that we cannot make a neat division of those things that are and those that are not systems; rather, we shall have to recognize varying degrees of "systemness." And if we also recognize that the "substances" or "entities" that the various scientific disciplines study—nuclear "particles," atoms, molecules, solar systems, cells, organs, organisms, ecological communities, societies—are all subsumable under a definition of system, then we seem forced to accept the notion of varying degrees of "entitivity." If we continue to think in terms of "real substances" this does not seem to make much sense, for how can there be degrees of "substance"? But if substances or entities represent systems whose characteristics or properties are due to a particular *organization* of lower-level components, and if we admit of varying degrees of organization, the mystery disappears. For we can understand that it is the *organization* that ceases to exist or is formed when, for example, a nuclear particle is "annihilated" and

33

another "created," or water is broken down into hydrogen and oxygen or table salt built up from sodium and chlorine atoms, or a living cell dies and becomes nothing but its constituent molecules while a new living cell is synthesized from such constituents, or a social group dissolves into its constituent individuals as another is created out of previously unrelated persons.

Thus, if social groups are not "real entities" then neither are individual organisms, organs, cells, molecules or atoms, since they are all "nothing but" the constituents of which they are made. But this "nothing but" hides the central key to modern thinking—the fact of *organization* of components into systemic relationships. When we say that "the whole is more than the sum of its parts," the meaning becomes unambiguous and loses its mystery: the "more than" points to the fact of *organization*, which imparts to the aggregate characteristics that are not only *different* from, but often *not found in* the components alone; and the "sum of the parts" must be taken to mean, not their numerical addition, but their unorganized aggregation.

What we have led up to is a way of viewing the hoary problem of sociological nominalism vs. realism. Herbert Spencer, facing the question of the nature of this thing called "society," offered a criterion for an "entity" which is also basic to the concept of system.

Until we have decided whether or not to regard a society as an entity; and until we have decided whether, if regarded as an entity, a society is to be classed as absolutely unlike all other entities or as like some others; our conception of the subject matter before us remains vague.

It may be said that a society is but a collective name for a number of individuals . . . But . . . it is the permanence of the relations among component parts which constitutes the individuality of a whole as distinguished from the individualities of its parts.[2]

Though acceptable, Spencer's statement requires several comments. First, we cannot take too literally the criterion of *"permanence* of the relations," for although some stability is necessary to constitute a persisting system, we have to allow for the possibility that aspects of a system's structure may change from time to time or even continuously without the dissolution of the system itself. Secondly, the question of whether society is absolutely unlike or like some other entities cannot be taken to imply a black or white distinction, for we can probably always find both similarities and differences between any two systems. Spencer argued cogently that since the constant relations among its parts make society an entity, then between a society and any other entity "the only conceivable resemblance must be one due to parallelism of principle in the arrangement of components."[3] He then went on to draw the analogy between society and organism. . . .

The grounds for his jump from society to organism, however, were not very solid, and modern systems theory is now in a position to advance his line of reasoning in a more acceptable direction.

Generally speaking, we might say that the modern concepts of system and organization are now taking over the duty of the overworked and perhaps retiring concept of the "organic." This concept, along with that of mechanical equilibrium, has performed the essential job of bringing the social scientist to full recognition of the fact that the parts of society are not independent, that society is to some degree an interrelated whole. But further advance required that we come to appreciate the important ways in which society differs from the organic or the mechanical.

An important shift of focus occurred with the growing recognition of the fact that, while phenomena of widely differing kinds are wholes constituted by more or less permanent relations of parts, a crucial distinguishing feature is *the particular nature of those relations*. After Spencer, it became clearer and clearer that whereas the relations of parts of an organism are physiological, involving complex physico-chemical *energy* interchanges, the relations of parts of society are primarily psychic, involving complex communicative processes of *information* exchange, and that this difference makes all the difference.

As Becker and Barnes have noted,[4] the shift from the "organismic" view to the later "organic" view gradually led such students as Schäffle, Tarde, and Worms to the psychosocial perspective of "mental interactionism," developed in illuminating detail by Baldwin, Cooley, and G. A. Mead. It was only after their analysis of the nature and dynamics of the psychic interrelations of the components that the underlying nature of the wholeness of society, which even Durkheim comprehended but vaguely, was understood to a point where a truly fundamental resolution of the so-called Hobbesian problem of order and disorder became possible. Their insight was summed up in the notion that the individual is truly social and society truly psychical. Thus it was no longer a question of the individual *vs.* society; it was no longer relevant to ask how group unity or societal order is possible when we only experience discrete individuals. The answer emerging was that society's "individuals" are *not* discrete. What is discrete to the human observer's limited sensory apparatus is simply the physical organism. The behaving individual—the psychological person—is essentially an organization that is developed and maintained only in and through a continually ongoing symbolic interchange with other persons. Some of these interchanges become repetitive and expected in certain situations—and we then refer to a "structure" of relatively stable social interrelationships comprising organizations and institutions. It is these psychosocially developed and supported webs of communicative interrelations of varying degrees of permanence that give society some degree of wholeness, or make it an "entity" in its own right, to be studied by techniques and perspectives different from those used in studying the entity called "the individual."

It is not necessary to trace the often tedious and unrewarding nominalist-realist argument. What is of interest to us is the recent transition of the question from one of either–or to the problem of *degrees* of wholeness or unity, *degrees* of integration, *degrees* of "entitivity" or "systemness." The psychologist Donald T. Campbell[5] in a recent paper to which our discussion is already indebted, argues that it is methodologically improper to assume axiomatically that the social groups we are studying constitute entities or systems. This is, rather, an hypothesis to be tested. To this end he addresses himself to the general psychological problem of how we perceive entities. . . .

Campbell then goes on to set forth a number of criteria of "entitativity," derived in part from Wertheimer's principles of perceptual organization, which lead discrete elements to be perceived as parts of a whole. Among these are: proximity, similarity, common fate, and "pregnance" or completed boundary. To the principles of Gestalt psychology are added criteria determined by 1) reflection or resistance to intrusions of external energy, matter, or diagnostic probes (for example, for groups, the sentry's challenge, indoctrination procedures, or permeability), and 2) internal diffusion, transfer, or communication rates and boundaries." Campbell recognizes, however, that some of these criteria may be relatively superficial or less essential when it comes to social groups or societies. But his analysis in general should go a long way in breaking down the naive epistemology underlying much of social science.[6]

We shall not take up here the question of exact specification and measurement of degrees of systemness, organization, or "entitativity." Current statistical techniques of association, correlation and variance analysis, and the like, can be considered, of course, crude measures of these. However, the problem of specifying and measuring the degree of organization or structure seems solvable in principle by such techniques as those of information theory and graph theory, though the era of their application to social organization has barely begun. . . .

COMPARATIVE SYSTEMS

We turn now to a more detailed consideration of the nature of the organization characterizing and differentiating types of systems. Our purposes are

1. To probe somewhat deeper into the intricacies of analysis of the nature of organization—beyond the mere interdependence of parts which characterizes any system;
2. To promote a deeper appreciation of the differences between the organization and dynamics of mechanical, organic, and sociocultural systems;
3. To introduce some key conceptions of modern systems analysis.

Since the types of systems we discuss here represent only three points along a series of possible system levels, our generalizations will only approximate any particular empirical system. And especially in the case of the mechanical system, our model is sometimes the man-made Machine enthroned in the eighteenth and nineteenth centuries, the prototype often being the clock, rather than natural physical systems. The Machine in this context will refer to the pre-cybernetic type, without deviation-regulating feedback loops. But to represent a system in equilibrium, our model may be a collection of gases or other substances at different temperatures, pressures, or concentrations, interacting in isolation from other influences long enough to reach an equilibrium state.

System Parts: Simple to Complex

The *nature of the parts* or components of a mechanical system are, typically, relatively simple in their own structure, stable, and not appreciably or permanently affected by being part of the system. By contrast, as we proceed up through the organic and sociocultural levels the components that are interrelated become more complex in their own organization, more and more unstable (more easily subject to change by small forces), and more fundamentally alterable by the workings of the system of which they are a part. These features, of course, are all prerequisite to the very development of higher levels of organization.

Systemic Relations: Energy Links to Information Links

The *nature of the relations* among components varies importantly along many dimensions for different types of system. In mechanical systems of the machine type the interrelations are typically narrowly restricted, with very few degrees of freedom in the behavior of the components. The structure of the system is rigid, and we have an example of what Rapoport calls "organized simplicity."[7] In the typical equilibrium system of particle mechanics we find conditions at the opposite extreme, "chaotic complexity."[8] There are so many degrees of freedom in the relations of components that states of the system can only be specified statistically, and there is little or no stable structure.

Organic and sociocultural systems are examples of "organized complexity."[9] As we proceed up the various levels, the relations of parts become more flexible and the "structure" more fluid with process as the set of alternative behaviors open to the components increases. Whereas the relations among components of mechanical systems are a function primarily of spatial and temporal considerations and the transmission of energy from one component to another, the interrelations characterizing higher levels come to depend more and more on the transmission of *information*—a principle fundamental to modern complex system analysis ... Though "information" is dependent on some physical base or energy flow, the energy component is entirely subordinate to the particular form or structure of variations that the physical base or flow may manifest. In the process of transmitting information, the base or carrier energy may change in many ways—as in the production and reproduction of phonograph records—but the structure of variations in the various media remains invariant over the carrier transformations. This structured variation—the marks of writing, the sounds of speech, the molecular arrangement of the genetic code substance DNA, etc—is still only raw material or energy unless it "corresponds" to, or matches in some important way, the structure of variations of other components to which it may thereby become dynamically related. A person speaking a language foreign to a companion is emitting only noise or vibrating energy as far as the latter is concerned, because there is no mapping of the structured variety of the vocal energy with the repertoire of meaningful sounds structured in the mind of the companion. If the latter did understand the language, however, and the information spoken was, "Look out, a car is coming at you!"—the very small amount of vocal energy would trigger off a large amount of energy in the companion who is acting as the receiving system.[10]

Thus, "information" is not a substance or concrete entity but rather a *relationship* between sets or ensembles of structured variety—to put it very generally. The implications of this shift from energy flow to information flow as a basis for the interrelations of components in higher level systems are of central importance in distinguishing the nature and behavioral capabilities of the latter, as against lower-level systems. Thus, a minute amount of structured energy or matter from one component of a higher system is able to "trigger" selectively a large amount of activity or behavior in other components in the system, at the same time overcoming limitations of temporal and spatial proximity as well as availability of energy. The components of systems thus become more autonomous in certain respects while still maintaining intimate and more intricate interrelation with one another. The structure of the system becomes more and more "fluid" as it merges with process—the communication process which is its predominant feature. At the higher ecological, social, and sociocultural system levels, the component individuals need come into physical contact in the manner of mechanical systems only or principally in sexual union and physical combat.

Interactions among components mediated by the selective "triggering" of information flows are possible, of course, only because 1) the system components are themselves organized and relatively unstable, or "sensitive," or in "tension," such that they react easily to a small influence of the correct type (or code) and can release much larger amounts of bound energy than that embodied in the triggering signal; and 2) each of the alternative behaviors open to the system components have somehow become associated with one of the structural arrangements embodying the information code.

Donald M. MacKay is one of the small number of systems theorists who have tackled the question of *semantic* information from the perspective of modern information theory,[11] and his work enlightens our present discussion. He begins by suggesting that so little progress is being made on the semantic side of information theory because of a failure to study the communicative process within a wide enough context to embrace, not only the channel and the nature of the signals flowing through it, but the terminal sender and receiver as goal-directed, self-adaptive systems. In a manner that strongly suggests the pioneering work of G. H. Mead . . . MacKay then conceptualizes an organism as a system with a repertoire of basic acts that, in various combinations, make up its behavior. . . . Within this conceptual framework, MacKay then goes on to define information, meaning, and communication, in a generalized way that we believe to be especially congenial to, and an important theoretical underpinning for, the social interactionist perspective in sociology.

Though oriented particularly toward the human, adaptive level, this conceptualization is broad enough to embrace the various evolutionary levels of the process of communication of information, from the genetic, biochemical information processes directing the formation or maintenance of organic structure, through tropistic and instinctual matchings with the environment, to individual learning and cultural accumulation processes. The key underlying notions in all cases . . . are: 1) the matching of two or more sets of structured things or events; and 2) the selectivity thus made possible on the action of a subset of one by a subset of another. In a real sense, then, information can "represent" structure or organization, and thus can preserve it, transmit it over space and time, and change it. The evolution of levels leading up to the sociocultural system show greater and greater dependence on indirect, arbitrary, or symbolic communication linkage of components and less and less on substantive and energy linkages, until at the sociocultural level the system is linked almost entirely by conventionalized information exchange, with *process* overshadowing any rigid substantial structure such as is found at organismic levels.

From Closed to Open Systems

The transition from mechanical systems to adaptive, information-processing systems is closely related to the transition from the relatively *closed* to the *open* type of system. That a system is *open* means, not simply that it engages in interchanges with the environment, but that this interchange is *an essential factor* underlying the system's viability, its reproductive ability or continuity, and its ability to change. As L. J. Henderson was at great pains to point out in his book, *The Fitness of the Environment*, the environment is just as basic as the organic system in the intimate system-environment transactions that account for the particular adaptation and evolution of complex systems.[12] In fact, of course, the system and its environment make up sub-parts of a wider system which often must be treated on its own level. Indeed, this is a key principle underlying the field or transactional approach.

The typical response of natural, closed systems to an intrusion of environmental events is a loss of organization, or a change in the direction of dissolution of the system (although, depending on the nature and strength of the intrusion, the system may sometimes move to a new level of equilibrium). On the other hand, the typical response of open systems to environmental intrusions is elaboration or change of their structure to a higher or more complex level. This is due to factors discussed above: the environmental interchange is not, or does not long remain, random or unstructured, but rather becomes selective due to the mapping, or coding, or information-processing capabilities (that is, its adaptiveness) inherent in this type of system. This is true whether the system is the lowliest biological organism or a complex sociocultural system. And as we proceed up the system levels we find the systems becoming more and more open in the sense that they become involved in a wider interchange with a greater variety of aspects of the environment, that is, are capable of mapping or responding selectively to a greater range and detail of the endless variety of the environment. At the sociocultural level the details of the natural environment become subordinate to the social, gestural, symbolic environment which is now mapped and responded to selectively in greater detail as the basis of group life.

The important distinction between open and closed systems has often been expressed in terms of "entropy": closed systems tend to increase in entropy—to "run down"; open systems are "negentropic"—tending to decrease in entropy, or to elaborate structure.[13] To apply the concept of equilibrium to open systems is to miss this important distinction.

System Tension

As we noted earlier, the source of action and interaction of the parts of mechanical systems is expressed in the physical concept of energy, whereas in complex, adaptive systems raw energy plays a less and less important role as it gives way to a more complex form of organized and directed motive force that we refer to as the inherent "irritability of protoplasm," tension or stress in animals, and psychic energy or motive power in men. "Tension," in the broad sense, of which "stress" and "strain" are manifestations under conditions of felt blockage, is ever present in one form or another throughout the sociocultural system—sometimes as diffuse, socially unstructured strivings, frustrations, enthusiasms, aggressions, neurotic or normative deviation; sometimes as clustered and minimally structured crowd or quasi-group processes, normatively constructive as well as destructive; and sometimes as socioculturally structured creativity and production, conflict and competition, or upheaval and destruction. As Thelen and colleagues put it:

1. Man is always trying to live beyond his means. Life is a sequence of reactions to stress; Man is continually meeting situations with which he cannot quite cope.
2. In stress situations, energy is mobilized and a state of tension is produced.
3. The state of tension tends to be disturbing, and Man seeks to reduce the tension.
4. He has direct impulses to take action . . .[14]

Thus it can be argued that, far from seeing any principle of "inertia" operating in complex adaptive systems, with "tension" occurring only occasionally or residually as a "disturbing" factor, we must see some level of tension as characteristic of and vital to such systems though it may manifest itself as now destructive, now constructive.

Feedback and Purposive Systems

Given the open, negentropic, information-processing nature of complex adaptive systems, we still need a more exact delineation of the mechanisms whereby these systems come to behave in a characteristic manner so different from physical systems—a manner usually expressed by the concept of "purposive." It is generally agreed among systems theorists that a basic principle underlying these purposive, or goal-seeking mechanisms is embodied in the concept of "feedback."[15] The notion of feedback is seen as finally removing the ancient mysticism associated with teleology by redefining it in operationally respectable terms. As Anatol Rapoport has argued, the trend is definitely toward explanation in terms of "efficient" causes operating here and now, and not of "final" causes (or future events, system "requirements," or ultimate functions). Today we can treat "purpose" causally in the former sense of forces acting here and now; if we can build a model of purposefulness, we can explain it.[16]

The concept of feedback has now been vulgarized, and is very often equated simply with any reciprocal interaction between variables. As a principle underlying the goal-seeking behavior of complex systems, however, it involves much more than that. As used here, it applies particularly to an open system:

1. Whose characteristic features depend on certain internal parameters or criterion variables remaining within certain limits;
2. Whose organization has developed a selective sensitivity, or mapped relationship, to environmental things or events of relevance to these criterion variables;
3. Whose sensory apparatus is able to distinguish any deviations of the systems' internal states and/or overt behavior from goal-states defined in terms of the criterion variables;
4. Such that feedback of this "mismatch" information into the system's behavior-directing centers reduces (in the case of negative feedback) or increases (in the case of positive feedback) the deviation of the system from its goal-states or criterion limits.

Even the simple thermostat meets these basic requirements: it is a system of components open to one aspect of the environment, and contains: 1) A criterion variable representing the particular temperature setting selected, 2) An element sensitive to the temperature of the surrounding air such that 3) The system responds to deviations of the air temperature on either side of the setting by 4) Turning on or off the heating component such that the deviation is reduced (hence, an example of negative feedback). We shall refer to simpler closed causal loops, lacking in internal variables, as "pseudo-feedback" loops.

Feedback-controlled systems are referred to as *goal-directed*, and not merely *goal-oriented*, since it is the deviations from the goal-state itself that direct the behavior of the system, rather than some predetermined internal mechanism that aims blindly. The significance of feedback control for complex systems can be partially expressed by a comparison of "pre-cybernetic" machines with modern servomechanisms. In the former, the designer had to attempt to anticipate all the contingencies the machine was apt to meet in performing its task, and to build counteracting features into the design; the modern machine, however, uses these very contingencies themselves as information which, fed into the machine, directs it against them. The great gain in capabilities is easily understood in these terms.

Of particular interest to us here in dealing with the evolution of complex adaptive systems is the development of more and more complex criterion-testing subsystems. Our concern is not so much with homeostatic mechanisms, which may or may not be made more comprehensible by translation into feedback terms, but rather with mechanisms that direct system behavior. These latter mechanisms run the gamut from tropistic, instinctual, and reflexive feedback testing mechanisms, to learned, conscious, symbol-actuated subsystems, to the mechanisms of social planning. It may be questionable whether all mechanisms on each of these levels involve true feedback, but it seems clear that higher levels of control, from cortical learning on, can only be adequately understood in terms of complex, often higher order feedback transaction. . . .[17]

Karl W. Deutsch has provided a very useful discussion of the advances in social system analysis provided by the concept of feedback as contrasted with the notions of equilibrium or homeostasis. . . . For Deutsch, feedback

is a more sophisticated notion than the simple mechanical notion of equilibrium, and it promises to become a more powerful tool in the social sciences than the traditional equilibrium analysis.[18]

In Deutsch's view, to say that a social system is in equilibrium implies that: 1) it will return to a particular state when disturbed; 2) the disturbance is coming from outside the system; 3) the greater the disturbance the greater the force with which the system will return to its original state; 4) the speed of the system's reaction to disturbance is somehow less relevant—a sort of friction, or blemish having no place in the "ideal" equilibrium; 5) no catastrophe can happen within the system, but once the equilibrium is disturbed, almost nothing can be said of the future of the society. Such equilibrium theories, Deutsch points out, are based on the very restricted field of "steady state dynamics," and are not well suited to deal with transient events, to predict the consequences of sudden changes. "Altogether, in the world of equilibrium theory, there is no growth, no evolution, no sudden changes, no efficient prediction of the consequences of 'friction' over time."[19]

Feedback theory, on the other hand, does not push "friction" into the background, but can deal specifically with the "lag" and "gain" between impinging events. Large "lag" can be conceptualized as a swing away from common goals so far before feedback correction occurs that only violent reaction, for example, revolution, can bring the social system back to a more viable, goal-oriented state.

A full appreciation of the role and nature of feedback permits a relatively objective attack on the problem of assessment and correction of the "lag" in the system.

Deutsch further promotes our conception of feedback by suggesting the kinds of information required to "steer" a society, the kinds or levels of feedback underlying system effectiveness, and the successive levels of purpose thereby made possible. For effective "self-direction" a sociocultural system must continue to receive a *full flow* of three kinds of information: 1) information of the world outside; 2) information from the past, with a wide range of recall and recombination; and 3) information about itself and its own parts. Three kinds of feedback, which make use of these types of information, include: 1) *goal-seeking*—feedback of new external data into the system net whose operational channels remain unchanged; 2) *learning*—feedback of new external data for the *changing of these operating channels themselves*, that is, a change in the structure of the system; and 3) *consciousness*, or "self-awareness"—feedback of new *internal* data via secondary messages, messages about changes in the state of parts of the system itself. These secondary messages serve as symbols or internal labels for changes of state within the net. Finally, four successively higher orders of purposes can be recognized: 1) seeking of immediate satisfaction; 2) self-preservation, which may require overruling the first; 3) preservation of the group; and 4) preservation of a process of goal-seeking beyond any one group. These orders of purpose, of course, require successively higher-order feedback nets.[20]

These suggestions, of course, need extensive development but may serve here to make the point that, whereas the concept of "equilibrium" is restricted to descriptions of steady states, the cybernetic view is based on full dynamics, including change of state as an inherent and necessary aspect of complex system operation. In particular, it can be seen that cybernetics offers to restore the problem of purpose to a fuller share of attention, and even to help us make a much needed distinction between the attainment of actual external goals, and the reduction of goal-drive merely by internal readjustment that provides an ersatz satisfaction (or short-circuit), such as scapegoating, drug addiction, or other so-called "mechanisms of control." In Deutsch's view, more complex, goal-changing, feedback conceptions take this distinction into account. . . .

Morphostasis and Morphogenesis

The various features of complex adaptive systems sketched so far—openness, information-linkage of the parts and the environment, feedback loops, goal-direction, and so forth—provide the basic conceptual elements that underlie the general features characteristic of systems referred to as "self-regulating," "self-directing," and "self-organizing." These concepts all point to the fact that the behavior of complex, open systems is not a simple and direct function of impinging external forces, as is the case with colliding billiard balls or gravitational systems. Rather, as open systems become more complex there develop within them more and more complex mediating processes that intervene between external forces and behavior. At higher levels these mediating processes become more and more independent or autonomous, and more determinative of behavior. They come to perform the operations of: 1) temporarily adjusting the system to external contingencies; 2) directing the system toward more congenial environments; and 3) permanently reorganizing aspects of the system itself to deal perhaps more effectively with the environment. The "self" in "self-regulation," "self-direction," and "self-organizing" points, of course, to these mediating processes, though we tend to use the term "self" in its full sense only on the human level. However, the perspective we are taking argues that an understanding of the mediating processes on lower system levels should help us understand their nature and workings on the higher level: sharp discontinuities are not to be found.

Some of the connotations of these concepts of "self-regulation" and the like are misleading, whether applied to modern machines, men, or groups, since the tendency is to overemphasize the independence of the internal system at the expense of situational or environmental variables. For this reason it might be profitable to utilize more neutral terms for the two basic processes of interest to us here, namely, *morphostasis* and *morphogenesis*. The former refers to those processes in complex system-environment exchanges that tend to preserve or maintain a system's given form, organization, or state. Morphogenesis will refer to those processes which tend to elaborate or change a system's given form, structure, or state. Homeostatic processes in organisms, and ritual in sociocultural systems are examples of "morphostasis"; biological evolution, learning, and societal development are examples of "morphogenesis."

We have already discussed morphostatic processes in dealing with equilibrium, homeostasis, and negative feedback. These conserving, deviation-counterbalancing processes have come to be emphasized in the literature at the expense of structure-elaborating, deviation-promoting processes that are central to an understanding of higher level systems such as the sociocultural. Just as the concept of negative feedback has provided insight into the mechanisms underlying homeostatic processes, the concept of positive feedback provides insight into the mechanisms underlying structure-building, or morphogenesis. Magoroh Maruyama has recently argued very effectively the case for greater concern with the latter. . . . [21] Maruyama gives as one example the development of a city in an agricultural plain. A farmer starts a farm at some chance spot on the homogeneous plain. Other farmers are attracted and follow suit. Someone opens a tool shop, someone else a food stand, and gradually a village grows. The village facilitates the marketing of crops and attracts more farms. The increased activity and population necessitates the development of industry, and the village becomes a city.

One of the many evolutionary examples is the adaptation of varieties of a species to colder and colder climates. In the beginning some mutants are enabled to live at a somewhat colder temperature than normal for the species. They move to a colder climate, where further mutations occur. Some of these are unfit for the colder climate and die off, but other mutants can stand even colder surroundings than their parents and move to a still colder climate. This deviation-amplifying process continues until some limit is reached.

Many illuminating examples in the sociocultural realm could also be given. Besides the above processes of growth or adaptive structural change, there are the often nonadaptive processes such as those embodied in Myrdal's "vicious circle" theory of racial discrimination, whereby initial prejudice generates those personal and social characteristics of Negroes that are then seen to justify further discrimination which, in turn, aggravates further the Negroes' condition.[22] Another example is the process by which the malfunctioning of bureaucratic organizations may occur. March and Simon have traced out, in *Organizations*, a model of Robert Merton's theory of bureaucracy which, in simplified form, starts with the demand for control made on the organization by upper management. This demand takes the form of an emphasis on the reliability of behavior of lower-level administrators, operationalized in terms of accountability and predictability of behavior. This, in turn, leads to a rigid adherence to rules and mutual defense of members' positions. But this creates difficulties in administrator-client relations, which lead to a felt need for defensibility of individual action. The net effect of client pressure on lower and higher officials is to tighten further the top official emphasis on reliability, thus closing the positive feedback loop leading back to a more rigid adherence to rules and a more vigorous defense of status. In sum, deviation from the goal of satisfying clients tends to reinforce the very factors creating the deviation.[23]

As Maruyama points out, there are a number of methodological implications to be drawn from the consideration of these morphogenetic processes. The classical principle of causality held that similar conditions produce similar effects, and consequently dissimilar results are due to dissimilar conditions.[24] Bertalanffy, in analyzing the self-regulating, or morphostatic, features of open biological systems, loosened this classical conception by introducing the concept of "equifinality."[25] This holds that, in ontogenesis for example, a final normal adult state may be reached by any number of devious developmental routes. Morphogenetic processes, however, go even further and suggest an opposite principle that might be called "multifinality":[26] similar initial conditions may lead to dissimilar end-states. Thus, two cultures developing in very similar ecological environments may end up with very different sociocultural systems. In the example of city growth, Maruyama suggests that if a historian should try to find the "cause" of the city's growth in that particular spot he will be unable to do so either in terms of the initial homogeneity of the plain or the decision of the first farmer.

The secret of the growth of the city is in the process of deviation-amplifying mutual positive feedback networks rather than in the initial condition or in the initial kick. This process, rather than the initial condition, has generated the complexly structured city. It is in this sense that the deviation-amplifying mutual causal process is called "morphogenesis."[27]

Such considerations provide a more precise and basic methodological rationale for the transactional approach to the study of complex adaptive systems. For example, the classical approach to the study of delinquent or criminal behavior was to look either at personality or at the environing situation. We now, however, can appreciate more fully the possibility that some deviation-amplifying transaction operating between the personality system and the situation has *generated* the deviant outcome. The initial conditions in either the personality or the situation may or may not be relevant or causally dominant.

A partial generalization of the morphogenic process is suggested in Maruyama's discussion of the biologist's puzzlement over the fact that the amount of information stored in the genes is much too small to specify the detailed structure of the adult individual. The puzzle can be resolved if we find that it is not necessary for the genes to carry all the detailed information, but rather that it suffices for them to carry *a set of rules to generate the information*. This can be conceptualized, for example, in terms of rules specifying the general direction and amount of cellular growth in terms of the immediate spatial and cellular environment of the growing tissues; the details are then generated by the *interactions* of the cells, tissues and other limiting boundaries and gradients. Thus, though the total process is deterministic, it is not possible or necessary to specify in the initial condition whether, for example, a particular part of an embryo is to become eye-tissue or skin tissue. . . .

This principle applies equally to the sociocultural system. There is not enough information, knowledge, or decision-making power when simply summed over all the relevant individuals or groups to account for the full-blown complex organization, the metropolitan agglomeration, the body of scientific theory, or the developed religious dogma. The sociocultural pattern is generated by the rules (norms, laws, and values—themselves generated in a similar manner) *and by the interactions* among normatively and purposively oriented individuals and subgroups in an ecological setting. Full understanding and explanation can appeal, alone, neither to early history nor common human characteristics (initial conditions), nor to final structure and functions. Attention must finally be paid to the interactions generated by the rules, seen as only limiting frameworks of action; to the new information, meanings, and revised rules generated by the interactions; and to the more or less temporary social products that represent the current state or structure of the on-going process. Only one-sided, highly selective observation and conceptualization could lead us to see a principle of "social in-ertia" or a predominance of morphostatic processes operating in the sociocultural realm.

NOTES

1. A good statement of the concept of "system" may be found in Arthur D. Hall and R. E. Fagen, "Definition of Systems," *General Systems*, 1 (1956), 18–28.

2. Herbert Spencer, *Principles of Sociology*, 3rd ed. (New York: Appleton-Century-Crofts, 1897), p. 447.

3. Ibid., p. 448.

4. Howard Becker and Harry E. Barnes, *Social Thought from Lore to Science*, 3rd ed., 2 (New York: Dover, 1961), pp. 688–92.

5. Donald T. Campbell, "Common Fate, Similarity, and Other Indices of the Status of Aggregates of Persons as Social Entities," *Behavioral Science*, 3 (1958), 11.

6. See also Ralph W. Gerard, "Entitation, Animorgs, and Other Systems," in Mihajlo D. Mesarović, ed., *Views on General Systems Theory* (New York: Wiley, 1964), Chap. 8.

7. Anatol Rapoport and William J. Horvath, "Thoughts on Organization Theory," *General Systems*, 4 (1959), 89.

8. Ibid.

9. Ibid.

10. A more pertinent example for the social researcher is the central methodological problem of mapping the researcher's scientifically oriented cognitive structure into the re-search subject's common-sense mapping (interpretive understanding) of the structured va-riety of the external situation of action. This example is suggested by the extensive dis-cussion of the problem in Aaron V. Cicourel, *Method and Measurement in Sociology* (New York: Free Press, 1964).

11. Donald M. MacKay, "The Informational Analysis of Questions and Commands," in *Information Theory: Fourth London Symposium*, ed. Colin Cherry (London: Butterworth & Co., Publisher, Ltd., 1961).

12. Lawrence J. Henderson, *The Fitness of the Environment* (New York: Macmillan, 1915).

13. See Erwin Schrödinger, *What Is Life?* (London: Cambridge University Press, 1945); and Leon Brillouin, "Life, Thermodynamics, and Cybernetics," *American Scientist*, 37 (1949), 554–568.

14. Herbert A. Thelen, "Emotionality and Work in Groups," in Leonard D. White, ed., *The State of the Social Sciences* (Chicago: University of Chicago Press, 1956), pp. 184–186. Such a conception also underlies the pragmatism or social behaviorism of William James, John Dewey, and G. H. Mead.

15. Arturo Rosenblueth, Norbert Weiner, and Julian Bigelow, "Behavior, Purpose, and Teleology," *Philosophy of Science*, 10 (1943), 18–24; Arturo Rosenblueth and Norbert Wei-ner, "Purposeful and Non-Purposeful Behavior," *Philosophy of Science*, 17 (1950), 318–326; W. Ross Ashby, *An Introduction to Cybernetics* (London: Chapman & Hall, 1956); C. W. Churchman and R. L. Ackoff, "Purposive Behavior and Cybernetics," *Social Forces*, 29 (1950), 32–39. For a critical review, see Richard Taylor, "Comments on a Mechanistic Con-ception of Purposefulness," and "Purposeful and Non-Purposeful Behavior: A Rejoinder," *Philosophy of Science*, 17 (1950), 310–317, 327–332.

16. Anatol Rapoport, in Roy Grinker, ed., *Toward a Unified Theory of Human Be-havior* (New York: Basic Books, 1956), Chap. 17.

17. See, for example, Derek H. Fender, "Control Mechanisms of the Eye," *Scientific American*, 211 (July 1964).

18. Karl W. Deutsch, "Mechanism, Teleology, and Mind," *Philosophy and Phenom-enological Research*, 12 (1951), 185–222. Quote is on p. 198.

19. Ibid.

20. Ibid., p. 201.

21. Magoroh Maruyama, "The Second Cybernetics: Deviation-Amplifying Mutual Causal Processes," *American Scientist*, 51(1963), 164–179.

22. Gunnar Myrdal, *An American Dilemma* (New York: Harper & Row, 1944), pp. 75–78.

23. James G. March and Herbert A. Simon, *Organizations* (New York: Wiley, 1958), pp. 37–41.

24. Myrdal, *An American Dilemma.*

25. Ludwig von Bertalanffy, *Problems of Life* (New York: Harper & Row, Torchbook ed., 1960), pp. 142 ff.

26. This concept is perhaps implied in the biological notion of "equipotential."

27. M. Maruyama, "The Second Cybernetics," p. 166.

CHAPTER 2

NEOPOSITIVISM AND THEORY CONSTRUCTION

Introduction

In terms of the number of conscious (or perhaps unconscious) adherents, neopositivism is the largest "school" in contemporary sociology. Neopositivism's major premise is that sociology is, or should be, a science and should, therefore, follow the methods of the natural, or more commonly, the physical, sciences. According to Wagner (1963), "It largely identifies scientific procedure with quantification and measuring.... Advanced forms ... are based on systems of interlinked causal (instead of functional) propositions which are expected to lend themselves to an eventual mathematical restatement of theory" (p. 737). With recently available computer techniques—factor, regression, and path analysis—this can lead to the generation of theory directly from empirical data. The more common approach for sociology students is the research scheme usually propounded in methodology classes: Hypotheses are deduced from theory, usually a classical one, and operationalized. Data are then collected and analyzed to verify the theory. Brief perusal of major sociological journals reveals the preponderance of these mathematical-verification styles.

Neopositivism has deep roots in sociological thought. August Comte laid the foundation for a sociology based on a philosophical positivism, but the modern variety stems more from a statistical tradition that may be traced to the Belgian Quételet (1796–1874). Three bases have been discerned by Timasheff (1967:139–140): *quantitativism*, which stresses measurement, whose main proponents were Galton (1822–1911) and Pearson (1857–1936); *behaviorism*, which stresses the exclusive study of observable behavior and is represented by the work of J. B. Watson (1878–1958) and contemporary exchange theory; and what he calls *positivistic epistemology*, derived from the philosophy of James (1842–1910) and Dewey (1859–1952).

The most eminent (and radical) recent neopositivist was George A. Lundberg (1895–1966). He insisted on the importance of measurement, on the necessity for operational—that is, measurable—definitions. His work contributed to the mathematical sociology developed by Dodd,

47

Zipf, and Hart. (For a full treatment of this period see Timasheff, 1967: 193–209.)

Part of contemporary neopositivism stems directly from the rather atheoretical survey research of the 1950's. Under the proddings of Merton's previously cited urgings for "theories of the middle range," researchers became much more attuned to the theoretical implications of their work. Although this often only meant adding a few citations to classical theorists in research reports, it did lead to serious attempts to collate and generalize research findings. Zetterberg (1965), for example, has suggested the development of what he calls "axiomatic theory," which would build from verified hypotheses to interrelated sets of propositions. The hypotheses would be developed from originating axioms and postulates, so the scheme is both inductive and deductive. Zetterberg's scheme, however, has not been universally accepted as adequate for theory construction (see, for example, Movahedi and Ogles, 1973).

Contemporary theory constructionists are more inductive in their approach and utilize modern computer techniques. There is still a strong emphasis on the scientific nature of the discipline (see, for example, Wallace, 1971), but it is less unitary than the image projected by Zetterberg. Much attention has been given to the process of theory construction (Dumont and Wilson, 1967; Stinchcombe, 1968; Dubin, 1969; and Mullins, 1971). Blalock (1964, 1966, 1969, 1971) and others (for example, Costner, 1969) have moved theory construction toward the mathematical investigation of causal relationships, which has stimulated the increasing sophistication in methodology (see Leik and Grove, 1969; Borgatta and Bohrnstedt, 1969, 1970). Path analysis has been applied to theory construction (Duncan, 1966; Werts, 1968) and has produced major new analyses of substantive areas of sociology (for example, Blau and Duncan, 1967, on stratification), and mathematical sociology has developed apace (White, 1970).

The criticism of neopositivism has been continuous and often heated. What some might see as the flowering of a truly cumulative and scientific sociology is seen by others in the discipline as "quantaphenia," or as a meaningless jumble of numbers and formulas which add little to our understanding of social life. Bierstedt (1974:133–149) has thoroughly critiqued empiricism on this score and Lundberg in particular (1955:41–71). Mills (1959) described the survey research of the 1950's as "abstracted empiricism" that would never add to significant knowledge. McHugh (1970) and Churchill (1971) have recently criticized neopositivism from the perspective of ethnomethodology, and Hampden-Turner (1970) has produced a radical attempt to demolish the foundations of scientism.

In his presidential address to the American Sociological Association in 1975, Lewis A. Coser singled out ethnomethodology and what is here labeled neopositivism for this attack. In an update of Mills' (1959) critique of "abstracted empiricism," Coser argues that the new methods are too often deflecting sociologists from theoretical tasks. They become, he claims, "Frankenstein monsters when they are applied indiscriminantly and, above all, when their availability dictates the problem choices of the investigator so that trivial problems are treated with the utmost refinement" (Coser, 1975:692). "Too often," he continues "they are used as 'magic helpers' as a shortcut to, or even replacement for, theoretical analysis rather than as a means for furthering it" (p. 693). Such use of these methods (for example, path analysis) is encouraged by leading journals, graduate training, and professional pressures to publish (Coser, 1975:592–693). Coser is not opposed to the methods in themselves, but to the distortions produced by their misuse and to the neglect of study not amenable to their techniques—for example, in studies of stratification (pp. 694–95).

Two sociologists have responded to Coser's harsh critique. Featherman (1976) argues that conventionality in the field, rather than stifling creativity, in fact aids "cumulative scientific exchange in sociology" (p. 22). While not defending poor work, he maintains that quantitative methods have led to major contributions. In sum, Featherman is "dismayed by Coser's caricature of quantitative sociology, annoyed by his inaccurate attributions about path analysis of stratification, and struck by the ultimate untenability of his stance toward empirical assessments of social relations and institutions" (1976:23). He believes that theory should be developed, but like Treiman (1976) he holds that the new methods aid rather than hinder this process. Both responders note that Coser overstresses the bad rather than good work in this style.

Treiman argues that the development of scientific theory "requires, first, precision of measurement, and second, precision in the specification of expected relationships among variables, that is, theoretical precision" (p. 28). He contends that there have been contributions in areas of stratification research that Coser claimed were lacking. Treiman concludes that Coser's type of "theorist" might do well "to learn a little statistics; for then they not only would be able to carry out research on problems more to their own taste, but also would be able to read the journals of their profession and thus discover what others have already done" (p. 32). Coser has replied that even the most sophisticated models actually explain less than they leave unexplained. He remains, therefore, unconvinced of their past and potential contributions to our understanding of society.

The readings begin with two selections from theory construction books. Reynolds deals with the basic rationale for scientific procedure. Scientific knowledge should give us ways of organizing social phenomena, permit prediction and explanation, foster understanding of causal processes, and heighten our ability to control events. Reynolds examines the use of the term "theory," provides a scientific definition of it, and explains how concepts and statements become accepted as scientific knowledge. Scientific knowledge, he concludes, should be abstract and intersubjective and should have empirical relevance. Mullins examines the basic building blocks of scientific theory, concepts, and variables and the way they are linked in definitions. Finally, he deals with the next step in theory construction, the analysis of relations. Blalock continues this line of thought and distinguishes between axioms and testable theorems. He demonstrates how the latter can be converted from verbal to mathematical statements and models. The last selection, by White, is an example of this type of work and the refinements in model building that now characterize "neopositivism" in sociology.

References and Suggested Readings

Berger, Joseph, Morris Zelditch, and Bo Anderson, eds. *Sociological Theories in Progess*. Vol II. Boston: Houghton Mifflin, 1972.

Bierstedt, Robert. *Power and Progress*. New York: McGraw-Hill, 1974.

Blalock, H. M., Jr. *Causal Inferences in Nonexperimental Research*. Chapel Hill: University of North Carolina Press, 1964.

———. "The Identification Problem and Theory Building: The Case of Status Inconsistency," *American Sociological Review*, 31 (February 1966), 52–61.

———. *Theory Construction: From Verbal to Mathematical Formulation*. Englewood Cliffs, N. J.: Prentice-Hall, 1969.

Blalock, H. M. Jr., ed. *Causal Models in the Social Sciences*. Chicago: Aldine-Atherton, 1971.

Blau, P. M., and O. D. Duncan. *The American Occupational Structure*. New York: Wiley, 1967.

Block, Fred, "Alternative Sociological Perspectives," *Catalyst*, 7 (Winter 1973).

Borgatta, Edgar F., and George W. Bohrnstedt, eds. *Sociological Methodology*. San Francisco: Jossey-Bass, 1969.

———. *Sociological Methodology*, San Francisco: Jossey-Bass, 1970.

Churchill, Lindsey. "Ethnomethodology and Measurement," *Social Forces*, 50 (December 1971), 182.

Coser, Lewis A. "Presidential Address: Two Methods in Search of Substance," *American Sociological Review*, 40 (1975), 691–700.

———. "Reply to My Critics," *American Sociologist*, 11 (February 1976), 33–38.

Costner, Herbert L. "Theory, Deduction, and Rules of Correspondence," *American Journal of Sociology*, 75 (1969), 245–263.

Dubin, Robert. *Theory Building*. New York: Free Press, 1969.

Dumont, Richard G., and William J. Wilson. "Aspects of Concept Formation, Explanation and Theory Construction in Sociology," *American Sociological Review*, 32 (1967), 985–995.

Duncan, O. D. "Path Analysis: Sociological Examples," *American Journal of Sociology*, 72 (July 1966), 1–16.

Featherman, David L. "Coser's 'In Search of Substance,'" *American Sociologist*, 11 (February 1976), 21–27.

Hampden-Turner, Charles. *Radical Man*. Cambridge, Mass: Schenkman, 1970.

Lazarsfeld, Paul F., Ann Pasanella, and Morris Rosenberg, eds. *Continuities in the Language of Social Research*. New York: Free Press, 1972.

Leik, Robert K., and Walter R. Grove. "The Conception and Measurement of Asymetric Monotonic Relationships in Sociology," *American Journal of Sociology*, 74 (1969), 696–709.

Lundberg, George A. *Social Research*. New York: Longmans, Green and Co., 1949.

———. "The Natural Science Trend in Sociology," *American Journal of Sociology*, 65 (November 1955).

McHugh, P. "On the Failure of Positivism," in J. D. Douglas, ed., *Understanding Everyday Life*. Chicago: Aldine, 1970.

Martindale, Don. "Limits to the Uses of Mathematics in the Study of Sociology," in James C. Charlesworth, ed., *Mathematics and the Social Sciences*. Philadelphia: American Academy of Political and Social Science, 1963.

Mills, C. Wright. *The Sociological Imagination*. New York: Oxford University Press, 1971.

Movahedi, Siamak, and Richard H. Ogles. "Axiomatic Theory, Informative Value of Propositions and 'Derivation Rules of Ordinary Language,'" *American Sociological Review*, 38 (1973) 416–24.

Mullins, Nicholas C. *The Art of Theory: Construction and Use*. New York: Harper & Row, 1971.

Stinchcombe, Arthur L. *Constructing Social Theories*. New York: Harcourt, Brace, and World, 1968.

Timasheff, Nicholas. *Sociological Theory*, 3rd ed. New York: Random House, 1967.

Treiman, Donald J. "A Comment on Professor Lewis Coser's Presidential Address," *American Sociologist*, 11 (February 1976), 27–33.

Wagner, Helmut R. "The Types of Sociological Theory," *American Sociological Review*, 28 (1963), 735–42.

Wallace, Walter L. *The Logic of Science in Sociology*. New York: Aldine, 1971.

Werts, Charles E. "Path Analysis: Testimonial of a Proselyte," *American Journal of Sociology*, 73 (1968) 509–512.

White, H. C. *Chains of Opportunity: System Models of Mobility in Organizations.* Cambridge, Mass.: Harvard University Press, 1970.

Zetterberg, Hans. *On Theory and Verification in Sociology.* Totowa, N. J.: Bedminster Press, 1965.

CONCEPTS, STATEMENTS, AND SCIENTIFIC KNOWLEDGE

PAUL D. REYNOLDS

From *A Primer in Theory Construction* by Paul D. Reynolds, copyright © 1971 by Paul Davidson Reynolds and the Bobbs-Merrill Company, Inc. Reprinted by permission of the publisher.

Paul D. Reynolds is associate professor of sociology at the University of Minnesota.

The purpose of this [paper] is to describe the characteristics of scientific knowledge. In order to explain and justify these characteristics, two issues will have to be discussed first: the purposes science ought to serve and the procedure scientists use in evaluating the usefulness of concepts and statements.

FOR WHAT SHOULD SCIENTIFIC KNOWLEDGE BE USEFUL?

While scientific knowledge is basically a system for description and explanation, not everything can be explained by science.

Such questions as "How does the moon affect the oceans of the earth?" "What changes a person's status in a social system?" or "Under what conditions does 'life' (an organism capable of reproduction) exist?" can be approached with scientific knowledge—and frequently answered. All of these questions are related to how or why certain events occur. Such questions as "Why is there a moon?" or "Why are there societies?" or "Why is there life?" are beyond the capacity of science. These "Why does it exist?" questions are more of a religious or philosophical nature and cannot be resolved with an empirically based science. For this reason, [we] will *not* treat "why things exist" but will emphasize "why things happen," the major focus of science.

Assuming that scientists have completed the task of building a scientific body of knowledge designed to describe "things" and explain why "events" occur, which is obviously not going to happen very soon, what should such a body of knowledge be useful for? Most people would probably want scientific knowledge to provide:

1 . A method of organizing and categorizing "things," a *typology;*
2 . *Predictions* of future events;
3 . *Explanations* of past events;
4 . A *sense of understanding* about what causes events.

And occasionally mentioned as well is:

5 . The potential for *control* of events.

Each of these will be discussed in turn.

Typologies

Of all these purposes, the first is the easiest to achieve, because any set of concepts can be used to organize and classify. For example, rocks can be classified by color, size, weight, strength, crystalline structure, or any number of other characteristics; individuals can be classified by color, size, weight, strength (physical condition), the nature of their cognitive structure, and so on; and social systems can be classified by size, strength (commitment of members to the system), the form of the internal organization, and so on.

Since there is such a large number of ways to organize and classify phenomena or "things" the problem becomes one of determining which typologies (methods of classifying) are the most useful. This leads to a major issue: What criteria should be used to evaluate the usefulness of typologies? Two of the more obvious criteria are that the application of a typology to phenomena should result in, first, its *exhaustiveness*—of all the "things" being classified, there is no item that cannot be placed in the scheme—and, second, its *mutual exclusiveness*—that there is no ambiguity about where each "thing" is to be placed in the scheme. A third and perhaps more important criterion is that typologies should be consistent with the concepts used in the statements that express the other purposes of science.

Prediction and Explanation

Predicting events that will occur in the future and explaining events that have occurred in the past are, except for a difference in temporal perspective, essentially the same activity as long as scientific statements are abstract. Consider, for example, the following statements:

(i) If the volume of a gas is constant,
then an increase in temperature will be followed
by an increase in pressure.

(ii) If the rate of succession (changes in membership) in an organization is
constant,
then an increase in organizational size will be followed
by an increase in formalization (of the structure and procedures).

Both of these statements have the same form:

Under certain conditions (constant volume, rate of succession) a change in one variable (temperature of a gas, organizational size) is followed by a change in another variable (pressure of the gas, formalization of the organization).

Statements of this form compose a scientific body of knowledge and can be used for prediction and explanation of scientific events, using a form of explanation adopted from symbolic logic. . . .

For example:

If the volume of a gas is constant, and the temperature increases, then the pressure increases.

In situation Z the volume of gas R is constant, and the temperature increased.

Therefore, the pressure of gas R increased.

This is a form of explanation adopted from symbolic logic. Notice that no mention of time (in a historical sense, a particular time in history) enters into the first statement in the explanation. Abstract statements of this sort and, therefore, explanations based on them, are independent of historical time. In other words, these statements can be used to explain past events and to predict future events.

Using an identical logical form, statement ii can be used to explain a change in organizational characteristics.

If the rate of succession is constant, and organizational size increases, then organizational formalization increases.

In situation Y the rate of succession in organization Q is constant, and organizational size increased.

Therefore, the formalization of organization Q increased.

Again, this logical deduction is independent of historical time because statement ii is independent of historical time and applies to past and future situations alike.

When a statement is useful for explanation and prediction, the concepts contained in the statement can be used to organize and classify. Gases can be classified according to their volume, temperature, and pressure; and organizations can be classified according to their rate of succession, size, and degree of formalization. Therefore, it seems reasonable to expect that, if a statement can be used to explain or to predict, the concepts contained in that statement can be used to organize and to classify (provide a typology).

Sense of Understanding

A further purpose of scientific knowledge, providing a sense of understanding, is both the most difficult to achieve and the most controversial. It is the assumption of this author ... that a sense of understanding is provided only when the causal mechanisms that link changes in one or more concepts (the independent variables) with changes in other concepts (the dependent variables) have been fully described. If a person feels ambiguous or uncertain about an explanation, it is because some part of the causal linkage has been omitted from the description.

In the previous examples, predictions and explanations about gases and organizations were logically derived from statements that are best described as empirical generalizations. Under certain conditions, when scientists have a great deal of confidence in the truth of such statements, they are called laws. However, despite the fact that these examples meet all the requirements of logical explanations, it is difficult to consider them complete, for they do *not* provide a sense of understanding.

A complete explanation would require several such statements that together provide a description of the causal process.

In relation to the example of the gas at a constant volume subjected to an increase in temperature, the following causal process, based on the conception of a gas as a collection of molecules in constant motion, might be proposed to explain this relationship.

> An increase of temperature increases the kinetic energy of the gas molecules.
>
> The increase of kinetic energy causes an increase in the velocity of the motion of the molecules.
>
> Since the molecules are prevented from traveling further by the vessel of constant volume, they strike the inside surface of the vessel more often. (Since they travel faster, they cover more distance and bounce off the vessel more often.)
>
> As the molecules strike the sides of the vessel more frequently, the pressure on the walls of the vessel increases.

The results of this process are summarized in the empirical relationship: as the temperature increases, the pressure increases. There may be other processes that will "explain" the relationship between a change in temperature and a change in pressure and perhaps this one process could be made more explicit, but nevertheless such descriptions seem to provide a sense of understanding.

In a similar fashion the process that relates an increase in organizational size to an increase in formalization might be described as follows:

> An increase in organizational size is considered to be an increase in the number of organization members.
>
> An increase in the number of members will cause an increase in the variation of training and experience of the members.

As the members vary more in terms of their training and experience, their interpretation of rules and procedures will vary more.

An increase in the variance in interpretation of organizational rules and procedures will cause a decrease of coordination in organizational activities.

A decrease in coordination of organizational activities causes a decrease in organizational performance.

A decrease in performance disturbs organizational administrators.

Organizational administrators attribute poor performance to a decrease of coordination.

Organizational administrators attribute a decrease of coordination to ambiguous rules and procedures.

To reduce the ambiguity of organizational rules, the organizational administrators increase the number of rules and make the rules more detailed and specific.

An increase in the number of rules and their specificity is generally considered an indicator of an increase in formalization.

Again, the results of this process are summarized by the statement: as size increases, formalization increases. Again, it is likely that other processes may link changes in size and the degree of formalization.

Two ways of explaining events, derivation from a scientific statement (or law) and description of a causal mechanism, have been presented. Both succeed in explaining, but it is clear that the second procedure, the description of the causal mechanism, provides a sense of understanding that is absent from the first procedure, the derivation from a scientific statement.

If the description of a causal process is properly formulated, it can provide explanations and predictions, in the sense of logical derivations, as well as provide concepts for organizing and classifying phenomena of interest. If the development of descriptions of causal processes is considered the most important purpose of scientific activity, then any typology not consistent with these descriptions will only yield confusion rather than clarity.

Control

If the ability to control events is taken literally as a desirable characteristic of scientific knowledge, then much of the current subject matter of science would be excluded. For instance, both astronomy and geology are considered to be sophisticated sciences in which there exist useful typologies as well as statements that explain and predict while providing a sense of understanding. But to expect astronomers to control such events in the solar system as eclipses or geologists to control such events within the earth as earthquakes is unreasonable since such control is clearly beyond their present capabilities.

The issue is one of making a distinction between understanding how certain variables affect one another and being able to change the variables. In order to control events in a predictable fashion it is necessary to meet both conditions. There is no reason to believe that some social phenomena, such as characteristics of a status structure (e.g., social mobility) or an economic system (e.g., inflation), won't be as hard to control as eclipses or earthquakes, even though social scientists may be able to provide typologies, explanations, predictions, and a sense of understanding with their theories. . . .

[Thus] . . . control will not be treated as a necessary criterion for accepting knowledge as scientific. However, it will be assumed that, if a theory related to a particular phenomenon is scientifically useful, then scientists and "men of action" can examine their ability to influence the variables that will affect the events they wish to control.

THEORY

What is a theory? Thus far there has been little mention of scientific theory, partly because there is more than one concept of what a theory is. . . . Two conceptions of scientific theory currently dominate. One, the conception of scientific knowledge as a set of well-supported empirical generalizations or "laws," can be referred to as the "set-of-laws" form of theory. The other, the conception of scientific theory as an interrelated set of definitions, axioms, and propositions (that are derived from the axioms), is borrowed from mathematical conceptions of theory and is called the "axiomatic" form of theory. Although both the set-of-laws and the axiomatic conceptions of theory can be used to logically derive explanations, neither provides a sense of understanding in the form the theory is usually given.

If a sense of understanding is provided when a description of a causal process is presented, then it seems reasonable to consider a third conception of theory, as a set of descriptions of causal processes; this can be considered the "causal process" form of theory. Frequently, a set of statements in axiomatic form may be reorganized into a description of a causal process, but this is not always possible. Unfortunately, this is seldom the case with the statements in the set-of-laws form of theory.

The word "theory" is frequently used to refer to a number of other types of formulations, usually abstract, including 1) vague conceptualizations or descriptions of events or things, 2) prescriptions about what are desirable social behaviors or arrangements, or 3) any untested hypothesis or idea. To refer to any set of abstract concepts used to describe a phenomenon as a theory is an inappropriate use of the word if *only* a set of concepts is presented (e.g., the characteristics of a bureaucratic organization). At best, these concepts can only provide a typology but fail to achieve the other goals of scientific knowledge . . . . Much of past social and political theory describes the form of an ideal social system, with no relationship to the actual types of behaviors or arrangements that develop among the members of social systems. In this use of the term "theory," to refer to any untested hypothesis or idea, its meaning is the same as when it is said that any idea is "theory" until it is supported by empirical data, whereupon it becomes "fact" or "reality."

This and related uses of the word "theory"—be they conceptualizations, prescriptions for behavior, or untested ideas—will be avoided [here]. . . . The use of the term "theory" will refer to abstract statements that are considered part of scientific knowledge in either the set-of-laws, the axiomatic, or the causal process forms.

HOW DOES A CONCEPT OR STATEMENT BECOME PART OF A SCIENTIFIC BODY OF KNOWLEDGE?

In general, the degree of acceptance of an idea as part of scientific knowledge increases 1) as each individual scientist becomes more confident that the idea is useful for the goals of science, and 2) as the number of scientists that consider the idea useful for the goals of science increases. Notice that ideas are not accepted or rejected, either part of science or not part of science, but vary in *degree* of acceptance. Although this is generally the most appropriate way to view the process of accepting scientific ideas, occasionally confidence in one widely held theory will be so high that it is considered *the* truth, and anything that contradicts *the* truth is considered false. The rigid classification of ideas as true or false does not encourage the development or acceptance of new ways of thinking about phenomena.

Two factors are important in affecting an individual scientist's attitude toward a concept or statement:

1. The scientist's confidence that he understands the meaning of the concept or statement;
2. The scientist's confidence that the concept or statement is useful for achieving the purposes of science.

The second factor is generally dependent on the correspondence between the idea and the results of empirical research. The major importance of empirical research is in its effects on the degree of confidence that scientists have with respect to some aspects of scientific knowledge. This fact places one important restriction on statements or concepts proposed for addition to a scientific body of knowledge: there must be some way they can be compared to the results of objective empirical research.

If an idea cannot be compared with the results of empirical research, there is no way for other scientists to determine for themselves if the idea is useful for the goals of science. An untestable idea is, then, one scientist's view of the phenomenon, not knowledge that can be shared by all scientists. As long as scientific knowledge is that knowledge accepted by a group of individuals, the view of *one* individual cannot be considered scientific knowledge.

Of more importance to the present discussion is the consideration of how scientists determine whether or not they understand the meaning of a concept or statement. Like any individual in a situation of uncertainty, they check their interpretations by comparing them with the interpretations of someone else, another scientist. If there is substantial disagreement among scientists, then no one scientist can be sure that he has correctly understood the meaning of a concept or statement.

The importance of having agreement about the meaning of a scientific concept or statement can best be understood if the alternative is considered. First, if there were no shared agreement on meaning, then scientific knowledge could not be transmitted from one generation of scientists to the next. Each scientist would then have to build a body of scientific knowledge from the same starting point—complete ignorance. It would be impossible to build a very significant or useful body of scientific knowledge under these conditions.

Second, if scientific knowledge is considered to be that knowledge that scientists agree is useful for achieving the goals of science, then scientific knowledge is impossible unless there is agreement about the meaning of a concept or statement. For if there is no agreement about the meaning of a concept or statement, how can there be agreement about its usefulness in organizing, explaining, predicting, or providing a sense of understanding? Under such conditions the knowledge developed by each scientist would be indistinguishable from everyday knowledge about events in general. It would become part of the scientist's personal philosophy about the world and no different from such knowledge held by a nonscientist.

In summary, if scientific knowledge is that knowledge that scientists agree is useful for achieving the goals of science, there must be agreement on the meaning of the statements and concepts that express scientific knowledge, and it must be possible for any scientist to compare some aspect of his theory with empirical research.

DESIRABLE CHARACTERISTICS OF SCIENTIFIC KNOWLEDGE

The desirable characteristics of scientific knowledge are:

1. Abstractness (independence of time and space);
2. Intersubjectivity (agreement about meaning among relevant scientists);
3. Empirical relevance (can be compared to empirical findings).

This section will describe 1) why these characteristics are desirable for achieving the goals of science and 2) how they facilitate the adoption of concepts and statements as scientific knowledge.

Abstractness

In its simplest form, abstractness means that a concept is independent of a specific time or place. In other words, a concept is not related to any unique temporal (historical time) or spatial (location) setting. Why is it so important that concepts used in science be abstract? There are two reasons, one related to the purposes that scientific knowledge should serve and the other a matter of efficiency in developing a scientific body of knowledge.

It is considered appropriate for scientific knowledge to make predictions about the future. However, if the concepts in the statements used to make predictions are not independent of historical time, they must be unique to a specific time. If we assume that the most important basis for confidence in scientific statements is their correspondence with empirical findings (the results of research), then any statement unique to a temporal setting must be unique to a past temporal setting, because the research must have been conducted in the past. If the statement is unique to a time in the past, then it cannot be applied to situations in the future. In sum, any scientific statement supported by research that is specific to a temporal setting must be specific to the past and cannot be used to make predictions about the future. Quite simply, such statements are not useful for achieving all the goals of science (predictions about the future).

The second reason for requiring abstractness is efficiency. If a scientific concept or statement is developed that is specific to a particular spatial setting, a unique location in the universe, then it cannot be used for prediction and explanation at any other location. If this procedure were followed, each different location (or culture) would require a unique body of scientific knowledge. To say the least, this is an inefficient procedure, and the task of science is difficult enough without this additional complication.

However, there are often events of enough importance, even though they are unique to a particular time and location, that considerable effort is expended to explain their occurrence. Particular aircraft accidents, certain geological phenomena, and many historical events (such as the results of a particular election) fall into this category. In each case the event is specific to a particular location and place in historical time: Why did two planes collide over New York City on a certain date? Why is the Grand Canyon now in Arizona? Why did Nixon get more votes than Humphrey in the 1968 presidential election in the United States?

Such explanations, unique to one specific event, can be called *historical* explanations. The most complete and widely accepted historical explanations utilize general scientific knowledge in explaining the unique event of interest. If the use of these general principles is made explicit, it may be that the successful application to the unique event increases confidence in the general principles as useful scientific knowledge. However, many explanations of unique human events tend to neglect the general principles or fail to make them explicit and focus on the specific aspects of the event of interest. Not only does this distract from the use of general principles in explaining human events, it prevents such explanations from contributing to the development of a scientific body of knowledge, since the general principles are never made explicit.

Intersubjectivity (Meaning)

"Intersubjectivity" means shared agreement among relevant individuals with respect to 1) the events or phenomena encompassed by a concept, and 2) the relationship between concepts specified by one or more statements.

The notion of shared agreement with respect to the meaning of a concept is relatively easy to understand. If a scientist uses a term, such as "tree," "mass," or "attitude," and if his audience shares his definition (of "tree," "mass," or "attitude"), then there is intersubjective agreement with respect to the concept. This is most likely to occur when the scientist 1) attempts to be as explicit as possible in defining new concepts, and 2) makes sure that there is shared agreement on any terms used in defining a new concept.

Intersubjectivity (Logical Rigor)

The concept of intersubjectivity with respect to relationships between concepts is more complex. Any statement, at a minimum, describes a relationship between two concepts. Assuming that there is shared agreement about the meaning of the concepts, it is appropriate to consider the conditions under which there is shared agreement about the relationships specified in a statement.

If only one statement is under consideration, achieving agreement about the nature of the relationships is not a major problem. However, if there are a number of statements, which is usually the case, different combinations of statements can be used to develop a variety of predictions and explanations. The complexity of making predictions from sets of statements can cause disagreement among scientists unless there is some agreement as to how statements should be combined for predictions and explanations.

The solution to this problem is to have a logical system, independent of the substantive content, that can be used to specify the relation expressed in a single statement as well as the implications of combinations of statements. There should be shared agreement about the predictions made within this logical system independent of the content of the theory. In other words, the logical system could be used with different theories treating different phenomena.

A scientist has two alternatives for acquiring a logical system. First, he can develop a logical system for use with his theory and then present this system for the inspection of other scientists, independent of the substantive content of the theory. However, this is a major undertaking, and few scientists have been willing, or able, to develop their own logical systems. Second, the scientist can use a logical system that has been developed by others and is already shared by the relevant scientific audience. Fortunately, there is a rather large set of logical systems available for borrowing. Mathematics (essentially a set of logical systems), symbolic logic, and computer languages can be employed. Many of the logical systems in mathematics have been developed for the specific purpose of providing scientists with logical systems suitable for particular substantive theories, generally in the physical sciences.

The reason for requiring intersubjective agreement on the relationships within and between statements can be stated briefly. If scientists cannot agree on the predictions derived from combinations of statements, then there can be no agreement as to the usefulness of the statements for predicting or explaining phenomena. If scientists cannot agree on the usefulness of the statements for achieving the goals of science, the statements cannot be accepted as part of a scientific body of knowledge.

The requirement for shared agreement about the relationships among statements is usually referred to as the need for "rigor," which is generally taken to mean "logical rigor."

Empirical Relevance

The possibility of comparing some aspect of a scientific statement, a prediction or an explanation, with objective empirical research is what is meant by the criterion of empirical relevance. In order to understand the importance of this criterion we must consider a difference between perceiving an event and explaining it. Perceiving an event is having sensory experience of a particular state of nature.

Explaining why one event is associated with another, or what causes an event, is the basic purpose of a theory. Individual perception is a sensitive and delicate process, and often many subtle and unconscious factors may affect what an individual thinks he has perceived. If an individual has proposed a theory and the only source of supporting evidence is his perception of the phenomenon of interest, then it is not clear whether or not his desire for the theory to "work" affected his perception of the phenomenon.

For this reason, it is desirable that any scientist be able to examine the correspondence between a particular theory and objective empirical data. The important factor is that the potential for such a check be available, for very seldom is it initiated. But if a theory and the empirical evidence that supports it is presented in the appropriate fashion, in detail, other scientists feel that they can verify the results for themselves, and this increases their confidence in the usefulness of the theory.

Again it is fruitful to consider the alternative. If a theory cannot be compared with objective research by another scientist, then it becomes the private philosophy of the originator and hence cannot become part of a shared body of knowledge—part of science.

THE PARTS OF SCIENTIFIC THEORY

NICHOLAS C. MULLINS

Abridged from pp. 7–25 of "The Parts of Theory" in
The Art of Theory: Construction and Use by Nicholas
C. Mullins. Copyright © 1971 by Harper & Row,
Publishers, Inc. Used by permission of the publishers.

Nicholas C. Mullins is associate professor of sociology
at Indiana University. His major theoretical work to
date is *Theories and Theory Groups in Contemporary
American Sociology* (1973).

Theories provide a bridge between language and experience. The two major parts of theory are *concepts,* a part of language, and *variables,* a summary of experience. A theory uses concepts and variables plus various other assorted parts to span the gap between what we know as ideas and what we perceive as experience. A concept consists of 1) an idea and 2) a word associated with that idea in some language (e.g., a common language such as English; a technical language such as sociology; or a formal language such as FORTRAN). A variable is a set of classifications to which experiences may be assigned.

CONCEPTS

A concept begins as an idea expressed in words . . . Since theories are about concepts, you must first decide what ideas are sufficiently important to form the basis for your concepts. If, to take an example, you are studying cooperation and conflict among races, an examination of your references will probably extract ideas such as "races," "occupational levels," "marriage," "classes," "integration," "separatism," "racism," and so on, some of which may ultimately not prove to represent basic concepts. If you are developing a theory about "football ability," "grades," and "attitudes," however, your theory must include at least these three ideas.

But an idea expressed in words is only the beginning of a concept. As we will see in the next chapter, each word exists within a network of other words (those which define it and those assumed to be synonymous or antonymous) which help to set its meaning; and meaning is further affected by context, group usage, and other factors which distinguish among words and their appropriate use.

The *idea* called to mind by a word is much more important than the word itself. These ideas are of two sorts: 1) examples of the word that one has seen or thought about; 2) those things which come to mind along with any particular example. When we "free associate," both sorts of ideas can occur without restriction. As scientists, however, our goal is to employ a specific abstraction which will bring the same ideas to the minds of a specific set of people. We occasionally disagree as to which of several words is more useful; the word itself, however, is less important than the context of words and experiences implied by it.

This core idea, which can be expressed in several related ways, constitutes a *concept* as we will use the term. Concepts can be expressed in terms of empirical definitions or of other concepts. For example, a concept which we express as "education" has a set of subconcepts: elementary education, trade education, continuing education, higher education, and so on; each of these more specific concepts is connected both to the more general concept and to a specific case (class) of a variable. In principle it is possible to have many layers of subconcepts between the most general concept under consideration and its related variable (for example, "shop" is a subconcept of "trade education"); in this [article], however, we will limit ourselves to two levels: a general concept and several, more specific, subconcepts. Any general concept can be divided into subconcepts, and most sets of subconcepts can be collected into a more general concept, although not always usefully.

Concepts as you find them are often *raw*; that is, they are one of a series of ideas that may not be very clearly defined. *Refined* concepts, by contrast, have mutually exclusive and totally inclusive partitions of the concept into a set of subconcepts. A set of subconcepts constitutes one partition of the concept. The above division of "education" suggests one partition of that concept; another might include "discussion," "lectures," "laboratory practice," and "reading" as subconcepts. You will want to use refined concepts and just one partition at any time. "Education," for example, should not be divided into "seminars," "trade education," and "books" since these subconcepts overlap and empirical analysis would therefore be inconclusive.

NECESSARY PROPERTIES FOR
GENERAL CONCEPT SETS

Since theories are not about one concept, but rather sets of general concepts, we should consider the properties of these sets. One such property is *commonality*. Each concept applies to a specific range of real or potential empirical situations. If all concepts in a set apply to the same range of situations, the set has high commonality and can more easily be tested empirically (e.g., "education," "occupation," "political party preference," and "automobile preference" are all usable concepts for describing citizens of the United States; any sample of these citizens could provide a test of a theory using these concepts). A low-commonality set might include "length of men's lace cuffs" and "width of mastodon teeth."

You can achieve high commonality but have quite *uninteresting* concepts, a difficulty which can sometimes be remedied. A seemingly uninteresting concept may fit into a theory which already contains some intrinsically interesting or useful concept(s) (e.g., almost any concept would gain interest if it belonged to a theory which had "the probability of nuclear war" as another concept). Or it may fit a theory central to some field and therefore be interesting to some specific group of professionals. Concepts may also become interesting for very pragmatic reasons: Someone else is interested in them and may be providing financial support or other motivation for the research.

A concept may be interesting and common but still lack *clarity* with reference to other terms with which it is used. Each term's place in the language must be made as clear as possible. At this point the *community* which you are addressing becomes quite important, and this may be quite different from your personal community. If the generation gap holds, you and I do not share a language; in order to communicate with me, you may have to modify your language, and I, mine. For example, a social scientist is often writing for an audience of fellow professionals, and he will therefore use terms and phrases common to that body, such as "group" or "institution," which may or may not be what you think they are.

It might be helpful to keep a personal dictionary which records the meaning of various terms as defined by your own community.

Rule 1   Concepts may be subdivided into more specific concepts or
collected into more general ones.

Rule 2 *a*) Concepts in the same theory ought, in principle, to be able to occur
together; if they cannot, combine or divide them.

  b) Some of a theory's concepts ought to interest someone.

  c) Concepts should be clear and understandable by the intended
audience.

Example. If I were writing for an audience of high school teachers, my concepts
might include:

1. "Class size" divided into "too small to provide variation," "too large to
   control," and "adequate";
2. "Form of lesson" divided into "rote learning," "projects," "drills on
   skills," and "gimmicks";
3. "Content" divided into "hard," "easy," and "acceptable."

For the school board these concepts might be divided differently: The class
size might be expressed as "above present teacher-student ratio," "at present
level," or "below"; the form of lesson in terms of "needs extra help or equipment," or "does not need extra help or equipment," and so on.

VARIABLES

A variable is a set of classifications into which empirical experiences or reports
may be placed. We may associate names with these sets for convenience, but the
way in which we classify these experiences is a much more important determinant of meaning. For example, we may have a set of classifications which we call
"red, blue, green, and black," or "1, 2, 3, and 4." The meaning of these classifications, however, is settled not by the names, but rather by observing the placement of items (e.g., a puce carpet, a mauve chair) into these classifications. Each
experience must be classified into one and only one classification of each variable.
The purpose of classification is to generalize so that more than one experience
will presumably belong in each classification. A graphic representation is given
in Figure 1.

 . . . You should note that each experience must be classified, and the number
of classifications should be limited by determining either 1) the specific range
(for example, a "length of time" variable could have the range "from 1 year to 10
years") or 2) the actual set of classifications (for example, "1 to 3 years," "4 to
6 years," "over 6 years").

Figure 1. Variable Classifications of Experience

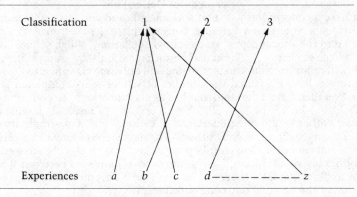

Types

Variables come in several types. Those having a range of just two values (e.g., "male" and "female"; "in office" or "out"; "guilty" or "not guilty") are termed *dichotomies* and constitute the simplest form. (A one-class variable simply doesn't vary.) A dichotomy may be either natural (e.g., "male" and "female") or an investigator's attempt to simplify the world. The simplification will often be done by defining a positive case (e.g., "American citizen") and then assigning all other cases to an "other" value of the variable.

A second level of variables can include several well-defined, definite, and known values; "hair color," for example, can be "blond," "dark," and "other" (three classes) or "blond," "dark," "red," "white," "auburn," and "others" (six classes). In any case, a relatively small number of values for the variable exist. These sets of values may be natural ones, or they may be created by the investigator. They may also have an implied order (e.g., "infant," "young," "middle-aged," "old"); the hair color set has no such order.

A third group of variables is termed *scales*. If a variable 1) has such a large number of values that for *all practical purposes* it can take every possible value from the lowest to the highest and 2) has an implied order to the classifications, it forms a scale. Age and income are examples of scales.

Rule 3 *a*) Variable sets must be *inclusive*. Always specify one residual classification (e.g., "other") for experiences that cannot be otherwise defined.

       b) Variable sets must have *one* and only one classification for each experience.

Rule 4 *a*) State both your variables and your concepts in dichotomous form during the early stages of theory building.

DEFINITIONS

So far we have discussed variables (e.g., "length of time" in three possible classification forms) and concepts (e.g., "experience," defined as "length of time on the job"). These two entities are joined in the theory-building process by a definition. A variable is a *potential empirical proxy* for a concept. It summarizes measurements of an attribute of a situation or thing. It must be a *proxy* because a concept cannot be directly measured but is rather associated with a variable that can be measured. It is a *potential* proxy because a variable must be explicitly associated by a definition with a concept before it can become that concept's proxy. Definitions are of two types: procedural and verbal.

Procedural Definitions

If you have a concept with several subconcepts and you wish to classify a series of individuals, you need a variable. For example, take the concept "education," divided into the subconcepts "grade school education," "high school education," and "college education." These can be measured only by using some *procedure* which will relate each subconcept to one and only one classification of a variable. Suppose you have measured the number of school years completed for a population. You then have a variable that has as classifications the counting numbers: 0, 1, 2, 3, . . . , 12, 13, 14, . . . , 20, 21, . . . , etc., plus a residual classification ("no answer," "other," "did not understand question," etc.) For simplicity call it 28 classifications, 0–26 years and "other." The next step is to map this variable onto the three subconcepts. One simple way to do this is to classify answers between 0 and 8 inclusive, or "other," as "grade school"; answers between 9 and 12 inclusive as "high school"; if over 12, as "college." This procedure maps every classification of the variable onto one subconcept.

Verbal Definitions

A verbal definition moves from a variable to a concept. If you begin with a variable such as the 28 classifications utilized above, you will want to know what concept this variable potentially indicates. Concepts that might possibly be associated with this variable are: experience, length of service, education, exposure, and so on. A dictionary and/or synonym list might help clarify exactly which concept to use. In creating the definition, take care to describe the variable in terms that will clearly indicate the specific concept to which you are relating it.

In trying to develop a verbal definition, you may find that a variable doesn't relate to any concept of any importance to your theory, in which case you should forget the variable. When using verbal definitions, you must balance the costs of getting data for those variables that exactly describe the concept in which you are interested against the theory's lessened importance if you conceptualize your variables narrowly. (For example, the variable "years in school" could be narrowly conceptualized as "time spent in an educational institution." A broader conceptualization of this variable would be "education.") Since the first cost is in dollars and the second difficult to measure, researchers have tended to conceptualize narrowly; the result has generally been trivial concepts and noncomparable results.

Concepts are not free floating; they cannot be assigned freely to any variable. They are embedded within networks of implication and meaning no matter how they are represented (e.g., as words or other symbols). Had you assigned the concept "intelligence" (instead of education) to the variable discussed at the beginning of this section, you would be questioned.

Using Definitions

As you examine [sociological] material, you will find that some sources have not produced concepts for the variables they measure while others give no procedures for their concepts. Several strategies are open to you at this point, each dependent on where you are in your research. I am assuming that, as a beginner, you will be using other people's data and generating your own theory. For you, then, variables are relatively fixed; you must search for adequate concepts. One example will illustrate this situation. If you wanted to examine the number of years of school completed by the whole American population, you would most likely use U.S. Census data. You may manipulate the Census figures to some degree, but you are limited to those variable classifications used by the Census; you must use "number of years completed in school" as the variable, not "information gained" or some other measure. Were you planning your own study, your choice of variables would be much freer.

When taking variables from someone else's work, you may find by examination that two or more fit naturally with one or more of the concepts you have already defined. If you have two indicators for the same concept, use both in order to reduce your chances for error. The matching of concepts and variables in definitions will also force you to make some crucial decisions. What is your theory about? If some variables do not attach to important concepts within your theory, you will probably want to set those variables aside.

Your concepts should also be considered. Do they have procedures? If not, do any of the variables indicate, however weakly or indirectly, the status of those concepts? Suppose, for example, that you are examining data and a theory about differences in medical care based on social class. You are not given income or occupational information, but you do know the number of school years completed. Although the education measure will be a poor proxy, you know that in American society education and class are generally closely related. You may decide, therefore, to let the number of school years completed indicate social class.

If even this fails, the concept should be dropped since at this point you are probably not prepared to design and execute a new data-gathering project.

Beyond these concerns, definitions must meet a validity criterion; that is, your definition must be accepted by some competent other person as a proper indicator of the concept and a proper conceptualization of the variable.

You may sometimes discover that a concept is little more than the variable specifications put into words. On other occasions you may find the reverse: a very narrow variable paired with a very general concept. If you were to use the price of candy in one hundred stores as a variable for the general concept "all retail prices," I would object to the difference in scale between the concept and the variable. You might try to remedy this deficiency by indicating *how* a smaller concept (e.g., candy prices) is actually being given a procedural definition and how this smaller concept links to the larger. (Candy prices are clearly a small part of retail prices.) You can link the concept "candy prices" with the concept "retail prices" because we do expect the price of candy and the total retail price index to be related (although not perfectly).

Even in the professional literature, not every concept/variable pair provides a good example of adequate definition. Nevertheless, the need for good procedural and verbal definitions is one reason the beginning student theorist should start with an existing theory or propositional inventory even though this rule limits, at least initially, the range of variables and concepts he can select. Until the student has some experience, he should use definitions from sources as much as possible. Beware of easy conceptualization.

Variable formulations must have built into them the power to discriminate between instances, and concepts must have subconcepts. Every definition must include points at which every level of discrimination in a variable relates to one and only one subconcept of the related general concept. Figure 2 shows the general pattern; specific examples will be presented later.

The pattern for definitions is quite simple: Each classification of a variable must be matched to one and only one subconcept of the associated concept. This pattern can be symbolized graphically (as in Figure 2), verbally, or by formula. Such precise definitions are absolutely essential to good theory.

To summarize:

Rule 5   Use definitions from your sources until you are experienced in handling definitions. Beware of easy conceptualizations.

Rule 6   In a definition, match each classification (value) of a variable to one and only one subconcept of the associated concept by means of graphic, verbal, or mathematical statement.

RELATIONS

To this point we have been building the "words" of a theory. These words are the concepts and variables connected by definitions. Having clarified the words

Figure 2. Concepts and Variables

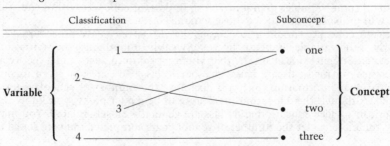

of your theory for future usability, you are now ready to explore the relations which will cement those words into a theory.

An abstract empirical relation[1] states that two concepts are related because they are defined as connected or not connected to two variables that are nonrandomly associated. For example, "age" and "education" are related because any reasonable variables for these two concepts are nonrandomly associated. The simple fact of association is generally not very interesting.

An abstract empirical relation can have three subtypes: positive, negative, and none. To produce these *signed relations,* you must give an order to the subconcepts of your general concepts; in arbitrary fashion you assign a "−" or "+" to one end of the order and the opposite sign to the other. A positive relation between concepts indicates that identically signed values of the connected variables tend to be associated; a negative relation, that values tend to be opposite in sign; and no relation, that the variables do not relate in any systematic pattern. We can symbolize five cases of related dichotomous concepts (see Table 1).

In analyzing concept relations you may find that several different relations between two concepts are actually proposed at different places in the same work. You can then build several alternative theories and test them against each other. And you may also find that not every concept will be linked to every other.

In addition to sign, you can assert an asymmetric relation when one of the following conditions pertains or is assumed to pertain among the concepts:

1. One can produce the change in y with changes in x but not vice versa.
2. There need be no change in any other variable for x to affect y (x is sufficient to change y).
3. The two variables have an unambiguous time separation, x occurring first (e.g., high school grades and college achievement).
4. x is a more permanant or lifelong characteristic (e.g., race, sex), and y can change over time (e.g., political beliefs, religious affiliation).
5. x is stated as the "cause" of y.

After linking some of your concepts, say x and y, you can symbolize that x is asymmetrically associated with y (x precedes y), and not vice versa, either by writing a word sentence to that effect or by graphing and using arrows: "$x{\to}y$," and not "$y{\to}x$" (see Table 2). This notation indicates simply that "x," a generalized name for one concept, and "y," the generalized name for another concept, are related such that, subject to the rules below, a change in the value of x is associated with a change in the value of y. You will find some proposed relations that do not fit any of these rules. You will find others explicitly labeled as situations in which the two concepts are related but not in any causal way. Both are symbolized by the signed but directionless lines discussed above (e.g., "x- - - - -y"; translates x and y are negatively related). If you are not certain which case you have, I suggest that you produce one model containing the first alternative and a second containing the other.

Table 1. Symbolization of Dichotomous Concepts

Case	Concept 1	Concept 2	Sign of Relation	Symbol
I	+	+	+	———
II	+	−	−	------
III	−	+	−	------
IV	−	−	+	———
V	No pattern (+ and −)	No pattern (+ and −)	0	

Table 2. Sentences to Symbolization

Sentence	Symbolization
x causes y.	
x and z cause y and both are necessary.	
x or z cause y and either can.	

These relations are basically asymmetric, signed associations between pairs of concepts graphed to show all known connections among the set of concepts under consideration. . . . [To] summarize:

Rule 7 a) If you think two concepts are associated, draw a graph linking them. Not all pairs of concepts need be linked.

b) If the identically signed subconcepts of two concepts tend to be associated, then link the two concepts with a positive relation (solid line). If differently signed, link them negatively (broken lines).

Rule 8 We assert an asymmetric relation when one of the following conditions pertains or is assumed to pertain:

a) One can produce a change in y with changes in x but not vice versa.

b) There need be no change in any other variable for x to affect y (x is sufficient to change y).

c) The two variables have an unambiguous time separation, x occurring first (e.g., high school grades and college achievement).

d) x is a more permanent or lifelong characteristic (e.g., race, sex), and y can change over time (e.g., political beliefs, religious affiliation).

e) x is stated as the "cause" of y.

NOTE

1. Relations could be of many types (logical, aesthetic, symbolic, etc.), but here we are interested only in abstract empirical relations.

AXIOMS AND THEOREMS

HUBERT M. BLALOCK

From Hubert M. Blalock, Jr. *Theory Construction: From Verbal to Mathematical Formulations,* © 1969. Reprinted by permission of Prentice-Hall, Inc., Englewood Cliffs, New Jersey.

Hubert M. Blalock is professor of sociology at the University of Washington. He is the author of six books and numerous articles on methodology, statistics, and theory construction.

A deductive theory must contain both axioms and theorems. Axioms are propositions that are assumed to be true. Theorems, on the other hand, are derived by reasoning, or *deduced*, from the axioms. Let us assume that a theorist has stated a number of specific propositions, some of which he wishes to take as axioms and the remainder as theorems. The focus of this [article] will be on two very important questions: How does one decide which propositions to select as axioms? Are there any differences in the ways in which axioms and theorems should be stated, given that the theorems are to be deduced from the axioms?

A distinct though related question involves the issue of testability. Conceivably, all axioms and theorems could be more or less directly tested.[1] Usually it will not be possible to test all propositions, however. We shall be specifically concerned with theoretical systems in which the axioms are inherently untestable but at least some of the derived theorems can be tested. The argument that will be developed [here] is essentially as follows: Our axioms should be causal assertions that strictly speaking will be untestable because of the fact that it will never be possible to control for all "relevant" variables. For example, if we assume that a change in X causes or produces a change in Y, even if we observe covariations and temporal sequences we can never be sure that these have not been produced by some extraneous factor.[2] But if our axioms contain such causal assertions, and if we make certain additional assumptions concerning the operation of extraneous factors, we shall then be in a position to derive from our axioms testable theorems about covariances and temporal sequences.

In geometry and other branches of mathematics an axiom is a statement the truth of which is taken for granted. Of course, in the strict sense, the axioms of geometry need not apply to the real world. That is, their "truth" in terms of their empirical validity is not at issue. They are simply a set of assumptions that generate theorems, once a set of rules and definitions has been added to the theoretical system. But the notion of "axiom" has been borrowed by the empirical sciences and used in the sense of an assumption that is almost universally accepted. It is of course rare in the social sciences to find very many unquestionable assumptions, and therefore we need to recognize that the term "axiom" is used in the sense of an untested (or untestable) assumption, rather than as an assumption the truth of which is taken for granted. Obviously it would be very much to our advantage if we could discover universal propositions the truth of which was not in question. There undoubtedly are a few such propositions, such as "all men are mortal," or "all men are motivated by self-interest." The question is whether such propositions can be combined with enough more specific ones to generate deductive theories that take us very far beyond the obvious. For a considerable period of time, social scientists will have to settle for highly tentative theories based on axioms that are really nothing more than rather plausible assumptions.

Tests of the theories in these instances will involve empirical tests of the derived theorems.[3] Clearly, if the theorems prove false the theory must be modified or the axioms of the theory even abandoned. But if they are true, one cannot claim that the theory has been "verified" unless all possible competing alternatives can be rejected. In the case of causal theories, it will always be possible to state alternative explanations by the simple device of introducing additional variables. Where one allows for measurement error, a second kind of alternative explanation can always involve the possibility that results might have been different had there been no such measurement error. Therefore we shall be in the unfortunate situation of having to proceed by eliminating inadequate theories, rather than ever really establishing any of them. This is of course a very general situation that is not peculiar to the social sciences. Since we shall not be concerned with the details of testing procedures, but rather with the process of theory construction itself, it is sufficient to merely note this fact in passing.[4]

COVARIANCE STATEMENTS

Many of the empirical generalizations found in the social science literature are stated in simple covariance form. Where both X and Y are continuous variables, the prototype statement of a covariance relationship would be of the form, "the greater the X, the greater the Y." Where both variables are attributes, the prototype statement would be of the form, "A's tend to be associated with B's." These covariance statements may or may not be testable, depending on whether each of the variables in the proposition has been measured. The question we shall deal with in the present section, however, is that of how one goes about deducing one covariance statement from another. How can one build a deductive theory on the basis of such propositions?

Let us consider a specific example of a theory, given by Zetterberg, consisting of ten propositions as follows:

1. The greater the division of labor, the greater the consensus.
2. The greater the solidarity, the greater the number of associates per member.
3. The greater the number of associates per member, the greater the consensus.
4. The greater the consensus, the smaller the number of rejections of deviants.
5. The greater the division of labor, the smaller the number of rejections of deviants.
6. The greater the number of associates per member, the smaller the number of rejections of deviants.
7. The greater the division of labor, the greater the solidarity.
8. The greater the solidarity, the greater the consensus.
9. The greater the number of associates per member, the greater the division of labor.
10. The greater the solidarity, the smaller the number of rejections of deviants.[5]

Zetterberg selects the last four propositions (7–10) as axioms and claims that the remainder can be deduced from this combination of four propositions.[6] He does not, however, adequately discuss the crucial question of why these particular four were selected. The reader is left with the impression that *any* set of propositions that could imply the remainder would be satisfactory. Presumably, a deductive theory which involved the smallest number of mutually consistent axioms, and which also implied all of the theorems, would be most satisfactory by virtue of the criterion of simplicity.

We cannot come to grips with this problem unless we first discuss a criticism of this approach given by Costner and Leik.[7] These authors make two main points. First, propositions of the form "the greater the X, the greater the Y" are ambiguous in that it is often not clear whether causal asymmetry is implied. Second, if one finds error or unexplained variation in an empirical attempt to test the theory, the strict deductive argument implied by an axiomatic theory (such as that relating propositions 1–10) will not apply unless one adds a set of auxiliary assumptions about the behavior of uncontrolled variables. Let us consider each of these points and then return to the question of how one chooses his axioms.

As Costner and Leik emphasize, causal asymmetry is often implied in propositions of the form, "the greater the X, the greater the Y." Sometimes a theorist is very explicit about this question. More often, it seems, the symmetry or asymmetry has to be inferred by a careful reading of an author's discussion of the proposition. I would infer, in the case of Zetterberg, that for each of these ten propositions the first variable mentioned in each pair is to be taken as causally prior. Yet, as we shall see below, this is probably not what is actually intended in the case of propositions 2 and 4, which are taken as theorems. Let us consider some additional examples.

Homans, in *The Human Group*, usually makes it clear to the reader whenever he wishes to imply a reciprocal relationship.[8] He states his propositions in several different ways, examples of which are as follows (with emphasis added):

If the frequency of interaction between two or more persons increases, the degree of their liking for one another will increase, *and vice versa.*[9]

. . . persons who feel sentiments of liking for one another will express those sentiments in activities over and above the activities of the external system, *and these activities may further strengthen the sentiments of liking.*[10]

The more frequently persons interact with one another, the more alike in some respects both their activities and their sentiments tend to become.[11]

In the case of the last proposition, there is no explicit mention of reciprocal causation, but in the very next sentence (which is not, however, part of the formal proposition), Homans goes on to say: "Moreover, the more a person's activities and sentiments resemble those of others, the more likely it is that interaction between him and these others will increase."[12] Thus Homans is reasonably explicit about the direction of causality, and one would therefore infer that a single direction is implied whenever no mention is made of relationships working in both directions. For example, if the phrase "and vice versa" were omitted from the first proposition cited above, one would infer that interaction affected liking but *not* vice versa.

Consider now a series of propositions given by Ralf Dahrendorf:

The intensity of class conflict decreases to the extent that classes are open.[13]

The violence of class conflict decreases to the extent that the conditions of class organization are present.[14]

The radicalness of structure change in an association covaries with the intensity of class conflict.[15]

Since most of Dahrendorf's propositions are stated in a language similar to that used in the first two of the above propositions, the reader might infer that the third proposition has been deliberately worded so as to mean something very different. Judging from the context of the propositions, I would infer that in the case of the first two propositions, Dahrendorf is implying that the first-mentioned variable is affected by the second. The notion of "covaries with" in the third proposition would not seem to imply the same asymmetry, however. Unfortunately, different readers are likely to draw different inferences from these statements.

The question of causal symmetry or asymmetry is not a moot point. . . . The simple phrase "and vice versa" can be tacked onto a theoretical proposition with great ease—but it can also lead to numerous verification problems. Here it will suffice to emphasize a point made by Costner and Leik. If statements of the form, "the greater the X, the greater the Y" are *not* meant to imply causal asymmetry, it is very easy to make erroneous deductive arguments. Consider, for example, propositions 7, 8, and 1 in Zetterberg's set. Presumably, theorem 1 follows from axioms 7 and 8. But suppose 8 were reversed to read: "the greater the consensus, the greater the solidarity." We would then have a theory of the form:

7. The greater the X (division of labor), the greater the Y (solidarity).
8'. The greater the Z (consensus), the greater the Y (solidarity).
1. Therefore, the greater the X (division of labor), the greater the Z (consensus).

Most readers will undoubtedly object that proposition 1 does not obviously follow from 7 and 8', and in so doing will in effect admit that the symmetry-asymmetry question is crucial. In terms of asymmetric causal models, one might wish to distinguish between the situations:

I (Original version)   II (Revised version)

$$X \rightarrow Y \rightarrow Z$$

In model I we expect X and Z to be related, since an increase in X will produce an increase in Y, which in turn will increase Z (assuming all relationships to be positive).[16] But in model II, there is no reason to suppose a specific relationship between X and Z merely because they have a common effect Y.

The more general point is that statements of the form, "the greater the X, the greater the Y" do not really permit one to deduce implications unless they are meant to be more than mere covariance statements. In many instances common-sense applications of verbal language will not lead one astray. But as the theory becomes more and more complex, there will be increasing opportunities for ambiguities of the above type, as well as for erroneous "deductions."

There is another point about "causal chain" relationships that has been noted by several authors, including Costner and Leik.[17] If one uses a number of intervening links, and also admits that at any point in the chain other uncontrolled factors may be operating, then the correlations between non-adjacent variables may be extremely weak. If so, the assumptions one makes about the ways that disturbing influences operate become crucial.[18] Consider the following theory, as stated by Gibbs and Martin:

1. The suicide rate of a population varies inversely with the stability and durability of social relationships within that population. (Postulate 1)
2. The stability and durability of social relationships within a population vary directly with the extent to which individuals in that population conform to the patterned and socially sanctioned demands and expectations placed upon them by others. (Postulate 2)

3. The extent to which individuals in a population conform to patterned and socially sanctioned demands and expectations placed upon them by others varies inversely with the extent to which individuals in that population are confronted with role conflicts. (Postulate 3)
4. The extent to which individuals in a population are confronted with role conflicts varies directly with the extent to which individuals occupy incompatible statuses in that population. (Postulate 4)
5. The extent to which individuals occupy incompatible statuses in a population varies inversely with the degree of status integration in that population. (Postulate 5)
6. The suicide rate of a population varies inversely with the degree of status integration in that population. (Derived theorem)[19]

The theory would seem to imply that suicide rates should vary inversely with the relative frequency with which status combinations are occupied. But given the fact that at each stage there will be numerous variables operating, over and above those specified by the theory, it is by no means obvious that one can deduce even the sign or direction of the relationship between the two end variables.[20] Deductions of this sort require one to commit himself on the causal asymmetry question and also to make explicit assumptions about error terms produced by variables left out of the system. Furthermore, the plausibility of the latter assumptions depends upon whether one allows for reciprocal causation or feedback, or whether he restricts himself to one-way causation.[21] Suffice it to say that the problem is not a simple one; purely verbal formulations will not enable us to deal with subtleties of this sort.

A RESOLUTION

Let us return to the original problem of choosing one's axioms by asking what many authors seem to be doing when they state their arguments in verbal or paragraph form. In most of the attempts I have made to reconstruct or infer an author's argument, I have concluded that his rationale for stating a proposition linking two variables is that he is assuming a direct causal connection between the two. The notion of "directness" is of course relative. An author may or may not attempt to spell out intervening links, some of which he may later omit from his formal theory. But when he states a proposition of the form, "the greater the X, the greater the Y," this is usually preceded or followed by a discussion of why the predicted relationship should hold. Sometimes, this discussion implies a reciprocal causal relationship, as is the case with many of the propositions in The Human Group. In other instances, the author is tracing out a causal chain argument, in which causal asymmetry is definitely implied. Sometimes, unfortunately, the language may be so ambiguous that the direction of causality cannot be inferred. Rarely, however, does an author link two variables in a proposition where no causal connection whatsoever is implied.

It is often difficult to infer exactly what an author has in mind by relying solely on the way he words his propositions. Sometimes propositions are stated as though they refer to total correlations, rather than direct causal links. But if one merely says that two variables should be correlated, without spelling out the mechanisms producing this correlation, then it will be difficult to deduce additional propositions from the theory.

Whenever a theorist is ambiguous on this question, it will of course be easy to put words into his mouth by assuming, for example, that a failure to mention a connection between two variables indicates that there is supposed to be no direct causal link. Rather than debate the question of what the author really meant, it is advisable to go ahead with a more explicit formulation according to whatever line of theoretical reasoning seems most sensible.

Given this ambiguity in statements of the form "the greater the X, the greater the Y," and given the desirability of stating axioms in such a way that they imply direct causal links among variables, I would suggest the following two rules for stating theories in verbal form:

Rule 1:   Select as axioms those propositions that involve variables that are taken to be directly linked causally; axioms should therefore be statements that imply direct causal links among variables.

Rule 2:   State theorems in terms of covariations and temporal sequences, thereby making them testable provided adequate measures of all variables can be obtained.

Axioms may be stated in such a way that reciprocal causation is implied. Ideally, the relative length of time required for the feedback should also be specified. Thus, an axiom might be stated somewhat as follows: "An increase in X will produce (cause) an almost immediate increase in Y; this increase in Y will, in turn, result in a further increase in X, but with a delayed reaction. . . . " This kind of verbal proposition could be translated reasonably easily into a set of simultaneous equations, one of which would be a differential or difference equation. . . . If, in addition, the verbal statement were to specify that the increases should be linear (or some specific nonlinear form, such as monotonically increasing with a decreasing slope), then the task of translating the argument into mathematical equations would be much less ambiguous.

To return to Zetterberg's ten propositions, let us first attempt to diagram what appears to be the argument behind selecting the last four propositions as axioms. Presumably, the causal model implied is that given in Fig. 1, in which the number of associations per member is assumed to affect the division of labor (proposition 9), which in turn affects solidarity (proposition 7). Solidarity then affects two variables, consensus (proposition 8) and the number of rejections of deviants (proposition 10). One might suppose that a theorist would have arrived at these axioms by means of a theoretical argument that specified such more or less direct linkages. Had he inserted intervening links at various points, he might also have elected to insert additional variables into the model. But if we are given only these five variables, we can assume that these particular linkages are taken as the "direct" ones, recognizing that no theoretical system can ever be complete.

The axioms might then be restated so as to make the direction of causal influence explicit:

1. An increase in the number of associates per member will produce an increase in the division of labor.
2. An increase in the division of labor will produce an increase in solidarity.

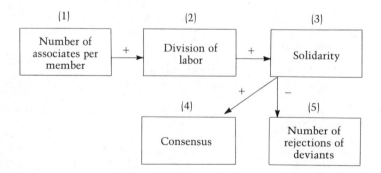

Figure 1. Causal model for Zetterberg's axioms.

3. An increase in solidarity will produce an increase in consensus.
4. An increase in solidarity will produce a decrease in the number of rejections of deviants.

As noted previously, these axioms will need to be supplemented by a set of auxiliary assumptions in order to derive statements about covariations among the variables, unless the theoretical system is taken to be completely closed (i.e., no disturbing influences whatsoever), and unless measurement is perfect. Even with complete closed theoretical systems, it will usually be true that several plausible models will all yield identical empirical predictions. Therefore, causal assumptions such as these can never be directly tested, though they can be used to derive testable theorems stated in terms of covariations.[22]

Assuming that the proper assumptions have been made about variables left out of the system, and about measurement errors, the above four postulates can now be used to derive ten propositions or theorems concerning the signs of the total correlations or covariances among the five variables. These can be represented in matrix form as follows:

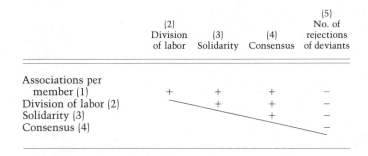

	(2) Division of labor	(3) Solidarity	(4) Consensus	(5) No. of rejections of deviants
Associations per member (1)	+	+	+	−
Division of labor (2)		+	+	−
Solidarity (3)			+	−
Consensus (4)				−

Each of these propositions could of course be stated verbally; for example: "There will be a positive correlation between number of associations per member and division of labor." Notice that we have not only restated Zetterberg's propositions 1–6 as theorems, but covariation statements have also been made about the variables directly linked by arrows in the four axioms (propositions 7–10).

But these are not the only deductions one can make from the theory. If one adds the assumption that all effects are linear and additive, then the model predicts that several partial correlations will also be zero. In particular, one would predict that apart from sampling error all of the following partial correlations should be zero: $r_{13.2}, r_{14.2}, r_{14.3}, r_{15.2}, r_{15.3}, r_{24.3}, r_{25.3},$ and $r_{45.3},$ where the variables have been numbered as in Fig. 1.[23] These predictions are based on the assumption that there are no direct links except as indicated by the arrows. For example, it is assumed that number of associates per member does not affect solidarity except through the division of labor.

If the theorist has spelled out a simple causal chain, as for example in the Gibbs-Martin formulation, one might take as a first approximation a model in which there could be at most one path between any two variables. In some instances, however, an author may explicitly note that there may be several paths connecting one variable to another. If so, this can be incorporated into the causal diagram, as in Fig. 2. It is now more difficult to make specific predictions regarding the sign of the total correlation between the two end variables X_1 and X_5 unless, of course, the products of the signs via each path are the same. One can predict that $r_{15.234}$ should be approximately zero, however. In general, the more complex the model the more difficult it will be to make definitive statements

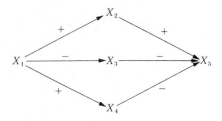

Figure 2. Causal model with alternative paths from x_1 to x_5

about total correlations. Furthermore, the task of evaluating the relative contributions via the different paths becomes more technical. . . .[24]

One additional point about causal chain models seems worth noting in the present context. If a theorist attempts a retrospective analysis of some historical sequence, he may very well reach the conclusion that the outcome was "inevitable." For example, he may conclude that a change in W (say, technology) led to a change in X (economy), which in turn affected Y (belief systems), which finally produced a change in Z (socialization patterns). He may fail to note that variations in other factors—which he has elected to ignore—might have affected the sequence at almost any point. The inevitability of such sequences seems much less obvious when one attempts to predict outcomes in advance of data collection. Likewise, an awareness of the existence of several alternative paths between variables would seem to reduce the likelihood of an analyst's using the inevitability argument.

NOTES

1. Strictly speaking, of course, direct tests will almost always be impossible because of the necessity of making untestable assumptions regarding measurement error.

2. This point is discussed more thoroughly in H. M. Blalock, *Causal Inferences in Non-experimental Research* (Chapel Hill: University of North Carolina Press, 1964), Chap. 1.

3. It is also possible that the axioms of a theory may be tested, or well established, whereas the theorems may not.

4. Procedures for testing relatively simple models involving one-way causation are discussed in Blalock, *Causal Inferences in Nonexperimental Research*, Chap. 3. In the case of more complex models, the reader is referred to the econometrics literature cited in H. M. Blalock, *Theory Construction* (Englewood Cliffs, N.J.: Prentice-Hall, 1969), Chap. 4.

5. Zetterberg, *On Theory and Verification in Sociology* (Totowa, N.J.: Bedminster Press, 1965), pp. 159–160.

6. Ibid., p. 160.

7. See Herbert L. Costner and Robert K. Leik, "Deductions from Axiomatic Theory," *American Sociological Review*, 29 (December 1964), 819–835.

8. George C. Homans, *The Human Group* (New York: Harcourt, Brace and Company, 1950).

9. Ibid., p. 112.

10. Ibid., p. 118.

11. Ibid., p. 120.

12. Ibid.

13. Ralf Dahrendorf, *Class and Class Conflict in Industrial Society* (Stanford: Stanford University Press, 1959), p. 239.

14. Ibid.

15. Ibid., p. 240.

16. In [this] diagram, and in all diagrams that follow, an arrow linking a given pair of variables indicates that there is assumed to be a *direct* causal link between these variables, with "directness" always being relative to the variables that explicitly appear in the model. For further discussion of this point see Blalock, *Causal Inferences in Nonexperimental Research*, Chaps. 1 and 2.

17. Costner and Leik, "Deductions from Axiomatic Theory." See also O. Dudley Duncan, "Axioms or Correlations?" *American Sociological Review*, 28 (June 1963), 452.

18. Perhaps the simplest set of such assumptions is that neglected factors produce only random disturbances.

19. Jack P. Gibbs and Walter T. Martin, *Status Integration and Suicide* (Eugene, Ore.: University of Oregon Press, 1964), p. 27. See also Jack P. Gibbs and Walter T. Martin, "On Assessing the Theory of Status Integration and Suicide," *American Sociological Review*, 31 (August 1966), 533–541.

20. Costner and Leik, "Deductions from Axiomatic Theory," refer to this kind of simple deduction as providing a "sign rule." In the case of a simple causal chain, one may multiply the signs of the intervening relationships; an even number of negative signs will produce a positive predicted relationship between the two "end variables," whereas an odd number of negative relationships will yield a negative predicted relationship, as in the case of the Gibbs-Martin propositions.

21. Blalock, *Theory Construction*, Chap. 4.

22. For a more complete discussion of the kinds of predictions that are possible in the case of linear recursive models, see Blalock, *Causal Inferences in Nonexperimental Research*, Chap. 3.

23. The prediction $r_{ij,k} = 0$ can of course be stated in the alternative form $r_{ij} = r_{ik}\, r_{jk}$.

24. The interested reader is referred to the literature on structural systems cited in Blalock, *Theory Construction*, Chap. 4, and to discussions of path analysis. See especially, C. C. Li, *Population Genetics* (Chicago: University of Chicago Press, 1955), Chap. 12; Sewall Wright, "Path Coefficients and Path Regressions: Alternative or Complementary Concepts?" *Biometrics*, 16 (June 1960), 189–202; O. Dudley Duncan, "Path Analysis: Sociological Examples," *American Journal of Sociology*, 72 (July 1966), 1–16; and H. M. Blalock and Ann B. Blalock, eds., *Methodology in Social Research*, Chaps. 2, 5, and 6.

SIMON OUT OF HOMANS BY COLEMAN [1]

HARRISON C. WHITE

Reprinted from the *American Journal of Sociology*, 75 (March 1970), pp. 852–862. Copyright © by the University of Chicago. Used by permission of the author and publisher, The University of Chicago Press, 1971.

Harrison C. White is professor and chairman of the Department of Sociology at Harvard University.

Homans (1950) teased out of empirical studies of small groups a set of propositions relating interaction, friendliness, and activity in terms of the level of output required by the environment. He did much else—delved into the effects of status, the architecture of roles, perception, etc.—but Simon (1952) settled for the average levels of the first four "quantities" in building a model. Coupled linear differential equations are his first translation of Homans's interrelations.[2] Simon goes on to a dazzling derivation of much from almost nothing, showing that linearity in the equations is not necessary to the fundamental qualitative conclusions about viable equilibrium states. The sore spot throughout is the lack of any suggestion on how to measure the four variables. Most model builders when shod in operational variables will cheerfully carry the cross of linearity—perhaps too cheerfully. Coleman's monograph (1964) provides some leather.

Coleman's core idea has three parts:[3] use proportions of individuals with given attributes as state variables, represent causal interrelations in terms of rates of flow among cells in a cross-classification by different attributes, and focus on instantaneous rates—differential calculus instead of the discrete time approach —so that most of the rates can be set at zero a priori. The latter two parts distinguish his from most earlier models of movement among attributes.[4] Coleman aims for the economy and clarity of random-walk models and avoids the proliferation of parameters in Markov chain models (see Feller, 1968). Coleman emphasizes stochastic interpretations of his models, but the core idea fits as well into a determinist model for aggregates.[5]

Simon's equations serve as guides in structuring a Coleman model for flows of individuals. There is no guarantee that every detail in Simon's interpretation of Homans will be consistent with a model for flows of individuals in an attribute space. Step by step, the most general set of linear differential equations compatible with Homans's topic will be specialized until Simon's particular equations emerge. It will be easy, if necessary, to alter Simon's equations.

Simon's linear model will be extended to include statements about individuals and thus about correlations of attributes over individuals, by interpreting each variable as the proportion of individuals with a given attribute. No longer is the sole concern in tracing the consequences of the set of postulates Simon finds in Homans. A successful search is made for a set of postulates about individual behavior which yield these postulates about group averages.

Operationalizing the model remains the central contribution. Not only must the variables be measurable, as proportions, but also the parameters must be few enough to be manageable. A useful by-product is to show the form a Coleman model of a cross-classification must take to yield valid dynamic equations in terms of marginals alone, here the equations of the Simon-Homans model. Results for correlations are then additional to, rather than subversive of, equations in group averages, and they permit additional tests of the model.

SIMON'S MODEL AS A SPECIAL CASE

Simon extracts from Homans the idea of mutual interrelations among the levels of friendship, interaction, and activity in a concrete group of people subject to very strong pressure from the environment to carry out some level of purposeful activity. Neither proposes measures for these variables, denoted F, I, A, and E, respectively. Simon (1952: 3d sec.) shows how mere ordinal scales for the variables are sufficient to derive useful results about equilibria and paths of change from a nonlinear model stipulating only qualitative functional relations among the variables. Even ordinal scales for group levels, however, could only be constructed as averages of variables and interactions for individuals if the latter were given as cardinal measures (see Simon, 1957: 100, last paragraph). One may as well assume cardinal measures, and in the next section operational definitions are proposed.

Like Homans, Simon assumes that the group does not instantly reach equilibrium so that paths over time must be specified. Simon goes beyond Homans to assume that, given cardinal measures of the group levels, all relations among these variables are linear. Moreover, Simon assumes that rates of change are determined by the levels of the four group variables at the preceding instant—memory, history, and anticipations play no independent role.

Make the simplest possible assumption: the rate of change of each variable equals the sum of all four variables, each multiplied by some constant parameter. The trick is in specifying the signs and relations among parameters.

1. Since E by definition is arbitrary, imposed from the outside, each parameter in the equation for dE/dt is zero, and the equation can be ignored.
2. Each other variable if left to itself—all other variables being zero—will dwindle to zero. That is, people are intrinsically inert, at least in the groups studied; they cannot sustain any level of activity, friendship, or interaction just for its own sake. Hence in the equation for rate of change of each variable, the coefficient of that variable in the sum on the right side is negative.
3. The effect of each other variable on the rate of change of a given one depends on how far the two existing levels are from being in harmony. Harmony means being in a given ratio, and the given variable changes so as to tend to return to that ratio, with a speed proportional to the deviation from that ratio. Harmony between two variables may be one ratio when viewed by the first, in *its* rate-of-change equation, and a different ratio when viewed by the second. Another, simpler way to put the matter is that in the equation for rate of change of a given variable the coefficients of all *other* variables on the right are positive; this, together with point 2, immediately permits one to gather terms as follows:

$$\frac{dF}{dt} = b(I - \beta F) + b_1(A - \beta_1 F) + b_2(E - \beta_2 F), \tag{1}$$

$$\frac{dA}{dt} = c(I - \gamma' A) + c_1(F - \gamma A) + c_2(E - \gamma'' A), \tag{2}$$

$$\frac{dI}{dt} = d(F - \delta I) + d'(A - \delta_1 I) + d''(E - \delta_2 I). \tag{3}$$

Points 2 and 3 state in effect that all coefficients in these equations are positive. The English letter coefficients outside the parentheses determine speed of adjustment. The Greek letter coefficients reflect the "harmony" levels: note that the harmony ratio $A/F = \beta_1$ need not be the same as the other harmony ratio $A/F = 1/\gamma$.

Substantive insight is required beyond these general ideas for any set of interdependent variables. Simon in effect extracts from Homans' text the following restrictions on parameters:

4. The rates d and d' can be treated as infinite: that is, the level of interaction adapts extremely quickly compared with activity and friendship levels.
5. The rate d'' is zero: that is, the rate of talking and other interaction is not directly responsive to the externally imposed level of activity E.

From points 4 and 5 it follows that I will instantaneously adapt to the levels of F and A in such a way as to make the right side of equation (3) equal zero. Express this as a new equation,

$$I = a_1 F + a_2 A , \tag{4}$$

where the a's are just new names for combinations of coefficients; for example, $a_2 = d'/(\delta + \delta')d$.

6. The rates b_1 and b_2 are zero. This is Simon's crucial step in specifying the causal order among the variables as Homans discusses them. Neither imposed activity level or actual activity level directly affects the change in friendliness. Thus interaction is the (sole) intervening variable through which activity affects friendliness.
7. Next, $\gamma'' = 1$. (Since E and A are both activity levels, γ'', unlike other Greek letters, need not contain a conversion from one kind of unit to another.) "Malingering factor" is a reasonable name for γ''; a squad of city street repairmen in Boston would surely have $\gamma'' > 1$, whereas one would hope a graduate seminar would have $\gamma'' < 1$.
8. Finally, $\gamma' = 0$: that is, the group's activity level is not directly responsive to the level of interaction.

Points 6–8 plus equation (4) simplify equations (1) and (2) to the form Simon (1952: eqs. 1.1–1.3) proposes from the beginning (and with the same notation):

$$\frac{dF}{dt} = ba_2 A - b(\beta - a_1)F , \tag{5}$$

$$\frac{dA}{dt} = c_1(F - \gamma A) + c_2(E - A). \tag{6}$$

Since there are no operational definitions of the variables, much less any estimates of the parameters, it is silly to derive the detailed path followed by the variables from the initial state, specified fully by F and A at time zero. Instead Simon first proves there can never be an oscillation in the time path given merely that all the parameters are indeed positive. Then he shows the variables will settle at some equilibrium values, instead of soaring up indefinitely, if and only if

$$(\beta - a_1)(c_1\gamma + c_2) > a_2 c_1. \tag{7}$$

Equation (7) can be stated in an intuitively plausible way: the geometric average of the damping rates must exceed the geometric average of the cross-excitation rates. Note that the imposed activity E does not figure, nor does the rate b.

The equilibrium levels of A and F (and thence I) are proportional to E as expected. If nothing is required of a group, it becomes completely inert. If required activity is doubled from a given level, activity, friendliness, and interaction double. The equations are easy to derive:

$$A_o = \frac{c_2(\beta - a_1)}{(c_1\gamma + c_2)(\beta - a_1) - c_1 a_2} E \tag{8}$$

and

$$F_o = \frac{a_2}{\beta - a_1} A_o. \tag{9}$$

Simon attaches plausible labels to parameters—for example, $1/\gamma$ measures "spontaneity"—and shows how various changes in parameters produce the kinds of changes in equilibrium values one would expect and can often find in Homans's descriptions. Simon emphasizes the comparison of A_o and E, the only two variables with the same units, and denotes $A_o < E$ as a situation of "positive morale." This discussion of the requirements for and effects of positive morale seems shaky because it depends crucially on assumption 7, which would itself seem to be plausible only for medium levels of morale.

A MODEL FOR PROPORTIONS WITH CORRELATION

The simplest possible way to operationalize average variables for a group is to equate each with the proportion of the group that has a corresponding attribute. Individuals are dichotomized as having or not having the attribute; naturally, information about differences among individuals may be lost in this simplification. Hereafter interpret A, F, and I as such proportions.

A new dimension obtrudes itself: correlation. Simon's model says activity and friendliness mutually influence one another as averages, and it seems implausible that possession of one attribute by an individual would not influence the likelihood of his having other attributes. At a deeper level one would argue for contextual effects in which the state of each individual is influenced by the number and proportion of others which have each attribute (see Coleman, 1964: sec. 11.6). Here only the minimal assumption is investigated, so that individuals change independently of one another. Can the average interrelations Homans describes and Simon formalizes be the aggregate result?

My main goal is developing, in Coleman's words (1964: 105–106), "a model which has precisely the characteristics for problems involving discrete states that the usual differential-equations model has for problems involving continuous variables"—that is, a model which derives from a conception of causal relations acting through time. Here E is an arbitrary exogenous force and I, although at the center of the causal nexus, adapts so fast that one need treat explicitly only the dynamics of A and F. Variable E is the external driving force, F is the internal driving force, and A is the measure of performance and in a sense the dependent variable, while I reflects intervening mechanisms and can be treated as a hidden variable. (Coleman [1964: 123–127] at one point sketches a model for Homans's propositions relating just friendliness and interaction, but it seems clear he made this awkward choice in order to tie the discussion to his own data on friendship and interaction among printers.)

Figure 1 reproduces Coleman's most general diagram (1964: 124) for flow rates of persons among cells in a 2×2 table. Treat friendliness and activity as dichotomous attributes, the former present when in the upper half and the latter when in the left half of the plane.[6] The rate q_{12}, for example, is for men in cell 1 moving to cell 2, that is, changing from the state of being active and friendly to that of being active and nonfriendly. The essential point is the lack of diagonal arrows: there is no chance of changing both attributes simultaneously.

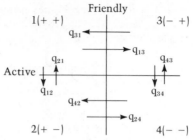

Figure 1. Rate parameters in the general case; from Coleman (1964, p. 124, labels supplied).

Let the fraction of men, or the probability of a man being in state i be labelled p_i. It is easy to write down the equations for Figure 1; a typical one is

$$\frac{dp_1}{at} = -(q_{12} + q_{13})p_1 + q_{21}p_2 + q_{31}p_3. \tag{10}$$

Only three are needed, since

$$p_1 + p_2 + p_3 + p_4 = 1, \tag{11}$$

and this equation can be used to eliminate, say, p_4 in the other three equations. The operational definitions of F and A are

$$F = p_1 + p_3 \text{ and } A = p_1 + p_2. \tag{12}$$

Through combinations of equations one obtains

$$\frac{dF}{dt} = -(q_{12} + q_{43})p_1 - (q_{34} + q_{43})p_3 + (q_{21} - q_{43})p_2 + q_{43}, \tag{13}$$

$$\frac{dA}{dt} = -(q_{13} + q_{42})p_1 - (q_{24} + q_{42})p_2 + (q_{31} - q_{42})p_3 + q_{42}. \tag{14}$$

To match equation (13) with equation (5), it must be possible to group all terms on the right into a constant times the sum of p_1 and p_2 and another constant times $(p_1 + p_3)$. Inspection shows rates must be constrained as follows:

$$q_{34} = q_{12} + q_{21} \tag{15}$$

and

$$q_{43} = 0. \tag{16}$$

Equation (16) is required because there is no exogenous term in equation (5). To match equation (14) with equation (6), inspection shows

$$q_{24} + q_{42} = q_{13} + q_{31} \tag{17}$$

and

$$q_{42} = c_2 E \tag{18}$$

must hold. Equations (15)–(17) say that the sum of the opposed rates (absolute values) across an axis in Figure 1 must be the same on both halves of the axis. It is convenient to relabel some rates in a manner parallel to Coleman's usage (1964: 169):

$$q_{31} = q_{42} + \theta ,$$ (19)

$$q_{24} = q_{13} + \theta .$$ (20)

Five independent parameters remain. There were eight independent rate parameters in the general case of Figure 1.[7] The special case which must hold for Simon's equations to be consistent with the equations for proportions is shown in figure 2. Equations (5) and (6) become in the new notation

$$\frac{dF}{dt} = q_{21}A - q_{34}F$$ (21)

$$\frac{dA}{dt} = \theta F - (q_{13} + q_{42} + \theta) A + q_{42}.$$ (22)

From (22) it is clear that θ must be positive.

A final, more subtle restriction becomes apparent from equation (22). The term not proportional to a variable, namely, q_{42}, is proportional to E; yet the coefficient of A, which contains q_{42} must be independent of E to conform to equation (6), for the Simon model. Hence one must assume q_{13} varies in such a way as to prevent variation with E of the coefficient of A.[8] One interpretation is that persons have a fixed total capacity for change on the A attribute so that, if external forces build up the rate in one direction (equation [18]), the rate in the other is decreased commensurately.

The parameter θ represents interaction effect; one more quickly changes from inactive to active when friendly than otherwise, and also one less quickly changes from active to inactive when not friendly than when friendly. The parameter q_{21} is parallel to θ; it represents the interaction effect of activity level on rate of change of friendliness state. In the absence of external forces and interaction effects, all movements in Figure 2 would be down or to the right toward complete absence of activity and friendliness.

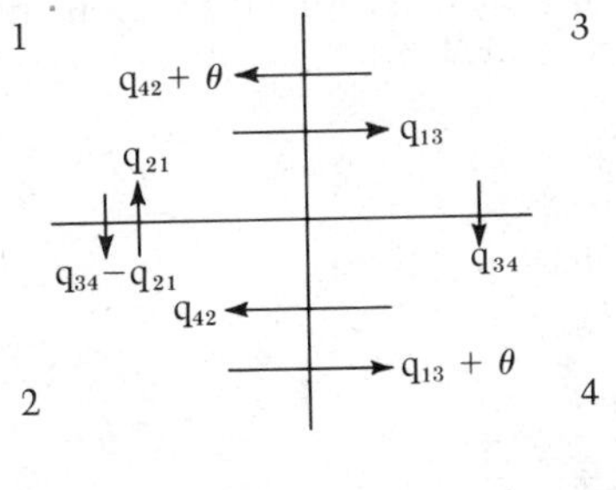

Figure 2. Rate parameters which yield the Simon equations in marginal totals. The variable q_{42} is proportional to the external level of activity E imposed, and q_{13} must change when E changes so as to keep fixed the sum $q_{42} + q_{13} + \theta$ (call it T).

Expressions for parameters in terms of Simon's constants are clear:

$$q_{21} = ba_2, \quad q_{34} = b(\beta - a_1), \quad \theta = c_1,$$

$$T = c_2 + c_1\gamma, \quad \text{and} \quad q_{42} = c_2E, \tag{23}$$

where $T \equiv q_{42} + q_{13} + \theta$. But the new parameters must be interpreted in the context of proportions with correlation, not averages of continuous variables in different units. Simon's condition for stability, equation (7), carries over and becomes in translation

$$q_{34}(q_{13} + q_{42} + \theta) > q_{21}\theta. \tag{24}$$

This is a tautology in the new model, since $q_{34} > q_{21}$ is required (equation [15]) if all the rate parameters q_{ij} are to be positive. Instability in Simon's sense is meaningless, since A and F must by their definition as proportions remain between 0 and 1. The equilibrium equations (8) and (9) for Simon carry over into

$$A_o = \frac{q_{42}q_{34}}{[q_{34}(q_{13} + q_{42}) + \theta(q_{34} - q_{21})]} \tag{25}$$

and

$$F_o = \frac{q_{21}}{q_{34}}A_o. \tag{26}$$

These predicted equilibrium sizes are always between 0 and 1, as required. The fact that A and F cannot tend to increase without limit even in extreme circumstances is a limitation of the new model.

When Simon's variables are identified with marginal totals in a cross-tabulation of men on activity and friendliness, his equations can be recovered from equations for proportions in the cross-tabulation. Instead of Simon's seven parameters, there are five independent transition parameters. These must be positive and must combine into seven positive rates between states, as shown in Figure 2; also, the sum $q_{42} + q_{13} + \theta$ must be a constant independent of the rate of activity E imposed from outside, whereas q_{42} is proportional to E. Instability, like oscillation, is impossible in this new form of the model, wherein the state variables are pure numbers confined between zero and 1.

To compute the correlation between attributes over individuals, one needs the proportions in single cells. Equilibrium levels (as well as time paths) of F and A, the marginals, are already determined; so, as in any 2×2 table, only one cell entry, say p_1, is undetermined. From equation 10, in equilibrium

$$(q_{34} - q_{21} + q_{13})p_1 = q_{21}p_2 + (q_{42} + \theta)p_3. \tag{27}$$

Substitutions from equation (12) lead to

$$p_1 = \frac{q_{21}}{q_{34}}\left(1 - \frac{q_{13}}{T + q_{34}}A_o\right) \tag{28}$$

If the correlation were zero, p_1 in equilibrium would be just the product of F_o and A_o.[9] Comparison of equations (28) and (26) makes it clear that correlation will not be zero in general.

DISCUSSION

Estimates of parameters and tests of the new model will be most convincing when based on observations of changes of state by all individuals in the group during very short periods.[10] Bales (1951) has shown how to code reliably the stream of communicating flashes in a small group as friendly (or hostile, neutral, etc.) and according to target of the interaction; presumably one could code instantaneous changes in attitudes and activity of these individuals with some reliability.[11] Joel Cohen (1968) reports this kind of observation: he judged change in membership in small play groups in a nursery every thirty seconds from a judgment of mutual orientation as well as physical proximity.

Questionnaires are the most common and possibly most reliable way to assess attitudes. Then estimates and tests would have to be made more indirectly because data could be gathered only at considerable intervals, in a panel study. The hypothesized absence of diagonal rates in Figures 1 and 2 could not be tested directly, and the other rates would not be simply proportional to observed turnover components in panel data.

The easiest but most limited tests and estimates would use only observation of the proportions p_i in equilibrium,[12] that is, of A_0, F_0, and p_1—equations (25), (26), and (28). The proportionality between q_{42} and E (eq. [18]), together with the independence between E and the coefficient of A insisted upon in equation (22), could be tested by seeing if A_0 were indeed simply proportional to E as stated in equation (25). There would remain the difficult problem discussed by Simon (1957: 100, n. 3) of estimating E numerically: one estimate might be the fraction of men who perceive the environment as requiring activity of the group. There would remain the task of estimating five independent parameters, one now being q_{42}/E rather than q_{42}. The three equations (25), (26), and (28) can yield estimates only of three combinations of parameters—variation of E would yield only a test of whether A_0, F_0, and p were each proportional to E as hypothesized.

One additional assumption of some plausibility would reduce the independent parameters required in the three equations for equilibrium to three. Suppose the total rate of movement in both directions across the activity boundary, the same for both levels of friendliness, is the same as q_{34}, the corresponding total rate across the friendliness boundary in Figure 2. Divide each parameter by this common total, and indicate this normalization by a bar over the symbol. Then from equation (26) $\bar{q}_{21}$ can be estimated:

$$F_o = \bar{q}_{21}A_o ; \qquad (29)$$

and thence from equation (28) $\bar{q}_{13}$ can be estimated:

$$p_1 = \bar{q}_{21}\left(1 - \frac{\bar{q}_{13}}{2}\, A_o.\right) \qquad (30)$$

The remaining parameter $\bar{q}_{42}$ can then be extracted from (25):

$$A_o = \frac{\bar{q}_{42}}{1 - (1 - \bar{q}_{13} - \bar{q}_{42})\bar{q}_{21}}. \qquad (31)$$

It will surely happen with many types of groups that the model is not valid. A return to the successive special assumptions listed earlier in specifying Simon's model may suggest ways to vary and enlarge the scope of the model.

NOTES

1. Financial support under grant GS-448 from the National Science Foundation is gratefully acknowledged. Students in a course on mathematical models, especially John Fitts and Paul Levitt, made valuable contributions.

2. In footnotes and text Simon cogently discusses both what he does and what he does not utilize from Homans in the actual model.

3. This is my assessment and may not be shared by others; Chapters 4 and 5 of Coleman (1964) are the core of his work for this interpretation.

4. Most notably, models for predicting the evolution of voting. Coleman himself draws the contrast with earlier models (e.g., Coleman, 1964: 53).

5. Stochastic interpretation provides a natural framework for assessing deviations between predicted and observed averages. It is hard, in any case, to conceive of behavior in a small group as having no chance components. Examples of sophisticated uses of stochastic aspects of a model, treated as integral with the model, can be found in Goodman (1962, 1964).

6. The cells might better be represented by four points, corners of a square, as in a random-walk model. One cannot assume the same model could describe moves of persons among quadrants if the attributes were truly continuous variables; I failed to find any bivariate distribution which permitted such an assumption.

7. Coleman (1964: 162) calls this the "opposing effects" case. The other case Coleman singles out, "presence and absence," does not hold here—it would, for example, require $q_{24} = q_{13}$ instead of equation (20).

8. The problem is not with the linearity of the equations: E as an exogenous level can be treated much like a parameter, as long as it does not vary rapidly, but the model then would become hopelessly complex.

9. In a 2×2 table a useful measure of association which is independent of the marginals is

$$\nu = \frac{p_1 p_4}{p_2 p_3}.$$

(See Levine, 1967; Mosteller, 1968.) From equations (11) and (12), ν can be expressed in terms of p_1 together with F_0 and A_0 (and thence E).

10. The essence of the difference between the new model and Simon's is that the former assumes individuals are changing constantly even though in the aggregate the proportions in different cells may stay near equilibrium values. Correlations across individuals do not appear in Simon's model because individuals are thought to reach equilibrium (though each at different levels of the variables).

11. The fundamental crudeness of the model, in either the new form or Simon's form, is manifest in their reduction of interaction phenomena to variables on individuals.

12. This is the familiar method of comparative statics (see Simon, 1957: 105).

REFERENCES

Bales, R. F. *Interaction Process Analysis*. Reading, Mass.: Addison-Wesley, 1951.

Cohen, Joel E. "The LOST Model." Unpublished manuscript, Society of Fellows, Harvard University, 1968.

Coleman, James S. *Introduction to Mathematical Sociology*. New York: Free Press and Macmillan, 1964.

Feller, W. *An Introduction to Probability Theory and Its Applications*. Vol. 1. 3d. ed. New York: Wiley, 1968.

Goodman, Leo. "Statistical Methods for Analyzing Processes of Change," *American Journal of Sociology*, 68 (July 1962), 57–78.

———. "Mathematical Methods for the Study of Systems of Groups," *American Journal of Sociology*, 70 (September 1964), 170–192.

Homans, George C. *The Human Group*. New York: Macmillan, 1950.

Levine, Joel H. "Measurement in the Study of Intergenerational Mobility." Ph.D. dissertation, Harvard University, 1967.

Mosteller, C. F. "Association and Estimation in Contingency Tables," *Journal of the American Statistical Association*, 63 (March 1968), 1–28.

Simon, Herbert A. "A Formal Theory of Interaction in Social Groups," *American Sociological Review*, 17 (1952), 202–211. Reprinted in Herbert A. Simon, *Models of Man* (New York: Wiley, 1957).

CHAPTER 3

SYMBOLIC INTERACTIONISM

Introduction

Symbolic interactionism is the dominant social psychology that informs sociologists and has permitted them to generally ignore Freudian psychology. Symbolic interactionism stresses that the self is developed by the exchange of meaningful symbols with other individuals and that social life and its rewards stem from such exchanges. Indeed, reality itself is an emerging product of interaction (see Berger and Luckmann, 1966). Theorizing is generally limited to this "micro" level, although some (such as Warriner, 1970) have attempted to bridge the gap between it and "macro" theorizing about society.

Mullins (1973) has called symbolic interactionists the "loyal opposition" to standard American sociology, approximately the schools discussed in Chapters 1 and 2. But, as he notes, symbolic interactionists have largely been able to coexist with the establishment sociologies. Some, however, have not and have launched critiques of standard sociology (see Glaser and Strauss, 1967). Indeed, most introductory textbooks in sociology draw heavily on symbolic interaction for social psychological concepts and their view of man in society. Symbolic-interaction oriented studies of deviance and the works of symbolic-interaction founders are also widely cited. Nonetheless, some symbolic interactionists have always felt themselves apart from the mainstream of sociology, and there is now a recently formed society to symbolize their separateness. Few academic departments, however, would be outraged by one of their faculty declaring that he is, and has always been, a symbolic interactionist.

There are identifiable "schools" within symbolic interactionism, the most common division being between the Chicago school and the Iowa school (see Meltzer and Petras, 1970; Vaughan and Reynolds, 1968). The former is derived directly from the work of symbolic-interaction founders and their followers, while the latter centers around the more quantitative approach of some University of Iowa sociologists, preeminently Manford Kuhn (1964). Mullins outlines the core members of both schools (1973:75), while others have pointed to the methodological differences between them (see Reynolds and Meltzer, 1973). Meltzer, Petras, and Reynolds (1975) note that others have discerned as many as ten varieties of symbolic interaction, but they themselves limit the division to the Chicago and Iowa schools together with ethnomethodology and dramaturgical varieties. The latter is a category designed primarily to envelop the work of Erving Goffman (1959, 1963, 1967, 1969, 1971), while ethnomethodology has now established an identity separate from symbolic interaction, despite the call for synthesis made by Denzin (1969).

Although it is possible for symbolic interaction to claim some heritage from the German sociologists Max Weber and Georg Simmel or the French psychology of Gabriel Tarde, the primary founders were Americans. The most widely recognized founders are Charles H. Cooley, W. I. Thomas, and especially, George H. Mead. (Meltzer, Petras, and Reynolds, 1975, in a comprehensive chapter on origins, also cite philosophers James and Dewey as founders.)

Although Cooley(1864–1929)worked on an organic theory of society, he is best remembered for his concepts of primary group and "looking-glass self"—the idea that our self-perception is derived from how we believe others to see us. W. I. Thomas (1863–1947) is remembered for emphasizing the importance of the "definition of the situation"—the notion that in terms of social consequences it is the person's perception of reality, not reality per se that counts. Unlike the other founders, Thomas was a pioneer in applying the theoretical perspective to substantive topics (for example, his studies of the adaptive problems of Polish peasants in the United States and of delinquent girls).

Mead (1863–1931) taught at the University of Chicago (hence the name "Chicago School" of symbolic interaction). Although he wrote little (his major works are edited versions of his papers and lectures—see Mead, 1934, 1938, 1956, 1964), he was an inspiring teacher and the center of the symbolic-interaction circle that included Herbert Blumer. According to Blumer (1966), sociology has not yet fully appreciated and absorbed Mead's teaching, and as with other founders of sociology (such as Weber and Durkheim), there is a continuing evaluative literature (see, for example, Miller, 1973a, 1973b; Petras, 1973).

The first selection in this chapter outlines the basis of symbolic interaction by its leading exponent, Herbert Blumer. None of the founders of symbolic interaction, he claims, worked out a fully "systematic statement of the nature of human group life." His attempt is, therefore, to set out the "basic premises" of symbolic interaction. Blumer stresses the symbolic nature of human interaction, the existence of the self (which is capable of "self-indication") and the conscious construction of interaction within a social context. Much of sociology, claims Blumer, ignores these realities and views individuals as organisms driven by external social forces. Society, he adds, should be seen as acting units made up of individuals, not as abstract structures. Too often, then, symbolic interaction is *not* taken into account by the sociologist.

Denzin's article that follows deals with the application of symbolic-interaction perspectives to the study of deviance and thereby counters the most common criticism of symbolic interaction—that it cannot be readily applied to social research. Denzin begins along lines similar to

Blumer, outlining the basic assumptions of symbolic interaction; he then derives a set of basic concepts from them. Deviant acts are viewed as "interactional productions." He then discusses the method—"natural-istic behaviorism"—by which they are best studied. The last stage of re-search—how to generate general explanations from richly detailed epi-sodic accounts—remains problematic for symbolic-interaction research. One derivation from symbolic interaction, "labeling theory," has been widely applied to the study of deviance but not without considerable dif-ficulty and criticism (see, for example, Trice and Roman, 1970; Mankoff, 1971).

Huber next provides a thoroughgoing critique of symbolic-interac-tion-inspired research. Theory is generated from the research setting it-self, he says, but it is biased by the researcher's personal perspective and the power relations between researcher and researched. This claim gen-erated considerable reaction among sociologists. Schmitt (1974) argues that Huber's treatment of symbolic interaction is "inadequate"and that symbolic-interaction methodology cannot be equated to participant ob-servation. The problem of bias is, for Schmitt, overdrawn, and alterna-tive, deductive explanations offer less hope of understanding social life. Stone, et al. (1974) question Huber's critique of the philosophical foun-dation of symbolic interaction and symbolic-interaction methodology. Huber's (1974) reply indicates that she still has serious reservations about the potential of symbolic-interaction research. Blumer's response and Huber's rejoinder are reprinted in this chapter, and they demonstrate well the heat of theoretical debate in sociology and the something-short-of-full-acceptance of symbolic interaction by other sociologists.

References and Selected Readings

Berger, Peter, and Thomas Luckmann. *The Social Construction of Reality*. Garden City, N.Y.: Doubleday, 1966.

Blumer, Herbert. "Sociological Analysis and the Variable," *American Sociological Review*, 21 (1956), 683–90.

———. "The Sociological Implications of the Thought of George Herbert Mead," *American Journal of Sociology*, 71 (1966), 535–44.

———. *Symbolic Interactionism: Perspective and Method*. Englewood Cliffs, N.J.: Pren-tice-Hall, 1969.

Cooley, Charles H. *Social Organization*. New York: Schocken, 1962.

———. *Human Nature and the Social Order*. New York: Schocken, 1964.

Denzin, Norman, "Symbolic Interactionism and Ethnomethodology: A Proposed Synthe-sis," *American Sociological Review*, 34 (1969), 922–34.

———. "The Methodologies of Symbolic Interaction. A Critical Review of Research Tech-niques," in Gregory P. Stone and Harvey A. Farberman, eds., *Social Psychology Through Symbolic Interaction*. Waltham, Mass.: Ginn-Blaisdell, 1970, pp. 447–65.

Glaser, Barney G., and Anselm L. Strauss. *The Discovery of Grounded Theory*. Chicago: Aldine, 1967.

Goffman, Erving. *The Presentation of Self in Everyday Life*. New York: Anchor, 1959.

———. *Behavior in Public Places*. New York: Free Press, 1963.

———. *Interaction Ritual*. New York: Anchor, 1967.

———. *Strategic Interaction*. Philadelphia: University of Pennsylvania Press, 1969.

———. *Relations in Public*. New York: Basic Books, 1971.

Huber, Joan. "The Emergency of Emergent Theory," *American Sociological Review*, 39 (1974), 463–67.

Kuhn, Manford H. "Major Trends in Symbolic Interaction Theory in the Past Twenty-five Years," *The Sociological Quarterly*, 5 (Winter 1964), 61–84.

Manis, Jerome G., and Bernard N. Meltzer. *Symbolic Interaction: A Reader in Social Psychology*. 2d ed. Boston: Allyn and Bacon, 1972.

Mankoff, Milton. "Societal Reaction and Career Deviance: A Critical Analysis," *The Sociological Quarterly*, 12 (Spring 1971), 204–18.

Mead, George H. *Mind, Self and Society from the Standpoint of a Social Behaviorist*. Edited, with an Introduction, by Charles W. Morris. Chicago: University of Chicago Press, 1934.

————. *The Philosophy of the Act*. Edited, with an Introduction, by Charles W. Morris, in collaboration with John M. Brewster, Albert M. Dunham, and David L. Miller. Chicago: University of Chicago Press, 1938.

————. *The Social Psychology of George Herbert Mead*. Edited, with an Introduction, by Anselm Srauss, Phoenix Books. Chicago: The University of Chicago Press, 1956.

————. *Selected Writings*. Edited, with an Introduction, by Andrew J. Reck. Indianapolis: Bobbs-Merrill, 1964.

Meltzer, Bernard N., and John W. Petras. "The Chicago and Iowa Schools of Symbolic Interactionism," in Tamotsu Shibutani, ed., *Human Nature and Collective Behavior: Papers in Honor of Herbert Blumer*. Englewood Cliffs, N.J.: Prentice-Hall, 1970, pp. 3–17.

Meltzer, Bernard N., John W. Petras, and Larry T. Reynolds. *Symbolic Interactionism: Genesis, Varieties and Criticism*. London: Routledge and Kegan Paul, 1975.

Miller, David L. "George Herbert Mead: Symbolic Interaction and Social Change," *Psychological Record*, 23 (1973), 294–304. (a)

————. *George Herbert Mead: Self, Language, and the World*. Austin: University of Texas Press, 1973. (b)

Mullins, Nicholas C. *Theories and Theory Groups in Contemporary American Sociology*. New York: Harper & Row, 1973.

Petras, John W. "George Herbert Mead's Theory of Self: A Study in the Origin and Convergence of Ideas," *Canadian Review of Sociology and Anthropology*, 10 (1973), 155.

Reynolds, Larry T., and Bernard N. Meltzer. "The Origins of Divergent Methodological Stances in Symbolic Interactionism," *The Sociological Quarterly*, 14, (Spring 1973), 189–99.

Reynolds, Larry T., Red R. Vaughen, Janice M. Reynolds, and Leon Warshay. "The Self in Symbolic Interaction Theory: An Examination of the Social Sources of the Conceptual Diversity," in Larry T. Reynolds and Janice M. Reynolds, eds., *The Sociology of Sociology*. New York: McKay, 1970, pp. 422–38.

Schmitt, Raymond L. "Symbolic Interaction and Emergent Theory: A Reexamination," *American Sociological Review*, 39 (1974), 453–56.

Shibutani, Tamotsu. *Society and Personality*. Englewood Cliffs, N.J.: Prentice-Hall, 1961.

————. *Human Nature and Collective Behavior: Papers in Honor of Herbert Blumer*. Englewood Cliffs, N.J.: Prentice Hall, 1970.

Stone, Gregory P., and Harvey A. Farberman. *Social Psychology Through Symbolic Interaction*. Waltham, Mass: Xerox Publishing, 1970.

Stone, Gregory P., David R. Maines, Harvey A. Farberman, Gladys I. Stone, and Norman K. Denzin. "On Methodology and Craftsmanship in the Criticism of Sociological Perspectives," *American Sociological Review*, 39 (1974), 456–63.

Trice, Harrison M., and Paul M. Roman. "Delabeling, Relabeling and Alcoholics Anonymous," *Social Problems*, 17 (1970), 539–46.

Vaughan, T. R., and L. T. Reynolds. "The Sociology of Symbolic Interactionism," *American Sociologist*, 3 (1968), 208–14.

Warriner, Charles K. *The Emergence of Society*. Homewood, Ill.: Dorsey Press, 1970.

SOCIETY AS SYMBOLIC INTERACTION

HERBERT BLUMER

From *Human Behavior and Social Processes*, edited by
Arnold M. Rose. "Society as Symbolic Interaction" by
Herbert Blumer. (Boston: Houghton Mifflin Company,
1962). Reprinted by permission of Houghton Mifflin
Company and Routledge & Kegan Paul Ltd.

Herbert Blumer is professor of sociology at the
University of California, Berkeley.

A view of human society as symbolic interaction has been followed more than
it has been formulated. Partial, usually fragmentary, statements of it are to be
found in the writings of a number of eminent scholars, some inside the field of
sociology and some outside. Among the former we may note such scholars as
Charles Horton Cooley, W. I. Thomas, Robert E. Park, E. W. Burgess, Florian
Znaniecki, Ellsworth Faris, and James Mickel Williams. Among those outside the
discipline we may note William James, John Dewey, and George Herbert Mead.
None of these scholars, in my judgment, has presented a systematic statement
of the nature of human group life from the standpoint of symbolic interaction.
Mead stands out among all of them in laying bare the fundamental premises of
the approach, yet he did little to develop its methodological implications for sociological study. Students who seek to depict the position of symbolic interaction
may easily give different pictures of it. What I have to present should be regarded
as my personal version. My aim is to present the basic premises of the point of
view and to develop their methodological consequences for the study of human
group life.

The term "symbolic interaction" refers, of course, to the peculiar and distinctive character of interaction as it takes place between human beings. The
peculiarity consists in the fact that human beings interpret or "define" each
other's actions instead of merely reacting to each other's actions. Their "response" is not made directly to the actions of one another but instead is based
on the meaning which they attach to such actions. Thus, human interaction is
mediated by the use of symbols, by interpretation, or by ascertaining the meaning
of one another's actions. This mediation is equivalent to inserting a process of
interpretation between stimulus and response in the case of human behavior.

The simple recognition that human beings interpret each other's actions as
the means of acting toward one another has permeated the thought and writings
of many scholars of human conduct and of human group life. Yet few of them
have endeavored to analyze what such interpretation implies about the nature
of the human being or about the nature of human association. They are usually
content with a mere recognition that "interpretation" should be caught by the
student, or with a simple realization that symbols, such as cultural norms or
values, must be introduced into their analyses. Only G. H. Mead, in my judgment,
has sought to think through what the act of interpretation implies for an understanding of the human being, human action, and human association. The essentials of his analysis are so penetrating and profound and so important for an un-

derstanding of human group life that I wish to spell them out, even though briefly.

The key feature in Mead's analysis is that the human being has a self. This idea should not be cast aside as esoteric or glossed over as something that is obvious and hence not worthy of attention. In declaring that the human being has a self, Mead had in mind chiefly that the human being can be the object of his own actions. He can act toward himself as he might act toward others. Each of us is familiar with actions of this sort in which the human being gets angry with himself, rebuffs himself, takes pride in himself, argues with himself, tries to bolster his own courage, tells himself that he should "do this" or not "do that," sets goals for himself, makes compromises with himself, and plans what he is going to do. That the human being acts toward himself in these and countless other ways is a matter of easy empirical observation. To recognize that the human being can act toward himself is no mystical conjuration.

Mead regards this ability of the human being to act toward himself as the central mechanism with which the human being faces and deals with his world. This mechanism enables the human being to make indication to himself of things in his surroundings and thus to guide his actions by what he notes. Anything of which a human being is conscious is something which he is indicating to himself —the ticking of a clock, a knock at the door, the appearance of a friend, the remark made by a companion, a recognition that he has a task to perform, or the realization that he has a cold. Conversely, anything of which he is not conscious is, *ipso facto*, something which he is not indicating to himself. The conscious life of the human being, from the time that he awakens until he falls asleep, is a continual flow of self-indications—notations of the things with which he deals and takes into account. We are given, then, a picture of the human being as an organism which confronts its world with a mechanism for making indications to itself. This is the mechanism that is involved in interpreting the actions of others. To interpret the actions of another is to point out to oneself that the action has this or that meaning or character.

Now, according to Mead, the significance of making indications to oneself is of paramount importance. The importance lies along two lines. First, to indicate something is to extricate it from its setting, to hold it apart, to give it a meaning or, in Mead's language, to make it into an object. An object—that is to say, anything that an individual indicates to himself—is different from a stimulus; instead of having an intrinsic character which acts on the individual and which can be identified apart from the individual, its character or meaning is conferred on it by the individual. The object is a product of the individual's disposition to act instead of being an antecedent stimulus which evokes the act. Instead of the individual being surrounded by an environment of pre-existing objects which play upon him and call forth his behavior, the proper picture is that he constructs his objects on the basis of his on-going activity. In any of his countless acts—whether minor, like dressing himself, or major, like organizing himself for a professional career—the individual is designating different objects to himself, giving them meaning, judging their suitability to his action, and making decisions on the basis of the judgment. This is what is meant by interpretation or acting on the basis of symbols.

The second important implication of the fact that the human being makes indications to himself is that his action is constructed or built up instead of being a mere release. Whatever the action in which he is engaged, the human individual proceeds by pointing out to himself the divergent things which have to be taken into account in the course of his action. He has to note what he wants to do and how he is to do it; he has to point out to himself the various conditions which may be instrumental to his action and those which may obstruct his action; he has to take account of the demands, the expectations, the prohibitions, and the threats as they may arise in the situation in which he is acting. His action is built up step by step through a process of such self-indication. The human individual pieces together and guides his action by taking account of different things and interpreting their significance for his prospective action. There is no instance of conscious action of which this is not true.

The process of constructing action through making indications to oneself cannot be swallowed up in any of the conventional psychological categories. This process is distinct from and different from what is spoken of as the "ego"—just as it is different from any other conception which conceives of the self in terms of composition or organization. Self-indication is a moving communicative process in which the individual notes things, assesses them, gives them a meaning, and decides to act on the basis of the meaning. The human being stands over against the world, or against "alters," with such a process and not with a mere ego. Further, the process of self-indication cannot be subsumed under the forces, whether from the outside or inside, which are presumed to play upon the individual to produce his behavior. Environmental pressures, external stimuli, organic drives, wishes, attitudes, feelings, ideas, and their like do not cover or explain the process of self-indication. The process of self-indication stands over against them in that the individual points out to himself and interprets the appearance or expression of such things, noting a given social demand that is made on him, recognizing a command, observing that he is hungry, realizing that he wishes to buy something, aware that he has a given feeling, conscious that he dislikes eating with someone he despises, or aware that he is thinking of doing some given thing. By virtue of indicating such things to himself, he places himself over against them and is able to act back against them, accepting them, rejecting them, or transforming them in accordance with how he defines or interprets them. His behavior, accordingly, is not a result of such things as environmental pressures, stimuli, motives, attitudes, and ideas but arises instead from how he interprets and handles these things in the action which he is constructing. The process of self-indication by means of which human action is formed cannot be accounted for by factors which precede the act. The process of self-indication exists in its own right and must be accepted and studied as such. It is through this process that the human being constructs his conscious action.

Now Mead recognizes that the formation of action by the individual through a process of self-indication always takes place in a social context. Since this matter is so vital to an understanding of symbolic interaction it needs to be explained carefully. Fundamentally, group action takes the form of a fitting together of individual lines of action. Each individual aligns his action to the action of others by ascertaining what they are doing or what they intend to do—that is, by getting the meaning of their acts. For Mead, this is done by the individual "taking the role" of others—either the role of a specific person or the role of a group (Mead's "generalized other"). In taking such roles the individual seeks to ascertain the intention or direction of the acts of others. He forms and aligns his own action on the basis of such interpretation of the acts of others. This is the fundamental way in which group action takes place in human society.

The foregoing are the essential features, as I see them, in Mead's analysis of the bases of symbolic interaction. They presuppose the following: that human society is made up of individuals who have selves (that is, make indications to themselves); that individual action is a construction and not a release, being built up by the individual through noting and interpreting features of the situations in which he acts; that group or collective action consists of the aligning of individual actions, brought about by the individuals' interpreting or taking into account each other's actions. Since my purpose is to present and not to defend the position of symbolic interaction I shall not endeavor in this essay to advance support for the three premises which I have just indicated. I wish merely to say that the three premises can be easily verified empirically. I know of no instance of human group action to which the three premises do not apply. The reader is challenged to find or think of a single instance which they do not fit.

I wish now to point out that sociological views of human society are, in general, markedly at variance with the premises which I have indicated as underlying symbolic interaction. Indeed, the predominant number of such views, especially those in vogue at the present time, do not see or treat human society as symbolic interaction. Wedded, as they tend to be, to some form of sociological determinism, they adopt images of human society, of individuals in it, and of group action which do not square with the premises of symbolic interaction. I wish to say a few words about the major lines of variance.

Sociological thought rarely recognizes or treats human societies as composed of individuals who have selves. Instead, they assume human beings to be merely organisms with some kind of organization, responding to forces which play upon them. Generally, although not exclusively, these forces are lodged in the make-up of the society, as in the case of "social system," "social structure," "culture," "status position," "social role," "custom," "institution," "collective representation," "social situation," "social norm," and "values." The assumption is that the behavior of people as members *of a society* is an expression of the play on them of these kinds of factors or forces. This, of course, is the logical position which is necessarily taken when the scholar explains their behavior or phases of their behavior in terms of one or other of such social factors. The individuals who compose a human society are treated as the media through which such factors operate, and the social action of such individuals is regarded as an expression of such factors. This approach or point of view denies, or at least ignores, that human beings have selves—that they act by making indications to themselves. Incidentally, the "self" is not brought into the picture by introducing such items as organic drives, motives, attitudes, feelings, internalized social factors, or psychological components. Such psychological factors have the same status as the social factors mentioned: they are regarded as factors which play on the individual to produce his action. They do not constitute the process of self-indication. The process of self-indication stands over against them, just as it stands over against the social factors which play on the human being. Practically all sociological conceptions of human society fail to recognize that the individuals who compose it have selves in the sense spoken of.

Correspondingly, such sociological conceptions do not regard the social actions of individuals in human society as being constructed by them through a process of interpretation. Instead, action is treated as a product of factors which play on and through individuals. The social behavior of people is not seen as built up by them through an interpretation of objects, situations, or the actions of others. If a place is given to "interpretation," the interpretation is regarded as merely an expression of other factors (such as motives) which precede the act, and accordingly disappears as a factor in its own right. Hence, the social action of people is treated as an outward flow or expression of forces playing on them rather than as acts which are built up by people through their interpretation of the situations in which they are placed.

These remarks suggest another significant line of difference between general sociological views and the position of symbolic interaction. These two sets of views differ in where they lodge social action. Under the perspective of symbolic interaction, social action is lodged in acting individuals who fit their respective lines of action to one another through a process of interpretation; group action is the collective action of such individuals. As opposed to this view, sociological conceptions generally lodge social action in the action of society or in some unit of society. Examples of this are legion. Let me cite a few. Some conceptions, in treating societies or human groups as "social systems," regard group action as an expression of a system, either in a state of balance or seeking to achieve balance. Or group action is conceived as an expression of the "functions" of a society or of a group. Or group action is regarded as the outward expression of elements lodged in society or the group, such as cultural demands, societal purposes, social values, or institutional stresses. These typical conceptions ignore or blot out a view of group life or of group action as consisting of the collective or concerted actions of individuals seeking to meet their life situations. If recognized at all, the efforts of people to develop collective acts to meet their situations are subsumed under the play of underlying or transcending forces which are lodged in society or its parts. The individuals composing the society or the group become "carriers," or media for the expression of such forces; and the interpretative behavior by means of which people form their actions is merely a coerced link in the play of such forces.

The indication of the foregoing lines of variance should help to put the position of symbolic interaction in better perspective. In the remaining discussion I wish to sketch somewhat more fully how human society appears in terms of symbolic interaction and to point out some methodological implications.

Human society is to be seen as consisting of acting people, and the life of the society is to be seen as consisting of their actions. The acting units may be separate individuals, collectivities whose members are acting together on a common quest, or organizations acting on behalf of a constituency. Respective examples are individual purchasers in a market, a play group or missionary band, and a business corporation or a national professional association. There is no empirically observable activity in a human society that does not spring from some acting unit. This banal statement needs to be stressed in light of the common practice of sociologists of reducing human society to social units that do not act —for example, social classes in modern society. Obviously, there are ways of viewing human society other than in terms of the acting units that compose it. I merely wish to point out that in respect to concrete or empirical activity human society must necessarily be seen in terms of the acting units that form it. I would add that any scheme of human society claiming to be a realistic analysis has to respect and be congruent with the empirical recognition that a human society consists of acting units.

Corresponding respect must be shown to the conditions under which such units act. One primary condition is that action takes place in and with regard to a situation. Whatever be the acting unit—an individual, a family, a school, a church, a business firm, a labor union, a legislature, and so on—any particular action is formed in the light of the situation in which it takes place. This leads to the recognition of a second major condition, namely, that the action is formed or constructed by interpreting the situation. The acting unit necessarily has to identify the things which it has to take into account—tasks, opportunities, obstacles, means, demands, discomforts, dangers, and the like; it has to assess them in some fashion and it has to make decisions on the basis of the assessment. Such interpretative behavior may take place in the individual guiding his own action, in a collectivity of individuals acting in concert, or in "agents" acting on behalf of a group or organization. Group life consists of acting units developing acts to meet the situations in which they are placed.

Usually, most of the situations encountered by people in a given society are defined or "structured" by them in the same way. Through previous interaction they develop and acquire common understandings or definitions of how to act in this or that situation. These common definitions enable people to act alike. The common repetitive behavior of people in such situations should not mislead the student into believing that no process of interpretation is in play; on the contrary, even though fixed, the actions of the participating people are constructed by them through a process of interpretation. Since ready-made and commonly accepted definitions are at hand, little strain is placed on people in guiding and organizing their acts. However, many other situations may not be defined in a single way by the participating people. In this event, their lines of action do not fit together readily and collective action is blocked. Interpretations have to be developed and effective accommodation of the participants to one another has to be worked out. In the case of such "undefined" situations, it is necessary to trace and study the emerging process of definition which is brought into play.

Insofar as sociologists or students of human society are concerned with the behavior of acting units, the position of symbolic interaction requires the student to catch the process of interpretation through which they construct their actions. This process is not to be caught merely by turning to conditions which are antecedent to the process. Such antecedent conditions are helpful in understanding the process insofar as they enter into it, but as mentioned previously they do not constitute the process. Nor can one catch the process merely by inferring its nature from the overt action which is its product. To catch the process, the student must take the role of the acting unit whose behavior he is studying. Since the interpretation is being made by the acting unit in terms of objects designated and appraised, meanings acquired, and decisions made, the process has to be seen from the standpoint of the acting unit. It is the recognition of this fact that makes the research work of such scholars as R. E. Park and W. I. Thomas so notable. To try to catch the interpretative process by remaining aloof as a so-called "objective" observer and refusing to take the role of the acting unit is to risk the worst kind of subjectivism—the objective observer is likely to fill in the process of interpretation with his own surmises in place of catching the process as it occurs in the experience of the acting unit which uses it.

By and large, of course, sociologists do not study human society in terms of its acting units. Instead, they are disposed to view human society in terms of structure or organization and to treat social action as an expression of such structure or organization. Thus, reliance is placed on such structural categories as social system, culture, norms, values, social stratification, status positions, social roles and institutional organization. These are used both to analyze human society and to account for social action within it. Other major interests of sociological scholars center around this focal theme of organization. One line of interest is to view organization in terms of the functions it is supposed to perform. Another line of interest is to study societal organization as a system seeking equilibrium; here the scholar endeavors to detect mechanisms which are indigenous to the system. Another line of interest is to identify forces which play upon organization to bring about changes in it; here the scholar endeavors, especially through comparative study, to isolate a relation between causative factors and structural results. These various lines of sociological perspective and interest, which are so strongly entrenched today, leap over the acting units of a society and bypass the interpretative process by which such acting units build up their actions.

These respective concerns with organization on one hand and with acting units on the other hand set the essential difference between conventional views of human society and the view of it implied in symbolic interaction. The latter view recognizes the presence of organization in human society and respects its importance. However, it sees and treats organization differently. The difference is along two major lines. First, from the standpoint of symbolic interaction the organization of a human society is the framework inside of which social action takes place and is not the determinant of that action. Second, such organization and changes in it are the product of the activity of acting units and not of "forces" which leave such acting units out of account. Each of these two major lines of difference should be explained briefly in order to obtain a better understanding of how human society appears in terms of symbolic interaction.

From the standpoint of symbolic interaction, social organization is a framework inside of which acting units develop their actions. Structural features, such as "culture," "social systems," "social stratification," or "social roles," set conditions for their action but do not determine their action. People—that is, acting units—do not act toward culture, social structure or the like; they act toward situations. Social organization enters into action only to the extent to which it shapes situations in which people act, and to the extent to which it supplies fixed sets of symbols which people use in interpreting their situations. These two forms of influence of social organization are important. In the case of settled and stabilized societies, such as isolated primitive tribes and peasant communities, the influence is certain to be profound. In the case of human societies, particularly modern societies, in which streams of new situations arise and old situations become unstable, the influence of organization decreases. One should bear in mind that the most important element confronting an acting unit in situations is the actions of other acting units. In modern society, with its increasing crisscrossing of lines of action, it is common for situations to arise in which the actions of participants are not previously regularized and standardized. To this extent, existing social organization does not shape the situations. Correspondingly, the symbols or tools of interpretation used by acting units in such situations may vary and shift considerably. For these reasons, social action may go beyond, or depart from, existing organization in any of its structural dimensions. The organization of a human society is not to be identified with the process of interpretation used by its acting units; even though it affects that process, it does not embrace or cover the process.

Perhaps the most outstanding consequence of viewing human society as organization is to overlook the part played by acting units in social change. The conventional procedure of sociologists is 1) to identify human society (or some part of it) in terms of an established or organized form, 2) to identify some factor or condition of change playing upon the human society or the given part of it, and 3) to identify the new form assumed by the society following upon the play of the factor of change. Such observations permit the student to couch propositions to the effect that a given factor of change playing upon a given organized form results in a given new organized form. Examples ranging from crude to refined statements are legion, such as that an economic depression increases solidarity in the families of workingmen or that industrialization replaces extended families by nuclear families. My concern here is not with the validity of such propositions but with the methodological position which they presuppose. Essentially, such propositions either ignore the role of the interpretative behavior of acting units in the given instance of change, or else regard the interpretative behavior as coerced by the factor of change. I wish to point out that any line of social change, since it involves change in human action, is necessarily mediated by interpretation on the part of the people caught up in the change—the change appears in the form of new situations in which people have to construct new forms of action. Also, in line with what has been said previously, interpretations of new situations are not predetermined by conditions antecedent to the situations but depend on what is taken into account and assessed in the actual situations in which behavior is formed. Variations in interpretation may readily occur as different acting units cut out different objects in the situation, or give different weight to the objects which they note, or piece objects together in different patterns. In formulating propositions of social change, it would be wise to recognize that any given line of such change is mediated by acting units interpreting the situations with which they are confronted.

Students of human society will have to face the question of whether their preoccupation with categories of structure and organization can be squared with the interpretative process by means of which human beings, individually and collectively, act in human society. It is the discrepancy between the two which plagues such students in their efforts to attain scientific propositions of the sort achieved in the physical and biological sciences. It is this discrepancy, further, which is chiefly responsible for their difficulty in fitting hypothetical propositions to new arrays of empirical data. Efforts are made, of course, to overcome these shortcomings by devising new structural categories, by formulating new structural hypotheses, by developing more refined techniques of research, and even by formulating new methodological schemes of a structural character. These efforts continue to ignore or to explain away the interpretative process by which people act, individually and collectively, in society. The question remains whether human society or social action can be successfully analyzed by schemes which refuse to recognize human beings as they are, namely, as persons constructing individual and collective action through an interpretation of the situations which confront them.

THE METHODOLOGICAL IMPLICATIONS OF SYMBOLIC INTERACTIONISM FOR THE STUDY OF DEVIANCE

NORMAN K. DENZIN

Reprinted from the *British Journal of Sociology*, 25 (September 1974), 269–282. Used by permission of Routledge and Kegan Paul Ltd.

Norman Denzin is professor of sociology at the University of Illinois, Urbana.

While the general theoretical and methodological implications of symbolic interactionism are commonly understood, there have been few attempts to directly apply this perspective to the study of deviance and deviant behavior. It is my intention to briefly review the major theoretical and methodological assumptions of symbolic interactionism[1] and then to indicate how an interactionist view of deviance and what may be termed the *labeling encounter* can be implemented through close-up naturalistic studies.

The Assumptions of Symbolic Interactionism

Theoretically symbolic interactionism rests on three primitive assumptions. Reality as it is sensed, known, and understood is a social production. As such it consists of social objects, the meanings of which arise out of the behaviors persons direct toward them. Humans are granted the capacity to engage in "minded," self-reflexive behavior. In the course of taking their own standpoint and fitting that standpoint to the behaviors of others, humans interact with one another. Interaction is seen as an emergent, negotiated, oftentimes unpredictable concern. Interaction is symbolic simply because minded, self-reflexive behavior demands the manipulation of symbols, words, meanings, and diverse languages.

Methodologically, symbolic interactionism directs the investigator to take, to the best of his ability, the standpoint of those studied. It demands that he situate his observations by time and place, and that he attempt to grasp the shifting relationship between attitudes and acts.

A Conceptual Proposal

These few assumptions can be dissected into the following concepts:

1. Language. Language refers to all the utterances, gestures and movements one interactant communicates to self or other. It is viewed as a conversation of gestures arising out of the interaction process. Interactants can communicate in a silent-gestural language or in a set of personally specific vocal utterances. Their languages may transcend situations (the language of the law). They may be sacred or profane, formal or informal, vulgar or polite.

2. Interactional setting and interactional arena. These two concepts differentiate the concrete setting wherein interaction occurs (setting) and the behavior that occurs within settings (arena). Every physical setting, whether bounded by walls or not, is automatically transformed into an arena given the presence of more than two actors. Settings are immovable; arenas are produced by social selves.

3. Self. Self is defined as all the thoughts and utterances any person has with himself as a distinct object. It is a process and arises out of covert, silent conversations and is behaviorally observed through one's communicative acts, through the conversation of gestures.

4. Joint act describes any behavior where one interactant takes account of at least one person besides himself. It represents the joining of at least two separate lines of action into a joint, interactional production. (Joint acts take many forms, to be discussed below.)

5. Interactional occasion designates all the behaviors that occur between more than one actor during that self's presence in an interactional arena. Interactional occasions are temporally bounded units of behavior that have beginnings, middles, and ends. The occasion describes that period of time in which interactants are in one another's physical, if not symbolic presence.

6. Encounter. Inside interactional arenas during interactional occasions encounters occur. Occasions set the stage for encounters, which may be defined as any joint act between two or more persons where the interactants are maintaining symbolic, visual, auditory, and at times tactile contact.[2] Encounters last only as long as two or more persons sustain a mutual co-orientation of action and activity. Co-present encounters end when interactants leave one another's physical presence, although they may be subsequently sustained symbolically. *Encounters of significance* describe these moments of co-presence where one or both interactants carry from the encounter an image of other such that 1) symbolic, non-co-present encounters are produced, and 2) the probability of future encounters is increased. *Dangling encounters* describe all those co-present episodes that carry over into the future. They reflect some consensus among selves that there is unfinished business at hand and future interactions are necessary to get that business done.

Labeling encounters describe those encounters of significance where one actor is defined in new, novel, and typically deviant ways. Apprehended in the middle of a deviant act, he or she is publicly branded deviant, or morally unacceptable. Labeling encounters describe those moments when one class of interactants exercise their authority and power over another class of actors.

7. A social relationship is defined as any situation where two or more persons symbolize one another in distinct terms and sustain and display those symbolizations through their interactional encounters. They may occur with physically absent others, or with those an actor sees on a routine co-present basis. Two classes of others may be taken account of: those whose influence transcends setting—arena (orientational others); and those whose effect is setting arena specific (setting specific others). Studies of the labeling encounter must untangle the relationship between these two classes of others. Typically labelers—members of official social control agencies—act as setting specific others for the deviant, or the pre-deviant. Having been defined as deviant, the individual finds himself in a social relationship with a labeler that attempts to make the labeler a trans-setting, orientational other.

8. Rules of conduct represent any recipe for action that guides behavior between two or more persons in a concrete situation. They specify the dimensions and conditions under which the set of actions can be and will be carried out. Rules of conduct take three forms: civil-legal rules protect selves and their properties; ceremonial rules protect the occasions of interaction and keep selves apart; relational rules bring selves together and represent complex mixtures of one and two. It can be seen that labeling encounters—those moments when one or more selves are classed as inadequate, impropitious, or deviant—involve an application of rules of conduct. An act, built up under one set of rules, is judged from the standpoint of another set of rules. Typically civil-legal rules brand relationally specific rules deviant; and the obverse occurs. Most labeling encounters involve rule and other juxtapositioning.

9. Social objects are social constructs. They represent anything a person can designate in an unitary fashion and hence act toward. They can be other people, bottles, chairs, or rules of conduct. Their meaning arises out of the interaction process. Social relationships can be viewed as unique configurations of social objects and relational rules of conduct.

10. Ritual and routine. To the extent that social relationships sustain themselves across time as distinct interactive units their participants will develop networks of ritual and routine to stabilize and make predictable the actions of their members. Ritual can be defined as a joint act, involving two or more persons, that is frequently repeated in the lives of those members. It is endowed with special, often sacred meaning, is focused around a set of clearly defined objects. It is enacted within the same interactional setting (a church, courtroom, police station), and is subjected to pressures of normalization. It admits of few variations. When performed, the ritual serves to legitimate the selves of the participants and to solidify their positions in that relationship's divisions of labor. Ritual can grow out of any segment of relational life (sexual, economic, political, religious, etc.). *Routine*, on the other hand, is a solitary act, given to less ceremony, likely to admit of more variations. It can be performed by interchangeable categories of selves. Ritual and routine are behaviorally observed in dangling encounters. Relationships sustain themselves over time through an ability to stage and repeatedly produce dangling encounters of a trivial, routine nature.

Labeling encounters will be subjected to pressures of normalization, and may become ritualized, as in the booking procedures police employ when defining an adolescent as delinquent. Indeed it is likely that one participant in most labeling episodes will be operating from a set of highly ritualized rules of conduct. Negotiation in the encounter involves the modification and application of these rituals and rules.

11. Behavioral repertoire. In taking account of one another, interactants engage in self-or-role taking. They orient their behavior to alter's standpoint and emerging line of action in the interactional arena. These lines of action represent unique configurations of meaning each person has lent to the occasion and the role at hand. They are termed *behavioral repertoires*. They are characteristic lines of action associated with a particular self or person. When a class of selves across situations display the same or similar repertoire, it is appropriate to speak of interactional roles—that is, roles fitted to a particular occasion and situation. In making these assessments, it is important not to explain behavioral similarity through recourse to the effect the role has on the behavior.

A Merger of Concepts: Interaction and Deviance as Process

These concepts can be combined to yield the following picture of interaction and deviance. A deviant act and a deviant individual, as Becker[3] argued, can now be seen as interactional productions. They are situated productions, occurring in interactional arenas, arising during the occasion of the interaction, and located in labeling encounters. These productions involve the application of rules of conduct by selves differentially bound to one another in a variety of social relationships. The following propositions are suggested:

1. The social relationship, whether friendly or hostile, fleeting or permanent, collegial or competitive, loving or spiteful, jealous or proud, binds man and his fellows into those collective fabrics called societies. These relationships merge into common worlds of social experience. Membership in them gives persons grounds for predictable and orderly interaction.
2. Man is an active constructor of reality and he constructs his worlds and realities inside social relationships.
3. Persons, deviant or ordinary, are variously defined and variously define themselves inside their intimate everyday interactional worlds.
4. That which a relationship and group takes to be problematic and troublesome will be subjected to pressures to make those problematic objects, acts, and events predictable and routine.
5. All interactants, at various junctures in their moral careers, will be viewed as problematic and troublesome by their fellow interactants.
6. Deviance and trouble are constant, yet negotiated features of all social groups.
7. At the heart of organized groups rests a complex network of ritual and routine which, if successfully communicated, will lead to systematic ways of processing and defining deviants and troublemakers.
8. Deviance and trouble are routine features of human group life and these features of daily interaction will be observed in the encounters and occasions of the group members.
9. The empirical study of deviance involves an examination of these behaviors in the lives and days of the group, with particular emphasis on their labeling, dangling, and perceived encounters of significance.

The Logic of Naturalistic Behaviorism: Toward the Study of Deviance and Deviants in Their Native Worlds

Central to interactionist studies of deviance is the method of *naturalistic behaviorism* which represents the studied commitment to actively enter the worlds of native persons so as to render those worlds understandable from the standpoint of a theory that is grounded in the *behaviors, languages, definitions, attitudes,* and *feelings* of those studied. Naturalistic behaviorism attempts a wedding of the covert private features of the social act with its publicly observable counterpart. It works back and forth between word and deed, definition and act, definer and defined. It endeavours to move beyond ethnographic description to explanatory theory.

Problems with Naturalistic Behaviorism

Most sociological methods work best in the study of persons most like the sociologist. They typically assume articulate respondents. They work least well on those persons who do not share the sociologist's perspective. They confront real problems when those studied are inarticulate. From the perspective of many sociologists deviants are not well understood. Those in drug or drinking cultures may deliberately slur their speech, or talk in a private language. Those in criminal occupations deliberately avoid the polite respectable worlds of the sociologist. Those of a race, ethnicity, or religion different from the sociologist may hold to a world view that gives neither respect nor credence to the social sciences. Those incarcerated behind the closed walls of jails, penitentiaries, mental hospitals, and drug clinics are not readily available for sociological study. (If they are studied, it is typically at the caretaker's, not the sociologist's, convenience.)

Requirements of a Naturalistic Study of Deviance

A naturalistic account of deviance, labeling encounters, and the deviant should 1) permit entry into the closed worlds of the actor and be lodged in those worlds, whether these be homes, sidewalks, prisons, taverns, mental hospitals, stores, or police stations; 2) be sufficiently reliable and valid so as to permit future investigators to build upon such accounts; 3) be grounded in a theory which attempts to explain and organize that which has been observed. In addition, these accounts must 4) take those studied seriously and attempt to understand and comprehend them on their own grounds; 5) give equal attention to all the relevant participants in the labeling-interaction process: family, peers, friends, police, psychiatrists, neighbors, etc. It should not be a one-sided account which stresses only the deviant's, or the definer's perspective.

Unit of Analysis

The *joint act* is the basic unit of analysis for naturalistic studies. Applied to the field of deviance this suggests that the investigator focus on labeling encounters whether between deviants and deviants, labelers and labelers, or labelers and deviants. The outcome of these encounters would be charted and recorded. An actor may have a deviant identity applied, but reject it. A previous presumption of deviance may be affirmed, or the label itself is negotiated. The joint acts that compose the labeling encounter would be situated in the interactional arenas of the actors in question. Two types of behavior settings can be initially distinguished: home or private settings and public *locales*. These types can be further separated into 1) publicly defined open situations which are treated as open — parks and beaches; 2) places which are open, yet kept private — grocery stores, plazas, malls; 3) places which are kept private — homes; and 4) private places which are made open — bars, open houses, neighborhood parties. It would be assumed that the character of the labeling encounter would vary by setting, as would the participants.

Finding the Relevant Behavioral Unit: The Day and Its Encounters

If the social act, symbolic, solitary, joint, covert, or public is the basic analytic unit in the naturalistic study of deviance, then the observer must fit that unit to the behaviors of those studied. What joint acts are naturally recurring phenomena in the subject's world? A naturally recurring time cycle for all actors, deviant or non-deviant, child or adult, is the 24-hour day. The day is a temporally and physically bounded unit. It can be behaviorally observed; it has a beginning, a middle, and an end. It is the *occasion* for multiple *encounters* and these encounters typically occur between a finite, if not predictable set of others. The naturalist begins with the occasion of the day. He examines the encounters of the day, whether focused or unfocused, sociable or solitary, potentially deviant, labeling or non-labeling, joint, private or public. The situations and interactional arenas of the day are isolated, and then the *participants* of the day are recorded.

Behavior Specimens

Naturalistic behaviorism directs the investigator to collect *behavior specimens* of interactive episodes as these acts arise in the natural settings and times of group, relational, and organizational life. The analyst attempts to reproduce in a rich and detailed fashion the experiences, thoughts, and languages of those studied. These specimens must reflect the actual temporal sequence of behavior under inspection, and they will show how each interactant influenced and was influenced by all others in the interactional arena. These specimens will be examined from multiple perspectives: from the points of view of the interactional participants and from the standpoint of social and psychological theory. The investigator compares native accounts of their behavior with his own behavior specimens and his emerging sociological scheme.

The naturalist fits sampling and observational strategies to the temporal, ritual, and moral features of the worlds studied. He couches measurement procedures around the collection of *naturalistic indicators* which are behaviors routinely engaged in by natives in the course of a day's or week's activities. These are behaviors that have high native relevance (e.g., chipping drugs on weekends, exchanging drinks in a bar, etc.). These behaviors are then treated as indicative of theoretical concepts. Ritual patterns of dress, hair-style, and body spacing can be treated as indicators of self-image and relational familiarity. Special languages, codes, and dialects reflect group boundaries and relational solidarity. Prized social objects (needles, weapons, belts, pipes, garments, records, etc.) are treated as observable extensions of the person's self, and they indicate prestige, esteem, and dignity structures in the subject's world of experience. Moments of interrogation, derogation, praise, and reward are seen as indicators of socialization and labeling strategies. Group talk around tables, in bars and living rooms is dissected for what it reveals about political, cultural, and economic struggles in relational circles. Quarrels, fights and battles among group members (and members of labeling agencies) are inspected for what they reveal about definitional and situational power in the group.

Specimen Format

The format for collecting and presenting behavior specimens is dramaturgical. The full specimen would 1) give each individual a short biographical history relevant to the encounter at hand; 2) clothe he or she in the garments appropriate to the occasion and the biography; 3) note any particular speech and behavior patterns (e.g., stutters, is abrasive, whines, shouts, slurs, etc.); 4) specify the actual times each actor comes into the interaction; 5) specify how each self is to respond to the other persons in the arena during the occasion of the interaction; 6) attempt to reveal what each actor is thinking and ultimately thinks of the behavior in question; 7) indicate what objects are to be acted on in the situation; 8) indicate the salient interactional features of the situation, separating situation from encounter; 9) take the encounter and occasion to conclusion (e.g., show its outcome).

Behavior specimens separate act, object, intention, situation, and interactants for special attention. Like their literary counterpart, the intent is to establish *verisimilitude*—to produce in the reader the same perceptual and experiential state sensed by the original observer; to give the illusion that the same experiences would have been (and could be) sensed were the reader there. They are reconstructive efforts to move the reader to take the role and self of the acting other.

IMPLEMENTING NATURALISTIC STUDIES OF DEVIANCE

Sampling Strategies

The naturalist samples interactions between people as these behaviors are forged into publicly observable moments of joint co-presence. He studies labeling encounters, interactions between deviants and normals, normals and normals, deviants and deviants. Sampling involves a set of procedures that take the observer into the social situations where observations will be made.

The first step in naturalistic sampling is to identify the class of joint acts and situational arenas that appear to have theoretical and empirical relevance for the investigator and the native. Students of deviance might examine those times in a group's daily routine when the deviant act in question is most likely to be performed (e.g., drug-use, drinking, stealing, fighting, etc.). Having identified the joint act and the situations of its occurrence, the naturalist then determines which members of the interactive unit routinely engage in those specified behaviors. He then stations himself in situations where those actions can be recorded.

Before the naturalist can begin to collect behavioral specimens, he must gain a working knowledge of the settings and arenas that constitute the native's world. He notes what situations are routinely entered, with whom, for what purposes, at what times, and for what duration. He then links the subject's behaviors to those situations so as to construct a *representational map* of that world. These maps detail 1) the temporal features of that social order—when it starts, stops, comes together, lags, etc.; 2) its network of interactive others—who enters and in what relationship do they stand to one another—peers, aliens, friends, police, etc.; 3) its setting locations—what rooms, alleys, bars, offices, etc.; 4) the typical objects found, or brought into each place. With this knowledge the observer is in a position to selectively sample behaviors of key theoretical concern.

The Timing of Actions

Many behaviors central to the native's world occur at irregular intervals. Some happen only once. The divorce, the first crime, and the first confrontation with drug dealers are examples. The behaviors cannot be experimentally reproduced. If the observer was not present when they occurred, he is forced to rely on the native's reconstruction of the event. Hopefully, alternative accounts of the behavior can be secured, perhaps from the native's peers, family members, friends, or from members of official social control agencies. Ideally, the naturalist would be present when these irregular actions transpire. This is crucial in the study of labeling encounters. He may locate himself in police stations, emergency rooms of hospitals, the offices of in-take personnel in mental hospitals, or the corridors of schools. He then records the labeling encounter in its natural setting.

Forming Generalizations

In the process of building up causal propositions, based on his representational maps and behavior specimens, the naturalist must demonstrate how representative his behavior specimens actually are. That is, do these specimens faithfully respect the character and frequency of the joint acts he wishes to generalize to and describe. If concerned with police brutality toward members of minority groups, for example, he must offer a frequency count of these acts over his observational period, compare the brutality rates of police toward members of the majority group, and then present behavior specimens which describe such episodes.[4] Similar strictures would hold for studies of discrimination in high schools, patterns of interracial contact in ghetto areas, rates of crime and deviance for particular social groups, the use of drugs by middle-class teenagers on weekends, swinging or group sex for married couples, or the hustling of whites by blacks in tourist sections of metropolitan areas. In short, the study of deviance and the labeling encounter must do more than record the fact that deviance has occurred, or that persons have been labeled deviant. The frequency, form, and content of these acts must be presented, analyzed, and shaped into an explanatory scheme that accounts for variations and stabilities over time, across persons and situations.

Knowing the Population

It is frequently the case that the population from which the behavior specimens have been drawn is unknown. While statistical-demographic data can be easily assembled to describe the age, sex, educational, and occupational structure of a community or a mental hospital, data on the *interactive relationships* among the members of those organizations are seldom available. They remain unrecorded. There are, for example, no concrete data on such behaviors as 1) the number of fights and arguments gang members have in an average day, week, or month; 2) the number of hustling activities street-gangs engage in during a week's time; 3) the number of focused conversational huddles police have with members of the criminal underworld during a month's time. The frequency and form of inter-active relationships are at issue in these examples. The unknown population is acutely problematic in the study of acts that go unnoticed by official recording agencies. Deviant acts and labeling encounters exist in a world that is neither systematically charted nor known. Students of these behaviors must modify, if not rewrite, the usual canons of sampling theory and develop alternative proce-dures for describing the populations they have sampled from.[5]

Alternative Sampling Units

Several approaches can be suggested. As Becker[6] suggests, the observer may em-ploy the situation as his observational unit and argue that his sample is drawn from observations of all persons who passed through that setting for a specified period of time. Here he or she must have data on the representativeness of the situation for the natives who pass through it.

Time may be employed as an observational unit. A particular day out of the native's week, month, or year may be selected for study. Members of social con-trol agencies work on a calendar of days that may bear little relationship to other calendars (e.g., a fiscal, or political calendar). They may hasten or slow down their recording and labeling behaviors depending on where they stand in their overall calendar. Finding an excess of money in the budget, as they approach the end of the fiscal year, they may inflate or increase their admissions of deviants. (This appears to operate for many mental hospitals and drug treatment clinics.) The observer of official labeling encounters would find, then, that rates of institu-tionally defined deviance would vary temporally. Hence, time by itself may not be sufficient as a basis for gaining insight into the population the analyst wishes to generalize to.

The naturalist may attempt to hold time and setting constant by selecting as his observational unit a social organization which processes and produces the types of labeling behaviors he is interested in. Here the organization, not its par-ticipants, becomes the sampling unit. Police precincts, mental hospitals, prisons, schools, alcoholic treatment centers, and family counseling agencies may be se-lected for the natives he observes. Lacking information on the frequency and dis-tribution of these organizations throughout the native's world he is left with little more than an ethnographic account of one or more institutional setting.

The observer may decide to employ an *interactive relationship* as his unit of analysis. He could focus on families, friendship groups, ghetto gangs, hustlers and pimps, teachers and students, police and juveniles, deviants and deviants, or labelers and those they label. (See Cicourel for a study of the latter and Brede for a study of police-juvenile encounters.[7])

There are advantages to selecting the interactive relationship as the sampling unit. It combines the variables of time and setting with a focused observational unit.

Progress could be made through the careful construction of representative maps for different classes of acting units (e.g., types of families, gangs, police patrol teams, psychiatrists and social workers, teacher and students, etc.). The temporal rhythms of specific classes of social organization (grocery stores, police stations, mental hospitals, wards in hospitals, schools, neighborhoods, etc.) could be detailed and then sampling would proceed at a pace fitted to the organization's temporal order. Observations of juvenile gang members in public places (street corners, bars, taverns, recreation centers, etc.) could follow from such a procedure. Here the analyst would fit the temporal structure of the interactive unit to the temporal order of the organizations that unit regularly passes through.

Types of Behavior Specimens

A naturalistic theory of social organization is grounded in the behavior specimen. Situated by time, place, and participant, the specimen presents in vivid detail the form and content of natural interactive relationships in the arena under inspection. Unlike its statistical counterpart in more quantitative studies, which strips behavior of time, place, and meaning, the specimen maintains a commitment to presenting behavior as it occurs. As a theory takes shape empirical regularities in the native's world emerge. It is the naturalist's task to identify these regularities and to forge theoretical propositions which account for their shape and form. Similarly, irregularities and episodic acts will be identified. Acts and actions which clearly nullify or challenge the emerging theory will be encountered. These three classes of behavior (regular, irregular, and deviant) must be detailed in behavior specimens and they must be theoretically accounted for. From his behavior specimens, the naturalist selects those which are most *representative* of the native's behavior. Representative specimens describe regularities in native behavior. The "booking" of a juvenile for a criminal offense in a police precinct station assumes a regular, routine form. The "booking" encounter has a predictable beginning, middle, and end. It has a predictable set of participants, occurs in a fixed setting, and is subject to pressures of normalization. An analysis of the "booking" encounter would involve a presentation of representative behavior specimens that detailed the temporal, ritual, and routine features of that interactive pattern. Negative, or deviant specimens—those which challenge the typical pattern found in the representative specimen—provoke revisions in the naturalist's emerging theory. While the booking encounter in police precincts is a relatively orderly concern, with power asymmetrically distributed, on occasion a citizen takes control away from the booking officer and completely overturns the routinized pattern of interaction. Such actions must be carefully noted and recorded. Not only do they suggest alterations in the booking encounter, but they reflect behaviors which do occur. To the extent that the naturalist's account of the social organization of police work is accurate and reflective of behaviors in that arena it must include these negative, or deviant specimens.

Triangulating Methods, Perspectives, Data Sources, and Observers

The naturalistic observer commits himself to the use of any and all sociological methods which will better reveal the dynamics of the situation under study. This demands an intimate familiarity with the native's world, and it assumes a methodological flexibility on the part of the observer. He or she should be skilled in direct and indirect interviewing procedures. A knowledge of unobtrusive methods should be possessed, whether this involves the analysis of body movements and spacing rituals, language analysis, time-sampling, studies of exterior body signs, or an inspection of documents and archival deposits.[8] The naturalist should be sensitive to the problems of life-history construction and would be knowledgeable in the various strategies involved in direct participant observation. Such a combination of methods and data sources is termed triangulation. While not without flaws and weaknesses (see, for example, Blalock, and the remarks of Phillips)[9] triangulation simply reflects the fact that no method will ever reveal all that is to be known (or can be known) about any social process. Thus, while as yet there are no firm rules for discounting the findings from one method that contradict the findings of another, and while the logics of some methods are better developed than others, the naturalist is committed to collecting any and all data that are ethically allowable, and that when combined yield a more processual view of the labeling encounter.

Developing Sociological Theory: A Concluding Note

A naturalistic theory of deviance and the labeling encounter will be multivariate and sequential. Based on a close inspection of representative, episodic, and negative behavior specimens, such a theory will stress the necessary conditions that produce labeling encounters. The phases these encounters pass through, and variations in participants and outcomes will be noted. The naturalist assumes that no event or process is the product of any single sufficient condition. Deviance production is negotiated from setting to setting, and its outcome is nearly always problematic. Faced with this fact, the naturalist assumes both a retrospective and prospective view of social action. Retrospectively, or historically, he collects behavior specimens that describe the outcomes of labeling encounters. He takes booking encounters to conclusion, or he observes the final negotiations between husbands and wives when they define a child as retarded or deviant. These specimens, which describe the final temporal phases of the labeling encounter are then dissected, and propositions concerning the phases the participants passed through to reach this end-point are formulated. These outcome specimens are then modified as the naturalist observes new classes of participants engaged in labeling encounters. Having formulated a set of propositions concerning the production of "police-booking" encounters, based on observations of the last phase of this act, the naturalist now attempts to trace the complete evolution of these acts from their beginnings, through their middles, to their negotiated conclusions.

The multivariate feature of naturalistic propositions is set by the number of episodic and deviant acts observed. Each of these nonrepresentative behaviors describe variations on the labeling encounter. They must be accounted for, if the naturalist is to produce a theory that explains all of the observed cases.

NOTES

1. Herbert Blumer, *Symbolic Interactionism* (Englewood Cliffs, N.J.: Prentice-Hall, 1969).

2. Erving Goffman, *Encounter* (Indianapolis: Bobbs-Merrill, 1961).

3. Howard S. Becker, *Outsiders: Studies in the Sociology of Deviance* (New York: Free Press, 1963).

4. Donald J. Black and Albert J. Reiss Jr., "Police Control of Juveniles," *American Sociological Review*, 35 (February 1970), 63–77; Richard Brede, "The Policing of Juveniles in Chicago," Ph.D. dissertation, University of Illinois, 1972.

5. Howard S. Becker, "Practitioners of Vice and Crime," in Robert W. Habenstein, ed., *Pathways to Data* (Chicago: Aldine, 1970), pp. 30–49.

6. Ibid., pp. 35–36.

7. Aaron V. Cicourel, *The Social Organization of Juvenile Justice* (New York: Wiley, 1968); Brede, "Policing of Juveniles in Chicago."

8. Eugene J. Webb, Donald T. Campbell, Richard D. Schwartz, and Lee Sechrest, *Unobtrusive Measures: Nonreactive Research in the Social Sciences* (Chicago: Rand McNally, 1966).

9. Hubert M. Blalock, "Aggregation and Measurement Error," *Social Forces*, 50 (December 1971), 151–165; Derek L. Phillips, *Knowledge from What?* (Chicago: Rand McNally, 1971).

SYMBOLIC INTERACTION AS A PRAGMATIC PERSPECTIVE: THE BIAS OF EMERGENT THEORY

JOAN HUBER

Reprinted from the *American Sociological Review*, 38 (1973), 274–284. Used by permission of Joan Huber and the American Sociological Association.

Joan Huber is associate professor of sociology at the University of Illinois, Urbana-Champaign. She is co-author of *Marxist Theory and Indian Communism, Income and Ideology,* and *The Sociology of Poverty.*

As a socially based approach to the relation of the individual and society, symbolic interaction (SI) has always been an important perspective in American sociology. Kuhn (1970:83) suggested that, unlike psychoanalysis, field theory, and learning theory, SI is logically consistent with basic social science propositions. As a research tradition, SI has produced insightful accounts of human interaction in natural settings. Yet even its adherents are doubtful about its methodology and the status of its findings. Blumer (1969:1) pointed out that the position of SI had never been clearly formulated and no reasoned statement of the methodological approach existed.

The SI tradition is related to a number of other approaches and techniques such as labeling theory, sociological phenomenology and existentialism, participant observation, qualitative sociology, and naturalism. No attempt to deal with the differences and similarities of these approaches to the SI tradition will be made in this paper, which is concerned, rather, with the overall historical drift. Yet their relationship to SI is important because even if, as Ehrlich (1972) asserts, what was scientifically most useful in the SI approach has already been absorbed into the mainstream of social psychology, many of the problems of SI methods still plague these other approaches.[1]

Events in the last decade have thrown the problems of SI methods into even greater relief. Many young sociologists are unhappy with the direction of the discipline, particularly with what they see as an overemphasis on quantification. They feel that social science has failed to come to grips with the real world (Blumer, 1966: vii).[2] Such concern has led to increasing criticism of standard methodology; the procedures which methodologists found so intriguing have not had the desired impact on research because the methodologists failed to communicate the substantive relevance of the tools they admired so much (Hill, 1970:18, 19). Apparently the SI tradition and similar approaches answer a need in the discipline; and, whatever their inadequacies, they will probably be around for some time.

The main thesis of this paper is that the SI tradition shares with the philosophy of pragmatism,[3] from which it originates, an epistemology which makes it reflect the social biases of the researcher and of the people whose behavior is observed. In a benignly liberal climate of opinion this outcome tends to go unnoticed; but in the long run, this kind of methodology is sensitive to the forces of social control. So far as I have been able to discover, SI methods have not been

criticized from this point of view. The explication of this thesis begins by showing the relationship of SI and pragmatism.

The progenitors of the SI tradition include Dewey, Cooley, Baldwin, and
Znaniecki, among others; but the chief architect was George Herbert Mead
(Manis and Meltzer, 1967:1; Kuhn, 1970:71). Most of the published materials on
which knowledge of his position is based were not originally intended for publication (Meltzer, 1959:27). His books, based on student notes, were published
posthumously (Stevens, 1967:553). His articles were scattered in journals and out-
of-print books until Reck's (1964:v) selection appeared. Mead was not a systematic writer. He found extemporaneous speaking to be his best medium and felt
that men do their best thinking in conversation (Lee, 1945:v). Dewey (1932:xl)
observed that at about the time of his death Mead was beginning to get a command of his ideas which made communication to others easier and more effective. SI thus began with an oral tradition which tended to persist. By the early
sixties neither Faris, Thomas, nor Blumer had presented a rounded theoretical
conception; hence much time was devoted to casuistical debating over questions
of orthodoxy (Kuhn, 1970:71–2).

Mead was one of the leading figures of pragmatism (Shibutani, 1968:83; Gallie, 1966:31). Dewey, its main expositor, became a close friend of Mead's at the
University of Michigan and their intellectual exchange continued at the University of Chicago where Mead taught from 1893 to 1931. Dewey provided the range
and vision, Mead, the analytical depth and precision (Morris, 1934:xi). Dewey's
daughter reported that the influence of Mead on Dewey, from the nineties on,
ranked with that of James (Mills, 1966:296). Yet Dewey is usually ignored as a
major influence on American sociology (Petras, 1968:18). Likewise, Mead tends
to be ignored by philosophers (Mills, 1966:464). Possibly one reason for their neglect is that Mead's ideas were not readily accessible in his lifetime (Shibutani,
1968:83). However, American sociologists typically take little interest in philosophy and philosophers show little interest in the output of sociologists.[4]

Pragmatism, as Durkheim (1960:386) observed, was a reaction to the ideas
of traditional rationalism.[5] Dewey and Mead, like Marx before them, thought
that traditional philosophy was arid, formal, and useless. Moreover, the dominant
social view held that customs derived from a fixed human nature which was,
in turn, derived from an immutable god. Such ideas supported a rigid legal system which shored up a privileged social order. To use material and social factors
to explain human arrangements unveiled the conservative bias of traditional
ideas. Ironically, pragmatism had a similar bias, although Dewey and Mead and
their followers were not aware of it. Nevertheless, all sociologists owe a debt
to the pragmatists (and to Marx) for what now appears to be common sense: men
make their own social world.

But pragmatism went far beyond this general assumption. According to Kaplan (1964:36, 42), pragmatism is a variant of semantic empiricism which, in turn,
was a development of epistemic empiricism. From Locke through Kant, epistemic
empiricism was the doctrine which held that experience was a necessary condition of knowledge. Semantic empiricism, developed in the last hundred years,
holds that not only knowledge but also meaning must necessarily include an
experiential component. Two of the three major variants of semantic empiricism,
logical positivism and operationism, ask the same question of any scientific assertion: Can its meaning be established and, if so, how? That is, can sense data
be used for verification and, if so, what kind of rules govern such use? Pragmatism
asks what difference it would make if a statement were true. The meaning of
objects is the effect they produce (Dewey, 1916:309). That is, whether a belief is
good or bad depends upon whether the activities which it inspires in the organism
entertaining the belief have consequences which are satisfactory or unsatisfactory
to it (Russell, 1945:825). What counts is not the origin of a proposition but its

outcome, not the connections with experience antecedently given but with those to be instituted. Truth is thus dependent on human action. Those who feel that human beings are not always rational see pragmatism as a step on the road to madness, an intoxication with power (Russell, 1945:828) or as an all-out assault on human reason (Durkheim, 1960:363). SI shares this stress on the outcome of human action as a criterion of scientific truth.

Why should the stress on the outcome of an event as a criterion of truth render knowledge susceptible to social control? Briefly, because the future, unlike the past, is subject to manipulation by those who currently have power. "The past cannot be affected by what we do, and therefore, if truth is determined by what has happened, it is independent of present or future volitions; it represents, in logical form, the limitations on human power. But if truth, or rather 'warranted assertibility,' depends upon the future, then, in so far as it is in our power to alter the future, it is in our power to alter what should be asserted" (Russell, 1945:826).

In order to clarify the line of argument, I shall outline it here. In the SI approach, as in the pragmatic, formal logic has an ambiguous status. The place of the rational (logico-theoretic) component in validation is never spelled out clearly. When the place of theory is unclear, when the theoretical expectations are not explicated, then the social givens of the present serve as an implicit theoretical formulation. In pragmatic doctrine, scientific truth is defined as whatever works best in a given situation, as judged by the investigator who observes the emergent outcome. A belief is judged by its effects; if the effects are good, then the belief is true, or has warranted assertibility. Later formulations held that truth is the emerging consensus of the participants in an interactive situation. All of these formulations have a status quo bias for, when no theoretical expectations are specified, and when truth is expected to emerge from interaction, then what is taken to be true tends to reflect the distribution of social power among the participants.[6] This assertion is supported by theory and research in group ranking and conformity (Zajonc, 1968:253–60). Dewey and Mead avoided confronting the power implications of the pragmatic model because they thought that the world was evolving from worse to better. Therefore, whatever worked was bound to be right, at least in the long run. However, the views of the latterday adherents of SI and related approaches are not explicitly evolutionary, nor is the implication of defining truth as an emergent social consensus of participants systematically confronted. I shall now discuss the main threads of this argument in detail, first, the relevant views of Dewey and Mead.

THE PRAGMATISM OF DEWEY AND MEAD

An aspect of pragmatism and SI basic to their sensitivity to social control is the ambiguous status of formal logic (Huber and Loomis, 1970). Philosophers of science distinguish between the logically necessary and the logically contingent, i.e., between mathematics-theory-logic and empirical observations; both are necessary for scientific knowledge (Braithwaite, 1963). A common sense translation of this statement says that facts do not speak for themselves. But the status of the logico-theoretic component is not clear in SI and pragmatism. The difficulty derives from the influence of Hegel's dialectic.

Hegel claimed that the dialectic was a new logic, but this claim is false if one uses the usual definition of the word "logic" (Mills, 1962:130). Hegel wanted to know if history had any meaning and posited the dialectic as a formal device to enable him to explain social change. In dialectical form, knowledge moves in stages from thesis, to antithesis, to synthesis; history obligingly repeats these stages empirically. "Process" and "emergent" are key words. To understand the result, one must understand the entire process because each stage contains the earlier stages in solution, so to speak; all have their place in the final whole. Because only the Whole is Reality, nothing partial can be quite true. Hence truth and falsehood are not sharply defined opposites. In Aristotelian logic, an entity can be defined as A or non-A. That is, entities can be analytically and empirically distinguished from one another. In the dialectic, entities simply merge into one another. Reality is one great Whole. One ought not study the eye of John Jones for Jones is an organic whole and to study his eye alone is pointless. Described in this fashion, the dialectic may strike some observers as nonsense. Most of the writers who use the word today leave it undefined, which is probably just as well.

In his early days Dewey was a Hegelian (Mead, 1936:151) and Hegel remained the chief source of Dewey's logic (Mills, 1966:357). The contradictions between thesis and antithesis became conflicting elements in a problematic situation (White, 1943:152). Dewey confused logic and empiricism; logic was thought to be both empirical and normative (Dewey, 1920:137), and ultimately derived from the acts performed (Dewey, 1929:163). But Dewey's view of what was good differed from that of William James in a way that was important for sociology. James had equated truth with what was good for the individual. Dewey saw the difficulties with this idea and declared that truth was public. A belief was to be judged by the consequences it had for many persons, not for just one person. This aspect of pragmatism may be what led Stone and Farberman (1970:15) to comment that pragmatism carried social psychology away from the psychologistic fallacy. From the standpoint of the present critique, it matters little whether the warranted assertibility of a proposition is based on the way it works out for one person or many.

Unlike Dewey, Mead was well aware of contemporary developments in symbolic logic (1934:202; 1936:Ch. 15; 1964:199 ff). Although he once claimed that the theory of the intelligent act fell within the realm of Hegel's logic (1964:8), and passages in his later work still indicate a strong dialectical aroma (1964:189), he finally concluded that the dialectic was a scientifically useless device that could be used to prove anything (1936:143). Yet his thought shows the influence of Hegel in a number of ways. His idea of sociality is basically holistic:

The principle of sociality is that in the present within which emergent change takes place, the emergent object belongs to different systems in its passage from the old to the new because of its systematic relationship with other structures, and possesses the characters it has because of its membership in these different systems. (Mead, 1932:65)

With this concept Mead attempts to avoid some of the difficulties of Aristotelian logic. Perhaps a clearer statement of the concept is the assertion that sociality is the capacity of being several things at once. "The animal traverses the ground in pursuit of his prey and is at once a part of the system of distribution of energies which makes his locomotion possible and a part of the jungle system which is a part of the life system on the surface of the inanimate globe" (Mead, 1932:49).

In addition to glossing over the distinctions between entities which characterize Aristotelian logic, Mead tended to ignore the logico-theoretic component in his notion of scientific methodology. His prescriptions for the practice of science sound very like the methods that Willer (1970:19) has described as empirical or magical thinking, when events A and B are connected only at the observational level. Mead's example of science indicates that he is discussing empirical thinking:

A child's explanation of the conduct of others and the savage's appeal to magic are uncritical uses of a method which requires only analysis and recognition of the implications of its technique to become scientific. (Mead, 1938:91)

The basic difficulty is that Mead fails to make a sufficient distinction between a hypothesis and a theory, with the result that his work fails to describe the theoretical component adequately. Facts define themselves in scientific problems (Mead, 1964:260). Like Dewey, Mead sees science as beginning with an immediate problem, with an exception that conflicts with a law and leads to the appearance in the mind of the scientist of a hypothesis that will solve his problem (Mead, 1936:136). The test of an hypothesis is that the conduct that was going on can be continued. "It is the same sort of test which the animal finds. If it finds itself in a difficult situation and sees escape, it rushes off in that direction and gets away. This is a fair test of what we call a hypothesis" (Mead, 1936:349). An animal and a scientist do the same thing when they face a problem. They select some element in the situation to carry the act through to its completion. "The only test the animal can bring to such a reconstruction of its habits is the ongoing of its activity. This is the experimental test; can it continue in action? And that is exactly the situation found in science" (Mead, 1936:346). The test of truth is the ability to continue a process which has been inhibited (1936:350; 1964:328). If an hypothesis works, it becomes an accepted theory (Mead, 1936;353). The test of truth is ongoing conduct and truth is synonymous with the solution of a problem (Mead, 1964:328).

His view of the relationship of a scientific law to an hypothesis is much the same:

You are undertaking to set up another law in place of the one which has been overthrown. The new law is tentatively set up as a hypothesis. You test it. When you have tested it, it becomes a working hypothesis. And if others test it and it works, it becomes an accepted theory. (Mead, 1936:825)

To illustrate the scientific method, almost all of Mead's examples refer to the natural or physical sciences where consensus on goals is high and the solutions are technological. In a rare discussion of a social problem, Mead (1964: 261–262) says that various cult values—which are incommensurable—will prevent a solution; hence the scientist must learn to state, as far as possible, our social customs in terms of their functions. What the scientist is supposed to do when this much is accomplished Mead does not say. Because his works are cast in a phylogenetic frame of reference (Petras, forthcoming) and because, like Dewey, Mead assumes that evolutionary processes will make the world better, the problem is minimized. Indeed, Mead often expressed the view that history was on the side of progress; inevitably the brotherhood of men on earth would emerge (Lee, 1945:75; Shibutani, 1968:87). If this assumption were true, then consensus on goals would trouble neither scientist nor citizen alike.

The scientific method, Mead thought, was only the evolutionary process grown self-conscious; scientific technique is simply doing "consciouslessly" what takes place naturally in the evolution of forms (Mead, 1936:371). As an example, Mead mentions the food problem, by which he means digesting materials that have cellulose coverings. Humans had to work out a means to get rid of the covering, i.e., milling. But Mead never mentions the problem of distribution. His position tends to be a purely analytical scheme which lacks content (Meltzer, 1959:29).

In addition to assuming that evolution was progressive, Mead and Dewey both assumed that men were naturally rational. In making inquiries, men "naturally" test and improve the operations in the course of what they are doing (Dewey, 1929:124). Mead (1934:379) thought that men were rational, capable of logical thinking, because they were social. Ethical judgments can be universal because the voice of all is the universal voice; that is, everyone who can rationally appreciate the situation will agree. Social reconstruction would presuppose a basis of common social interests, by all of those whose minds bring about the reconstruction:

And the way in which any such social reconstruction is actually effected by the minds of the individuals involved is by a more or less abstract intellectual extension of the boundaries of the given society to which these individuals all belong, and which is undergoing the reconstruction—the extension resulting in a larger social whole in terms of which the social conflicts that necessitate the reconstruction of the given society are harmonized or reconciled, and by reference to which accordingly, these conflicts can be solved or eliminated. (Mead, 1934:308–309)

The Hegelian influence appears in this passage. The conflicts are somehow going to dissolve in the larger social whole that is created. Mead simply did not allow for irreconcilable conflict. He felt that every interest involved would be considered, but added that "you cannot lay down in advance fixed rules as to just what should be done" (Mead, 1934:388). Indeed, were all men rational and evolution progressive, rules would not be very important. As Dewey put it, the educative process is all one with the moral process, since the latter is a continuous passage of experience from worse to better (Dewey, 1920:183). Science, reason, and progress were isomorphic and inevitable.

The problems of the pragmatic model would be less obvious in a small community with a high level of education and homogeneity of the values that people often squabble over. If people can agree on the way things are supposed to work, it is not so difficult for them to agree on whether things really do work out that way. On technological matters the degree of agreement is often high. It is on social matters that fights occur.

LATER FORMULATIONS[7]

Of the subsequent attempts to provide a methodological basis for SI, Blumer's (1969) is the most sophisticated. But he shows a Meadian ambiguity when he describes the theoretic component. He generally uses words from the vocabulary of the hard-science methodologist, such as "theory" and "concept," but he gives them different meanings. Blumer (1969:24) says that a "prior picture" of the empirical world is an unavoidable prerequisite for its study. The four customary means for empirical validation (proper research design, replication, hypothesis testing, and operational procedures) are claimed to be inadequate because they can give no assurance that premises, problems, data relations, and so forth are empirically valid.[8] Since these four usual means will not do, Blumer concludes that the only way to get this assurance is to go directly to the empirical social world (Blumer, 1969:35). Blumer does not mean that the investigator should consult census data or surveys but rather that he or she should directly inspect group life. Direct familiarity is necessary, he says, because most sociologists hold their theoretical positions tenaciously; and they gratuitously accept concepts and beliefs as inherently true. These images shape inquiry and become a substitute for direct experience. But Blumer does not explain how scientists can approach reality with blank minds nor does he offer evidence to show that persons who follow the SI tradition hold to their concepts and positions any less tenaciously than those who do not. Nor is his conclusion at this point consistent with his earlier statement that a prior picture is necessary in order to study the world.

What the investigator should do, Blumer says, is to conduct an exploratory study, seeking acute, well-informed observers. The investigator should also aim to cast the problem in a theoretic form for analysis. But the usual theoretical procedures used in sociology will not do. What is needed is "inspection," an intensive focused examination of the empirical content of whatever elements are used for analysis, and the same kind of examination of the empirical nature of the relations between such elements (Blumer, 1969:43). The prototype of inspection is represented by the handling of a strange physical object. "We may pick it up, look at it closely, and test it in one way or another. Inspection is not preset, routinized; it is free and flexible, the antithesis of inquiry as outlined in current methodology" (Blumer, 1969:44).

The crucial deficiency of social theory, Blumer (1954:5) says, is the ambiguous nature of its concepts.[9] There are two ways to solve the problem. First, to develop precise procedures that will yield a definitive empirical content, relying on standardized techniques and mathematical categories. This way will not establish genuine concepts related to the natural world. The other way is to accept sociological concepts as sensitizing rather than definitive. This approach is spared the logical problems confronting the first, but it forfeits the achievement of definitive concepts with specific objective bench marks. It depends on faithful reportorial depiction and analytical probing; and it remains in close and continuous relation with the natural social world (Blumer, 1954:9–10).

Thus theory is seen to emerge from direct observation, with little specification of the rules of logic or procedure to be used. The investigator is urged to use well-informed observers. But if the observers fail to agree among themselves, on what grounds does the investigator choose one view rather than another? Do the observers ultimately shape the theory that emerges? What ensures the objectivity or reliability of the investigator? Many scholars currently involved in SI and related research styles ignore some of these questions and disagree on others. Let us examine some responses to these questions.

The Meadian tradition requires the researcher to maintain both his own and the actor's perspective. Unless he addresses this problem, he cannot warrant his findings on scientific grounds and will be open to the charge that they are no different from those of a lay actor (Cicourel:1964:52). But those who do sociology in this style do not always confront this issue clearly. For example, researchers are advised to cultivate close relationships with those they study because such persons can check on the emerging theory (Denzin, 1971:168). Equal weight cannot be given to informants because their motives for aiding the observer shape the character of their information. But the reader is not told how the researcher knows which informants to drop. Becker (1970) avoids the problem of separating his views from those of the participants by opting for the side of the underdog. Because values are said to be an implicit part of any scientific enterprise, nothing is gained by not frankly taking sides. This solution fails to distinguish the findings of sociologists from the findings of anyone else, and hence is unsatisfactory to those who hold that sociologists can claim special competence. Gouldner (1968:105) notes that the problem of identifying an underdog is ignored, as well as the problem of knowing which dog to side with in a hierarchy of stratified dogs.

The phenomenologists encourage a complete merging of the views of the researcher and the interactive situation, for fear that a scientific hypothesis will create the very reality that the scientist defines in his design. As Bruyn (1966:271, 273) notes, the traditional empiricist sets up preconceived realities which he seeks to verify; the phenomenologist wants to keep his preconceptions to a minimum and avoid anticipating causal relationships. Research interests are to be guided by the subject as given. The ambiguous view of theory which characterized the Meadian tradition is thus made consistent by eliminating the need for theory.

The objectivity of the scientist is also a source of difficulty. Dewey's (1939:775) criterion of truth was a method, to be used by intelligent men who would have a sympathetic regard for persons of differing views. The guarantee of objectivity was the social sensitivity of the observer to the needs of others (Dewey, 1920:147). To judge the credibility of grounded theory, Glaser and Strauss (1967:230) use a criterion based on the feelings of empathy aroused in the observer: if the reader is so caught up in the description that he feels as if he were in the field, he is more likely to be convinced of the accuracy of an account than if the description were flat and unconvincing. The judgment is also based on the assessment of how the researcher came to his conclusions, whom he interviewed, and how he might have appeared to those he studied. Douglas (1970:13 ff) advised that a "review" of the experience taken for granted by the natural, or everyday-life stance, will enable the researcher to understand what is going on. What the review should consist of and how the researcher knows that he has done it properly is not explained.

Summarizing earlier efforts, Denzin (1970:26) concluded that no single method will ever meet the requirements for the validation of interaction theory and therefore recommended multiple methods. The proper strategy cannot be derived solely from principles in research manuals because it is an "emergent" process, contingent on the investigator, the research setting, and his theoretical perspective (Denzin, 1970:310). The formulation appears to be a mixture of standard methods added to a derivative of the research prescription advanced by Dewey and Mead.

DISCUSSION

A major legacy of pragmatism to the Meadian tradition is the ambiguity toward the logico-theoretic component in scientific research. When the theoretical formulation is primitive, when it "emerges" from the research, or when it is absent, then investigators will tend to use implicitly their own social givens as a theory. When the subjects studied by the sociologist participate in the formulation of emerging theory, then their own givens are added to the emerging theory. The subjects studied by sociologists in the SI tradition have made such problems less obvious. Much of the research has focused on people who have little social power or influence: little children, skid row bums, drug addicts, mental patients, immigrants, delinquents, and assorted deviants.[10] The investigators are typically persons who are deeply sympathetic to and understanding of the underdogs they study, but the fact remains that any lack of consensus among the participants in such situations can be settled by the researcher with little backtalk from the participants.

The problem of scientific objectivity raised by lack of a prior theoretical formulation, by the absence of clear-cut criteria for selecting credible informants would be highlighted were the researcher to inspect a group of topdogs, say, the executives of a major corporation. In this situation, the researcher's colleagues might be uneasy if the researcher could not distinguish between theoretical concepts and observed behavior, if the hierarchy of credibility of the informants were arbitrary, and if other such judgmental procedures could hardly be replicated. Which of the participants in an interactive setting is to have most influence in determining the shape of an "emerging" theory is a question that the SI model has not confronted.

The most important way to improve the practice of SI sociology would be for its adherents to confront the problems raised by their ambiguity toward the logico-theoretic component in their work. Their use of the customary vocabulary of methodology illustrates the ambiguity. Often such words as theory, hypothesis, concept are given meanings which are quite different from those they have when used by conventional methodologists. In this situation, the rational discussion of important issues in the discipline is difficult. Every group, of course, has a right to define words any way it chooses; but when words already have a consensual definition, to give them a different one obfuscates communication.

Furthermore, nothing prevents a detailed observational account from being informed with notions from a stratification theory or any other theory. For the researcher to spell out in advance and in detail what is expected and why it is expected is more work than transcribing events with the atheoretical simplicity of a blank mind. But such preliminary spadework would help to integrate the findings into a larger body of work, hence make them more meaningful. To be sure, the production of theory in sociology is beset with many unsolved problems. Nevertheless, the prior construction of logically related propositions is important in science because it gives the researcher a chance to lose the game. A theoretical formulation forces researchers to bet on a particular outcome and to explain why they bet the way they do. In the absence of such a formulation, the researcher always wins, for any outcome is permissible.

This paper has criticized the SI tradition, one of the most important approaches in the discipline of sociology. Along with ethnomethodology and other styles in the holistic tradition, however, SI has retained a freshness in its approach to data which is often lost when aggregate data emerge from the bowels of the computer. Blumer's injunction to look at real people makes good sense. The detailed accounts of the way people behave make good reading. Some of these rich reports may well survive studies awash with mathematical formulations.[11] But the practitioners of SI remain nervous lest their reports be confused with mere journalism. Their fear is justified. What is needed is a frank confrontation with a major legacy of pragmatism. In the absence of theory, the social givens of the researcher and the participants serve as a theoretical framework, giving the research a bias which reflects the unstated assumptions of the researcher, the climate of opinion in the discipline, and the distribution of power in the interactive setting. Much SI research reflects a kindly concern for the people who are studied because SI methods attract those who delight in observing the nuances of human behavior. Nevertheless, when the criterion for truth is what people do, when theory emerges from practice, then the biases of those who do and act are embedded in the theory.

NOTES

1. For example, Becker (1958:653) points out that the observational researcher faces the problem of convincing others of the validity of his findings; Bruyn (1966:174) says that there is currently no method to do this. Lofland (1971:vii) notes that, strangely, few instructions are available to show how qualitative observation and analysis is done.

2. Filstead (1970:1, 8) cites Blumer, Clinard, Bruyn, Deutscher, Becker, Gouldner, and Horowitz as showing a concern with the current direction of the field.

3. The paper refers mainly to Dewey's version of pragmatic philosophy. Peirce's conception is different (Lewis, forthcoming). He thought that other pragmatists misunderstood his theories and his dominant attitude toward them was one of contempt. From Kant's *pragmatisch* Peirce adopted the name pragmatism, which became popular. This so irritated Peirce that he referred to his own formulation as "pragmaticism," a name which he thought was so ugly that no one would use it (Wennerberg, 1962:14–15). In this opinion he was correct.

4. Mills' (1966) doctoral dissertation, a rare exception, is a sociological analysis of pragmatism rather than an assessment of the impact of pragmatic philosophy on sociology. Such an analysis is yet to be made. Mills (1966:464) omitted a detailed consideration of Mead's work but felt that the omission was intellectually unwarranted.

5. Durkheim lectured on pragmatism at the Sorbonne, 1913–14. He wanted to find a formula that would preserve the essentials of rationalism but at the same time answer the valid criticisms that pragmatism had made. Stone and Farberman (1970:100–12) see Durkheim as more sympathetic to pragmatism than I do.

6. The claim that SI methods have a status quo bias does not imply that scholars in this tradition are more conservative than other sociologists. I am arguing only that the model is especially susceptible to influence. Whether scholars in this tradition have a distinctive political viewpoint is a question I have not examined. I have no reason to suppose that they are anything but humanitarian liberals. Dewey was a kindly and admirable man. But this fact has no bearing whatsoever on the susceptibility of these methods to social bias.

7. In recent years the two foremost exponents of the SI point of view have been Herbert Blumer and the late Manford Kuhn (Manis and Meltzer, 1967:vi), and four major varieties of the tradition have been identified (Petras and Meltzer, forthcoming).

8. Blumer's criticism of the discipline is extraordinarily persuasive. As a critic, he is without peer.

9. Willer and Webster (1970) also conclude that the amount of theory in sociology is small because sociologists conceptualize incorrectly. Their prescription is unlike Blumer's. Rather than using the concepts of everyday experience, observables, or descriptive terms, sociologists should define constructs expressing abstract properties of entities for use in theories.

10. Meadian sociology has been accused of ignoring the reality of social stratification. The labeling theory of deviance, a derivative of the SI approach, is an apparent exception. Deviance occurs because some powerful groups can impose their rules on subordinates (Becker, 1963:17). The focus of research shifts from types of deviance to the processes by which people become deviant (Kitsuse, 1964:87). This development shows great promise but thus far a detailed analysis of the institutional arrangements which enforce definitions has not been made. That is, the theoretical approach has not been well developed.

11. Many of the studies using the latest techniques of quantification are also examples of empirical thinking (Willer, 1970), and are relatively atheoretical.

REFERENCES

Becker, Howard S. "Problems of Inference and Proof in Participant Observation," *American Sociological Review*, 23 (December 1958), 625–660.
———. *Outsiders: Studies in the Sociology of Deviance*. New York: Free Press, 1963.
———. "Whose Side Are We On?" in William H. Filstead, ed., *Qualitative Methodology: Firsthand Involvement with the Social World*. Chicago: Markham, 1970, pp. 15–25.
Blumer, Herbert. "What Is Wrong with Social Theory," *American Sociological Review*, 19 (February 1954), 3–10.
———. "Foreword" to Severyn T. Bruyn, ed., *The Human Perspective in Sociology*. Englewood Cliffs, N.J.: Prentice-Hall, 1966, pp. iii–vii.
———. *Symbolic Interactionism: Perspective and Method*. Englewood Cliffs, N.J.: Prentice-Hall, 1969.
Braithwaite, R. B. *Scientific Explanation*. New York: Cambridge University Press, 1963.
Bruyn, Severyn T., ed. *The Human Perspective in Sociology*. Englewood Cliffs, N.J.: Prentice-Hall, 1966.
Cicourel, Aaron V. *Method and Measurement in Sociology*. New York: Free Press, 1964.
Curtis, James E., and John W. Petras. *The Sociology of Knowledge: A Reader*. New York: Praeger, 1970.
Denzin, Norman K. *The Research Act: A Theoretical Introduction to Sociological Methods*. Chicago: Aldine, 1970.
———. "The Logic of Naturalistic Inquiry," *Social Forces*, 50 (December 1971), 166–182.
Denzin, Norman K., ed. *Sociological Methods: A Sourcebook*. Chicago: Aldine, 1970.
Dewey, John. *Essays in Experimental Logic*. Chicago: University of Chicago Press, 1916.
———. *Reconstruction in Philosophy*. New York: Henry Holt, 1920.
———. *The Quest for Certainty*. New York: Minton, Balch, 1929.
———. "Prefatory Remarks," in George Herbert Mead, *The Philosophy of the Present*. Chicago: Open Court, 1932, pp. xxxvi–xl.
———. "Experimentation in Moral Theory," in Joseph Ratner, ed., *Intelligence in the Modern World: John Dewey's Philosophy*. New York: Modern Library, 1939, pp. 775–778.
Dewey, John, A. M. Moore, H. C. Brown, G. H. Mead, et al. *Creative Intelligence*. New York: Henry Holt, 1917.
Douglas, Jack D., ed. *Understanding Everyday Life: Toward the Reconstruction of Sociological Knowledge*. Chicago: Aldine, 1970.
Durkheim, Emile. "Pragmatism and Sociology," in Kurt H. Wolff, ed., *Emile Durkheim, 1858–1917: A Collection of Essays with Translations and Bibliography*. Columbus: Ohio State University Press, 1960, pp. 386–436.
Ehrlich, Howard. Personal communication, 1972.
Filstead, William H., ed. *Qualitative Methodology: Firsthand Involvement with the Social World*. Chicago: Markham, 1970.
Gallie, W. B. *Peirce and Pragmatism*. New York: Dover, 1966.
Glaser, Barney G., and Anselm L. Strauss. *The Discovery of Grounded Theory: Strategies for Qualitative Research*. Chicago: Aldine, 1967.
Gouldner, Alvin W. "The Sociologist as Partisan: Sociology and the Welfare State," *The American Sociologist*, 3 (May 1968), 103–116.
Hill, Richard J. "On the Relevance of Methodology," in Norman K. Denzin, ed., *Sociological Methods: A Sourcebook*. Chicago: Aldine, 1970, pp. 12–19.
Huber (Rytina), Joan, and Charles Loomis. "Marxist Dialectic and Pragmatism: Power as Knowledge," *American Sociological Review*, 35 (April 1970), 308–318.
Kaplan, Abraham. *The Conduct of Inquiry: Methodology for Behavioral Science*. San Francisco: Chandler, 1964.

Kitsuse, John I. "Societal Reactions to Deviant Behavior: Problems of Theory and Method," in Howard S. Becker, ed., *The Other Side: Perspectives on Deviance.* New York: Free Press, 1964, pp. 87–102.

Kuhn, Manford. "Major Trends in Symbolic Interaction Theory in the Past Twenty-five Years," in Gregory P. Stone and Harvey A. Farberman, eds., *Social Psychology Through Symbolic Interaction.* Waltham, Mass.: Xerox, 1970, pp. 70–87.

Lee, Grace Chin. *George Herbert Mead: Philosopher of the Social Individual.* New York: King's Crown, 1945.

Lewis, J. David. "Peirce, Mead, and the Objectivity of Meaning," *Kansas Journal of Sociology,* forthcoming.

Lofland, John. *Analyzing Social Settings: A Guide to Qualitative Observation and Analysis.* Belmont, Calif.: Wadsworth, 1971.

Manis, Jerome G., and Bernard M. Meltzer. *Symbolic Interaction: A Reader in Social Psychology.* Boston: Allyn and Bacon, 1967.

Mead, George Herbert. *The Philosophy of the Present.* Edited by Arthur E. Murphy, with prefatory remarks by John Dewey. Chicago: Open Court, 1932.

———. *Mind, Self & Society.* Edited, with introduction, by Charles W. Morris. Chicago: University of Chicago Press, 1934.

———. *Movements of Thought in the Nineteenth Century.* Edited by Merritt H. Moore. Chicago, University of Chicago Press, 1936.

———. *The Philosophy of the Act.* Edited, with introduction, by Charles W. Morris in collaboration with John M. Brewster, Albert M. Dunham, and David L. Miller. Chicago: University of Chicago Press, 1938.

———. *Selected Writings.* Edited, with introduction, by Andrew J. Reck. Indianapolis: Bobbs-Merrill, 1964.

Meltzer, Bernard N. *The Social Psychology of George Herbert Mead.* Kalamazoo, Mich.: Western Michigan University Press, 1959.

Mills, C. Wright. *The Marxists.* New York: Dell, 1962.

———. *Sociology and Pragmatism: The Higher Learning in America.* New York: Oxford University Press, 1966.

Morris, Charles W. "Introduction" to George H. Mead, *Mind, Self & Society.* Chicago: University of Chicago Press, 1934.

Petras, John W. "John Dewey and the Rise of Interactionism in American Social Theory," *Journal of the History of the Behavioral Sciences,* 4 (January 1968), 18–27.

———. "George Herbert Mead's Theory of Self: A Study in the Origin and Convergence of Ideas," *The Canadian Review of Sociology and Anthropology,* forthcoming.

Petras, John W., and Bernard N. Meltzer. "Theoretical and Ideological Variations in Contemporay Interactionism," *Catalyst,* forthcoming.

Reck, Andrew J., ed. *George Herbert Mead: Selected Writings.* Indianapolis: Bobbs-Merrill, 1964, pp. v–lxxii.

Russell, Bertrand. *A History of Western Philosophy.* New York: Simon and Schuster, 1945.

Shibutani, Tamotsu. "Mead, George Herbert," in David L. Sills, ed., *International Encyclopedia of the Social Sciences.* Vol. 10. New York: Macmillan and Free Press, 1968, pp. 83–87.

Stevens, Edward. "Biographical Note: G. H. Mead," *American Journal of Sociology,* 72 (March 1967), 551–557.

Stone, Gregory P., and Harvey A. Farberman, eds. *Social Psychology Through Symbolic Interaction.* Waltham, Mass.: Xerox, 1970.

Wennerberg, Hjalmar. *The Pragmatism of C. S. Peirce: An Analytical Study.* Lund, Sweden: CWK Gleerup, 1962.

White, Morton C. *The Origin of Dewey's Instrumentalism.* New York: Columbia, 1943.

Willer, David, and Murray Webster Jr. "Theoretical Constructs and Observables," *American Sociological Review,* 35 (August 1970), pp. 748–757.

Willer, David, and Judith Willer. *Systematic Empiricism: Critique of a Pseudo-Science.* Englewood Cliffs, N.J.: Prentice-Hall, 1970.

Willer, Judith. *The Social Determination of Knowledge.* Englewood Cliffs, N.J.: Prentice-Hall, 1970.

Zajonc, Robert B. "Conformity," in David L. Sills, ed., *International Encyclopedia of the Social Sciences.* Vol. 3. New York: Macmillan and Free Press, 1968, pp. 253–260.

A NOTE ON SYMBOLIC INTERACTIONISM

HERBERT BLUMER

Reprinted from the *American Sociological Review*, 38
(1973), 797–798. Used by permission of the author and
the American Sociological Association.

"Symbolic Interactionism as a Pragmatic Perspective: The Bias of Emergent Theory" . . . [which first appeared] in the April 1973 issue of the *American Sociological Review*, misrepresents the position of pragmatism, the views of George Herbert Mead, and my own views which Professor Huber has addressed. The readers of the ASR are entitled to a correction of the misrepresentations.

The central contentions of Professor Huber are the following. 1) Under the precepts of pragmatism and symbolic interactionism, the act of scientific inquiry is initiated without any theory; thus, the position of the investigator is that of the "atheoretical simplicity of a blank mind" [116]. 2) Because of this initial absence of theory the symbolic interactionist investigator is forced back on his own views and those of his informants; thus bias is introduced and objectivity lost: "In the absence of theory, the social givens of the researcher and the participants serve as a theoretical framework, giving the research a bias which reflects the unstated assumptions of the researcher, the climate of opinion in the discipline, and the distribution of power in the interactive setting" [117]. I wish to discuss briefly each of these two contentions.

1) Surely, Professor Huber cannot be serious in asserting that pragmatism and symbolic interactionism treat the act of scientific inquiry as beginning with a "blank mind." Neither Mead nor I ever advanced such an absurd position. Mead's view on the matter is stated unequivocally in his classical article, "Scientific Method and the Individual Thinker"; mine is given in the article, "The Methodological Position of Symbolic Interactionism." As a reading of these articles should show beyond question, both Mead and I see the act of scientific inquiry as beginning with a problem. Any reasonable consideration of what is involved in the experience of the investigator when he perceives, poses, and addresses a scientific problem should show how ridiculous it is to characterize this experience as starting with a "blank mind." Confronted with a problem, the investigator must note given empirical happenings that give rise to the problem; he must pay attention to the prevailing generalizations or beliefs being challenged by the noted empirical happenings; he must give shape to the problem as it emerges before him; he must identify an area of inquiry implied by the problem; he must form some idea of the kinds of empirical data relevant to clarifying and possibly resolving the problem; and he must sketch out lines of empirical inquiry. To imply that these vigorous orienting actions, essential to the detection, posing, and addressing of the problem, are the actions of a "blank mind" is to do violence to meaningful language.

Obviously, Professor Huber's contention reduces to something else. As I interpret her discussion this "something else" is that the symbolic interactionist approach lacks a "logico-theoretic component" and that this lack is equivalent to an absence of theory. Professor Huber's reasoning on this point is gratuitous and quaint. She apparently identifies the "logico-theoretic component" with the use of Aristotelian logic [112], with the consequence that an approach using a different type of logic is automatically lacking in theory! Professor Huber fails to see that posing, clarifying, and addressing a scientific problem constitute theoretical action in its own right. In the effort to *shape the problem* for empirical attack, the investigator has to develop premises as to the nature of the empirical world, cut out relevant empirical objects, impute connections between classes of such objects, and form initial conceptions as to the nature of the relationship of these connected classes. To shunt aside this complex of activity as not being theoretical is unwarranted.

The real issue raised by Professor Huber's charge is not that the symbolic interactionist approach lacks theory but, instead, how the scientific problem is to get its theoretical shape. My impression is that she believes that this shaping must precede empirical observation; in this belief she is definitely in line with the dominant methodological position in our discipline today. My own view is that in studying human conduct or human group life the theoretical shaping of the problem must be done through an on-going, flexible, shifting examination of the empirical field, itself, in order to set the problem correctly. Charles Darwin is the appropriate model for this type of scientific procedure. This is no place to rehearse the differences between these two types of study. I merely wish to point out that Professor Huber is not justified in contending that under the precepts of pragmatism and symbolic interactionism the act of scientific inquiry begins with a blank mind and is devoid of theory.

2) Professor Huber's second contention is that scientific theory under the framework of pragmatism or symbolic interactionism is bounded by the views of the investigator and his informants and thus becomes a prey to these views. She holds that (a) the investigator is unable to test his assumptions, (b) there is no way to tell which of the informants has the correct views, and (c) the view that triumphs depends on the relative power position of the given informants or the investigator. I suppose that one could find an instance of symbolic interactionist study that fits what Professor Huber is saying; but if so it would be a caricature of proper procedure. There is no reason why the investigator who follows the symbolic interactionist approach cannot test his assertions and hypotheses about his empirical world by a careful, continuous examination of that world; his position is no different from that of Darwin or scores of competent ethnographers. The investigator who is sincere and sensitive to empirical observation is in the same position to find that his given ideas are untenable (and thus "lose the game") as is the researcher operating with a "prior construction of logically related propositions" [116]. I can find no basis for Professor Huber's peculiar assertion of this point. Similarly, why is it not possible to test the respective validity of informant views when such views conflict with each other? There are various ways of approaching such a problem, the chief of which is to have the informants thresh out their difference through joint confrontation and hence renew collective examination of the empirical area in dispute. In no sense is this problem inevitable or insoluble as Professor Huber seems to imply. Finally, the notion that the respective power position of informants or of the investigator determines which views among them emerge as "empirically valid" is not backed up by any evidence submitted by Professor Huber. Any conscientious observer who is aware of what is going on, whatever his philosophical persuasion, would not allow himself to fall into such a trap; and if he is sufficiently intelligent and skilled, he will know what is going on. I must conclude that these three boo-

geymen that Professor Huber gratuitously sees in symbolic interactionist research are in no sense indigenous to or greater in such research. In my judgment, the real source of social bias (as well as the source of its correction) lies in the procedure by which the scientific problem is constructed. The likelihood of introducing unwitting bias is much less when the problem is developed through a close, flexible and reflective examination of the empirical world than when the problem is formed by using a model not derived through such intimate, empirical examination.

A brief comment is due one other questionable line of treatment in Professor Huber's article. I refer to the theme that the test of truth in pragmatic doctrine is whether the given proposition or hypothesis "works." This hoary characterization of pragmatism easily lends itself to absurd interpretation. One should not assume that this crude notion means that the pragmatist fails to examine meticulously the empirical world. The opposite is the case.

REPLY TO BLUMER: JOAN HUBER
BUT WHO WILL
SCRUTINIZE THE
SCRUTINIZERS?

Reprinted from the *American Sociological Review*, 38
(1973), 798–800. Used by permission of the author and
the American Sociological Association.

In considering Professor Blumer's thoughtful comments, let us begin where he left off, since the final issue needs the fewest words. An earlier ASR article (Huber and Loomis, 1970:309) specifically disclaimed the notion that pragmatism involves only the idea that it is important to see how things work out in practice. I had not thought it necessary to repeat the disclaimer. Apparently I was wrong.

The first issue concerns my reference to the blank mind with which the SI researcher approaches data. This metaphor, harking back to Locke's *tabula rasa*, describes a mind whose knowledge derives from experience. The founder of empiricism, Locke characterized the mind as a sheet of white paper and asked how it came to be furnished. His answer was that all knowledge derives from experience alone because the mind has no innate ideas. But this view fails to account for formal logic and mathematics, neither of which can be derived from experience. Kant corrected Locke by observing that, although the mind contains no innate ideas, it can generate the categories of logic and mathematics which thus arise neither from the mind alone (as rationalists claimed) nor from experience alone (as empiricists claimed). Current philosophy of science also separates logic from sense data and holds that both are necessary for scientific theory. Although no one disputes that Lockeans and SI researchers can *think* about problems, or that thinking and the "vigorous orienting actions" Professor Blumer lists may be theoretical *actions*, they are not theory (Lewis, 1973). The issue is whether scientific knowledge can be produced without a prior logical framework. Professor Blumer (1969:43, 44) feels that the conventional analytical schemes in science force data into an "artificial framework" that seriously impairs "genuine empirical analysis." He recommends instead a procedure whose "essence" is "close, shifting scrutiny." Thus he rejects conventional use of a prior logical structure in favor of empirical procedures used with a "different type of logic" which is not described, so far as I have been able to discover, anywhere in his work. The mind of Blumer's observer, like Locke's, is thus a *tabula rasa* because it is furnished by means of empirical observation.

Because I charged that inadequate testing and replication procedures in the SI model permit the influence of power and personality on findings, the real issue between us concerns the rules for deciding whether a proposition is true. In the initial stages of research, abductive reasoning (including observational statements) helps put a problem into testable form. But what is the purpose of all this "theoretical" activity? At what point do you pin something down precisely so that it can be tested? Precise concepts are unsuitable, Professor Blumer (1954:8,

9) holds, because of the varying nature of reality. Instead, researchers should rely on "sensitizing concepts" grounded on sense instead of on explicit objective traits; such concepts are formulated and communicated by ". . . exposition which yields a meaningful picture, abetted by apt illustrations which enable one to grasp the reference in terms of one's own experience." But the rules for deciding whether one picture is more "meaningful" than another are not discussed.

In order to learn how SI research should be tested, let us examine the description of methods that Professor Blumer (1969:1–60) recommends, using his phrasing as much as possible. The page numbers in parentheses will help the reader to assess whether the following summary is accurate.

Since the researcher usually does not know at first hand the sphere of life he wants to study (35), Blumer says, he unwittingly forms a picture of it, using images he already has (36). This is all right if the images are revised and tested by first hand experience, but this motif does not prevail in social science (37). Instead, images substitute for experience; the researcher relies on starting with a theory, an hypothesis, and a mode of inquiry to test it. Thus the protocol of inquiry becomes the unwitting substitute for direct examination of the real world (38).

What the study of the ongoing real world requires, Blumer says, is a high order of careful and honest probing, creative yet disciplined imagination, resourcefulness, flexibility, pondering, and a constant readiness to recast one's images (38). This world can best be studied by two modes of naturalistic inquiry: exploration and inspection (40). Exploration is a flexible procedure whose purpose is to lead to a clearer understanding of how to pose the problem (40). Such direct examination sets the need for another procedure, inspection or analysis, in order to cast the problem in theoretical form and formulate theoretical propositions, the aim of empirical science. [In this passage Blumer is insensitive to what Peirce called the ethics of terminology for, as we shall soon see, inspection does not constitute scientific analysis as that phrase is customarily used.]

How is scientific analysis to be done in direct examination of the real world? By inspection, Blumer says, an intensive focused examination of the empirical content of whatever analytical elements are used (43), such as "integration" and "social mobility" (44), and of the relations between such elements. Inspection proceeds by subjecting such elements to meticulous examination by careful, flexible scrutiny of the empirical instances covered by the analytical element; it is not preset, routinized, or prescribed, for ". . . it only becomes such when we already know what it is and thus can resort to a specific test, as in the case of a technician" (44). The antithesis of scientific inquiry in the current methodology (45), inspection is appropriate for pinning down and testing the relations between analytical elements by flexible scrutiny of empirical instances (46). Without inspection one is captive to one's prior image of the relationship (46).

Thus SI research should be tested by scrutiny. If the scrutiny is not sufficiently intense and flexible, the researcher presumably remains captive to prior images. How researchers know that they have scrutinized hard enough, Professor Blumer does not say. Although SI researchers may scrutinize harder than others, the injunction to look again is an inadequate prescription for testing or replication. Conspicuously, the people who write about SI research don't do it, and the people who do it do not use the basic SI paradigm; if they are good sociologists, they throw in other components, as appropriate (Bucher, 1973). Logical analysis of the SI model shows that its use gives the researcher no rules to decide whose picture of reality is most meaningful, and hence allows the intrusion of power and personality factors into the picture that is drawn.

The pragmatic model also lacks clear rules for deciding what is a "satisfactory" outcome. Mead (1964:341–342) claims that the pragmatic criterion of truth is the continuance of the common world; the test is the ability to act where the action was formerly stopped. Thus Mead implicitly accepts the given distribution of power. Problems arise, Mead says, because the common world continually breaks down when the natural processes of men are inhibited. The solution is found in resolving the inhibitions. Thus Mead sees the ongoing world as unproblematic; the problem arises when the action stops, and the solution is to get it started again. Mead and Dewey avoid the implications of this model by using examples of technological rather than social problems to illustrate their methods.

What is best about the SI or pragmatic formulation is the injunction to inspect the real world; too often students engage in secondary analysis with little first hand knowledge of the situation. But nothing guarantees that sociologists will scrutinize more carefully than other people. A sensitive essay may be a delight to read, but a word picture that can be refuted only by a more "sensitive" word picture leaves unanswered the main question: on what grounds does one choose one picture rather than another? Professor Blumer's suggestion that, in case of disagreement, the informants simply settle the matter by threshing out their views in joint confrontation supports my criticism of the SI model better than anything I could say.

REFERENCES

Blumer, Herbert. "What Is Wrong with Social Theory," *American Sociological Review*, 19 (February 1954), 3–10.

————. *Symbolic Interactionism: Perspective and Method*. Englewood Cliffs, N.J.: Prentice-Hall, 1969.

Bucher, Rue. Personal communication, 1973.

Huber (Rytina), Joan, and Charles P. Loomis. "Marxist Dialectic and Pragmatism: Power as Knowledge," *American Sociological Review*, 35 (April 1970), 308–318.

Lewis, J. David. "The Methodology of Herbert Blumer." Unpublished paper, 1973.

Mead, George Herbert. *Selected Writings*. Edited, with introduction, by Andrew J. Reck. Indianapolis: Bobbs-Merrill, 1964.

CHAPTER 4

EXCHANGE THEORY

Introduction

Exchange theory is a synthesis of animal psychology, behavioral psychology, and elementary economic theory and yields a view of man as rational and calculating. George Homans is the recognized "founder" of exchange theory in sociology. Homans (1958) begins by noting that the behavior of pigeons undergoing conditioning parallels that of humans: We persist in behavior that is rewarded. In interaction, people try to maximize their "profit" by seeking the most "rewards" while minimizing "costs." This, concludes Homans, is the most obvious way of viewing behavior, although we often neglect the economic view of behavior implied by the everyday terms "reward" and "costs." "What's in it for me?" is surely a much asked, if silent, question.

The impact of exchange theory has been great, but without massive destructiveness on other theoretical approaches. This may be attributed in part to the "founders," Homans and Blau. Each had eminence and strategic positions in sociology *before* they embraced the exchange paradigm. Despite Homans' (1964) critique of functionalism, neither man alienated nonfollowers. Indeed, both were elected to the presidency of the American Sociological Association. While, as noted by Gouldner (1970:395–96), their theoretical model is "significantly different from the Parsonian," they have only provided an alternative theory, without demolishing the old. Exchange is eminently compatible with neopositivism (Homans, 1964, called for the development of scientific deductive theory) and with the burgeoning field of behavior modification in psychology. Its research implications, then, fit well into traditional modes of sociological (and psychological) research.

The economic interpretation of human behavior is not new to social thought. Precursors of exchange theory include the English "classical" economist Adam Smith (1723–1790) and, more closely, the utilitarians, Jeremy Bentham (1748–1832) and John Stuart Mill (1806–1873). For Smith, human motivation was not, however, primarily for economic gain, but for prestige. Bentham set forth the principle that behavior is shaped by the human preference for pleasure over pain. Individuals are motivated by maximizing their personal utility (gain). The responsibility of government is to provide "the greatest good for the greatest number." Mill subscribed to this view of man and insisted on the development of a science of society adhering to the rules of scientific method.

Exchange theory has been used to guide behavior modification research and also to tackle theoretical problems usually dealt with by different approaches. Blau (1964), for example, has attempted to extend exchange theory from Homans' "elementary forms" of behavior to a theory of social structures. He takes into account unequal exchange and the possession of sanctions (ultimately of force)—that is, power relations. Burns (1973) has extended the theory to embrace more "social" everyday interaction by taking into account "the structural and temporal context of interaction." Meeker (1971) has developed the theory to encompass decision making, while Kunkel and Nagasawa (1973) have revised exchange theory in light of recent findings in behavioral psychology, particularly those of Bandura (1969). Ellis (1971) has attempted to answer the "Hobbesian problem" of how the existence of organized society is possible, and finds exchange theory superior to normative approaches to the task. That exchange theory can be a powerful tool in modifying behavior is attested by the work of Hamblin, et al. (1971) with autistic and "problem" children.

Despite the demonstrated utility of exchange theory in behavior modification, there has been some criticism of it on philosophical grounds. (There are, of course, ethical problems inherent to its application in behavioral modification.) The criticism, however, has been muted: It is apparently not perceived as a threat to other theories. Abrahamson (1970) has provided perhaps the most complete critique of Homans, summarizing earlier negative responses (for example, Boulding, 1961; Davis, 1961; and Sorokin, 1966). Homans' theory, Abrahamson claims, has "shortcomings with regard to its deductive and inductive aspects." This, and the tautological usage of the concept "reward" makes the theory untestable. Insofar as the theory is hedonistic, Abrahamson concludes, it is open to established antihedonistic criticisms.

To its practitioners, exchange theory is a separate paradigm in sociology. (Mullins, 1973, withholds such recognition, subsuming exchange under standard American sociology as a variety of structural functionalism.) An attempt to synthesize exchange with symbolic interactionism (Singelmann, 1972) was rejected by some followers of exchange theory as inappropriate and fruitless (Abbott, et al. 1973). Exchange may, however, be compatible with modern systems theory (see Burns, 1976, and Baumgartner et al. 1975). While exchange theory is not being readily absorbed into most introductory texts in sociology, it is developing a distinct research tradition "on the sidelines"—that is, without unduly threatening the discipline from within.

The first reading in this chapter is an updated version (1974) of the general propositions of exchange theory as formulated by George C. Homans. These propositions all relate to the behavior of individuals and are not extended to encompass whole societies. They urge that the social scientist focus on *behavior*, not on the norms and values that are so often stressed by sociologists.

The second article deals with the potential impact of behavioral psy-chologist B. F. Skinner on sociology. Homans is in basic agreement with Skinner's work; as he admits, "I am a Skinnerian and have long been known as one" (Homans, 1974:296), but clearly he is one who has res-ervations about some of Skinner's "extreme" behaviorism. Other soci-ologists have reacted more strongly to Skinner's work. See, for example, Swanson (1972) and Berger (1972). Staats (1976) has noted that within psychology, Skinner is considered a "radical." Friedrichs' article, then, is dealing not just with Skinner but with the future of exchange theory in sociology. He argues that the behavioral paradigm may be able to com-bine the "system" and "conflict" paradigms, or rather subsume them, and become the dominant "orthodoxy" of sociology. This will most likely occur if the paradigm is merged with policy research and with what has been termed "neopositivism" in this volume. Friedrichs nominates James Coleman for the task. He lists by name the prominent behaviorists within contemporary sociology and their likely success in grant getting.

Frederick Lynch's paper takes issue with Friedrichs. Lynch questions the changes in Friedrichs' predictions since 1972 and prefers his prior prediction of an emergent "Comtean positivism" or, as Lynch calls it, the positivist establishment) as closer to the truth. Indeed, notes Lynch, Homans is as well known for his philosophy of science as for his be-haviorism. Coleman, too, is better known for his positivism than for his covert behaviorism. He finds little evidence of the emergence of the be-havioral paradigm in policy research, nor is behaviorism particularly compatible with functionalism. Lynch concludes that more promising and healthy new paradigms will not be swamped by any new "orthodoxy." Friedrichs' response, which follows, maintains that unlike positivism, the emerging behaviorism *does* mediate several major theoretical con-flicts, although Friedrichs adds that he does not favor the establishment of any orthodoxy himself.

References and Selected Readings

Abbott, Carvell W., Charles R. Brown, and Paul V. Crosbie. "Exchange as Symbolic Inter-action—For What," *American Sociological Review*, 38 (1973), 504.

Abrahamson, Bengt. "Homans on Exchange; Hedonism Revisited," *American Journal of Sociology*, 76 (1970), 273–285.

Bandura, Albert. *Principles of Behavior Modification.* New York: Holt, Rinehart and Win-ston, 1969.

Baumgartner, Tom, Walter Buckley, and Tom R. Burns. "Meta-power and Relational Con-trol in Social Life," *Social Science Information*, 14 (1975), 49–78,

Berger, Bennett M. "Review Symposium on *Beyond Freedom and Dignity* by B. F. Skinner," *American Journal of Sociology*, 78 (November 1972), 705–708.

Blau, Peter M. *Exchange and Power in Social Life.* New York: Wiley, 1964.

Boulding, K. E. "Critique of Homans' Social Behavior—Its Elementary Forms: An Econo-mist's View," *American Sociological Review*, 26 (1961), 458–461.

Burns, Tom R. "A Structural Theory of Social Exchange," *Acta Sociologica*, 16 (1973), 188–208.

————. "The Structuring of Unequal Exchange Patterns and Social Structure," *Acta So-ciologica*, 1976, forthcoming.

Burgess, R. L., and D. Bushell, eds. *Behavioral Sociology.* New York: Columbia University Press, 1969.

Davis, J. A. "Critique of Homans' Social Behavior—Its Elementary Forms: A Sociologist's View," *American Sociological Review*, 26 (1961), 454–458.

Ellis, Desmond P. "The Hobbesian Problem of Order: A Critical Appraisal of the Normative Solution," *American Sociological Review*, 36 (August 1971).

Emerson, R. M. "Exchange Theory, Part I: A Psychological Basis for Social Exchange," in J. Berger, B. Anderson, and M. Zelditch, eds., *Sociological Theories in Progress*, Vol. II. Boston: Houghton-Mifflin, 1972.

Gouldner, Alvin W. *The Coming Crisis of Western Sociology*. New York: Basic Books, 1970.

Hamblin, Robert L., David Buckholdt, Daniel Ferritor, Martin Kozloff, and Lois Blackwell. *The Humanization Processes: A Social, Behavioral Analysis of Children's Problems*. New York: Wiley, 1971.

Homans, George C. "Social Behavior as Exchange," *American Journal of Sociology*, 63 (1958), 597–606.

———. "Bringing Men Back In," *American Sociological Review*, 29 (1964), 809–918.

———. "Review Symposium on *Beyond Freedom and Dignity* by B. F. Skinner," *American Journal of Sociology*, 78 (November 1973), 696–702.

———. *Social Behavior: Its Elementary Forms*. Rev. ed. New York: Harcourt Brace Jovanovich, 1974.

Krasner, Leonard, and Leonard P. Ullmann, eds. *Research in Behavior Modification*. New York: Holt, Rinehart and Winston, 1965.

Kunkel, John H. *Society and Economic Growth: A Behavioral Perspective of Social Change*. New York: Oxford University Press, 1970.

Kunkel, John H., and Richard H. Nagasawa. "A Behavorial Model of Man: Propositions and Implications," *American Sociological Review*, 38 (1973), 530–543.

Maris, Ronald. "The Logical Adequacy of Homans' Social Theory," *American Sociological Review*, 35 (1970), 1069–1081.

Meeker, B. F. "Decisions and Exchange," *American Sociological Review*, 36 (1971), 485.

Mullins, Nicholas S. *Theories and Theory Groups in Contemporary American Sociology*. New York: Harper & Row, 1973.

Singelmann, Peter. "Exchange as Symbolic Interaction: Convergences Between Two Theoretical Perspectives," *American Sociological Review*, 37 (1972), 414–424.

Staats, Arthur W. "Skinnerian Behaviorism: Social Behaviorism or Radical Behaviorism?" *American Sociologist*, 2 (February 1976), 59–60.

Sorokin, P. A. *Sociological Theories of Today*. New York: Harper & Row, 1966.

Swanson, Guy E. "Review Symposium on *Beyond Freedom and Dignity* by B. F. Skinner," *American Journal of Sociology*, 78 (November 1973), 702–705.

Thibaut, John W., and Harold H. Kelley. *The Social Psychology of Groups*. New York: Wiley, 1959.

THE GENERAL PROPOSITIONS OF EXCHANGE THEORY

GEORGE C. HOMANS

George C. Homans teaches at Harvard University.

. . . A proposition states a relationship between properties of nature. The propositions we shall use will avoid each of two extremes. On the one hand, they will not take the form of saying merely that there is *some* relationship between the properties, that x is *some* function of y, for logic is unable to draw any definite conclusions from propositions of this sort. Nor, on the other hand, will they take the form of saying that x is a definite function of y, such as $x = \log y$, for the data rarely justify any such precision. Instead they will take the form of saying that, for instance, as x increases in value, so does y (or in the case of some of the propositions decreases), without saying how much y increases. Propositions of this form do say something, though obviously they say it pretty crudely. They are only approximate truths, but an approximate truth is far more valuable than no truth at all. If even our general propositions take this form, the conclusions in logic we are entitled to draw from them cannot be of a higher degree of precision. Luckily the propositions to be explained are as crude as the general ones. Though certainly a science, social science is certainly not an exact science.

THE SUCCESS PROPOSITION

"In the beginning was the act," said Goethe. . . .[We] shall be much more interested in men's actions than in their attitudes, especially if attitudes do not lead to action. We are sick of a social science in which men are always "orienting" or indeed "orientating" themselves to action, but never acting. Yet we shall not be concerned with all the actions of men. Our propositions will not refer to reflex action, such as the familiar knee jerk, but will refer to what Skinner (1938) calls *operants* and we might call voluntary actions to distinguish them from reflexes, which are clearly involuntary. Our first proposition relates a man's (or woman's) action to its success in getting a favorable result. In classical psychology it is called "the law of effect." Because we believe another name will make its meaning more obvious, we shall call it the *success proposition*.

We may state it as follows:

I. *For all actions taken by persons, the more often a particular action of a person is rewarded, the more likely the person is to perform that action.*

The proposition in itself says nothing about the reasons why the person performed the action in the first place. In the case of an experimental animal like a pigeon, its repertory of innate behavior seems to include a tendency to explore or investigate its environment by pecking at the objects within it. The psychologist may have so arranged its cage that the motion of a metal key will release a grain of corn to the pigeon. If, in the course of exploring its cage, the pigeon happens to peck at the key and thus get the corn to eat, the probability that the pigeon will peck the target again will increase. Not until then will the psychologist be able to use the pigeon's tendency to repeat its action for the purposes of further experimentation. The same sort of behavior is characteristic of men. What the success proposition says is that, whatever be the reason why a person performs an action, once he has in fact performed it, and the action has proved successful—the result has for the person what we shall later call positive value—then the person is apt to repeat the action.

The result of an action is what follows it. The success proposition holds good even if success was not, in the eyes of some informed observer, caused by the action but was rather a matter of chance. Much of the magic men have performed has been maintained by fortuitous success, especially when success is much desired and alternative means of producing it are not known. After all, rain usually does follow the magic of rainmaking—sooner or later.

The proposition may sound as if it said that an action were caused by its result, which is absurd to those of us who do not believe in teleology. But it does not say that. What we observe is a sequence of at least three events: 1) a person's action, which is followed by 2) a rewarding result, and then by 3) a repetition of the original action or, as we shall see, by an action in some respects similar to the original. It is the combination of events 1 and 2 that causes event 3, and since the former two precede the latter in time, we are saved from teleology. It is natural to call the original sequence of three events a learning process, and therefore the general propositions we shall use are often called the propositions of "learning theory." We believe this to be a mistake, since the propositions continue to hold good long after the behavior has in every ordinary sense of the word been learned.

The fact that a person's action has been rewarded on one occasion makes it more probable that he will repeat it on the next occasion. If there are many such occasions, the probability that he will perform the action will vary directly with the frequency with which it has been rewarded, and we have deliberately cast the proposition so that it takes this form. Remember that we are particularly concerned ... with the process by which social behavior gives rise to relatively enduring social structures. Without repeated social actions there are no enduring social structures.

The proposition implies that an increasing frequency of reward leads to an increasing frequency of action, but it is obvious that such an increase cannot go on indefinitely. It has built-in limits, as we shall see later when we consider satiation. The proposition also implies that the less often an action is rewarded, the less often it is apt to be repeated. At the extreme, if an action once rewarded is never rewarded thereafter, a person tends in time never to perform it at all. In the technical language of behavioral psychology, it eventually becomes *extinguished*. But the time required for extinction may be very long indeed, and a single occasion on which the action is rewarded may be enough to *reinstate* it at full strength.

Let us now consider some qualifications of the success proposition. The shorter the interval of time between the action and the reward, the more likely the person is to repeat it—the more likely, to use the language of everyday life, he is to "see" the connection between his action and its reward. If we wish a person to learn, we shall do well to reward his correct responses promptly. This is the principle on which "teaching machines" are based. The reason why we do not use ordinary language but a proposition which merely sums up the facts is that everyday language is apt to embody assumptions about human behavior that are not always justified. Thus prompt reward is apt to make action more probable even if the person does not "see" the connection between his action and its reward in any conscious sense. The greater, moreover, is the value of the reward, the more likely is the person to make the connection, but we shall have much more to say about that value later.

The frequency with which the person performs the action depends also on the pattern in which the reward comes. (On this matter see especially Ferster and Skinner, 1957.) For a given total number of rewards within a given period of time, it looks as if man, like an experimental animal such as a pigeon, will repeat an action less often if it is rewarded regularly—for instance, if it is rewarded every time it is performed— than he will if it is rewarded at irregular intervals of time or at irregular ratios between the number of times he performs the action and the number of times it is rewarded. Furthermore an action once regularly rewarded will, when the reward ceases, become extinguished sooner than one rewarded irregularly. One reason why people are willing to work so hard at gambling, fishing, or hunting, even when they have little success, is that such actions are characteristically rewarded irregularly. Indeed the tendency to repeat an action more often if its reward comes irregularly may have arisen in animals, including the ancestors of men, because of its survival value. If one depends for one's food on activities such as fishing and hunting, one had better not give up too easily if one is unsuccessful, but persist. The tendency implies that animals will do just that.

Though we take note of these relationships subsidiary to the success proposition, we shall have little more to say about them. They do not render invalid the success proposition itself. Even in its crude form, the latter holds good over a wide range of behavior. In gross and in a first approximation it will serve us well in explanation. . . .

We stated the success proposition as if it applied to a single kind of act and a single kind of reward at a time: the higher the absolute frequency of the reward, the higher the absolute frequency of the action. It is both true and convenient to state the proposition in this way. But men, like other organisms, are not usually so constrained that they can perform one kind of action and one only. Alternative kinds of action, which get men alternative rewards, are open to them. In this case we may be less interested in the absolute frequencies with which they perform actions and receive awards than in the relative frequencies, or how they distribute their actions among alternatives. The success proposition implies that the relative frequencies with which a man performs alternative actions should equal the relative frequencies with which the actions are rewarded. This proposition, though plausible, has not been experimentally demonstrated for men. But Herrnstein (1971) has demonstrated it experimentally for pigeons. . . .

THE STIMULUS PROPOSITION

We turn now to the second of our general propositions—but remember that they are "our" propositions only in the sense that we use them and not that we discovered them. This proposition concerns the effect on action of the circumstances attending it. Since in many accounts of operant or voluntary behavior these attendant circumstances are called *stimuli*, we call this the *stimulus proposition*.

We may state it as follows:

II. *If in the past the occurrence of a particular stimulus, or set of stimuli, has been the occasion on which a person's action has been rewarded, then the more similar the present stimuli are to the past ones, the more likely the person is to perform the action, or some similar action, now.*

In formulating their theories some psychologists include the reward of the action itself among the stimuli, referring to it as a *reinforcing stimulus*. We believe it is confusing to do so. It is true that the sight of some object that we have coveted and obtained earlier is a stimulus to our efforts to obtain it again; but it is the sight of the object, not the success in obtaining it, that is the stimulus. If we confuse the two, proposition II would seem to say the same thing as proposition I, whereas they really say something different.

Proposition II says that the reappearance of the circumstances attending successful action make more probable the repetition of the action. Thus a fisherman who has cast his line into a dark pool and has caught a fish becomes more apt to fish in dark pools again. The connection between the stimuli and the action is subject to both *generalization* and *discrimination*. If our fisherman has been successful in a dark pool, he may come to fish more often in any pool that is to some degree shady. Indeed his action itself may generalize. If he has been successful at one kind of fishing, he may become prepared to try other kinds and even other related sports, such as hunting. On the other hand, he may learn to fish only under very specific conditions of water, light, and shade, provided he has been successful under these but not under other conditions. In this case, the stimuli that govern his behavior have become highly discriminated. Should the conditions under which success is alone possible become complicated, they may not establish themselves at all as stimuli for his action. He is, as we say, unable to recognize them. As in the case of reward, the temporal relationship between stimulus and action makes a difference: if the crucial stimulus precedes the action by too long a time, the actor may not make the connection. The greater the value of the reward, the more sensitive to stimuli the person may become —so much so that if the value to him of a potential reward is very high, he may become oversensitive and, until corrected by failure, respond to irrelevant stimuli. Finally, alertness to stimuli or attentiveness to stimuli is itself an action which, like any other kind of action, a person may perform more often if it has brought him reward. All of these relationships should be looked on as subsidiary to the main stimulus proposition.

In social behavior persons and their attributes become crucial stimuli. Did this person, rather than another, reward a man's action? If he did, his identity was one of the circumstances attending successful action, and his presence on some new occasion is a stimulus making it more likely that the man will once more direct similar action toward him. Does this person display the cold blue eyes that a man's father did when the father punished him long ago? Then the grown man may show some slight tendency to avoid such a person. In human social behavior, what complicates the stimuli even more is the fact that they are largely verbal. The use of language sets the behavior of men further apart from that of animals than does anything else. The same general propositions apply to the behavior of both, but within these propositions the complexity of the stimuli available to men in their interaction with each other makes possible a higher order of complexity in their behavior.

The crucial variable in the stimulus proposition is obviously the degree of similarity between present stimuli and those under which an action was rewarded in the past. Yet similarity may not vary along a single dimension but along many, and indeed it may depend on a complicated pattern of measures. The ways in which persons discriminate among, or generalize across, combinations of stimuli is the subject of the field of psychology called *perception* or *cognition*. So various and so many are the findings in this field that in this book we shall only state the stimulus proposition, though we shall feel free to use more specific findings *ad hoc* to explain particular cases. The real intellectual danger is not that the findings are complex but that some social scientists should believe perception and cognition to be essentially different from other behavior and thus require a different type of explanation. They are not essentially different. The ways in which men perceive and think are just as much determined by the results they achieve as are other kinds of behavior.

Yet we do not wish to appear so rigidly behaviorist as to deny reality to some processes in which perception plays a large part and which are of great importance in social behavior. Our view of these processes has been greatly influenced by the work of Bandura (1969).

Men, like many animals, often imitate the behavior of others of their kind. Imitation of others naturally requires some degree of observation of their behavior. We believe that a tendency to imitate others is genetically inherited and not initially learned through operant conditioning. Yet, whatever its origin, a man will not persist in performing an action he has imitated unless that action eventually brings him reward. If it is successful in bringing him reward, he will not only be apt to repeat it but also to adopt imitation as a generalized form of behavior. Then his practical success will support the genetic tendency; and the persons he has imitated will become stimuli in whose presence he will be especially likely to carry out imitative actions again.

Evidence is also accumulating that men can learn to act in a certain way even when, at first, the reward they get from the act is only vicarious. Suppose that a child sees another child put a box against a wall and use it to climb successfully out of his yard. At the moment, the first child has no occasion for climbing a wall himself, but if he does have such occasion later, the evidence suggests that he is much more likely to look for a box than he would have been if he had not observed the other child, even though he has yet received no reward himself. Naturally he will not go on repeating the action unless sooner or later he is personally rewarded for performing it, but the initial stimulus to the action is the observed success of the other child, not his own. This kind of learning has been called *model learning*. The success of any one action originally modeled on the action of another may lead to a generalization of modeling behavior. As Bandura and Walters put it (1963:5): "Most children develop a generalized habit of matching the responses of successful models." They cannot help developing at the same time a generalized habit of observing those who are successful, or indeed of observing others to discover whether they are successful. The matching presupposes the observation.

If we did not accept the reality of model learning, we should be hard put to it to account . . . for the effect of a man's behavior not only on the others with whom he is in immediate contact but also on members of an audience, who take no part in the social behavior themselves but only watch it.

THE VALUE PROPOSITION: REWARD AND PUNISHMENT

In proposition I we stated the effect of the success of an action in obtaining a reward on the probablity that a person will repeat it. In speaking of the reward, we assumed that the value to the person of the result of his action was greater than zero—that is, he was not indifferent to it nor did he find it actually punishing. But the proposition had nothing to say about *how* rewarding the person found it. This variable, the degree of reward, we shall now bring in and call it *value*. The value in question is always that of a given unit of reward, no matter how that unit be defined, since, as we shall see, the values of successive units may change. The gross effect of this variable upon behavior may be expressed by the *value proposition:*

> III. *The more valuable to a person is the result of his action, the more likely he is to perform the action.*

The variable, *value*, may take either positive or negative values (now used in the mathematical sense of the term). The results of a person's actions that have positive values for him we call rewards; the results that have negative ones, punishments. The zero point on the scale is where the person is indifferent to the result of his action. The proposition implies that just as an increase in the positive value of the reward makes it more likely that a person will perform a particular act, so an increase in the negative value of the punishment makes it less likely that he will do so. And by an obvious extension of the stimulus proposition, if the occurrence of a particular stimulus was the occasion on which an action was punished, the recurrence of the stimulus on a new occasion makes it less likely that the person will perform the action. All of this is obvious enough.

Any action that has the result of allowing a person to avoid or escape punishment is rewarded by that result, and the person becomes more likely to perform the action. Thus there are two classes of reward: intrinsic reward and the avoidance of punishment. Similarly, there are two classes of punishment: intrinsic punishment and the withholding of reward.

The use of punishment is an inefficient means of getting another person to change his behavior: it may work but it seldom works well. On the other hand, it may give great emotional satisfaction to the man who does the punishing, and that is something not altogether to be despised. Punishment may be enough when all that is required is that the person stop doing something. Even then, if his action has otherwise brought him valuable reward, it will soon reinstate itself unless the punishment is often repeated and severe. Much more efficient as a means of eliminating an undesirable activity is simply to let it go unrewarded and thus eventually become extinguished, but applying this method sometimes takes strong nerves. Suppose we wish to stop a child's crying, when we suspect he cries only because it gets him attention. The best thing for us to do would be to ignore him when he cried. But a mother often finds it heart-rending to carry out a policy like this. What if there really were something wrong with him?

Punishment or its threat is still less efficient when it is used not just to stop a person from doing something but to get him to perform a particular action. Then we punish him if he does *not* perform the action. The difficulty here is that punishment makes rewarding *any* action that allows him to avoid or escape the punishment and not just the one we have in mind. Accordingly, we must also be prepared to punish or otherwise block off all avenues of escape except that one. Doing so is apt to prove a costly business, especially if we add the cost of surveillance to determine whether he is really doing what we wish him to do. Punishment, moreover, is apt to produce hostile emotional behavior in the person punished, and we must be prepared to cope with it. . . . To get a man to perform an action by rewarding him if he does it, rather than by punishing him if he does not do it, avoids these costs—but then the positive rewards may not be available. We must face the fact that positive rewards are always in short supply. Accordingly, while recognizing its disadvantages, there are times when we shall use punishment, for lack of anything better, as a means of controlling behavior.

The things that men find rewarding—their values—are infinitely varied. Some of them are innate—that is, genetically determined and therefore shared by many men, such as the value set on food and shelter. Even some social values may be innate. It now looks as if men had evolved from apes that hunted in packs in open country. As a result, we seem today to be more "social" in our behavior than our cousins, the present anthropoid apes, just as wolves, who hunt in packs, are more "social" than their cousins, the jackals. Men could hardly have maintained pack behavior if they did not find social life as such innately rewarding. But this is speculation, and in any event, the capacity to find reward in social interaction must be highly generalized, not tied down to specific kinds of social reward.

What makes values infinitely varied is that, besides being born in men and animals, they can also be learned. A value is learned by being linked with an action that is successful in obtaining a more primordial value. (See especially Staats and Staats, 1963:48–54.) Suppose a mother often hugs her child—and getting hugged is probably an innate value—in circumstances in which the child has behaved differently from other children and, as the mother says, "better." Then "behaving better" than others is a means to a rewarding end and is apt to become, as we say, "rewarding in itself." In other words, it is an *acquired* value. The reward may generalize, and the child may be well on the way to setting a high value on status of all kinds. By such processes of linking, men may learn and maintain long chains of behavior leading to some ultimate reward. Indeed apart from obvious anatomical differences and the use of language, the chief difference between the behavior of men and that of other animals may lie in the capacity of men to maintain longer chains relating, as we say, means to ends. For the animals the ultimate reward cannot long be postponed, if the sequence of behavior is not to fall to pieces. And even for men the ultimate reward must come sooner or later. Note that the process by which values are acquired and linked to one another is the same for men as for other animals, but the number of links that can be put together in a chain is greater for the former than for the latter. As usual, the differences are not differences in kind but in degree.

Since different individuals may encounter different circumstances in the course of their upbringing and thus acquire different values, men are apt to be more unlike one another in their acquired than in their innate values. Yet there are some values that men in particular kinds of society would have difficulty in *not* acquiring. These are the so-called *generalized values*, good examples of which are money and social approval. The act of fishing can be made more probable only by its success in getting a rather specific reward, that is, by the catching of fish—though some men seem to use fishing only as an excuse for daydreaming or admiring the scenery. But money and social approval can serve as rewards for a wide variety of actions and not just for some single kind. It is for this reason that they are called generalized values. . . .

So numerous are the values men can acquire, and so varied are the circumstances in which they acquire them, that it is idle to make any general statement about which ones they will hold. But if the particular values held by particular individuals in particular circumstances are known or can be reasonably inferred from the attendant circumstances (if the values in question can be taken as given —and they often can be) then this variable can certainly be used in accordance with our propositions to predict or account for other aspects of behavior. But let no one talk about human values in abstraction from the past history and present circumstances of particular men.

In spite of all this talk about rewards, the reader should never assume that our theory is a hedonistic one, concerned only with materialistic values. The values a man acquires may perfectly well be altruistic. All our theory asks is that the values in question be a man's own values, not those that somebody else thinks he ought to have. A man's success in obtaining altruistic values has just the same effect on his behavior as his success in obtaining egotistical ones: he becomes more likely to perform the actions that have proved successful, whatever they may be. My sisters and I once knew a woman who set a high value on doing good to others, including ourselves. People sometimes say that virtue like hers is its own reward, that no external reward, no change in the behavior of others, is needed to maintain it. We soon discovered that this was not true in her case. Her high-minded behavior did require an external reward, and it was nothing less than our willingness to allow her to do good to us. Strangely enough, we were sometimes unwilling, and then she got as angry as the most materialistic of women deprived of the most material of goods. The language she used was more likely to disguise her anger, but we soon became aware that it was anger just the same. We suspect that the same sort of thing may be true of other persons who hold altruistic values, which does not in the least mean that we must be cynical about them or admire them less. They are out to help others, and why should the fact that in so doing they also reward themselves be held against them?

THE DEPRIVATION-SATIATION PROPOSITION

It is something to know what a man finds rewarding or punishing, what his values, positive or negative, *are*. But the value proposition (III) is not really concerned with what a person's values *are*. It is concerned rather with *how valuable* they are, how valuable a person finds a particular reward in comparison with other rewards. This question in turn must be divided into two separate ones. First: Is the same kind of reward more valuable on one occasion than on a different occasion? Does a person find catching fish more rewarding, for instance, this morning than he will this afternoon? Second: Is one kind of reward more valuable than a different kind on the same occasion? Does, for instance, a person this afternoon find catching fish more rewarding than the results of working in his garden?

What we shall call the *deprivation-satiation proposition* deals only with the first question. We may state it as follows:

IV. *The more often in the recent past a person has received a particular reward, the less valuable any further unit of that reward becomes for him.*

If a man has received the reward often, he is beginning, as we say, to be satiated with it. Its value for him decreases, and by the value proposition (III), he becomes less apt to perform an action that is followed by this reward. The proposition emphasizes the "recent past" because there are many rewards with which a man can only temporarily be satiated. Food is the best example. If, on the other hand, a man has learned to value a particular kind of reward, but has received it only rarely in the recent past, we say he is deprived of it. For him, its value increases, and by the value proposition he becomes more apt to perform an action that is followed by this reward.

Obviously the deprivation-satiation proposition is not very precise and states only a very general tendency. What constitutes the recent past within which deprivation or satiation takes place must be different for different kinds of rewards. Food can satiate men quickly, but it soon recovers its value. Most persons are not so easily satiated with money or status, if indeed they ever can be wholly satiated. The reason is that these are *generalized rewards*, which can be used to obtain a large number of more specific ones. Unless a person is satiated with all the things that money can buy, he will not be satiated with money itself.

As for the second question—whether one kind of reward is more valuable than a different kind on the same occasion—we can state no general proposition that will help us to answer it. We can only try to deal with particular cases. The number of possible comparisons is infinite, and in each case we must rely as best we can on the accumulated experience and knowledge that men have of other men and even at times of our own knowledge of particular persons. We know, for instance, that a man caught out in a chill rain without a coat is likely for the moment to set a relatively high value on shelter compared to other rewards, but that even then he would stay out in the rain if seeking shelter meant losing his life. Again, we know that a man who is new to his job is likely to set a relatively high value on getting good advice on how to do it. At the other extreme, there are preferences, differences in value, which are far from obvious. Thus we are told that the Chinese, faced with a choice of drinks, do not like milk and far prefer tea. It is easy to say that they have been taught to like tea and not milk, but that is not really an answer to the question. Why should they have been taught the preference? The ultimate answer may lie in differences between the traditional agriculture of China and that of the West. Yet if we have some confidence that we know what the values of a man or of a group of men *are*, even if we do not know why they hold these values—if we can take their values as given in given circumstances—we can, with the help of our general propositions, make some good bets on what their other behavior is apt to be.

We have begun by separating the two kinds of questions about relative values. In the end we may have to bring them together again, so that we do not leave the different values of the same reward at different times wholly unrelated to the different values of different rewards at the same time. In general, a man's satiation with a particular reward renders all his other rewards relatively more valuable to him. Moreover, it may turn out that the values can be placed in some kind of rank order, or hierarchy, of values, such that unless a man is first satiated with a particular kind of reward, the next higher kind in the hierarchy will have little value for him. Or rather, to bring in the success proposition (I), the man, if not actually satiated, must be pretty sure of getting enough of the first kind before he can set much store by the next (see Maslow, 1954). Thus unless a man knows where his next meal is coming from, he is unlikely to set a high value on some other reward such as status: he can forgo status more easily than he can food. Americans are said to set a high value on democratic processes. Would they do so if democracy got in the way of their getting enough to eat? One may guess that democracy would be the loser, but fortunately most Americans have not had to make the choice. There are some intangible and ideal rewards on which men will set a very high value—but only if other "lower" needs are being met. We can only raise the question here. We know too little about the ways in which men rank values in a hierarchy of this sort.

COST AND PROFIT

One reward is an alternative to another when it is not a perfect substitute for the other in the sense in which two nickels are usually a perfect substitute for a dime. Now that we have brought up the question of alternative rewards, we are in the position to go back to the value proposition (III) and restate it in a different, and sometimes more useful, form. Indeed there may be more than one such form. Some actions that get a man reward necessarily incur him punishment at the same time. Thus if a fisherman is to get a successful day's fishing, he may have to scramble through thickets or wade into a pool and get soaked to the skin. We may go even further and argue that, since the withdrawal of a reward is itself a punishment, most actions must incur punishment. For when a man chooses to perform one of two alternative actions followed by two alternative rewards, he necessarily withdraws from himself or, as we shall now say, forgoes the reward to be gotten from the action he did not perform. Thus the fisherman who scrambles through thickets to cast his fly in a secluded pool forgoes the reward he would have received from any alternative action that would have gotten him out of being scratched.

Following the economists, we shall say that the *cost* of any action performed is the forgone reward of an alternative action not performed. There may, of course, be several alternatives, though never an infinite number of them. We have in mind the best alternative, the one that would have brought the most valuable reward. And we shall call the excess of the reward a person gets from an action over the cost he incurs his *profit* or net reward from the action. . . .

Since reward tends to increase the frequency with which a man performs an action and cost, being a punishment, tends to decrease it, we are now in a position to reformulate the value proposition by saying: the greater the profit a person receives as a result of his action, the more likely he is to perform the action. The reformulation does not bring in anything essentially new, it merely makes explicit the effect of alternative rewards forgone and incidentally, we believe, conforms to the intuitive notions men have concerning what determines their actions.

A still better formulation may be one which puts the matter in terms of the relative frequency at which men perform alternative actions. At the risk of gross oversimplification, let us suppose that a man can perform two alternative actions, 1 and 2. The frequency with which he performs one let us call A_1 and the frequency with which he performs the other, A_2. Similarly, the value of a unit of reward that he receives from one is V_1 and the value of such a unit that he receives from the other is V_2. Then according to the value proposition (III), if the frequencies with which the actions are rewarded are equal:

$$\frac{A_1}{A_2} = \frac{V_1}{V_2}$$

Profit has been defined as $V_1 - V_2$ in the case of action 1, that is, as its reward less its cost, the forgone value of the alternative reward, and as $V_2 - V_1$ for action 2. As V_1 and V_2 tend toward equality, the profit of either action tends toward zero, which now must be looked on as the profit of either action *relative* to that of the other. Under this condition, equation (1) does not imply that the man will cease to perform either action but only that he will perform one just as often as the other; in this sense, he is indifferent between the two.

If a particular kind of action is repeated in successive units, each with its associated units of reward and cost, and if the value of the reward of successive units decreases (as is usual in satiation) while their cost increases (as, for instance, in fatigue), then the science of economics would say that a man would maximize his total reward from this kind of action if he stopped repeating it when the value of the reward from its latest unit just equaled the cost associated with that unit. Or, marginal cost should equal marginal return. But this statement helps little in explaining or predicting human behavior in the cases, not often studied by economics, in which action does not meet these conditions and men cannot assess the value of successive units of reward and cost in money but only by far grosser processes. In this book we need not assume that men try to maximize their rewards. For us they need not be maximizers but only meliorizers. They do try to make their rewards greater. Whether they ever really try to make them the greatest possible is another question, and one which it would be exceedingly difficult to answer.

The value proposition, in the present way of putting it, implies that the probability of a man's performing one action rather than another depends only on their relative values, on the excess of reward over cost, and not at all on the absolute values of either. It implies that if the profit is the same, the probability remains the same whether the costs and rewards are absolutely high or low. At extreme values this does not remain true. If the value of the reward of an action is very high, but the cost is very high too, especially if both the reward and the cost are uncertain, then a man may be overcome by anxiety and "freeze up"—he may be unable to perform any action at all. An example of extreme values would be a great prize that can only be obtained at the risk of great danger. Nevertheless the value proposition, as stated now in terms of the relation between reward and cost, holds good in its crude way over a wide range of values, and if we do not press it beyond its limits it will serve us well.

For an action to incur cost, an alternative and rewarding activity must be on hand to be forgone. Unless a real alternative is open to a man, so that he is able to forgo it, his action costs him nothing, and he is apt to perform it even if the absolute value of its reward is low. Great captains try to arrange, if they can, that their soldiers shall have no alternative to fighting the enemy, as Cortez did when, before his advance into Mexico, he burnt his ships behind him. Nor should we overlook here a special and weighty kind of cost. If a man has chosen a certain course of action, and it is one that will take time to accomplish—if he has, as we say, committed himself to this course—one of the costs he incurs, one of the values he forgoes, is that of availing himself of other opportunities, which might turn out later to be even more attractive, but which are incompatible with his chosen course. As Marshal Foch, the generalissimo of the Allied armies at the end of World War I, put it: "One should not sell one's freedom of action except for a high price."

The value proposition, some scholars argue, must, if it is valid, imply that a man can rank all his values on a single scale. In fact, efforts to get a man to do just that by means of a questionnaire of some sort often results in inconsistencies: the man will rank value A higher than value B, and B higher than C, but then rank C higher than A. Whatever may happen in the abstract and in answer to a questionnaire, the issue is not one of great importance in real life. Again, for example, once the fisherman has gone off to fish and left the camp far behind, once he has committed himself to fishing, he cannot easily go back to the camp and play bridge, especially if others, his possible partners in bridge, have made the same choice he has made. It is idle then for him to compare the rewards of fishing with those of playing bridge. The only choice now open to him may be between fishing in one pool and fishing in another. The fact that a man never has to choose among all his values but only between those open for him to gain at a particular point in time makes it easier for others, including social scientists like ourselves, to predict his behavior. For many purposes, indeed, we only need to know which of two or three rewards has the greatest value for him. We need not know, if indeed we could possibly find out, just how much greater it is. This characteristic of human behavior may, on the other hand, make trouble for the man who is doing the choosing. Once a man has committed himself at a series of choice points to particular courses of action, he may find himself in the end, even if he chose the better alternative at every point, in a position he would not have intended or preferred if he could have foreseen the whole sequence from the beginning. Nothing in the human condition leads to greater tragedies than this. . . .

THE AGGRESSION–APPROVAL PROPOSITION

So far we have had nothing to say about the emotional behavior of men, and thus have left out much that makes them human. A fuller psychology than ours pretends to be would include several propositions about emotional behavior, among the most important of which would be statements about the causes and effects of anxiety. But . . . in order to keep the treatment as simple as possible, we shall introduce only one proposition about emotional behavior, the only one we shall badly need in order to explain the findings about social behavior. . . . This proposition we call the *aggression-approval proposition* and we can perhaps state it most conveniently by dividing it into two parts, one concerned with aggression and the other with approval.

The first part is usually called the *frustration-aggression* hypothesis (Miller and Dollard, 1941):

> Va. *When a person's action does not receive the reward he expected, or receives punishment he did not expect, he will be angry; he becomes more likely to perform aggressive behavior, and the results of such behavior become more valuable to him.*

Let us now comment on each clause of this complicated proposition.

When a person does not get what he expected, he is said to be frustrated. A purist in behaviorism would not refer to the expectation at all, because the word seems to refer, like other words such as "purpose," to a state of mind. Yet if we did not use it we could only replace it by a long circumlocution, without any offsetting gain in rigor. Nor need the word refer only to an internal state; it can refer to wholly external events, observable in principle not just by the person himself but by outsiders. What a man expects to get by way of reward or punishment under a given set of circumstances (stimuli) is what he has in fact received, observed, or was told others received, under similar circumstances in the past; and none of these things are private events confined within the individual's head. This is what we shall mean by the word *expectation*. . . .

When a man is frustrated, he is apt to feel some degree of the emotion we call anger. Again, a purist in behaviorism might not refer to anger in his version of the proposition but only to the aggressive behavior; we keep the anger in so that we may not do too great violence to the common sense of men. Men show that the experience of anger has much the same meaning for all of them through the ease with which they can communicate to others the fact that they are angry. No doubt the more valuable to a person is the reward he expected or the more painful the punishment he did not expect, the greater is his frustration and hence his anger.

When a man is frustrated, he is apt to perform aggressive actions. These are actions that attack, break, hurt, or threaten the source of the frustration, whether the real source or what the man perceives it to be. If for any reason the real source cannot be attacked, almost any target will do in a pinch. The target may of course be an inanimate object. We do not kick a stuck door just because a kick will help to open it, for it usually will not. We kick the door in order to hurt it. But [here] we are naturally much more interested in human sources of frustration and targets of aggression. In anger, moreover, the successful results of aggressive action reward a man as they would never have done without the anger. When we are furious at someone and hit him, the sight of his wincing under our blow becomes intensely rewarding.

In our first four propositions we were dealing with voluntary or, as the behaviorists call it, operant behavior. Operant behavior and emotional behavior such as aggression differ in the initial conditions that make their appearance more probable. No previous stimulus can automatically get a man to perform an operant the first time. He must just happen to perform it, even as a matter of chance, and be rewarded by it before he will perform it again. Only after he had been rewarded will the attendant stimuli begin to get some control over his action. Aggressive behavior can, on the contrary, be automatically produced the first time by a stimulus—the failure of an action to get the expected reward. In this respect, its initial release by a stimulus, aggression resembles a reflex like the familiar knee jerk.

Yet in another and more important respect aggression differs from a reflex. A reflex cannot be learned—one cannot learn to do a convincing knee jerk—but aggression can be learned. That is, an aggressive action, originally purely emotional, can become voluntary. Whatever the conditions of frustration that led a man to perform an aggressive action in the first place, if in fact his aggression is followed by a reward, wholly apart from the satisfaction of his anger, he becomes more likely to perform it again, just as if it were an ordinary operant. As we all know to our cost, aggression may pay, and if it does will be repeated. Many men and groups use aggression simply as an instrument for attaining practical results. In their case, the aggression may create the anger, not the anger, the aggression. But by the same token, a man may come to perform aggressive actions less often if they have not been successful or have actually resulted in punishment. He may learn to get his outward aggression, if not his inward anger, under control. Or he may still attack but may learn to displace his attacks from targets that respond with punishing reprisals to less dangerous ones. In this book aggression and the like will be treated as if they were, at one and the same time, both emotional and voluntary activities.

Let us now turn to the second part of the aggression-approval proposition. We have long believed that the special emphasis psychologists have placed on the first part, that is, the frustration-aggression hypothesis, has tended to give a one-sided view of the emotional behavior of men since it has pointed only to their negative emotions. But if they can be frustrated and hate, they can also be fortunate and love. Let us therefore propose with some diffidence the following as the second part of the aggression-approval proposition:

> Vb. *When a person's action receives reward he expected, especially a greater reward than he expected, or does not receive punishment he expected, he will be pleased; he becomes more likely to perform approving behavior, and the results of such behavior become more valuable to him.*

If the reader is not altogether happy with the words *pleased* and *approving* which we have used in the proposition—and we confess we are not altogether happy ourselves—let him find his own opposites to *angry* and *aggressive*.

Many of the comments that we have made about the first part of the proposition we may repeat, *mutatis mutandis*, for the second part. Two points are of particular importance. First, though men often give what we call their spontaneous admiration to others who have provided them with unusual reward, they obviously can also learn to give approval to others simply as an instrument for getting further reward from them, apart from the expression of the admiration itself. Approval can become such an instrument because many men find the approval they receive from others rewarding, just as they find aggression punishing. In short, approval like aggression may become a voluntary as well as an emotional action. In later chapters we shall have a great deal to say about approval as one of the most important rewards of social behavior. Second, if what was once an unexpected and unusual reward becomes by repetition an expected and usual one, the person's original emotional reaction will tend to decline in strength, which need not mean that he will cease to use approval instrumentally. . . .

THE PROPOSITION AS A SYSTEM OF PROPOSITIONS

Now that we have stated the general propositions . . . we must make one or two comments on the set of propositions as a whole. We have stated each proposition baldly, without qualifications, without adding the escape clause that each holds good only under the condition that "other things are equal." The reason we have done so is that what these "other things" are and where they are "equal" are determined for each proposition by the other propositions in the set. The effects that would be predicted by any one of the propositions may, in concrete cases, be masked or modified by the effects of other propositions in the set. That is, the set must be taken as a whole system of propositions.

Let us offer just one crude illustration. The success proposition (I) says that the more often an action is rewarded, the more often a man will perform it. But this relationship certainly does not always hold good in real life. For if the reward comes often enough, the value the man sets on a further unit of it will, by the satiation proposition (IV), decline, perhaps even to the extent that he is indifferent to it for the time being. But as the value of the reward decreases, then the man, according to the value proposition (III), becomes less likely to perform it and not more likely. What follows from the three propositions taken together is that a man will perform an action at the fastest rate when the action is rewarded only just enough to keep him slightly deprived of it. If he were wholly deprived, it would mean that his action was utterly unsuccessful in getting the reward; and complete lack of success leads to inaction just as much as satiation does.

THE HISTORICITY IMPLIED BY THE PROPOSITIONS

The propositions imply, if we did not know it already, that the past history of men makes a big difference to their present behavior, and not just the recent past but often the past of long ago. A man's past history of success, of stimulation, of the acquisition of values all affect the way he behaves now. The choices he made in the past may still be limiting the opportunities available to him today, or he may perceive them as limiting; hence the great weight attached to a man's early experience by all schools of modern psychology. The ill effects of some early experiences may of course be overcome, but it may be difficult to do so—there is something to *be* overcome.

The effect of past experience extends beyond the history of individuals to the history of societies. Since children learn much of their behavior and values from parents and other members of the older generation, the past culture of a society tends to perpetuate itself. We need not believe that a society maintains itself by teaching its members just those actions it is prepared to reward, just those values it is prepared to satisfy. If a child acquires at his mother's knee a value like independence, he may, when he grows up, try to change his society radically instead of preserving it. Indeed we know that old values and actions whose success in attaining these values were learned long ago may, in new circumstances, lead to radical, unforeseen, and quite unintended social change. . . . Yet there is always some tendency for past behavior to maintain itself, at least in the sense that every new generation has to start from something that already exists; it can never make a wholly fresh start. Indeed the men of the past may, in pursuit of the values of their time and by its methods, have created institutions to which their descendants are committed, at least to the extent that they cannot change all their institutions at once. Past institutional commitments have the same effect on the history of societies that past choices often have on the history of individuals. . . .

This may be a useful point at which to enter a warning. Although the general propositions we shall use are often called the propositions of "learning theory," we are far from believing that men are equally likely to learn anything in the way of behavior, provided only that they encounter in the social and physical enviornment the appropriate stimuli and rewards. They do not, so to speak, start life as blank sheets of paper on which the environment can readily write whatever occurs to it to write in the way of learning. Not only their experience but their genetic endowment—not only nurture but nature, to use the neat antithesis—determines what they learn.

It is not a question of which is the more important, nurture or nature, though that was the question psychologists asked themselves for several decades. The real question is how the experience of men interacts with their genetic inheritance. . . .

THE RATIONALITY PROPOSITION

We have less need to bring in past history in explaining some kinds of behavior than others. In order to understand this point let us begin by looking at a proposition that in effect sums up the first three of our propositions, those concerned with success, stimuli, and value. (As for the last two propositions, the *deprivation-satiation* proposition (IV) states one of the causes for a change in the value of a reward and the *aggression-approval* proposition (V) states the conditions under which the results of certain kinds of actions become valuable.) The proposition has been called the principle of rational choice or the *rationality proposition.* (See, for instance, Harsanyi, 1967.) It may be stated as follows:

> VI. *In choosing between alternative actions, a person will choose that one for which, as perceived by him at the time, the value, V, of the result, multiplied by the probability, p, of getting the result, is the greater.*

In so acting, a person is said to maximize his expected utility (Ofshe and Ofshe, 1970:3). . . .

Just as the rationality proposition has nothing to say about why a man perceives his chances of success as high or low, so it has nothing to say about why he has acquired certain values and not others, why he sets a higher value on one reward than he does on another, or why he values a particular reward more highly on one occasion than he does on another. A more fully developed psychology, and one that deals with the effects of a man's past history on his present behavior, is needed to account for these things.

Yet we must always remember that, besides what a man perceives to be his chances of success in various actions, there are always the actual chances of success as given by the outside world independent of his perceptions, including at the extreme the certainty that some kinds of actions will be successful. Suppose we have reason to believe that a man's perceptions of the outside world are accurate, that the outside world and his map of it coincide. Suppose we can assume further that his values are common values, values that most persons share, or that are common to a class of men to which he is known to belong. Then, in explaining his behavior, we can neglect the details of his past history. . . .

Much human behavior, of course, meets these conditions and can be explained in this way. But much behavior cannot be explained by the rationality proposition. If a man's values are somewhat queer . . . and if his chances of success are not given by the outside world, or at least not accurately known by him, then the rationality proposition by itself may not help us much. Our favorite example, among the enormous number that could be cited, is the decision by William the Conqueror (then simply the Bastard), Duke of Normandy, to invade England in 1066. That he set a high value on the result of successful conquest, becoming king of England, those of us who have some knowledge of other feudal lords will find no difficulty in accepting. But what about the other term in the rationality proposition, his chance of success as perceived by him? He could not know what his chances were. As the economists would say, his condition was one of uncertainty and not of risk. In risk the odds on success are accurately known; in uncertainty they are not known. Even if he were fairly sure he could get an army and a fleet together, there remained for him the dangers of a sea voyage, of landing on a hostile shore, and of battle with an English army under the experienced and hitherto successful command of Harold Godwinsson. Defeat in battle would almost certainly mean death. William's contemporaries might well have judged his chance of success to be small. On the record, we have no reason whatever to believe that he was a foolish man. Why then did he go ahead with the enterprise? In trying to answer this question it is surely relevant to point to the almost unbroken series of his military victories over the preceding twenty years. It is not the rationality proposition but the success proposition that will account for the effect of these victories on his decision. Past success in military action made his future military action more probable. Or, as we say in ordinary language, past success had given him confidence.

Certainly, if we keep the rationality proposition firmly in mind, we shall never forget that human action is determined by two kinds of factors, not one. Many persons, including many social scientists, talk as if what determines a man's action was his "motivation" alone—in our terms, the value he sets on the result of his action. But a man may be highly motivated in this sense and still not take action, if his similar actions in the past have been uniformly unsuccessful. Again, some social scientists talk as if the reason why some lower-class groups, like blacks in the United States, remain unassimilated to the larger society in which they live is that their values are different from those of other groups in the society. Their values may be just the same as those of the rest of society, but if their actions have been, for whatever reason, unsuccessful in obtaining those values, they will turn to alternative actions. If these alternative actions are successful in obtaining a different kind of reward, their actions may keep them as effectively cut off from the rest of society as if their values had been different all along. The rationality proposition serves to remind us that action is determined by success and value jointly.

REFERENCES

Aristotle. *Politics*. Translated by H. Rackham. Cambridge, Mass.: Harvard University Press, 1967.

Bandura, Albert. *Principles of Behavior Modification*. New York: Holt, Rinehart and Winston, 1969.

Bandura, Albert, and Richard H. Walters. *Social Learning and Personality Development*. New York: Holt, Rinehart and Winston, 1963.

Ferster, C. B., and B. F. Skinner. *Schedules of Reinforcement*. New York: Appleton-Century-Crofts, 1957.

Harsanyi, John C. "A General Theory of Rational Behavior in Game Situations," *Econometrica*, 34 (1967), 613–634.

Herrnstein, Richard J. "Quantitative Hedonism," *Journal of Psychiatric Research*, 8 (1971), 399–412.

Maslow, Abraham H. *Motivation and Personality*. New York: Harper & Row, 1954.

Miller, Neal E., and John Dollard, *Social Learning and Imitation*. New Haven: Yale University Press, 1941.

Ofshe, Lynne, and Richard Ofshe. *Utility and Choice in Social Interaction*. Englewood Cliffs, N.J.: Prentice-Hall, 1970.

Skinner, B. F. *The Behavior of Organisms*. New York: Appleton-Century-Crofts, 1938.

Staats, Arthur W., and Carolyn K. Staats. *Complex Human Behavior*. New York: Holt, Rinehart and Winston, 1963.

THE POTENTIAL IMPACT OF B. F. SKINNER UPON AMERICAN SOCIOLOGY

ROBERT W. FRIEDRICHS

Reprinted from *The American Sociologist*, 9 (1974), 3–8. Used by permission of the author and the American Sociological Association.

Robert W. Friedrichs is professor and chairman of sociology at Williams College. He is author of *A Sociology of Sociology* (Free Press, 1970), which won the Sorokin Award of the ASA in 1971.

It has been argued elsewhere (Friedrichs, 1970, 1972) that the 1950's witnessed proximate consensus within American sociology over the "orthodoxy" of a "systemic" image of the nature of our subject matter and that this in turn was supported by a self-image in which the sociologist identified himself with the value-free stance he associated with the natural scientist (a posture characterized as "priestly").

It was also suggested that, confronted by the obstinate anomaly that is fundamental social change, a miscellany of alternative paradigms flowered in the 1960's. They were dominated, however, by "system's" polar opposite—"conflict"—and an associated self-image which identified the sociologist as an agent of change (the latter termed, in contrast, a "prophetic" stance).

The analysis concluded with the observation that a "dialectical" paradigm might, for a wide variety of reasons, ultimately inherit the field so hotly contested by "system" and "conflict," since it would appear capable of granting essentially equivalent status to both as well as opening the way to a dialogical relationship between the "priestly" and "prophetic" modes of self-understanding.

What was almost completely overlooked was the possibility that the two sets of contending paradigms—"system" versus "conflict" and "priestly" versus "prophetic"—might be combined as well under the aegis of a renaissant behaviorism. Indeed, it would appear that the latter may be in an even better position to inherit the claim of sociological "orthodoxy" in the latter half of the 1970's.

The charismatic point of reference for the new behavioral dispensation appears clearly to be B. F. Skinner. Psychologist though he may be, it is worth recalling that Talcott Parsons, orthodoxy's dominant spokesman in the 1950's, was trained and received his earliest appointment at Harvard not as a sociologist but as an economist and that the first review symposium of the American Sociological Association's official journal of reviews, *Contemporary Sociology*, focused upon Skinner (Marwell and Boguslaw, 1972). Furthermore, the latter's fundamental posture is ably served by two of sociology's most highly respected and strategically placed practitioners, is claiming the allegiance of a rapidly growing group of younger sociologists and social psychologists, and is remarkably in tune with the ethos of a national research establishment upon whose funds the major graduate faculties (and thus graduate training) in the discipline depend.

What is in the Skinner box of tricks that glistens with such attractiveness? From a paradigmatic point of view its fundamental strength lies in its combination of the hard, natural scientific proclivities of the scientific "priest" with the conscious commitment to change of the social scientific "prophet." And, through the mediation of his foremost disciples within sociology, the "systemic" assumption that adheres to the logic of natural science is seen as secondary to an essentially "conflict" image of fundamental human social behavior.

Little need be said in defense of the first observation. Skinner's life-long marriage to an austerely natural scientific epistemology is as self-evident as his fathering of an operant behaviorism that focuses immediately upon the change that can be brought about through positive reward. The very anomaly that was the fatal flaw of the "system" presumption—change—becomes operant conditioning's fundamental aim. Furthermore, the posture is graced by a proper claim to extreme conceptual parsimony, to logical adequacy (Maris, 1970), and to at least provisional experimental success with subject-settings (psychotics in mental hospitals and children in ghetto schools, among others) that have largely eluded the sustained efforts of social and behavioral scientists employing other models. And *Walden II* and *Beyond Freedom and Dignity* clearly register Skinner's "prophetic" commitment.

But the complexity and subtlety of the larger social scene—impossible of capture within the neat limits and controls of a Skinnerian laboratory—lie, it has been contended (Back, 1970), far beyond the conceptual or instrumental apparatus of operant conditioning as presented to date by the behavioral psychologist. Still it is not my intention to argue that the latter will or could serve as immediate exemplar for social research in the years ahead. I speak rather of Skinner's potential impact upon "significant others" within the highest ranks of our discipline and of the ethos of a research-funding establishment that will encourage their emulation.

MANIFEST AND LATENT SUPPORT AT HIGHEST LEVELS

Skinner's foremost advocate within sociology is, of course, George Homans, strategically placed as he has been of late as chairman of Harvard's Department of Sociology. Even the departure of that program from the umbrella of "Social Relations" created by Parsons would seem to encourage the possibilities of which I speak, for it has allowed Social Relations' center of gravity to slip toward a psychological perspective in which Skinner has been afforded a privileged place and has granted Homans freer rein within the Sociology Department itself. His own lofty stature and influence within the discipline is suggested by the fact that, of all past presidents of the ASA, only three stand above him—with only one among the three (Robert Merton) neither retired nor deceased—in a sampling of ASA membership "familiarity" with the ex-presidents' works (Westie, 1973). The sociologist of sociology would also note that social theorists trained at Harvard have been taken with considerable seriousness: the majority elected to the presidency of the ASA since World War II who have specialized in theory received their Ph.D.s there. One is also tempted to repeat the well-worn observation that "converts" typically turn out to be the most zealous of spokesmen for the new orthodoxy; and, as all are aware, George Homans' early volume, *The Human Group*, stood for many as exemplar for the earlier functionalist paradigm, just as his presidential address, "Bringing Men Back In" in 1964, as well as his *Social Behavior: Its Elementary Forms* (1961) stand as potential exemplars for the new.

But there are two substantive features that Homans has added to the Skinnerian frame that are of even more interest to the sociologist of sociology. The first is that he begins, not with the assumption of "system," but with an appreciation of the fact that men's interests (and, as he would say in Skinnerian terms, the rewards they seek) fundamentally conflict (Homans, 1971:367). Add to this his admonition that "if you would know why institutions are what they are today, look at the historical record of their development" (Homans, 1971:377). The two postures combined speak directly to the basic objections "conflict" theorists have had with the sociology deemed orthodox in the 1950's: that it treated social conflict as a secondary category and was essentially ahistorical. In other words, Homans places a "conflict" image of man firmly beneath Skinner's necessarily systemic natural scientific epistemology and states that the final source for verification of theories concerning social man lies in an examination of the historical record. These modifications not only place "conflict" on an essential par with "system"—as Skinner had himself added the "prophetic" dimension to the "priestly"—but could serve to undermine much of the contemporary sociologist's immediately negative reaction to Skinner's self-evidently ahistorical utopianism.

In all likelihood, however, the neo-behaviorism of which I speak will demand a subtler mediator than Homans, to say nothing of Skinner, to make the headway I predict for it: someone identified with the methods and mathematical models deemed appropriate to the relatively macroscopic settings and problems faced by most sociologists, at least as strategically located professionally, and immediately conversant with the increasingly applied and policy research orientation of the current federal research bureaucracy. He need not have identified his conceptual apparatus with Skinner's and/or Homans'; the clue should lie with his comparable ability to link "conflict" with "system" and the "prophetic" with the "priestly." I—and I think Homans himself—would nominate James Coleman.

No one can claim a more "systemic" methodology than the founding chairman of a graduate program specializing in the elicitation of models of complex and ongoing social interaction from sociology's beast of burden, the digital computer. Yet he, too, quite explicitly deems Hobbes' "war of all against all" as sociology's appropriate point of departure (Coleman, 1971:272–73). And, though natural scientific in epistemological stance, he is currently the discipline's most powerful advocate for, and probably its most experienced participant in, policy research—that is, of research aimed directly at the resolution of societal problems. For Coleman has shared Skinner's sensitivity to the currents that are in process of reframing the behavioral and social scientific marketplaces. Sociology —at least from the vantage point of a sociologist of sociology—must itself be increasingly viewed as a dependent variable: a function of the economic, political, and social currents that throb through the larger body politic from which sociology derives its material sustenance. Talcott Parsons was shaped by a time in which the sociologist still played his academic game largely of, by, and for himself —reflecting the relatively parochial ethos of the academy in the pre-World War II years and the independent, relatively isolated professional goal it fostered. Skinner, on the other hand, represents perhaps the first major behavioral scientist of his generation to recognize that his discipline's resources, if one expects them to be replenished and expanded by public monies, must be focused directly upon the resolution of what that public, through its representatives, deems its most oppressive societal problems. And James Coleman is but a short step behind.

Coleman is, however, a step ahead in terms of personal involvement in ameliorative research and in having codified the lessons he would have the social and behavioral sciences learn from such involvement. Indeed, he has thought through, and offers a very sophisticated resolution of, perhaps the weakest link in the Skinnerian program: the role the social and behavioral scientist is to play vis-a-vis representatives of the body politic in establishing societal—and thus research —goals and in the communication and implementation of research findings. His conclusion that policy makers should reserve to themselves the right to commission research cannot but help in the longer run to make the funding of policy research more attractive to those who, through the power of the purse, are indeed society's policy makers. And his contention that such research can best be done through independent research organizations may well be equally propitious: it could provide a rapidly expanding source of employment that would be in a position to absorb the professional talent spilling from our graduate programs, which our colleges and universities are no longer able to accommodate (Coleman, 1972).

"System" and "conflict," the "priestly" and the "prophetic": Coleman would join Homans in the mutuality of their contributions. Indeed, he explicitly identifies with the Homans of exchange theory. Coleman states that his central postulate is "that of rational man attempting to pursue his selfish interest," followed by the acknowledgement that "the introduction of this approach into sociological theorizing was carried out by Homans" (Coleman, 1971:272). Homans in turn would carry that identification up to the present—"Coleman only thinks there is a difference" (Homans, 1971:367), with but a modest disclaimer regarding what he believes to be Coleman's over-rational image of man.

Homans now sits astride a department that has been the dominant force in sociological theory over the past generation while Coleman has returned to that wellspring of American sociology (and still by far its largest producer of Ph.D.s), the University of Chicago. Hardly unsuggestive as well was the National Academy of Science's choice of two sociologists to add to the two already on its rolls in the Spring of 1972. Who were they? George Homans and James Coleman. Another fact that impresses itself upon the eye of the sociologist of sociology is that 70 percent of the presidents of the ASA over the quarter century following World War II received their graduate training either at Chicago or Harvard.

EXEMPLARS AND DISCIPLES

Some will protest with the observation that Skinner's operant conditioning is far from dominant within the discipline of psychology itself, even in America. But here the sociologist of science (and, perhaps, education) is impressed by John Finley Scott's conclusions that the posture has, for good institutional reasons, less bright an immediate future in psychology than in sociology:

Were it to be established as legislative for academic psychology, large numbers of psychologists who now make the analysis of mentalistic constructs ... their life work would find their efforts to be redundant. Whole specialties in psychology, each with its own traditions, would come to an end. . . Since Skinner's program would radically change psychology, most psychologists who value their tradition oppose it. . . (Scott, 1971:17)

This need not be the case in sociology, for the discipline grounds itself upon the very assumption that makes Skinner anathema to so many of his colleagues: that the behavior of the individual is to be viewed as dependent variable, that of the environing social context the independent variable.

Scott's recent *Internalization of Norms: A Sociological Theory of Moral Commitment* (1971) may in fact serve as a more persuasive exemplar for the new dispensation than Homans' *Social Behavior: Its Elementary Forms* (1961) or "Bringing Men Back In" (1964b). This is because the nature of an *exemplar*—if one would follow current usage as established by Thomas Kuhn in *The Structure of Scientific Revolutions* (1970:187)—is to serve as a concrete model or example which can replace rules within the activity of normal science. Homans has largely limited himself to the exegesis of the new "rules." Scott, on the other hand, actually demonstrates the manner in which those "rules" may be applied to a major issue of traditional concern to the sociologist: the internalization of moral norms. And he does so freed from the socially abnormal constraints—the laboratory setting and the controls demanded by the experimental method—that typically have provided the context for Skinner's research. In other words, he has provided an *example* rather than mere rhetoric in support of the manner in which the sociologist can transplant operant conditioning analysis from the microscopic environs traditional to the research of the learning theorists to the field of everyday life that is the primary focus of the sociologist. And along the way he offers operant analogues for terms as central to the contemporary sociologist's vocabulary as "social structure," "role" and "role expectation," and "ascribed" and "achieved" status.

Many a sociologist will, of course, reject the Skinnerian model—and its near relatives in sociology—because of their antipathy to the ideological implications of Skinner's apparent unwillingness to grant empirical content to the term "freedom." The animus is not altogether easy to maintain, however, when one stops to recall that such a "humanistically" oriented sociologist as Peter Berger admits much the same: that the affirmation of freedom by man poses "a priori difficulties within the framework of a sociological argument . . . [since] . . . freedom is not empirically available" (Berger, 1963:122). Indeed, the functionalist tradition within sociology had transformed "freedom" into but a "feeling state" long before the discipline confronted the Skinnerian project. As A. K. Davis put it, freedom was but "a subjective feeling of personal well-being which results from the objective fact of living in a functioning society" (Davis, 1953:443). There is, then, a worthy tradition within sociology itself that has reified the assumption of recurrence that adheres to the logic of natural science. If it would turn upon Skinner in this regard, it will have to turn upon itself as well.

Robert L. Burgess and Don Bushell, editors and contributors to *Behavioral Sociology: The Experimental Analysis of Social Process* (1969), exemplify the fact that Skinner's sociological disciples tend to cluster as "invisible colleges" at institutions where his influence is strong among their colleagues in psychology: the University of Washington in Burgess' case (where he is joined by David Schmitt) and the University of Kansas in Bushell's (along with Keith Miller). But those whose work evidences kinship with Skinner can be found scattered widely across the nation's campuses, with James Wiggins and John Burchard at the University of North Carolina, Sidney Bijou and Robert Peterson at the University of Illinois, Bruce Chadwick at Brigham Young, John Finley Scott at the University of California, Davis, John Kunkel at Western Ontario, and Robert Hamblin chairing the increasingly impressive department at the University of Arizona. G. E. Swanson (once Hamblin's mentor at Michigan and now at Berkeley), though certainly not a professed Skinnerian, has demonstrated a long-standing interest in learning—particularly reinforcement—theories.

Kenneth Goodall (1972) has plotted the locations of the psychology departments that are significant proselytizing centers: in addition to the above, the University of Oregon, Stanford, Arizona State, Florida State, Southern Illinois, the University of Minnesota, Indiana University, Western Michigan (Kalamazoo is also the site of *Behavioradelia*, a media center using Skinnerian principles), Stony Brook, Columbia, and of course Harvard. Two "Behavior Modification" conferences—hoping to continue as annual gatherings—have already been held in Colorado, while Elliott McGinnies and C. B. Ferster have brought together for publication over seventy relevant papers, most of which reported experimental results (1971). Hamblin's *The Humanization Process* (1971), summarizing five years of experimentation in St. Louis, was in the running for a recent Sorokin Award.

The Federal research establishment has, in the meantime, nearly tripled its funding of applied research commissioned at colleges and universities over the previous decade, with the largest increases attributable to HEW. The ASA took the cue and organized, with NIMH monies, a conference of seventy persons in late 1972 to explore concrete steps to shift funding from "basic" to "policy" areas and to make commensurate changes in graduate training. Not long thereafter graduate departments were inundated with announcements of new NSF-funded programs for "policy-related research." Some academicians had sensed the new direction for some time, initiating an International Association of Applied Social Sciences, and organizing outlets for their publications such as the new journal, *Policy Sciences*. The University of Pennsylvania has recently announced a Ph.D. program in "Public Policy Analysis."

Yet just as the actual term "dialectical" is unlikely to gain ascendancy within American sociology in the foreseeable future because of the ideological burden it has been forced to carry in our political and philosophic discourse, so one would not expect a Skinnerian vocabulary to be directly honored by a discipline that is periodically threatened by reductionism (Webster, 1973). What one may expect is that *synonyms* of such terms as "positive reinforcement," "reward," and "non-aversive control" will find their way increasingly into the sociologist's vocabulary.

One of the intriguing aspects of a shift from a Parsonian to a Skinnerian-inspired orthodoxy is that it would reflect a measure of underlying continuity as well—just as, for all the highly touted (yet largely symbolic) "revolutions" of the 1960's, the ethos that undergirds the public expression of our larger culture's norms has remained remarkably stable. This should not be altogether surprising, for that ethos not only lies deeply imbedded within American history, but is evidenced in Parsons' and Skinner's biographically formative years as well. It is the reason the new sociological dispensation is likely to taste so similar, after we've had it on our tables for a time, to the old.

FUNCTIONAL EQUIVALENCE TO PARSONIAN PARADIGM

Both Skinner and Parsons appear to have been the product of essentially middle class Protestant households. Parsons' father served for a time as a Congregational minister, while Skinner's autobiographical reminiscences are even more revealing: a mother with "rigid standards of what was 'right' "; attendance at a Presbyterian Sunday school, with heavy emphasis upon the Old Testament; a mouth washed out with soap in response to a forbidden utterance; a father who viewed a trip with his son through the county jail and attendance at a program of slides on life at Sing Sing as essential to the boy's education; and a grandmother who "made sure that I understood the concept of hell by showing me the glowing bed of coals in the parlor stove" (Skinner, 1967:387–91). Both Parsons and Skinner would seem to provide functional equivalents to the Protestant ethic's predestinarian asceticism, expressed by the mature Skinner's rejection of any "freedom" or independent "dignity" to man and, in Parsons' case, through the conceptual priority and presumptive status his later work granted "system." Both responded to the tension which history has all too often documented as the metaphysic's concomitant by preaching a startlingly similar "inner-worldly asceticism": Parsons in his "voluntaristic" insistence upon "effort" and "the exercise of will," Skinner by his commandment that thou shalt "control." The end result of both of their historical projections is, as with Weber, a rationalized, impersonal world devoid of conflict or autonomy. Theirs is not the harsh imagery of a 1984; rather, it reflects the paternalistic transposition of a Calvinist communitarianism into a cybernetic secularism, with program-bearing behavioral scientists standing as "functional equivalents" to scripture-bearing men of the cloth.

Thus, the "prophetic" side of the reversible mantle that would cloak a Skinnerian-informed sociology could expect, as with Comte's visions of a new Parisian Jerusalem, to be overwhelmed by its "priestly" subordination to those within the body politic in position to frame immediate policy. This, together with an epistemology that denies man any empirical meaning to his dreams of "freedom" and "dignity"—though not likely to prevent the posture's ascension to the behavioral and sociological thrones over the decade ahead—promises at the very least to nourish in its wake a less orthodox but competing paradigm that refuses to root itself in the radical subject-object dichotomization that is the presumptive soil of natural science.

REFERENCES

Back, K. W. Review essay on Robert L. Burgess and Don Bushell Jr., eds., *Behavioral Sociology: The Experimental Analysis of Social Process, American Sociological Review*, 35 (December 1970), 1098–1100.

Berger, Peter L. *Invitation to Sociology: A Humanistic Perspective.* Garden City, N.Y.: Doubleday Anchor, 1963.

Burgess, Robert L., and Don Bushell Jr., eds. *Behavioral Sociology: The Experimental Analysis of Social Process.* New York: Columbia University Press, 1969.

Coleman, James S. "Collective Decisions," in Herman Turk and Richard L. Simpson, eds., *Institutions and Social Change: The Sociologies of Talcott Parsons and George C. Homans.* Indianapolis: Bobbs-Merrill, 1971.

———. *Policy Research in the Social Sciences.* Morristown, N.J.: General Learning Press, 1972.

Davis, A. K. "Review of Robert A. Nisbet, Quest for Community," *American Sociological Review*, 18 (August 1953), 443.

Friedrichs, Robert W. *A Sociology of Sociology.* New York: Free Press, 1970.

Goodall, Kenneth. "Shapers at Work," *Psychology Today*, 6 (November 1972), 53–63.

Hamblin, Robert L. *The Humanization Process.* New York: Wiley, 1971.

Harris, T. G. "All the World's a Box," *Psychology Today*, 5 (August 1971), 33–35.

Homans, George C. "Social Behavior as Exchange," *American Journal of Sociology*, 62 (May 1958), 597–606.

———. *Social Behavior: Its Elementary Forms.* New York: Harcourt, Brace and World, 1961.

———. "Contemporary Theory in Sociology," in R. E. L. Faris, ed., *Handbook of Modern Sociology.* Chicago: Rand McNally, 1964, p. 951–977. (a)

———. "Bringing Men Back In," *American Sociological Review*, 29 (December 1964), 808–818. (b)

———. *The Nature of Social Science.* New York: Harcourt, Brace and World, 1967.

———. "Commentary," in Herman Turk and Richard L. Simpson, eds., *Institutions and Social Exchange: The Sociologies of Talcott Parsons and George C. Homans.* Indianapolis: Bobbs-Merrill, 1971, pp. 363–379.

Kuhn, Thomas S. *The Structure of Scientific Revolutions.* Chicago: University of Chicago Press, 1970.

McGinnies, Elliott, and C. B. Ferster, eds. *The Reinforcement of Social Behavior.* Boston: Houghton Mifflin, 1971.

Maris, R. "The Logical Adequacy of Homans' Social Theory," *American Sociological Review*, 35 (December 1970), 1069–1081.

Marwell, G., and R. Boguslaw. "Skinner: Pro and Con," *Contemporary Sociology*, 1 (January 1972), 19–29.

Scott, John Finley. *Internalization of Norms: A Sociological Theory of Moral Commitment.* Englewood Cliffs, N.J.: Prentice-Hall, 1971.

Skinner, B. F. *Walden Two.* New York: Macmillan, 1948.

———. *Science and Human Behavior.* New York: Macmillan, 1953.

———. *Verbal Behavior.* New York: Appleton-Century-Crofts, 1957.

———. "B. F. Skinner," in E. G. Boring and Gardner Lindzey, eds., *A History of Psychology in Autobiography.* New York: Appleton-Century-Crofts, 1967, pp. 387–413.

———. *The Technology of Teaching.* New York: Appleton-Century-Crofts, 1968.

———. *Contingencies of Reinforcement.* New York: Appleton-Century-Crofts, 1969.

———. *Beyond Freedom and Dignity.* New York: Knopf, 1971.

Webster, M., Jr. "Psychological Reductionism, Methodological Individualism, and Large-Scale Problems," *American Sociological Review*, 38 (April 1973), 258–273.

Westie, F. R. "Academic Expectations for Professional Immortality: A Study of Legitimation," *American Sociologist*, 8 (February 1973), 19–32.

IS THERE A BEHAVIORIST BANDWAGON?

FREDERICK R. LYNCH

Reprinted from *The American Sociologist*, 10 (1975), 84-91. Used by permission of the author and the American Sociological Association.

Frederick Lynch teaches at Pitzer College.

Sociology does not resemble a symphony, a harmonious blend of patterns and chords. It is, particularly at present, something of a raucus cacophony of differing theoretical themes and methodological melodies without consistent rhythm, order, or form. This bothers a good many members of our discipline who long for a firm disciplinary identity. They are convinced, just as Talcott Parsons' children were a generation ago, that "The sociology is about to begin said the man with the loudspeaker" (Parsons, 1954:349). Convention chatter is full of references to "developing trends" in sociology and necks are craned whenever important personages in the profession pronounce upon sociology's True Destiny. We are ready to board the scholarly bandwagon—if only someone can point it out to us.

Therefore, it seems likely that Robert Friedrichs' (1974) latest prophecy regarding the profession will receive due notice. For Friedrichs thinks he has seen the bandwagon and it is driven by B. F. Skinner, George Homans, and James S. Coleman: the bandwagon is behaviorism.

Friedrichs contends that a "renaissant behaviorism" may well become the sociological "orthodoxy" of the latter half of the 1970's. This is likely to be so, he feels, because 1) the ideas of B. F. Skinner have influenced the theories and methodologies of "significant others" in our profession, such as George Homans and James S. Coleman; 2) increased research funding for applied or "policy-oriented" studies will be conducive to behaviorism, which has shown success in dealing with social problems; and 3) there is a basic continuity in a shift from a Parsonian to a Skinnerian-inspired orthodoxy. Furthermore, Friedrichs maintains that a behavioristic paradigm could unite the two heretofore divergent images of sociological subject matter, which he has named "system" and "conflict." The emergent behaviorism could also combine the different sociological self-images that accompany the system and conflict paradigms, which Friedrichs respectively labels "the priestly mode" of the natural scientist and the "prophetic mode" of the agent of social change (Friedrichs, 1974).

Unfortunately, Friedrichs fails to define a key term: behaviorism. This is regrettable because it makes it difficult to distinguish his 1974 prophecy from one which he advanced in late 1972. In the preface to the paperback edition of his book, *A Sociology of Sociology*, Friedrichs supplanted his first prophecy (1972a) of a "dialectical sociology" with a forecast that a revised "Comtean positivism" might be on the way (1972b). What he meant by this term is not entirely clear, but the seeds of the movement, Friedrichs stated, could be found in "Homans' regression" to Skinnerian categories and William Catton's more sophisticated extrapolation of the deceased Lundberg's infatuation with man as "mechanism"

(1972b:xxxix). Is "Comtean positivism" synonymous with "behaviorism"? If so, why did Friedrichs employ the first term at all?

It is my contention that Friedrichs' third prophecy is, at best, only partially perceptive and that his second vision of a revival of "Comtean positivism" is hinting at a broader truth. The question needs to be raised as to whether Friedrichs believes the trend he has most recently perceived is truly toward a Skinnerian-style of behaviorism, a type of social inquiry premised upon 1) a mechanistic model of man; 2) the central importance of operant conditioning; 3) psychological reductionism; 4) natural science epistemology; and 5) the measurement of overt forms of behavior and the dismissal of subjective, "private events" as largely irrelevant.[1] Or, rather, are we witnessing the continuing maturation of a more broadly based Positivist Establishment, a growing union of those practicing sophisticated methodological techniques with the proponents of logical positivism?

In many respects the dogma of the Positivist Establishment is similar to that of behaviorism. Behaviorism might be said to represent something of a radical sect, while the United Positivist Establishment is one of the major churches. Like the behaviorists, contemporary positivism tends to emphasize a rational model of man, the epistemology of the natural sciences, and the precise measurement of behavior. However, a belief in psychological reductionism is not required for membership nor is the absolution of Skinner. Sociologists of almost any theoretical bent are eligible for membership in the Positivist Establishment, and to publish in the journals controlled by it, so long as those sociologists adhere to good "scientific" forms.

So much for preliminary definitions—I shall return to the Positivist Establishment and its intellectual roots in a moment. To try to answer the main question of the study, that is, whether Friedrichs is observing a trend towards behaviorism or simply the crystallization of contemporary positivism, it is necessary to examine the social structure and theoretical aspects of his study. It must be asked: 1) for *which aspects* of their works are such "significant others" as George Homans and James Coleman well known? 2) is an increase in policy-oriented research funding likely to significantly advance behavioristic research? and 3) to what extent is Skinner's theoretical framework congruent with that of Parsons?

WILL THE REAL GEORGE HOMANS PLEASE STAND UP?

Homans' behavioristic theory of social exchange appeared at the end of the 1950's, a decade which had been dominated by functionalism, and by the atheoretical research of the abstracted empiricists (Cf. Mills, 1959; Gouldner, 1970.) The question of why behaviorism did not attract a large following during the early and mid-1950's—as theoretical backing for the abstracted empiricists—is an intriguing one. Surely, with Marxist and other critical perspectives largely driven underground, behaviorism would have been ideally suited to a society in which sociologists became fascinated with the Organization Man and the structures within which he worked. Yet it was not behaviorism that bloomed, but Parsonian functionalism. And, though Parsonian theory incorporated many behavioristic tenets and terms (as Friedrichs himself is aware—1972b:233–234), it was not congenial to abstracted empiricism. Parsons' theoretical concepts, it was assumed, could not be effectively "operationalized" for purposes of empirical research.

It was into this gap between theory and research that George Homans rushed with his theory of social exchange in 1958. His union of Skinnerian behaviorism with the logico-deductive form of explanation was then expanded into a book with the publication of *Social Behavior: Its Elementary Forms* in 1961. Yet *Social Behavior* was Homans' *third* book. While his first book (and also his personal favorite—Homans, 1968a) has been overlooked, Homans has obtained considerable influence in the profession as the author of the less polemical *The Human Group* (1950). In fact, this book was Homans' chief source of influence in the profession through 1962, according to Cloyd and Bates (1971). In their analysis of footnote citations in six professional journals from the years 1951 through 1962, they concluded that "clearly *The Human Group* had been the chief source of influence on other authors by the end of 1962. . . . So far as journal publications reflect the influence of Homans, then, this single volume was the major source of his influence in the period we studied" (Cloyd and Bates, 1971:95).

Therefore, when Friedrichs (citing a study by Westie, 1973) finds that George Homans is one of the best known American sociologists, it is necessary to ask *for what* is Homans known and admired? Is it George Homans, author of *The Human Group*? Is it Homans the Behaviorist? Or is it Homans the Philosopher of Science, the Homans who stridently calls for and attempts to build logico-deductive schemes of explanation?

First, the temporal limits of the Cloyd and Bates study must be acknowledged: their data were collected only through the year 1962—which considerably handicapped *Social Behavior* (published in 1961) in the footnote sweepstakes. Therefore, in a effort to partially supplement their findings, I have recorded the footnote citations to Homans' work in the *American Sociological Review*, the *American Journal of Sociology*, and *Sociometry* for the period 1963 through 1973. The findings for the three journals during the eleven year period are presented in Table 1.[2]

Clearly, *Social Behavior* has made a significant impact: nearly half of all citations to Homans' work are to this book. There are slightly more than twice as

TABLE 1. Frequency of Citations of Homans' Works in *ASR*, *AJS*, and *Sociometry*, 1963–1973

Reference cited	63	64	65	66	67	68	69	70	71	72	73	Total	%
English Villagers (1941)	1							2				3	
Human Group (1950)	3	4	3	3	7	7	3	3	1	1	5	40	23.4
"Psychological Aspects of Social Structure" (1954)	3	1						1				5	2.4
"Social Behavior as Exchange" (1958)						2	1	2	1	1		7	4.1
"Calling Things by Their Right Names" (1960)		1										1	.6
Social Behavior: Its Elementary Forms (1961)	7	5*	9	7	10	6	9	6	9	8	8	84	49.1
Sentiments and Activities (1962)		1										1	.6
"Small Groups" (1963)									1			1	.6
"Bringing Men Back In" (1964)			1	4	2			3	2		2	14	8.3
"Contemporary Theory in Sociology" (1964)						1		2	1	1		5	2.4
"Effort, Superstition, and Productivity" (1965)							1					1	.6
The Nature of Social Science (1967)						1	3	1		1	2	8	4.7
"The Study of Groups" (1968b)									1			1	.6
"The Relevance of Psychology to the Explanation of Social Phenomena" (1970)									1			1	.6

---

*Homans footnoted his own book in his Presidential address which appeared in the December 1964 issue of the *ASR*. I did not include that citation as it is only natural that Homans influences himself.

many citations to *Social Behavior* than there are to *The Human Group*. Yet the durability of the latter work is evident: nearly one quarter of all citations to Homans' work in the period from 1963 through 1973 are to *The Human Group*. That there were only three more citations to *Social Behavior* in the year 1973 further attests to the continuing influence of *The Human Group*.

When the frequency of citations for *Social Behavior* and *The Human Group* are examined in each of the three journals an interesting finding appears. The impact of *Social Behavior* is much more marked upon those social scientists who published in Sociometry. Of the total citations to both books in that journal, 76.3 percent were to *Social Behavior* and 23.7 to *The Human Group*. In the *American Sociological Review,* the respective percentages are 64.1 and 35.9, while in the *American Journal of Sociology, Social Behavior* obtains only 55.5 percent of the total citations for the two works. In the latter journal, in fact, from the year 1967 through 1973, the number of citations to *The Human Group* exceeds those to *Social Behavior*—a work which is not cited at all in 1971, 1972, or 1973. Clearly if Homans' brand of behaviorism is nearly upon us, the *AJS* has not been informed.

Returning to Table 1, it can be seen that "Bringing Men Back In" (1964a) and *The Nature of Social Science* (1967) are third and fourth, respectively, in the number of citations. In both these works, as in *Social Behavior*, Homans mixes his call for behaviorism with a strident affirmation of the logico-deductive form of explanation. Homans almost always invokes the logico-deductive scheme of explanation to buttress his behavioristic position. In fact, in his comment upon an essay by a fellow exchange theorist—Peter Blau—Homans stresses "scientific explanation" much more than he does behaviorism or psychological reductionism (see Homans, 1969). It is "The Logical Adequacy of Homans' Theory" upon which Maris (1970) focused his attention in his lengthy analysis in the *American Sociological Review*. Therefore, I think it can be argued that Homans the Philosopher of Science is as well known as Homans the Behaviorist—and probably a good deal more popular.

HOMANS AND THE UNITED POSITIVIST ESTABLISHMENT

Homans the Philosopher of Science joins a growing chorus of social scientists and philosophers who advocate and occasionally practice a rigorous, formal, logico-

Table 2. Number of Citations to *The Human Group* and *Social Behavior* in *ASR, AJS,* and *Sociometry* During the Period 1963–1973

	Year of Citation												
Journal	63	64	65	66	67	68	69	70	71	72	73	Total	%
ASR													
Human Group	2	2	2	2	1	1	1	1	0	0	2	14	35.9
Social Behavior	1	0*	2	1	2	2	3	1	4	3	6	25	64.1
AJS													
Human Group	0	1	0	0	5	1	0	2	0	0	3	12	44.5
Social Behavior	0	1	2	4	4	1	2	1	0	0	0	15	55.5
Sociometry													
Human Group	1	1	1	1	1	5	2	0	1	1	0	14	23.7
Social Behavior	6	4	5	2	4	3	4	4	5	5	2	42	76.3

*Homans' reference to his own book was not included.

deductive style of "explanation." Hempel and Oppenheim, 1948; Braithwaite, 1953; Hempel, 1953, 1965; Popper, 1959; Nagel, 1961; Zetterberg, 1965; Rudner, 1966; Stinchcombe, 1968; Blalock, 1969; Blau, 1970; and Reynolds, 1971 are works which exemplify the "philosophy wing" of the Positivist Establishment. The general message in these works is that propositions "of the general form 'x varies as y' " (Homans, 1961:9) should be tested against empirical data. Ideally, these propositions are deduced in a formal, logical manner from more general theoretical statements which, in turn, may be deduced from still more general statements.[3] This constitutes "explanation."

The obsession with method and measurement which characterized the work of the "abstracted empiricists" (Mills, 1959) is still a central focus in today's more sophisticated "systematic empiricism" (Willer and Willer, 1973), but methodolatry is less and less *the* central ritual in the Positivist Establishment.[4] For the abstracted empiricists of the 1950's have seen anew the organizational power and coherence offered by the deductive form of explanation (again, see Blau, 1970). Methodology and the philosophy of science are allied in nearly co-equal partnership in the Positivist Establishment. Whether explicitly stated or not, all those regression tables, the path analysis models, and the smallest-space analyses are aimed at the goal of deductive "scientific" explanation.

COLEMAN AND THE POSITIVIST ESTABLISHMENT

A renewed emphasis upon theory construction and model-making, however, hardly means that leading methodologists and mathematical sociologists, such as James S. Coleman, will yield influence or even leadership—far from it!

Friedrichs contends that James Coleman is a second "significant other" in the discipline who has been influenced by Skinner—through the work of George Homans. Coleman claims to reject Homans' emphasis on operant conditioning (see Coleman, 1964a), though Homans (1971) argues that there is little difference in their views. However, even if it is true that Coleman is something of a covert behaviorist, I think it can be argued that such an orientation is overwhelmed by his commitment and skills in mathematical sociology (Coleman, 1964b, 1973) and methodology (Coleman, 1966, 1969). Several of his colleagues at Chicago have similar leanings: Edward O. Laumann, in fact, has employed his methodological skills to operationalize *Parsons'* A.G.I.L. scheme (see Laumann and Pappi, 1973). Though not cast in the logico-deductive form, Laumann's study illustrated both the power and appeal of contemporary positivism: its methods and its eventual aims are compatible—at least ostensibly—with diverse perspectives. It is the *form*, not necessarily the contents which is stressed. With its doctrinal flexibility and the continued emphasis on measurement, it would seem more likely that a broader contemporary positivism, rather than a narrower behaviorism, would stand to benefit the most from a boost in funding for policy-related research.

APPLIED RESEARCH AND BEHAVIORISM

Friedrichs notes that "The Federal research establishment has . . . nearly tripled its funding of applied research commissioned at colleges and universities." This development, he maintains, is likely to bring sociology and society closer together as sociologists are called to respond to social currents and social problems in the wider society:

Sociology—at least from the vantage point of a sociologist of sociology—must itself be increasingly viewed as a dependent variable: a function of the economic, political and social currents that throb through the larger body politic from which sociology derives its material sustenance. (1974:5)

And with neo-behaviorists such as James Coleman being strongly attuned to developments in policy research, the argument goes, then we may expect the increasing use of behavioristic methods in just those areas of endeavor.

The research of Galliher and McCartney (1973) lends credence to such contentions, though they found that federal funding of delinquency research has served to bolster the *positivist* approach in that field. In their survey of delinquency articles in three journals (*ASR, AJS,* and *Social Problems*), they observed that researchers concentrated upon "hypothesis-testing, the active collection of data (questionnaires, interviews), measurement and scientific methodologies, and a nearly exclusive focus on the criminal behavior of individuals" (1973:80). Now, this last-mentioned finding might seem like fertile ground for the seeds of a "renaissant behaviorism," but Galliher and McCartney do not so indicate. They do not mention behaviorism. On the contrary, they hint that, with the rising suspicion and distrust of government in the United States, then "we might expect a blossoming use of the interactionist and conflict perspectives, which do not necessarily rely on official definitions and official data" (1973:88).

Scott and Shore (1974) have recently discussed the problems they encountered in policy-related research. They suggest the existence of a considerable gap between social scientific knowledge and policy research. Furthermore, they find that "there is a real paucity in sociology of independent variables that are both predictively powerful and amenable to control and manipulation in the context of operational social programs" (1974:53). And, though they cite Coleman's 1972 work on policy research, they do not mention any behaviorist or neo-behaviorist solution to these problems.

A tacit implication of both of the above studies is that behavioristic method may be confined to highly controlled settings such as the laboratories in which Hamblin, et al. (1971) carried out those startlingly effective experiments on the behavior modification of "problem" schoolchildren. Yet, even when behaviorists do get the chance to apply their techniques in prisons, mental hospitals, and so on, they must expect that their own behavior may be "modified" by agents of the society in which they are operating. Thus, the exploits of various practitioners of behavioristic programs in prisons have been subjected to muckraking attacks and legal action in several states (see Mitford, 1973). There is, undoubtedly, more of this on the way. (In addition, it would be interesting to know how many such programs have failed by their own "scientific" criteria.)

Finally, there have been but three references to Homans' *Social Behavior* during the past five years in one of the leading "applied" journals: *Social Problems*. This, too, would seem to argue against an increasingly close relationship between behaviorism and policy-oriented, "social problems" research.

FROM PARSONS TO SKINNER: THE QUESTION OF CONTINUITY

Would a "shift from a Parsonian to a Skinnerian-inspired orthodoxy . . . reflect a measure of underlying continuity" (Friedrichs, 1974:7)? This a difficult and complex question to answer largely because Parsons' theoretical framework has undergone a number of subtle revisions (see Martindale, 1960; Scott, 1963). Furthermore, Parsons' scheme was formulated as something of a Grand Synthesis of several theoretical traditions. Hence, it is not surprising that one can find aspects of classical functionalism, Weberian action theory, conflict theory, symbolic interactionist theory, the phenomenological perspective, and even behaviorism in the vast outpouring of Parson's writing.

Therefore, there probably would be "a measure" of continuity in a shift from a Parsonian to *any* kind of paradigm—including a Skinnerian one. Friedrichs has taken note of some superficial parallels in the Parsonian and Skinnerian schemes

(1972b:232–234). And the synonyms for behavioristic concepts that Friedrichs says are likely to creep into our lexicon (Friedrichs, 1974) have been present in the Parsonian taxonomy for quite some time. John Finley Scott has been particularly adept at teasing out the behavioristic nuances in Parsons' terminology (Scott, 1971:21). However, according to Scott, Parsons' scheme cannot fully qualify as a truly behavioristic one because Parsons is "unwilling to depreciate the subjective point of view" (1971:21).

Indeed, Parsons cannot depreciate the subjective point of view. Subjective elements have always been at the conceptual heart of his theory. From *The Structure of Social Action* (1937) to *Societies* (1966), shared values—an intersubjective consensus on meaning and evaluation—are seen as crucial in the maintenance of the stability of social action. This central commitment to subjective phenomena must be rejected by behaviorists such as Scott, who maintains that "attention to subjective events has not, in my opinion, been heuristically valuable: more often it has led behavioral scientists away from the development of *good objective theories*" (Scott, 1971:21, my emphasis).

SUMMARY AND CONCLUSIONS

Prophecies of a behaviorist bandwagon gathering momentum in sociology are at best premature. Any heightened visibility of behaviorism in sociology more likely reflects the maturation of a Positivist Establishment, a union of "systematic empiricists" and philosophers of science who share a natural science epistemology with the behaviorists.

Major figures in sociology who might be identified with behaviorism, such as George Homans and James S. Coleman, owe their influence as much or more to their advocacy of "scientific explanation" or to their achievements in mathematical sociology and methodology.

It seems doubtful that an increase in applied research funding will significantly benefit the advance of behaviorism. Behavioristic programs, heretofore largely confined to laboratories and prisons, are beginning to meet legal and cultural resistance in a society in which *1984* and *Brave New World* are regarded as antitheses of utopia. It is questionable whether behaviorism can break free of the "bad press" it has had (Hamblin, et al. 1971:xi–xii). Furthermore, a recent study on sociology and social policy makes no mention of behaviorism (Scott and Shore, 1974), and a behaviorist boom in delinquency research is not forecast in Galliher and McCartney's survey of literature.

Parsons' theoretical scheme has absorbed elements of so many theoretical perspectives that there probably would be a minor degree of continuity in any shift from a Parsonian to a Skinnerian orthodoxy. But such a changeover would represent more of a real revolution because subjective phenomena, central to Parsons' action frame of reference, would be totally purged in the behaviorist framework.

The ultimate fate of any trend either toward positivism or toward behaviorism will heavily depend upon how sociologists choose to deal with subjective phenomena—with ideas, feelings, motives, and other phenomena of the mind. Behaviorists and positivists alike tend to eschew such phenomena since these things are difficult to measure in any precise, quantitative manner. But theoretical viewpoints that *are* concerned with mental phenomena and the problem of meaning—symbolic interactionism, phenomenological sociology, ethnomethodology, radical sociology, the sociology of knowledge, the dramaturgical perspective of Goffman, and the critical framework of Habermas—seem more acceptable and more exciting than ever. So long as these schools of sociology continue to thrive, a new dominant paradigm based upon either positivism, behaviorism, or any other overly objective perspective on the one hand or any overly subjective orientation, on the other, seems unlikely. The day of the dominant paradigm or disciplinary "orthodoxy" in a field as diverse and specialized as sociology may be over. The healthy amount of conflict and creative confusion that presently characterizes our discipline is likely to continue into the future. And perhaps that is as it should be.

NOTES

1. There are, perhaps, as many versions of behaviorism as there are behaviorists. The term behaviorism as employed in this study, however, specifically refers to the "hard core" behaviorism of Skinner and Homans.

2. Of course, the counting of citations is but one indicator of the influence of a specific scholar or a particular school of sociological endeavor. This type of indicator would undoubtedly underestimate the influence of a Lewis Coser or a Robert Nisbet, to name just two examples. Nor might the findings obtained by this method reflect the influence of all the varieties of behaviorism in sociology. In the case of Homans and his brand of behaviorism, however, I think such measurement yields some degree of face validity.

3. In some versions, notably Hempel's, the testable proposition may also be a general "law-like" statement.

4. It is for this reason I chose to employ the term "United Positivist Establishment" rather than the Willers' "systematic empiricism." The Willers, in my opinion, did not give sufficient emphasis to the increasing importance of logical positivism as the organizational framework of the systematic empiricists.

REFERENCES

Blalock, Hubert. *Theory Construction.* Englewood Cliffs, N.J.: Prentice-Hall, 1969.

Blau, P. "Justice in Social Exchange," *Sociological Inquiry,* 34 (Spring 1964), 193–206.

———. "A Formal Theory of Differentiation in Organizations," *American Sociological Review,* 35 (April 1970), 201–218.

Braithwaite, R. B. *Scientific Explanation.* Cambridge: Cambridge University Press, 1953.

Cloyd, J. S., and A. P. Bates. "Homans' Transactional Theory in Footnotes," in Herman Turk and Richard L. Simpson, eds., *Institutions and Social Exchange.* Indianapolis: Bobbs-Merrill, 1971, pp. 93–101.

Coleman, James S. "Collective Decisions," *Sociological Inquiry,* 34 (Spring 1964), 166–181. (a)

———. *Introduction to Mathematical Sociology.* New York: Free Press, 1964. (b)

———. *Equality of Educational Opportunity.* Washington, D.C.: U. S. Department of Health, Education and Welfare, 1966.

———. "The Methods of Sociology," in Robert Bierstedt, ed., *A Design for Sociology: Scope, Objectives, and Methods.* Philadelphia: The Academy of Political and Social Science, Monograph 9, 1969.

———. *Policy Research in the Social Sciences.* New York: General Learning Press, 1972.

———. *Mathematics of Collective Action.* Chicago: Aldine, 1973.

Friedrichs, Robert W. "Dialectical Sociology: Toward a Resolution of the Current 'Crisis' in Western Sociology," *British Journal of Sociology,* 23 (September 1972), 263–375. (a)

———. *A Sociology of Sociology.* New York: Free Press, 1972. (b)

———. "The Potential Impact of B. F. Skinner Upon American Sociology," *American Sociologist,* 9 (February 1974), 3–8.

Galliher, J. F., and J. L. McCartney. "The Influence of Funding Agencies on Juvenile Delinquency Research," *Social Problems,* 21 (Summer 1973), 77–89.

Gouldner, Alvin W. *The Coming Crisis of Western Sociology.* New York: Basic Books, 1970.

Hamblin, Robert, David Buckhold, Daniel Ferritor, Martin Kozloff, and Lois Blackwell. *The Humanization Process.* New York: Wiley, 1971.

Hempel, Carl G. "The Logic of Explanation," in Herbert Feigel and May Brodbeck, eds., *Readings in the Philosophy of Science.* New York: Appleton-Century-Crofts, 1953, pp. 319–52.

———. *Aspects of Scientific Explanation.* New York: Free Press, 1965.

Hempel, Carl G., and P. Oppenheim. "The Logic of Explanation," *Philosophy of Science,* 15 (1948), 135–175.

Homans, George C. *English Villagers of the Thirteenth Century.* Cambridge, Mass.: Harvard University Press, 1941.

———. *The Human Group.* New York: Harcourt, Brace, and World, 1950.

———. "Social Behavior as Exchange," *American Journal of Sociology,* 63 (May 1958), 597–606.

————. "Calling Things by Their Right Names." Paper read at the 55th annual meeting of the American Sociological Association, 1960.

————. *Social Behavior: Its Elementary Forms.* New York: Harcourt, Brace, and World, 1961.

————. *Sentiments and Activities: Essays in Social Science.* Glencoe, Ill.: Free Press, 1962.

————."Small Groups," in Bernard Berelson, ed., *The Behavioral Sciences Today.* New York: Basic Books, 1963, pp. 165–175.

————. "Bringing Men Back In," *American Sociological Review*, 29 (December 1964), 809–818. (a)

————. "Contemporary Theory in Sociology," in Robert D. Faris, ed., *Handbook of Modern Sociology.* Chicago: Rand McNally, 1964, pp. 951–977. (b)

————. "Effort, Superstition, and Productivity," in R. Dubin, G. C. Homans, F. C. Mann, and D. C. Miller, eds., *Leadership and Productivity.* San Francisco: Chandler, 1965, pp. 51–67.

————. *The Nature of Social Science.* New York: Harcourt, Brace, and World, 1967.

————. "A Life of Synthesis," *American Behavioral Scientist*, 12 (September–October 1968), 2–8. (a)

————. "The Study of Groups," *International Encyclopedia of the Social Sciences*, 6 (1968), 259–65. (b)

————. "Comment on Blau's Paper," in Robert Bierstedt, ed., *A Design for Sociology: Scope, Objectives, and Methods.* Philadelphia: The American Academy of Political and Social Science, Monograph 9, 1969, pp. 80–85.

————. "The Relevance of Psychology to the Explanation of Social Phenomena," in R. Borger and F. Cioffi, eds., *Explanation in the Behavioral Sciences.* Cambridge: Cambridge University Press, 1970, pp. 313–329.

————. "Commentary," in Herman Turk and Richard L. Simpson, eds., *Institutions and Social Exchange.* Indianapolis: Bobbs-Merrill, 1971, pp. 363–379.

Laumann, E. O., and F. U. Pappi. "New Directions in the Study of Elites," *American Sociological Review*, 38 (April 1973), 212–229.

Maris, Ronald. "The Logical Adequacy of Homans' Theory," *American Sociological Review*, 35 (December 1970), 1069–1080.

Martindale, Don. *The Nature and Types of Sociological Theory.* Boston: Houghton Mifflin, 1960.

Mills, C. Wright. *The Sociological Imagination.* New York: Grove Press, 1959.

Mitford, Jessica. *Kind and Unusual Punishment.* New York: Knopf, 1973.

Nagel, Ernest. *The Structure of Science.* New York: Harcourt, Brace, and World, 1961.

Parsons, Talcott. *The Structure of Social Action.* New York: McGraw-Hill, 1937.

————. *Essays in Sociological Theory.* New York: Free Press, 1954.

————. *Societies: Evolutionary and Comparative Perspectives.* Englewood Cliffs, N.J.: Prentice-Hall, 1966.

Popper, Karl. *The Logic of Scientific Discovery.* New York: Basic Books, 1959.

Reynolds, Paul Davidson. *A Primer of Theory Construction.* Indianapolis: Bobbs-Merrill, 1971.

Riecken, Henry W., and George C. Homans. "Psychological Aspects of Social Structure," in G. Lindzey, ed., *Handbook of Social Psychology.* Vol. 2. Reading, Mass.: Addison-Wesley, 1954, pp. 786–832.

Rudner, Richard S. *Philosophy of Social Science.* Englewood Cliffs, N.J.: Prentice-Hall, 1966.

Scott, John Finley. "The Changing Foundations of the Parsonian Action Scheme," *American Sociological Review*, 28 (October 1963), 716–735.

————. *The Internalization of Norms.* Englewood Cliffs, N.J.: Prentice-Hall, 1971.

Scott, Robert A., and A. Shore. "Sociology and Policy Analysis," *American Sociologist*, 9 (May 1974), 51–59.

Stinchcombe, Arthur. *Constructing Social Theories.* New York: Harcourt, Brace, and World, 1968.

Westie, F. "Academic Expectations for Professional Immortality: A Study of Legitimation," *American Sociologist*, 8 (February 1973), 19–32.

Willer, David, and Judith Willer. *Systematic Empiricism: A Critique of a Pseudoscience.* Englewood Cliffs, N.J.: Prentice-Hall, 1973.

Zetterberg, Hans. *On Theory and Verification in Sociology.* Totowa, N.J.: Bedminister Press, 1965.

REPLY TO LYNCH

ROBERT W. FRIEDRICHS

Reprinted from *The American Sociologist* 10 (1975),
91–92. Used by permission of the author and the
American Sociological Association.

Neither Lynch nor I claim to be sociological "seers." What each has done is to share an unavoidably partial vision of what *might* lie ahead of us as a discipline.

I find his argument relatively compelling, one which certainly deserves as wide a hearing as my own. Indeed, I am almost ready to admit that my projection was but one species of the larger genus he described. But if I were to do so, I might deny the special genius of the Homans-Coleman paradigm in responding to the anomalies that led to the revolt against structural-functionalism in the 1960's: its capacity (*not* present in Lynch's "United Positivist Establishment") 1) to combine the "priestly" and "prophetic" self-images that have battled for dominance throughout sociology's biography, 2) to supplement a "conflict" image of the fundamental nature of our subject matter with an essentially natural scientific epistemology that presumes "system," 3) to focus upon change per se in a day in which policy and applied research rides high among those upon whom most within the discipline have come to rely for funding, and 4) to breathe life once again into history as both subject matter and criterion for our activity as sociologists. Though Lynch notes the "creative confusion" that entered the discipline with the 1960's, he seems to have largely ignored the *substantive* nature and significance of the "revolution" that was taking place. The pluralism we have both noted and encouraged is, from my point of view, far from idiosyncratic. And, though Parsons continues to grant lip service to the "subjective" dimension in social action he highlighted in his initial work, his lengthy odyssey has carried him deeper and deeper into the accommodating analogies available within—and thought patterns appropriate to—the natural sciences of physics and biology.

I cannot and would not dispute the evidence Lynch brings to bear suggesting that others do not share the projection I contributed, for it was offered precisely because *I knew they did not* and had only recently seen the jig-saw begin to fall together myself.

But what I am afraid might be at the heart of Lynch's (and many another's) apparent misreading of the intent of the modest trial balloon I lofted is that I rejoice in the appearance of any evidence (Lynch's included) that sociologists are not taking and will not take the path I described as a tempting new "orthodoxy."

For it must be obvious by now to the attentive that there are those of us who are wed to the task of revealing those patterned portions of the social past and present which, by their very revelation, may assist us in avoiding them (or at the very least in mitigating their impact) in the future. Ours, in other words, is the task of self-defeating prophecy. Insofar as Lynch has assisted—however unconsciously—toward that end, we are grateful.

CHAPTER 5 CONFLICT THEORY

Introduction

The emergence of conflict theory in contemporary sociology has raised the hopes of antifunctionalists for a new theoretical basis for the discipline. Unfortunately, there has been a considerable gap between the promise and the development of such a theory. There is considerable confusion over the nature of conflict theory and over who can and cannot be validly claimed a conflict theorist. There are at least three fairly distinct varieties of conflict theory. The first is the conflict paradigm or model of society. This paradigm posits that society is composed of individuals who compete for scarce resources. As such, it is diametrically opposed to functionalist imagery, which sees order, not conflict, as the central reality of societies. The second set of claimants to the title of "conflict theory" are theories of conflict—that is, explanations of conflict phenomena. These theories may or may not be drawn from the conflict paradigm. In fact, functionalism, exchange, or symbolic-interaction perspectives can be employed to explain conflict phenomena. Third, "conflict theory" can be used to describe conflict as a methodology or political strategy. This view sometimes implies that knowledge demands action, usually radical. It is currently more often the view of those sociologists who prefer the radical, critical, or neo-Marxist labels dealt with in Chapter 6. Karl Marx, who is usually considered the primary founder of conflict theory, fits all three types.

The history of conflict theory, in the first and second varieties discussed above, is a long one, and awareness of the tradition has been revived in recent years. Martindale's (1960) text on the history of social thought devotes a chapter to the conflict paradigm from early Greek and Asian writings through medieval Arab and European thought to the Scottish moral philosophers (pp. 127–149). The more modern development, Martindale writes, was toward "conflict ideologies," which approximates the third variety of conflict theory discussed above. Under this rubric are Marxian socialism, social Darwinism, and Nazism (see Martindale, 1960:150–175). Martindale concludes with a chapter on "sociological conflict theories" (pp. 176–207) formulated around 1880–1950. These, he explains, aspired "to be an explanation rather than a social program" (p. 206). By stripping away the ideological component, he adds, they fostered a clear advance in social thought.

Ralf Dahrendorf (1959) is the best-known recent advocate of a conflict theory expressly opposed to functionalism (without, according to Turner, 1973, avoiding some of its weaknesses).

Dahrendorf bases his theory on an updated Marxism coupled with elements from Weber and Michels and considerable original thought. The coercive nature of society, he claims, gives rise to authority relations, and subsequent role interests may lead to organized conflict groups. Thus, wherever there is organization, there is a potential for conflict, and social life is inherently conflictive. Dahrendorf's work, then, is both a conflict paradigm and a specific theory of conflict.

The fullest development of a conflict paradigm to date has been achieved by Randall Collins (1975), who argues for the development of a truly scientific sociology and believes that the elements of such a causative theory are already existent in organization and stratification theories. (Another useful recent work is Duke, 1976). In the first selection reprinted here, Collins outlines the historical basis of such a theory. Much of value can be drawn from Marx and Weber and the present continuation of their studies.

Several scholars have commented on the need to synthesize the "order" and "conflict" paradigms—the views that see stability and competition as the central realities of social life. Van den Berghe (1963) and Ossowski (1963) believe such a synthesis desirable, while Frank (1966) and Horton (1974) are critical of such attempts. Friedrichs (1972) has claimed that an emerging "dialectical" sociology might transcend this problem.

The second meaning of "conflict theory" actually refers to theories about the social phenomenon of conflict. Theorists who hold the view that conflict is endemic to society, of course, often develop theories about the causes of conflict. Clearly, though, they need not do so—they can merely take conflict as a "given." Nor, of course, need one hold a conflict world view to theorize about the phenomenon: Conflict can be seen as abnormal to society. Thus, both Simmel—who held that conflict may be functional to group life—and Marx established traditions in the study of conflict. Indeed, Turner (1975) has argued that a synthesis of their approaches would provide "the broadest foundation for the sociology of conflict."

Bottomore (1971) has traced the history of such studies. Modern proponents of theories of conflict include the functionalist approach of Coser (1956), who explicitly follows Simmel [in anthropology, Gluckman (1964), has followed similar lines], and Dahrendorf (1958). The reading by Turner attempts to synthesize the work of these two theorists. Turner believes that sociology would benefit from focusing on theoretical propositions rather than on ideologies. When this is done for the work of Coser and Dahrendorf, we are still considerably short of a comprehensive theory of conflict.

The concluding reading, by Lehmann and Young, traces the emergence of a conflict paradigm in recent American sociology. This paradigm has developed out of dissatisfaction with society and established sociology on the part of politically aware sociologists. The new theoretical orientation, they claim, needs a new methodological approach to the subject matter—one that is antithetical rather than supportive of elites and that will yield hitherto unresearched areas of knowledge.

References and Suggested Readings

Bottomore, Thomas B. "Sociological Theory and the Study of Social Conflict," Indian Journal of Sociology, Vol. 2, No. 1 (1971).

Collins, Randall. Conflict Sociology. New York: Academic Press, 1975.

Coser, Lewis. The Functions of Social Conflict. Glencoe, Ill: Free Press, 1956.

———. "Social Conflict and Social Change," British Journal of Sociology. Vol. 7, No. 3 (September 1957).

———. Continuities in the Study of Social Conflict. New York: Free Press, 1967.

Dahrendorf, Ralf. "Toward a Theory of Social Conflict," Journal of Conflict Resolution, 2 (June 1958), 170–183.

———. Class and Class Conflict in Industrial Society. Stanford: Stanford University Press, 1959.

Duke, James T. Conflict and Power in Social Life. Provo, Utah: Brigham Young University Press, 1976.

Frank, Andre G. "Functionalism and Dialectics," Science and Society, 30 (Spring 1966), 62–73.

Friedrichs, Robert W. "Dialectical Sociology: Toward a Resolution of the Current 'Crisis' in Western Sociology," British Journal of Sociology, 23 (September 1972), 263–274.

Gluckman, Max. Custom and Conflict in Africa. New York: Barnes and Noble, 1964.

Horton, John. "Order and Conflict Theories in Sociology," American Journal of Sociology. Reprinted in R. Serge Denisoff, Orel Callahan, and Mark H. Levine, eds., Theories and Paradigms in Contemporary Sociology. Itasca, Ill.: F.E. Peacock, 1974, pp. 53–60.

Kriesberg, L. The Sociology of Social Conflict. Englewood Cliffs, N.J.: Prentice-Hall, 1973.

Martindale, Don. The Nature and Types of Sociological Theory. Boston: Houghton Mifflin, 1960.

Oberschall, Anthony. Social Conflict and Social Movements. Englewood Cliffs, N.J.: Prentice-Hall, 1973.

Ossowski, Stanislaw. Class Structure and the Social Consciousness. Translated by Sheila Patterson. New York: Free Press, 1963.

Swingle, Paul G. The Structure of Conflict. New York: Academic Press, 1970.

Turner, Jonathan H. "From Utopia to Where? A Strategy for Reformulating the Dahrendorf Conflict Model," Social Forces, 52 (December 1973), 236–244.

———. "Marx and Simmel Revisited: Reassessing the Foundations of Conflict Theory," Social Forces, 53 (June 1975), 618–27.

van den Berghe, P. L. "Dialectic and Functionalism," American Sociological Review, 28 (1963), 695–705.

THE EMPIRICAL VALIDITY OF THE CONFLICT TRADITION

RANDALL COLLINS

Reprinted from *Theory and Society*, 1 (Summer 1974), 147–78. Used by permission. Copyright © Elsevier Scientific Publishing Company, Amsterdam.

Randall Collins is associate professor of sociology at the University of California, San Diego. He is co-author of *The Discovery of Society* and author of *Conflict Sociology: Toward an Explanatory Science*.

The history of sociology remains alive in a peculiar sense not found in other disciplines. The classic sociologists are studied today, not for their purely historical interest, but because in important respects we haven't yet gone beyond them. In relation to major figures like Marx and Weber (and others), we are like the scholars of the Renaissance rediscovering the Greeks—not that we seem destined never to move past them, but that we have yet to move through them in their full depth. Add to this the clash of self-definitions that characterizes contemporary sociology, and we see another reason why sociology's classics should be brought into contention. Different figures are favored and their different facets turned toward the modern eye, depending on current interests in social criticism and social reconstruction, historicist interpretation, epistemological argument, justification for research techniques, or the construction of an explanatory science.

I am concerned here with the last: the prospects of sociology as a science, that is to say a system of causal generalizations borne out by empirical test. The ideal has sustained considerable attack, above all on epistemological grounds. But most of this battle has been fought out over programmatic and methodological claims; critiques of the *possibility* of scientific sociology would look rather different directed against an existing set of empirically validated generalizations.

My claim is that sociology does contain a solid core of explanatory principles, but they are not to be found in the places where they are most often sought. The scientific tradition in sociology has usually been considered to be the positivist tradition, especially its organic side from Comte through Durkheim to contemporary functionalists. The failure of this tradition to produce much more than a-causal categorizations and post-facto justifications of dominant institutions has been a major reason for the declining prestige of the scientific ideal. Another version of positivism has given science a bad name by stressing raw induction and purely technical canons of data-gathering, again without producing serious generalizations. Other versions of sociology—the interpretive social psychologies and philosophies, along with sociological historicism and various forms of political activism—have, of course, rejected the aim of producing a sociological science.

But these contending positions do not exhaust the field. There is another line of development, interrelated with some of the above, but cutting a distinctive path of its own: conflict theory. It is a distinctive tradition in that it proceeds along a certain line of insight worn steadily deeper over time; it is a scientific tradition, both in that the ideal of social science was developed within it, and in that we may draw from it a consistent network of causal generalizations of considerable empirical power.

The basic stance of conflict theory was taken by Machiavelli. Its fundamental element is a capacity for naturalistic realism, for sustained periods of intellectual detachment from the rhetoric of popular controversy. Men follow their own interests; success breeds honor; power breeds ambition; morality is based on violence, but works best by deception, especially through the deliberate staging of dramatic gestures; mass support is useful in the struggle of elites, and can be manipulated by show, especially of the externals of religion. This line of analysis was advanced by Marx's sociology, which specifies the conditions shaping interests and conflicts, describes the resources that enable particular interests to dominate, and generalizes about the relationship between the ideological surface of public consciousness and the real events below. Parallel developments were made by the realism of modern historiography, by the German theorists of *realpolitik* and of the conquest theory of the state. A sophisticated synthesis of these lines of thought with elements of Marxian sociology was accomplished by Max Weber, and applied to more limited topics of modern politics by Robert Michels and his successors.

This constitutes the main line of conflict theory on the macro level. There is also a development on the micro level, a tradition of tell-it-like-it-is in private life that extends from Schopenhauer through Nietzsche to Freud. Here again we find explanation in terms of amoral self-interest, with morality interpreted as the effect of external social pressures, and an interplay between a surface of deceptive ideals and an underworld of real interests. Standing somewhere between macro and micro levels is Georges Sorel, with his recognition of the interrelations of violence and moral solidarity, of the ideological surface and the realm of real satisfactions. However, Darwin is in the background for all of the later nineteenth-century conflict theory. It reflects not so much his evolutionism as his picture of man as an animal in a situation of biological struggle upon which civilization is only a veneer.

What I am interested in here is an abstraction from the whole body of their work: what this tradition has accomplished in the way of explanatory generalizations borne out by empirical research. The most important figures of the conflict tradition are very famous; their thought pulled together many strands, and they have contributed to many different lines of subsequent development. Some of these lines—especially those that have recently been prominent—have obscured the aspect of their thought that I wish to concentrate upon. I am not necessarily concerned here with their philosophies or methodological orientations, nor with the total body of their substantive theories, but only with what we can take from them that will bear fruit in subsequent research.

Above all, I wish to put to one side the political positions of these thinkers and the political interpretations that have been placed upon them. The importance of such detachment is especially clear in the case of Weber. Weber has been taken up by liberal anti-Marxists and presented first as a one-sided idealist who gave a religious explanation of capitalism and a legitimist interpretation of politics; then as a multi-causal pluralist who invalidates any emphasis on class influences, and above all as the proponent of a doctrine of value-neutrality that justifies obliviousness to conceptual and methodological choices which can make seemingly objective research into covert propaganda for particular value positions. Thus Weber has been made into both an idealist and a positivist, and the object of polemical attack by the philosophical Left in contemporary sociology.

As a result, Weber's most significant work remains obscured. His early work on the Protestant Ethic is only a fragment of his full analysis of the preconditions for capitalism. Throughout his main writings, Weber develops a complex and sophisticated version of the conflicting interests, material resources, and organizational forms that make up the stuff of history. Religious ideas play an important part, not as incursions from a transcendent realm, nor yet as unmediated reflections of a class structure; with his good command of historical detail, Weber shows ideals as created by religious practitioners and sustained by religious organizations, their affinity with the interests of various classes and status groups, and their use as weapons in struggles for political control. In stratification, organizations, and elsewhere, far from being the proponent of idealized abstractions, Weber provides some of our sharpest insights into the processes of conflict and the weapons of domination.

It has been the political interests of both liberals and radicals that has obscured Weber's main accomplishments for so long; the history of the reception of his own work is one of the strongest arguments for Weber's conception of scholarly detachment. For it should be noted: Weber's doctrine of value neutrality is no naïve shutting of the eyes to the sources of hidden value-bias. It is, on the contrary, a deliberate choice in favor of a difficult form of self-discipline, a continual effort to rise above political factions and toward the maximally powerful line of scholarly explanation. The orientation of conflict theory facilitates this, as its emphasis on the nature of conflicting factions warns the analyst against being caught in their self-serving argumentation. The strategy does not preclude taking sides at some point; but it calls for every effort to do this in full consciousness, while preserving a separate realm of scholarship, whose standards are not those of the world of politics.

The same applies to Marx. I am concerned here with his sociology, not his political philosophy, nor with the aspects of his economic system that seem to be molded by the historical aspirations of his era. I do not claim to be inclusive, nor am I interested here in arguments as to what is the "authentic" Marxism. My criterion is purely pragmatic: to pick out those theoretical generalizations that can explain the evidence and lead to even more powerful conceptual refinements. Hence I deliberately emphasize the broadly materialistic stance that flows so naturally from Marx, but give this a sociological focus rather than identifying it with the system of economic evolution presented in *Capital*. The most fruitful explanatory principles are those that give the conditions for class consciousness and political mobilization, with their implications for explaining organized conflict and dominance in all spheres. This kind of pragmatism about sociological ideas from the past is the most appropriate epistemological method for conflict theory; "truth" is always historically situated, and advances by continual reformulations, as thinkers strive for maximal explanatory coherence of ideas and evidence. Conflict theory can recognize that the existence of an intellectual community with sufficient autonomy from external pressures to carry this on depends on particular historical circumstances; as long as we have those conditions, there is nothing contradictory about making use of them to further the development of the most detached and coherent theory possible.

My aim, then, has been to take up the universal side of Machiavelli, rather than his schemes for the Florentine state; the leading insights of Nietzsche and Freud, without their biologism and their sexism. Conflict theory is Machiavelli without the Prince; Marx without Hegel; Darwin without Spencer; Weber without idealism; Freud without Victorianism—better yet, Freud restored to his Nietzschean historical premises. With sufficient detachment, the main line of explanatory accomplishment in sociology should come into view.

My contention is that conflict theory has been vindicated by empirical evidence to an extent approached by no other sociological theory. This involves understanding several things. First, that the body of conflict theory does contain a network of causal, testable explanatory generalizations, although they must often be abstracted from specific historical discussions, and above all, from the political and philosophical polemics that have obscured them. Second, that there is a fair amount of sociological research, on both contemporary and historical materials, that bears out the main propositions of conflict theory, and enables us to add refinements to them. Again, one must abstract out the relevance of this research, for it is seldom presented as explicitly bearing on conflict theory—or for that matter, on any explanatory generalizations at all. This is particularly true of research on stratification, which has been primarily descriptive, and its larger relevance has usually been taken in terms of social problems or ideological controversies.

The task now is to put together the pieces, to treat the evidence as it bears on explicitly formulated conflict theory, and thus to recognize where we stand. Sociology has accomplished a good deal more than is usually recognized. It is the prominence of the a-causal abstractions of functionalism and of interpretive social psychologies that give such a widespread impression that sociology has no real explanatory power. The materials of stratification and of organizations do fall into a fair degree of order around the propositions of conflict theory, and there is little within the scope of sociology that cannot be treated as a variant on stratification and/or organizational principles. The evidence is not as precise as one might wish, but the overall pattern is clearly there; and after all, it is the broad coherence of theory and research that is the basic criterion of validity. The theoretical obliviousness of ultra-positivist methodologists and of the more solipsistic ethnomethodologists alike are nothing more than polemical defenses of over-specialization; the only path towards a science, and the only way of resolving methodological ambiguities, is to see specific researches in the context of the largest possible system of generalizations. Conflict theory hardly provides a complete science, but it is firmly on the path toward one. Theory-building in a science is always a dialectic between gathering evidence and conceptual organization; in the history of conflict sociology, these poles have been pulled rather far apart, but the underlying connections are nevertheless strong. The important task now is to recognize them. The evidence we have now, for all its imperfections, supports more than a program.

OUTPOSTS OF A NATURALISTIC REALISM

The dominant forms of thought about the social world have been idealistic throughout most of history. Religion was the mode of legitimizing the state and stratification in most societies until the modern era, and even the more rationalistic systems that emerged from time to time—those of Plato and Aristotle, for example—legitimized some ideal form of social structure on the basis of transcendent forms. The emergence of a realistic conflict theory thus required special conditions, especially a situation of sustained political struggle among interests of approximately equal strength, so that no single legitimization could claim undisputed reality. Thus we find brief outcroppings of naturalistic realism in the most conflictful periods of ancient civilization.

In China, the long period of warring states preceding the Han dynasty produced a variety of intellectual factions, among them the followers of Mo Ti (ca. 400 B.C.), who taught a doctrine not unlike Hobbes: that self-interested conflict was the natural state, and only complete obedience to a ruler who set all standards of truth and morality could bring social order. In India, the period during which the ancient tribal republics were giving way to a series of petty kingdoms and to the rigidification of the caste system produced a variety of heterodox reactions: these ranged from asceticism and mysticism to materialist cynicism, and Gautama Buddha himself (ca. 560–480 B.C.) taught that the world as ordinarily experienced is nothing but conflict among creatures following their sensual appetites. In Greece, the chaotic period of democratization and balance of power among warring city-states saw the doctrine of Heraclitus (ca. 500 B.C.), whose cryptic pronouncements included the doctrine that strife is the basis of all things, and of the Sophists, who taught that standards of truth and morality are socially created by self-interested parties. In the 4th century B.C., these efforts at realism crystallized in Epicureanism, which incorporated the atomic theory of matter to argue against the existence of gods and sought happiness in a kind of anarchist intentional community.

These insights into the world of material conflict led to no sustained explanatory analysis. For the most part, although existing doctrines of religious legitimation were rejected, recognition of social conflict was only a stepping stone to a new practical solution. The Mohists became a quasi-military sect; the Buddhists' cynicism was simply the counterpart of a thorough-going mystical rejection of the world; the Sophists were content to teach rhetorical tactics; and the Epicureans, for all their espousal of the major scientific achievement of ancient society, became a conservative and anti-intellectual sect. What was necessary to produce a conflict theory was not only a detached realism, but an effort at systematic generalizations as well, and an effort to test generalizations against a range of empirical evidence. The third of these conditions had to await modern times; the second—the effort at stating general laws—was found primarily among the idealists. The doctrines of Plato, Pythagoras, Plotinus, Hermes, and Aristotle (the last incorporating material science in a position subordinate to ideal forms) carried the intellectual field, and all but obliterated the more realistic insights of their opponents for future generations.

KAUTILYA, THUCYDIDES, MACHIAVELLI

The most explicit and secularized expositions of social conflict came from three men whose careers were in the heart of political struggle: one of them a successful revolutionist, the other two ending up as exiles. Kautilya (ca. 320 B.C.), living at the end of the period of intensive doctrinal struggle in north India, engineered a coup d'etat to bring Chandragupta Maurya to the Nanda throne, and as his chief minister directed the policy of war and alliance that produced the Maurya empire —the only state of premodern times to conquer all of India. Kautilya's *Arthashastra*, like Machiavelli's *The Prince*, is designed to express the principles of realistic statecraft. Its tone is completely secular and pragmatic, recognizing military force as the *sine qua non* of the state, and recommending rational calculation of strengths in deciding on wars and alliances, tactics of trickery and stirring up dissension among enemies, and a system of spies for domestic order. Nothing is ever at rest, asserts Kautilya, and the power of a state is always increasing or decreasing; he details a dynamic policy to ensure military expansion. Yet the *Arthashastra* falls short of a scientific treatise. It is a handbook for a king, and its great length includes an entire legal and administrative system, ranging from marriage customs to taxation; the doctrines of political conflict are put only in the form of tactical admonitions, without historical examples or any effort at empirical explanation. It falls short, as well, of the major insight of modern conflict theory: the importance of ideological superstructure as a weapon in conflict —the religious legitimation whose manipulation Machiavelli was to stress. Kautilya's tone, indeed, is on a level of cynical realism scarcely approached since.

Thucydides (ca. 456–396 B.C.) was an Athenian general put in command of an expedition early in the Peloponnesian war (431–404 B.C.); the expedition ended in disaster, and Thucydides went into exile rather than face the wrath of Athenian democracy. In a position of enforced detachment, he wrote a history of the war based on his observations and interviews on both sides of the conflict. The result founded the discipline of serious historiography. Thucydides is the first historian to be concerned about his sources, and to make efforts to check them from alternative accounts; in his work, too, the usual allusions to divine intervention, to omens and portents, are completely missing. History for the first time reveals what a thoroughly secular and realistic account of the world looks like; even the distortions of patriotism are strained out in Thucydides' detachment from his city's losing cause. The world that is revealed is one of conflict and brute force. Athenian imperialism is taken for what it is, and its leaders put aside moralizing to justify it in terms of *realpolitik*. The class struggles within the city-states, the realities of slavery, the maneuvering of political factions, the intolerance of the victors towards their opponents, are displayed without disguise. With Thucydides begins a line of development whose importance for conflict theory cannot be overestimated: the discipline of realistic history-writing itself. For history is largely a record of conflict of a very un-ideal sort, and it is out of familiarity with serious historiography that most of the modern conflict theorists have drawn their insights. Thucydides, moreover, is the one exemplar of ancient realism whose works came down to the modern era as an accepted classic; Hobbes' first work was a translation of the *Peloponnesian War*, and it is from its realism that Hegel and Marx apparently drew their insights into the conflicts of ancient Greece.

Machiavelli (1469–1527) was another individual who danced precariously on the chopping block of history. As a youth, he lived through the popular uprising led by the fanatical monk, Savonarola, which overthrew the rule of the Medicis in Florence and established the Florentine republic; in 1499, after the fall and execution of Savonarola, Machiavelli served as Secretary of State for the new government, in charge of military reforms as well as foreign diplomacy. Thus he had first-hand dealings with the Borgias, the most worldly and corrupt of the Renaissance popes, with the shifting alliances in a period of foreign invasion and domestic Italian rivalries, as well as with popular revolts and internal *coups* in his native city. In 1512, the Florentine republic was overthrown and the Medicis returned to power; Machiavelli was tortured and then exiled. *The Prince* (1513), in his immediate response to this change of fortune, was both the distillation of his experiences, and an effort (which proved unsuccessful) to offer his services to the new Medici power. This work, together with his later ones, which included a history of Florence, expressed a realistic insight into the mechanisms of power and conflict to a degree not seen for two thousand years. His historical work, together with that of his countryman Guiciardini, began the modern tradition of realistic historiography; in its pages, the class conflicts of Florence were laid bare for all who wished to see. Yet this beginning was not followed up. Machiavelli's attack on the conventional religious pieties concerning statecraft brought him only infamy; his analysis of the mechanisms of conflict was too tightly interwoven with his political advice to be easily separable. For Machiavelli was not yet in the scientific tradition; for him the world was a matter of *Fortuna* and *virtu*, not of explanatory principles and empirical evidence. The transformation of realistic insight into conflict theory awaited the work of Hobbes and the post-Reformation free thinkers.

HOBBES AND VOLTAIRE

Hobbes (1588–1679) and Voltaire (1694–1778) are important figures in the conflict tradition, not so much because of the actual content of their doctrines about conflict, but because they established a tradition of naturalistic social realism within the emerging ideal of science. Personally, their lives show a similar pattern with that of other thinkers who had the necessary detachment to understand conflict. Both of them were exiles: Hobbes, an aging tutor attached to a royalist family during the English civil war, published his *Leviathan* (1651) while at the exiled court of Charles II; Voltaire, exiled to England as a young man (1726–28) over a personal quarrel with an aristocrat, returned to publish his *Lettres Philosophiques sur les Anglais* (1734), the subversiveness of which banished him from Paris again for most of the rest of his long life. Their political aims were similar only in a common opposition to the existing state of affairs; Hobbes put forth his arguments against the libertarian doctrines which led to civil war, Voltaire attacked religious superstition and aristocratic privilege in the name of tolerance. Their crucial point of agreement was in removing religious justifications as a basis for understanding the state, although they did this in the context of different political opponents and allies—Hobbes' position deriving from his conservative attachments in a civil war where the rebels were religious fanatics, Voltaire's from a parvenu's antagonism to traditionalistic elites, and his hope of preferment by the rationalist bureaucracies of the new absolutist monarchs.

For different political reasons, both men drew the intellectual battle lines at science versus religion. Hobbes was already a follower of Galileo and an acquaintance of Descartes before the outbreak of civil war in 1640; political events motivated him to produce a thoroughly materialistic social philosophy to counter the religious, moralistic, and legalistic doctrines of the rebels. Thus the immortal soul and the kingdom of heaven are irrelevant in a material world, where worldly power alone rules; morality is reduced to obedience to social conventions, and these in turn are nothing if not upheld by the state. The state is organized violence, and that is its basis for keeping order; laws are upheld only because the state controls violence, and cannot be a basis for it. Material interest in individual self-preservation is the basic driving force; good and evil are reduced to appetite and aversion—reward and punishment. Hobbes' analytical notion of a state of nature in which there is conflict of all against all, is taken to be the logical consequence of these axioms; the resulting "contract" which produces order by providing absolute obedience to a sovereign who controls violence is Hobbes' doctrinal conclusion, justifying royal absolutism.

What was important about Hobbes' doctrine was not this conclusion, which in fact drew very little assent, even from royalists (who preferred the cloak of religious legitimacy to this strange new justification). For despite much vilification on this score and for his atheism, Hobbes succeeded in popularizing the doctrine that scientific method and materialism apply to society as well as elsewhere. For the most part, they were watered down to eliminate the conflict elements; in the hands of Locke, the material interests of different individuals are seen as adjustable through a common interest in upholding private property, and the social contract becomes a benign agreement. The recognition of stark political violence underlying the state was muted; Hobbes' axiom-following political man was transformed into the utilitarians' economic man.

Hobbes' political conclusions had little importance for conflict theory, and his immediate followers took something of a detour from the path of social realism. For, if Hobbes formulated the ideal of social science, the victorious British liberals who appropriated this ideal made it into another doctrine which served to protect privileged interests and hide the harsh realities of social conflict. In the hands of Locke and his utilitarian successors, Hobbes' conflictful materialism became utopian positivism. The label emerges later, but the doctrine appears here. From Locke onward, and culminating in the economics of Adam Smith, the rationalist reformism of Bentham and John Stuart Mill, the evolutionism of Spencer, and eventually the associationist and behaviorist psychologies, the ideal of scientific materialism is taken to imply peaceful progress in a world of mutually self-adjusting individuals. The sharp teeth of Hobbes' realism were hidden by a superficial smile.

Voltaire, a rebel of a later generation and from a more autocratic state than the one that succeeded Hobbes, illustrates the ambivalence of the conflict tradition in the 18th century. For although he is the archenemy of superstition and pretense, he believes that victory is so close that his criticisms become muted in an appreciation of the coming rational order. His jokes and slogans keep the spirit of atheism alive, and with it, the recognition of the arbitrariness of traditional stratification; but he feels it necessary in his later works to support a rationalistic deism to replace the old dogmas. He writes world history as a record of quarrels and follies, but he cannot resist the urge to propagandize for a long-term evolution that is about to usher in the Age of Reason. The presence of England on the European scene gives him an ideal society whose internal conflicts are invisible to him; along with the doctrines of Newton, Voltaire popularizes Locke's positivism. It is only one step further to the *philosophes*, to Turgot and Condorcet, with their claims that science shows an evolution of reason, manifested alike in technology and in social progress, that inevitably (and without conflict) brings with it the better age of the future. The militant atheism of the 17th century underground was gradually becoming transformed into the bourgeois rationalism of the 19th.

The ideal of social science as it emerged in the 17th century contained the fundamentals of conflict theory. As long as religion was a powerful enemy, the connection was maintained. As modern states and political factions began to provide for their own secular justification, however, the cutting edge of science toward a realistic view of social conflict was blunted; the ideal (if not the substance) of science became subverted into a screen to hide social conflicts. The thinkers of the French Revolution, where science became the slogan of a victorious faction, contribute nothing to conflict theory; their successors, Saint-Simon and Comte, establish the theories of technocracy, social organicism, and benign evolutionism that have made up the positivist tradition in sociology ever since.

Yet, an iconoclastic cutting edge remained sheathed within the scientific tradition. Behind the liberal economists lurked Hobbes' doctrine of conflict and the violence of the state; behind Saint-Simonian evolutionism lurked Voltaire's religious iconoclasm. Karl Marx, in synthesizing these traditions, was to gather them together at their roots.

THE MARXIAN SYNTHESIS

It is a commonplace that Marx integrated British economics, French history, and German philosophy. What these labels conceal, however, are much wider traditions; Marx pushed through to the underlying conflict theories in each of them. (He also incorporated elements that are not part of the conflict tradition.) The English economists exemplified by Ricardo, for example, were but the forward edge of the entire movement of liberal rationalism, with its faith in science and its belief in the rational calculability of individual motives. In the early 19th century, it still carried the critical, anti-Establishment tone of bourgeois radicalism. And more importantly—for this utilitarian thought was even then turning into an Establishment ideology of its own (or at best a genteel reformism)—it carried beneath its surface the realistic insights of Hobbes and the unguarded class interests of Locke. It is from this that Marx acquired a full-blown materialism, and a model of society proceeding entirely from the pursuit of individual self-interest. In the background is Hobbes' bold assertion of the fundamentality of conflict, and of the violence upholding the state. From Locke comes the revelation that the basic purpose of the state is to uphold property, as well as the labor theory of value. And from Adam Smith himself proceeds the implicit contradiction within an economic system: for Smith's self-adjusting market moves men and resources inevitably in a chase for profits as long as supply and demand are out of balance, until a profit-free equilibrium is reached; it only remained to show that the empirical existence of long-term stratification and economic growth implied terrible convulsions within this system.

The French historians who influenced Marx are usually taken to be the bourgeois radicals, Thierry and Guizot. Behind them stood the whole evolutionist tendency of the late Enlightenment, which was made immediately relevant by Saint-Simon's claims for industrialism as the underlying reality of the post-1789 era. And one stage behind this was a more radical note, the attack by Voltaire and the free-thinkers on religious superstition; Marx's own father was an ardent Voltairian. The theme of science versus the supernatural was to be brought up to date in Marx's hands as economics versus ideology.

German philosophy means above all Hegel, whose idea of the movement of the spirit into greater and greater self-consciousness Marx was to stand on its feet as the historical dialectics culminating in communism. It is striking, however, how explicitly Marx's conflict theory is expressed already in Hegel. The *Phenomenology of the Spirit* (1807), takes the pattern of world history to be reflected in the history of philosophy, but Hegel's mode of exposition is remarkably "Marxian." The initial problem of Greek philosophy, Hegel asserts, can be found in the conflict of slave and master; successive philosophical systems are seen as different mental maneuvers in that conflict, producing a series of one-sided views, which are finally united in Hegel's own philosophy. Ideas are seen as reflecting the social conditions of each historical epoch, although for Hegel this contributed to an idealist conclusion because ideas were finally revealed to be the underlying reality of the entire world. In Hegel's dialectic, history moves by conflict, by ironical reversal, by the extension of each phase into an extreme at which it breaks, and although his references are most often to the history of ideas, he is well aware that history itself is a record of violence and bloodshed. "History [is] the slaughter bench at which the happiness of peoples, the wisdom of States, and the virtue of individuals have been victimized."[1]—although the End of history justifies its sacrifices, Hegel is one of the first great realists of the ordinary experiences of human events.

How did Hegel attain this insight? The man did not stand alone, nor was he merely reacting to Kant, Fichte, and Schnelling. "German philosophy" is a gloss on a larger movement of scholarship: the rise of modern historiography. Philosophy was not the only subject which came alive in the refurbished German universities of the turn of the 19th century: the study of classical languages, the history of law, political and religious history were undergoing the quantum leap that constitutes the beginning of critical modern historical scholarship.[2] Hegel was the philosopher who took fullest advantage of this movement; and as always, the revelation of an even mildly informed historical view was of the enormous importance of conflict, the violence and ironic deflections of human aims, the sense of larger forces beyond the ken of the ideas that accompanied them. Hegel is of the same milieu as Niebuhr and von Ranke with their effort to tell history "as it really happened." In the German tradition, then, Marx is heir to the emerging discipline of historical realism; and his own mentors—David Strauss and Bruno Bauer—were historical scholars who unmasked Biblical Christianity precisely in their capacity as critical researchers in religious history.

What, then, does Marx represent for the development of conflict theory? He brought together for the first time the major sources of the conflict tradition: the revelations of historical scholarship, the effort at a materialist theory of society, the iconoclasm of the freethinkers. Along with this, he incorporated elements that have proven misleading. He was too willing to accept the closed economic system of the utilitarian positivists, too sanguine about some historically inevitable version of Saint-Simon's industrial utopia, too wedded to secularized equivalents of Hegel's spiritual trends. Marx's work as a whole is multi-sided, and subsequent traditions have emphasized quite different implications, including a version of positivist scientism, an economic evolutionism, and most recently a realistic version of idealist philosophy. My intention is to pick out another theme: the implications of Marx's work as the first comprehensive expression of a scientific conflict sociology.

This means emphasizing, in a broad sense, Marx's materialism, and his positive orientation toward science in general, and putting aside highly abstract dialectics. The basic premise is that sociological explanation is grounded in the physical world. It is the action of human bodies in space and the material things amid which they move, that are the basic elements of explanation; all else is to be related to these. This is the Hobbesian program again, in which laws are understood in terms of the process of enforcement, and the state in the threat of violence. What Marx added, of course, is a special emphasis on the principles of economics. But even more important for sociological explanation are two other implications of the materialist principle: first, that human action depends on its material setting, and on the material resources available; second, that motivation is to be understood in terms of the material desires of human bodies. Marx couched this primarily in terms of the need to stay alive as prerequisite to everything else, the fundamentality of the economic system in society, and of the individual's place in it as the source of his most basic outlook. This principle is capable of further extension, however; maneuvering for physical dominance, for emotional satisfaction, and for sexual pleasure all fall within its purview, when understood as behavior of an organism. On this abstract level, the materialist principles are general and programmatic, directing us toward the sources of explanation. More specific applications give the conditions for various empirical outcomes.[3]

(1) *Property and the State.* The crucial characteristic of any society, Marx asserted, is its form of property; and the crucial determinant of any individual's behavior is his relation to property. Marx thus characterized ancient Mediterranean societies in terms of slavery, feudal societies in terms of landed estates with attached laborers, capitalist society in terms of industrial equipment. From these proceed the distinctive interests and cultures of slave-owners and slaves, lords and serfs, capitalists and workers. There are other property relationships as well; one might be outside the prevailing ones, such as freemen in slave societies, urban groups in feudal societies; petit bourgeoisie who work their own property in industrial societies; and besides, there are usually *several* kinds of property in any society. Marx's interest in picking out the principal form of property was to explain the predominant form of *political* action, but this need not detain us from examining the full implications of the analysis. Nor are we limited to the few historical types Marx stressed, as any empirical society is amenable to the same principles. These have three specifiable components.

(1a) *Property is Upheld by the Violence of the State.* It is for this reason that property classes are involved in politics. Control over material goods and human labor (which is either a direct form or an indirect result of property) is based upon violent threat, whether administered personally, by the army, or by the police. The state, as the organization of violence, is the necessary prop under every property system. Marxian analysis has usually emphasized the causal link from economic interest to political action; this was bolstered by the corollary emphasis on technology as setting the conditions for the type of property system possible. But there is another direction of causality implied, which is of immense importance: the conditions of political organization (i.e., the organization of violence) directly control the form of property. The connection of property with state violence is reciprocal, and material conditions can be invoked in both spheres to explain causal processes in each direction.

I have stressed an implication that is somewhat contrary to many of Marx's own assertions. Marx was at pains, in *The German Ideology* and elsewhere, to attack the idealist notion of the state as a manifestation of *Geist*, of the People, or an abstract ideal of Justice, and to contrast this ideologizing with the real world of economic goods over which men struggled. And since his major scientific effort was to create a comprehensive economic theory, he tended to stress economic dynamics above all else. But the same logic tends to uncover a realm of the state which is engaged in actual material activity: guarding property, arresting thieves, issuing money, regulating transactions, and the like. It is not a great shift from

Marx's own formulations to regard the state, in these material activities, as part of the relations of production, and to see them in reciprocal interplay with the specific technology involved in the means of production.[4] It does go beyond Marx to give political factors a crucial place in determining important variations in the economic system, even *within* a given type of technology; but as we shall see, this is a realistic and important implication. It helps us to understand the very existence of the 20th century communist revolutions, and it provides the embryo of a theory for the shaping of all aspects of earning a living—the system of credit, the media of exchange, the boundaries of occupational positions—by political power.

(1b) *Property is the Basis of Class Division.* What men do and think always takes place in a physical world in which they must assure their physical survival. Making a living is the one unavoidable necessity, even if this is done indirectly by attaching oneself to others who provide sustenance. Thus, one's relationship to property—which for Marx summarized the whole complex of earning a living —is the most important thing in one's life, and it takes up the biggest portion of one's time, as well. By a complex of influences, it shapes class cultures:[5] the characteristic outlooks of persons who spend major portions of their lives at particular tasks, with their peculiar worries and insecurities, their particular personal associations, their particular kinds of consumption and leisure. Moreover, since property is inherently connected with state violence, it implicitly invokes threat, domination and conflict. The experiences of different social classes are different not only because their daily lives are different, but because cross-class encounters involve the inherent antagonism of those who can successfully call on state violence to back them up, as opposed to those who are dominated by such threats.

This confrontation is more explicit between slave owners and slaves, lords and serfs, than between employer and employee, and these historical variants add degrees of specificity to the kinds of class cultures found in each case. The general principle also holds: cultural differences not only proceed from differences in livelihood, but take an important part of their content from the implicit amount of conflict in the dominance relationships in that sphere. This is the basis of a conflict theory of stratification.

(1c) *Property Divisions Are the Basis of Political Action.* Property creates political interests as being part of the ongoing process by which it is upheld. Thus, political attitudes and behavior are predictable from class divisions. The analysis may be refined as far as one wishes. There are as many economically motivated political factions in a particular society as there are discernible kinds of property. There is also a further level of political analysis: within the *general* interest of a class in upholding a particular form of property (or other economic arrangement), individuals struggle for state influence on behalf of themselves alone—for franchises, land-grants, monopolies, gifts, exemptions. For Marx himself, the problem of predicting political alliances among different property sectors, and the transition points between class-wide political action and individual self-seeking within an economic class, was solved by concentrating on periods of economic crisis and transition from one system to another. For the short run of everyday politics, Marx's own theory was underdetermined, and he himself analyzed particular historical events with retrospective rather than predictive clarity. This is not entirely necessary, for there are additional principles buried in Marx's work and obscured by his concentration on economics, which go some way toward the necessary specificity.

(2) *Material Conditions Determine Mobilization of Interests.* Material conditions determine the degree to which class interests are effectively brought into action. Property relationships thus not only shape political interests, but determine the degree to which men may participate in the struggle to control the state.

In Marx's own work, this principle is expressed in two places: in the *Communist Manifesto*, the famous phrase about capitalism producing its own gravediggers follows a discussion of the factory system as bringing the workers together to organize with the full weight of numbers; in the *Eighteenth Brumaire*, Marx explains the lack of effective political participation of the peasantry by their ecological dispersion, which results in their having no more organizational unity than "potatoes in a sack."[6] Social ecology, conditions of transportation, and the effects of property systems and disposable wealth are all crucial conditions that determine which interests win out to what degree. Small elites can control large numerical majorities precisely because of the unequal distribution of facilities for mobilization. Marx tended to focus on the major economic changes which brought about periods of revolutionary mobilization, but the principle has much wider applicability in the explanation of politics, and does not depend for its validity on a doctrine of economic evolution. By implication, the principle of mobilization also serves to refine the theory of stratification by showing the processes through which conditions of social ecology and communication affect class outlooks. This leads to another principle.

(3) *Material Means of Mental Production Determine Consciousness.* The dominant ideas of an historical period are those of the dominant class (Marx asserted in *The German Ideology*), because they control the means of mental production. This introduces an intervening variable between property itself and the ideological superstructure; although the theory was not explicitly worked out on this point, in principle it allows for considerable refinements in the way the means of mental production are organized, and hence in the varieties of consciousness. The theory of mental production applies to two different areas. It is an extension of the theory of interest mobilization, specifying another set of material resources—writing materials, printing presses, wealth to pay for secretaries, teachers, publicists, priests, entertainers, and so on—which, when unequally distributed, result in the formulation of the ideas that dominate public discourse, official definitions of reality. It also has implications for the theory of class cultures taken in themselves: those classes which have the greatest control of the means of mental production are correspondingly "cultured," in the popular sense of the term, whereas those with little such control are less intellectual, less taken up in playing with symbols.

Marx presents us with principles which can be formulated sharply enough so that we may fruitfully compare them with the empirical evidence accumulated since Marx's day. To do so is to recognize how serious a start upon a scientific sociology is provided by conflict theory at this stage of formulation; even where the principles have been modified, the direction of movement proves that it is on the right track.

(3a) *Property Upheld by State.* This principle implies a theory of wealth: variations in the conditions of political organization have corresponding systems of property distribution. This is the line of analysis taken by Lenski; in his model, the technology of material production (and certain other resources and conditions affecting political/military mobilization) determines both the sheer amount of wealth in a society, and its distribution via intervening effects on the organization of the state.[7] The theory is successfully tested by Lenski on a broad set of societal types covering all of world history, and has been borne out by contemporary cross-national comparisons.[8] This is a striking achievement, above all, since it is the *only* theory of the distribution of wealth which has proven successful by empirical test. The various functional theories of wealth, for all the argument that has surrounded them (e.g., the Davis-Moore-Tumin debate) have yet to be even formulated in sufficiently causal terms to bear testing; nor has neo-classical economics produced any general theory of the distribution of wealth.[9]

By extension, not only property but other distributive features of economic life are influenced by the organization of political power. This approach has not yet culminated in explicit hypotheses relating particular political variables to particular features of economic life, but there are moves in this direction. Occupational "position" is being de-reified, understood as a sphere of action that may be divided up more narrowly or combined with other actions and hedged with varying degrees of tenure;[10] just where occupational boundaries are drawn (and with them their corresponding controls over remuneration, possibilities of promotion, and degree of monopolization over recruitment procedures) depends on maneuverings which are ultimately backed up by the law—i.e., the coercive threat of the state. The theory of professions—where political enfranchisement is particularly obvious—is moving in this direction.[11]

It is also worth noting that conflict theory has issued explicit propositions in the area of crime which recognize the political-power/property-defense connection;[12] it only remains to cast this model in a sufficiently historical and comparative form to provide a firm empirical test of its power.

(3b) *Property and Class Cultures.* In a general sense, Marx's principle that the means of earning a living determine cultural distinctions has been overwhelmingly borne out by the evidence. Community studies, whether sympathetic to Marx or not, have inevitably (and sometimes inadvertently) turned out to be descriptions of stratification among occupational levels; and survey studies have proven occupational class to be the most ubiquitous of all independent variables, predicting political attitudes and participation, personal associations, marriage, childrearing practices, work attitudes, career patterns, leisure activities, consumption styles, sexual behavior—the list is endless.

In a more specific sense, however, the Marxian formulation is inaccurate. For the strongest break between categories of the variable are between white-collar and blue-collar classes, even though a great deal of the former are on the *property-less* side of the dividing line proposed by Marx.[13] The principle required reformulation; this was done by Dahrendorf, who proposed distinctions of power, between order-givers and order-takers, as the most general determinant of class cultures, and property ownership as an historically specific form of power relation.[14] This accounts for the modern blue-collar/white-collar line, for analogous cultural distinctions in socialist societies, for the dominant-class orientation of management even where separated from ownership, as well as for the tendency for similar splits in outlook to appear between leaders and followers within voluntary associations.

In this form, the conflict principle of stratification is strongly buttressed by empirical evidence. But the general form is capable of much further specification to account for various forms of power relationship—for the difference between the upper class whose face-to-face encounters consist almost entirely of giving orders, and the middle class who experience both giving orders (to some) and taking orders (from others), for differences in ethos between more independent and more centrally controlled occupations, and between occupations experiencing varying degrees of explicit control and the different kinds of sanctions applied. Many of the empirical variations may doubtless fall into this conceptual order.[15]

It remains the case that occupational variables are not the only ones which affect attitudes and behaviors: education, sex, age, ethnicity, religion, parental background, personal associations also have their effects. The theory of stratification must have many causal links; but the multiple variables can be integrated around common principles of conflict theory. Many of these variables are themselves indirect transmitters of occupational class cultures; influences of parents, spouse, and acquaintances add further occupational variables to the individual's own, whether to reinforce it or dilute it. Other variables represent non-occupational influences. In both cases, the shaping of individual cultures is very much in the realm of the conditions formulated under the principles of mobilization and of mental production.

(3c) *Class Divisions and Political Action.* The Marxian principle (especially as reinterpreted by Dahrendorf, to account for white-collar/blue-collar distinction) has had considerable success in survey research on political behavior.[16] Other variables affect political behavior as well; but to understand that this principle is part of a *set of principles* goes some distance towards accounting for this —above all, the principle of mobilization of interests helps account for much political behavior not in keeping with the class model.[17]

Another source of validation comes from comparative/historical approaches. Barrington Moore has demonstrated the success of a refined application of the principle of property interest in determining the structural form of the state.[18] Focusing on the period of commercialized agriculture which precedes industrialization, Moore proposes that class interests vis-a-vis opposing forces determine political orientation; the peasants, landowning aristocracy, bourgeoisie, industrial workers, and government bureaucracy are characterized in terms of their preference for democracy, fascism, or communism as means of enhancing their economic positions. The particular mode of agricultural property, in turn, is a crucial variable specifying the orientation of the aristocracy (the most mobilized class of the period); from this, and from historical violence which forcibly removes particular classes from the line-up of contenders, Moore is able to explain the main historical divergences of the modern period. The analysis is bolstered by Stinchcombe's independent comparison of the political tendencies of various agricultural property arrangements, which arrives at similar conclusions.[19] The extension of this mode of analysis to the constellation of class interests upholding the entire range of variations in political structures, in view of this success, is quite plausible.

(4) *Resources For Interest Mobilization.* The principle that power is proportional to the degree of mobilization of interests has recently received a number of applications. Mann shows that the evidence supports the view that it is not only the higher classes who keep the modern working class from defending its political interests, but its lesser command of the resources of mobilization as well;[20] Pinard, that the capacity for concerted political action depends on organizational ties on the informal level;[21] Burstein and Portes, that class-consciousness depends on class community structure as well as work relations;[22] Domhoff, on the national level, and Perrucci and Pilisuk, on the community level, give descriptive evidence of the ties of intercommunication which are correlated with effective power;[23] Lieberson explains areas of elite control in government policy in terms of their sole mobilization of interests in those areas.[24] The interaction of material interests with the resources mobilizing such interests begins to introduce some theoretical order into the overly descriptive and polemical area of the study of political influence.

The principle of mobilization also adds further specification to the process by which class cultures are shaped. Gans, on the basis of an empirical summary, demonstrates that a crucial distinction between working-class and middle-class culture is in the degree of localization and personalization of world views, which in turn rests on the actual conditions of work participation in networks of communication; similar principles account for the outlook of highly localized peasants in traditional rural society.[25] Analogous principles may be extended to account for the ultra-cosmopolitanism of the most highly mobilized occupations, such as professions oriented toward national networks.

(5) *Means of Mental Production.* This principle was formulated originally on the political level, and although systematic comparative tests are lacking, there are several studies of the mass media which describe the mechanisms by which

class interests affect public "reality" by affecting the material means of its production.[26] Education has also been shown to reflect the resources and cultural
stances of dominant classes.[27] Such analyses explicitly introduce intervening
variables into the process of cultural production, which point the way toward a
theory of variations in the "superstructure"; and they add refinements to the
stratification model, by showing how cultural selection, the process by which
occupational careers are mediated, is itself the product of interest groups and their
unequal resources for producing culture. More remotely, the means of intellectual production are being analyzed in the relatively autonomous communities of
natural science, where studies have shown the importance of the struggle for
advancement in the context of variations in the availability of positions and research equipment, and in the number of rivals;[28] these variables explain both the
ethos of particular intellectual disciplines and the innovativeness and some of
the directions of scientific ideas.

The most far-reaching extension of the principle of the means of mental production has occurred in the study of organizations. Michels' *Political Parties*
(1911) was among the first works to show not only the existence of internal conflicts of interest within voluntary organizations, but a principle that accounts for
the outcomes of such conflicts: power is proportional to a factions' control over
the technical means of administration, not only as it provides for the superior
intercommunication (i.e., mobilization) of that group, but also as means of controlling the information upon which opponents operate. Subsequent studies in
this tradition have borne out the importance of variations on this dimension.[29]
The same general principle emerges in the studies of Crozier, who finds that organizational power goes to those groups which preserve autonomous control over
areas of uncertainty, which they alone can define to the rest of the organization;[30]
a similar principle has been borne out by Wilensky.[31] It reappears again in comparative studies of the conditions which enable an occupational group to achieve
monopolistic control over its own recruitment, work practices and advancement
—i.e., to "professionalize."[32] Much of the area of organizations is thus unified
around a set of variations on the principle that power is proportional to control
over the material means of defining the cognitive reality within which other organizational members act.

The Marxian synthesis of conflict theory traditions is unquestionably—if
retrospectively—the take-off point for a sociology with empirical scope and explanatory success. Its flaws came largely from elements extraneous to the conflict
tradition, above all from its overly evolutionist treatment of the economy, and
from its idealized conception of a final historical stage. Yet even within its own
bounds, Marxian sociology left major areas of omission. The next major step toward filling them in was taken by Weber.

WEBER AND GERMAN HISTORICAL SOCIOLOGY

Marxian thought remained in the underground through most of the 19th century,
and began to receive sustained intellectual attention only in the 1890's, in the
controversy over Marxian economics and the related issue of revisionism that
followed from the adoption of Marxism as the official doctrine of the German
Social Democratic Party. Weber, as an academic economist, and a member of the
reformist *Verein für Sozialpolitik*, was one of the first generation of non-socialist
intellectuals to become aware of Marx's accomplishments, and to take account
of them in his own work. There were, of course, other important influences on
his thought. There were the doctrines of neo-Kantian idealism, which Weber
made the basis of his methodology, and which have given the impression to readers who know little of Weber first-hand besides his methodological essays that
Weber was primarily an idealist. More importantly, Weber was at the heart of
the German historicist tradition, the part that emphasized cold-blooded under-

standing of the role of violent conflict in world history. The tradition of critical realism in history that we already found in Hegel's background had made tremendous advances during the century in recovering ancient and non-European history; one difference between Marx and Weber, accordingly, was that the latter knew a great deal more history than the former, and was in a position to formulate principles with a good deal more scope and precision. The German economic tradition in which Weber worked, moreover, followed historical rather than the classical (Ricardian) lines taken up by Marx; where Marx emphasized the laws of the market and fell back on technological development as the principal exogenous determinant of change, Weber stressed the organizational arrangements that underlay the rise of a market in specific historical periods. (Weber, in other words, was an institutional economist, of the sort represented in the United States by Veblen and Commons.) More generally, the German tradition of historiography was oriented toward conflict, but along military rather than economic lines; this was reflected in contemporary sociology in the conflict theories of Gumplowitz, Ratzenhofer, and Oppenheimer, with their special emphasis on conquest in the origins of the state, and in the theory of geopolitics put forward by Ratzel. Not least was the influence of the political doctrine of *realpolitik*, a revival of Machiavellian realism fostered by Bismarck and transmitted to Weber by personal experience and by observation of his father's parliamentary career.

Weber, then, was in an auspicious position to develop the conflict tradition, through his acquaintance with Marxism, his thorough exposure to indigenous German conflict theories, and his broad knowledge of the accomplishments of mature historiography. For my purposes here, I shall not even attempt to sketch his overall position (which was primarily concerned with world economic history), but only to deal with those propositions that Weber adds to the conflict theory which first came to maturity with Marx. This means ignoring Weber's historicism—his expressed limitation of generalizations to aid in the analysis of unique historical sequences. But we are not bound by this aspect of Weber, any more than we are by Marx's economic evolutionism; once we take the step of formulating Weber's principles more sharply than he did himself, and comparing them with Weber's own evidence and with subsequent research, it is apparent that Weber achieved a second stage of synthesis in the conflict tradition.

Weber's Congruence with Marxian Sociology

It should be noted first that Weber's sociology not only accords with, but builds upon Marxian fundamentals. The primacy of self-interested conflict, the importance of material conditions, the effects of interests on ideology, the existence of economic class struggle—all of these are found in Weber. Indeed, Weber gives an even sharper formulation of economic conflict, pointing out conflicting class interests in the credit and commodity markets as well as the labor market; as Wiley points out, these help us understand class conflict in historical contexts, where it is usually glossed over by the more conventional emphasis on worker/ employer conflict alone.[33] The principles of property interacting with the state, of interest mobilization, and of the means of mental production are illuminated by Weber's work; his contributions to conflict theory may be understood as amplifying them in regard to the technical conditions of violence and of administrative organization, to internal conflict within organizations, as well as adding another principle that we may refer to as the "means of emotional production," which subsumes the contributions Weber made under the labels of "legitimacy" and "status groups," and in his sociology of religion.

Means of Violence and Its Administration

Weber was highly aware of the role of military force in history, and his theory of political organization proposes a set of conditions under which it takes different forms.[34] There is an inherent struggle for power wherever coercion is involved. Hence states are unified or break apart depending on the technical means available for keeping administrative control over the organization of violence. Coercive power is maintained by a network of mutual threats among the bearers of arms, and the control goes to whoever can control the network of surveillance through which this operates, and the sources of military supply.

Weber's model of bureaucratic *and patrimonial* organization gives the main variations in technical resources and their political results. There is the *military technology* itself: weapons such as firearms which must be centrally supplied and administered favor a unified organization, whereas weapons such as those of self-equipped knights foster decentralization. *Technology of transportation and communication* determines the extent to which centralized control over supplies may be maintained. *Literacy* and the *material resources for written records*—the availability of paper, files, writing implements of varying degrees of cumbersomeness—affect the ease of centralized administration, and hence the size of the geographical area that can be controlled. The availability of *literate* administrators has a similar effect. The *mode of household organization* also affects the problem of control: the key to patrimonial type is the billeting of troops in the personal household of leaders, caring for them from a common larder, and thus making no distinction between personal and public relationships; the accompanying structural tendency is for superiors to lose control whenever their subordinates must administer a distant territory, especially when they appropriate land there to support themselves. Bureaucratic organization is an effort to counter this tendency; in addition to the technical resources noted above, it depends on a system of recruitment from outside of household and family ties. Universal churches have been important politically because they provide just such a form of organization, and governments of any degree of bureaucratization have depended on this form—initially by directly using the priests as administrators, later by wholesale imitation of church organization through a secular bureaucracy.[35]

Organizational Power Struggles

Weber explicitly saw organizations as sites of conflict. The tendency of subalterns to assert their autonomy whenever distance permitted was the main theme of patrimonial regimes; a parallel struggle goes on in bureaucracies due to the control by subordinates over the administrative machinery. (Weber's protégé Robert Michels provided a fairly straightforward application of this principle to modern parties, and Weber's own writings on modern politics emphasize similar observations.) As Roth points out, Weber's use of ideal types implies that bureaucracy is only one of several strategies employed in struggles for control; personalistic (patrimonial) networks of individual loyalties remain part of the structure within formally bureaucratic organizations because of their utility in the ongoing struggle.[36] The history of organizational theory since Weber has thus included much rediscovery of insights already formulated by Weber.

This is made explicit in Etzioni's theory of organizational control, which summarizes evidence showing that coercion, material rewards, and normative control—applications of Weber's "party," "class," and "status" dimensions—each have their distinctive consequences for compliance, and hence for the kinds of tasks that can be achieved with them.[37] Etzioni's synthesis draws on a great deal of organizational research from Mayo and Barnard onward, which reveals organizations to be sites of continual maneuvering for control, even though these studies have tended to be interpreted within the framework of managerial ideologies that obscure their relevance for conflict theory.[38] But some studies have gradually brought about the explicit recognition of conflict as a major determinant of organizational phenomena.[39] Together with the advances in formulating explanatory principles mentioned above (as extensions of the principle of the means of mental production), this work adds up to a fairly refined and empirically well-grounded conflict theory of organizations.

The Means of Emotional Production

Weber is best known for a series of contributions that apparently break the Marxian mold. These include the importance of status groups—the dimension of stratification into communities distinguished by life style and ranked by prestige, communities which are built up over and above class lines, and sometimes cutting across them; the importance of religion in setting personal attitudes and social change; the importance of legitimacy as the basis of stable political order. These are indeed important and original contributions by Weber; but they remain within the conflict tradition, and supplement rather than negate the model of conflict over material goals and through material resources. To make this clear, I have reformulated the underlying principle under the term, *the control of the means of emotional production:* i.e., the conditions in the material world whereby individuals are influenced to experience emotions, especially social solidarity, fear, awe, or a sense of purpose. The implication is that these are resources to be used in conflicts (for goals of power and wealth as well as for emotional gratification), and that the control of these means is itself affected by the distribution of resources resulting from other forms of conflict.

That is, Weber made a discovery analogous to those of Durkheim and Freud (and above all Nietzsche, on which he drew), when he recognized that people have emotional desires and susceptibilities, and that these are crucial for their social lives. Weber saw that particular conditions excite emotional dynamics; above all, conditions of conflict, deprivation, and threat on one hand, and on the other ceremonies and displays which arouse emotions and resolve them into feelings of solidarity and awe. Manipulation of the settings of such face-to-face encounters is the basis of religion. Weber does not reduce religion to economic interests, although he shows that social classes have their typical religious propensities;[40] rather, it is to be understood as a distinctive area of emotional gratification, and the product of a distinctive group, the priests. With his sense of the internal conflicts of organizations, Weber recognizes religious developments as proceeding from the interests of religious elites themselves in struggling for dominance both vis-a-vis each other (in which the outcomes are influenced by the material conditions of church organization, analogous to the principles of political struggle), and in relation to the public and to the state, which makes use of religion in its own struggles.

Weber's underlying theory of status groups is that the means of emotional production affect the organization of interest groups as communities, and serve as resources in social conflict. The means of emotional production include the ecological conditions and material resources that bring people together for emotional encounters, the material resources for putting on ceremonial display, and the resources to communicate and monopolize accumulated techniques for emotional manipulation. Control over these resources means control over people's physical mobility, and over the stage-settings on which they meet. Analogous to what has been said above regarding the means of intellectual production, the means of emotional production determine: a) the formation of groups with varying degrees of internal solidarity; b) the domination of the ceremonial standards of some groups over others, due to their greater resources for putting on emotionally compelling displays, and thus creating an order of prestige. Such communities can be based upon economic classes, and this occurs to the extent that the distribution of the means of emotional production coincides with class lines. But since ecological propinquity and standards of communication (a common language and symbolic tradition) are important means of emotional production, migration or conquest by cultural aliens produces community splits which may cross economic lines, and whose immediately determining variables are in the distribution of the means of emotional production rather than in economics per se. Such cultural solidarities, which are now to be called "ethnic groups," in turn produce continuing conflicts over political and economic goals, and further reinforce lines of cultural distinction. In *The Religion of India* above all, Weber lays down the fundamental of a theory of cultural stratification, upon which the variations of caste, feudal estate, educationocracy, or modern "high society" may be seen as the results of different distributions of the resources for producing status solidarity and domination.

The theory of legitimacy should be read in this light. Empirically, Weber's concept of traditional legitimacy refers to the uses that governments historically have made of religious ceremony in order to manipulate emotional support; rational-legal legitimacy is an appeal to secular ceremonial equivalents. The *goals* of politics remain the struggle for material advantage and power; legitimacy refers to another set of *techniques* to be manipulated in this struggle. The same applies within organizations; Etzioni's category of normative control refers to the manipulation of particular kinds of techniques for emotional solidarity.[41] Goffman, who builds his original model of "frontstage" ceremony and "backstage" solidarity upon the same empirical results of industrial relations research, can be seen as specifying some of the mechanisms by which the production of emotional effects is achieved.[42]

Many of Weber's theoretical propositions have been tested by empirical evidence inadvertently rather than consciously and deliberately. The area of organizations has been ordered, however, around his underlying model of conflict and control under different conditions of administrative and technological resources and means of emotional manipulation. The area of ethnic and other kinds of status communities has been well described in research, but has only recently begun to be subjected to comparative analysis aimed at testing causal propositions. Bonacich formulates principles based upon comparative evidence which bear out the thrust of the above argument, with special emphasis on the types of economic conflicts that sustain ethnic antagonisms.[43] Weber's political sociology has only slowly emerged into broader understanding. Cast in more explicit form, and seen in conjunction with the principles established in the Marxian synthesis, we can find in Weber the development of conflict theory to a considerable level of sophistication.

CONCLUSION

The conflict tradition does not end with Max Weber, but there is room for only the barest sketch of subsequent or even contemporary developments. We have already covered many of the follow-ups of the Marx-Weber line of conflict sociology. Among these, there is the important line of influence in which Michels served as the link between Weber's historical theory of organizational politics and the organizational studies of the 1940's–1960's. Studies of stratification, although often pursued with naive theoretical categories, have gradually accumulated a great deal of evidence bolstering and refining the classical principles explained above; and some work, especially since the time of C. Wright Mills (but not necessarily influenced by him) has made a conscious effort to build on classical theory.

Some other lines of conflict theory must at least be mentioned. The social-psychological tradition of conflict theory originating with Schopenhauer and Nietzsche, of course, has Freud as its most famous representative. This level of analysis, despite various theoretical attempts, has not yet been convincingly related to the organizational/stratification level outlined above, nor has it had as much empirical support. But this social-psychological conflict tradition continues to have great potential importance. It holds out the promise of a model for the shaping of the individual psyche by the emotional and symbolic interchanges involved in struggles for interpersonal advantage to replace the artificially one-sided and relatively static models of psychological learning theory. Its premises move toward replacing adult-centered "socialization" theory with a two-sided view of age conflict under conditions of unequal resources. And when cast in an explicitly historical form, its insights into sexual repression become the basis of a comparative theory of sexual stratification.[44]

Many other interesting figures have been slighted in this brief history. Some, like Simmel and Pareto, appear isolated from the main stream, as they subordinated their insights about conflict to principles which led in quite different directions: neo-Kantian idealism and liberal positivism respectively. Others, like Sorel, came closer to the main line, above all, in Sorel's emphasis that conflict is *the* basis of moral solidarity, a point which resonated with Weber's understanding of group ceremony as the basis of legitimacy and solidarity *precisely* in situations of conflict and domination. From here, the possibility exists for appropriating the main achievements of the Durkheimian tradition—the understanding of the ceremonial bases of social reality-constructing—into a comprehensive conflict theory.

For the arena encompassed by conflict theory is not only the moments of obvious strife in society, but the systematic explanation of the entire social structure. The central focus is on the organization of material arrangements into a system of power which divides society into interest groups struggling for control. Such material conditions operate not only through the sphere of economic production, but also directly condition the mobilization of interest groups for political action, as well as the production of ideas and of emotional ties.We need no longer rest with an abstract assertion of the determination of structure by contending interests with varying material resources; refined principles of conflict theory may explain specific outcomes in all areas of society.

NOTES

1. G.W.F. Hegel, "Introduction to the Philosophy of History," in J. Loewenberg, ed., *Hegel Sections* (New York: Scribner's, 1957), p. 365.

2. Underlying the sudden outpouring of creativity in the German universities, especially in the period 1780–1820, was a structural change. The philosophical faculty, previously only an undergraduate preparation for the higher facilities of theology, medicine, and law, struggled for and finally achieved upgrading to advanced status. The battle centered on the effort to show that preparatory fields could become subjects of scholarship, with the field of classical studies leading the way; the classics seminars at Göttingen and Halle in the late 18th century set the model for critical historical method in other fields.

3. It should be noted that this broad conception of materialism is not equivalent to vulgar positivism, with its claim that only material *objects* exist and that all ideas are impressions of them. Marx himself emphasized (in *Theses on Feuerbach*), rather, that it is human beings as *material subjects* who do thinking—a formulation that enables us to recognize the crucial importance of the material world as a setting for thought, while also keeping conscious thought as an *activity* with a crucial part to play in the material world. This is an especially appropriate viewpoint for a conflict sociology, with its emphasis on active, self-interested maneuvers in the world, in which mental action plays a crucial part, while yet constrained by the material conditions which surround it.The idealist versions of Marxism which have become popular in the mid-20th century are reactions against a rigidly evolutionist economic interpretation of Marx, one that has proven an embarrassment both as a predictive instrument and as a favorite viewpoint of bureaucratic Communist Party interests. A broader materialism, which takes into account the conscious material actor, and does not limit the material world to economic system, is a more fruitful path for recovering the sociological contributions of Marx.

4. Cf. L. Althusser, *Lenin and Philosophy and Other Essays* (London: New Left Books, 1971), pp. 123–73.

188   CONFLICT THEORY

5. Again, we discover that Marx's model has implications, in this case in terms of individual social psychology, which have sociological value outside of the context of his original formulation on the level of the economic system.

6. K. Marx, *The Eighteenth Brumaire of Louis Bonaparte* (New York: International Publishers, 1963).

7. G. E. Lenski, *Power and Privilege: A Theory of Social Stratification* (New York: McGraw-Hill, 1966).

8. P. Cutright, "Inequality: A Cross-National Analysis," *American Sociological Review*, 32 (1967), 562–78.

9. In fact, the Davis-Moore theory, carried to its logical conclusions, does not imply any inequality at all, but the reverse; since it envisions a market for talent flowing to the socially most desirable services, it falls prey to an implication that was explicit in Adam Smith: that the flow of labor supply to areas of greatest demand would tend to produce equality of all wages. (See L. Thomas, *The Occupational Structure and Education,* Englewood Cliffs, N. J.: Prentice-Hall, 1956.) This paradoxical result actually leads to a new application of the Davis-Moore type of theory, although in a different sense than originally intended: if the *pure* tendency of the market is toward equality, then inequalities must indicate areas of *constraint* on the market—which again tends to emphasize the importance of political power in shaping the property and occupational system.

10. A.L. Stinchcombe, "Social Structure and Organizations," in J. G. March, ed., *Handbook of Organizations* (Chicago: Rand McNally, 1965), pp. 162–63.

11. E. Friedson, *Profession of Medicine: A Study of the Sociology of Applied Knowledge* (New York: Dodd, Mead, 1970).

12. R. Quinney, *The Social Reality of Crime* (Boston: Little, Brown, 1970).

13. J. A. Kahl, *The American Class Structure* (New York: Rinehart, 1957); N.D. Glen and J.P. Alston, "Cultural Distances among Occupational Categories," *American Sociological Review*, 33, (1968), 365–82.

14. R. Dahrendorf, *Class and Class Conflict in Industrial Society* (Stanford: Stanford University Press, 1959). It should be stressed, however, that property distinctions *also* exist in modern societies, and continue to influence political attitudes above all; this is important for the difference between socialist and capitalist societies, a difference which Dahrendorf was at pains to obliterate in the *applications* of his theory to contemporary issues.

15. Cf. M. L. Kohn, and C. Schooler, "Class, Occupation, and Orientation," *American Sociological Review*, 34 (1969), 659–78.

16. E.g., S. M. Lipset, *Political Man* (Garden City, N.Y.: Doubleday, 1960), pp. 230–278; W. Korpi, "Working Class Communism in Western Europe: Rational or Nonrational," *American Sociological Review*, 36 (1971), 971–84.

17. It should be apparent that this principle does not stand or fall on predictions of revolutions; that involves not only class attitudes, but also their mobilization, and above all the military weakness of the state. Marx, in another part of his overall system, attempted to tie all of these to an *economic* model predicting economic crises, but that is beside the *sociological* point presented here.

18. B. Moore, Jr., *Social Origins of Dictatorship and Democracy: Lord and Peasant in the Making of the Modern World* (Boston: Beacon Press, 1966).

19. A. L. Stinchcombe, "Agricultural Enterprise and Rural Class Relations," *American Journal of Sociology*, 67 (1961), 165–76.

20. M. Mann, "The Social Cohesion of Liberal Democracy," *American Sociological Review*, 35 (1970), 423–39.

21. M. Pinard, "Mass Society and Political Movements: New Formulation," *American Journal of Sociology*, 73 (1968), 682–90.

22. P. Burnstein, "Social Structure and Individual Political Participation in Five Countries," *American Journal of Sociology*, 77 (1972), 1087–1110; A. Portes, "Political Primitivism, Differential Socialization, and Lower-Class Leftist Radicalism," *American Sociological Review*, 36 (1971), 820–34.

23. G. W. Domhoff, *Who Rules America?* (Englewood Cliffs: Prentice-Hall, 1967); R. Perrucci and I. Pilisuk, "Leaders and Ruling Elites; The Interorganizational Bases of Community Power," *American Sociological Review*, 35 (1970), 1040–56.

24. E. Lieberson, "An Empirical Study of Military-Industrial Linkages," *American Journal of Sociology*, 76 (1971), 562–84.

25. H. J. Gans, *The Urban Villagers,* (New York: Free Press, 1962).

26. W. Breed, "Social Control in the Newsroom," *Social Forces*, 33 (1955), 326–35; G. Tuchman, "Objectivity," *American Journal of Sociology*, 77 (1972), 660–79.

27. P. Bourdieu and J. C. Passeron, *La Reproduction: Eléments pour une Théorie du Système d'Enseignement* (Paris: Editions de Minuit, 1970); R. Collins, "Functional and Conflict Theories of Educational Stratification," *American Sociological Review*, 36 (1971), 1002–19.

28. W. O. Hagstrom, *The Scientific Community* (New York: Basic Books, 1965); J. Ben-David, "Scientific Productivity and Academic Organization in Nineteenth Century Medicine," *American Sociological Review*, 25 (1960), 828–843; J. Ben-David, *The Scientist's Role in Society* (Englewood Cliffs: Prentice-Hall, 1971); J. Ben-David and R. Collins, "Social Factors in the Origins of a New Science: The Case of Psychology," *American Sociological Review*, 31 (1966), 451–63.

29. P. Selznick, *TVA and the Grass Roots* (Berkeley: The University of California Press, 1949); P. Selznick, *The Organizational Weapon: A Study of Bolshevik Strategy and Tactics* (New York: McGraw-Hill, 1952); S. M. Lipset, M. A. Trow and J. S. Coleman, *Union Democracy*, (Garden City, N.Y.: Doubleday, 1956).

30. M. Crozier, *The Bureaucratic Phenomenon* (Chicago: University of Chicago Press, 1964).

31. H. L. Wilensky, *Intellectuals in Labor Unions* (New York: Free Press, 1956).

32. H. L. Wilensky, "The Professionalization of Everyone?" *American Journal of Sociology*, 70 (1964), 137–58.

33. N. Wiley, "America's Unique Class Politics: The Interplay of the Labor, Credit, and Commodity Markets," *American Sociological Review*, 32 (1967), 529–40.

34. See M. Weber, *Economy and Society* (New York: Bedminster Press, 1968), Part II, Chapters 9-16; and the introduction by G. Roth, pp. lxxviii–xciv.

35. These principles have been applied to various historical contexts by R. Bendix, *Nation-Building and Citizenship* (New York: Wiley, 1964); G. Roth, "Personal Rulership, Patrimonialism, and Empire-Building in the New States," in R. Bendix, ed., *State and Society* (Boston: Little, Brown, 1968); W. F. Wertheim "Sociological Aspects of Corruption in Southeast Asia," in Bendix, *State and Society*.

36. G. Roth, "Personal Rulership."

37. A. Etzioni, *A Comparative Analysis of Complex Organizations* (New York: Free Press, 1961).

38. A. Carey, "The Hawthorne Studies: A Radical Criticism," *American Sociological Review*, 32 (1967), 403–417, shows that the so-called "Hawthorne effect" is a myth, and that the original evidence shows that material incentives, not good "human relations," were the effective variables in boosting production.

39. A. W. Gouldner, *Patterns of Industrial Bureaucracy* (New York: Free Press, 1954); M. Dalton, *Men Who Manage* (New York: Wiley, 1959); Crozier, *The Bureaucratic Phenomenon*.

40. Weber, *Economy and Society*, pp. 468–86.

41. Etzioni, *A Comparative Theory*.

42. E. Goffman, *The Presentation of Self in Everyday Life* (Garden City, N.Y.: Doubleday, 1959).

43. E. Bonacich, "A Theory of Ethnic Antagonism: The Split Labor Market," *American Sociological Review*, 37 (1972), 547–559; E. Bonacich, "A Theory of Middleman Minorities," *American Sociological Review*, 38 (1973), 583–94.

44. R. Collins, "A Conflict Theory of Sexual Stratification," *Social Problems*, 19 (1971), 2–21.

A STRATEGY FOR REFORMULATING THE DIALECTICAL AND FUNCTIONAL THEORIES OF CONFLICT

JONATHAN H. TURNER

Reprinted from *Social Forces*, 53 (March 1975). "A Strategy for Reformulating the Dialectical and Functional Theories of Conflict" by Jonathan H. Turner. Copyright © The University of North Carolina Press.

Jonathan Turner is professor of sociology at the University of California, Riverside.

The growing disenchantment with structural-functional theory has been marked by the rise of alternative theoretical perspectives over the last two decades. One of the most conspicuous of these alternatives has been "conflict theory" which has presumably rediscovered for the discipline such phenomena as power, force, coercion, constraint, and change in social systems. Despite the excessive polemics which have often accompanied this rediscovery (Dahrendorf, 1958b; Horowitz, 1962; Lockwood, 1956; Rex, 1961) there have been a number of impressive attempts at developing systems of theoretical statements on certain conflict processes (e.g., Blalock, 1967; Coser, 1967a; Dahrendorf, 1957; Mack and Snyder, 1957; Williams, 1947). One of the drawbacks of this accumulated body of theoretical statements is that attempts at synthesizing, reconciling, and integrating them into a more adequate system of propositions have not been often undertaken. The result is that sets of propositions exist side by side in the literature yet in virtual isolation from one another.

In this paper, I seek to begin redressing this oversight by examining the propositional inventories of two prominent conflict schemes, the functional conflict theory of Lewis Coser (1956, 1957, 1962, 1966, 1967a, 1967b, 1968, 1969a, 1969b) and the dialectical perspective of Ralf Dahrendorf (1957, 1958a, 1958b, 1961, 1967). The functional and dialectical schemes of these thinkers are singled out for examination because they are often presumed to be contradictory; and thus, if some tentative guidelines for synthesis can be suggested for these perspectives, then other conflict schemes should be more readily reconciled—thereby allowing for the development of a more unified theory of conflict processes.

In this effort, I will draw attention to how Coser's and Dahrendorf's assumptions have been translated into highly suggestive propositions. Emphasis is placed upon the respective propositions of these two conflict theorists, because it is in this form that: 1) the causal relations between concepts can be accurately discerned, 2) the points of compatibility and incompatibility between schemes can be readily visualized, and 3) the promise of operationalization and empirical investigation are greatest. Thus, I have chosen to focus on propositions because it is only when assumptions are translated into statements of covariance among explicitly stated variables that theoretical schemes become sufficiently clear to allow for tentative attempts at synthesis. Such a synthesis is, of course, only an uncertain first step in what will be a long process of converting theoretical schemes into propositional inventories, and then, critically examining them to see what they have to offer sociological theory.

DIVERGENT ASSUMPTIONS

In his efforts to direct sociological theory out of a "functional utopia," Dahrendorf has reformulated in even more extreme form some of Marx's key assumptions: 1) social life is typified by opposed interests cohering around differences in the distribution of power; 2) opposed interests will inevitably result in conflict between those who have and do not have power; 3) conflict is dialectical since the resolution of one set of conflict relations establishes the conditions of opposed interests for subsequent conflict; 4) social change ensuing from conflict dialectics is therefore an inevitable feature of social systems.

Much like Dahrendorf, Coser (1967a:141) also views functional theorizing as having "too often neglected the dimensions of power and interest." But in contrast to Dahrendorf, he has not followed Marx's emphasis on conflict dialectics and their consequences for perpetual reorganization of social systems. On the contrary, Coser has sought to correct for Dahrendorf's one-sidedness with another one-sidedness emphasizing the "integrative" and "adaptive" functions of conflict for social systems. In so doing, Coser has been led to embrace many of the organismic assumptions of Simmel's (1955) earlier analysis of conflict: 1) social life tends to be organized into systems, whose interrelated parts reveal imbalances, tensions, and conflict of interests; 2) under different conditions, processes in social systems operate to maintain, change, and increase or decrease not only the system's integration but also its "adaptability"; and 3) some of these processes—notably violence, dissent, deviance, and conflict—can, under certain conditions, strengthen the system's basis of integration as well as its adaptability to the environment.

These two sets of assumptions would both seem one-sided, emphasizing some phenomena while excluding other key processes. As such, they project a seriously distorted vision of social reality. However, such indictments have little meaning when stated at the assumptive level, for one can endlessly argue over assumptions. More meaningful criticism, especially from the point of view of building a theory of conflict, comes when the propositions inspired by these assumptions are examined. For in the end, theoretical disputes can only be resolved at the propositional level.

DIVERGENT PROPOSITIONS

In anticipating the following discussion of Coser's and Dahrendorf's propositions,[1] I should emphasize that while both thinkers at times conceptualize similar variables, they appear at different junctures in their propositional inventories —thus revealing divergent conceptions of the impact of similar variables on the course of conflict. To analyze these difference, I have grouped Coser's and Dahrendorf's propositions under the following headings: 1) the causes of conflict; 2) the intensity of conflict; 3) the violence of conflict; and 4) the outcomes of conflict.[2] While there are some conceptual merits to this ordering of propositions, I think that these headings are too simple and arbitrarily partition interrelated conflict processes. Hence, the grouping of the propositions under these headings follows the intent of both Coser and Dahrendorf. But as I will argue, this ordering creates some conceptual problems in building a theory of conflict.

(1) The Causes of Conflict

In Comparison 1, I have summarized Dahrendorf's and Coser's propositions on the underlying causes of conflict. In their first proposition, both Dahrendorf and Coser assert that the cause of conflict in a social system ultimately resides in the dissatisfaction of the deprived. However, Dahrendorf visualizes this dissatisfaction in terms of awareness of interests, while Coser's analysis focuses on the question of legitimacy. Presumably Dahrendorf would argue that awareness of their true interests would lead the deprived to withdraw legitimacy, while Coser

Comparison 1. The Causes of Conflict

DAHRENDORF	COSER
I. The more members of quasi groups in ICAs can become aware of their objective interests and form a conflict group, the more likely is conflict to occur.	I. The more deprived members of a system question the legitimacy of the existing distribution of scarce resources, the more likely they are to initiate conflict (1956, 1957).

A. The fewer the channels for redressing grievances over the distribution of scarce resources by the deprived, the more likely they are to question legitimacy (1967a).
   1. The fewer internal organizations there are segmenting emotional energies of the members of the deprived, the more likely are deprived groups without grievance alternatives to question legitimacy (1967a).
   2. The greater the ego deprivations of those without grievance channels, the more likely they are to question legitimacy (1967a).
B. The more membership in privileged groups is sought by the deprived, and the less mobility allowed, the more likely they are to withdraw legitimacy (1956).

II. The more deprivations are transformed from absolute to relative, the more likely are the deprived to initiate conflict (1957, 1967b).

A. The less the degree to which socialization experience of the deprived generate internal ego constraints, the more likely they are to experience relative deprivation (1967b).
B. The less the external constraints applied to the deprived, the more likely they are to experience relative deprivation (1967b).

A. The more the technical conditions of organization can be met, the more likely is the formation of a conflict group.
   1. The more a leadership cadre among quasi groups can be developed, the more likely are the technical conditions of organization to be met.
   2. The more a codified idea system, or charter, can be developed, the more likely are the technical conditions of organization to be met.
B. The more the political conditions of organization can be met, the more likely is the formation of a conflict group.
   1. The more the dominant groups permit organization of opposed interests, the more likely are the political conditions of organization to be met.
C. The more the social conditions of organization can be met, the more likely is the formation of a conflict group.
   1. The more opportunity for members of quasi groups to communicate, the more likely are the social conditions of organization to be met.
   2. The more recruiting is permitted by structural arrangements (such as propinquity), the more likely are the social conditions of organization to be met.

would maintain that interests are only laid bare and articulated when the deprived withdraw legitimacy from the system. Now these are more than terminological quibblings, since they have implications for subsequent propositons. If awareness of interests is considered the key causal variable, then additional propositions need only specify the conditions raising levels of awareness. Thus for Dahrendorf, the major theoretical task is to list the "technical," "political," and "social" conditions fostering awareness of deprived groupings' "true interests." In contrast, Coser's first group of propositions addresses the structural conditions which would lead the deprived to question the legitimacy of existing structural arrangements. Coser follows up on this analysis in his second proposition in Comparison 1 by attempting to indicate that the withdrawal of legitimacy, per se, will not necessarily lead to conflict. A threshold of emotional arousal is also necessary, with this threshold being a result of unspecified structures involved in socialization and social control.

Dahrendorf's and Coser's divergent propositions reflect their differing assumptions about the nature of social organization. Dahrendorf's dialectical assumptions lead him to visualize conflict as smoldering just beneath the surface of all structures; and thus, it is to be expected that his propositions will be loaded in the direction of isolating those forces which will merely *release* inherent conflict potential. Coser's more organismic assumptions, borrowed from Simmel, dictate a concern with what forces would be involved in *overcoming* the "inertia" and organic interdependence of the system; and hence, it is likely that his propositions would focus, first of all, on the conditions causing the breakdown of the legitimacy holding the body social together, and then on the conditions causing the sudden mobilization of actors' emotional energies to pursue conflict in the system.

My ordering of the propositions in Comparison 1 is intended to suggest tentative guidelines for synthesis. I believe it is reasonable to hypothesize that conflict initiated by the deprived will be likely only after an initial withdrawal of legitimacy has occurred (Coser's Proposition I). Withdrawal of legitimacy, however, is not sufficient to initiate conflict, for the questioning of legitimacy must also be accompanied by a sudden arousal of the deprived's emotional energies (Coser's Proposition II). Thus, Coser's analysis directs sociologists to seek the causes of conflict in the structural conditions leading to a questioning of legitimacy and a sudden jump in emotional arousal. It also seems reasonable to predict that the conflict ensuing from these conditions will be spontaneous and expressive, lacking in a high degree of organization. Dahrendorf's propositions specify some of the conditions under which conflict will become more organized and instrumental, but I think it likely that the withdrawal of legitimacy and escalating emotions of relative deprivation must precede this organization. For it can be questioned whether mere awareness, even as fanned by technical, political, and social conditions, is enough to induce the deprived to join in costly organized conflict with those in power. In sum, then, by examining Dahrendorf's and Coser's combined propositional formats, it is possible to suggest how different *types* of structural variables lead to different *types* of psychological states among the deprived which in turn, under additional *types* of structural conditions, cause different *types* of conflict. Coser's and Dahrendorf's combined propositions go a long way toward suggesting some of the generic classes or types of variables involved in developing a theory of the causes of conflict in social systems.

(2) The Intensity of Conflict

For Dahrendorf, the concept of intensity refers to the degree of psychological commitment of parties to pursue conflict. While Coser is less explicit, he appears to define intensity in a similar manner. In Comparison 2 I have listed, as in the previous table, Dahrendorf's and Coser's propositions on the conditions promoting intense forms of conflict. For Dahrendorf, the more the conditions of organization are met, the more the distribution of scarce resources are correlated, and the less the mobility of the deprived, the more intense will be the conflict. For Coser, the conditions causing conflict also affect conflict intensity, as is emphasized in his Proposition II on the conditions heightening emotional involvement. Further, Coser's Proposition III appears to parallel Dahrendorf's on the technical conditions found in Comparison 1.

The most striking divergence in Dahrendorf's and Coser's propositions can be seen in Dahrendorf's failure to incorporate propositions into his scheme on emotional involvement as either a cause or a condition leading to greater conflict intensity. As Coser's propositions underscore, emotional involvement is critical in both the initiation and the willingness of the parties to become committed to the conflict. However, Coser apparently fails to make explicit the feedback of different types of conflict, for it can be hypothesized that, once initiated, conflict intensity will be necessary for Dahrendorf's conditions of social organization to be met. Thus, intensity of conflict is as much a cause as an effect of the technical, political, and social conditions of organization. Individuals are not likely to be moved by technical, political, and social conditions of organization to form conflict groups unless their questioning of legitimacy and escalated sense of relative deprivation (see Comparison 1) is sufficient to generate an emotionally charged commitment to and willingness to be involved in *organized* efforts at conflict.

Comparison 2. The Intensity of Conflict

DAHRENDORF	COSER
I. The more the technical, political, and social conditions of organization are met, the more intense is the conflict.	I. The more the conditions causing the outbreak of conflict are realized, the more intense the conflict (1967a).
	II. The greater the emotional involvement of members in a conflict, the more intense the conflict (1956).

    A. The more primary the relations among parties to a conflict, the more emotional involvement (1956).
      1. The smaller the primary groups where conflict occurs, the more emotional the involvement (1956).
      2. The more primary the relations among parties, the less likely the open expression of hostility, but the more intense the expression in a conflict situation (1956).
    B. The more secondary relations among parties to a conflict, the more segmental their participation and the less emotional involvement (1956).
      1. The more secondary relations, the more frequent the conflict, but the less the emotional involvement (1956).
      2. The larger the secondary group, the more frequent the conflict, but the less the emotional involvement (1956).

                III. The more conflicts are objectified above and beyond individual self-interest, the more intense the conflict (1956).

    A. The more ideologically unified a group, the more conflicts transcend self-interest (1956).
      1. The more ideologically unified is a group, the more common are the goals of a group, and the more they transcend individual self-interest (1956).
      2. The more ideologically unified is a group, the more will conflicts be entered with a clear conscience, and the more they transcend individual self-interest (1956).

II. The more the distribution of authority and other rewards are associated with each other (superimposed), the more intense is the conflict.

III. The less the mobility between super- and subordinate groups, the more intense is the conflict.

Coser's propositions in Comparison 2 on the structural conditions leading to emotional involvement thus provide a further specification of the causes of organized conflict, since they give a tentative indication of the structural conditions necessary for emotionally aroused individuals to seek further organization. In turn, as Dahrendorf's proposition on the conditions of organization (Comparison 1) emphasizes, a given level of organization can increase intensity as conflict groups become ideologically unified, develop clear leadership structures, and actively recruit members.

Thus, a theory of conflict must analyze conflict processes over time by focusing on the conditions leading to the withdrawal of legitimacy, the escalation of relative deprivations, the initial increase in conflict intensity, the organization of conflict groups, and the subsequent increases (or decreases) in conflict intensity. Only in this way can the causes of different types of conflicts be understood. Figure 1 is an attempt to use Dahrendorf's and Coser's combined propositional legacy on causes and intensity to develop a tentative model describing the major classes or types of variables, and the sequential and feedback relations among them, which will need to be incorporated into a theory on the causes of conflict. The arrows connecting the seven stages of conflict denote the key causal chains in the initiation of conflict. These causal relations could be phrased propositionally, but my efforts are so tentative that they can be adequately expressed diagrammatically. Some of the key propositions denoted by the arrows in Figure 1, which are not given sufficient attention in Coser's and Dahrendorf's inventories, concern the feedback relations among variables at different stages of conflict. As I have represented in Figure 1, stages 5, 6, and 7 are particularly critical for stages 2, 3, and 4, feeding back and accelerating the withdrawal of legitimacy, the aware-

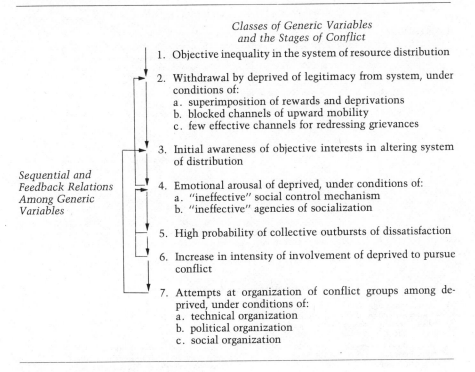

*Classes of Generic Variables
and the Stages of Conflict*

*Sequential and
Feedback Relations
Among Generic
Variables*

1. Objective inequality in the system of resource distribution

2. Withdrawal by deprived of legitimacy from system, under conditions of:
   a. superimposition of rewards and deprivations
   b. blocked channels of upward mobility
   c. few effective channels for redressing grievances

3. Initial awareness of objective interests in altering system of distribution

4. Emotional arousal of deprived, under conditions of:
   a. "ineffective" social control mechanism
   b. "ineffective" agencies of socialization

5. High probability of collective outbursts of dissatisfaction

6. Increase in intensity of involvement of deprived to pursue conflict

7. Attempts at organization of conflict groups among deprived, under conditions of:
   a. technical organization
   b. political organization
   c. social organization

Figure 1. The causes of conflict.

ness of interests, and the emotional deprivation which will cause both spontaneous outbursts and the resulting increases in intensity of commitment ultimately driving the deprived to become organized to pursue conflict.

(3) The Violence of Conflict

As Dahrendorf makes explicit, violence denotes the degree of combativeness between parties to a conflict. Coser is less explicit in his formulation of the violence dimension in conflict, but it is nevertheless possible to isolate some propositions which pertain to conditions under which conflict will be violent. In Comparison 3, I have listed as in previous tables, the propositions developed by Dahrendorf and Coser with respect to the violence of conflict.

Dahrendorf's Proposition I restates the conclusion reached in the discussion of the causes of conflict: if the technical, political, and social conditions of organization cannot be met, conflict will be less structured and regulated. But why should it be violent, involving open combat between the privileged and deprived? Dahrendorf then specifies a proposition on relative deprivation which Coser included in his analysis of the causes of conflict. Thus, for Dahrendorf, conflict will be violent when the parties are emotionally aroused, the conditions of organization are not met, and as Proposition III indicates, the conflicting parties cannot develop regulatory agreements. What Dahrendorf fails to recognize in these propositions is that emotional arousal is also necessary for the conditions of organization to be met (see earlier discussion) and that unregulated conflict need not necessarily be violent. Coser's propositions provide more insight into what structural conditions would make violent conflict more likely. For Coser, whether conflict is over objective interests represents an important set of conditions fa-

Comparison 3. The Violence of Conflict

DAHRENDORF	COSER

I. The less the technical, political, and social conditions of organization are met, the more violent is the conflict.

    I. The more groups engage in conflicts over their realistic (objective) interests, the less violent the conflict (1956).

      A. The more groups conflict over realistic interests, the more likely they are to seek compromises over means to realize their interests (1956).
        1. The greater the power differentials between the groups in conflict, the less likely alternative means are to be sought (1956).
        2. The more rigid the system where conflict occurs, the less availability of alternative means (1956).

    II. The more groups conflict over nonrealistic issues (false interests), the more violent the conflict (1956).

      A. The more conflict occurs over nonrealistic issues, the greater the emotional involvement of the parties in the conflict, and the more intense the conflict (1956).
        1. The more intense previous conflict between groups, the greater the emotional involvement in subsequent conflicts (1956, 1967a).
      B. The more rigid the system where conflict occurs, the more likely is the conflict to be nonrealistic (1957).
      C. The more realistic conflict endures, the more nonrealistic issues emerge (1956, 1967c).
      D. The more the conflicting groups have emerged for purposes of conflict, the more nonrealistic the subsequent conflicts (1956).

II. The more the deprivations of the subjugated over the distribution of rewards shift from an absolute to relative basis of deprivation, the more violent is the conflict.

III. The less the ability of conflict groups to develop regulatory agreements, the more violent the conflict.

    III. The more rigid the social structure, the less will be the availability of institutionalized means for absorbing conflict and tensions, and the more violent the conflict (1956).

      A. The more primary the relations among parties where conflict occurs, the more rigid the structure (1956).
        1. The less stable the primary relations, the more rigid the structure of those relations (1956).
        2. The more stable the primary relations, the less rigid the structure of those relations (1956).
      B. The more secondary (based on functional interdependence) the relations among parties where conflict occurs, the more likely are institutionalized means for absorbing conflict and tensions, and the less violent the conflict (1956).
      C. The greater the control mechanism of the system, the more rigid the structure and the more intense the conflict (1957).

    IV. The more the conflict in a group occurs over core values and issues, the more violent the conflict (1956).

      A. The more rigid the structure where conflict occurs, the more likely is conflict to occur over core values and issues (1956).
      B. The more emotional involvement in a situation where conflict occurs, the more likely it is to occur over core values and issues (1956).

cilitating or inhibiting violence. Dahrendorf recognizes this condition in his discussion of how awareness of true interests is a result of the conditions of organization being met. But Coser specifies additional conditions which can supplement Dahrendorf's limited discussion. Furthermore, Coser's inventory has already incorporated the relative deprivation hypothesis at a more appropriate place in the overall inventory of propositions on conflict (see Comparison 1 and Figure 1). Also, Coser's inventory specifies some of the conditions under which Dahrendorf's "regulatory agreements" inhibiting violent conflict will be likely to emerge between conflict parties. And finally, Coser places more significance on the impact of values on conflict—a variable Dahrendorf only implicitly acknowledges in discussion of the technical conditions of organization.

Thus, for both Coser and Dahrendorf the degree of organization of the conflict parties, the capacity of the more inclusive system to institutionalize conflict relations, and the ability of conflict parties to articulate their interests independently of core values will influence the degree of violence in the conflict between the deprived and privileged. In turn, these variables are influenced by those variables first initiating conflict relations as well as by a series of only partially specified structural arrangements of the system in which the conflict occurs. In Figure 2, I have again sought to represent diagrammatically the classes of variables and the general types of interrelations among them which the Dahrendorf and Coser schemes offer a theory of conflict violence. Figure 2 should be visualized as an extension of the variables and interrelations outlined in Figure 1. As indicated in Figure 2, attempts at organization (stage 7 in Figure 1) will result in conflict of varying degrees of violence, depending upon a series of causally related conditions. In turn these conditions display both sequential and feedback relations which need to be incorporated into propositions on conflict violence.

(4) The Outcomes of Conflict

I have listed as in earlier tables Dahrendorf's and Coser's propositions on the outcomes of conflict in Comparison 4. For Dahrendorf, the only outcome of conflict is social change, with only the amount and the rate of such change visualized as varying. In contrast, Coser has developed propositions on integrative and adaptive outcomes of conflict for both the parties to a conflict and the social whole within which the conflict occurs. In the first group of propositions conflict can cause a shoring up of group boundaries, centralization of decision-making, ideological solidarity, and increased social control. As with previous propositions, these events occur only under specified conditions, including the degree of rigidity and differentiation in social structure, the intensity of the conflict, and the extent to which conflict is perceived to affect all factions of the group. Of particular interest is the fact that only in Proposition IV-A is there a clear statement about the potential dysfunctions of conflict for each respective conflict group. Furthermore, in this particular inventory it is not immediately evident that stating the inverse of the propositions would reveal the conditions under which conflict would lead to disintegration of conflict groups. For example, taking Proposition III, it would be difficult to maintain that if all group members did not perceive the conflict as affecting them, ideological disunity or some other less positively functional state would be forthcoming. Clearly, additional propositions would be necessary to establish the conditions under which less benign outcomes could be expected. Thus, by choosing to focus primarily on the *positive functions*

Classes of Generic Variables

7. Attempts at organization of conflict groups among deprived

	8a. More violent conflict, under conditions of:	8b. Less violent conflict, under conditions of:
Sequential and Feedback Relations Variables	a. failure to realize technical, political, and social conditions of organization.	a. capacity to realize technical, political, and social conditions of organization.
	b. failure to define clearly true interests, independently of core values.	b. articulation of true interests, independently of core values.
	c. incapacity of inclusive system to regularize conflict relations.	c. capacity of system to regularize conflict relations.

Figure 2. The degree of violence in conflict.

or *outcomes* of conflict for social integration, the net effect of the propositions as they now stand is to convey an overly integrated view of the social world, even in the face of open conflict among groups.

This unfortunate connotation is buttressed by Propositions V through IX in which conflict in loosely structured systems is seen as promoting integration, innovation, creativity, release of hostilities, and attention of elites to system maladjustments. Furthermore, under conditions of conflict frequency and intensity, conflict can promote varying degrees and types of equilibrium, normative regulation, and associative coalitions. While the inverse of some of these propositions perhaps reveals a few of the conditions promoting disequilibrium, anomie, and antagonisms among subgroups, the propositions still remain overly loaded in the direction of emphasizing system integration and adaptability.

In reviewing Coser's and Dahrendorf's propositions on the outcomes of conflict, then, I think that the one-sidedness of their assumptions about the social world has greatly diminished the power of their propositional inventories. We may applaud Coser and Dahrendorf for undertaking an analysis of conflict outcomes, but the two schemes ignore more than they include. Probably the most obvious problem with these propositions is that they fail to conceptualize adequately the conditions under which conflicts of varying degrees of violence cause certain outcomes in the short and long run for both conflict parties and the more inclusive system. For example, does violent conflict always result in rapid change of a system? It is clear that such a proposition would hold true only under conditions which would have to specify the causal impact of such variables as the duration of the violence, the repressive powers of the privileged, the nature and composition of the deprived who initiate the conflict, the issues over which the conflict is fought, the values involved to justify the violence, and so on. Coser's propositions would seem to provide a list of variables influencing outcomes; but unfortunately the variables of "intensity" and "violence" are not clearly defined in this context. Hence, the propositions on outcomes are not systematically linked to the conditions causing conflict of varying degrees of violence. To take another example from Dahrendorf's analysis of outcomes: Does organized conflict of high intensity necessarily lead to "more structural change"? Or, could not the regularization of conflict among highly organized groups result in forms of competition which maintain the status quo? This possibility is, of course, the point to be emphasized by Coser's propositions, and a number of suggestive variables are introduced to explain when such an outcome is likely. But Coser's inventory again raises as many theoretical questions as it answers. For example, does frequent and violent conflict in flexible social systems which have clear-cut mechanisms for regulating conflict lead to change? or to counter reactions maintaining the status quo? And could one objectively describe either outcome as increasing integration or adaptability?

These, then, are the kinds of problems presented by Coser's and Dahrendorf's propositions on the outcomes of conflict. Seemingly, the one-sided assumptions underlying their analysis forced *evaluative* conclusions about the desirable outcomes of conflict—for Coser, integration and adaptability, and for Dahrendorf, social change and reorganization. As such, the analysis of outcomes is not easily connected to their more interesting analysis of the causes of conflicts of varying degrees of violence. Thus, in contrast to Coser's and Dahrendorf's propositions on the causes, the intensity, and the violence of conflict, I do not think that the propositions on outcomes suggest any leads for synthesis. Coser provides a suggestive list of variables: but no clear causal relations can be inferred from this list because they are not clearly linked to the conditions affecting the causes and violence of conflict. And yet, Coser's propositions do have an intuitive plausibility, as they apparently did for Simmel. Indeed, it does seem that conflict groups do become clearly bounded, more centralized, and more ideologically unified and

Comparison 4. The Outcome of Conflict

DAHRENDORF

I.   The more intense the conflict, the more structural change and reorganization it will generate.
II. The more violent the conflict, the greater the rate of structural change and reorganization.

COSER

I.   The more intense the conflict, the more clear-cut the boundaries of each respective conflict party (1956).
II. The more intense the conflict and the more differentiated the division of labor of each conflict party, the more likely each is to centralize its decision-making structure (1956).
   A. The more intense the conflict, the less differentiated the structure and the less stable the structure and internal solidarity, the more centralization is despotic (1956).
III. The more intense the conflict and the more it is perceived to affect all segments of each group, the more conflict promotes structural and ideological solidarity among members of respective conflict groups (1956).
IV. The more primary the relations among members of respective conflict groups, and the more intense the conflict, the more conflict leads to suppression of dissent and deviance within each conflict group and to forced conformity to norms and values (1956).
   A. The more conflict between groups leads to forced conformity, the more the accumulation of hostilities and the more likely internal group conflict in the long run (1956).
V.   The less rigid the social structure where conflict between groups occurs and the more frequent and less intense the conflict, the more likely is conflict to change the system in ways promoting adaptability and integration (1956).
   A. The less rigid the system, the more likely is conflict to promote innovation and creativity in the system (1957).
   B. The less rigid the system, the less likely is conflict to involve displacement of hostilities to alternative objects and the more likely is conflict to confront realistic sources of tension (1956, 1967a).
      1. The more a system is based on functional interdependence, and the more frequent and less intense the conflict, the more likely it is to release tensions without polarizing the system (1956).
      2. The more stable the primary relations in a system, and the more frequent and less intense is the conflict, the more likely it is to release tensions without polarizing the system, but not to the extent of a system based on secondary relations (1956).
   C. The less rigid the system, the more likely is conflict to be perceived by those in power as signals of maladjustment that need to be addressed (1966, 1967a).
VI. The more frequently conflict occurs, the less likely it is to reflect dissensus over core values and the more functional for maintaining equilibrium it is likely to be (1956).
   A. The more a conflict group can appeal to the core values of a system, the less likely the conflict to create dissensus over these values and the more likely it is to promote integration of the system (1968).
   B. The more a conflict group does not advocate extreme interpretations of core values, the less likely a counterconflict group to form and the less disruptive the conflict for the system (1968).
VII. The more frequent and less intense are conflicts, the more likely they are to promote normative regulation of conflict.
   A. The less rigid a system, the more frequent and less intense the conflict (1956, 1957).
      1. The less rigid the system, the more likely conflict is to revitalize existent norms (1956).

(continued)

Comparison 4—Continued

    2. The less rigid the system, the more likely conflict is to generate new norms.
  B. The more frequent and less intense conflicts, the more likely are groups to centralize in an effort to promote conformity of each group's membership to norms governing the conflict (1956).
    1. The more equal the power of conflict groups, the more likely is conflict to generate centralization promoting normative conformity (1956).
VIII. **The less rigid system, the more likely it is that conflict can establish balances and hierarchies of power in a system (1956).**
  A. The less knowledge of the adversary's strength and the fewer the indexes of such strength, the more likely is conflict between two groups vying for power to promote a balance of power relations in a system (1956).
IX.   **The less rigid the system, the more likely is conflict to cause formation of associative coalitions that increase the cohesiveness and integration of the system (1956).**
  A. The more other parties in a system are threatened by coalitions of other parties, the more likely they are to form associative coalitions (1956).
  B. The more a system is based on functional interdependence, the more likely coalitions are to be instrumental and less enduring (1956).
    1. The more a system reveals crosscutting cleavages, the more likely groups in a coalition are to have their own conflicts of interests, and the more likely is the coalition to be instrumental (1956).
    2. The more a coalition is formed for purely defensive purposes, the more likely it is to be instrumental (1956).
  C. The more tightly structured and primary the relations in a system, the more likely coalitions are to develop common norms and values and form a more permanent group (1956).
    1. The more coalitions are formed of individuals (or more generally, the smaller the units forming a coalition), the more likely they are to develop into a permanent group (1956).
    2. The more interaction required among the parties of a coalition, the more likely it is to form a permanent group (1956).

---

that frequent conflicts between such groups in less rigid systems do increase the level of system integration. Or, as hypothesized in Dahrendorf's analysis, extensive and perhaps rapid structural change will ensue from conflict between groups of varying degrees of organization in rigidly structured systems. But these propositions represent only crude hypotheses which will require considerably more refinement through delineation of the conditions under which violent or nonviolent, long or short, and frequent or infrequent conflict among variously organized groups over differing issues variously charged by values in systems of varying degrees and forms of rigidity influence diverse outcomes, including change, stasis, reaction, integration, or adaptability. It is to the specification of the causal relations among at least these variables, so conspicuous in Coser's and Dahrendorf's inventories, that true theoretical synthesis must be directed.

CONCLUSIONS

In this paper I have tried to bring together the disparate and yet suggestive propositions of Coser's and Dahrendorf's continuing work on conflict processes. In focusing on their propositions, I hope that I have avoided the tendency to debate the assumptions from which the propositions are derived, since sociological theorizing has too long argued over assumptions about the relative degrees of conflict, consensus, change, stasis, equilibrium, and disequilibrium in social systems. The more important task of theory is to begin to specify the conditions under which different events can be expected to occur. Dahrendorf and Coser have provided an important set of theoretical statments on the conditions under which conflict of varying degrees of violence is likely. By not focusing on their divergent assumptions, but rather on the propositions these inspire, we may achieve considerably more theoretical pay-off.

In Dahrendorf's and Coser's works, the Marxian and Simmelian legacy has been recast in an important list of theoretical statements that complement not only each other, but also inventories developed elsewhere. These tentative suggestions for synthesis with respect to the causes and violence of conflict can, I hope, provide some clues as to how a more adequate set of theoretical statements on conflict processes can be developed. If the combined inventories of Coser's and Dahrendorf's propositions still seem sparse and inadequate to the task of explaining even some conflict processes, I suspect that other schemes will appear the same when boiled down to their generic propositions. This inadequacy is the result of an unwillingness by theorists to integrate, reconcile, and synthesize their inventories so as to create a more comprehensive body of theoretical statements on conflict processes. Until this difficult task is more frequently undertaken, the propositions of any one conflict theorist, whether Dahrendorf, Coser, or anyone else, will continue to appear impoverished.

And thus, the substance of this paper is perhaps less important than the strategy advocated: *to examine propositional inventories and to seek reconciliation at this level.* For only by focusing on explicit propositions will a body of true sociological theory be possible. While few would argue with such a platitude, its dictates have not always been translated into vigorous theoretical activity.

NOTES

1. One drawback to Coser's propositional inventory is that it has never been delineated in a formal or logical format. Rather, the propositions appear in a number of discursive essays and in his analysis of Simmel's essay on conflict. While each discrete proposition is usually stated quite clearly, it is often necessary to interpret with some danger of misinterpretation the exact interrelationships among the various propositions. This fact makes the attempt at a systematic presentation of Coser's propositions an *ad hoc* exercise that may do injustice to some propositions and over- (or under-) estimate Coser's intended significance of others. Dahrendorf's propositions have been rephrased so as to facilitate comparison with Coser's. However, the rephrasing has not in any way distorted their intended meaning. The propositions were taken from Dahrendorf's most formal statement of his "theory" (1957:236–40). See also Turner (1974b).

2. One of the problems with both Coser's and Dahrendorf's theoretical schemes is their extremely broad and vague definitions of conflict. For example, Dahrendorf uses the term "conflict" for examining "contests, competitions, disputes, and tensions as well as for manifest clashes between social forces" (1957:135). Coser's definition is equally inclusive. This failure to define more specifically the key variable in their theories makes it difficult to know just *what type* of conflict is being addressed in a particular set of propositions.

REFERENCES

Blalock, Hubert M. *Toward a Theory of Minority Group Relations.* New York: Wiley, 1967.

Coser, Lewis A. *The Functions of Social Conflict.* New York: Free Press, 1956.

———. "Social Conflict and the Theory of Social Change," *British Journal of Sociology,* 8 (September 1957), 197–207.

———. "Some Functions of Deviant Behavior and Normative Flexibility," *American Journal of Sociology,* 68 (September 1962), 172–81.

———. "Social Functions of Violence," *Annals of the American Academy of Political and Social Science,* 364 (March 1966), 8–18.

———. *Continuities in the Study of Social Conflict.* New York: Free Press, 1967. (a)

———. "Violence and the Social Structure," in Lewis A. Coser, ed., *Continuities in the Study of Social Conflict.* New York: Free Press, 1967. (b)

———. "The Functions of Dissent." in Lewis A. Coser, ed., *The Dynamics of Dissent.* New York: Grune & Stratton, 1968.

———. "The Visibility of Evil," *Journal of Social Issues,* 25 (Winter 1969), 101–09. (a)

——. "Unanticipated Conservative Consequences of Liberal Theorizing," *Social Problems*, 16 (Summer 1969), 263–72. (b)

Dahrendorf, Ralf. *Class and Class Conflict in Industrial Society*. Stanford: Stanford University Press, 1957.

——. "Toward a Theory of Social Conflict," *Journal of Conflict Resolution*, 2 (June 1958). (a)

——. "Out of Utopia: Toward a Reorientation of Sociological Analyses," *American Journal of Sociology*, 64 (September 1958), 115–27. (b)

——. *Gesellschaft und Freidheit*. Munich: Piper, 1961.

——. *Essays in the Theory of Society*. Stanford: Stanford University Press, 1967.

Horowitz, I. L. "Consensus, Conflict and Cooperation: A Sociological Inventory," *Social Forces*, 41 (December 1962), 117–88.

Lockwood, D. "Some Remarks on 'The Social System,' " *British Journal of Sociology*, 7 (June 1956), 134–46.

Mack, R. W., and R. C. Snyder. "The Analysis of Social Conflict—Toward an Overview and Synthesis," *Journal of Conflict Resolution*, 1 (January 1957).

Rex, John. *Key Issues in Sociological Theory*. London: Routledge & Kegan Paul, 1961.

Simmel, Georg. "Conflict," in K. H. Wolff, trans., *Conflict and the Web of Group Affiliations*. Glencoe, Ill.: Free Press, 1955.

Turner, Jonathan H. *The Structure of Sociological Theory*. Homewood, Ill.: Dorsey, 1974. (a)

——. "From Utopia to Where? A Critique of the Dahrendorf Conflict Model," *Social Forces*, 52 (December 1974), 236–44. (b)

Williams, Robin M., Jr. *The Reduction of Intergroup Tensions: A Survey of Research on Problems of Ethnic, Racial, and Religious Group Relations*. New York: Social Science Research Council, 1947.

FROM CONFLICT THEORY TO CONFLICT METHODOLOGY: AN EMERGING PARADIGM FOR SOCIOLOGY

TIMOTHY LEHMANN
AND
T. R. YOUNG

Reprinted from *Sociological Inquiry*, 44 (1974), 15–28. Used by permission.

Timothy Lehmann is associate professor and director of program evaluation, Office of Research and Evaluation, Empire State College, Saratoga Springs, New York. T. R. Young teaches at Colorado State University and is director of The Red Feather Institute.

When we first began to develop our ideas on conflict methodology, we had not considered the broader context of conflict methodology in terms of the development of American sociology, the rise of the post-industrial society and the particularly explosive events of the 1960's. Since that time we have been expanding the scope of our ideas about conflict methodology and would like to lay out the significance of conflict methodology in the broader social context.

We have been influenced by Kuhn's *The Structure of Scientific Revolutions* and Friedrichs' application of Kuhn's basic ideas to life cycle of sociology as a science (Kuhn, 1962; Friedrichs, 1970). Agreeing with Kuhn and Friedrichs that the development of American sociology is not a linear accumulation of one verified hypothesis after another, we propose that contemporary sociology has entered a revolutionary period of scientific development that transcends the functionalist paradigm—the normal science of the past several generations of sociologists.

It is our position that sociology is entwined in a revolutionary crisis with its past paradigm. At present, a state of paradigmatic anarchy has developed. Crucial problems confront the discipline that no longer can be resolved with past theories and past research methods. The functionalist paradigm and allied consensus methodologies have reached the end of their creative usefulness. The talents and skills of a new generation of sociologists are needed to reinvigorate conflict theory which, when linked up with strategies and tactics of conflict methodology, offers an alternative paradigm and a new set of standards to meet the theoretical and empirical tasks that lie ahead of the profession.

SOCIOLOGICAL PARADIGMS: NORMAL AND REVOLUTIONARY SCIENCE

A paradigm is the fundamental image of a discipline's subject matter. Normal science proceeds within the confines of a single paradigm that has been sufficiently compelling to shape a discipline's sense of where its problems lie, what its appropriate methods are, and what kinds of solutions are possible. A paradigm, then, is grasped before a conceptual schema, a theory, or a set of methodological postulates are articulated. Without such a paradigmatic foundation, all problems, all methods, all facts and all criteria for identifying solutions are likely to appear equally relevant.

Kuhn argues that paradigms are shattered as fundamental anomalies between hard empirical data and paradigm-derived theories and methods appear and persist. When anomalies first arise, they usually are treated as counter-instances that require adjustment of the old paradigm. Difficult evidence by itself does not trigger the rejection of a paradigm. If the anomalies resist resolution, the focus of attention will shift to meet the problems inherent in the old paradigm. The stage is set then for the introduction of a new paradigm, an acceptable alternative to the old one which resolves the serious anomalies plaguing it and which presents a new jigsaw puzzle as the normal science for the next generation of students. This is the point of the present paper: to push the dialectic of science in the direction of a new, more productive paradigm.

Revolutionary science manifests a sharp break from normal science. There is no longer a clearcut path to guide one's choice of problems and corresponding methods. Hypotheses that might have been rejected at other times as extravagant are condoned; the scientific arena—professional meetings, the journals, etc.—are filled with dissent. The actual revolution occurs, however, only when an alternate paradigm is ready and its advocates and supporters are sufficiently coherent. This is a revolution in the sense that the new paradigm is incompatible with its predecessor and there is no framework that will encompass and mediate between the two. It is also revolutionary in that the acceptance of a new paradigm is likely to call forth a new definition of the discipline itself. Old answers will be discarded as unscientific or relegated to the gray zone of applied science. Methods and tools will change as well as the standards and criteria for identifying solutions (Kuhn, 1962: Chaps. 9 and 10; Lakatos and Musgrave, 1970).

Contrasting Paradigms in the Development of Sociology

When we examine the development of American sociology during the twentieth century, we find that certain paradigms have presented sociology with its key theoretical tasks and that related styles of sociological training have dominated the discipline. Drawing upon the work of Mills (1959), Coser (1956), Hinkle and Hinkle (1954), Friedrichs (1970), Bramson (1961), Martindale (1960), and others, we can categorize the paradigms of twentieth-century sociology into four periods.

(1) *Pre-paradigm—prophetic period (1890–1920).* The first period was dominated by the concerns of the prophetic reformers. The first generation of sociologists saw themselves as reformers, as activists and advocates not only of a newly emerging academic discipline but as major spokesmen on the problems of American society engulfed by waves of immigrants, by a major world war, and by turmoil in the cities as urbanization and industrialization continued. For many of these sociologists, social conflict provided the central explanatory orientation for the analysis of social change and of progress (Hinkle and Hinkle, 1954: Ch. 1; Coser, 1956: 16–19). The fathers of American sociology were troubled by the social problems of their day and sought melioristic solutions. They held an image of science as an instrument of social reform and were optimistic that sociology could make a contribution to a more intelligent reordering of human affairs. In the writings of Ward, Veblen, Ross, Small and Cooley, social conflict was an inherent and constructive part of all social organization. This generation of activist sociologists stressed the need for basic structural reforms rather than piecemeal adjustment to existing societal requirements.

(2) *The quest for a scientific sociology (1920–1940).* Although the Chicago School, notably under the influence of Park, Ogburn, and Wirth, continued the orientation of the first generation of sociologists into the second period, the conflict perspective lost its central place. To secure sociology within the walls of the university as a scientific discipline, this generation of sociologists addressed themselves to academic and professional rather than reformist audiences and

sought support for research activities from government agencies and private foundations.

Perhaps Lundberg's positivist position most clearly and strongly indicates the shift away from the first period. Lundberg argued that sociologists as scientists should in no way make value judgments in their work; instead they should be objective and politically neutral. Using the natural sciences as models, sociologists must concentrate on discovering empirical uniformities that could be used to predict and control empirical phenomena. Lundberg and a new generation of sociologists ushered in a neopositivist era, stressing the utility of a social science modeled upon investigations in the natural sciences where attitude scales, opinion thermometers and operationally defined concepts would achieve the maximum predictive value (Lundberg, 1947).

A second line of work at a more theoretical level also marked the transition from the conflict perspective to the functionalist paradigm of the third period. We find sociologists during this time focusing on problems of stability and social order, upon the maintenance of existing structures and the mechanisms to insure their smooth functioning. Perhaps the capstone work of this genre was Parsons' *The Structure of Social Action*, published in 1937, which sought the laws of social order and cohesion. Parsons viewed conflict as primarily disruptive, dysfunctional, and a kind of social disease which should be dealt with therapeutically (Parsons, 1954; Coser, 1956: 160).

Coser points out an important shift in orientation from the first period by noting changes in terminology launched by Parsons and picked up by Mayo, Warner, Lundberg, and Roethlisberger among others. Instead of discussing social conflict, class conflict, and social change, we find a substitution of system language couched in medical metaphors using such labels as tensions, strains, psychological malfunctioning, disequilibrium, and disintegration. Conflict thus became a phenomenon exclusively disruptive, negative, and dissociative—a phenomenon to be contained and reduced.

(3) *The consolidation of the functionalist paradigm (1940–1960)*. This period saw the consolidation of the functionalist paradigm through the training and work of several generations of sociologists led by Parsons, Merton, Davis, Levy, Williams, Selznick, Moore, Gouldner, Lipset, and Blau. Adding to the frame developed in 1937, Parsons and his colleagues produced three more volumes in the early 1950's which provided the model of a morphostatic system for the discipline (Parsons, 1951a, 1951b, 1953). Reinforcing the functionalist paradigm after World War II was the development of survey research, cybernetics, and the electronic computer. Social theorists and methodologists were quick to see the potentials of these devices to reinforce the system-like qualities of the discipline: simulation studies, game theory, and cybernetic modeling allowed sociologists to use conceptual and technical tools of similar precision to those of the natural sciences. Daniel Bell pronounced all was well at the end of the decade with his appropriately titled work, *The End of Ideology* (1959).

The normal science of the post World War II period was clearly that of the functionalist paradigm. Such issues as power, valuable and irreducible conflict as well as basic change were not easily contained by the paradigm and were put aside as the price paid for clarity of focus. Explicit dedication to value neutrality made the commitment of the sociologist to his science complete. By the end of this period sociology was a firmly established scientific discipline possessing its own body of knowledge.

(4) *Toward a conflict paradigm (1960–1973)*. The conservative functionalist paradigm was challenged during this period. The major anomaly resisting solution was fundamental social conflict and change. What was striking about the news events of this period was the rise of massive social conflict. The civil rights

movement and the drive for human equality, the Cuban missile crisis and the breakup of the Cold War ideology, the Vietnam War and ensuing antiwar movement, the revelations of the Pentagon Papers, Project Camelot, and the ITT affair, and the manipulating role of corporate organizations in the political arena—all typify events that required basic change in the fabric of society (Lowi, 1971). The underlying significance of these movements was the fact that they were manipulated and controlled by the managerial cadre in large-scale organizations who were responsible for the policies of the welfare state, the warfare state, and the dramaturgical society (Young, 1972).

The 1960's provided a decade of debate over alternative paradigms to the functionalist one. (For a review of these efforts, see Friedrichs, 1970: 36–45; Gouldner, 1970.) There are at least five types of evidence that lead us to believe a conflict paradigm will emerge as the dominant paradigm in the years ahead. First, a wave of "radical" and conflict sociology texts, readers, and other publications have appeared on the market (Colfax and Roach, 1971; Hampden-Turner, 1970; Deutsch and Howard, 1970; Horowitz, 1971; Kriesberg, 1973; Oberschall, 1973; and special issues of *Sociological Inquiry*, 1970, and *American Journal of Sociology*, 1972). Second, younger sociologists have brought their pervasive discontent with the functionalist paradigm before ASA meetings and the discipline's journals. Starting in 1967, activist sociologists have sought Association approval of various resolutions on the war, civil rights, violations of academic freedom, etc. (Nicolaus, 1969; Brown, 1970; Colfax, 1970). Furthermore, in 1970 a new journal, *The Insurgent Sociologist*, was established as an outlet for ideas of those sociologists unhappy with the discipline's past paradigms. Third, certain more established sociologists such as Gouldner (1970), Friedrichs (1970), Birnbaum (1971), and others (Demerath and Peterson, 1967; Becker and Horowitz, 1972) have written seminal books which reported the crisis of American sociology and endorsed the call for a reinvigorated conflict paradigm to meet the sociological tasks of the 1970's. Fourth, ASA presidents themselves have sensed the paradigm crisis and have addressed the study of conflict, force, and protest as a major agenda item for the discipline. We find it significant that five of the past six ASA presidents have focused on the paradigm crisis in sociology calling for new directions in research by the profession (Loomis, 1967; Rose, 1969; Turner, 1969; Bendix, 1970; Goode, 1972a). Finally, a brief examination of *The American Sociologist* over the past few years shows some evidence that younger sociologists are pursuing new specializations in the areas of political sociology, race, sex, and ethnic relations, deviance, and stratification that are linked to interests in a conflict paradigm (Stehr and Larson, 1972; Goode, 1972b; Brown and Gilmartin, 1969; Dorn and Long, 1972; Gouldner and Sprehe, 1965). Although we recognize these changes in professional activities and interests are suggestive and not systematic, they do indicate a beginning reorientation toward a conflict paradigm for the field. What this review of twentieth century sociology has shown, then, is that Kuhn's basic ideas about paradigms can be fruitfully applied to the ontogeny of American sociology.

THE FUNCTIONALIST PARADIGM
AND RECIPROCITY

By the end of the 1950's leading sociologists displayed a remarkable convergence concerning the capabilities of the functionalist paradigm to handle the basic problems of the discipline: ranging from Merton's (1957) essay on manifest and latent functions wherein the functionalist paradigm, postulates, and methodological difficulties were assessed, to Davis' (1958) [1959] presidential address proclaiming the end to useless debates by declaring that the functional analysis is simply sociological analysis writ small, to Bell's (1959) declaration that the end of ideology has arrived, and to Dahrendorf's (1958) claim that the functional paradigm depicts the structural characteristics of status quo utopian societies. The end of ideology was in fact the end of the functionalist paradigm as the social movements of the 1960's revealed.

If we can take Dahrendorf's statement on the basic characteristics of the functionalist paradigm as representative, we find that the model of society depicted is one where "universal consensus on prevailing values and institutional arrangements" exists, where "structurally generated conflict" is absent, where social harmony is a key factor used to account for social stability, and where "social processes follow recurrent patterns and occur within, and a part of the design of the whole" (Dahrendorf, 1958). The functionalists were preoccupied with a social system that emphasized problems of socialization, role allocation, and an appropriate division of labor where deviants are unique fallouts from the institutionalized normative patterns of society.

The norm of reciprocity occupies a special place in the functionalist paradigm and needs clarification if our argument in later sections is to be understood. The norm of reciprocity means that the parts of a given social system are functionally interrelated and engaged in mutually supportive interchanges. These interdependent reciprocities provide an equilibrium to the social system over time. Although more sophisticated functional theorists have gone beyond earlier statements of rather simple symmetrical reciprocities (to moving equilibriums, compensating mechanisms, functional alternatives, etc.), the norm of reciprocity implies a certain moral character and social balance that is healthy for the whole system (Gouldner, 1959). When the norm of reciprocity is circumvented, denied, or is unevenly observed, then the entire functionalist paradigm is invalidated.

Below the surface of the major news events and protest movements of the 1960's was a new set of social conditions that many social scientists argued indicated a shift away from the structure of society depicted by the functionalist paradigm. The structural changes underlying the development of the post-industrial society necessitate a different conceptual paradigm—conflict theory—and new research strategies—conflict methodology. Let us examine some of these basic changes quickly as a way to highlight the evasion of reciprocity, itself central to functionalism.

First, the post-industrial society and its dominant structural feature, the large-scale organization, now stand in overt hostile contrast to the public interest and the general welfare of society. Although corporate organizations still cling to a free enterprise ideology which extols consumer sovereignty and the virtues of a competitive decentralized industrial system, the dominant trend of the past 30 years has been one of the massive growth and consolidation of large organizations (Galbraith, 1967; Zeitlin, 1970; Mintz and Cohen, 1971).

The Nader study report on antitrust enforcement shows that the 200 largest corporations in 1950 controlled 47 percent of the total manufacturing assets in the United States. By 1967, these corporations controlled 67 percent of all manufacturing assets and over 33 percent of the assets of the free world (Green, 1972: 8). This consolidation in asset size understates considerably the extent of industrial concentration since joint ventures are common and interlocking managements and directorships predominate. For example, in 1967 some 49 banks were trustees of $135 billion in assets and held 5 percent or more of outstanding shares of stock in 5,270 companies (108 per bank). These same 49 banks had interlocking directorates with 6,591 companies or 164 per bank (Green, 1972: 9; Domhoff, 1967). During the 1962–1968 period, 110 of *Fortune* magazine's top 500 corporations disappeared through mergers with other giants. According to Nader's study, the monopoly and oligopoly costs to the consumer in lost production and excessive prices are about $80 billion yearly. Furthermore, a recent Federal Trade

Commission report states that if the government deconcentrated industries to a level of four companies with less than 40 percent of the sales, the prices of consumer products would fall by 25 percent (Green, 1972: 14).

Let us look at a few strategic examples of how the large corporations operate under the closed enterprise system, starting with the automotive industry. Since the passage of the 1966 Federal Highway Safety Act by Congress, the automobile industry has been forced to recall some 36 million cars out of about 60 million produced during 1966–1972 period for shoddy workmanship and serious factory defects. Thus 60 percent of the cars produced in this country have been found to contain serious enough defects to warrant recall (Moskin, 1973; Nader, 1973; Kelley, 1973). What does this brute fact tell us about quality control in the auto industry, about the level of government inspection prior to car sales, and about the thousands of Americans killed needlessly because of product deficiencies?

Take another example, the subsidy and tax system, which favors disproportionately the interests of large scale organizations. Recently, the Joint Economic Committee released a report which identified 170 subsidy programs maintained by the federal government that cost the consumer $63 billion in fiscal 1970. Of course, there are many subsidized programs of great value to the nation but the committee raised serious questions regarding the merits of many programs (Heinemann, 1972). Another kind of subsidy that seems increasingly costly to the consumer is found in the Vanik testimony presented to the Joint Economic Committee. In a study of the biggest 145 corporations, utilities, and banks drawn from the *Fortune* magazine list in the years 1969–1971, Vanik found that 21 corporations paid *no* federal corporate tax on incomes of $1.9 billion. Another 29 corporations paid an effective federal tax rate of less than 10 percent on incomes of $8.7 billion (Vanik, 1972: 1). Although these large corporations theoretically are in the 48 percent tax bracket, the average effective corporate tax rate paid in 1969 was 26 percent. Thus, enormous sums of corporate incomes are lost to society as a result of subsidies, tax breaks, legal loopholes, and other privileges.

One final example will complete our look at how large organizations maintain and enhance their overall position in the post-industrial society at the expense of the average citizen. What is important to examine here are the basic trends in the data. There was some reduction in income inequality during the depression, during World War II and during the 1960–1968 period. However, the degree of inequality has not changed much from 1946 to 1970. The fact that the top and bottom fifths receive about the same percent of income in 1970 as in 1946 needs to be qualified. During these years income has risen for each person but the absolute gap between the rich and the poor has increased (Jencks, 1972: 211; Domhoff, 1967: 38–62).

The development of a new elite structure is a special condition which also affects the flow of reciprocity. The basic trends in the labor force have been known for some time. Agricultural workers have declined sharply. There has been an enormous expansion of the lower reaches of the white-collar work force, surpassing for the first time the number of blue-collar workers in the mid-1950's. The skilled occupations of the blue-collar workers have also been rapidly growing. The census-designated category of professional, technical, and managerial workers has grown remarkably in the post World War II period (Price, 1965; Bell, 1967). Behind these familiar trends is a concentration of certain industries, often referred to as the knowledge producing and disseminating industries (Machlup, 1962; Drucker, 1968). So crucial have the knowledge industries become to our advanced economy that Bell among others considers knowledge as a new factor of production which must be exploited to keep the post-industrial society moving ahead. Thus technical and scientific knowledge has been integrated into the power positions of society to a far greater degree than ever before.

Accompanying the changes in the composition of the labor force and the changes in production technology itself are vital questions of organizational power, property, and control. Following Galbraith's analysis, we concur that the mode of exercising organizational power has shifted from stockholders to professional managers to the technostructure, from overt coercion by entrepreneurs to the subtle manipulation by corporate managers and technicians (Galbraith, 1967). Those large-scale organizations which are well served by the information industry technicians (sociologists, economists, psychologists, accountants, computer scientists, engineers, and so on) gain structure and survival potential at an order of magnitude far in excess of those segments of society still dependent upon a stone-age information flow technology.

Sociologists are intrigued with the effects of this new elite structure. Those adhering to the functionalist paradigm have argued that the rise of a technocratic elite has diminished ideological politics, has led to new levels of affluence for all social classes and a more rational and pragmatic kind of decision making. In fact, the functionalists argue that the political and economic systems can function within their present boundaries, that the competition of a plurality of interest groups is preferred to the general confrontation of social classes, that apathy on the part of voters and workers is beneficial to the system, and that, indeed, the corporate interest is synonymous with the conception of society's general welfare.

Those sociologists adopting the conflict paradigm argue that application of computer science and the use of our technological capabilities has reinforced a highly inequitable distribution of society's wealth, income, and goods and services. Furthermore, the structure of decision making in the post-industrial society generates additional social problems on a magnitude that exceeds the resources of the consensus oriented technostructure to resolve. Thus a major and growing cleavage exists between the vested interests of large-scale organizations supported by the federal government, the multiversities, big military and big labor and the average citizen and consumer, the small businessman, the non-unionized laborer and powerless minorities of blacks, women, chicanos, and students. There are some signs of citizen awakening to reclaim rights of participation in governance matters. The politics of the Kennedy, McCarthy, Wallace, and McGovern campaigns, the national meat boycott of April 1973, and the voters' decision not to host the Olympics in Colorado manifest a search for new ways to control corporate elites and national centers of decision making.

It is our position that while the technostructure has assumed dominance in the acquisition of production of knowledge and does indeed control the command hierarchies in these areas, the more traditional political and corporate elites still retain much control over the key decision-making hierarchies of society. These decision centers move the economy, determine the time, place, and manner of military and corporate intervention in the world, and shape governmental policy in the interests of large-scale organizations at home and in violation of the reciprocity norm.

The major conclusions we draw from the illustrative data presented are as follows: that large-scale organizations are consolidating their position in the political economy of the nation, that the closed enterprise system provides special incentives to corporations which utilize a disproportionate amount of the technological advances of post-industrial society for their own interests.

For sociologists, there is a more personal and professional default on the norm of reciprocity implicit in our relation to the people and the system which sustains us. The work of consensus methodologists has not met the information needs of the general public and individual citizen. In the early days of consensus methodology, advertising, media research and public opinion polling, and labor relations provided the subject matter for many researchers. Since then, attitude surveys, voting behavior studies, consumer preference polls, opinion sampling, sociometric methods, projective techniques, content analysis, sophisticated scaling devices, and computerized factor analyses have provided the consensus methodologist with social and psychological data extracted from the compliant respondents. All of these types of studies provide the corporate world with a treasured reservoir of useful product information. This kind of quantitative empiricism provides decision makers with a useful portrait of the American voter, tastemaker, consumer, and worker. The development of consensus techniques fits nicely into the functionalist paradigm with its stress on harmony, equilibrium, manipulated consensus, and social control. When viewed in the larger social context, consensus methodology facilitates evasion of the norm of reciprocity as between large-scale organizations and their publics while (at the same time) ignoring the obligations of reciprocity between social research and society.

The major strength of functionalists and consensus methodologists has been to meet the voracious needs of the post-industrial society for accurate, detailed, and reliable information about those sectors of society in need of "proper" management and control. Although claiming a value neutral stance, functionalists and consensus methodologists have had their work revealed as furthering the interests of the powerful at the expense of the powerless. Becker and Horowitz have succinctly stated the issue in terms of riot control at home and civic action abroad:

Prison research has for the most part been oriented to the problems of jailers rather than those of prisoners; industrial research, to the problems of managers rather than those of workers; military research, to the problems of generals rather than those of privates. Greater sensitivity to the undemocratic character of ordinary institutions and relationships (ironically fostered by social scientists themselves) has revealed how research frequently represents the interests of adults and teachers instead of those of children and of the lower class blacks, chicanos, and other minorities; of the conventional straight world instead of freaks; of boozers instead of potheads. Wherever someone is oppressed, an "establishment" sociologist seems to lurk in the background, providing the facts which make oppression more efficient and the theory which makes it legitimate to a larger constituency. (1972:48)

We apply our argument here to the research technology or data collection phase of consensus methodologies to illustrate these points but contend that the argument can be extended to all steps in the research process. We have examined a number of textbooks and position statements which reveal the linkages between the functionalist paradigm and consensus methodologies that prevail in the field (Lazarsfeld, 1959, 1970, 1972; Merton, 1959; Selvin, 1963; Friedrichs, 1970; Hammond, 1964; Cicourel, 1964; Phillips, 1973).

In the process of social research and its legitimization by society, the social scientist is granted by that society the authority to conduct his work with the long run objective of promoting the general welfare of the people. Thus the sociologist has certain reciprocity obligations that must be fulfilled if his science contract with society is to be equitable. The ultimate justification for the science of society is an improved society, a society which minimizes the negative consequences of its stratification system and enhances the quality of life, including equalizing opportunities in a wider range of basic institutions. Furthermore, it ensures a system of accountability wherein the general public is properly informed so that it can make better decisions about its own welfare and future. In terms of the norm of reciprocity, the professional sociologist must take an active role in creating the social conditions under which reciprocity is maximized.

CONFLICT METHODOLOGY

Based on the previous material, we make a basic assumption that social scientists who are skilled at using the strategies of consensus methodologies have supported and advanced the basic interests of large-scale organizations. The record of research and policy recommendations promoted by the scientific management school, the human relations school, and the decision-making school have heavily reinforced the functionalist paradigm which favors managers, stockholders, and policy makers at the expense of the interests of blue-collar workers, white-collar workers, and the public in general (Mouzelis, 1967; Perrow, 1972a; Baritz, 1960). Social scientists have all too frequently been coopted by enticing research projects. Project Camelot, the Pentagon Papers, and the activities of the Rand Corporation or Stanford Research Institute are familiar examples (Sjoberg, 1967; Horowitz, 1967; Perrow, 1972b; Bauer and Cleaver, 1969). Adherence to the canons of corporate professionalism and consensus methodology make it very difficult for sociologists to investigate large-scale organizations and assess their social, political, economic, and psychological impacts on society (Szymanski, 1970; O'Toole, 1971).

The consensus norms surrounding the development of rapport, the exercising of research tact and persuasion, the protecting of privacy and confidentiality over the source of data, the securing of sponsorship of establishment funding, and the value neutral stance of the entire enterprise—all serve to enhance the collection of safe and valuable data. The point of interest here about the consensus norms of data collection is that the respondent is usually unaware of the objectives of the research, is coaxed often against his own interests into giving out information used to legitimate the sponsor's or researcher's interests, and receives little or no feedback from the study as to what he can do to improve his own social situation. Furthermore, if a curious respondent should inquire into social research findings, the statistical language that fills most methods texts and sociological journals is incomprehensible, unavailable to the average citizen, and of little direct use to him (Bode, 1972).

If the above mentioned strategies of data collection fail, then sociologists frequently resort to unobtrusive measures and selected forms of outright deceit to insure the success of their research efforts (Dalton, 1968; Denzin, 1970a; Webb, et al., 1966; Filstead, 1970; Sjoberg, 1967). Such tactics raise serious ethical and practical questions about the relationship of the researcher to the respondent under the norm of reciprocity. Under the guise of some legitimating rationale, the sociologist often dupes the respondent into supplying information later put to use hostile to the respondent's own interests.

We argue that there are other ways to do research than under conditions of cooperation with and sponsorship by the large-scale corporation. We argue that modern large-scale organizations are designed to withhold quality information from their putative publics while using information specialists to acquire quality information from those publics. This twofold constraint on information flow necessarily restricts the social researcher to exploiting the information sets of the unorganized public while excluded from the rich information resources about the large-scale organization.

One can ask, where are the sociological studies of GM, GE, ITT, ATT, Department of Defense, and the Bank of America? It is sad to discover that the reservoir of work here is very shallow and superficial. To the student of large-scale organizations, sociology has provided almost no tradition of research investigation into this world which has such massive impact on our lives except upon terms of cooperation. What we do know is that large-scale organizations are deeply involved in a corporate-governmental network which insures their continued stability, subsidy, and prosperity. Corporations have become very sophisticated in selling an ideology of consumerism to the public by hiding the facts and costs of control from those over whom power is exerted.

It is our point here that each paradigm is made complete with the development of its related and compatible technology. A conflict paradigm will be complete only when new technologies of research are invented and used by which to breach the barriers to quality information erected by a secretive administration, a conspiring oil industry, an ambitious war department, or a slick commercial operation. These methods we term conflict methodology: the techniques by which quality information is obtained from organizations in hostile contrast to the researcher or his client.

The fatal argument against conflict methodologies heretofore has been that "real" science does not intrude into its domain of study. Three points from Seeley are relevant here. Sociologists borrowed rather uncritically this argument of a "neutral" science from the physical and biological sciences. But of critical importance to sociology is the fact that the *very discovery* of social uniformities represents a new and unique event. Seeley (1963) has called this fundamental paradox of social science the *action theorem*. Whatever a social scientist does in his research, he inevitably intervenes in the very process he is studying. All new science is in conflict with existing science and, when introduced into an information system, is an act of conflict with existing social knowledge.

Merton in his famous essay on "The Self-Fulfilling Prophecy" put forth the proposition that prediction "peculiar to human affairs . . . will enter into the situation as a new and dynamic factor, changing the very conditions under which the prediction initially held true" (Merton, 1957: 129–130). But unfortunately Merton did not apply this insight to the process of social research itself.

In addition to the action theorem, Seeley presents two more theorems which support the general argument here. The *inexhaustibility theorem* states that the sociologist can never exhaust the content of his subject matter by his description of it because the very act of description adds to it. Thus the process of research itself provides sociology with an unlimited horizon as basic to its subject matter.

A third theorem is the *freedom theorem*. Every theory regarding human behavior enters into human behavior as a new factor, an assertion which makes necessary its own qualification. The freedom theorem moves beyond Merton's self-fulfilling and self-denying prophecies since it involves an inevitable dialectical principle operative in every piece of social research. In combination, these three theorems of action, inexhaustability, and freedom result in an implicit assumption of *social change* in the research process. If we take Seeley's theorems as valid for the science of sociology, we find the traditional image and role separation of the sociologist no longer holds: the professional research role is indelibly fused with the political role. The real question is what social change is to be the product of research methodology rather than how to avoid change by the researcher. Our argument is that consensus methodology restricts sociology to such change as has led to the warfare, welfare, and managed society. Conflict methodology is necessary to control big business, big government, and the other sophisticated information consumers.

CONFLICT METHODOLOGY IN PRACTICE:
THE ADVERSARY PRINCIPLE

In this paper we do not intend to provide an exhaustive set of strategies of conflict methodology. Instead, we shall develop several strategies we believe hold great promise as points of cognitive orientation. The first strategy is found in the adversary principle and the legal model. In contrast to the overwhelming reliance among sociologists upon the scientific method as the means to collect and analyze data and ascertain the truth, the adversary principle offers a different approach. Let us clarify our use of the term adversary principle. In its narrow courtroom meaning, the adversary principle refers to a form of interaction and a specialized set of rules with different functions performed by advocates, litigants, judges, and jurors in making a decision involving the parties to a dispute. Basic to the adversary principle of information acquisition is the practice of partisan advocacy (Frank, 1949). The advocates of the parties in a dispute can put witnesses on the stand, sort out conflicting testimony at deeper levels of contextual meaning, recall hostile witnesses and force them to respond, and construct alternate frames of meaning by which to understand "facts." The proceedings of a court trial offer the sociologist a new model for data collection which is beyond the techniques used by consensus strategies. Since significant social issues are fought out in courts, sociologists also can make use of the court setting as a place to collect new types of information.

A second way in which sociologists can use the courts is to become litigants and advocates themselves. Resort to the legal model can provide the sociologist with new types of problems, and new types of clients (Vose, 1958; Nussbaum, 1970). We are assuming here that most large-scale organizations, whether they be public agencies or private corporations, are not willing to air before the public their critical decisions. Therefore, they close the doors to information of value for serious analysis by sociologists. The use of law suits, injunctions, and petitions filed under the Freedom of Information Act can secure data about the operations and impact of these superstructures which otherwise is foreclosed to the outside researcher (Wellford, 1970).

One other important value can be claimed for the adversary method. By institutionalizing a distinction between the rules and functions of the litigants, their lawyers, and the judge, a certain guarantee in the "internal morality" of courtroom adjudication is established. By such role insulation and division of labor, the impartiality of the judge can be better preserved with the consequence of increased fairness in his decisions. Under the scientific method, the professional sociologist sets himself up as the investigator, advocate, judge, and jury of what he will study, how he will carry out his research, and what he will do with his findings. This kind of autonomy and role dominance is rarely challenged by his colleagues, and there is no formal appeals structure to provide for serious controversies to be reopened. Thus sociologists are freed from facing the value implications and moral responsibilities of their social research, especially when the subject under review is a controversial one.

Fuller argues that the principle competence of the adversary method is to enhance the rationality and legitimacy of policy choices. By providing a forum wherein alternative and competing arguments, data, and values may be expressed, a more effective decision can be reached (Fuller, 1961: 30–44; 1964). Under conditions where rules and norms are unclear or even absent, or where issues of policy are at stake, the adversary process is an indispensable part of any decision-making process.

One important trend in the post-industrial society has been the proliferation of administrative agencies, boards, bureaus, and commissions. Such administrative bodies are performing executive, legislative, and judicial functions which formerly were handled in a more restricted courtroom setting. In varying degrees, the administrative agencies have the power to make rules, to decide controversies, to grant licenses, and to render particular kinds of services (Auerbach, 1961, Part 3; Reich, 1964). These administrative bodies and the power they exert over our society provide a lucrative arena for social research and social action. Joseph Sax has demonstrated in *Defending the Environment* (1971) the use of the lawsuit as a strategy which *produces* information and clarifies positions which would otherwise be hidden from public view. Sax provides us with insight on the advantage of a trained researcher acting as an adversary in seeking out information on behalf of the public using such legal instruments as the public hearing, the injunction, the interrogatory, the court order, as well as the public record laws. Sax stresses that a request for information by a private person or by a sociologist can be ignored by administrators of large-scale organizations while a court order for documents cannot so readily be discounted. By means of this kind of conflict methodology, the canons of bureaucratic secrecy are set aside or seriously challenged on behalf of the public which such agencies purport to serve.[1] As a strategy to elicit data and to bring about change, the lawsuit is clearly superior under these conditions to questionnaires, surveys, interviews, unobtrusive measures, and other consensus tactics.

Sax's book is most eloquent when he seeks to reinvigorate the idea of public trust and develop a charter for citizen environmental rights. Today the balance has been tipped by the rise of large-scale organizations and the institutionalization of private property rights over public rights. Conflict methodology links up readily with the adversary principle to provide the cutting edge for social researchers and other agents of social change to begin restoration of public rights.

Public Advocacy, another significant example of conflict methodology in the legal arena, is the work that Ralph Nader's Center for the Study of Responsive Law has been using to introduce consumerism into public consciousness. The people who have authored the flow of studies and published reports of the Center have taken seriously the "consumer perspective" in the law (Cahn, 1963; Cahn and Cahn, 1964). In sharp contrast to the official perspective on the relation of law to society, the advocates of the consumer perspective articulate the grievances of the public with the goal of increasing the responsiveness of public officials and corporations to a more equitable and just distribution of social goods and social services.

What is needed is an expansion of advocacy on behalf of the public interest. Lawyers designed at least three new strategies of advocacy in the 1960's. First, they developed strategies of class-based advocacy to represent the collective interests of certain groups such as the poor, tenants, ghetto neighborhoods, welfare recipients, and students on the campus (Carlin and Howard, 1965). Second, lawyers refined strategies of selective advocacy which challenged certain official practices by focusing on the rules, regulations, and discretion of police departments, welfare agencies, finance companies, and the like. Third, lawyers promoted strategies of organizational advocacy as an important force for social change. The formation and deployment of consumer councils and such defense organizations as NAACP, CORE, Common Cause, National Welfare Rights Organization, NOW, public interest law firms, and Alinsky's Industrial Areas Foundation highlighted the struggle for civil and civic rights. Sociologists working with lawyers may play a special advocate role in restoring the norm of reciprocity to citizens that have been excluded from the mainstream of American life.

Ethnomethodology as a Special Type of Conflict Methodology

We see ethnomethodology as another type of conflict methodology. Ethnomethodologists are interested in discovering the tacit understandings that undergird the ongoing social world. This is an effort to understand the social world as it is interpreted by people in their daily lives. Thus the ethnomethodologist seeks to discover the "methods" that people use in their everyday life in constructing social reality and to discover the nature of the realities they have constructed. In order to penetrate this social reality, ethnomethodologists poke, probe, and puncture normal situations of interaction to uncover the rules and rituals participants take for granted.

Garfinkel and his students have introduced a new tactic of social research called "demonstration experiments." In demonstration experiments, the researcher disturbs the ongoing social situation or introduces "nasty surprises" in interaction in order to demonstrate the presence of much that was taken for granted (Garfinkel, 1967; Denzin, 1970b). Garfinkel disturbed others by simply not performing those acts which they expected—or by performing acts which others did not have any "reason" to expect at all. For example, his students were instructed to treat their parents at home as though they were boarders in the home. The politeness and small acts of kindness they performed were then taken by their parents to be signs of hostility, antagonism, fatigue, etc.

What Garfinkel's techniques do is place the researcher in direct hostile contrast to his subjects so that the taken-for-granted presuppositions of everyday life are exposed and can be studied. Ethnomethodologists unveil elements of the "silent dialogue" that underlie a great deal of face-to-face encounters. The grounds of man's social existence can be discovered and that discovery can have tremendous possibilities not only for understanding particular social worlds but for changing them altogether.

Of key importance to our interest in conflict methodology are those studies by ethnomethodologists of large scale organizations. Sudnow (1967), Cicourel (1968) and Douglas (1967) have reported studies which highlight the special nature of organizational records and dramatized the basic finding that members of any social organization develop special perspectives for handling their clients and the public at large. Utilizing this approach, ethnomethodologists have argued that

1) organizations perpetuate themselves through time by generating fictitious records and public ideologies of legitimacy; 2) comparable organizations differ in the meaning they assign to the same events (birth, death, mental illness, cured, etc.); 3) the production of organizational records is basically an interactional process based on rumor, gossip, overheard conversations, discrepant information and biographically imperfect bookkeeping. (Denzin, 1970b: 272)

Cicourel has demonstrated, for example, that agencies created to process juvenile delinquents routinely create delinquents by piecing together long series of conversations between the predelinquent, his parents, the arresting officer, the counselor, and the judge. The sum total of these conversations, which became translated into official reports, became the organizational documentation that a delinquent act had or had not occurred. Ethnomethodologists like Cicourel show in their work that deviance may be as much an artifact of organizational processing as it is of interactions among significant others.

Ethnomethodologists have found that members of large-scale organizations, in piecing together their official reports and other documents, relied upon open-ended categories of meaning and interpretations to classify ambiguous cases. Garfinkel has identified this pattern as the et cetera clause because people always struggle to fit events into a pattern that complements their ongoing action (Garfinkel, 1967: 73–75). As we well know, large-scale organizations often manipulate data in their records which will justify the organization's existence, enhance more favorable budget allocations, or strengthen its spheres of authority.

From the perspective of conflict methodology, the fact that the ethnomethodologist stands in hostile contrast to the subject of his research means that he will be able to unravel deeper layers of social reality and extract a different kind of data than would be the case with consensus methodologies. Although most ethnomethodological studies to date have been micro-sociological in nature, ethnomethodology offers the conflict theorist several strategies for extracting information from large scale organizations. We see the application of ethnomethodological strategies to large-scale organizations as an important arena for future research.

Community Organizing: Conflict Strategies for Facilitating Organizational Reciprocity

Another example of conflict methodology in action is demonstrated in the work of Saul Alinsky (1946; 1971). The purpose of Alinsky's efforts to build community-controlled organizations where native leadership is uncovered and conflict tactics are employed is to restore the norm of reciprocity to those social groups previously excluded from the existing community institutions. Pioneering in the strategies and tactics of confrontation politics, Alinsky believed in the long run that the ordinary citizen was capable of reaching good decisions if given the opportunity to act. The task, therefore, of the community organizer is to develop those strategies which give deprived citizens new ways to participate in collective decision making, new methods to hold existing community organizations accountable for their actions and to realize the values of a more humane social order (Kahn, 1970).

Starting from the people's own experience, from their own self-interests, and from an inventory of community grievances, the community organizer assists the development of protest organizations. In order to redress the grievances of deprived social groups, Alinsky sought out indigenous community leaders who could utilize conflict strategies and organizational power to make existing social institutions more responsive to local needs. In the perspective of this paper Alinsky's contribution lies in his awareness that conflict strategies of community organizing were necessary in order to introduce new types of information into the existing community's institutions. Usually this type of conflict information is defined as "noise" by the target institutions. The task then of the applied sociologist is to restore the norm of reciprocity between the citizens of the community and those organizations, both public and private, which have responsibility for community services, employment opportunities, educational opportunities, and land use policies. By introducing new information into the existing system, the community organizer alters the imbalance of vested interests and forces incumbent leaders to recognize and act in different ways.

Technological Accidents and Technostructure Scandals: Research Sites for Conflict Methodology

The social characteristics of the post-industrial society offer strategic sites for research that sociologists are just beginning to utilize. Molotch has pioneered in the use of the technological accident as a research site for studying the nature of corporate power (Molotch, 1970; Molotch and Lester, 1972; Galbraith, 1967). Technological accidents are unplanned events which reveal the inner workings of large-scale organizations which by mistake or miscalculation caused a breakdown in the conception of public order. Such an accident pierces the service myth of large-scale organizations by revealing to the public hidden and antithetical power interests.

In his study of the Santa Barbara oil spill, Molotch revealed that, although the oil companies never intended to cause the huge blow out, their vested interests in securing the continuation of offshore drilling had to be preserved. As the technological accident unfolded, Molotch shows how the Santa Barbara community united to fight the oil companies and the federal government to stop the drilling; how the regulatory agencies and Congress abandoned the public interest to protect the vested interests of the oil companies; and how the science and technology establishment abdicated responsiblity for deciding the outcome of further offshore drilling. Molotch argues that technological accidents provide a useful site for conflict methodology as such miscalculations lead to the breakdown of public order exposing the structure of power behind it.

Technostructure scandals provide a second research site for the study of large-scale organizations. Scandals are planned events, usually set off by some informer or insider of an organization who leaks embarrassing news to the public. Scandals, like technological accidents, provide the sociologist with insights into the normally protected world of organizations by providing access to a type of data beyond the province of the usual research techniques.

A scandal, then, is a deliberately planned event which is promoted by a party different from the interests of the technostructure responsible for maintaining business-as-usual decision making. Two recent scandals of this type have headlined the news stories of the past two years—the release of the Pentagon Papers by Ellsberg and the Watergate affair. As Molotch puts it:

What makes the scandal a type of event in its own right is the *way* in which it becomes a public event. Scandals involve persons who have at least some access to private sectors and who for one reason or another provide outgroups with information about that private sector. That is, scandals require "leakers" or "informants" and thus are contingent upon some dispute or disagreement among persons who are supposed to operate in substantial harmony. The scandal can only emerge when some insider is pissed-off, when some conflict methodologist manages to get placed inside, and only when the media is willing to be a party to the exposure. The amazing thing about the Pentagon Papers is thus not that Presidents tell lies, but that *The New York Times* was willing to so dramatically expose that fact. (1972: 18)

Thus we argue that technological accidents and technostructure scandals provide strategic vantage points for the conflict theorist and conflict methodologist. By carefully studying such accidents and scandals, sociologists can accumulate otherwise hidden data on groups and large-scale organizations; sociologists can penetrate the decision-making activities of the technostructure and corporate-governmental elites; and sociologists can provide important research reports on the vested interests of large-scale organizations that comprise the structure of the post-industrial society.

SUMMARY

Contemporary sociology is undergoing a crisis in paradigmatic orientation. Four paradigmatic periods are identified. The functionalist paradigm is being challenged by a conflict paradigm made complete by the development of a conflict methodology. Consensus methodology, developed under the perspective of functional analysis, is inadequate to meet the information needs of the whole system. Its limitations are noted.

The social conditions supporting conflict theory and methodology are outlined briefly. Examples of conflict methodology in practice are provided. The role of accidents and scandals is emphasized as a more suitable research site for sociologists than those sites determined by sponsors of consensus methodologies.

The position of the authors is that professional sociologists must take an active role in creating the social conditions under which reciprocity is maximized. Under conflict conditions of social organization, we argue that conflict methodology is necessary to constrain the corporate-dominated society. Conflict methodology comprises those strategies and techniques by which information is obtained from and introduced into systems under conditions of hostile contrast. By proper use of conflict methodology strategies, the norm of reciprocity between sociologist and his subject of research and between the individual citizen and his society can be restored and a more equal and just social order created.

NOTE

1. For detailed documentation of the cooptation of governmental agencies by the corporations they are supposed to regulate, we cite the studies produced by Nader's Center for Responsive Law: *Vanishing Air*, 1969, a study of the National Air Pollution Control Administration; *The Federal Trade Commission*, 1969; *The Interstate Commerce Commission*, 1970; *The Chemical Feast*, 1970, a study of food regulation by the Food and Drug Administration; *Sowing the Wind*, 1971, a report on pesticides and the Department of Agriculture; *The Water Lords*, 1971, a study of pollution in the Savannah River; *The Closed Enterprise System*, 1972, a report on antitrust enforcement.

REFERENCES

Alinsky, Saul D. *Reveille for Radicals*. New York: Vintage, 1946.
———. *Rules for Radicals*. New York: Random House, 1971.
———. "Playboy Interview," *Playboy*, March 1972, 59–178.
Auerbach, Carl A., et al. *The Legal Process*. San Francisco: Chandler, 1959.
Baritz, Loren. *The Servants of Power*. Middletown, Conn.: Wesleyan University Press, 1960.

Bauer, Ann, and Harry Cleaver. "Minority Report," Campus Report Supplement, Stanford University Relations Office, April 14, 1969, 37–52.

Becker, Howard S. "Whose Side Are We On?" Social Problems, 14 (Winter 1967), 239–48.

Becker, Howard S., and Irving L. Horowitz. "Radical Politics and Sociological Research: Observations on Methodology and Ideology," American Journal of Sociology, 78 (July 1972), 48–67.

Bell, Daniel. The End of Ideology. New York: Collier, 1959.

———. "Notes on the Post-Industrial Society," Public Interest, 6 (Winter 1967), 24–35.

Bendix, Reinhard. "Sociology and the Distrust of Reason," American Sociological Review, 35 (October 1970), 831–43.

Birnbaum, Norman. "Is There a Post-Industrial Revolution?" in Birnbaum, Toward a Critical Sociology. New York: Oxford University Press, 1971, pp. 393–416.

Bode, Jerry G. "The Silent Science," American Sociologist, 7 (May 1972), 3, 5–6.

Bramson, Leon. The Political Context of Sociology. Princeton: Princeton University Press, 1961.

Brown, Carol. "A History and Analysis of Radical Activism in Sociology," Sociological Inquiry, 40 (Winter 1970), 27–35.

Brown, J. S., and B. G. Gilmartin. "Sociology Today: Lacunae, Emphasis and Surfeits," American Sociologist, 4 (November 1969), 283–91.

Cahn, Edgar S., and Jean C. Cahn. "The War on Poverty: A Civilian Perspective," Yale Law Journal, 73 (July 1964), 1317–52.

Cahn, Edmond. "Law in the Consumer Perspective," University of Pennsylvania Law Review, 112 (November 1963), 1–21.

Carlin, Jerome, and Jan Howard. "Legal Representation and Class Justice," UCLA Law Review, 12 (January 1965), 381–437.

Cicourel, Aaron V. Method and Measurement in Sociology. New York: Free Press, 1964.

———. The Social Organization of Juvenile Justice. New York: Wiley, 1968.

Coleman, James S., et al. Equality of Educational Opportunity. Washington, D. C.: U. S. Department of Health, Education and Welfare, 1966.

Colfax, David. "Knowledge for Whom? Relevance and Responsibility in Sociological Research," Sociological Inquiry, 40 (Winter 1970), 73–85.

Colfax, David, and Jach Roach, eds. Radical Sociology. New York: Basic Books, 1971.

Coser, Lewis. The Functions of Social Conflict. New York: Free Press, 1956.

Dahrendorf, Ralf. "Out of Utopia: Toward a Reorientation of Sociological Analysis," American Journal of Sociology, 64 (1958), 115–27.

Dalton, Melville. Men Who Manage. New York: Wiley, 1968.

Davis, Kingsley. "The Myth of Functional Analysis as a Special Method in Sociology and Anthropology," American Sociological Review, 24 (December 1959), 757–72.

Demerath, N. J., and Richard A. Peterson. System Change and Conflict. New York: Free Press, 1967.

Denzin, Norman K. The Research Act. Chicago: Aldine, 1970. (a)

———. "Symbolic Interactionism and Ethnomethodology," in Douglas, ed., Understanding Everyday Life. Chicago: Aldine, 1970. (b)

Deutsch, Steven E. "The Radical Perspective in Sociology," Sociological Inquiry, 40 (Winter 1970), 85–95.

Deutsch, Steven, and John Howard. Where It's At: Radical Perspectives in Sociology. New York: Harper & Row, 1970.

Domhoff, G. William. Who Rules America? Englewood Cliffs, N.J.: Prentice-Hall, 1967.

———. "Equality of Educational Opportunity," Harvard Educational Review, 38 (Winter 1968).

———. The Higher Circles. New York: Vintage, 1970.

Dorn, D. S., and G. L. Long. "Sociology and the Radical Right: A Critical Analysis," American Sociologist, 7 (May 1972), 8–9.

Douglas, Jack D. The Social Meaning of Suicide. Princeton: Princeton University Press, 1967.

———. Understanding Everyday Life. Chicago: Aldine, 1970.

Drucker, Peter F. The Age of Discontinuity: Guidelines to Our Changing Society. New York: Harper & Row, 1968.

Etzioni, Amitai. Modern Organizations. Englewood Cliffs, N.J.: Prentice-Hall, 1964.

Filstead, William J. Qualitative Methodology. Chicago: Markheim, 1970.

Frank, Jerome. Courts on Trial. New York: Atheneum, 1949.

Friedrichs, Robert W. A Sociology of Sociology. New York: Free Press, 1970.

Fuller, Lon L. "The Adversary System," in Harold Berman, ed., *Talks on American Law.* New York: Vintage, 1961, pp. 30–44.
———. *The Morality of Law.* New Haven, Conn.: Yale University Press, 1964.
Galbraith, John. *The New Industrial State.* Boston: Houghton Mifflin, 1967.
Garfinkel, Harold. *Studies in Ethnomethodology.* Englewood Cliffs, N.J.: Prentice-Hall, 1967.
Goode, William J. "The Place of Force in Human Society," *American Sociological Review,* 37 (October 1972), 507–19. (a)
———. "Report of the President," *American Sociologist,* 7 (August 1972), 24. (b)
Gouldner, Alvin W. "Reciprocity and Autonomy in Functional Theory," in Gross, ed., *Symposium on Sociological Theory.* New York: Harper & Row, 1959.
———. *The Coming Crisis of Western Sociology.* New York: Basic Books, 1970.
———. "Varieties of Political Expression Revisited," *American Journal of Sociology,* 78 (March 1973), 1063–94.
Gouldner, Alvin W., and T. J. Sprehe. "The Study of Man: Sociologists Look at Themselves," *Transaction,* 4 (May 1965), 42–44.
Hammond, Philip, ed. *Sociologists at Work.* New York: Basic Books, 1964.
Hampden-Turner, Charles. *Radical Man.* Cambridge: Schenkman, 1970.
Heinemann, H. E. "170 Subsidy Programs Cost $63 Billion in 1970," *Denver Post,* 13 December 1972.
Hinkle, Roscoe C., and Gisela Hinkle. *The Development of Modern Sociology.* New York: Random House, 1954.
Horowitz, David, ed. *Radical Sociology: An Introduction.* San Francisco: Canfield Press, 1971.
Horowitz, Harold. "Equal Protection Aspects of Inequalities in Public Education and Public Assistance Programs from Place to Place Within a State," *UCLA Law Review,* 15 (1968), 750–92.
Horowitz, Harold, and Kenneth Karst. "The Proposition Fourteen Cases: Justice in Search of a Justification," *UCLA Law Review,* 14 (1966).
Horowitz, Irving L. *The Rise and Fall of Project Camelot.* Cambridge, Mass.: M.I.T. Press, 1967.
Horton, John. "Order and Conflict Theories of Social Problems as Competing Ideologies," *American Journal of Sociology,* 71 (May 1966), 701–14.
Jencks, Christopher, et al. *Inequality: A Reassessment of the Effect of Family and Schooling in America.* New York: Basic Books, 1972.
Kahn, Si. *How People Get Power: Organizing Oppressed Communities for Action.* New York: McGraw-Hill, 1970.
Karst, Kenneth. "Serrano vs. Priest: A State Court's Responsibility and Opportunity in the Development of Federal Constitutional Law," *California Law Review,* 60 (May 1972), 720–57.
Kelley, Ben. "Our Booby-Trapped Highways," *World,* 2 (March 1973), 30–32.
Kriesberg, Louis. *The Sociology of Social Conflicts.* Englewood Cliffs, N.J.: Prentice-Hall, 1973.
Kuhn, Thomas S. *The Structure of Scientific Revolutions.* Chicago: University of Chicago Press, 1962.
Lakatos, Imre, and Alan Musgrave, eds. *Criticism and the Growth of Knowledge.* London: Cambridge University Press, 1970.
Lazarsfeld, Paul F. "Problems in Methodology," in Merton, et al., *Sociology Today: Problems and Prospects.* New York: Basic Books, 1959, pp. 39–81.
———. "Sociology," in *Main Trends of Research in the Social and Human Sciences.* Paris: UNESCO, 1970.
———. *Qualitative Analysis: Historical and Critical Essays.* Boston: Allyn & Bacon, 1972.
Loomis, Charles P. "In Praise of Conflict and Its Resolution," *American Sociological Review,* 32 (December 1967), 875–90.
Lowi, Theodore J. *The Politics of Disorder.* New York: Basic Books, 1971.
Lubenow, Gerald. "The Action Lawyers," *Saturday Review,* 26 August 1972, 36–42.
Lundberg, George A. *Can Science Save Us!* Longmans, Green, 1947.
Machlup, Fritz. *The Production and Distribution of Knowledge in the United States.* Princeton: Princeton University Press, 1962.
Martindale, Don. *The Nature and Types of Sociological Theory.* Boston: Houghton Mifflin, 1960.
Merton, Robert K. *Social Theory and Social Structure.* New York: Free Press, 1957.

————. "Notes on Problem Finding in Sociology," in Merton, et al., *Sociology Today: Problems and Prospects.* New York: Basic Books, 1959.

Mills, C. Wright. *The Power Elite.* New York: Oxford University Press, 1956.

————. *The Sociological Imagination.* New York: Grove Press, 1959.

Mintz, Morton, and Jerry Cohen. *America, Inc. Who Owns and Operates the United States.* New York: Dial Press, 1971.

Molotch, Harvey. "Oil in Santa Barbara and Power in America," *Sociological Inquiry,* 40 (Winter 1970), 131–45.

Molotch, Harvey, and Marilyn Lester. "Accidents, Scandals and Routines: Resources for Conflict Methodology." Paper read at ASA meetings, New Orleans, 1972.

Moskin, Robert. "Life and Death in Your Automobile," *World,* 2 (March 1973), 14–20.

Mosteller, Frederick, and Daniel Moynihan, eds. *On Equality of Educational Opportunity.* New York: Random House, 1972.

Mouzelis, Nicos. *Organization and Bureaucracy.* Chicago: Aldine, 1967.

Nader, Ralph. "Who Wants Safer Cars?" *World,* 2 (March 1973), 24–26, 59.

Nicolaus, Martin. "The Professional Organization of Sociology: A View from Below," *Antioch Review,* 29 (Fall 1969), 375–87.

Nussbaum, Michael. *Student Legal Rights.* New York: Harper & Row, 1970.

Oberschall, Anthony. *Social Conflict and Social Movements.* Englewood Cliffs, N.J.: Prentice-Hall, 1973.

Orleans, Harold. *Contracting for Knowledge.* San Francisco: Jossey-Bass, 1973.

O'Toole, Richard, ed. *The Organization, Management, and Tactics of Social Research.* Cambridge: Schenkman, 1971.

Parsons, Talcott. *The Social System.* New York: Free Press, 1951. (a)

————. *Essays in Sociological Theory.* New York: Free Press, 1954.

Parsons, Talcott, et al. *Toward a General Theory of Action.* Cambridge: Harvard University Press, 1951. (b)

————. *Working Papers in the Theory of Action.* New York: Free Press, 1953.

Perrow, Charles. *Complex Organizations: A Critical Essay.* Glenview, Ill.: Scott, Foresman, 1972. (a)

————. *The Radical Attack on Business.* New York: Harcourt Brace Jovanovich, 1972. (b)

Phillips, Derek. *Abandoning Method.* San Francisco: Jossey-Bass, 1973.

Price, Don K. *The Scientific Estate.* Cambridge: Harvard University Press, 1965.

Reich, Charles. "The New Property," *Yale Law Journal,* 13 (April 1964), 733–87.

Rose, Arnold. "Varieties of Sociological Imagination," *American Sociological Review,* 34 (October 1969), 623–30.

Sax, Joseph L. *Defending the Environment: A Strategy for Citizen Action.* New York: Knopf, 1971.

Seeley, John R. "Social Science? Some Provocative Problems," in Stein and Vidich, eds., *Sociology on Trial.* Englewood Cliffs, N.J.: Prentice-Hall, 1963, pp. 53–65.

Selvin, Hanan C. "The Teaching of Sociological Methodology in the United States of America," *International Social Science Journal,* 15 (1963), 2–20.

Sethi, S. Prakash. *Up Against the Corporate Wall.* Englewood Cliffs, N.J.: Prentice-Hall, 1971.

Sjoberg, Gideon, ed. *Ethics, Politics and Social Research.* Cambridge: Schenkman, 1967.

————. "Some Radical Perspectives in Sociology," *Sociological Inquiry,* 40 (Winter 1970), 3–167.

Stehr, Nico, and Lyle Larson. "The Rise and Decline of Areas of Specialization," *American Sociologist,* 7 (August 1972), 3, 5–6.

Sudnow, David. *Passing On: The Social Organization of Dying.* Englewood Cliffs, N.J.: Prentice-Hall, 1967.

Szymanski, Albert. "Toward a Radical Sociology," *Sociological Inquiry,* 40 (Winter 1970), 3–13.

Thio, Alex. "Class Bias in the Sociology of Deviance," *American Sociologist,* 8 (February 1973), 1–12.

Turner, Ralph H. "The Public Perception of Protest," *American Sociological Review,* 34 (December 1969), 815–31.

Vanik, Charles. "Corporate Federal Tax Payments and Federal Subsidies to Corporations." Testimony before Joint Economic Committee, Congressional Record, 19 July 1972. (a)

————. "Varieties of Political Expression in Sociology," *American Journal of Sociology,* 78 (July 1972), 1–221. (b)

Vose, Clement. "Litigation as a Form of Pressure Group Activity," *Annals of the American Academy of Political and Social Science,* 519 (September 1958), 20–31.

Webb, Eugene, Donald T. Campbell, Richard D. Schwartz, and Lee Sechrest. *Unobtrusive Measures.* Chicago: Rand McNally, 1966.

Wellford, Harrison. "On How To Be a Constructive Nuisance," in DeBell, ed., *The Environmental Handbook.* New York: Ballantine, 1970.

Young, T. R. "The Politics of Sociology: Gouldner, Goffman and Garfinkel," *American Sociologist,* 6 (November 1971), 276–81.

———. "Conflict Methodology." The Red Feather Institute, 1972.

Young, T. R., and Jeanne Boland. "The Dramaturgical Society." Paper read at ASA meetings, New Orleans, 1972.

Zeitlin, Maurice, ed. *American Society, Inc.: Studies of the Social Structure and Political Economy of the United States.* Chicago: Markham, 1970.

CHAPTER 6 RADICAL, CRITICAL, AND NEO-MARXIST SOCIOLOGY

Introduction

In this chapter we deal with a set of sociologies whose chief distinguishing point is their radical critique of society and of "established" sociology. They are not well unified with each other, although they are recognizable as an emergent group in sociology (see Mullins, 1973: Chapter 11, whose subtitle "Here There Be Tygers" indicates a mocking stance toward their style rather than substance). Annual meetings of the American Sociological Association in recent years have accommodated meetings of a Radical Caucus that provides concrete identification for sociologists of this type. Above all, perhaps, these sociologists are concerned with the *use* of sociology and opt for personal and social liberation tasks.

There is, of course, a long tradition of social criticism in sociology (see Bottomore, 1968), with Marx as exemplar. The contemporary radical movement, however, began as non-Marxist with the work of C. Wright Mills, who in turn was more influenced by the American social critic Thorstein Veblen (1857–1929). The movement's origins were, first, a discontent with established sociology over values, ethics, and its incomplete (or nonexistent) understanding of society—particularly its blindness to power; and second, participation in social movements—civil rights, black power, women's liberation, anti-war, and new left—and, belatedly, the rediscovery of intellectual, predominantly European, Marxism.

The foundation for radical sociology was what was briefly known as the "new sociology," the collective efforts of the followers of C. Wright Mills (see Horowitz, 1964). Mills, while rejecting the abstract theorizing of Parsons (Mills, 1959), insisted on the study of large-scale sociological problems that take the individual, social structure, and history into account. His study of power elites in the United States (1956) is illustrative of this aim. Mills argued that such has been the "true" sociological tradition (1960b). His followers retained an interest in "big range" sociology and the need to politicize the public with possible solutions to society's problems (see Horowitz, 1964). Radical sociology has built on the "new sociology" while perhaps losing the structural model that Mills employed (see Scimecca, 1976), becoming more political than scholarly.

Contemporary radical sociology is generally consciously opposed to the established order of society. To Deutsch

radical sociology is a perspective, an approach which is applicable to social phenomena . . . [It] may well lead to calls for action: but first it will muster a perspective which calls for basic change, not minor alterations in social structures which are dysfunctional for masses of people, inhumane, and which inevitably generate massive societal problems. (1972:210)

According to Szymanski, the radical sociologist should maintain "1) a driving and relentless curiosity to understand man and society; 2) a deep and healthy skepticism toward all received and established ideas . . . 3) a fundamental compassion for people, and an identification with the victims of the routine workings of social structures" (1971:100–101).Colfax (1971) has outlined the varieties of sociology that claim the radical label. Other sociologists have reacted to the radical challenge in sociology, particularly to its disruptive style (see Hauser, Robbins, Gramson, and Barton, reprinted in Colfax and Roach, 1971).

Rather than methodology, or even perhaps theory (Young, 1975, has found radical dimensions in modern systems theory), it is *intent* that makes a sociology radical. This is the subject of the first selection in this chapter, written by two sociologists at the Mills ("new sociology") end of the radical spectrum. They first sketch the turmoil created by the radical movement when it raised the question of the political dimension of sociological work. To be truly radical—that is, politically effective—radical sociology must be *good* sociology. In other words, it must accurately portray the social world, be able to explain why it is so, and provide viable alternatives. The best way we have for establishing "approximate truths," although imperfect, is standard methodology. What is often labeled biased (conservative, status quo) is often only *bad* sociology, inadequate in its own terms. While the authors are committed to radical political aims, they take a conciliatory approach to sociology and insist that radicals need *quality* work, not meaningless slogans.

Richard Flacks takes up the problem of the agenda for a radical sociology. He, too, notes that sound intellectual backing is often absent in radical politics, and he adds that radical goals and programs (or utopias) have not been clearly articulated at present. He describes the consensus arrived at by a group of radical sociologists: Sociology should be committed to a humane socialist America. Marxism and the study of power provide a first step in understanding contemporary America. The radical must investigate the political constituencies, class and others, for the propagation of socialism and find ways to make socialism a credible alternative to the present social organization of the United States.

The term "critical theory" has both a general and specific meaning in sociology. It can refer to any sociology that is critical—in the everyday meaning of the term—of society. This is the meaning in which the word is used by Bottomore (1968). A recent text (Hansen, 1976) sees critical sociology as "an effort to come to grips with the nature of individual consciousness and its relation to social order and change" (p. 244). This clearly parallels Mills' view of the sociological imagination. Hansen finds these qualities in the work of the "founders" of critical sociology, Karl Marx, Max Weber, and George Mead. He does not attempt to synthesize their work into a unified theory of society, but rather demonstrates their shared attitude toward the study of self and society.

"Critical" is also used as a synonym for Marxist sociology. The most specific usage refers to the variety of neo-Marxism propounded by the German "Frankfurt school," whose most prolific current theorist is Jurgen Habermas. The work of the "school" has been introduced into American sociology by emigrés Erich Fromm and Theodor W. Adorno (who has returned to the Frankfurt Institute for Social Research), and it has been rediscovered and developed by American sociologists (for example, Birnbaum, 1971). The revived interest has encouraged new translations of the Frankfurt school work of the pre-war and immediate post-World War II periods and rapid English language editions of recent works (see Frankfurt Institute, 1973; Horkheimer, 1972; Habermas, 1971, 1973, 1976). The article by Trent Schroyer reprinted here draws on the work of Habermas to sketch the distinct logic that underpins the emerging critical science.

Neo-Marxist sociology has been developed largely outside of the United States. It ranges from the orthodox Russian variety to the critically informed East European type to free-hitting West European traditions. The latter two have gained an increasing impact on American sociology (see Birnbaum, 1971). Marx has become more prominent and respectable in history-of-theory texts, and his work is being reexamined by "conventional" sociologists. Zeitlin (1967:159), for example, claims that "Marx's work taken as a whole is invaluable for an understanding of whole societies in the process of historical change." He concludes, however, that there is no need for a special Marxist sociology since "Many of Marx's ideas have been incorporated into present day social science and have become its permanent acquisition" (p. 162).

Permanent acquisition or not, current interest in Marx has encouraged a growing literature. Foreign works such as Lefebvre's (1968) have been translated for the American reader. Texts in introductory sociology and stratification using a Marxist orientation are now on the market (for example, Anderson, 1974a, 1974b). While some sociologists doubt the value of Marxist perspectives (see Dotson, 1974), they are likely to receive open rebukes in established journals (see Roach and Roach, 1975, and Dotson's reply, which together indicate considerable hostility between the two sides). Meanwhile, journals of avowed critical orientation are airing the tensions and different positions within neo-Marxist sociology (see Gouldner, 1974; Piccone, 1975). Others are reexamining the work of earlier Marxists (see, for example, Salamini, 1975, on the Italian Marxist Antonio Gramsci) and are developing something approaching a sociology of Marxism. Gouldner's article, which concludes this chapter, investigates the part played by ideology in Marxist theory. While stressing the importance of ideas, Marxist theory has masked the part played by intellectuals.

References and Suggested Readings

Anderson, Charles H. *The Political Economy of Social Class.* Englewood Cliffs, N.J.: Prentice-Hall, 1974. (a)
———. *Toward a New Sociology.* Rev. ed. Homewood, Ill.: Dorsey Press, 1974. (b)

Birnbaum, Norman. *Toward a Critical Sociology.* New York: Oxford University Press, 1971.

Bottomore, Thomas B. *Critics of Society: Radical Thought in North America.* New York: Pantheon, 1968.

Colfax, David. "Varieties, and Prospects of 'Radical Scholarship' in Sociology," in David Colfax and Jack L. Roach, eds., *Radical Sociology.* New York: Basic Books, 1971, pp. 81–92.

Deutsch, Steven E. "The Radical Perspective in Sociology," in John F. Glass and John R. Staude, eds., *Humanistic Society.* Pacific Palisades, Calif.: Goodyear, 1972, pp. 202–14.

Domhoff, G. Williams. *Who Rules America?* Englewood Cliffs, N.J.: Prentice-Hall, 1968.

———. *The Higher Circles: The Governing Class in America.* New York: Random House, 1970.

Dotson, Floyd. "Marx and Engels on the Family: Retrospect with a Moral," *American Sociologist,* 9 (1974), 181–86.

Frankfurt Institute for Social Research. *Aspects of Sociology.* Boston: Beacon, 1973.

Gouldner, Alvin W. "The Metaphoricality of Marxism and the Context-Freeing Grammar of Socialism," *Theory and Society,* 1 (1974), 387–414.

Habermas, Jurgen. *Knowledge & Human Interests.* Boston: Beacon, 1971.

———. *Theory and Practice.* Boston: Beacon, 1973.

———. "Some Distinctions in Universal Pragmatics," *Theory and Society,* 3 (1976), 155–167.

Hansen, Donald A. *An Invitation to Critical Sociology.* New York: Free Press, 1976.

Horkheimer, Max. *Critical Theory.* New York: Herder and Herder, 1972.

Horowitz, David. *Radical Sociology: An Introduction.* San Francisco: Canfield Press, 1971.

Horowitz, Irving L., ed. *The New Sociology.* New York: Oxford University Press, 1964.

Lefebvre, Henri. *The Sociology of Marx.* New York: Random House, 1968.

Marcuse, Herbert. *Eros and Civilization.* Boston: Beacon, 1955.

———. *Negations: Essays on Critical Theory.* Boston: Beacon, 1969.

———. *Counterrevolution and Revolt.* Boston: Beacon, 1972.

Milibrand, Ralph. *The State in Capitalist Society.* New York: Basic Books, 1969.

Mills, C. Wright. *White Collar.* New York: Oxford University Press, 1951.

———. *The Power Elite.* New York: Oxford University Press, 1956.

———. *The Sociological Imagination.* New York: Oxford University Press, 1959.

———. *Listen, Yankee: The Revolution in Cuba.* New York: Ballantine, 1960. (a)

———. *Images of Man.* New York: Braziller, 1960. (b)

———. *The Marxists.* New York: Dell, 1962.

———. In Irving Louis Horowitz, ed., *Power, Politics and People: The Collected Essays of C. Wright Mills.* New York: Ballantine Books, 1964.

Mullins, Nicholas C. *Theories and Theory Groups in Contemporary Sociology.* New York: Harper & Row, 1973.

Piccone, Paul. "Reading the Grundrisse: Beyond 'Orthodox' Marxism," *Theory and Society,* (Summer 1975), 235–55.

Roach, Jack L., and Janet K. Roach. "Marx and Others on the Family: Will the Real Sociologist Stand Up?" *The American Sociologist,* 10 (August 1975), 186–89.

Ryan, William. "Some Radical Perspectives in Sociology," *Sociological Inquiry,* 40 (Winter 1970).

Salamini, Leonardo. The Specificity of Marxist Sociology in Gramsci's Theory," *The Sociological Quarterly,* 16 (Winter 1975), 65–86.

Scimecca, Joseph A. "Paying Homage to the Father: C. Wright Mills and Radical Sociology," *The Sociological Quarterly,* 17 (Spring 1976), 180–96.

Szymanski, Albert. "Toward a Radical Sociology," in David Colfax and Jack L. Roach, eds., *Radical Sociology.* New York: Basic Books, 1971, pp. 93–107.

Young, T. R. "Radical Dimensions of Modern Systems Theory: Social Change." Paper presented at the ASA meetings, San Francisco, 1975.

Zeitlin, Irving M. *Marxism: A Reexamination.* New York: Van Nostrand Reinhold, 1967.

RADICAL POLITICS AND SOCIOLOGICAL RESEARCH: OBSERVATIONS ON METHODOLOGY AND IDEOLOGY

HOWARD S. BECKER AND IRVING LOUIS HOROWITZ

Reprinted from the *American Journal of Sociology*, 78 (July 1973), copyright © 1972 by the University of Chicago.

Howard Becker is professor of sociology at Northwestern University. Irving Louis Horowitz is professor of sociology and political science at Rutgers University, director of *Studies in Comparative International Development*, and editor-in-chief of *Transaction/Society*.

With the increasing polarization of political opinions and positions in the United States, sociologists have become increasingly concerned about the political import of their work. Until recent years, most sociologists probably believed that sociology was somehow above politics, even though sociologists had often engaged in political activity, and political and sociological discussion had often overlapped. Events have now made it impossible to leave that belief uninspected. The disclosure that social scientists have undertaken research designed to further the interests of the powerful at the expense of those of the powerless (e.g., riot control at home and "civic action" abroad) showed how even apparently innocent research might serve special political interests. Prison research has for the most part been oriented to problems of jailers rather than those of prisoners; industrial research, to the problems of managers rather than those of workers; military research, to the problems of generals rather than those of privates. Greater sensitivity to the undemocratic character of ordinary institutions and relationships (ironically fostered by social scientists themselves) has revealed how research frequently represents the interests of adults and teachers instead of those of children and students; of men instead of women; of the white middle class instead of the lower class, blacks, chicanos, and other minorities; of the conventional straight world instead of freaks; of boozers instead of potheads. Wherever someone is oppressed, an "establishment" sociologist seems to lurk in the background, providing the facts which make oppression more efficient and the theory which makes it legitimate to a larger constituency.

The belief that members of the sociological discipline are guilty as charged helps to account for the way many sociologists have responded to the attacks. They have not dismissed the charges. On the contrary, professional associations, scientific societies, the periodical literature, and foundations from Ford to Russell Sage have reviewed the political tenor of sociological work. Younger men have debated whether it was moral to be affiliated with the sociological enterprise. Older sociologists have searched their work and their consciences to see if, far from being the political liberals they imagined themselves, they were in fact lackeys of capitalist repression.

In the midst of these reconsiderations, positions hardened. The language of scholarly journals became increasingly polemical. Meetings thought to be scientific were disrupted by political protests and discussion. Presidential addresses at national and regional meetings were interrupted. All this was accompanied by, and in some cases was intimately connected with, political uprisings on entire campuses, in more than one of which sociology students played a key role. Some teachers found themselves unable to bear the discourtesies of their radical students. Some professors saw attempts to change the hierarchical relations of a department as an attack on the very idea of scholarship. They assumed that a student who called their ideas "bullshit" was attacking rational thought, and not simply using in public a critical rhetoric usually reserved for private meetings. Sometimes they were right, for some students seemed intent on cutting off debate and substituting for the free play of intellect a vocabulary designed exclusively to conform to a political position. The distinction was not always easy to make, and those making affronts were often as unsure of what they were about as those receiving them.

In situations of collective upheaval, persons and groups move to maximize their private interests. In this case, some sociologists tried to further their professional careers by judiciously taking one side or the other. Groups moved to secure power within professional associations. Some radicals seriously discussed taking over professional associations or university departments, having convinced themselves that worthwhile political goals might be served by such acts—though the resemblance of such maneuvers to similar careerist actions by doctrinaire groups of quite different persuasions in the same associations and departments was obvious. Elder sociological statesmen of every political stripe appeared, trying to gather "unpredictable youth" into their own sphere of influence. The rhetoric of radicalism appeared in every area of sociology.

Participants in these events found themselves confused. Members of the older "straight" factions, however, failed to note the confusion. They saw the actions as concerted expressions of radical or left sentiment. They could not see the conflicts of interests among radicals, blacks, chicanos, women, and other "liberation" groups. The persistent emergence of differences among these groups made it obvious that the mere assertion of radical sympathies guaranteed neither concerted political action nor a uniform style of sociological analysis. The differences and confusions demonstrate the need for a clearer analysis of the political meaning and relevance of sociology.

Good sociology is often radical. A sociology which is not good, however, cannot be radical in any larger sense. But moral sentiments do not determine scientific quality. The reverse is more often true: the quality of sociological work determines the degree to which it has a radical thrust.

We insist on the isomorphism between radical sociology and good sociology in order to dissuade those who think political sloganeering can substitute for knowledge based on adequate evidence and careful analysis; to persuade others that their work has suffered from a conventional social and political attitude, expressed in the way they frame problems and in the methods of research they choose; and to demonstrate that there is a tradition of good sociology worth preserving, that the expression "good sociology" has meaning, and that the possibility of doing good sociology is not tied irrevocably to contemporary academic institutions.

GOOD SOCIOLOGY

Good sociology is sociological work that produces meaningful descriptions of organizations and events, valid explanations of how they come about and persist, and realistic proposals for their improvement or removal. Sociology based on the best available evidence should provide analyses that are likely to be true in the

linguistic sense of not being falsifiable by other evidence, and also in the ontological sense of being "true to the world."

In the first sense, generations of methodologists have developed procedures
and techniques by which approximate truth can be reached. The sociologist
achieves partial truths, always open to correction. While methodologists have
dealt only with a small part of the problem of arriving at propositions and inferences likely to be true, the techniques they recommend as warranted are all we
have; we will have to use them until we invent something better. With all their
faults, interviews, participant observation, questionnaires, surveys, censuses, statistical analyses, and controlled experiments can be used to arrive at approximate
truth. While the results to date are modest, some things are known because sociologists have employed these techniques.

Sociologists have done less well by truth in the second sense. While they
know some things well, they can predict few things with accuracy. Humanists
and scientists alike complain that sociology tells them only a tiny part of what
they really want to know. Men want to know how the world is; sociologists give
them correlation coefficients. Coefficients do help us know how the world is, and
one need not accept the humanistic contention that unless sociology can reproduce the world in full living color it is worthless. Nonetheless, the charge stings.
Sociologists' knowledge about real problems in society does not take them far.

If essentials are left out, the work cannot pass the tests that science poses
for itself. The work cannot, to use the language of statistical analysis, account
for much of the variance in the phenomena under study. In addition, sociological
work loses its potential practical importance if it does not encompass the major
processes and actors involved in those parts of the world to be changed. Therefore,
work that is not true to the world has neither scientific nor practical value.

Why does so much sociological work fail to be true both to its own scientific
standards and to the larger world? Some radical sociologists have insisted that
political ideologies blind us to the truth because our political masters have paid
us to produce research that will be useful in a different direction, or (more subtly)
because our standard methods and concepts, reflecting political biases and pressures, prevent us from seeing what would be politically inconvenient. Many failures in sociological research result from simple ignorance, having little to do with
either ideological bias or utopian fantasy. But we should examine those instances
in which sociological research has been severely blemished not so much by ignorance as by bias.

Consider the charge that the concept of "accommodation," applied to racial
relations, had a conservative effect (Myrdal, 1944). It implied that blacks accepted
their lower position in American society and that therefore, because blacks did
not complain, the situation was not unjust. But to say that racial relations in a
given place at a given time were accommodative means only that the racial
groups involved had achieved a modus vivendi and does not imply that the actors
were happy or the system just. Whether any or all actors considered the system
pleasant or righteous is a matter for empirical investigation. If the description of
the situation as accommodative were true to the world, no evidence of conflict
and resistance could be discovered because none would exist. To assume consensus would be bad sociology insofar as it assumed that, since there is evidence
of accommodation, we can rule out the the possiblity of conflict. The concept of
accommodation can be objectionable only if we insist that its use will necessarily
cause sociologists to overlook or ignore conflict, exploitation, or resistance to
change where they occur. But a full exploration of possibilities, as in Robert
Park's description of the race relations cycle (Park and Burgess, 1921), applied
evenhandedly, should spare sociologists such errors.

Much contemporary sociology is not true even in the narrow scientific sense.
It is falsifiable by evidence contained in its own data or by evidence that could

have been obtained had the investigator bothered to look for it. Sociologists tend to ignore the degree to which they fail to abide by their own methodological standards and consequently fail to achieve the scientific rationality to which they pretend. Where sociology allows political biases and generalized expression of wishful thinking to affect its conclusions, it lacks truth in either of the two meanings discussed.

RADICAL SOCIOLOGY

An immense variety of political positions have been announced as radical. Since the actual consequences of the label are so important to all the people involved, one cannot expect any definition to go undisputed. But most arguments over definitions turn on questions of the means by which agreed-on goals can be achieved or of the correct diagnosis of the ills that afflict society, rather than on the goals that radicals ought to strive for. Thus, most radicals will agree that a key feature of any radical political program is the reduction and eventual removal of inequalities in society, whether the inequality is of power, economic resources, life chances, or knowledge. Likewise, most radicals will agree that a radically reconstructed society should maximize human freedom, especially when that is conceived as dialectically related to social order.

Radicals may not so universally agree on the necessity of permanent change and revolution as an ideal. We ourselves believe that every society and every set of social arrangements must be inspected for their potential inequalities and interferences with freedom, even those which seem to conform to one or another blueprint for a socialist utopia. The radical, so defined normatively, is never satisfied, never prepared to abandon the struggle for an even more egalitarian and free society. At the least, the better is the critic of the good.

Where circumstances compel a choice between individual interests, self-expression, and personal welfare, on the one hand, and social order, stability, and the collective good, on the other, such a radical politics acts for the person as against the collectivity. It acts to maximize the number and the variety of options people have open to them, at the expense of neatness, order, peace, and system. It regards conflict as a normal concomitant of social life and a necessary element in political action. Clearly, some definitions of radicalism are based precisely on collectivism. While we look for the convergence of personal and public goals, when we are compelled to make a choice, it is on behalf of persons.

The radical sees change as permanent and inevitable, but he need not accept all changes as good. Rather, he sides with the powerless against the powerful, and renounces coercion, terror, and control as methods of establishing truths about the world.

The posture of a radical sociology overlaps considerably with that of a radical politics. Radical sociology also rests on a desire to change society in a way that will increase equality and maximize freedom, and it makes a distinctive contribution to the struggle for change. On the one hand, it provides the knowledge of how society operates, on the basis of which a radical critique of inequality and lack of freedom can be made. On the other hand, it provides the basis for implementing radical goals, constructing blueprints for freer, more egalitarian social arrangements, the working plans for radical utopias. These constructive aspects are rooted in the positivist tradition, just as the critical aspects are rooted in the Marxist tradition. Both involve an explanation of radical goals, and both involve a repudiation of all forms of mystical, theological, and supernaturalist interpretations of events.

A radical sociology thus looks for explanations of social life and theories of society which assume that radical change is at least possible, and resists those theories which root inequality in "inescapable facts" of biology or social structure (Horowitz, 1968). Since such assumptions are seldom subjected to empirical test, a radical sociology can just as reasonably assume possibilities that more conservative or pessimistic sociologies do not.

In the controversy between Davis and Moore (1945: 242–49) and Tumin (1953: 387–93), the real difference of opinion was not over the fact of social stratification in American life, or even over the existence of inequality. There were indeed differences of opinion at the factual level, but the core controversy concerned the tendencies of American society: whether the direction of the democratic society carried with it as a central agenda item the reduction and finally the elimination of inequality. If inequality is rooted in the nature of man, with only the forms of inequality changing and the types of oppressors shifting, then the goal of equality is itself suspect. Any radical sociology must explore the nature of inequality fully, and beyond that must assume the possibility of abolishing inequality and describing the machinery necessary to implement a more egalitarian social order (Dumont, 1969).

It might be objected that this equation of radicalism and the search for equity itself represents a liberal "bourgeois" model rather than a radical paradigm, that true radicalism must uphold the banner of a particular social system, such as socialism. While this formulation is abstractly appealing and in fact is often employed by radical theorists, it omits the most important fact of our times: the need for a social scientific judgment of *all* available political systems. Any equation of radical perspectives with the demand for equity implies the universal claim to priority of equality in socialist systems such as the Soviet Union, no less than in capitalist systems such as the United States. To demand allegiance to any social system as the mark of a radical perspective is to ignore the 100-year history of inequality within what has passed for socialism, as well as the far longer history of inequality under capitalism.

But the search for equity is only one side of the radical thrust. At least equal in importance is the investigation of the ability of society, as presently organized, to deliver equity. It is the assessment of that ability that divides radical and liberal analysts. The ability of established society to absorb new social demands of disenfranchised groups becomes a major concern of the radical. The historic concern of radicalism with problems of revolution expresses a pessimistic view of the present social and economic order's ability to absorb change.

No matter which of these several tasks a radical sociology undertakes, it finds itself providing the facts, theories, and understandings that a radical politics requires for its implementation. For a radical political posture without reliable facts and analyses is no more than insurrectionary art incapable of predicting its own successes or failures. Radical sociology provides relevant and trustworthy data, intellectual resources for measuring costs as well as benefits in realizing the insurrectionary act.

CONFLICT BETWEEN RADICAL SOCIOLOGY AND RADICAL POLITICS

Radical sociology may create a tension with radical politics, pure and simple, by indicating the high cost of some desired act. For example, it may analyze the special features of the Cuban-Castro revolution and produce an explanation of why guerrilla insurgency was successful in Cuba in 1959 but tragically unsuccessful in Bolivia in 1969. It is by no means a simple matter to counsel the gathering of evidence instead of performing a revolutionary act. But the gathering of evidence distinguishes a radical sociology from a radical politics, without necessarily destroying the basis for their mutual interaction.

A radical sociology will base itself either explicitly or implicitly on the premises of a radical politics. In either case, it will produce knowledge that serves the purposes of radical politics, in any of a variety of ways.

Every group in power is bent on the protection of privilege. Therefore, every radical sociology must expose the nature of such privilege, unmasking forms of domination. This unmasking process creates dilemmas. It implies a ruthless stripping away of all mystery and cant, not just that of the Department of Defense but also that of the Nation of Islam. One task of a radical sociology is thus to persuade the oppressed and radicals of the need for as total a dedication to what is true as to what they may deem good. It is here too that the issue between most contemporary forms of radical sociology and radical political action becomes enmeshed in controversy, since many forms of radical politics are themselves bound to canons of secrecy, perhaps more benign than conservative politics but ultimately no less destructive of the search for truth in society.

Every status quo—societal, organizational, or factional—thrives on myth and mystification. Every group in power—in a nation, a government, an economy, a political party, or a revolutionary cadre—tells its story as it would like to have it believed, in the way it thinks will promote its interests and serve its constituencies. Every group in power profits from ambiguity and mystification, which hide the facts of power from those over whom power is exerted and thus make it easier to maintain hegemony and legitimacy. A sociology that is true to the world inevitably clarifies what has been confused, reveals the character of organizational secrets, upsets the interests of powerful people and groups. And while uncovering error does not necessarily aid the interests of those exploited by an organization or society, it does at least permit equal access to the evidence upon which action must be based. Only if sociological work is good in the sense of explaining actual relationships of power and authority can it provide a force for change. Thus, work which is true to the world and explains the actual relations of power and privilege that envelop and determine what goes on in society will be politically useful to radicals, even though (importantly) those who do such work may not themselves be committed to radical political goals.

Sociologists already know the difficulties that come from doing work which exposes the operations of powerful groups in society (see the various accounts in Vidich, Bensman, and Stein, 1964). In operating explicitly in behalf of radical goals and in cooperation with people engaged in radical political action, the sociologist will experience other characteristic difficulties. For instance, a good sociological analysis, explored fully for its political implications, may undermine one's own position of superiority and privilege. Thus, a radical sociological analysis of universities entails exposing the myths by which the professor who makes the analysis supports his own privileged position of tenure and income. Similarly, white sociologists find themselves producing work which undermines their unequal privileges vis-à-vis blacks; men undermine the bases of their social superiority to women; and so on. This is why the poor and downtrodden are never "radical"—what they do is "natural," in keeping with their "interests." The radical violates the canon of self-interest or group interest. The good sociologist carries radicalism a step further: he makes it a principle to transcend parochialism and patriotism in investigating the social context.

The radical sociologist will also find that his scientific "conservatism"—in the sense of being unwilling to draw conclusions on the basis of insufficient evidence—creates tension with radical activists. This results from the differing time scales of the two activities. The social scientist takes time to collect evidence, but the political activist must often make decisions prior to the compilation of adequate evidence. Under such circumstances, the political man will act; the sociologist can give him the best available evidence. Radical activism is not the same as the know-nothingism underlining the irrationalist "will to act," but rather a recognition that action may be induced by needs that cannot possibly await the supply of the social scientist's information. The lag between action and information explains, in part, the peculiar tension between the political man and the social scientist, a tension that often leads the activist to disregard the sociologist's advice and, correspondingly, often leads the sociologist to an overconservative estimate of the potential success of a dramatic political action.

Since radical politics and radical sociology are not the same, the two may conflict. What is the relation between political radicalism and sociological radicalism? Rosa Luxemburg acted as a revolutionist and as a leader of the Spartacists of the German Left Socialist movement, but at the same time she functioned as a radical, as a critic of Lenin and of the dogma of proletarian dictatorship. She did this at a moment of revolutionary euphoria when serious thinking was at a premium. It is her criticism which is now best remembered. The same can be said of Eugene V. Debs, whose importance in the Socialist movement lay precisely in his being above the fraticidal struggles for control of the Socialist party apparatus. Debs, the radical man, had little organizational power in American socialism. Far less concerned with organization than DeLeon, Debs alone emerged as the ecumenical figure for the Socialists (see Ginger, 1949).

Radicalism, then, entails a critique of organizational constraints. Yet revolution can only be made on the basis of a theory of organization. This is why the roles of radical sociologist and revolutionary activist, while they may coexist, cause considerable tension within the person and between the organization and the individual. If the activist joins forces with other advocates for rapid change, the sociologist points out how limited the practical effects of these changes may be. The activist, achieving his goals, seeks to enjoy the fruits of his victory; the radical sociologist looks for new sources of inequality and privilege to understand, expose, and uproot.

The difference between political radicalism and sociological radicalism deserves further elaboration. While the two can be linked, they can also occur independently and may be quite distinct. Radical action and rhetoric are one thing, and a radically informed sociology is another. Confusing the two opens leftism to any professional opportunism of the moment. Political sloganeers can easily tailor their doctrine to the changing fortunes of political sects. Serious sociologists find it much harder to change their sociological practice to match their changing political beliefs. To teach the same courses in theory and method one taught 20 years ago, while shifting from support for the government to opposition, does little to change the political thrust of contemporary social science. One can use radical rhetoric and engage in radical political action while one's sociology, because of its failure to be good, leaves established myths and institutions untouched. This is only the radical manifestation of the dualist distinction between "fact" and "value" adhered to by most conservatives. The "values" shift and become anti-establishment rather than pro-establishment. But the world of "fact," or, as is more nearly true, the fantasy that passes for sociological fact, remains unaltered.

RADICALISM AND CAUSAL ANALYSIS

The intersection of sociological and political analysis, the common ground which allows a characterization of various kinds of sociology as having one or another political cast, lies in their mutual concern with causes of events. It seems clear that any necessary condition for the occurrence of an event may be considered a cause of that event, at least in the limited sense that if the condition were not present, the event would not occur. From this point of view, there is an infinite or at least a very large number of causes of any event. To use a *reductio ad absurdum*, the presence of oxygen in the atmosphere is a cause of class exploitation, since without oxygen there would be no people, and without people there could be no exploitation. All such physical conditions of human action are, in this extended and vacuous sense, causes. In a more restricted and less trivial way, the actions of every person and group that contribute, however remotely, to a social event occurring in the way it did can be seen as a contributing cause of the event, since in their absence things would have occurred differently. To take a not-so-absurd example, the actions of slaves constitute one of the causes of slavery, since they could (and sometimes did) refuse to act as slaves (even though the price might be death).

Even though there are a multitude of causes of any event, both scientific and political analysis concentrate on only a few of them—different analyses emphasizing different causes. How do sociologists choose from among the many possible causes those they will emphasize in their political analysis or investigate in their research? Sometimes they look for those potential causes which vary, or might vary, in the specific cases observed. Thus, social scientists ignore the presence of oxygen as a cause of social events, since it is a constant in human affairs—except, of course, for those rare situations in which its presence becomes problematic, as in a recent study of social relationships among the men who climbed Mount Everest (Emerson, 1966). Sometimes they choose causes for investigation with an eye to the "usefulness" of results. Insofar as analysis is meant to be useful as a guide to someone's action, sociologists look to causal analysis for the clues as to how things might be changed, how they might be kept the same, and what the cost of either course is.

These guidelines help somewhat but do not go far enough in cutting down the number of causes the analyst pays attention to. On further inspection, we can see that the assignment of causes to events has a political aspect. The way sociologists assign causes, both in setting up hypotheses to be studied and in announcing conclusions, exhibits the influence of a political point of view, however implicit or hazy.

When sociologists link a cause to an event or a state of affairs, they at the same time assign blame for it. An event occurred because certain actors did something that helped to make it occur; had they acted differently, the event would not have occurred as it did. If the event is judged to be morally or politically reprehensible, the sociological analysis, by isolating those actors as the cause of the event, blames them for its occurrence.

An analysis may also implicitly or explicitly place the blame for events on impersonal forces beyond personal control—human nature, the human condition, or the social system—and thus excuse the people whose actions appeared to be morally suspect by suggesting that they could not help doing what they did. Deterministic sociologies of every description perform this service for the villains they identify.

If sociology allows for choice on the part of human actors, then it can blame, by the way it assigns causes, any of the people involved, since they could have chosen not to do what they did. This has consequences for the political character of a sociological analysis. Volitional sociologies perform this service for the heroes they identify.

The sociological analysis of causes has practical importance. When some object or action is labeled as the cause of the event or situation, the analysis suggests what would have to be influenced or altered in order to make a significant change in that event or situation. Some things will be easier to change than others. The analysis may suggest that, under the circumstances, it is virtually impossible to change what must be changed in order to affect the situation. Alternatively, the analysis may focus on things easily changed in themselves but which have little chance of changing the situation. Every combination of the feasibility of intervention and of the magnitude of the expected effect can occur in a particular analysis.

When sociologists, in their investigation of causes, implicitly or explicitly assign blame for events and when they suggest what must be done to cause meaningful social change, they speak of matters that are also the subject of political analyses. Their analyses can be judged to be radical, liberal, or conservative by the same criteria used to judge political analyses.

In general, radicals will judge a sociological analysis as radical when its assignment of causes, and thus of blame, coincides with the preferred demonology of the political group making the judgment. Radicals will denounce analyses as conservative (and conservatives will denounce analyses as radical) when the assignment of causes blames people who "don't deserve it." Similarly, radicals may criticize analyses that suggest causes which, when we take action, are too easily influenced and will not produce sufficiently profound results (right-wing reformism or opportunism), or are too difficult to influence, thus leading to disillusionment and low morale (left adventurism).

Since radical political positions are more "unusual" and thus more visible in contemporary social science, it is radical sociologists who are most aware of these political connotations of sociological work. Most discussions of the problem have therefore been conducted by sociologists who conceive of themselves, or would like to conceive of themselves, as radical and who therefore focus on ferreting out the political implications of work that is not politically self-conscious. Both because of our own political position and for the sake of congruence with current discussions, we will take the same tack. It should be understood, however, that in a society where some version of radical politics was more common and dominated research in an unselfconscious way, a similar critique might be mounted from the center or right. In our own society, political judgments of the results of sociological work could as easily be made from those positions, though they could scarcely be designed to uncover hidden radical assumptions, since radical sociologists tend to make these quite explicit.

Examples of the political import of causal analysis are easily available. It is common knowledge that most black Americans live less well than most white Americans. Something ought to be done about it; people mostly agree on that as well. What causes this situation? Some explanations explicitly blame the victims themselves, by finding, for instance, that their own inherited defects lead to all their trouble (see the critique in Ryan, 1971: 3–30). Many people found fault with Moynihan's explanation that some of the trouble lay in the disorganization of the black family (Rainwater and Yancey, 1967). That explanation seemed implicitly to blame blacks for their own troubles by suggesting that they need not have been so disorganized. It did not emphasize the causes of that disorganization, which, when revealed, placed the blame on their oppression by the white community. The same analysis further suggested that it would be difficult to change things because it is quite difficult to change family patterns. The Moynihan analysis might thus be interpreted as having a conservative political thrust.

Consider the rash of ideological interpretations of student protest movements. Investigators may locate the causes of those protests in some characteristic of students themselves (e.g., Shils, 1969; Feuer, 1969), and thus implicitly suggest that it is the actions of students which, without the help of any of the other involved parties, produce all the trouble. Students are to blame while, by implication, others whose behavior we do not regard as a cause are not to blame. Alternatively, we can interpret campus disorders as political phenomena which arise in the same way as other political phenomena, and serve as a mechanism by which subordinate groups make hierarchical superiors pay attention to their demands for change (e.g., Becker, 1970; Horowitz and Friedland, 1970). In such a case, the difficulty can be located in the disparity between what one group wants and what the other group is willing to give, and it becomes equally possible to blame those who refuse to give students what they want, since that refusal is one of the necessary conditions for the occurrence of the disorderly events.

Political and sociological analyses both operate under a potent constraint, which is that actions based on them should have the anticipated consequences. That remains a major test of any *scientific* proposition. If an analysis is factually incorrect, then political predictions will not come to pass and strategies will be discredited. Science will not validate propositions just because they appear ethically worthwhile; the propositions must be correct in the real world. In this sense, radicalism is a necessary, but not a sufficient, condition of good sociology.

The production of factually correct analyses involves a paradox. What sociologists need to know about any institution or organization in order to achieve radical goals is usually similar to what they must know to achieve conservative ends as well. Consider research on consumer behavior. Advertising and marketing experts, presumably lackeys of the capitalist system, have done research to discover how to make advertising more effective, that is, how to manipulate people so that they will buy what they might not have bought otherwise. Simultaneously, radicals have complained, though they have not done research on the topic, that advertising makes people desire commodities they do not need. Radicals agree that advertising works the way marketing people say it does. Radical sociologists presumably want to know how to lessen the impact of advertising and make people's choices free; they might be interested in how the process of choice would work in a situation devoid of the artificial influence of advertising.

Apart from the difference in the moral animus of the language used by opposing groups, both conservative businessmen and radical activists need, to further their opposing ends, the same knowledge about the process by which consumers choose products. If we had a decent theory of consumer behavior, empirically validated, then the radical, knowing how advertising works, would know where to intervene so that it would not work, and the marketing expert would know why his techniques fail and how to improve them. An adequate analysis of how things stay the same is thus at the same time an analysis of how to change them. Conventional, presumably conservative, analyses often fail to take into account matters radicals think important. If those matters are indeed important, then the conservative analysis which ignores them will be faulty and its predictions will not prove true.

Political commitment is revealed by the kind of causes sociologists include in their analyses, by the way blame is assigned and the possibilities of political action evaluated. It is revealed most clearly by ignoring causes conceived of as incapable of change when in fact they could be changed under certain conditions, and by regarding a situation as easily subject to change when in fact there are substantial forces perpetuating it. Such false assumptions make it likely that plans of action resting on them will fail. In fact, although it is often charged that American social science is (presumably successfully) engaged in helping oppressors keep subject populations in their place, the actions which are supposed to be based on these analyses often fail, precisely because they have failed to take into account important causes suggested by more radical sociological analyses.

OBSTACLES TO RADICAL SOCIOLOGY

If the foregoing analysis of causality is correct, it ought to be no more difficult to create radical sociology than other varieties already available. Yet, for all the stated need for a more radical sociology, we find mostly programmatic statements and little substantive work that could reasonably be so labeled. It cannot be that there are no radical sociologists, for they have made their presence known. Indeed, as we have suggested, even those who call themselves radical have trouble knowing what their sociology ought to look like; in fact, we can see that it often differs in no observable way from nonradical sociology.

Some radicals in sociology claim that there is no truly radical sociology because most sociologists, being liberals or worse, are on the take from the establishment and naturally do not wish to make analyses that will subvert their own material interests. These radicals further suggest that the organizations which distribute research funds and control publication are so dominated by liberals and conservatives that radical work cannot be supported or published. If we accept such statements as radical sociological work, the ease with which they too achieve publication and professional recognition suggests that they are not true (see Nicolaus, 1969).

Those who conceive of themselves as radical sociologists find it hard to do identifiably radical research, while politically neutral sociologists do research useful for radical goals (in the sense that they discover causal relationships which can be used as guides for radical political action). That demands explanation. There seem to be three chief reasons for this lack of connection between radical sociology and radical politics: 1) the conservative influence of conventional technical procedures, 2) common-sense standards of credibility of explanations, and 3) the influence of agency sponsorship. Each of these, in its own way, deters the sociologist's full exploration of the range of necessary conditions that ought to be considered as potential causes of the situation he studies.

Most commonly used research techniques require the investigator to have worked out his hypotheses fully before he begins gathering data. If we conceive research as testing deductions made from existing theories (wherever those theories come from), then the data one gathers must be suitable for making such tests. One restricts what he finds out to what will be relevant to those hypotheses. Experiments, surveys, and paper-and-pencil testing necessarily restrict the range of causes eventually considered, by the simple technical fact of confining inquiry to what the researcher has in mind when he plans his research. But in doing research, we often find that we have failed to take into account many variables and causes that, on the basis of early findings, we see we should take into account.

With respect to the possibility of a radical sociology, what we leave out may not be important for the allocation of blame. But if what has been neglected, or made impossible to locate, is necessary to effect change, such research becomes less useful for radical political purposes by virtue of that gap. Even committed political radicals find themselves constrained by the research techniques they are familiar with. These techniques often leave out some things they would think important if they knew about them. Some techniques, indeed, require sociologists to leave out things they *know* might be important. Thus, it is difficult, though not altogether impossible, to study certain kinds of power relationships and many kinds of historical changes by the use of survey research techniques. If that is what one knows how to do, then he is stuck with what he can discover by that technique.

Another barrier to a radical sociology lies in common-sense conceptions of credibility. Every theoretical stance, including those defined as radical, makes assumptions about the character of the world. In particular, the sociological view of the world usually assumes that some people are more believable than others, that their stories, insights, notions, and theories are more worthy of being taken seriously than those of others. One of the chief reasons conventional sociology fails to uncover some important causes of events and situations is that it accepts the common-sense notion that the people who run organizations and are highly placed in communities know more about those organizations and communities than others, and therefore ought to be taken more seriously. The immediate effect of assuming the veracity of highly placed people is to leave out of consideration questions and problems that appear foolish from an elitist viewpoint (Becker, 1967).

Conventional sociologists might, for instance, find it reasonable to ask why some schools are more effective in teaching their students than others. But it violates common sense to suggest, even though research might show it to be true, that schools actually prevent people from learning what they are supposed to learn. We have similar official versions and analyses of most social problems.

When we study those problems, we find it hard to free ourselves from official analyses sufficiently to consider causes not credited in those versions. This is not to say that other causes are necessarily operative, but only that sociologists often fail to look at them because they seem unlikely or bizarre.

Radical politics has its own set of official explanations, its own set of preferred causes, and one can err as badly by taking these for granted as he can by taking conventional causes for granted. Of course, radically oriented research will seldom leave out of account what conventional sociologists include, if only because it wishes to demonstrate that those analyses are wrong. Therefore, research organized on radical lines will probably be more inclusive and therefore more useful.

Agency sponsorship tends to put conservative limits on the search for necessary conditions (Blumer, 1967). Although research is most commonly funded and sponsored by the government or foundations politically suspect from some radical point of view, the trouble does not necessarily arise from the political character of the sponsors. Rather, it occurs because, whatever their political persuasion, when agencies purchase research they are concerned with answers to particular questions, questions which arise for them as operational difficulties. They do not wish to spend their money on meandering investigations of God knows what. Therefore, the agreement between researcher and agency typically specifies a limited area of research, the limits set by the agency's conception of what the problem is and where its causes lie. Ordinarily, the agency will not see its own operations as one of the causes of the problem, and thus those operations will not be included in the area the researcher agrees to study; by implication, he agrees not to study them (see Platt, 1971).

This discussion of barriers to unconventional radical sociological analyses allows us to look critically at some common notions of what constitutes radical sociology. Most of the common definitions of a radical style in sociology bear some relation to making the kinds of analyses we have now identified as radical. In every case, however, the connection is contingent rather than necessary. We need to understand the circumstances under which the phenomenon in question actually leads to radical analysis and when it does not.

When one does research for a government agency, that agency will want the questions to be studied in a way that makes it difficult to come up with unconventional and radical conclusions. But refusing to accept government funds does not guarantee a radical analysis, nor is all research paid for by the government by definition conservative. If a federally funded researcher has arranged conditions so that he has maximum freedom, he may very well produce radical findings. Having done so, he may find it difficult to get further research funds from the same or similar sources. The remedy for that is to travel light, to avoid acquiring the obligations and inclinations that make large-scale funds necessary.

Studying radical groups from a sympathetic point of view, though one need not be particularly sympathetic with them to do so, may be of great use. Those groups might be exceptions to sociological wisdom, based on more conventional cases, and might make us aware of causal connections sociologists had not seen before. Thus, the study of communal living groups might allow sociologists to see certain possibilities of social organization that are ordinarily masked if we examine only longer-lasting and more stable institutions.

The influence of the sociologist's life style on his work becomes especially important in an era of theatrical politics. Wearing a Viet Cong button does not make one a radical any more than living in a suburb makes one a conservative. Nevertheless, wearing buttons, beads, or otherwise looking "freaky" may cause the person to have experiences (with police, fellow sociologists, or others) which will force him or her to question assumptions that might otherwise have been left uninspected. In the same way, living in a middle-class suburb might insulate the sociologist from some experiences and so lead him to incorrect assumptions about some matters of fact.

Personal involvement in political radicalism or affiliation with an organization that champions radical programs and positions does not necessarily lead one to do radical sociology. Such a political commitment might dispose a sociologist to search for causes and possible modes of intervention other analyses had left out. On the other hand, a radical sociologist might do research for his political allies which was no different in its style from the research other sociologists do for General Electric or Standard Oil. Such research might produce no more profound analysis of causes and would thus be no more useful to the movement than market research and an investigation of how to keep the native labor force happy have been for industry.

A radical rhetoric or ideological posture does not inevitably result in politically useful sociological work. Ideologically "correct" analyses cannot substitute for cogent, empirically verified knowledge of the world as a basis for effective action. Ideological radicalism cannot provide a workable understanding of the relative roles of China and India in the developmental process of Asia. Ideological radicalism cannot tell us how long it takes to make the transition from rural to urban life. Ideological radicalism cannot prove the merits or demerits of one or another form of economic investment. When radicalism without sociology is employed as a surrogate for truth, it becomes fanaticism—a foolish effort to replace substance with style. But when these limits are understood and expressed, sociological radicalism can help us measure the distance between where people are and where they want to go—between the society and the utopia.

In a period of railing and ranting against the social sciences, it is perhaps time once again to raise the matter of priorities for our age. It is the purpose of a meaningful sociology to demonstrate how it is that society and its institutions are on trial, and how it is that society and its organizations are undergoing crisis. When we keep this in mind and remember that sociology is part of society, and that sociology in itself means very little apart from the larger social tasks, then perhaps the sense and style of radical sociology will be enhanced, adding flesh and blood to its current programmatics and calling us back once again *first* to the criticism of society and only *second* to the criticism of other sociologists.

REFERENCES

Becker, Howard S. "Whose Side Are We On?" *Social Problems*, 14 (Winter 1967), 239–48.
———. "Introduction: The Struggle for Power on Campus," in Howard S. Becker, ed., *Campus Power Struggle*. Chicago, Aldine, 1970.
Blumer, Herbert. "Threats from Agency-Determined Research: The Case of Camelot," in Irving Louis Horowitz, ed., *The Rise and Fall of Project Camelot*. Cambridge, Mass.: M.I.T. Press, 1967.
Davis, Kingsley, and Wilbert E. Moore. "Some Principles of Stratification," *American Sociological Review*, 10 (April 1945), 242–49.
Dumont, L. "Caste, Racism and 'Stratification': Reflections of a Social Anthropologist," in André Béteille, ed., *Social Inequality: Selected Readings*. Baltimore: Penguin, 1969.
Emerson, Richard M. "Mount Everest: A Case Study of Communication Feedback and Sustained Group Goal-Striving," *Sociometry*, 29 (September 1966), 64–70.
Feuer, Lewis S. *The Conflict of Generations*. New York: Basic Books, 1969.
Ginger, Ray. *The Bending Cross*. New Brunswick, N.J.: Rutgers University Press, 1949.
Horowitz, Irving Louis. *Professing Sociology: Studies in the Life Cycle of a Social Science*. Chicago: Aldine, 1968.
Horowitz, Irving Louis, and William H. Friedland. *The Knowledge Factory: Student Power and Academic Politics in America*. Chicago: Aldine, 1970.
Myrdal, Gunnar. *An American Dilemma*. New York: Harper & Bros., 1944.
Nicolaus, Martin. "The Professional Organization of Sociology: A View from Below," *Antioch Review*, 29 (Fall 1969), 375–87.

Park, Robert E., and Ernest W. Burgess. *Introduction to the Science of Sociology.* Chicago: University of Chicago Press, 1921.

Platt, Anthony M. *The Politics of Riot Commissions.* New York: Collier, 1971.

Rainwater, Lee, and William L. Yancey. *The Moynihan Report and the Politics of Controversy.* Cambridge, Mass.: M.I.T. Press, 1967.

Ryan, William. *Blaming the Victim.* New York: Pantheon, 1971.

Shils, Edward. "Plentitude and Scarcity," *Encounter,* 32 (May 1969), 37–48.

Tumin, Melvin W. "Some Principles of Stratification: A Critical Analysis," *American Sociological Review,* 18 (August 1953), 387–93.

Vidich, Arthur J., Joseph Bensman, and Maurice R. Stein. *Reflections on Community Studies.* New York: Harper & Row, 1964.

TOWARD A SOCIALIST SOCIOLOGY

RICHARD FLACKS

Reprinted from *Insurgent Sociologist*, 2 (Spring 1972), 18–27. Used by permission.

Richard Flacks is chairperson and professor of sociology at the University of California, Santa Barbara.

Anyone who works as a radical in academic life experiences extreme intellectual isolation. This fact is probably important in explaining why radical intellectuals in America have been relatively effective at criticism and markedly deficient in working out coherent *alternatives* to established intellectual structures in the academic disciplines.

During the spring of 1971 in Santa Barbara, a few self-defined radical sociologists had the opportunity to break down some of that isolation since we all happened to be living or visiting in Santa Barbara. As a result of being together, we decided that we might fruitfully try to develop a program of intellectual work for radical sociologists in the hope of stimulating those who shared our perspective to orient toward a common set of problems—so that radical sociology could move beyond criticism of the discipline and become helpful in providing an intellectual basis for the movements for change in the U.S.

The members of our group included: William Domhoff, Milton Mankoff, Harvey Molotch, John Seeley, and Maurice Zeitlin. A radical economist, Andrew Winnick, participated in a number of our sessions. The following paper was written by me in an effort to summarize our sessions. It represents my own perspective on what was discussed; the others should not be held responsble for its many weaknesses, although it is infused with their ideas. A version of this paper was presented and discussed at the meetings of the American Sociological Association in Denver, August 1971.

This paper is intended to be part of a continuing discussion—not a finished product. I am therefore eager to have any thoughts it might stimulate, and suggestions about how this discussion can be institutionalized so that all who wish to can take part in it.

If there is a "crisis in Western Sociology" reflected in its increasing incoherence and its failure to apprehend central features of contemporary reality, those of us who claim to be radicals in sociology must nevertheless recognize our own failure to create alternative models of work for ourselves and for those who are attracted to our perspective. In fact, the "radical sociology" which emerged in the past decade appears to have completed its limited role. If we were mainly seeking to legitimate a socially critical, "anti-establishment," stance within the discipline, we have largely succeeded. There can be little doubt that sociologists now are increasingly sensitive to the over-commitment of the discipline to established power and the status quo; that social criticism of considerable range and depth is now more possible within the official forums of the discipline; that there has been a general loosening of theoretical and methodological inhibitions so that critical problems concerning conflict, change, power, and exploitation can more freely be addressed; that the Marxian tradition has a new acceptability within the discipline; and, that texts and other curricular materials embodying radical or critical perspectives are increasingly published and gaining use in undergraduate education. If it is not "safe" to be a radical in sociology, especially if one tries to act as a political radical, it is nevertheless increasingly intellectually respectable to work in the radical tradition.

The legitimation of "radical sociology" is part of the wider fact that the "adversary culture" has been reborn among American intellectuals generally. And, the impact of this rebirth has been very substantial. As exposure, dissent, fundamental political criticism have become increasingly legitimate and practiced by intellectuals, there has been a corresponding delegitimation of established elites, prevailing values and institutions.

Radical criticism contributes to widespread public disaffection, the articulation of discontent, and the declining self-confidence of the powerful. But, by itself, it has so far been unable to do two kinds of work which ought to be integral features of the role of radical intellectuals: first, to provide theoretical tools and empirical materials which would enable the forces of insurgency to map a strategy of social transformation; second, to formulate programs and visions which might make a social alternative credible.

Those of us who have participated in preparing these notes have been working as radical social scientists for a number of years. Each of us has worked in his own special area; the group as a whole represented a suprisingly diverse range of "specialties." Yet, if there is a common thread in our work, it has involved the effort to be critical—to expose the myths embodied in the ruling ideologies of advanced capitalism, and to interpret the historical meaning of new forces of opposition, domestic and international, to advanced capitalism. The fact that we have been in the same town and able to come together frequently during the past few months has helped us understand the need now to begin to clarify and change some of our intellectual priorities: to see that beyond criticism lies the work of positive formulation.

There are, no doubt, some important political differences among us; nevertheless, we agreed that we shared a commitment to what would best be called a "socialist" America (though several of us are uncomfortable with some of the historical connotations which that word conveys to Americans). That is, we agreed that the collective aspirations of Americans could have a chance of realization only if the capitalist system of privately controlled economic decisions made in terms of profit-maximization were to be replaced by a system in which such decisions were made by public bodies whose goals involved the maximization of social, economic, and political equality, the abolition of alienated labor, and the use of technology to promote public happiness. We also tended to agree that many of the material conditions for such a social transformation were coming into existence. Finally, we agreed that it was necessary to free socialism of its authoritarian, bureaucratic and technocratic implications, by opposing such tendencies within the socialist tradition, and by trying to work out concrete visions of a socialized economy which fostered decentralization, diversity, democracy, individuality, civil liberties, and personal initiative.

Finally, we agreed that virtually none of the necessary intellectual work needed for a socialist transformation was being done, but that the possibilities for doing such work had perhaps never been better. We decided that one way to promote such work was to try to lay out in some concreteness an inventory of the types of tasks which were needed. One way to phrase our objective was this: Let us imagine that an organized socialist movement or party existed in the U.S. What kinds of things would sociologists do who were allied to it?

In certain respects, we failed to fulfill our initial aspirations. We had hoped, initially, to produce a document which would not only sketch a few program-matic ideas, but would be a rather detailed review of the work being done by radical intellectuals, in an effort to summarize major contributions, highlight im-portant controversies and gaps in knowledge, call attention to work which pro-vides models. We hoped, too, to formulate some new perspectives on method. But to do such an exhaustive and systematic analysis required more commitment from each of us to the collective enterprise than any of us was willing to give. So, it turned out that none of us was ready to work in a collective way: in part, because each of us was highly involved in ongoing work of our own, but also, more fundamentally, because of the deeply ingrained individualism which is characteristic of each of us. The competitiveness and self-importance which each of us possessed was often a barrier to systematic discussion and cooperative work. In any case, this draft is considerably less, at this point, than what needs to be done. What we hope for, at least, is that it will stimulate those who share its perspective, including ourselves, to intensify the process of defining and fulfilling the role of the socialist intellectual in these times.

SOME CENTRAL THEORETICAL ISSUES

One of the marks of the radical intellectual is that he is someone who is blessed (and cursed) by a drive to make theory—theory which will comprehend the op-eration of society in its totality, link the present with the past organically, and reveal the necessary contradictions and unravellings of the established order. As Marx demonstrated, theory can have enormous power—to enable men to tran-scend the pressures of their particular existence, to guide the practice of move-ments, to provide men with the courage derived from seeing their struggles as historically meaningful, to offer a vision of a social alternative—an alternative made credible because it seems to flow out of the potentialities of the present. A theory can help men decide how to allocate their energies, justify their sacri-fices, undermine the confidence of the enemy, and, above all, learn from experience.

Radical sociologists have always criticized American sociology for its theo-retical barrenness and naivete. However, since its inception, the American left has exhibited its own share of theoretical weakness. There are, however, signs that this situation is changing. The international revival of creativity within Marxism has begun to have a substantial impact even in the U.S. The rise of the New Left within the U.S., combined with the emergence of neo-Marxian theorists internationally, has greatly improved the chances that a new critical theory, rel-evant to the situation of advanced capitalism, will be realized. In any case, we think the creation of such a theory is rightfully a central preoccupation of radical intellectuals.

The Problem of Agency

Perhaps the major achievement of the past decade, on the part of American radical social scientists, has been to attempt to apply Marxian theory to the analysis of the structure of power in America. The effort to demonstrate the existence of a power elite, acting in the interest of a capitalist class, is critical in a society whose political structure depends for its legitimacy so fundamentally on an ideology of democracy, and in which the leading social scientists have been so committed to the reality of the pluralist model. The effort to demonstrate that American foreign policy is rooted in imperialist drives is critical in a society in which both intellectuals and masses have believed that America's world role was limited to the defense of democratic principles. The effort to demonstrate that domestic social reform has largely been either limited by, or in the interest of, monopoly corporate power is critical in a society in which both workers and intellectuals have believed that the welfare state was an alternative to business domination and that welfare-reformism was made possible by the operation of the established political system. If American radicals, then, have devoted most of their energy to the exposure of the myths of power, it is because, perhaps unlike other peoples, Americans are unusually illusioned by such myths, and more likely to be radicalized when such illusions are broken.

In any case, although our understanding of the structure of the society has been clarified during the past decade, there has been little theoretical development with respect to what might be called the dynamics of American society.

A key question for radicals—perhaps the key one—with respect to dynamics is the question of "agency." If there is a ruling class, then what is its "negation"? Is there a definable social grouping which has the potential consciousness, and the potential means, to lead a struggle for the overthrow of established power?

Marx, of course, had a clear answer—the industrial proletariat is the agency for the overthrow of capitalism, just as the bourgeoisie had been the agency for the overthrow of feudalism. The empirical failure of that prediction in industrial capitalist countries has, of course, created Marxism's central theoretical problem. More importantly, the difficulties involved in defining the "agency" have posed the gravest strategic problems for the New Left and other radical movements in the advanced capitalist countries, and have been the source of bitter factional dispute within these movements.

Two broad hypotheses have emerged in contemporary Marxism which propose new agencies.

First, there is the view that the class struggle has been internationalized, and has become a struggle between the imperialist mother countries and the peoples of the colonized Third World. This view tends to argue that the standard of living of white Americans, and the viability of the capitalist system as a whole, depends on the maintenance and expansion of imperialist domination of the Third World. It thus tends to predict, on the one hand, continuing conservatism of the white industrial working class (as well as other strata within the mother country), but the eventual overthrow of their imperialist system through the combined and separate liberation struggles occurring in Third World Countries and among Third World minorities within the U.S.

Second, there is the more recent and rather less-well-known proposal which emanates from those who have tried to theoretically comprehend the student uprisings of the sixties. This view argues that the student movements of the advanced capitalist countries are harbingers of a new class-consciousness and class struggle internal to those countries—a situation resulting from the necessary creation of a "new" working class of educated workers in order to meet the needs of advanced technology and sophisticated system management. This view argues that the new working class is as crucial for advanced capitalism as the traditional proletariat was for an earlier stage, and that it can play a vanguard revolutionary role, not because of its material deprivation, but because of its openness to anti-capitalist ideology.

These notions are not mutually exclusive, but neither are they entirely compatible with each other. Moreover, in practice, they have led to rather severe differences in strategy within the left. What is important, for our purposes here, is that, although these ideas form the basis for much debate and action within the left, there has been little effort to study them systematically.

In a real sense, "Third World" and "mother country" liberation movements are interconnected. A powerful socialist movement within the U.S. is critical for the success of revolutionary movements in the Third World, just as successful resistance to imperialism internationally helps us to build support for fundamental change in America.

Although our group differed on the relative weight of emphasis to be given to these two sources of agency, my own bias is to stress the necessity for American radicals to comprehend the possibilities for change internal to the U.S., and particularly within the white population. The "new working class" notions require a deep scrutiny and are open to questions of many kinds. It would seem, therefore, that this is a very good time to launch a program of systematic research and theoretical analysis bearing on this question.

Among the relevant issues are these:

The question of definition. Just what are the boundaries of the stratum? What theoretical principles, if any, permit the establishment of boundaries? What internal differentiation exists within this stratum, and what political consequences are predicted as a result?

The question of consciousness. Is there any evidence, aside from the radicalization of students, that a new working class consciousness exists, and that it has or could have a socialist content? How is the consciousness of educated workers affected by considerations of status, career, income, working conditions? What features of educated work are "alienating"? To what extent do workers in this category identify themselves as workers? As members of an elite?

Linkages to the economic system. Just how central is the "knowledge industry"? What are the implications of the current contraction of job opportunities for the educated, and the cutbacks in investment in education, science, and military technology which underlie this contraction?

Class struggles of the educated. What is the fate of efforts to organize educated workers? Of radical caucuses and other political expressions?

The problem of "agency" would not, however, be settled simply by obtaining data which might support the socialist potential of the "new" working class. For that stratum contains within its very definition a limitation on its potential as agency. First, it does not constitute the majority in itself. Even if it were politically united, it would have to ally itself with other strata to achieve revolutionary aims. Second, its relative material well-being generates a crucial ambiguity—the educated are likely to *profess* a universalistic concern for the freedom and well-being of those more oppressed, but they surely cannot be trusted to speak and act for the more oppressed and less articulate masses. In theoretical terms, the issue is the extent to which the interests of "educated labor" coincide and conflict with other strata that are in motion. Is there any theoretical way to link, for instance, the radicalization of white students with the black revolt in the U.S. and with revolution in Third World countries? Clearly the revolts of the hungry have catalyzed and inspired the revolt of students and educated workers. But in practice the conflicts between the two are deep and glaring. What common interest do these groups share?

Meanwhile, in the background is the "white working class," the traditional proletariat, who exist for contemporary radical intellectuals as stereotypes, and whose articulate spokesmen are evidently opposed to both student and Third World revolutionaries. Is there, in theory, a basis for a unified working class?

Finally, there is the fact that much of the conflict in American society is not easily reduced to class struggle. It has become possible to analyze the student revolt in class terms, but what of the broader youth consciousness, which has certainly played a role in stimulating rebellion within the military and in prisons? What of the women's liberation movement? And what of the fact that serious revolutionaries, despite their Marxism, have typically found it necessary to recognize the revolutionary potentialities of nationalist and other "non-class" bases of solidarity?

All of these questions imply the need for deep conceptual clarification and systematic research. The problem of agency and the concept of class have always been, we suspect, more ambiguous in Marxism than many Marxists have recognized. These issues are not academic, for the answers to these questions determine very concretely how energies are used by political movements. Nor can the answers be arrived at through academic means alone. It may well be that by its very nature sociology as an academic enterprise cannot comprehend the social bases of rebellion in American society. It seems likely that without political practice intellectuals are largely incapable of anticipating possibilities for political motion. I shall return, briefly, to this issue below.

The Problem of Limits

Marx did not rest with the question of agency (although a sociologist might). His theoretical purpose was deeper: to uncover the main laws of motion of capitalist society—the inner contradictions and tendencies upon which predictions of future development might be based. The ultimate aim was to discover the limits of the system, the points at which it could develop no further without breaking apart.

The history of theoretical Marxism is in large part the history of efforts to elaborate and eventually revise the economic model which Marx began to develop in pursuit of these aims. Those efforts continue. Contemporary analysis of this question focuses on such issues as: the degree to which imperialism is a necessary component of American economic growth; the consequences for domestic growth of rising international trade competition; the degrees to which the state can effectively manage problems of unemployment and inflation; the fiscal problems of the public sector, etc. The analysis of political economy has at least two purposes: to demonstrate the underlying irrationality of capitalism—the fact that it *must* perpetuate one or another barbarity (imperialism, war, unemployment, poverty, urban squalor, militarism, etc.) to preserve its stability; secondly, such analysis helps solve the problem of agency, by suggesting likely sources of discontent. Ultimately, there is the hope of demonstrating a contradiction so overwhelming that the defeat of the system will be inescapable (but this hope is perhaps quixotic).

Sociologists *qua* sociologists have relatively little to offer such analytic work —a fact which illustrates the incompatibility between academic specialization and the task of theory-construction. But lately, there has begun to emerge a theoretical perspective within the Marxian framework which is more directly sociological (rather than economic)—a perspective which sees the limits of capitalism not primarily in economic terms but rather in terms which are broadly social, cultural, and psychological. Briefly, it is proposed that capitalism reaches its limit when it creates the material-technological basis for abolishing or greatly reducing alienated labor, but cannot implement that possibility.

Marx himself was aware of this as a theoretical possibility, but apparently believed that the socialist revolution would occur before this point was reached.

The idea that we are on the verge of a new historical stage, in which, for example, the production of goods will be secondary to other activity, in which the power of those who manage production will be subordinated to considerations of comprehensive planning, in which men will be freed from economic priorities —this idea in a variety of forms is being proposed by men of various persuasions. There is a technocratic version of "post-industrial" society and a variety of socialist versions. One can see how the notion of a "new working class" as a revolutionary agency is derivable from such a perspective. That a "post-industrial" society is now (or shortly to be) materially possible fits with the yearnings of alienated youth and gives such yearnings historical meaning. It also fits with certain tendencies of the environmentalist movement and the quest for a limit on the exploitation of natural resources.

There is an idea here, and if intellectual convergence means anything, it is an idea whose time has come. So far, as we are aware, it is little more than a speculation—and not very well worked out at that.

Here are some basic issues raised by the "post-industrial" perspective:

To what extent is it true that existing technology can liquidate routinized human labor?

What are the political, economic, cultural, and social barriers to such a development under capitalism?

To what extent is the technocratic vision of decisive power in the hands of experts and a system of comprehensive planning a plausible one? How can it be criticized?

Is post-industrialization possible within one country? Can "post-scarcity" be achieved without imperialism?

Is the goal of reduced economic growth and labor time compatible with the goal of abolishing poverty and inequality of living standards?

Does post-industrialism imply a reduction in the production of consumer commodities and a reallocation of resources to the creation of better public services, environmental values, and collectively shared goods? If so, to what extent are Americans prepared to trade certain kinds of possessions and commodities for reduced labor, improved natural and urban environments, a richer community life, education, health, and other social services? Which Americans are most and least resistant to such a trade? Why?

These are some of the researchable questions which have occurred to us in trying to formulate our thoughts on the "post-industrial" notion. If this notion is at all plausible, it is decidedly appealing, not only as a conceptual lever for comprehending important trends in advanced capitalism, but as the keystone for the construction of a socialist vision with direct relevance to such a society. But it is crucial that, at this point, serious analysts not accept the concept as given, but attempt to work out its underlying assumptions and implications, and the means to test empirically the major assertions which flow from it. It is also important for radicals to pay serious attention to the elitist and technocratic versions of the post-industrial image of the future, and to sharply distinguish these from socialist and humanist images.

CULTURE, CHARACTER AND CONSCIOUSNESS

An important development of the past decade in critical theory has been the revival and development of work on the ways in which processes of socialization, mass communication and other means of control operate to undermine (and facilitate) revolutionary forms of consciousness. The efforts to link Marx and Freud, to study the consciousness-molding effects of schooling, mass media, and other institutions represent the theoretical side of this work, while an enormous range of practical efforts have been made to deal with the same issues in the real world. (We are referring here, of course, to many of the efforts to create forms of communal living, to develop alternate media, to attack consumerism and sexism, to develop new forms of education and child-rearing, to develop new forms of therapy). Many of these experiments are justified precisely as part of an effort to free individuals from cultural and psychological constraints, not only because that is held to be intrinsically desirable, but because of the political consequences of eradicating some of the bases of "false consciousness."

The theoretical and practical importance of studying consciousness cannot be overemphasized. It is clear that one of the deficiencies of classical Marxism was its failure to develop this theme. But the question has never been more pressing, given the steady elaboration of the means of control and the many ways in which the existence of material abundance can serve to deplete social solidarity.

For a socialist movement in this country at this time there is a critical need to develop modes of activity which can link the personal, the cultural, the social, and the political. In part, such modes must arise from practice. But, in part, we suspect that clues to some answers will be derivable from theory. American social scientists have much to learn on this topic from recent European work, but radicals in sociology, social psychology, ethnomethodology, and related fields could make an important contribution by, for instance, reinterpreting much of the "micro" and abstractedly empiricist work in this area in terms of the "macro," the "critical," and the political.

THE NEED FOR RADICAL RESEARCH

One suspects that radical intellectuals do not need much encouragement to engage in theorizing. A primary intent of this paper is to encourage much more systematic engagement in empirical-practical work by radical sociologists; to urge that we go beyond the endless elaboration of polemical criticism of sociology, to produce systematic inquiry that has real use for movements for social change.

We keep asking—what would a hypothetical socialist movement in America demand of its members who had been trained in sociology? In our discussions we did not get as far as we would have liked in formulating concrete answers to such a question, but here are some:

(1) *The development of a process of mapping the structure of power in the United States.* Such a process involves, on the one hand, the continuous collection of data on the membership of the "power elite," and on the other hand, the use of sophisticated methods of data analysis to depict patterns of interlock, the structure of corporate interest groups, linkages between corporate and political elites, possible sources of cleavage and connection, etc., as well as efforts to define the relationships between specific corporate interests and specific policies and issues. This is already the most typical kind of research in which radicals are engaged, and has been the basis for a considerable amount of effective anti-corporate activity. In addition to expanding and deepening the "data bank" concerning corporate-political structure, however, there is a need to attempt more systematic efforts at broad mapping—in which case we may find some radicals seeking to acquire skills which they previously disdained—e.g., computer programming, advanced methods of data reduction, and statistical analysis.

(2) *The study of constituencies for socialism.* Despite the enormous elaboration of opinion and attitude research in America, there is precious little systematic study which provides detailed knowledge about which sectors of the population are likely to support various kinds of social change. Furthermore, it is likely that whatever conclusions can be drawn from the extant body of such research are likely to be wrong. There is no doubt that survey research contains inherent limitations as a tool for predicting changes in consciousness; nevertheless, we are convinced that its potentialities have not been fully tested by any means. There is, at best, only a handful of radicals who have used survey methodology as a way into research on class consciousness, and, although fruitful and suggestive, even their work is relatively primitive.

The practice on the movements of the sixties has taught us far more about the potentialities for consciousness-raising in America than all the academic research on public opinion and political behavior. And yet, we feel that it ought to be possible to combine techniques of survey, depth interviewing, and political organization to increase our comprehension.

How do various potential constituencies react to proposals for fundamental structural reform? To visions of alternative social organization? To anti-capitalist sentiments and slogans? What are the sources of support for and resistance to existing movements for change? What latent and explicit hostilities exist to established elites, authorities and institutions? Under what conditions do people see their private discontents as rooted in social conditions and political processes? Under what conditions would people undertake what kinds of political action themselves?

This is just a sample of the kinds of questions which a socialist movement needs to answer, and which sociologists are supposed to have the skill to answer, concerning political consciousness and behavior. In the absence of "professional" assistance, a movement will attempt to supply answers using its own methodologies. One of the critical questions for sociology is to comprehend the process by which social movements do in fact formulate and test hypotheses about the social environment in which they must operate, about political behavior of potential constituents, about social control, about the political psychology of potential recruits, and about their own successes and failures. Not only is that process intrinsically interesting, it seems crucial for sociological method—since movements are often more "correct" than academic sociologists in predicting certain events and outcomes. We did not in our discussions go deeply into this question, but I believe it is crucial. To wed the practical understanding of movement activists to the systematizing skills of the sociologist would represent a major breakthrough in the struggle to understand the conditions which give rise to collective revolt in a society like ours.

(3) *Making socialism credible.* But the main problem for a socialist movement—the reason that none exists—is not the problem of defining its agencies or constituencies. Rather, it is the fact that all existing ideas of what socialism means are discredited or irrelevant for Americans (including American radicals). In our time, socialism has come to mean either an authoritarian system applicable to the situation of pre-industrial society, a welfare state which seems ineffective in coping with the deepest problems of advanced industrial society, or a system to increase and even totalize the control apparatus of the modern state.

Nevertheless, we centered our discussion around the need for a commitment to socialism. We did so because we know of no other word which encompasses the vision of a society organized so that production is carried on for use rather than profit, class-based privilege and inequality is abolished, and men have equality of access to power and to the fruits of human labor.

The question is—how to make such a vision relevant to the conditions, problems and discontents of our time? How to demonstrate to ourselves and to people generally that the abolition of capitalism is possible, and that an alternative to it can be constructed which provides the means to solve the problems presented by capitalism?

An element of an answer lies in the development of concrete models. Such models are not proposals for reform of the existing system, but hypotheses about how activities would be organized assuming the abolition of the private corporate system. For example, can we imagine concretely how any of the following might "work" in "advanced industrial society"?

1. The allocation of resources at the national, regional, and local level is determined through a process of public debate and popular decision-making.

2. Self-determination and personal initiative are maximized within a system in which resource allocation is centrally planned and co-ordinated.

3. Civil liberties are guaranteed within a system of collective ownership.

4. Access to the full benefits of advanced technology is provided while routinized human labor is abolished, reduced, and shared.

5. Americans are not deprived of material well-being despite massive redistribution of control over resources internationally.

6. The distinctions between "town" and "country" are abolished without destroying the positive values of either.

7. All people have maximum and equal opportunity to work creatively, fulfill their intellectual, aesthetic, and sensual potentialities, and govern themselves, etc.

Marxists have always, with good reason, opposed the effort to create blueprints. The substance of socialist society will be a product of practical struggles, not speculation by an intellectual elite. What is here being proposed is not the elaboration of blueprints, in the sense that one is trying to manufacture panaceas for society's ills. Instead, what we are suggesting is a kind of work which might be called mental experimentation—the development of hypothetical models of reconstructed social relations in order to stimulate debate and analysis, in order to catalyze practical experiment—all for the purpose of making alternatives to the status quo credible. The creation of credible theoretical alternatives is an important aspect of criticism; in fact, after a period in which increasing numbers of people have learned to oppose or mistrust the existing order, criticism, as such, can lead to despair unless it is coupled with reasons for hope. We sense that the New Left has reached a dead end, precisely because it has been effective at criticism and negation, but simultaneously unable to provide grounds for hope. It is not so much that the constituencies in favor of basic change are lacking, it is that they have no idea what change might mean. Sociologists and other intellectuals cannot provide *the* answer, but we can help to provide the concrete ideas from which answers can be constructed.

Another function of such models is that they provide material for the development of programs for fundamental structural reform. By "structural reform" we refer to popular demands for institutional change which cannot in fact be met "under capitalism." Socialist movements search for such demands because popular movements around them tend to experience radicalization as their aspirations are frustrated. It is not up to us as sociologists to formulate such programs (although popular movements may find our ideas useful), but the effort to concretize the meaning of socialism can help movement activists figure out the kinds of programs which will be both relevant to the felt needs of people and fundamentally challenging to the system.

Finally, utopian thinking is relevant to the effort to build "counter-institutions." For the latter makes sense politically to the extent that it is defined as a conscious struggle to establish a piece of the future in the present. Such practice —the building of communes, the counter-institutional movements in education, health, childcare, the movements for self-determination in the black and youth ghettoes, etc.—provides an important ground for learning about the problems and potentialities of recreating social relations. The efforts to build counter-institutions are then a major source of "data" for "model-building"—while at the same time these efforts can be stimulated and influenced by the theoretical models which are devised.

In general, both the source and the test of the ideas of radical intellectuals lies with the movements for social change. As sociologists, what we bring to such movements is this: some knowledge of the "literature" which might be relevant to political work; a certain degree of training to generalize from particular experience, to synthesize diverse experiences, to confront discomforting data, to examine underlying assumptions, to entertain alternative explanations for events; possibly some factual knowledge which might be of use. One of the critical questions which we, as a group, evaded was just this—how to integrate a socialist sociology with the movements for change. This question is not simply an "organizational" problem—it strikes to the heart of sociology's conception of itself as a discipline. The fact that it is evaded here does not mean that we thought that a socialist sociology would be organized and conducted in the ways which have been characteristic of academic sociology. On the contrary. Our failure to confront this question was partly due to our feeling that we, as a group, could never achieve consensus on the issue; partly because the question cannot really be decided by a small group of relatively established types—but only through a continuous effort at practical redefinition on the part of all those who seek to build a socialist movement.

If such a movement already existed, the task of self-definition would be greatly simplified. Perhaps radicals in sociology and other disciplines will have the chance to take part in building such a movement. But, in the meantime, to *imagine that one exists* seems a good way to begin to give form and direction to our collective work. Such an act of imagination might turn out to be a self-fulfilling fantasy.

A RECONCEPTUAL- IZATION OF CRITICAL THEORY

TRENT SCHROYER

Pages 132–149, Chapter 8, "A Reconceptualization of Critical Theory," by Trent Schroyer, from *Radical Sociology*, edited by J. David Colfax and Jack L. Roach, © 1971 by Basic Books, Inc., Publishers, New York.

Trent Schroyer is lecturer in anthropology, graduate faculty of the New School for Social Research and professor of sociology at Ramapo College. He is author of *The Critique of Domination*.

INTRODUCTION: THE NOTION OF A CRITICAL THEORY

A critical theory of society derives from the philosophical tradition of the critique of appearances. Such a totalizing theory cannot emerge from a compilation of empirical facts. It is by now clear to all that the methodological rationales of established social science predefine the reality investigated. In nailing down the facts about society, the activity of men is reified into a thing-like facticity. A critical theory, on the other hand, transcends its facts, rendering them meaningful, but at the same time placing them in the context of the tension between the given and the possible. Construction of a critical theory follows the principle of an immanent critique. By first expressing what a social totality holds itself to be, and then confronting it with what it is, a critical theory is able to break down the rigidity of the object. Hence, Marx's identification of the ideology of "equivalence exchange" as the self-image of capitalist society is contradicted by the formulation of the "developmental laws of capitalism." The phenomenal appearance of capitalism is negated by its own internal dynamics. Marx's critical theory is, in his mentor's terms, a "determinate negation" of capitalism, and has remained till our time the foundation for critical research.

During the 1960's the young German philosopher-sociologist Jürgen Habermas had reformulated critical theory. Taking late capitalism's image of itself as a society in which social change is managed rationally, Habermas has been demonstrating that the immanent dynamic negates the self-image of late capitalism.

What is the relationship of Jürgen Habermas' developing critical theory to the critical theory of Marx? Are we to believe that Habermas' theory is a sublation of Marx? Or is it possible that he simply redirects critical research to another focus—that of the quality of symbolic communication in advanced industrial society? In either case the relationship of the two critical totalizations must be explained. This is the concern of this paper.

I

Habermas tries to reformulate critical theory through an immanent development of Marx's categories.[1] Capitalism is the first society in history where the extension of the forces of production forces a questioning of traditional authority systems. For the first time in history emancipation from the repression of nature (necessity) becomes at the same time a liberation from moral authority. The unleashed powers of men, however, embodied in the new forces of production are themselves transformed into a new mode of moral authority. This technical authority is at the same time a more effective mode of repression. Habermas' theory focuses upon the fantastic potential of this new form of technical repression, which now can be seen as possibly stilling the dialectic of morality itself. What this means is the disappearance of the age-old attempt to logically objectify the conditions of human life, and through public communication generate a principle of justice.

In an era of technical transcendence a technocratic ideology becomes the new basis for the rationalities of behavior. Habermas' critical insight is the recognition that this new scientific culture does not allow for actual individualization of persons. Habermas thus continues the tradition of dialectical analysis and is able to express the immanent contradictions of a distorted dialogue, or in other terms, the analysis of disrupted communication in a moral community. In our epoch the power of material negativity negates the technological optimism of the Enlightenment. The advance of human technics does not necessarily result in the emancipation of men.

Habermas has restored to a critical theory the traditional distinction between techne and praxis; between technics and symbolic communication. This distinction can be elaborated logically and methodologically, as the following sections will demonstrate. Anthropologically it illuminates the self-forming processes that derive from symbolically mediated interaction. Habermas' systematic elaboration of the techne-praxis distinction results in a new framework for critical theory. Marx and Marcuse had held that language systems are linked to the process of work. Habermas, on the other hand, identifies the dialectic of symbolic communication as logically irreducible to the dialectic of purposive rational action. In this theory resides both the unique contribution of Habermas to critical theory and, perhaps, his sublation of Marx and Marcuse. Hence his critique of the technological utopianism of Marx and Marcuse:

Freedom from hunger and toil doesn't necessarily converge with freedom from slavery and degradation, because an automatic developmental connection between labor and interaction doesn't exist.[2]

II

Science and science-based technology have become more basic to the production processes of advanced industrial societies.[3] The institutionalization of science and technology as research and development has generated a knowledge industry that is itself a force of production. Knowledge production units become autonomous structures that are perpetuated beyond their originating goals. They link directly, or indirectly (technology transfer from state-financed research, e.g., space program), to corporate profit-making capacity.[4]

"Knowledge," however, is produced within the context of an instrumentally rationalizing society.[5] Thus, scientism increasingly becomes the prescriptive decision-matrice for ever new spheres of society.[6] Insofar as more spheres of decision making are construed as "technical problems" requiring information and instrumental strategies produced by technical experts, they are progressively removed from political debate.

The increased importance of the knowledge industry has led some social theorists to conceptualize "post-industrial" society as a self-regulating system in which information is the crucial input.[7] With this, and related images of contemporary society, we have an infinitely flexible ideology which can be interpreted in ways which legitimate public or private policy adopted by established power and privilege groups (e.g., theories of modernization applied to socioeconomic development).

Given this new aspect of the contemporary reproduction process we can see that the scientistic image of science becomes the dominant legitimating system of advanced industrial society. It has gradually replaced the ideology of equivalence exchange which had performed the legitimating function for early industrial society. Whereas Marx was able to show how equivalence of exchange between labor and capital was the major contradiction in capitalist society, it is now less precise as an expression of contemporary alienation. Where Marx was able to formulate his critical theory as a critique of the purest ideological expression of equivalence exchange, i.e., classical political economics, we are forced to broaden our critique to the positivistic theory of science itself. It is our thesis that the scientistic image of science is the fundamental false consciousness of our epoch. If the technocratic ideology is to loose its hold on our consciousness, a critical theory must lay bare the theoretical reifications of this scientistic image of science.

III

A reinterpretation of the nature of science and its relation to society has already begun in contemporary European Marxism, especially in the Frankfort school of critical sociology. This particular attempt to reinterpret Marx consists of searches for the first principles of a critical (or emancipatory) science that can respond in a contemporary manner to the methodology of the established social sciences. Jürgen Habermas has both inherited and extended the work of this school.

In Habermas' reconstruction of Marxism, science is conceived as part of the materialist model of society. But the materialist model of society is now reconceptualized as societal systems of action:

1. Instead of talking about the substructure, we refer to the systems of purposive rational action.
2. Instead of talking about the superstructure, we refer to the systems of symbolic interaction.
3. Instead of talking about the forms of social consciousness we can speak about the reflexive recognition of legitimate authority which is internal to societal modes of self-reflection.

By considering scientific inquiry as the formalization of the logics-in-action of society systems, we can achieve an insight into the prior orientations of scientific inquiry. We can express predefinitions of the object-of-knowledge in terms of the relation of cognition and interest. By analyzing the transcendental interests of cognition as they are linked to historically determined conceptual schemes and behavioral systems we can arrive at an understanding of the logical rules of the process of inquiry. The procedures of scientific inquiry are rooted in the prescientific processes of everyday life. The finding and inventing of hypotheses, the deduction of conditional predictions, and the testing of hypotheses are parallel to the practice of life itself.

Only within this mode of conceptualizing scientific inquiry and its rootedness in everyday life can we both see the validity of science and relate it to changing historical variables. Only by integrating a logic of inquiry within an empirically transforming life world can we achieve a dialectical theory of science and society. In so constructing a unified theory of the logics-in-use of scientific practice and the logics-in-action of societal systems we are able to show that cognition is never a neutral fact picturing. Since knowledge is never neutral, we can demonstrate that there are distinct scientific methods and that each requires a somewhat different explanatory model. In this way we are able to refute the theory of science inherent in scientism.

Our payoff is a new classification of the sciences and an analysis of the logical interest (or transcendental principle) presupposed in each practice. We then see three interests as fundamental to three kinds of sciences:

1. We conceive of the strict sciences as the mode of analysis which yields information that presupposes the interest of certainty and technical control.

2. We conceive of the hermeneutic sciences (or the historical-interpretive
    sciences) as that mode of interpretation which yields an understanding
    of the social cultural life world and which presupposes the interest of
    extending of intersubjective understanding.
3. We conceive of a critical science as that kind of inquiry which is
    capable of analyzing the supposed and actual necessity of historical
    modes of authority and which presupposes the interest of the
    emancipation of men from lawlike patterns of nature and history.

Established, official social science understands itself as having the interest
of the strict sciences. In practice, that means that established social science, although it conceives of itself as neutral, is actually an inquiry which has the theoretical interest and societal consequence of maintaining technical control.

Within the methodological debates of established social science, however,
there has emerged a recognition of a competing interest and a competing logics-
in-use of scientific inquiry. To cite a few of these debates in one sphere, sociology,
we can see emergent modes of analysis, such as phenomenology, ethnomethodology, a priorist sociology deriving from the late Wittgenstein, and symbolic interactionism. These debates are recognition of a competing practical interest
within social science methodology, that of the hermeneutic sciences. Despite
these new methodological reflections, the dominant trend is to continue to understand social inquiry in a way which identifies it with the strict sciences.

This idealization of strict science and its method is none the less an active
force in history and does transform the human world. Thus the greatest problem
that social theory faces is not whether behaviorism, game theory or systems analysis are theoretically valid, but whether they might not become valid through a
self-fulfilling prophecy justified by a technocratic ideology.

IV

In our time, with its dominant technocratic ideology, the point of a critical theory
of science will be to show that instrumental action is not the only interest that
guides research practice in the social sciences. More specifically, the concern of
a critical theory is to try to formulate a view of practical scientific interests and
relate these to the societal action systems. Toward that end we need a reconceptualization such as the following:

The Logic-in-Use of the Strict Sciences

In this direction we find that the pragmatic philosophy of science, especially that
of C. S. Peirce, has already developed an approach to this problem which is consistent with a dialectical epistemology.[8] The pragmatic tradition has focused
upon the logical analysis of the procedures and inquiry of science, and has not
restricted itself to formal methodology and the analysis of language as have the
positivists. Thus pragmatism has conceived of methodological rules as norms
guiding the practice of inquiry; the analysis refers to the communication and
interaction of the community of investigation. From this analysis we can make
a basic distinction between the logics-in-use and the reconstructed-logic of science. The former analysis explicates the rules guiding the practice of inquiry; the
latter formulates criteria validity and semantic meaning in relation to the results
of science. The positivist philosophy of science has worked primarily with the
reconstructed logic of science.

Thus Peirce gives us an analysis of the logical (transcendental) and empirical
conditions for the validity of strict science inquiry in the form of a logics-in-use
of strict science. Peirce argues that the research interest guiding strict science is
that of gaining and expanding control over objects which we have observed. Development of this logical argument cannot be dealt with here. What this means,
however, is that in the process of inquiry we ourselves behave *as if* the events

of reality were the products of a subject who, under contingent initial conditions, continuously draws conclusions from a definite valid set of rules and then decides to act, permanently conforming to the predictions thereby derived. Thus our research praxis is guided by *instrumental actions* which presuppose that reality is also an actor who has internalized a set of habits we call laws of nature. Peirce's analysis is unique and is parallel to Marx's analysis of the logic of the work process, in that both logical and empirical conditions are seen as determining the possibility of successful instrumental action. Whereas Marx's analysis can be construed as a general critique of Kant's notion of the world-constituting powers of human knowing, Peirce's can be seen as a similar critique of Kant, but dealing with the instrumental action procedures of the community of strict scientists.

Peirce has shown that the synthetic modes of reasoning, i.e., induction and deduction, are chains of inference whose validity can be accounted for only by referring to the norms of procedure that are sedimented into the research practice of a community of investigators. Within this frame of reference we are able to conceive of scientific reasoning as systems of purposive rational behavior which are essentially the habits of research practice. Their function is to fixate belief, to operate as guiding principles for the accumulation of new information, and to be revised when there are failures in anticipated results. Belief is secured again when there is a successful acting upon a new recipe which is repeatedly reconfirmed. Hence the systems of purposive rational behavior embedded in the research practice of a community of investigators function as the transcendental scheme that constitutes possible cognition. But this transcendental framework is within the system of instrumental action of a given historical context; the framework determines the conditions under which we objectify and experience reality as a possible object of a purposive rational action, or possible technical control.

Instrumental action is a form of purposive rational action which proceeds according to technical rules based on empirical knowledge. It includes predictions about observable events and these are true or false, thus providing us with knowledge whose adequacy depends on how efficiently man controls reality. A more recent variation of instrumental behavior is systems of rational choice which proceed from strategies that are based on analytical knowledge that include deductions from preference rules or general maxims and may be correct or not. Strategic behavior depends upon a correct evaluation of alternative possibilities of action by inferring from a given system of values and maxims. Systems of instrumental action are different forms of technical rules which are universal and not context based, and they can be formulated in context-free language. Thus the truly universal languages are the technologies produced by men.

We can therefore see that the work process and strict science inquiry are related. Both are constituted through an instrumental logic-in-use and linked to the instrumental action system of society. To put it another way we can say that they both presuppose (in the transcendental sense) a model of certainty for the successful control of observed processes. In short, the "interest" of instrumental praxis and strict science in this category of science would be interested in recurrent regularities of the social world toward the end of technical control, e.g., behaviorism.

Indeed the most advanced forms of social science inquiry, such as systems analysis and decision theory, are guided by the interest of technical control. But Habermas' theory of science shows that this is not the only interest that guides research in the established social sciences. In competition with the technical interest of strict science inquiry we can formulate, from the tradition of the Human Sciences (Geisteswissenschaften) a practical interest—that of the extension of communicative understanding toward the end of the formation of consensus. This interest is presupposed by the historical-interpretive sciences of the social-cultural life world such as cultural sociology, history of art, etc. We will refer to this category of science as "hermeneutic" sciences.[9]

The Logic-in-Use of the Hermeneutic Sciences

Identification of a unique method for the hermeneutic sciences requires a return to the debate about the differences between the natural and human sciences. At the very least, we must go back to the theory of science which preceded the neo-Kantian distinction between the empirical and the philosophical, the "is" and the "ought" dimensions.

An important beginning point for the rediscovery of a hermeneutic logic-in-use is the last essays of Wilhelm Dilthey.[10] In these essays, written between 1905 and 1910, Dilthey is putting the distinction between the natural and human sciences in a way which recaptures part of the Hegelian theory while addressing itself to a twentieth-century context. He points to the logical differences between perception and explanation in the natural sciences, and interpretation and understanding in the human sciences. The focus then is upon the different logic-in-use of these scientific processes. This focus suggests that concepts, theories, methods and principles of verification are related to the processes of inquiry for their validity.

Whereas in the strict sciences we are constrained by the range of our technical control over natural processes, in the hermeneutic sciences we are constrained by our socially established conventions which exercise a predefinition of how we understand symbolic communication. In this way the fundamental communality we have with others constitutes a transcendental presupposition of hermeneutic understanding. Thus in the systems of common symbols which are sedimented, first in an ordinary language and then in typical action patterns and typical attitudinal orientations, are the rules of the logic-in-use of hermeneutic understanding. In formulating rules of interpretation, we are trying to consciously recapture the process of interpretation which enables everyday actors to understand each other. The expression of these logic-in-use rules has been worked out by Dilthey's analysis of the "cycle of interpretation" and by what later writers call the Hermeneutic Circle. Recognition of the logical difference between the interpretation of symbolic systems has led to the programmatic ideals for the social sciences such as phenomenological sociology (e.g., Alfred Schutz)[11]; ethnomethodology (e.g., Garfinkel, Cicourel)[12]; symbolic interactionism (Herbert Blumer and others).[13] However, the result of hermeneutic inquiry in these paradigms can give us a little more than a Verstehen sociology's explanation.

But we are not concerned with a defense of the human sciences but with the existence of a competing interest in technical control in social inquiry. The question for social science is how to develop a mode of analysis which is both explanatory and able to interpret symbolic communication. This form of science would have a still different research guiding interest—that of emancipation.

Established social science is essentially manipulative because it has allowed itself to be conceived as having the same research-guiding interest as the strict sciences. Insofar as technical control is the guiding interest of social science, it is consistent with the technocratic trend and overtly legitimate class or elite exploitation. On the other hand a social science guided only by the practical interest would have very little explanatory power. Thus the need for the synthetic critical science.

Foundations of a Critical Science

Reflection about the subsystems of society, and their function as transcendental frameworks which link system interests and cognition requires a unique mode of analysis. Such methodological reflection tries to illuminate both human history and the practice of science as historical self-forming processes, and thereby restores to men an awareness of their position as the active, yet historically limited subject of history. To recognize the processes of historical self-formation of human history is to become aware of the mechanisms of historical negativity and therefore to be able to generate a critique of existing structures by objectifying the objective possibilities of a social totality.[14] Hence the generation of a critical theory of science and society is at the same time the broadest theoretical framework for a revolutionary theory.[15]

A critical science differs from the strict or hermeneutic sciences in that it presupposes that all self-conscious agents can become aware of the self-formative processes of society and self, and with this knowledge achieve a historically conditioned autonomy. Thus the character of a critical science is unique insofar as it is concerned with the assessment of the socially unnecessary modes of authority, exploitation, alienation, repression. The interest of a critical science is the emancipation of all self-conscious agents from the seemingly natural forces of nature and history.

How is a critical science related to human society? This linkage is to the capacity of men to be reflective about their own formative process. A critical science is linked to the dialectic of self-reflection that is present in all socialization processes, specifically in the reflective recognition of legitimate authority.[16] From the point of view of the strict or hermeneutic sciences, a critical science is a speculative science in that it tries to reflect about the necessity for the conditions of lawlike patterns in society and history.

At this point let us go back to Marx himself and reconstruct the beginnings of a critical science. Whereas Marx was grounded in classic philosophy and discovered the key to an emancipatory science of man, in Hegel we are often less aware of these foundations. We therefore need to fill in the philosophical dimensions of Marxism as a critical science, seeing it as a product of its time and perhaps being able to reconstruct its main elements more systematically than its founder.

Hegel provided for Marx the foundations of a critical theory of human development in that he formulated a science of the experience of consciousness as a historical self-forming process. Marx extended this analysis to the historical conditions of the self-formation of man by materializing the notion of dialectical synthesis. He thus transformed the critique of knowledge into the critique of society. It is in the reconstruction of this common link between Hegel and Marx that we will find the key to a Marxist theory of science and society, to Marxism as a critical science.[17]

The Marxian critique of Hegel's claim to absolute knowledge, or the deduction of all from the principle of Geist, is but an extension of this dialectic of reflection; Marx's *Capital* is a realization of Hegel's conception of a science of reason. Marx produced, however, not a dialectical ontology but a dialectical empiricism, i.e., a science of society which is rooted in the transcendental concept of reason, but realized that this form of science can be conceived only as an empirical science. In so refuting the residue of classical ontology in Hegel, Marx does not thereby banish Reason from an empirical science. Instead the Marxist science is different in that it retains this mode of historic-genetic conceptualization. The history of Marxist theory and struggle has too often denied or ignored the fact that a Marxist science is based upon a unique logic-in-use—that of Reason in the Hegelian sense. In so suppressing the foundations of a Marxist science or theory, Marxism has repressed its own logical foundations and has therefore fallen into a sterile distinction between science and philosophy which simply assimilates the scientistic image of science. The problem with much of contemporary Marxism is that it is unable to understand itself as a unique critical science. Beginning with Engels, Marxists have fallen into a scientistic understanding of the work of Marx.

Marx's unique contribution to critical science was his labor theory of value which was a self-reflexive model for the critical analysis of capitalist society.[18] In the classical form of the labor theory of value Marx discovered the basic ideology of a society based upon economic exchange. By distinguishing between living-labor and labor-power Marx broke the ahistorical equation of labor and value embedded in Ricardo's labor theory. As long as feudal production was organized through status authority it was primarily production for use. However, the emergence of a class society where economic exchange is liberated from status relations results in the gradual deterioration of production for use and its replacement by a universal exchange value. In this epoch the equivalence between labor and value is negated in the exchange between the seller of labor-power and the capitalist who appropriates it. Whereas the seller receives its market price, its exchange value, the capitalist appropriates the value-creating capacity of living labor. Hence Marx demonstrates the nonequivalence of the exchange between labor and capital by working out the developmental laws of capitalism. While being the basic legitimation of capitalist society the practice of equivalence exchange was also the source of the alienation of all labor.

... thus all the progress of civilization, or in other words, every increase in the production power of labor itself, does not enrich the worker, but capital, and thus increases the power that dominates labor.[19]

Equivalence exchange was then both the principle of justice and the practice of domination: reflection upon this fundamental contradiction of capitalist society liberated consciousness from the cultural reifications of the "commodity form." In the commodity form is found the record of the alienated work process and the immanent contradiction of capitalist society. To Marx, the dialectical analysis of the commodity form is a "Schein," or showing forth, of the essence of human production. That is, Marx's analysis in the first chapter of *Capital*, while seemingly couched in visual metaphor, is really attempting to make transparent the essential behind the appearance. At every point in *Capital*, Marx tries to keep the real (use value) in the foreground while dealing with the exchange-system of capitalism. In identifying the commodity form he has made the real nature of human work show forth to all so they can see through the appearance of capitalism. "Seeing" the commodity form is to reflexively understand its real nature. The moment of "show" is the moment of negation of the appearance and is the characteristic of a critical science. Marx thus restores the historical dimension to a whole social process, capitalist production, thereby enabling men to recognize the reified character of life practice under the domination of the commodity form.

All critical science attempts to restore missing parts of the self-formation process to men and in this way to force a process of self-reflection which will enable them to reinterpret the legitimacy of existing control systems. Insofar as these reconstructions are able to link repressed dimensions of historical structures to both individual and collective self-forming processes, and can be accepted as fitting all available facts, we can be liberated. That is, insofar as men become aware of the structuring of their self-formation they can distinguish between historically necessary modes of control and those that are but unnecessary patterns connected to distorted communicative systems. In this self-reflective recognition of a pseudo-"necessity" the conditions needed to perpetuate unnecessary behavioral orientations are removed and men can enter into the realm of self-discovery.

V

Habermas has argued that Marx's critical theory of capitalism no longer captures the basic contradictions of advanced industrial society. Emergent aspects of contemporary society that Marxist theory must confront are:

1. Extension of the forces of production does not, in itself, bring about the emancipation of men but has in fact become a run-away revolution whose manifold potentials increasingly threaten mankind with the possibility of total control of social change. Marx was unable to imagine the stage of technological development where control systems could begin to effectively contain social movements and reify symbolic communication through new scientific rationales, e.g., personality control through drugs and the institutionalization of an adjusting therapeutic system.

2. The interests that preserve the mode of production can no longer be seen as simple class interests. The complex integration of the base and superstructure of society suggests the emergence of a qualitatively new dynamic. The interests that guide the reproduction process of society involve now the subsystems of purposive rational action, i.e., contemporary technocratic consciousness confronts the reproduction process as a question the answers to which derive from technical necessities. Thus in the new ideological consciousness, the system *seems to* function according to structural constraints. Given this new complexity, expression of the basic societal contradiction as class exploitation oversimplifies the actual reproduction process of advanced industrial societies. That there continues to be an appropriation of surplus by class interests is true, but these are more difficult to locate now.

Not only have the forces of production necessitated an integration which approaches a refeudalization of society,[20] but they have generated a technical-administrative system which mediates the contradiction between capital and labor. Alienation of human activity is now not directly expressible as the appropriation of the surplus value but is more accurately conceptualized as the repressive results of instrumental rationalization. It is not simply the movement of economic change that is central to contemporary domination but the broader movement of a technical complex into which economic exchange is now embedded. Marx's critical theory was conceived during the transitional phase to industrial society and his critique centered on the rational mechanism—economic exchange—which undermined traditional society. We need a new critical totalization for an advanced epoch in which the character of rationalizing forces has become more fully developed.

By reconstructing Marx's critical theory in the terms of Habermas, we can illuminate a suppressed dimension of Marx's analysis. The appropriation of surplus requires that those who restrict the freedom of others render it just in the language of exchange relations. Hence the fetishism of commodities is a deformation of language; men are unable to communicate publicly about actual human relationships. Under the domination of the capitalist economy neither the laborer nor the employer can communicate about the actual nature of production.

Despite the principle of just exchange, however, the actual meaning of human production becomes a repressed ideal which presses on the minds of active men.

Like the specter that reappears to Macbeth and in so reappearing changes the meaning of kingship, the meaning of human activity is impossible to quell. In the capacity of everyday language to express the distinction between appearance and essential reality there resides a potential for emancipation. Men are able to express both a manifest message and a latent message that informs other men how that message is to be understood. Therein is a self-reflexive potential for expression of contradictions. Hence language is that device that allows men to combine their intellectual capacities and organize their interactionist systems.

It is only the utilization of intersubjective symbols which allow men to cope with an elaborate status system and yet maintain personal identity, to create adequate self-representations in novel situations and to maintain a flexible interpretation of internalized norms.

The self-reflexivity of language can thus be used to interpret repression. Unlike Marcuse who conceives repression as the repression of libido, Habermas has a broader conception of repressed experience. Rather than reading Freud's theory as pivoting on the libido theory, Habermas reconstructs Freud's "talking-cure" as a special type of hermeneutic inquiry.

The independence of intersubjective language games (or symbolic interaction systems) brings with it the logical possibility for a critical science. In the unique causality of an open system of linguistic communication there is latent a potential for a reflection process which can emancipate men from cultural reifications. Insofar then as Habermas' critical theory is based upon the liberating potential of self-reflexive language the new form of critical science is essentially a pathology of communication. Hence this form of critical research will focus upon class-specific socialization patterns and attempts to formulate a theory for the comparative study of repression in human organizations. These dimensions of Habermas' work are, to my knowledge, incomplete.

Many questions remain, however, for those who remain curious about the relationship of Habermas' new critical theory to that of Marx. For example, in order to update the materialist theory of history we would expect a reinterpretation of the historical constitution of the human world. Only in this way will the techne-praxis distinction gain the unique sociological significance that Habermas claims for it.

NOTES

1. Jürgen Habermas, *Technik und Wissenschaft als Ideologie* (Frankfurt: Suhrkamp, 1968).

2. Habermas, "Arbeit und Interaction . . ." *Technik und Wissenschaft*, p. 46.

3. ". . . knowledge has become a factor of production, in the form of the technological derivatives of scientific inquiry and in the indispensable contribution of other forms of knowledge . . . to the organization and maintenance of the productive process. Indeed, the ineluctable development of a fusion of administrative, political, and productive processes in neo-capitalism . . . has made it difficult to specify where precisely production stops and the administrative begins, and has rendered virtually impossible a distinction between 'political' and 'economic' decisions." Norman Birnbaum, "On the Idea of a Political Avant-Garde in Contemporary Politics: The Intellectuals and the Technical Intelligentsia," *Praxis* Nos. 1 and 2, 1969, pp. 234–35; also see Amitai Etzioni, *The Active Society* (New York: Free Press, 1968), Chapter 9.

4. At the moment the disproportionate allocation of state resources to the military and space research and development is legitimated by the concept of "technology transfer." Whatever the significance of such "transfer" (this constitutes an important area for research), there is no doubt that it presently legitimates an undiscussed commitment to a "defense economy." For example: "The exacting demands of the space program, which operates at the outermost limits of knowledge, have stimulated advances in almost every discipline of science and engineering. . . . These advances have spun off into business and industry." Wernher von Braun as quoted in the *Wall Street Journal* (July 9, 1969).

5. The concept of "instrumental rationalization" is used by Habermas in his critical reconceptualization of Max Weber's unitary concept of rationalization. Habermas is concerned with demonstrating that the extension of economic rationality to spheres of symbolically mediated interaction is a suppression of necessary communicative prerequisites for self-reflective consciousness. Habermas therefore reconceptualizes "rationalization" upon a twofold model of instrumental and symbolic interaction, seeing both modes of rationalization as necessary for a rational society.

6. Cf. Gerald Radnitzky, *Contemporary Schools of Metascience* (Goteborg: Akademeforfaget, 1968), pp.133ff.; Irene Taviss, "The Technological Society: Some Challenges for Social Science," *Social Research*, 35 (Autumn 1968), 521–39.

7. For example, Etzioni's *The Active Society*.

8. Cf. Jürgen Habermas, *Erkenntnis und Interesse* (Frankfurt: Suhrkamp, 1968), pp. 116–78.

9. The modern hermeneutic movement and its foundations are only now becoming known in the Anglo-American world. For its crucial significance for a critical science methodology see, Habermas, "Zurlogik der Sozialwissenshaft," *Philosophische Rundschau* (February 1967).

10. The key essay here is "The Construction of the Historical World of the Human Studies" which appears in a partial translation in *Pattern and Meaning in History* (Harper paper, 1962) or W. Dilthey, *Gessamalte Schriften*, Vol. VII (Stuttgart-Tubner Verlag, 1958).

11. Cf. Alfred Schultz, *Collected Papers*, Vols. I–III.

12. Cf. Harold Garfinkel, *Studies in Ethnomethodology* (Englewood Cliffs, N.J.: Prentice-Hall, 1967); Aaron Cicourel, *Method and Measurement in Sociology* (New York: Free Press, 1964).

13. Cf. Herbert Blumer, "Society as Symbolic Interaction" in A. Rose, ed., *Human Behavior and Social Processes* (Boston: Houghton Mifflin, 1962).

14. The possibility of a critical science depends upon a theoretical totalization which can function as both a framework for the analysis of contemporary society and at the same time serve as a hypothetical philosophy of history that can guide hermeneutic inquiry. Cf. Marlis Kruger, "Sociology of Knowledge and Social Theory," *Berkeley Journal of Sociology*, 14 (1969), 152–63.

15. However, to have a theory broad enough for a societal critique is not to have an "instrument to guide praxis." A historical theory must be interpreted in regard to specific historical conditions and hence between theory and praxis there is a crucial mediator of judgment. It is illusory to believe that any critical theory can simply be a tool in the hands of any class. Between theory and praxis there is a crucial phase of political program formulation which requires not only theoretical clarity but practical judgment about specific life-worlds.

16. This distinction is crucial for a critical science. Marcuse's concept for "surplus repression" (*Eros and Civilization* [Boston: Beacon Press, 1955], p. 32) is an attempt to turn it into a category of critical theory. It is also the focus of critical research done by the Frankfurt school, notably Max Horkheimer, ed., *Studien über Autorität und Familie*, (Paris: Alcan, 1936). Critical research now being carried on at Frankfurt focuses on the formation of ego identity, and class-specific socialization patterns.

17. Cf. Trent Schroyer, *"Alienation and the Dialectical Paradigm,"* Ph.D. dissertation, New School for Social Research, 1968.

18. Cf. Martin Nicolaus, "The Unknown Marx," *New Left Review*, 48 (March-April 1968), 41–61.

19. Quoted in Nicolaus, *ibid.*

20. Cf. John O'Neil, "Public and Private Space," in Trevor Lloyd and Jack McLeod, eds., *Agenda: 1970* (Toronto: University of Toronto Press, 1968).

MARXISM AND SOCIAL THEORY

ALVIN W. GOULDNER

Reprinted from *Theory and Society*, 1 (1974), 17–35.
Copyright © by Alvin W. Gouldner. Used by
permission of the author.

Alvin Gouldner is Max Weber Research Professor of
Social Theory at Washington University, St. Louis.

Marx's treatment of ideology and ideologues has certain symptomatic silences.
It possesses a "dark secret" in which the existence of the secret itself lays hidden.
Having focused its analysis on what is hidden in other theories and in bourgeois
society, Marxism may seem to some the embodiment of a healthy candor that
has no secrets of its own. The accusor, of course, classically diverts attention
from his own guilt by accusing another. That his accusation has this self-protec-
tive function, however, does not mean that it was intended to do so, nor does it
mean that his accusation is untrue.

While we are issuing caveats, add this: the analysis that follows focuses on
certain of the internal contradictions and mystifications of Marxism; but those
who have the illusion that the "normal" social sciences are devoid of corresponding contradictions and false consciousness will find no support here. The sectarian, of course, could not care less for such even-handedness. Sectarian and vulgar
Marxists—which is to say, *some* but scarcely all Marxists—will totally reject the
general point here, even while ritually nodding acceptance of it. Such Marxist
sectarians are the radical counterparts of "normal" sociologists; or, conversely,
normal sociologists (in Thomas Kuhn's sense) are the sectarians of academic social theory, bound by limits concerning which they lack reflexive awareness.
Neither can reject self-criticism openly; both must admit the possibility of self-
contradiction within their systems—at least, in principle. Neither will, therefore,
focus his attack on the general thesis that his system embodies a false consciousness. Rather, his response commonly takes the form of a rejection of the specific
cases held to exemplify his false consciousness, while never acknowledging the
truth of any particular specification of it. In short, both sectarian Marxists and
normal sociologists alike will admit that all men are mortal, but neither really
believes in his own mortality. For the unreflective, false consciousness like mortality is always the fate of the Other.

I

We may approach our problem by asking how ideology and ideologues—any ideology—commonly expect to change the world. The question is the Kantian one:
how is this surmounting "possible"; what are the assumptions that any ideology
necessarily makes, in proposing its public projects of social reconstruction? We
will focus here only on one such necessary assumption: ideology proposes to sur-
mount the present by (whatever else it also does) providing a new and allegedly
correct re-thinking that is expected to yield a re-ordering of the world. In other
words: ideology supposes that, if the world is to be changed, there must be a prior

change in thinking; that a change in thinking is a necessary condition for world reconstruction. However diverse the other assumptions made by ideologies, and however different their concrete projects, this premise is their common one, true of both revolutionary and reactionary ideologies alike.

The presence of this assumption is not always evidenced by what ideologues say expressly about the relations between thinking and world-changing. It is, however, (at least) commonly exhibited by the potency they tacitly attribute to ideas by the very act of communicating them emphatically through writing, by the importance they attribute to writing, by the sheer amount of time and energy they devote to writing. Not to speak, yet, of reading.

Whatever their politics or their public project—whether reactionary or revolutionary—all ideologies are regarded by their believers as having their definitive and authoritative exposition in a writing . A Socratic preference for the spoken word, and a corresponding rejection of writing, is inherently anti-ideological. It is, however, profoundly characteristic of ideological persuasion, discussions, or meetings, that there will commonly be, at some point, a reference recommending certain readings; there will commonly be the buying, lending, or borrowing of books or pamphlets or articles. And there will be talking about this reading and writing. (That this makes it difficult to distinguish between ideology and, say, academic social science, that it focalizes a rational dimension in ideology, is correct and was intended. It is difficult to distinguish the two and ideology *is* historically characterized by its rational mode of discourse and persuasion. But this is another problem that will not be explored here.) To bring the potential adherent to a reading is to bring him into what is taken to be a relation to the authoritative expression of the idea; with a highly valued, if not quasi-sacred, embodiment of the idea that may occur apart from the distracting presence of a surrounding troupe of believers. There is, however, some ambiguity here: from one standpoint, a man's isolation with a book can be a basis for a more rational appraisal of an idea, facilitating a more reflective judgment. From another standpoint, however, the printed object may be seen as a way the ideological group penetrates the person's private life, thus reinforcing their public pressure upon him.

II

To revert: the importance attributed by ideologues to writing and to written objects evidences, then, the great importance they attribute to ideas, in particular, and to ideas as instruments of social change. We may say, then, that the concept of ideas-as-potent constitutes the generic, underlying, common dimension of concrete ideologies. "Generic ideology," then, is a belief in the potency of ideas.

This estimate of the power of ideas, this *over*-estimate that is sedimented in the ideological vision and is the essence of generic ideology, may also be looked at ideologically. That is, one can ask: whose ideology is generic ideology? Which social stratum commonly overestimates the potency of ideas? Which group is more likely to have an interest (spiritual no less than material) in stressing the significance of ideas? Who holds that ideas can change the world? Once asked, these questions, as it were, point to their own answers: generic ideology is the ideology specific to the intelligentsia, to the intellectuals.

The overestimate of the power of ideas, the belief that the crucial thing in social change is to have correct ideas, the stress on the importance of theory, of explanation, of conceptual systems, on facts that concretize concepts or take shape with them, the stress on words, languages, speech, and on communication systems, all these are symptoms of the presence of a "generic ideology" that is more typical of intellectuals than of other social strata. The unstated but consequential premise of all intellectuals is the importance of writing and reading. The premise of all intellectuals is that people are changed by ideas: the intellectual's concrete paradigm of the idea; the model of its embodiment is the written or printed object.

Even among those intellectuals who seek to exorcise ideologies, the practitioners of "ideology-critique," there is the usually tacit, sometimes explicit, assumption that ideologies may be vanquished simply by exposing those who believe in them to true ideas. Ideologies, they sometimes seem to believe, can be defeated by brandishing true ideas before ideologists as one brandishes the cross before the vampire.

I have suggested, then, that "generic ideology"—the stress on the potency of ideas—is the ideology distinctive of (not limited to) the intellectuals. How do these views compare with Marx's classic formulation of this issue? They are for the largest part convergent and essentially continuous with his views. Clearly, Marx rejected any overestimate of the potency of ideas, and he did so polemically and repeatedly. Marx rejected the idealist assumption that consciousness determines being and he opted, instead, for the inverted formulation: man's consciousness is determined by his social being.

When Marx and Engels sought to clarify the essential and distinctive characteristics of "ideology" they stressed that it was a belief system made with a false consciousness. They held it was a false consciousness precisely in that thought saw its own origins only in thought and ideas were grounded only in ideas. In his famous letter to Franz Mehring (London, 14 July, 1893) Engels remarks that "ideology is a process accomplished by the so-called thinker consciously, indeed, but with a false consciousness . . . he imagines false or apparent motives." Specifically, adds Engels, ideology is a false consciousness because the thinker "derives both its form and its content from pure thought, either his own or that of his predecessors. He works with mere thought material, which he accepts without examination as the product of thought, he does not investigate further for a more remote process independent of thought . . . the tacit pre-supposition is that these facts themselves are also only the fruits of a process of thought. . . "

III

Clearly, then, there is a continuity between the Marxist view of ideology, as thought accomplished with a false consciousness, and the view of (generic) ideology as that which premises the potency of thought. There is, I say, a continuity but not an identity between these two views. For, in Marxism's view, the ideologist has a false consciousness because he only makes reference to thought and ideas, in grounding his own thinking; ideology, then is seen as something in the nature of a "limit" upon the ideologist's thought. Our own position, however, stresses the complementary view that thought is viewed (at least tacitly) by the ideologist in a certain positive way: as a locus of power. It is precisely this conception of it that makes it possible for the ideologist to accept ideas as a limit and not seek beyond them. For thought is conceived as sufficing to account for thought because it is defined as powerful. This was the tacit premise accepted by philosophical idealism and is implied in speaking of thought as *Geist*. (*Geist* was not so much a plan or blueprint, but was more like germinal matter with imprinting power.)

Another way of clarifying this: Marx does not unequivocally affirm that (in his own vocabulary) "idealism" is the essence of ideology. For he also wants to be able to speak of (certain vulgar or mechanical forms of) materialism as being ideologies. If he identifies the essence of ideology as idealism—the overestimate of ideas—he is then in the seemingly contradictory position of asserting: materialism is idealistic.

The difficulty is that Marx did not firmly establish a distinction between idealism as a technical philosophy, an extraordinary language, on the one side, and idealism as a part of ordinary language and everyday life, on the other. Had he done so, it might be seen more readily that there was no contradiction here, for these were different levels. It would be obvious—not as fugitive insight but as theoretical perspective—that even philosophers who are "materialists" may, in their tacit, everyday assumptions, overestimate the power of ideas—even when their theories affirm the contrary. Tacit, everyday idealism, is, then, compatible with theoretical materialism.

It is not that Marx is unaware of the presence of "idealism" in everyday life. It is, rather, that he has difficulty in speaking of it there. When Marx speaks of idealism, he mostly focuses on it as a technical theory of Mandarins rather than as an aspect of ordinary language. Correspondingly, when Marx focuses on ideology he is mostly focusing on the role of ideas and interests in everyday life. For Marxism, idealism is ideology written in a Mandarin technical language; and ideology is interest-corrupted idealism written in ordinary language.

Marx does not want to assimilate philosophical idealism to ideology because he does not see technical philosophy as "nothing but" the tool of the ruling class, which is how he saw ideology. As Marx's "Theses on Feuerbach" indicated, idealism properly saw the "active" side of cognition. He thus does not want to reduce idealism to ideology because he believes idealism does have a measure of truth and autonomy, but he correspondingly stressed the distorted character and bondage of ideology.

Failing to construct "ideology" and "idealism," so that both had a measure of autonomy, from one another as from other social forces, Marx sometimes failed to see that the tacit rules of everyday life were not simply a degenerate form of high culture and have a great degree of autonomy from the objects of Mandarin culture. He thus failed to see that one's everyday life might go its own way, remaining idealistic, for example, even as one's theoretical culture became materialistic. In this, however, there is a paradoxical and tacit overestimate of the importance that Mandarin languages are expected to have in everyday life. As a step toward a definition of Marxism we might say that it is: a philosophical "materialism" that is, in practice, grounded in the tacit idealism of an everyday culture.

In some large part, this is why much of Marx's study of *Das Kapital* is focused, not simply on capitalist society, but on *theories* about capitalism and on their technical vocabularies; *Das Kapital* is, after all, emphatically subtitled "A Critique of Political Economy." In Marx there is a decisive conflation between the technical categories of economic theory, on the one side, and the cultural categories of everyday life, on the other. In the result, there is also in Marx a conflation between the critique of political economy and the critique of capitalist society.

In thus focalizing the importance of Mandarin culture for everyday life, Marxism merely manifests once more an importance it always attributed to "theory"; Marxism once again exhibits its assumption that technical theory was vital for transcending everyday life. Indeed, what is *Das Kapital* but the most technical political economics? Marxism's concern is to subject everyday life to an extraordinary "theory," to a *praxis* informed and guided by this theory: this is what it means to affirm the "unity" of theory and practice. From such a standpoint, everyday life then inevitably loses its autonomy; indeed, the aim is to make it lose its autonomy; the aim is to subject everyday life to a high theoretical culture.

IV

The generic ideology of intellectuals that premises the power of ideas does so in a distinctive style of discourse and rhetoric. It does so "objectivistically," speaking as it does of the power of certain ideas or cultural objects, but saying nothing about the power of their producers, intellectuals themselves. It is precisely by dramatizing the importance of ideas that generic ideology functions to obscure the role of idea-producers. Generic ideology serves to hide the role of men in the shadow of the cultural objects that it accentuates.

Why is there such an objectivistic occlusion of intellectuals? Above all, it is indicative of efforts to resolve tensions between intellectuals and more dominant, hegemonic classes. The bourgeoisie and other dominant classes in bourgeois society conceive themselves to be "principals" acting on their behalf. They also want their agents to act on behalf of these interests. The hegemonic class rejects agents who want to govern.

So the newly emerging intelligentsia learned they had better bridle and disguise their ambitions, which soared beyond their modest social position. But this disguise could not be made so impregnable that no one could ever guess that they had something to offer. Intellectuals had, in short, prudently to flash their product without calling vulgar attention to *themselves*. The rhetoric of objectivism enabled them to do just that, to separate their ideas from their persons, thereby giving the social role of ideas emphatic yet anonymous endorsement.

It is on that level—i.e., on the level of this displaced objectivism—that Marxism joined the issue with idealism, addressing itself primarily to a critique of ideas rather of the intelligentsia. In the course of this polemic, Marxism introjected idealism's objectivism, the objectivism generally characteristic of ideology itself, even while disengaging itself from idealism on the technical, philosophical level.

In the language of this introjected objectivism, Marxism's announced method becomes "the unity of theory and practice" (or "praxis") rather than the unity of intellectuals and proletariat. The doctrine of a unity of theory and practice, is, tacitly, a call to the establishment (or re-establishment) of certain social relations between intellectuals and masses. The objectivistic focus on the unity of theory and practice thus permits socialists to avoid direct confrontation with the question of the role of intellectuals in their own cadres. The very emphasis on the role of "theory" leads discourse to the brink of that issue but stops it there, leaving it as a discussion of theory but not of intellectuals.

Behind Marxism's affirmation of the doctrine of the unity of theory and praxis there are unresolved fundamental questions about the role of intellectuals; and not only about their social role in the modern world in general but, more pointedly, about their role in the socialist movement, about their relations with the proletariat, and about their implication in communism and vanguard parties. Above all, there is the unresolved problem of the paradoxical authority of intellectuals in a "workers' movement." Marxism's stress on the role of theory and of a "scientific" socialism must inevitably invest theorists and intellectuals with a great authority. For it is they and they alone—with the rare exception of a working class autodidact such as Eugene Dietzgen[1]—that are the sources and origins of socialism's theory. If Marxism affirms the primacy of the proletariat as historical agent, it is clearly an agent that is expected to fill its historical mission only after it has freed itself from bondage to the immediacy of the status quo and this, in turn, is never possible except by submitting itself to the tutelage of "theory."

The doctrine of the unity of theory and practice has this silence: how can one submit oneself to the tutelage of theory without, at the same time, submitting oneself to the tutelage of theorists and intellectuals? Marxism's doctrine of the unity of theory and practice is therefore a doctrine tacitly functioning to conceal the actual social structure of the socialist movement; it is a tacit doctrine about the system of social stratification within the socialist movement, and serves to obfuscate its actual structure of domination, and the origins and character of its dominant strata of intellectuals.

Contrast this formulation with the characteristic self-understanding of Marxism. So far as its own grounding is concerned, Marx's and Marxism's self-understanding was that itself it was a theoretical standpoint based on the objective interests, and reflecting the historical emergence, of the proletariat. From this standpoint, Marxism was the critical philosophy guiding the proletariat's self-emancipation.

What this obscures is the role of the intelligentsia as the social grounding of Marxist theory and as the social strata whose own social character—and not only the proletariat's—shapes the nature of Marxism. If it was true that "social being" determines consciousness, as Marx and Engels insisted, then this question must arise: how could the consciousness of the proletariat emerge from the social being of the intelligentsia? How could the intelligentsia elude their own different social being to give expression to the consciousness of another strata, the proletariat? Did Marx and Engels really believe that they themselves were workers, even intellectual proletarians? There is not the slightest indication that they thought of themselves in that way. Rather, they seem to have thought of themselves as revolutionary intellectuals. But they never suggest how intellectuals could develop the consciousness of a revolutionary proletariat, except to remark that, on some few occasions, certain members of the ruling class go over to the proletariat.

Marxism had only the most fugitive and garbled account of its own origins. For it could not account for itself without the most obvious self-contradiction, and without revealing the dissonant presence of intellectuals as authoritative figures in a working class movement. The objectivism of Marxism functions to conceal the embarrassing presence and authority of intellectuals in a "working class" movement.

Marxism's unconsciousness, then, is an inability to face and mount rational discourse concerning the actual leading role of intellectuals in a proletarian, socialist movement; concerning the role of ideas in a movement committed to materialism; concerning the importance of voluntaristic commitment in a political theory stressing the primacy of social structures and formations.

V

Workers, says Marx writing to Sorge (London, 19 October 1877), who "give up work and become professional literary men, always set some theoretical mischief going and are always ready to attach themselves to some muddleheads from the alleged 'learned' caste." It was in this vein that one of the first to be purged from the young Marx's revolutionary circle in 1846 was Wilhelm Weitling, the uprooted German revolutionary leader, one of the few having authentically working class origins; in a near-ritual ceremony of status degradation, Weitling was upbraided by Marx and Engels for the poverty of his theoretical doctrine and denounced by them as an ignorant, "abject fraud."

To foster theory among workers, then, was to require something for which workers themselves clearly had little training or talent. With all its risks, the proletariat would have to get theory from social strata outside their own ranks —as Karl Kautsy would, years later, correctly infer from his Marxism—and to whom the working class would have to submit itself, if it were to achieve its historical mission.

Marxism was thus created, and remains, a paradoxical social theory in which those who create the theory itself do not clearly figure in it, but are hidden behind the objectivistic doctrine of the unity of theory and praxis. Paradoxically, it is the theorist, the intelligentsia, the intellectuals, who, although given short shrift in Marxist theory, are to be the source of the very theory which Marxism holds to be indispensable for the advent of socialism.

Still, it also needs to be stressed that there is a certain rationality in Marxism's impulse to conceal the presence of theorists, even while vaunting the importance of theory, in the socialist movement. For as the above quotation from Engels sees, on which theorists could socialism actually rely? If not the autodidacts among the workers and if not the academicians, then who? And if neither, then from where indeed will the continuing and cumulative development of Marxist theory come from?

If Marxism stresses the importance of theory for social transformation, on the one side, and if, on the other, it encourages an understandable suspicion of the autodidact and the academician, Marxism thereby ensures its own stasis. For if there are no social strata of intellectuals and theorists who can continue to develop Marxist theory how, then, is Marxist theory to provide a guide to the continually changing and new historical circumstances within which the transition to socialism would have to be made?

While vaunting theory, then, Marxism—and, quite properly so, given its revolutionary aspirations—is suspicious of theorists. If theorists are working class in origin and training, Marxism fears that they will either have the crudity of autodidacts or the susceptibilities of the *parvenu* to the merely cheap and fashionable. If, however, the theorists are academicians comfortably living a Mandarin life, Marxism greatly fears their conventional timorousness, their implication in the state civil service of the university, their middle-class family origins, their false consciousness and accommodation to the status quo. There is, therefore, in Marxism this ineluctable contradiction: theory is absolutely necessary for social transformation, but theorists may not be trusted. From Marx to Mao, that contradiction is fully exhibited in the continuing distrust of the intelligentsia. It is the contradiction, too, that is concealed by the doctrine of the unity of "theory" and "practice."

VI

Marxism's relation to theorists, then, must be profoundly ambivalent. It needs but cannot trust intellectuals and theorists. It copes with this ambivalence in part by affirming a commitment only to "theory" but not to the theorists. Marxism has a lucid and firm understanding that even its own theorists may bind it to the staus quo, that they may constantly serve as an unwitting "transmission belt" subverting Marxism's own revolutionary commitments.

For Marxists to be ambivalent to theory and theorists means that they must also be ambivalent to *Marxism itself*. It is precisely in this that we reach the deepest levels of Marxism's own secret: its own self-doubts about culture, intellectual activity, and theory itself. There is a level in Marxism, a level as perduring and strong as it is repressed, in which Marxism is anti-intellectual, anti-philosophical, anti-theoretical. There is a level in which Marxism's promised "abolition" of philosophy was not only some cerebral Hegelian *Aufhebung* but a hot fantasy of true aggression against theory. These are among the repressed proclivities of Marxism derivative of its own contradiction, of its simultaneous vaunting of theory and suspicion of theorists.

On this repressed level, Marxism glimpses itself as in part the seed of its enemy,[2] has an intimation that the enemy to be vanquished is in part within itself; begins to suspect that the "revolution in permanence" has its ultimate implication in a *self*-transcendence. Marxism begins to grasp that revolution in permanence must mean revolution against itself. The contradictions within Marxism, then, direct it blindly onto the path of theoretical parricide, inviting it to a rebel act that paralyzes it. Maoism has seen this more clearly than all other Marxisms. For this is the most fundamental (but hidden) object of its "cultural revolution."[3]

In its awareness of the vulnerability of theorists, of its own theorists, to ideological distortions emanating from the dominant institutions, Marxism achieves —even if recoiling from the ultimate implication—a substantial measure of genuine reflexivity. It has a certain sensitive and correct understanding of the dangers that threaten it. It can easily accept the reality of this enemy as an external object, even if sometimes resisting the idea that he is also inescapably internalized. Limited and precarious as its self-awareness is, Marxism seems more prudently self-critical of its own vulnerability to the status quo than does normal, academic social theory. Unlike the Marxist, the academic theorist is not committed to a rebel cause that brings him into conflict with the dominant ideologies around him, thereby making him aware of their pressure upon him and of his vulnerability to them. Commonly lacking such awareness-heightening tensions, the academic social theorist is more likely to fantasy himself a "value free" scholar.

VII

In vaunting theory, while warning about theorists, Marxism plainly implied that a special sort of theorist would be necessary for socialism. For the working class cannot be emancipated, Marxism held, without theory; but it can neither create theory itself nor hope to receive the theory it needs from the usual academicians. And if a special theorist thus becomes necessary, it is also necessary to create the social infra-structure that could produce and reproduce such special theorists. That special instrument was, of course, the organized "vanguard party," which came to full self-consciousness with Lenin's organization of the Bolshevik party and in his theoretical analysis, *What Is to Be Done?* It was the latent function of the vanguard party to overcome the contradiction between Marxism's insistence on the necessity of theory, and its critique of theorists.

The function of the vanguard party, then, cannot simply be conceived in terms of the needs and role of the proletariat alone. It cannot simply be conceived as the true "consciousness" of the working class of its historical mission—in Lukács terms. It is surely not the consciousness "natural" to the proletariat which, as Lenin suggested, is primarily that of economics or trade unionism. This consciousness of the vanguard party is largely articulated and directed by the intellectuals within the party and especially in its leadership cadres. As such, it is a consciousness open to the intelligentsia, open to its specific background, ongoing culture, and present situation, which are scarcely identical with those of the proletariat.

But the vanguard party is not just a transmission belt for the consciousness of the intelligentsia. It is not just the instrument through which the intellectuals give expression to a consciousness and ideology that they "bring with them" to the vanguard party; it is not a consciousness altogether anterior to that party. The vanguard party, then, is not just a disguise and an instrument for the intelligentsia, even though the vanguards' central cadres are essentially derived from and manned by the intelligentsia.

The vanguard party is the instrument of an intelligentsia transformed. It is, also, an instrument for the transformation of that intelligentsia's social character. In some part, this "transformation" of the consciousness of the intelligentsia by the vanguard party can be thought of as a "radicalization" brought about, in some degree, by involving the intelligentsia in an intensifying political struggle against the status quo. This is and always has been a unique kind of radicalization. It is a radicalization from above, born not of the intellectual's own experience but of his identification with the lowly and suffering; born not of his own economic deprivation so much as from the violation of his own Jacobin spirit, the violation of the intellectual's sense of his own dignity and self-worth, the violation of his cultural hope and values and, especially, of his emphatic belief in (a certain kind of) equality. This radicalization *precedes* the intellectual's involvement with the vanguard party and is the leverage through which he is cumulatively committed in the course of organized struggle. Through this, the intelligentsia are freed of an uncritical acceptance of the language and ideology of the status quo; freed of respect for its symbols of authority, of any assumptions about its "naturalness" or invulnerability to change.

Commitments are made via the vanguard party that make it difficult (or impossible) for the intelligentsia to pursue normal careers within conventional institutions. From one perspective, it might be said that an intelligentsia thus "radicalized" is one whose career prospects in the status quo are threatened. Its future is, therefore, tied increasingly to the struggle against and victory over the status quo. It is this "material" transformation that is part of the infrastructure of the ideological changes, the value transformations, the linguistic shift, and the consciousness-raising entailed by "radicalization."

A central function of the vanguard party is the management of this alienation of the intelligentsia from normal careers within the status quo by a series of successive tests and cumulative commitments until, at the end, a small section of the intelligentsia has and wants no way back into the status quo. Moreover, it is also an important function of the vanguard party to help intellectuals in such transition cope with their own anxieties and panics. These are to be expected, first, because such intellectuals enter into dangerous confrontation against powerful authority and, secondly, because they cut themselves off from conventional, security-giving careers that they and their families had at first often expected them to pursue.

One central function of the vanguard party, then, is managing the social transformation of the intelligentsia; promoting their alienation from conventional society and careers; facilitating their self-discipline in the face of often rampant anxiety. This is a view substantially different from a Pollyanna conception of the vanguard party as "radicalizing" the intellectual, as imparting sympathy for and a learning from the proletariat. It is also a conception totally at variance with a Lukácsian view of the vanguard as the embodiment of the proletariat's true historical mission and its proper class consciousness.

The vanguard party, then, is an agency for the selective assimilation and resocialization of the intelligentsia, alienating it further from its middle-class antecedents and culture. It is also an agency for the corresponding tutelary development of some of working-class origin, on the condition that they assimilate appropriate theory, subordinate their practice to it, and overcome the natural limits of working-class consciousness—economism and trade unionism. The latter thus escape the pressures of those institutional structures which, from their different quarter, would bind them back into conventional society.

The emergence of the vanguard party marks a new historical period in which a sector of the socialist movement no longer passively waits for the historical maturation of the objective socio-economic formations once deemed requisite for socialism. The emergence of the vanguard party marks the beginning of the long crisis of "scientific," evolutionary socialism. Now, it is the testing, the hardening, the combativeness, and the obedience of the vanguard party to its center that become the new operational definition of the existence of the objective requisites for revolution. The vanguard party's own development becomes the decisive objective condition for the revolution.

Thus one central organizational innovation of the Leninist vanguard conception was the stress it placed upon the political initiative of the vanguard, vis-à-vis the proletariat and the masses. The second organizational innovation, crystallized by Lenin in his well-known controversy with L. Martov (Iullii Osipovich Tsederbaum) over the formal requisites for party membership, was one in which Lenin successfully rejected a distinction between intellectuals and others, and imposed his requirement for their common submission to Party discipline.

The vanguard party is in continual peril from two fundamental organizational pathologies. One is "opportunism," in which it succumbs to bourgeois culture and politics, being no longer able to maintain an effective boundary between itself and its threatening surround. The second organizational pathology is "sectarianism" in which, because the boundary it has drawn is too impermeable, the vanguard isolates itself from social reality and, in protecting itself from outside influence, also fails to influence that outside. Both these pathologies demoralize and exhaust its forces. They are, we might say, the occupational hazards normal to the life of the professional revolutionary. But still, they are pathologies only, and they are by no means the entire sum and substance of his existence and his meaning.

VIII

Seen from the standpoint of ideology and theory, sectarianism means the breakdown of encounter with the Other. It means the corresponding distortion of theory, first, by its "monumentalization," by sacralizing the great books and other authoritative sources which, being written earlier, inevitably fail to do justice to an understanding of the present. Secondly, sectarianism means "subjectivizing" theory, by failing to discipline political fantasy and personal anxiety with a reality-test, with Other-encounter; here political needs and individual autisms govern social diagnosis.

Correspondingly, opportunism means surrender to an alien theory and ideology, not because it is more empirically sound, but because it is essentially stronger, politically and socially; it also means irrational discontinuities in theoretical development, the failure to build and develop theory cumulatively. Above all, opportunism means the fundamental transformation of revolutionary theory—it becomes academicized.

The transformation of the intellectual into professional revolutionary by the vanguard means the total instrumentalization of theory itself. On the one side, theory no longer serves as a wide-ranging effort to comprehend the culture as a whole but focuses on narrower issues implicated in the polemics concerning present party policy. Theory no longer concerns itself with the "big news," serving as an outpost and early warning system; theory comes to be subordinated to the very immediacy of the at-hand that it was, at first, intended to transcend. It now becomes the "market research" of the revolution.

There is, of course, always a powerful tendency for such market research to make its findings consistent with political commitments that had already been made and justified on other grounds. Far from providing information, theory then serves primarily to contribute legitimacy to policies formed without reference to it. It now constitutes an *ersatz* rationality.

Finally: theory becomes *Weltanschauung* in the context of the vanguard party—in its own internal relations, on the one side, and, on the other, in the vanguard's relations with the masses. In the vanguard, then, theory does not function as a grounding for a critical understanding of the larger social world; nor even as information instrumentally useful for managing it; nor even as window-dressing to persuade others to accept problematic policies. Theory also becomes a set of shared beliefs that maintain the social solidarity of the vanguard party and the personal security of its individual members.

Locked as it may be in fearsome rebellion against the powerful forces of the status quo, the vanguard party cannot easily look upon—or allow others to look upon—its theory with a cold reflective eye. For it needs this theory as a shared language to hold itself together; to enable it to mount cooperative effort; to fortify its solidarity and to fend off its members' threatening anxieties.

It is in this respect mistaken, I believe, to condemn the Soviet Union for having transformed Marxism into a *Weltanschauung*; or, at least, it is mistaken to impute a special culpability to them for this development. For this is inherent in the fact that, in the context of the vanguard party's absorbing and dangerous struggle to change the world, and to maintain its own organizational existence under pressure, it must have and maintain shared values. In effect, it derives these from its theory. Theory here, then, becomes culture subserving social solidarity and survival. To that extent, it must be removed from the calculating and rational appraisal necessary to develop, deepen, adjust, improve it, as an instrument for either understanding the social world or changing it.

Once theory becomes culture, the everyday culture requisite for vanguard social solidarity, theory can be neither "played with" nor instrumentallly revised without offending the vanguard cadre's sense of propriety, its conception of the sacred, and without threatening its very security. Affirmation of the doctrine of the unity of theory and practice all too often serves to conceal the fact that theory has died and has been replaced by ritual.

IX

Marxism, then, lives on two levels, which is not in the least to suggest that it is "two-faced"; nor, again, is it in the least to imply that it is in this respect one whit different from normal academic sociology. There is Marxism's manifest level as an extraordinary language, as a technical theory and philosophy, as a materialism on behalf of working-class emancipation. Marxism also lives on a deeper level, an unconscious level not easily spoken in its own community, in which there is an abiding commitment to theory, to ideas, to generic ideology, and the dissonant authority of intellectuals.

It is in terms of this two-layered structure of Marxism that we may be able to bring into focus the existence and the meaning of Marxism's metaphoricality. For it is only in the light of Marxism's two-fold structure that we may note how the proletariat for Marx was, indeed always was, a metaphor. It is because of this metaphoricality of the proletariat in Marxism that it has been capable of dropping the proletariat and searching out other historical agents to replace that tired "heart" of the revolution. Again, this also makes it understandable how Marxists can concretize "socialism" in such a surprising variety of forms, for example, as a "people's democratic dictatorship," presumably (perhaps only) capable of emerging even in societies with scarcely a proletariat.

To speak of the metaphoricality of Marxism is to make reference to the interchangeability, for Marxism, of vastly different concrete cases, so that "socialism" can be said to exist in Russia, China, or even (for some) Algeria and Albania. Correspondingly, the interchangeability of the "proletariat," of the people, of the peasantry, of colonially exploited, of the racially subjugated, means that the fundamental commitment that Marxism made was not to the "proletariat" as such but to some other, imprecisely defined value, which subsumes the proletariat but also allows inclusion of vastly different social stratas.

This metaphoricality of Marxism is one of its great adaptive factors. It allows Marxism to survive repeated contradictions of its manifest technical social theory and economics and to accommodate to falsified predictions without evoking, in many of its believers, a demoralizing sense of Marxism's nonrationality or inauthenticity.

Indeed, it is precisely Marxism's metaphoricality that signals the presence of its very rationality; that signals that its fundamental commitments are not to some historically limited social segment but primarily to certain values and ideas: the struggle against unnecessary suffering, exploitation, irrational scarcity, and any "surplus" inequality interpretable as unnecessary in the light of modern productivity—a struggle that was now no longer limited to capitalist societies with proletariats; a struggle whose universalism was primarily persuasive and meaningful to intellectuals.

This rationality of Marxism, its basic value commitment, abides on its deepest level as ideology justifying and fostering action against almost any form of inequality in the modern world.

This is Marxism's repressed underside; repressed because it is in direct contradiction with its technical level, where Marxism easily and frequently succumbs to a view of itself as a "science"; where Marxism becomes a materialism which grounds a political evolutionism, where it is not so much struggle, but the development of certain objective conditions, that is the requisite of revolution and socialism. This deeper and repressed level is an infra-structure of Marxism that cannot be self-reflected upon. Indeed, its sheer existence is scarcely acknowledgeable in the symbol system constituted by manifest Marxist theory. This deeper, repressed level is Marxism's final survival system and its ultimate meaning. It contains the last immanent code for interpreting messages on the technical level; for authoritatively resolving ambiguities and dissonance that could not be resolved on that manifest level. In short, the deeper level contains—among other things—the analytic of last resort.

X

The great Marxist revolutionaries are defined by their courage in establishing connections with this repressed and silent level in Marxism, by their ability to reestablish a revitalizing contact with the deeper Marxism. The invisible struggle of revolutionaries such as Lenin, Mao, and Castro has been a struggle to get beneath the manifest surfaces of "scientific" Marxism, beneath the objectivism and the passive evolutionism. Probing beneath manifest Marxism they risked the charges of revisionism, of political heresy, of leftism and the ostracism that follows. In short, they risked their Marxism and their lives. Having once found their way down to the repressed deeper levels, they could now mobilize and use latent Marxism's voluntarism, its conviction about the importance of ideas, and the potency of the subjective. The successes of the great revolutionary Marxists are due in part to the fact that they were able to work their way down to the repressed latent level of Marxism.

POSTSCRIPT

Our discussion of the tensions between the manifest level of Marxism, with its stress on the importance of socio-economic structures, and Marxism's latent level with its generic ideology and its stress on the importance of ideas, consciousness, and will, corresponds to the distinction I had earlier developed[4] between "Scientific Marxism" on the one side and "Critical Marxism" on the other. That distinction had been largely developed in a structural manner. Here, however, I begin to exhibit some of the dynamics of that structural differentiation. This was done by stressing, in effect, that critical and scientific Marxisms are different layers in one structurally integrated Marxism, although each may occupy a different position at different times.

As Marxism first emerged as an historical phenomenon, perhaps until the Second International, these two layers had a distinct relation to one another. In that structuring of Marxism, Scientific Marxism was the dominant layer and served to impose a repressive silence on Critical Marxism. That, we might say, was Marxism₁ and our analysis of the dynamics in Marxist theory has centered primarily on it. With the emergence of Leninism that specific structure of Marxism cracks. With the emergence of Mao's China and Castro's Cuba that structure of Scientific Marxism gives way to a radically new structuring of Marxism, in which the bottom rail has become the top; in this, Critical Marxism surfaces, becomes the controlling and dominant layer in Marxism, especially in underdeveloped nations, and there is a new repressed layer—Scientific Marxism itself.

Historically, what had first been publicly defined as Marxism was Marxism₁, Scientific Marxism. One may well wonder whether there is sufficient continuity between it and Marxism₂, Critical Marxism, to speak of the latter as being a Marxism at all. It is clear, however, why some will wish to pour new wine into old bottles, for to define oneself as a Marxist is to link oneself with that powerful and authentic tradition of determined, if not always revolutionary, resistance to established arrangements. With the movement toward Marxism₂, however, Marxism is pressed toward an increasing metaphoricality. Such increasing metaphoricality serves to liberate political action from the limits involved in Marxism₁ without, however, having to renounce one's claim to a Marxist identity and without having to sever one's connection with the long-standing anti-establishment tradition it names.

NOTES

1. Marx's own judgment of Dietzgen (in a letter to Engels of 4 October, 1868) was characteristically harsh and condescending: "My opinion is that J. Dietzgen would do best to condense all his ideas into two printer's sheets and have them published under his own name as a tanner." In his reply of 6 November, 1868, Engels was more generous and argued that Dietzgen be given much more space than Marx had advocated; but it was in character that Engels also doubted that the most brilliant part of Dietzgen's work was actually his own: " . . . if one could be *sure* that he had discovered it for *himself*."

2. As, for instance, in the idea that "capitalism creates the seeds of its own destruction."

3. For fuller development see my discussion of Maoism in "The Two Marxisms," in Alvin W. Gouldner, *For Sociology* (New York: Basic Books, 1973, and London: Allen Lane, 1973), pp. 444 ff.

4. Ibid., pp. 425–62.

CHAPTER 7 ETHNOMETHODOLOGY AND PHENOMENOLOGICAL SOCIOLOGY

Introduction

Ethnomethodology, or as it is now more fashionably called, phenomenological sociology, is a new approach to sociology. Mullins (1973:184) has defined it as "the study of the methods used by members of a group for understanding communication, making decisions, being rational, accounting for action, and so on." This approach is premised by the claim that we do not yet understand the basic processes of everyday interaction. Thus, the editor of an anthology of writings on communicative behavior notes that ethnomethodology "tends to cut off all macrosociological considerations for the time being in order to concentrate on the basic rules of everyday communication and interaction. Until we have understood how we do, in fact, understand each other, all further sociological inquiry will be useless" (Dreitzel, 1970:x). Introducing a more recent reader on ethnomethodology, Roy Turner (1974:7) claims that there is no longer an easy definition of this style of sociology, that it is best gleaned from reading the growing literature. There is, however, a common concern with "practical reasoning"—the ways in which people make sense of events and of interaction to themselves and others.

Ethnomethodology has had a broad impact on sociology. Mullins (1973:183–212) treats it as a cohesive specialty in sociology, while Jonathan Turner (1974:321–31) devotes a chapter to the question of its existence as a distinct theoretical paradigm. Ethnomethodology, since its beginning with the work of Garfinkel in the 1950s and 1960s, has been strongest in West Coast universities, with the phenomenological branch centered in the East around Alfred Schutz in New York (see Mullins, 1973; Wagner, 1975). The two wings are now largely merged under the latter title and have absorbed some underpinning from European phenomenological philosophy. They are loosely organized by informal and formal (e.g., the *Phenomenological Sociology Newsletter*) communication channels.

Although ethnomethodology has close affinity to the symbolic-interactionist perspective (see Denzin, 1969), it has not been warmly received by most sociologists. Many find it incomprehensible or irrelevant to their goals in the discipline. A few give it a sympathetic reading (see Gouldner, 1975) and, like Collins (1975), attempt to absorb it into their own theoretical perspectives. Many sociologists, however, are openly hostile to what they perceive as a subversive cult that would demolish all existing sociology and build a new one based on a radically new foundation.

In his 1975 presidential address to the American Sociological Association, Coser exemplifies the hostile reaction. To him, ethnomethodology "seems aggressively and programmatically devoid of theoretical content of sociological relevance" (1975:696). He ridicules ethnomethodology for its jargon and triviality and concludes that it is

a massive cop-out, a determined refusal to undertake research that would indicate the extent to which our lives are affected by the socioeconomic context in which they are embedded. It amounts to an orgy of subjectivism, a self-indulgent enterprise in which perpetual methodological analysis and self-analysis leads to infinite regress . . . (1975:698)

It is difficult to conceive of harsher words for a president of a scholarly association to address a minority faction of its membership. The function of Coser's induced conflict seems to be the degradation of ethnomethodology.

Zimmerman (1976), in a written response to Coser, denies that ethnomethodology is a closed "sect." It is Coser's inadequate reading and understanding that make work in this tradition appear trivial. In short, Coser has created "a crude caricature" (Zimmerman, 1976:7). Mehan and Wood (1976) provide a lucid summary of ethnomethodological themes to rebut Coser's attack: Much is being discovered about *social* life that is ignored by traditional sociology.

Current "phenomenological" sociology, as Mehan and Wood (1976) well document, is varied both in its subject matter and in the methods it uses. It is clearly still an emerging part of sociology that has yet to fully crystallize its foundations. Mehan and Wood (1975) have argued that it is a unique blend of the hermeneutic-dialectic and logico-empiricist traditions of doing science, but they urge practice rather than analysis of ethnomethodology. Ethnomethodology is clearly opposed to some varieties of sociology, especially the normative (see Wilson, 1970), and neopositive (see Churchill, 1971).

Clearly, phenomenological sociology has attracted considerable attention in recent years, both in the United States and in Europe. In Britain, Pivcevic (1972) denies the utility of phenomenology as a basis for sociology, while Hindess (1972) directly criticizes the value of the work of Alfred Schutz (Garfinkel's mentor, and widely recognized as a founder of phenomenological sociology). Similarly, Best (1975) denies the validity of the philosophical basis of current "phenomenological" sociology. In the United States much attention has been given to the political implications of this work, especially its alleged latent radicalism or conservatism (see Young, 1971; Morris, 1975; McNall and Johnson, 1975). Finally, ethnomethodology has been called on to defend its methods. To some, they are not very unique in sociology (see Gidlow, 1972); to others, they constitute the basis of a "new empiricism" (see Bruyn, 1967).

The selections in this chapter reflect three different varieties of ethnomethodology-phenomenological sociology. Heap and Roth deal with the philosophical underpinnings of the "school." They begin with a critique of the work of Tiryakian, Bruyn, and Douglas, who, they claim, misunderstand philosophical phenomenology. They attempt to rebuild phenomenological sociology on a new basis, first by showing that Husserl's philosophy is *not* followed by self-styled phenomenologists. They then outline three types of phenomenological sociology and ethnomethodology, which they conclude are compatible with phenomenological concerns. The second article, by Garfinkel and Sacks, represents "classic" ethnomethodology. They argue the position of the "West Coast school," introduce and illustrate ethnomethodological concepts such as indexical expressions and the phenomenon to be studied, and set an example of ethnomethodological analysis. The last article, by Blum and McHugh, investigates the term "motive" from a similar perspective (note the distinction they make in Footnote 1 between their "East Coast" work and ethnomethodology). They argue that motives are themselves socially constructed.

References and Suggested Readings

Attewell, Paul. "Ethnomethodology Since Garfinkel," *Theory and Society*, 1 (Summer 1974), 179–210.

Barnes, Barry, and John Law. "Whatever Should be Done with Indexical Expressions?" *Theory and Society*, 3 (Summer 1976), 223–37.

Best, R. E. "New Directions in Sociological Theory? A Critical Note on Phenomenological Sociology and Its Antecedents," *British Journal of Sociology*, 26 (June 1975), 133–43.

Bruyn, Severyn T. "The New Empiricists: The Participant Observer and Phenomenologist," *Sociology and Social Research*, 51 (April 1967), 317–22.

Churchill, Lindsey. "Ethnomethodology and Measurement," *Social Forces*, 50 (December 1971), 182–91.

Cicourel, Aaron V. *Method and Measurement in Sociology.* New York: Free Press, 1964.

———. *The Social Organization of Juvenile Justice.* New York: Wiley, 1968.

———. *Cognitive Sociology.* New York: Free Press, 1974.

Cicourel, Aaron V., K. H. Jennings, S. H. M. Jennings, et al. *Language Use and School Performance.* New York: Academic Press, 1974.

Collins, Randall. *Conflict Sociology: Toward an Explanatory Science.* New York: Academic Press, 1975.

Coser, Lewis A. "Two Methods in Search of a Substance," *American Sociological Review*, 40 (December 1975), 691–700.

Denzin, Norman K. "Symbolic Interactionism and Ethnomethodology: A Proposed Synthesis," *American Sociological Review*, 34 (December 1969) 922–34.

Douglas, Jack D. *Understanding Everyday Life: Toward the Reconstruction of Sociological Knowledge.* Chicago: Aldine, 1970.

Dreitzel, Hans Peter, ed. *Recent Sociology No. 2: Patterns of Communicative Behavior.* New York: Macmillan, 1970.

Garfinkel, Harold. *Studies in Ethnomethodology.* Englewood Cliffs, N.J.: Prentice-Hall, 1967.

Gidlow, Bob. "Ethnomethodology—A New Name for Old Practices," *British Journal of Sociology*, 23 (December 1972), 395–405.

Gorman, Robert A. "Alfred Schutz—An Exposition and Critique," *British Journal of Sociology*, 26 (March 1975), 1–19.

Gouldner, Alvin W. "Sociology and the Everyday Life," in Lewis A. Coser, ed., *The Idea of Social Structure.* New York: Harcourt Brace Jovanovich, 1975.

Hill, Richard J., and Kathleen Stones Crittenden. "Proceedings of the Purdue Symposium on Ethnomethodology," Monograph 1. Lafayette, Indiana: Institute for the Study of Social Change, Purdue University, 1968.

Hindess, Barry. "The 'Phenomenological' Sociology of Alfred Schutz," *Economy and Society,* 1 (1972), 1–27.

Korenbaum, Myrtle (ed.). *Phenomenological Sociology Newsletter.* Dayton, Ohio: Wright State University.

Lyman, S. M., and M. B. Scott. *A Sociology of the Absurd.* New York: Appleton-Century-Crofts, 1970.

McNall, Scott, and James Johnson. "The New Conservatives: Ethnomethodologists, Phenomenologists and Symbolic Interactionists," *The Insurgent Sociologist,* 4 (Summer 1975).

Mehan, Hugh, and Houston Wood. "The Morality of Ethnomethodology," *Theory and Society,* 2 (1975), 509–30.

————. "De-secting Ethnomethodology," *The American Sociologist,* 11 (February 1976), 13–21.

Morris, Monica B. "Creative Sociology: Conservative or Revolutionary?" *The American Sociologist,* 10 (August 1975), 168–78.

Mullins, Nicholas C. *Theories and Theory Groups in Contemporary American Sociology.* New York: Harper & Row, 1973.

Pivcevic, Edo. "Can There Be a Phenomenological Sociology?" *Sociology: The Journal of the British Sociological Association,* 6 (September 1972), 335–49.

Schegloff, Emanuel, and Harvey Sacks. "Opening Up and Closings," *Semiotica,* 8 (1973), 289–387.

Sudnow, David. *Passing On: The Social Organization of Dying.* Englewood Cliffs, N.J.: Prentice-Hall, 1969.

Sudnow, David, ed. *Studies in Social Interaction.* New York: Free Press, 1972.

Turner, Jonathan H. *The Structure of Sociological Theory.* Homewood, Ill.: Dorsey Press, 1974.

Turner, Roy, ed. *Ethnomethodology.* Baltimore: Penguin, 1974.

Wagner, Helmut R. "Sociologists of Phenomenological Orientations: Their Place in American Sociology," *The American Sociologist,* 10 (August 1975), 179–86.

Wieder, D. Lawrence. *Language and Social Reality.* The Hague: Mouton, 1974.

Wilson, Thomas P. "Conceptions of Interaction and Forms of Sociological Explanation," *American Sociological Review,* 35 (August 1970), 697–710.

Young, T. R. "The Politics of Sociology: Gouldner, Goffman and Garfinkel," *The American Sociologist,* 6 (November 1971), 276–81.

Zimmerman, Don H. "A Reply to Professor Coser," *The American Sociologist,* 11 (February 1976) 4–13.

ON PHENOMENO-LOGICAL SOCIETY

JAMES L. HEAP AND PHILLIP A. ROTH

Reprinted from the *American Sociological Review*, 38 (June 1973), 354–367. Used by permission of the authors and the American Sociological Association.

James Heap is assistant professor of sociology at the Ontario Institute for Studies in Education. Phillip Roth was in the graduate program at the University of British Columbia when the article was written.

There is increasing interest in something called "phenomenological sociology." If this interest is to be sustained, indeed if this sub-discipline is to contribute to our knowledge of the social world, we must become clear on what phenomenological sociology is and can become. At present serious problems exist in the writings of many sociologists who have contributed to, and implicitly defined, this approach to sociology. In general, they display only a metaphorical understanding of phenomenology as a philosophy and as a set of methods. In addition, and partly as a result, they fail to understand the relationship between sociology and phenomenology. However, if we go back to Edmund Husserl's original formulation of the relationship, we once again face serious problems. Our purpose in this essay is to explicate these problems and point out the existence of sociologies which do not share the shortcomings of what is called "phenomenological sociology," yet which make use of its perspective and approach. One of these sociologies, ethnomethodology as developed by Harold Garfinkel, will be briefly treated in our final section.

From the few authors who have contributed to phenomenological sociology we have selected the work of Tiryakian (1965), Bruyn (1966), and Douglas (1970) as representative. Tiryakian's study in the *ASR* of the affinity between phenomenology and the mainstream of sociological tradition is one of the earliest and most often quoted. Bruyn's discussion of social phenomenology appears in his book *The Human Perspective in Sociology*. Douglas' discussion of various phenomenological sociologies appears in one of the most important edited volumes in the field of ethnomethodology. In view of the availability of these statements, we take them to be important for how phenomenological sociology is understood and defined by sociologists.

THE PROBLEM OF METAPHOR

The one problem Tiryakian, Bruyn, and Douglas have in common is that *they use the concepts of phenomenology "metaphorically."* That is, they use the terms as understood in everyday conversation rather than as they are meant in phenomenology. They fail to recognize these terms' intended domain of reference and thus to recognize the transformation of meaning they undergo when used to refer to an utterly different domain. In the instances of conceptual confusion to be discussed, all three authors make claims which they present as consistent with the philosophy or methods of Husserl (1962). Our criticisms have therefore been formulated solely along Husserlian lines.

Intention

The concept of intention is greatly misunderstood and misrepresented by Tiryakian. He quotes W. I. Thomas as defining attention as " 'the mental attitude which takes note of the outside world and manipulates it' " (Tiryakian, 1965:682). Then we are told that the notion of attention "is equivalent to the phenomenological notion of 'intention' " (1965:682). In order to see how far afield Tiryakian is, it is worthwhile to cite what Thomas had to say about attention after he had defined it:

... attention does not operate alone; it is associated with habit on the one hand and crisis on the other. When the habits are running smoothly the attention is relaxed, it is not at work. But when something happens to disturb the run of habit the attention is called into play and devises a new mode of behavior which will meet the crisis. (1951:218)

Phenomenologically, intention is not something that at one point is "not at work" and at another point "called into play." As Husserl said "all experiences in one way or another participate in intentionality" (1962:222). Consciousness is fundamentally intentional: it is always consciousness of something, "*consciousness of* an object whether real or ideal, whether existent or imaginary" (Gurwitsch, 1966:124). One of the main points of Husserl's program was that Descartes' formulation was incomplete: *ego cogito* must be expanded to *ego cogito cogitatum* (Husserl, 1962:105). The relationship between *cogito* and *cogitatum* was worked out in terms of Husserl's theory of intentionality which transcends the objectivist and subjectivist positions by dealing with the object as perceived (the *noema*) and the perception of the object (the *noesis*), or better yet, "the intended object" and the act of consciousness which intends that object, "the intentional act." Thus the concept of intention must not be confused with Thomas' attention; for intention is an essential feature of consciousness prior to the operation of attention.[1]

The phenomenological concept of intention is also misunderstood by Douglas, although to a lesser degree, when he equates it with the concept of purpose. In his paper entitled "Understanding Everyday Life" he declares that

as Schutz, following Husserl and other phenomenologists, has argued so well, it is primarily intentions at any time—our purposes at hand—that order human thought, that determine the relevance of information and ideas about the world and ourselves. (1970:26)[2]

While it is true that intentionality can be equated with purpose, this is so only at the predicative level of experience, the level of judgment, of action in Weber's sense. However, Husserl's theory of intentionality refers also, and most significantly, to the pre-predicative level. This is the level of immediate experience, of perception (cf. Merleau-Ponty, 1962), of so-called non-meaningful behavior in Weber's sense (cf. Schutz, 1967:54–57).

Reduction

Husserl's concept of reduction is used only metaphorically by Tiryakian and Douglas. In demonstrating that "Durkheim's sociological analysis is really phenomenological" Tiryakian discusses the "implicitly phenomenological approach" taken by Durkheim in his study of suicide.

The "surface" manifestations of suicide establish its presence as a social phenomenon; these objective quantitative factors are then "reduced" phenomenologically to underlying layers of the social structure in which the act of suicide occurs ... (1965:681)[3]

We are told, however, that "Durkheim stops short of a 'transcendental reduction' " (1965:681). Tiryakian also takes the position that Simmel, "although he diverged from Husserl in some respects ... sought to reduce manifestly different concrete forms of social phenomena to their underlying characteristics ('forms')" (1965:680).

The reduction is misunderstood here as operating in the empirical realm. While there are at least three types of reduction—eidetic, psychological, and transcendental—all treat intended objects or intentional acts within the a priori realm of possibilities.[4] In this realm, through a method of imaginative variation, the phenomenologist can freely vary the objects or acts of consciousness. He does so to discover what is a priori, i.e., essential to every possible appearance of the object or act within the empirical world, the realm of actualities. To secure the a priori realm the empirical world must be "bracketed." In that Tiryakian footnotes Schutz's first volume of *Collected Papers*, it is surprising that he had not grasped the radical nature of the reduction, of "putting the world in brackets," as discussed by Schutz.[5]

The phenomenologist does not deny the existence of the outer world, but for his analytical purpose he makes up his mind to suspend belief in its existence—that is, to refrain intentionally and systematically from all judgments related directly or indirectly to the existence of the outer world. . . . What we have to put into brackets is not only the existence of the outer world, along with all the things in it, inanimate and animate, including fellow-men, cultural objects, society and its institutions . . . but also the propositions of all the sciences. (1962:104–105)

What is left after the initial reduction is the intended object and the intentional act. While the transcendental reduction is more complex in that it requires bracketing one's own mundane existence as a human being within the world, we shall not take our explication further; for by now it is clear that Durkheim and Simmel were hardly engaged in phenomenological reductions. One does not reduce quantitative factors "down" to "underlying layers of social structure," for social structure itself must be bracketed. The common nuclear meanings which Simmel induced from the repetitive aspects of social life could not have been grasped via reduction, for these meanings themselves have to be bracketed.

Besides those like Tiryakian who argue that the reduction has been used unknowingly by sociologists, there are others who suggest it as a research method.[6] Douglas declares that

accepting presuppositions as necessary, there obviously remains that vast realm of common sense, of everyday experience that can be phenomenologically *bracketed*, that is, toward which one can take a theoretic stance and reflect upon until the basic elements and relations of the phenomenal experience are discovered. (1970:22)

Not only does Douglas assume that his "theoretic stance" *is* a phenomenological reduction, but he also claims that "phenomenological interactionists," such as Blumer and Becker, as well as ethnomethodologists use the theoretic stance, i.e., phenomenological reduction (1970:19, 16). No sociologist brackets the existence of the world. Sociology's interests, problems, and solutions are not to be found in the realm of possibilities. While some ethnomethodologists do employ a transformed version of the reduction, they make it quite clear that theirs is not to be confused with phenomenological reduction. In the very volume which Douglas edited and within which his article appears, Zimmerman and Pollner (1970:98) state:

The term reduction is borrowed from Husserl (1962). While the notion of an occasioned corpus partakes of Husserl's program, the order of phenomena revealed by its use is by no means offered as equivalent to that which appears by virtue of the use of the phenomenological reduction.

In our final section we shall discuss the similarities and differences between phenomenological and ethnomethodological reduction. Suffice it to say that neither should be confused with methods used by symbolic interactionists.

Phenomenon

The concept of phenomenon is highly problematic. Would-be phenomenological sociologists (Psathas, 1971:2) seem drawn to Husserl's dictum "to the things themselves," by which Husserl meant a return to the phenomena as given in immediate consciousness. By phenomenon Husserl meant that "which, having been subjected to the phenomenological reduction, is purified from the reality attributed to it by naive consciousness" (Spiegelberg, 1971:722). A phenomenon qua phenomenon only becomes available when we cease to treat an object[7] as real, and begin to treat the object as meant, as intended, as it appears.

Sociologists (Schur, 1971:124), however, understand "things" and phenomena in a strictly mundane, and therefore metaphorical manner. Arguing that Durkheim's methodology is not antithetical to an existential-phenomenological viewpoint, Tiryakian (1965:680) declares that "On the contrary, 'consider social facts as things,' has for Durkheim the same import and meaning as Husserl's dictum 'to the things themselves' "! Furthermore, we are told that Durkheim's approach "is grounded in accepting social facts as *sui generis* phenomena of intersubjective consciousness, as products of social interaction" (1965:680). Social facts are hardly phenomena, for they are theoretic abstractions from what is given in experience within the empirical realm. They are not *"prior to all* 'theory,' " as Husserl (1962:95) required. They are not arrived at through phenomenological reduction.

Bruyn (1966:94–95) shares a similar problem when he suggests "phenomenological inquiry into the nature of social phenomena." By the latter he understands the referents of such sociological concepts as primary groups, social institutions, religion, society, etc. (1966:94). Since his discussion draws upon Husserl we feel warranted in inquiring how the referents of these concepts are to be phenomenologically reduced and examined. These referents transcend the immediate experience of any observer and furthermore would seem to have their existence through theoretical abstraction from immediate experience. Thus it is difficult to see how Bruyn can treat these referents as phenomena in Husserl's sense. *That is not to say that it cannot be done,* for Husserl (1962) held that all objects of consciousness can be reduced to phenomena. However it is no simple matter. Unless this point is made and understood it is almost inevitable that sociologists will read "phenomenon" in Durkheim's mundane sense of social fact (1938:14). Bruyn seems unaware of this point. Thereby he perpetuates the metaphorical misunderstandings he himself is involved in.

While Douglas takes his theoretical stance to be a phenomenological reduction, he does not seem to realize that phenomena are made available only through reduction. For Douglas (1970:15) the reduction is simply another (though preferred) stance toward the everyday world as a phenomenon. Other stances are the absolutist and the natural (1970:13–14). All stances, however, are presented as sharing phenomena: the "phenomena of everyday life," which Douglas (1970:4) argues to be social action, in Weber's sense (1968:4). Social actions "must be studied and explained in terms of their situations and their meanings to the actors themselves" (Douglas, 1970:4).

The problems involved are multiple. First, Douglas fails to recognize the radical difference between ethnomethodology's and conventional sociology's so-called phenomena. This is the same mistake which Denzin (1970) makes and to which Zimmerman and Wieder (1970) respond in articles appearing in the very book which Douglas edited and in which his article appears. Drawing from another article in that book we can say that whereas interpretive sociology seeks to interpret social action, ethnomethodology treats "the interpretive process itself as a phenomenon for investigation" (Wilson, 1970:78).

Secondly, from within the reduction how are we as observers able to grasp the subjective meanings of the acts of others? Douglas fails to mention or recognize this problem of intersubjectivity within the reduced sphere. For Husserl this problem required a transcendental solution, which he attempted, but failed (Schutz, 1966:51–91). Douglas does not even offer a solution at the mundane level. Without explicating intersubjectivity, it is difficult to understand how, from within the reduction, we are to study and explain observed social action as phenomenon. The difficulty lies in the fact that in order to treat social action as a phenomenon we have to bracket the existence of actors qua fellow-men. The difficulty subsides, however, if we understand phenomenon and reduction metaphorically.

Essence
Finally we come to the troublesome concept of essence. After discussing the work of the early phenomenological sociologists (cf. Martindale, 1960:267–282), Bruyn (1966:44) declares that "A conceptual contribution which European phenomenology may make to American field studies lies in the term *essence* . . . the work of the social phenomenologist becomes one of interpreting anew the meaning of essence in social theory." Thus he suggests that the term essence "may be applied to such concepts as primary group, social institutions, values, society, religion, beauty, morality, or whatever sociological phenomenon might be studied" (1966:94).

The questionable utility of the concept of essence for the sociologist will be clearer if the concept is clarified. Essence may be taken to be that intuited invariant quality without which the intended object, the phenomenon, would not be what it is (Husserl, 1962:45–51). This is not to be confused with any notion of the "defining characteristics" or "necessary features" of objects in the empirical factual world. Essence has as its reference the a priori realm of possibilities which precedes that of actualities (Husserl, 1962:213). As such, it is intuited from the intended object, the object as experienced, as perceived, the object as noema.[8] It is arrived at through the method of reduction and imaginative variation discussed above. Defining characteristics, on the other hand, are arrived at a posteriori, through logical operations (deduction, induction) based on factual knowledge about actual objects in the taken-to-be real world. Only the latter are the concern of empirical sociology, for it is in the real world that sociological problems and their solutions are to be found.

While it is not clear that Bruyn understands phenomenon in a phenomenological sense, it is quite clear that he misconceives the concept of essence. After having discussed Husserl, he distinguishes between seeking the essence of a construct and the essence of a social belief: "If it is a social belief, it should not be determined by the scientist's own theoretical musings, but rather by what is inherent in the minds of those who hold it" (1966:95). Nowhere does he discuss how this is to be done phenomenologically. No theory of intersubjectivity is provided nor is any mention made of reduction or imaginative variation.

While contrasting essences with ideal types he states that "Max Weber was uneasy about essences in ideal types and feared the value judgments implied in them" (1966:95). Bruyn makes no distinction, however, between Weber's and Husserl's use of essence. Later, in discussing Weber and essences, Bruyn (1966: 117–18) quotes Weber: "All expositions, for example, of the 'essence' of Christianity are ideal types enjoying only a necessarily very relative and problematic validity, when they are intended to be regarded as the historical portrayal of empirically existing facts" (Weber, 1949:97). Essences in Husserl's sense are a priori, formal, invariant, not relative, and of problematic validity. They exist and are to be discovered within the realm of possibilities, not within the empirical realm. Bruyn does not recognize the domain of reference of the concept essence. Hence his use of that concept is metaphorical.

Given the misuse of the major concepts in phenomenology, i.e., intention, reduction, phenomenon, and essence, by Tiryakian, Douglas, and Bruyn, we must conclude that Tiryakian's thesis of the affinity between phenomenology and leading figures in the sociological tradition, Douglas' discussion of various phenomenological sociologies,[9] and Bruyn's suggestions for a social phenomenology, are fundamentally flawed and misleading. The problem of metaphor, however, is not simply lexical. It betrays a thoroughgoing failure to recognize and grasp the radical nature of Husserl's enterprise. Any attempt to graft phenomenological concepts onto a sociology which has not been fundamentally reconstituted can only lead to a distortion, if not perversion, of both phenomenology and sociology.

THE PROBLEM OF EIDETIC SOCIOLOGY

Sociology's realm is the empirical world. Husserl, however, held the position that parallel and prior to every empirical science there could and should be an eidetic science, e.g., an essential sociology within the realm of possibilities (1962:55–57). This essential sociology would provide a rigorous foundation for empirical study, in line with the belief that the relation of phenomenology to social sciences is foundational.

Through the methods of reduction and imaginative variation, the essence and essential relationships of such objects of empirical sociology as society and the family, would be clarified. This essential sociology itself, however, would presuppose and be founded on an eidetic science of the structures of the life-world (cf. Kockelmans, 1967:104), the world within which empirical sociology finds its subject matter. Each and every eidetic science then would be ultimately founded on transcendental phenomenology, for only within the transcendental realm can the constitution of the world be clarified. Since all eidetic sciences would presuppose the world, this clarification is necessary. Only radical "presuppositionless," a priori knowledge could serve as an adequate foundation for science. Until such knowledge is attained the sciences would continue to have foundation problems[10] (Husserl, 1962:19). They would continue to be confused as to the human meaning and significance of their findings (cf. Husserl, 1970a).

Setting aside the program of transcendental phenomenology for a moment, we can ask whether an eidetic sociology is possible. In recommending the incorporation of essence into the corpus of sociological concepts, Bruyn presupposes this possibility. In fact, such a science was attempted by students and contemporaries of Husserl, most notably Max Scheler. In terms of strict Husserlian phenomenology though, they were unsuccessful (cf. Schutz, 1962:140–142, 150–179; Neisser, 1959:210–211; Spiegelberg, 1971:266–267). They often provided a wealth of insights (cf. Scheler, 1954), but their findings were not essential, not a priori. Scheler in fact was forced to reverse his position on findings he once held essential (Spiegelberg, 1971:266).

The question of an eidetic sociology is complex. This complexity follows from Husserl's theory of essence (1962:45–71; Levinas, 1967; Kockelmans, 1967:77–105), the changes it underwent (Merleau-Ponty, 1964a:43–95) and the cogency of the criticisms leveled at it (Dufrenne, 1966:75–84; Merleau-Ponty, 1969:105–129; Neisser, 1959; Schutz, 1966:92–115). Space does not permit a detailed discussion, nor is it our purpose to render a final judgment. Instead we wish to point to the thorny problems sociologists must face if they wish to do an eidetic sociology.

If we wished to describe the essence of a psychological phenomenon which did not imply the existence of others, e.g., action as experienced, it would be possible. Of course, such a description would be of our own experience of action within the reduced sphere. Indeed, Schutz (1967:45–96) provided such a description. Sociology's objects, however, are social. The existence of others are presupposed. If we wish to do an eidetic description of social action, even our own, we run into Douglas' problem, discussed above. A theory of intersubjectivity is required and implied.[11] By definition, social action takes account of, and is oriented to the behavior of others (Weber, 1968:4).

Within the empirical, mundane realm a theory of intersubjectivity seems possible (cf. Zaner, 1961). Husserl's approach (1970b:89–151), unfortunately, led him into the transcendental realm, where the problem of intersubjectivity seems insoluble (Lauer, 1965:148–62; Ricoeur, 1967a:115–42). Through the use of the phenomenological-psychological reduction Husserl (1970a:238) held that it is possible for the social scientist to understand and describe the intentional acts of his subjects. By extension, it would seem that the meaningful action of others can be grasped.

However, social scientists who wish to follow Husserl at this point are led into the problem of transcendental intersubjectivity. The social scientist must first perform the reduction on himself (1970a:253), which reveals the social scientist as the *"absolutely single ego"* (1970a:256), the transcendental Ego. In so doing, his subjects are transformed into a phenomenon. In order to account for the existence of others and a world in common, "there necessarily occurs a transformation of the phenomenological-psychological epoché and reduction into the *transcendental"* (1970a:256). The knotty problem must then be faced of how others are constituted in the social scientist (*qua* transcendental Ego) through his own intentional acts. As Schutz (1966:51–91) has skillfully argued, Husserl's theory of transcendental intersubjectivity not only fails, but is addressed to a psuedo-problem. Intersubjectivity "is not a problem of constitution which can be solved within the transcendental sphere, but is rather a datum (*Gegebenheit*) of the life-world" (Schutz, 1966:82).

If we withdraw from the transcendental sphere and treat the world and intersubjectivity as ontologically given, as do Schutz (1966:89) and Merleau-Ponty (1964b:151–181), we can still inquire as to the possibility of a strict eidetic sociology. A theory of intersubjectivity is still required, but only at the mundane level. Presupposing such a theory (cf. Schutz, 1967:97–138; Merleau-Ponty, 1962:346–365), a problem still remains.

An essence is always intuited from an "example," a phenomenon which corresponds to a factual or imaginary object. Husserl has said that immediately given phenomena are grasped and explicated according to types (1970a:220). That is, the life-world and all objects in it are experienced in their typicality, e.g., a typical house, a typical concert, a typical day, an atypical child (cf. Schutz, 1962:7–27). Natanson (1970:5) has called ours a "typifying consciousness." This leads to the question, though, of whether or not the essence is preconstituted by the type in terms of which we have experienced the object in the mundane world. Schutz (1966:115) argues that this is in fact the case, and that "there is indeed merely a difference of degree between type and eidos" (essence).

Since types are "vacillating approximations" generated in terms of actors' pragmatic purposes (cf. Schutz, 1970:63–64), they are not vehicles to be driven beyond their own pragmatic destination. Descriptions of the essence of typified social phenomena may very well go beyond how those phenomena are seen, experienced, and accomplished by the actors themselves. Furthermore, since types are contingent and somewhat arbitrary, there is no guarantee that the typified object with which one begins will bear any determinate and unequivocal relationship to the phenomena being sought.

Systematic sampling offers a solution, but to opt for that solution is to vitiate the search for eidetic knowledge. Reasoning from samples leads to a posteriori knowledge. If the promise of a strict eidetic sociology is to be fulfilled only the methods of phenomenology may be used, e.g., reduction and imaginative variation. If only these methods are used, though, it is difficult to see how we can ever arrive at a priori knowledge of the essential structure of social phenomena. On the other hand, if these are our sole methods, our approach begins to take on features of the very objectivism (cf. Schutz, 1964:4) which would-be phenomenological sociologists have opposed. We may be led to make claims about "what social phenomena really are" which run counter to claims put forward by actors.[12]

Clearly, the search for an eidetic sociology faces many seemingly insurmountable problems. The social presupposes a theory of intersubjectivity. Husserl required and formulated such a theory at the transcendental level, but was unsuccessful. Even if we refuse his transcendental invitation and remain on mundane ground, we find that the search for eidos is circumscribed and prejudiced by its origin: the typified life-world. To seek for the essence beyond the type is to risk forsaking interpretative understanding with little assurance of finding a priori knowledge. In the end, even if we put aside these problems, we might well ask whether it is even wise to assume that social phenomena have a Husserlian a priori.

PHENOMENOLOGICAL SOCIOLOGIES

The foregoing would seem to suggest that even properly understood, the possibility of a phenomenological sociology in the sense envisioned by Husserl is highly questionable. However, we should realize that Husserl actually knew little of the concrete problems of the social sciences (cf. Schutz, 1962:140). In fact some sociologies which have been called phenomenological are closer to the spirit, if not the letter of phenomenology than the pertinent statements of its founder. What distinguishes these sociologies from those we have criticized is that *the following involve and invoke no claim that what is done actually is, or is the same as, Husserlian phenomenology.*

Here we wish to discuss briefly three of these sociologies in terms of their phenomenological features. A fourth type, ethnomethodology, will be elaborated in our final section. These types are neither exhaustive nor strictly drawn. Rather, they are somewhat arbitrarily drawn analytical devices offered simply to point out and distinguish between different programs in what can be called phenomenological sociology.

Hopefully, in noting and distinguishing between types of phenomenological sociologies we may prevent further confusion among critics (Schur, 1971; Neisser, 1959; Goldstein, 1963; Pivcevic, 1972). So far, they have sought to question the possibility and utility of something they have called phenomenological sociology, usually without realizing their arguments are only aimed at one type. Or, worse yet, they are aimed unknowingly and indiscriminately at different types. Finally, and unfortunately, their arguments reveal a failure to understand completely any of the types they have addressed.[13]

Type I can be called phenomenological in a loose sense because, whether it is realized or not, it makes use of a phenomenological philosophical perspective. This perspective is one which stresses "the primacy of consciousness and subjective meaning in the interpretation of social action" (Natanson, 1962:157). Natanson (1962:165) has identified W. I. Thomas, Cooley, Mead, and Weber with this approach; but it would not be out of order to identify this as the perspective of those working within what Wilson (1970) has called the interpretive paradigm (cf. Shearing and Petrunik, 1972). Natanson (1962:157) cautions, however, that "Obviously the label 'phenomenological' is less than satisfactory for this total approach, since it neither derives directly from the philosophy of Edmund Husserl nor is always philosophically compatible with principles of Husserlian phenomenology." Neither intersubjectivity nor the natural attitude are thematized in Type I.

Type II adopts an explicit and clarified phenomenological philosophical perspective as its foundation. This phenomenologically founded sociology follows from the studies of Alfred Schutz (1967) in which the latter clarified Weber's concept of action and his method of ideal type construction. In his studies Schutz revealed the invariant formal structures of the life-world (cf. 1966:116): the realms of manipulation (1962:306) and of others (1962:15), and the systems of relevance and typification (1970).

This "ontology of the life-world," which Husserl had called for (1970a:173), provides a true a priori framework within which, and with reference to, sociologists necessarily discover and resolve their problematic. Though Schutz did an eidetic science, his was not an eidetic sociology, for he did not seek the essence of discipline-defined "social phenomena." Rather, he sought to elucidate the a priori structure of the world in which sociological phenomena are apprehended. Rather than seeking the essence, e.g., of corporations, the state or society, Schutz turned to the structures of the life-world which those phenomena presuppose, e.g., a world of contemporaries beyond our reach grasped through socially distributed and pragmatically generated typifications, etc.

For Schutz these structures included mundane intersubjectivity as an ontological given. He began, but never completed, a theory of intersubjectivity (1967: 97–138; Zaner, 1961). The life-world, intersubjectivity, and the natural attitude (cf. Husserl, 1962:91), that is, the attitude of naive belief in the existence of the world, were examined by Schutz through the eidetic science which he called the "constitutive phenomenology of the natural attitude" (1962:132). The type of sociology founded on Schutz's phenomenology is continued most notably by Berger and Luckman (1966) and Holzner (1968).

Type III also is phenomenologically founded on the structures of the life-world, but it uses what may be called a phenomenological approach. Traveling under the banner of reflexive sociology, Type III can be understood as a philosophically radicalized version of the type of sociology Gouldner (1970) called for (cf. Zaner, 1971). Drawing upon Husserl, Schutz, Merleau-Ponty (1964b:98–113; cf. O'Neill, 1970) and Garfinkel (1967), this first person approach is predicated on the recognition that sociology is in and about the very life-world that it studies. This leads to a rejection of the ideal of an absolute observer and requires that research be carried out in a manner which preserves the presence of the observer (cf. Darville, 1972). In so doing, this approach seeks to warrant its claims of knowledge through explicating the grounds for those claims.

This Type is phenomenological in the sense that it

purports nothing less than accounting for the world, its objectivity, and the unquestioned certainty of its existence in subjective terms, or to put it differently, revealing the world as a correlate and product of subjective functions, activities, and operations. (Gurwitsch, 1966:416)

Understood as critical in a phenomenological sense (cf. Zaner, 1970), reflexive sociology seeks "to make explicit those structures that remain merely implicit and taken for granted" (Zaner, 1970:82). It does so in the belief that "Unless the respondent's and researcher's decoding and encoding procedures are basic elements of the research enterprise, we cannot make sense of either the phenomena being studied or the materials labeled 'findings' " (Cicourel, 1968:3). Intersubjectivity and the natural attitude do become thematized in this approach. While there are wide differences in their work, O'Neill (1972), Smith (1972a, 1972b) and Cicourel (1968) can be identified with this approach.

PHENOMENOLOGY AND ETHNOMETHODOLOGY

Type IV, ethnomethodology, has a distinctive relationship to both sociology and phenomenology. It is a program of inquiry which combines certain phenomenological and sociological concerns while transforming them in such a way as to do violence to neither but, rather, to constitute for itself a unique and independent domain of study. Note, however, that the following exposition by no means deals with all of what currently travels under the rubric of ethnomethodology. Rather, our attention is restricted to explicating the ethnomethodological program of Harold Garfinkel (1967) as found in the writings of Pollner, Wieder, and Zimmerman (in Douglas, 1970). Using their formulations as a resource, we will now sketch some of the affinities of the ethnomethodological program with phenomenological concerns and the ways in which it transforms those concerns to establish its own distinctive domain of investigation.

To begin with, the attitude which constitutes the ethnomethodological domain differs from the "attitude of everyday life" (the natural attitude) which constitutes the domain common both to lay members and conventional sociological analysts in a manner akin to the way that the phenomenological attitude differs from the natural attitude. Under the natural attitude, the objects of the domain of everyday life are believed to exist independently of the mode of inquiry addressed to them. Both phenomenology and ethnomethodology suspend or "bracket"[14] the belief that such objects are independent of the mode of inquiry used to make the objects observable. The phenomena thus made available for phenomenological and ethnomethodological inquiry differ in their constitution from the phenomenon of the natural attitude. They also differ from each other by virtue of the particular form of reduction used by each (cf. Zimmerman and Pollner, 1970:98).[15] For phenomenology, objects in the "real" world are reduced to objects of immediate consciousness and are seen as constituted in and through intentional acts of consciousness. For ethnomethodology, the "objective" features of the social world are reduced to the interpretative procedures by which that world is assembled and accomplished in concrete, ongoing, social situations. For phenomenology, the foundational nexus of meaning in the world is immediate consciousness; for ethnomethodology, the foundational nexus of meaning in the social world is the immediately present, directly observed social situation.[16] For both, anything transcending this nexus ("real" objects "outside" of consciousness; "objective" features of society "outside" of situations wherein their sense is recognized by members) is bracketed or "put out of play" with regard to the task of describing or accounting for the features of their respective domains. The domain of phenomenological inquiry, then, consists solely of the recognizable structures of immediate consciousness; while the domain of ethnomethodological inquiry consists solely of members' situated practices which produce for themselves and for observers the *sense* of objective social structures.

Note also that the fundamental notion of intersubjectivity receives a characteristically different placement in these domains. In the phenomenology of Schutz, intersubjectivity is viewed as an ontologically given feature of the social world, and analysis is directed toward the constitutive attitudes and beliefs that make such a viewpoint possible for members of the social world. In contrast, intersubjectivity enters the ethnomethodological domain as the *sense* of intersubjectivity contingently accomplished by members' situated practices. The transformation here involves a shift from the realm of the a priori to that of the contingently actual—the a priori becomes a problematic feature of actual accomplishment. In contradistinction to both these conceptions, however, the question of intersubjectivity never enters the domain of the natural attitude in the thematized form as a topic or object of study in its own right. Rather, intersubjectivity resides at its foundation as an unexamined but essential presupposition.

Perhaps enough has been said to display yet another similarity between phenomenology and ethnomethodology: the structurally similar character of the misunderstandings to which both are often subject. These misunderstandings typically fail to recognize that the domains of reference and the language used to describe the objects of those domains are *radically* different in constitution (and, hence, meaning) from the domain of reference constituted by the natural attitude, i.e., the taken-for-granted reality of the commonsense world. The radical character of this difference may be indicated by the fact, paradoxical as it may seem, that the "same" question cannot be addressed to problems within these domains. This is so simply because the terms of any question (and, hence, the terms of any possible answer) undergo a thorough transformation of meaning as they pass from one domain to another. For example, under the auspices of the natural attitude a question may be asked about the manifest or latent function of some transsituational phenomena (phenomena whose existence is taken to reside outside any particular situation, i.e., objective phenomena). Under the auspices of the ethnomethodological attitude and its attendant reduction, however, a question about transsituational phenomena automatically becomes a question about the phenomenon of transsituationality (i.e., how *members* produce and sustain the sense of objective phenomena taken to exist outside the occasion where that sense is made collectively available).

Clearly the actual practitioners of the ethnomethodological program are explicitly aware of the radical character of their domain assumptions and that the order of phenomena which concerns them is entirely incommensurable with what it is usually taken to be. Thus, Zimmerman and Pollner state that "The reduction does not generate research that may be regarded as an extension, refinement, or correction of extant sociological inquiry. . . . The [ethnomethodological] reduction constitutes as its phenomenon an order of affairs that has no identifiable counterpart in contemporary social science" (1970:99).[17]

CONCLUDING REMARKS

It should be apparent that phenomenology, properly understood, can contribute to the sociological enterprises, properly understood. For this contribution to come about, and to save ourselves from the radical problems of what is called phenomenological sociology, we must make a systematic and disciplined inquiry into Husserlian phenomenologies and their derivatives (transcendental, psychological, hermeneutical, and existential phenomenologies). This alone, however, is not enough; for any contribution phenomenology can make presupposes and depends on a clear understanding of what sociology is and can become. Since there are many sociologies, the task is complex. The resolution, however, is an individual problem (cf. Gouldner, 1970) not only compatible with, but complementary to, phenomenological inquiry (cf. Zaner, 1971).

NOTES

1. Berger (1966) caught this misuse of "intention" but in doing so called into question whether Thomas in fact had ever used a concept called "attention." Tiryakian (1966:262) responded that Thomas had used the concept of "attention" and said that it certainly does "imply *intentional* direction of consciousness to the outside on the part of the subject." True, but not in a phenomenological sense: consciousness isn't "intentionally" directed —consciousness *is* intentional.

2. Parenthetically he adds that "John Heeren in Chapter 2 has provided the best analysis of this intentional theory of consciousness." Examining Heeren's article (in Douglas, 1970:45–46) we find no discussion of the "intentional theory of consciousness." Rather we find a discussion of the actor's purposes at hand, his pragmatic interest in the world of daily life.

3. For an "implicitly phenomenological approach" to suicide, with apropos criticisms of Durkheim's approach, see Jacobs (1967). While Jacobs seems to have tacked on the word "phenomenological" to the title of his study, a closer investigation reveals that his work satisfies Schutz's postulates of subjective interpretation and adequacy (1962:43–44). To the degree that this is the case, he can be said to be doing one form of "phenomenological sociology," or more precisely a *phenomenologically founded* sociology (cf. Schutz, 1967).

4. Strictly speaking, a reduction furnishes a reduced sphere which allows access to the realm of possibilities. See Lauer (1965:52). While somewhat misleading, for simplicity we shall treat the realm of possibilities as the domain of reference of all phenomenological concepts; but see Schutz (1962:113).

5. Husserl uses reduction and epoché interchangeably, but some phenomenologists treat the two as different sides of the same coin (Natanson, 1962:14). The epoché is negative in that it brackets reality; whereas the reduction is positive, having to do with the character of the phenomena obtained through bracketing (Lauer, 1965:50). For simplicity we shall not distinguish between the two.

6. George Psathas (1971:6) is quite explicit in making such a recommendation.

7. "Object" is to be understood in the widest sense, as any object of consciousness, including thought objects.

8. As Gurwitsch (1966:132), following Husserl, has explained, "The noema is to be distinguished from the real object ... the 'perceived tree as such' [the noema] varies according to the standpoint, the orientation, the attitude, etc., of the perceiving subject, as when for instance he looks at the tree from above, or at another time perceives it while in the garden." Whereas the real object, the tree, is known to be an oak, to have a root system, to have a more or less round trunk, to be losing its leaves, etc., the "perceived tree as such" consists of only that which I perceive, of that which is immediately given to me in my experiencing act (cf. Husserl, 1962:240–245).

9. Douglas (1970:32) treats Sacks and his followers as "linguistic phenomenological sociologists." This is unfortunate: 1) the compatibility of linguistic analysis and phenomenology is highly controversial (cf. Natanson, 1962:34–43; TeHennepe, 1965:133–146), 2) Sacks does not define his work as phenomenological, but instead 3) states in his dissertation that some of his work "may be viewed as somewhat analogous to the analysis of syntactic structures in formal linguistics, or componential analysis by anthropologists" (1966:14). For a critique of semiology from a phenomenological perspective and a discussion of recent developments in the phenomenology of language see Paul Ricoeur (1967b).

10. In sociology, the abiding problem has been the appropriate model of science. For a discussion of foundational problems in sociology see Wilson (1970).

11. That Scheler's findings were not a priori may be traceable partly to his defective theory of intersubjectivity (Scheler, 1954:213–264; Schutz, 1962:150–179) on which he based his search for essences. That theory involved the positing of a highly questionable supra-individual consciousness.

12. Koestenbaum's suggested use of phenomenology in the study of status (1966:336) seems to us, in fact, to suggest a type of result incompatible with Schutz' Weberian postulate of adequacy (1962:44).

13. Schur (1971:115–136) fails to distinguish and understand the differences between Types I, II, and IV. He misunderstands the latter in a rather common fashion (cf. Denzin, 1970; Zimmerman and Wieder, 1970). Neisser (1959) criticizes the major figure of Type II (Schutz) in terms of the inappropriate criteria of strict eidetic sociology. Goldstein (1963) misconceives phenomenological sociology as being solely a first person enterprise. In so doing he confuses features of Type III with Type II, and fails to grasp how the latter develops an observer's account of social action. Pivcevic (1972) confuses Type I, II, and III. He rejects rather than disproves Type II because he uses an objectivist notion of what is social (cf. Schutz, 1964:5–6). Thus he fails to grasp the meaning of social (action) within Weber's framework.

14. A distinction must be made here regarding the attitude assumed by the ethnomethodologist. That attitude brackets the ontological status of any social world "external" to the directly observed social situation, but takes as given the objective reality of the observed "situated practices." To the degree that it gives the latter ontological status, it parallels the natural attitude in having a mundane, objective, intersubjectively verifiable domain. As Pollner (1970) pointed out, however, it is a precondition of all forms of inquiry, including the phenomenological variety, to have an "objective" domain. Phenomenological inquiry differs from the other two which concern us in that its domain is intersubjectively verifiable, but no claim is made for the objective reality of that domain. The very question of "reality" is bracketed, but the resulting phenomena are treated as unquestionably given. Thus, naively speaking, the domain is "objective."

15. It is perhaps useful to observe that the term "reduction" derives from the Latin compound "reducere," which means "to lead back to origins."

16. While misleading in certain respects, the following formulations may be useful in grasping the character of the transformation of perspective involved in shifting from one attitude to another.

(a) the natural attitude views consciousness as an "object" in the world, while the phenomenological attitude views the "world" as an object of consciousness.

(b) The natural attitude views the features of particular social situations as products of the encompassing society, while the ethnomethodological attitude views the features of the encompassing society as products of particular social situations.

17. Note that Douglas (1970) is either unaware of or ignores the radical character of this transformation of meaning between the natural and ethnomethodological attitudes. Throughout his introduction he continually treats the goals of studying everyday life as establishing "objective transsituational knowledge." Yet this is precisely the sort of "knowledge" that is bracketed under the ethnomethodological attitude! In this, of course, Douglas is far from being alone, but it is curious to see such a viewpoint expressed by one who, among other things, purports to give a knowledgeable account of ethnomethodology.

REFERENCES

Berger, Peter. "On Existential Phenomenology and Sociology (II)," *American Sociological Review*, 31 (April 1966), 259–60.

Berger, Peter, and Thomas Luckman. *The Social Construction of Reality*. Garden City, N.Y.: Doubleday, 1966.

Bruyn, Severyn. *The Human Perspective in Sociology*. Englewood Cliffs, N.J.: Prentice-Hall, 1966.

Cicourel, Aaron. *The Social Organization of Juvenile Justice*. New York: Wiley, 1968.

Darville, Richard. "Sociologist and Person." Unpublished paper presented at the Annual Meetings of the Canadian Sociology and Anthropology Association, Montreal, Quebec, 1972.

Denzin, Norman. "Symbolic Interactionism and Ethnomethodology," in J. Douglas, ed., *Understanding Everyday Life*. Chicago: Aldine, 1970, pp. 259–84.

Douglas, Jack. "Understanding Everyday Life," in J. Douglas, ed., *Understanding Everyday Life*. Chicago: Aldine, 1970, pp. 3–44.

Dufrenne, Mikel. *The Notion of the A Priori*. Evanston, Ill.: Northwestern University Press, 1966.

Durkheim, Emile. *The Rules of Sociological Method*. New York: Free Press, 1938.

Garfinkel, Harold. *Studies in Ethnomethodology*. Englewood Cliffs, N.J.: Prentice-Hall, 1967.

Goldstein, Leon. "The Phenomenological and the Naturalistic Approaches to the Social," in M. Natanson, ed., *Philosophy of the Social Sciences*. New York: Random House, 1963, pp. 286–301.

Gouldner, Alvin. *The Coming Crisis of Western Sociology*. New York: Basic Books, 1970.

Gurwitsch, Aron. *Studies in Phenomenology and Psychology*. Evanston, Ill.: Northwestern University Press, 1966.

Heeren, John. "Alfred Schutz and the Sociology of Commonsense Knowledge," in J. Douglas, ed., *Understanding Everyday Life*. Chicago: Aldine, 1970, pp. 45–56.

Holzner, Burkart. *Reality Construction in Society*. Cambridge, Mass.: Schenkman, 1968.

Husserl, Edmund. *Ideas: General Introduction to Pure Phenomenology*. New York: Collier, 1962.

———. *The Crisis of European Sciences and Transcendental Phenomenology*. Evanston, Ill.: Northwestern University Press, 1970. (a)

———. *Cartesian Meditations*. The Hague: Martinus Nijhoff, 1970. (b)

Jacobs, Jerry. "A Phenomenological Study of Suicide Notes," *Social Problems*, 15 (Summer 1967), 60–72.

Kockelmans, Joseph. *A First Introduction to Husserl's Phenomenology*. Pittsburgh: Duquesne University Press, 1967.

Koestenbaum, Peter. "Phenomenological Foundations for the Behavioral Sciences: The Nature of Facts," *Journal of Existentialism*, 4 (Spring 1966), 305–41.

Lauer, Quentin. *Phenomenology: Its Genesis and Prospect*. New York: Harper & Row, 1965.

Levinas, Emmanuel. "Intuition of Essences," in J. Kockelmans, ed., *Phenomenology*. Garden City, N.Y.: Doubleday, 1967, pp. 83–105.

Martindale, Don. *The Nature and Types of Sociological Theory.* Boston: Houghton Mifflin, 1960.

Merleau-Ponty, Maurice. *Phenomenology of Perception.* London: Routledge and Kegan Paul, 1962.

————. *The Primacy of Perception.* Evanston, Ill.: Northwestern University Press, 1964. (a)

————. *Signs.* Evanston, Ill.: Northwestern University Press, 1964. (b)

————. *The Visible and the Invisible.* Evanston, Ill.: Northwestern University Press, 1969.

Natanson, Maurice. *Literature, Philosophy and the Social Sciences.* The Hague: Martinus Nijhoff, 1962.

————. "Phenomenology and Typification: A Study in the Philosophy of Alfred Schutz," *Social Research,* 37 (Spring 1970), 1–22.

Neisser, Hans. "The Phenomenological Approach in Social Science," *Philosophy and Phenomenological Research,* 20 (December 1959), 198–212.

O'Neill, John. *Perception, Expression and History: The Social Phenomenology of Maurice Merleau-Ponty.* Evanston, Ill.: Northwestern University Press, 1970.

————. *Sociology as a Skin Trade: Essays Towards a Reflexive Sociology.* New York: Harper & Row, 1972.

Pivcevic, Edo. "Can There Be a Phenomenological Sociology?" *Sociology,* 6 (September 1972), 335–49.

Pollner, Melvin. "On the Foundations of Mundane Reasoning." Ph.D. dissertation, University of California at Santa Barbara, 1970.

Psathas, George. "Phenomenological Sociology." Unpublished paper presented at the Annual Meetings of the American Sociological Association, Denver, Colorado, 1971.

Ricoeur, Paul. *Husserl: An Analysis of His Phenomenology.* Evanston, Ill.: Northwestern University Press, 1967. (a)

————. "New Developments in Phenomenology in France: The Phenomenology of Language," *Social Research,* 34 (Spring 1967), 1–30. (b)

Sacks, Harvey. "The Search for Help: No One to Turn To." Ph.D. dissertation, University of California at Berkeley, 1966.

Scheler, Max. *The Nature of Sympathy.* New Haven, Conn.: Yale University Press, 1954.

Schur, Edwin. *Labeling Deviant Behavior.* New York: Harper & Row, 1971.

Schutz, Alfred. *Collected Papers I: The Problem of Social Reality.* The Hague: Martinus Nijhoff, 1962.

————. *Collected Papers II: Studies in Social Theory.* The Hague: Martinus Nijhoff, 1964.

————. *Collected Papers III: Studies in Phenomenological Philosophy.* The Hague: Martinus Nijhoff, 1966.

————. *The Phenomenology of the Social World.* Evanston, Ill.: Northwestern University Press, 1967.

————. *Reflections on the Problem of Relevance.* New Haven: Yale University Press, 1970.

Shearing, Clifford, and M. G. Petrunik. "Normative and Phenomenological Approaches to the Study of Deviance." Unpublished paper presented at the Annual Meetings of the American Sociological Association, New Orleans, 1972.

Smith, Dorothy. "The Ideological Practice of Sociology." Unpublished paper presented at the Department of Sociology, Queens University, Kingston, Ontario, 1972. (a)

————. "The Intersubjective Structuring of Time." Unpublished paper presented at the Annual Meetings of the Canadian Sociology and Anthropology Association, Montreal, Quebec, 1972. (b)

Spiegelberg, Herbert. *The Phenomenological Movement: Volumes 1 & 2.* The Hague: Martinus Nijhoff, 1971.

TeHennepe, Eugene. "The Life-world and the World of Ordinary Language," in James Edie, ed., *An Invitation to Phenomenology.* Chicago: Quadrangle Books, 1965, pp. 133–46.

Thomas, W. I. *Social Behavior and Personality.* New York: Social Science Research Council, 1951.

Tiryakian, Edward. "Existential Phenomenology and Sociology," *American Sociological Review,* 30 (1965), 674–88.

————. "Reply to Kolaja and Berger," *American Sociological Review,* 31 (April 1966), 260–64.

Weber, Max. *The Methodology of the Social Sciences.* New York: Free Press, 1949.

————. *Economy and Society.* New York: Bedminster Press, 1968.

Weider, D. Lawrence. "On Meaning by Rule," in J. Douglas, ed., *Understanding Everyday Life.* Chicago: Aldine, 1970, pp. 107–35.

Wilson, Thomas. "Normative and Interpretive Paradigms in Sociology," in J. Douglas, ed., *Understanding Everyday Life.* Chicago: Aldine, 1970, pp. 57–79.

Zaner, Richard. "Theory of Intersubjectivity: Alfred Schutz," *Social Research,* 28 (Spring 1961), 71–93.

———. *The Way of Phenomenology.* New York: Pegasus, 1970.

———. "Solitude and Sociality: The Critical Foundations of the Social Sciences." Unpublished paper presented at the Annual Meetings of the American Sociological Association, Denver, Colorado, 1971.

Zimmerman, Donald, and Melvin Pollner. "The Everyday World as a Phenomenon," in J. Douglas, ed., *Understanding Everyday Life.* Chicago: Aldine, 1970, pp. 80–103.

Zimmerman, Donald, and D. Lawrence Wieder. "Ethnomethodology and the Problem of Order: Comment on Denzin," in J. Douglas, ed., *Understanding Everyday Life.* Chicago: Aldine, 1970, pp. 287–98.

ON FORMAL STRUCTURES OF PRACTICAL ACTIONS[1]

HAROLD GARFINKEL AND HARVEY SACKS

Harold Garfinkel and Harvey Sacks, "On Formal Structures of Practical Actions," in *Theoretical Sociology: Perspectives and Developments*, McKinney and Tiryakian, eds. © 1970, pp. 338–362. Reprinted by permission of Prentice-Hall, Inc., Englewood Cliffs, New Jersey.

Harold Garfinkel is professor of sociology at the University of California, Los Angeles. He is author of *Studies in Ethnomethodology*. Harvey Sacks teaches at the University of California, Irvine.

The fact that natural language serves persons doing sociology—whether they are laymen or professionals—as circumstances, as topics, and as resources of their inquiries furnishes to the technology of their inquiries and to their practical sociological reasoning *its* circumstances, *its* topics, and *its* resources. That reflexivity is encountered by sociologists in the actual occasions of their inquiries as indexical properties of natural language. These properties are sometimes characterized by summarily observing that a description, for example, in the ways it may be a constituent part of the circumstances it describes, in endless ways and unavoidably, elaborates those circumstances and is elaborated by them. That reflexivity assures to natural language characteristic indexical properties such as the following: the definiteness of expressions resides in their consequences; definitions can be used to assure a definite collection of "considerations" without providing a boundary; the definiteness of a collection is assured by circumstantial possibilities of indefinite elaboration.

Indexical features are not particular to laymen's accounts. They are familiar in the accounts of professionals as well. For example, the natural language formula, "The objective reality of social facts is sociology's fundamental principle,"[2] is heard by professionals according to occasion as a definition of association members' activities, as their slogan, their task, aim, achievement, brag, sales pitch, justification, discovery, social phenomenon, or research constraint. Like any other indexical expression, the transient circumstances of its use assure it a definiteness of sense as definition or task or whatever, to someone who knows how to hear it.[3] Further, as Helmer and Rescher[4] showed, on no occasion is the formula assured a definiteness that exhibits structures other than those that are exhibited by pointed references. This is to say that when the definiteness of the expression is analyzed with prevailing methods of logic and linguistics it exhibits few or no structures that available methods can handle or make interesting. Sociology's methods of formal analysis are differently disappointed by these expressions. Their definiteness of sense is without structures that can be demonstrated in the *actual* expressions with the use of available mathematical methods, to specify a sense, definitely. In a search for rigor the ingenious practice is followed whereby such expressions are first transformed into ideal expressions. Structures are then analyzed as properties of the ideals, and the results are assigned to actual expressions as their properties, though with disclaimers of "appropriate scientific modesty."

The indexical properties of natural language assure to the technology of sociological inquiries, lay and professional, the following unavoidable and irremediable practice as their earmark: Wherever and by whomever practical sociological reasoning is done, it seeks to remedy the indexical properties of practical discourse; it does so in the interests of demonstrating the rational accountability of everyday activities; and it does so in order that its assessments be warranted by methodic observation and report of situated, socially organized particulars of everyday activities, which of course include particulars of natural language.

The remedial practices of practical sociological reasoning are aimed at accomplishing a thoroughgoing distinction between objective and indexical expressions with which to make possible the substitution of objective for indexical expressions. At present that distinction and substitutability provides professional sociology its infinite task. . . .[5]

The remedial program of practical sociological reasoning is specified in such characteristic practices of professional sociological inquiry as the elaboration and defense of unified sociological theory, model building, cost-benefit analysis, the use of natural metaphors to collect wider settings under the experience of a locally known setting, the use of laboratory arrangements as experimental schemes of inference, schematic reporting and statistical evaluations of frequency, reproducibility, or effectiveness of natural language practices and of various social arrangements that entail their use, and so on. For convenience, we shall collect such practices of professional sociology's practical technology with the term "constructive analysis."

Irreconcilable interests exist between constructive analysis and ethnomethodology in the phenomena of the rational accountability of everyday activities and its accompanying technology of practical sociological reasoning. Those differences have one of their foci in indexical expressions: in contrasting conceptions of the ties between objective and indexical expressions, and in contrasting conceptions of the relevance of indexicals to the tasks of clarifying the connections between routine and rationality in everyday activities. Extensive phenomena that constructive analysis has missed entirely are detailed in the ethnomethodological studies of Bittner, Churchill, Cicourel, Garfinkel, MacAndrew, Moerman, Pollner, Rose, Sacks, Schegloff, Sudnow, Wieder, and Zimmerman. Their studies have shown in demonstrable specifics 1) that the properties of indexical expressions are ordered properties,[6] and 2) *that* they are ordered properties is an ongoing, practical accomplishment of every actual occasion of commonplace speech and conduct. The results of their studies furnish an alternative to the repair of indexical expressions as a central task of general theory building in professional sociology.

The alternative task of general theory building is to describe that achievement in specifics in its organizational variety. The purposes of this paper are to locate that achievement as a phenomenon and to specify some of its features, to describe some structures in the practices which make up that achievement, and to take notice of the obviousness, enormous interest, and pervasiveness which that achievement has for members, be they lay or professional analysts of ordinary activities. We do so with the aim of recommending an alternative account of formal structures in practical actions to those accounts that make up the work and achievements of practical sociological reasoning wherever it occurs—among laymen, of course, but with overwhelming prevalence in contemporary professional sociology and other social sciences as well, and in all cases without serious competitors.

MEMBERS' METHODS OF SOCIOLOGICAL INQUIRY

Alfred Schutz made available for sociological study the practices of common-sense knowledge of social structures of everyday activities, practical circumstances, practical activities, and practical sociological reasoning.[7] It is his original achievement to have shown that these phenomena have characteristic properties of their own and that thereby they constitute a legitimate area of inquiry in themselves. Schutz's writings furnished us with endless directives in our studies of the circumstances and practices of practical sociological inquiry. The results of these studies are detailed in other publications. They furnish empirical justification for a research policy that is distinctive to ethnomethodological studies. That policy provides that the practices of sociological inquiry and theorizing, the topics for those practices, the findings from those practices, the circumstances of those practices, the availability of those practices as research methodology, and the rest, are through and through members' methods of sociological inquiry and theorizing. Unavoidably and without hope of remedy the practices consist of members' methods for assembling sets of alternatives, members' methods for assembling, testing, and verifying the factual character of information, members' methods for giving an account of circumstances of choice and choices, members' methods for assessing, producing, recognizing, insuring, and enforcing consistency, coherence, effectiveness, efficiency, planfulness, and other rational properties of individual and concerted actions.

The notion of *member* is the heart of the matter. We do not use the term to refer to a person. It refers instead to mastery of natural language, which we understand in the following way.

We offer the observation that persons, because of the fact that they are heard to be speaking a natural language, *somehow* are heard to be engaged in the objective production and objective display of common-sense knowledge of everyday activities as observable and reportable phenomena. We ask what it is about natural language that permits speakers and auditors to hear, and in other ways to witness, the objective production and objective display of common-sense knowledge, and of practical circumstances, practical actions, and practical sociological reasoning as well. What is it about natural language that makes these phenomena observable-reportable, that is, *account-able* phenomena? For speakers and auditors the practices of natural language somehow exhibit these phenomena in the particulars of speaking, and *that* these phenomena are exhibited is thereby itself made exhibitable in further description, remark, questions, and in other ways for the telling.

The interests of ethnomethodological research are directed to provide, through detailed analyses, that account-able phenomena are through and through practical accomplishments. We shall speak of "the work" of that accomplishment in order to gain the emphasis for it of an ongoing course of action. The work is done as assemblages of practices whereby speakers in the situated particulars of speech mean something different from what they can say in just so many words, that is, as "glossing practices." An understanding of glossing practices is critical to our arguments . . .

I. A. Richards has provided a thematic example.[8] He suggests the use of question marks to bracket some spoken phrases or text. For example, ?empirical social research?, ?theoretical systems?, ?systems of sequences?, ?social psychological variables?, ?glossing practices? instruct a reader to proceed as follows. How a bracketed phrase is to be comprehended is at the outset specifically undecided. How it is to be comprehended is the task of a reading whereby some unknown procedure will be used to make the text comprehensible. Since nothing about the text or procedure needs to be decided for the while, we will wait for the while, for whatever the while. When and if we have read and talked about the text, we will review what might be made of it. Thus we can have used the text not as undefined terms but as a gloss over a lively context whose ways, as a sense assembly procedure, we found no need to specify.[9]

Richards' gloss consists of practices of talking with the use of particular texts in a fashion such that how their comprehended character will have worked out in the end remains unstated throughout, although the course of talk may be so directed as to compose a context which embeds the text and thereby provides the text's replicas with noticed, changing, but unremarked functional characters such as "a text in the beginning," "a text as an end result," "an intervening flow of conversation to link the two," and so on.[10]

Apparently speakers can, will, could, ought, and do proceed in the fashion for which Richards' gloss of a text is a thematic example, to accomplish recognizably sensible definiteness, clarity, identification, substitution, or relevance of the notational particulars of natural language. And apparently speakers can proceed by glossing, and do the immense work that they do with natural language, even though over the course of their talk it is not known and is never, not even "in the end," available for saying in so many words just what they are talking about. Emphatically, that does not mean that speakers do not know what they are talking about, *but instead they know what they are talking about in that way.*

Richards' gloss is merely one of these ways.[11] Glossing practices exist in empirical multitude. In endless but particular, analyzable ways, glossing practices *are* methods for producing observable-reportable understanding, with, in, and of natural language. As a multitude of ways for exhibiting-*in*-speaking and exhibiting-*for*-the-telling that and how speaking is understood, glossing practices *are* "members," *are* "mastery of natural language," *are* "talking reasonably," *are* "plain speech," *are* "speaking English" (or French, or whatever), *are* "clear, consistent, cogent, rational speech."

We understand mastery of natural language to consist in this. In the particulars of his speech a speaker, in concert with others, is able to gloss those particulars and is thereby meaning something different than he can say in so many words; he is doing so over unknown contingencies in the actual occasions of interaction; and in so doing, the recognition *that* he is speaking and *how* he is speaking are specifically not matters for competent remarks. That is to say, the particulars of his speaking do not provide occasions for stories about his speaking that are worth telling, nor do they elicit questions that are worth asking, and so on.

The idea of "meaning differently than he can say in so many words" requires comment. It is not so much "differently than what he says" as that *whatever* he says provides the very materials to be used in *making out* what he says. However extensive or explicit what a speaker says may be, it does not by its extensiveness or its explicitness pose a task of deciding the correspondence between what he says and what he means that is resolved by citing his talk verbatim.[12] Instead, his talk itself, in that it becomes a part of the selfsame occasion of interaction, becomes another contingency of that interaction.[13] It extends and elaborates indefinitely the circumstances it glosses and in this way contributes to its own accountably sensible character. The thing that is said assures to speaking's accountably sensible character its variable fortunes. In sum, the mastery of natural language is throughout and without relief an occasioned accomplishment.

ETHNOMETHODOLOGY'S INTERESTS IN FORMAL STRUCTURES OF PRACTICAL ACTIONS

Ethnomethodology's interests, like those of constructive analysis, insistently focus on the formal structures of everyday activities. However, the two understand formal structures differently and in incompatible ways.

We call attention to the phenomenon that formal structures are available in the accounts of professional sociology where they are recognized by professionals and claimed by them as professional sociology's singular achievement. These accounts of formal structures are done via sociologists' mastery of natural language, and require that mastery as the *sine qua non* of adequate professional readership. This assures to professional sociologists' accounts of formal structures its character as a phenomenon for ethnomethodology's interest, not different from any other members' phenomenon where the mastery of natural language is similarly involved. Ethnomethodological studies of formal structures are directed to the study of such phenomena, seeking to describe members' accounts of formal structures wherever and by whomever they are done, while abstaining from all judgments of their adequacy, value, importance, necessity, practicality, success, or consequentiality. We refer to this procedural policy as "ethnomethodological indifference."

Ethnomethodological indifference cannot be viewed as a position which would claim that no matter how extensive a volume like Berelson's might become, problems yet could be found. Nor, in that regard, would it be the case that insofar as the predictive efficacy of professional sociology had an asymptotic form, one could count on a margin of error as a stable property within which research could proceed. Counting on the fact that given the statistical orientations of professional sociology one would always have unexplained variance is not our way of locating yet unexplained phenomena. Our work does not stand then in any modifying, elaborating, contributing, detailing, subdividing, explicating, foundation-building relationship to professional sociological reasoning, nor is our "indifference" to those orders of tasks. Rather, our "indifference" is to the whole of practical sociological reasoning, and *that* reasoning involves for us, in whatever form of development, with whatever error or adequacy, in whatever forms, inseparably and unavoidably, the mastery of natural language. Professional sociological reasoning is in no way singled out as a phenomenon for our research attention. Persons doing ethnomethodological studies can "care" no more or less about professional sociological reasoning than they can "care" about the practices of legal reasoning, conversational reasoning, divinational reasoning, psychiatric reasoning, and the rest.

Given ethnomethodology's procedure of "indifference," by *formal structures* we understand everyday activities (a) in that they exhibit upon analysis the properties of uniformity, reproducibility, repetitiveness, standardization, typicality, and so on; (b) in that these properties are independent of particular production cohorts; (c) in that particular-cohort independence is a phenomenon for members' recognition; and (d) in that the phenomena (a), (b), and (c) are every particular cohort's practical, situated accomplishment.

The above development of formal structures contrasts with that which prevails in sociology and the social sciences in that the ethnomethodological procedure of "indifference" provides for the specifications (c) and (d) by studying everyday activities as practical ongoing achievements.

A further contrast between ethnomethodology's treatment of formal structures and that of constructive analysis is specified by the characteristic that it is as masters of natural language that constructive analysts recommend and understand that their accounts of formal structures provide aims and singular achievements of their technology of research and theory. It is as masters of natural language that constructive analysts understand the accomplishment of that recommendation to be constructive analysis' infinite task. Constructive analytic accounts of formal structures are thus practical achievements, through and through. Natural language provides to constructive analysis its topics, circumstances, resources, and results as natural language *formulations* of ordered particulars of members' talk and members' conduct, of territorial movements and distributions, of relationships of interaction, and the rest.

Ethnomethodologically, such practices whereby accounts of formal structures are done comprise the phenomena of practical sociological reasoning. Obviously those practices are not the monopoly of Association members. The remainder of this chapter takes that phenomenon under scrutiny, reviewing members' methods for producing and recognizing formal structures of everyday activities by examining members' practices of *formulating*.

THE PHENOMENON

In that inquiries are done that make use of or are about members' talk, an inquirer will invariably exhibit a concern to clarify that talk in the interests of the inquiry. So, for example, an interviewee's remark, "She didn't like it here so we moved," may provide a researcher occasion to do such things as give that utterance a name, tell who "she" is, where "here" is, whom the "we" covers. In the large literature in logic and linguistics such terms have been called indicators, egocentric particulars, indexical expressions, occasional expressions, indices, shifters, pronominals, and token reflexives. A list of such terms would start with "here, now, this, that, it, I, he, you, there, then, soon, today, tomorrow."

We begin with the observations about these phenomena that everyone regularly treats such utterances as occasions for reparative practices; that such practices are native not only to research but to all users of the natural language; that without knowing what a particular research dealt with one could list the terms that would need to be clarified, or translated, or replaced, or otherwise remedied, and that the terms could be located and their remedies proposed and demonstrated for all practical purposes, with or without research and with or without knowing how extensive are similar concerns of others. The large and ancient literature in logic and linguistics that bears on researchers' work is a minor tributary in the rush of that omniprevalent work.

We treat as fact that researchers—*any* researchers, lay or professional, naïve or well versed in logic and linguistics—who start with a text, find themselves engaged in clarifying such terms that occur in it. What should be made of that sort of fact? What do we, in this article, want to make of that fact?

If, whenever housewives were let into a room, each one on her own went to some same spot and started to clean it, one might conclude that the spot surely needed cleaning. On the other hand, one might conclude that there is something about the spot and about the housewives that makes the encounter of one by the other an occasion for cleaning, in which case the fact of the cleaning, instead of being evidence of dirt, would be itself a phenomenon.

Indexical expressions have been studied and have been dealt with in identical fashion times without end, not only in naïveté, but more interestingly, in apparently required disregard of previous achievements. The academic literature furnishes evidence of how ancient is that reparative work. The *Dissoi Logii*, a fragment of text from approximately 300 B.C., gives attention to the sentence "I am an initiate" because it presents difficulties.[14] The issue is that of the truth or falsity of a sentence when, if said by A it was true, but if said by B it was false; if said by A at one time it was true, but if said by A at another time it was false; if said by A from one status of A it was true, but if said by A from another it was false.

To the problems posed by sentences like this, programmatic solutions have long been available. One would begin by replacing "I" with a proper name, would add a date, would specify a status with respect to which the speaker was an initiate. A stupendous amount of work has been devoted to such phenomena. That work is briefly characterized in the following section.

A CHARACTERIZATION OF INDEXICAL EXPRESSIONS

An awareness of indexical expressions occurs not only in the earliest writing but in the work of major authors over the entire history of logic. Every major philosopher has commented on them. Consider for example Peirce and Wittgenstein,

Peirce because he is usually cited to mark the beginning of the interest of modern logicians and linguists in indexicals, and Wittgenstein because when his later studies are read to see that he is examining philosopher's talk as indexical phenomena, and is describing these phenomena without thought of remedy, his studies will be found to consist of a sustained, extensive, and penetrating corpus of observations of indexical phenomena.[15]

We borrow from the remarks by logicians and linguists to characterize indexical expressions. Edmund Husserl spoke of expressions (i) whose sense cannot be decided by an auditor without his necessarily knowing or assuming something about the biography and purposes of the user of the expression, the circumstances of the utterance, the previous course of discourse, or the particular relationship of actual or potential interaction that exists between the user and the auditor.[16] (ii) Bertrand Russell pointed out that descriptions involving them apply on each occasion of use to only one thing, but to different things on different occasions.[17] (iii) Such expressions, he said, are used to make unequivocal statements that nevertheless seem to change in truth value. (iv) Nelson Goodman wrote that each of their utterances constitutes a word and refers to a certain person, time, or place but names something not named by some replica of the word.[18] (v) Their denotation is relative to the user. (vi) Their use depends upon the relation of the use to the object with which the word is concerned. (vii) For a temporal indexical expression, time is relevant to what it names. (viii) Similarly, just what region a spatial indexical expression names depends upon the location of its utterance. (ix) Indexical expressions and statements containing them are not freely repeatable in a given discourse in that not all their replicas therein are also translations of them.[19]

In their explicit attempts to recover commonplace talk in its structural particulars, logicians and linguists encounter these expressions as obstinate nuisances.[20] The nuisances of indexicals are dramatic wherever inquiries are directed at achieving, for practical talk, the formulation and decidability of alternatives of sense, or fact, or methodic procedure, or agreement among "cultural colleagues." Features of indexical expressions have motivated among professionals endless methodological studies directed to their remedy. Indeed, the work by practitioners to rid the practices of *a* science, of *any* science, of these nuisances, because, and in the ways such work occurs in all sciences,[21] furnishes each science its distinctive character of preoccupation and productivity with methodological issues. Whatever the science, actual situations of practical investigative activities afford researchers endless occasions and motives for attempts to remedy indexical expressions. Thus methodological studies, wherever they occur, lay and professional, have been concerned, virtually without exception, with remedying indexical expressions while insistently holding as aims of their studies a programmatically relevant distinction between objective and indexical expressions, and a programmatically relevant substitutability of objective for indexical expressions. In these programmatic studies of the formal properties of natural languages and practical reasoning, the properties of indexicals, while furnishing investigators with motivating occasions for remedial actions, remain obstinately unavoidable and irremediable.

Such "methodological" concerns are not confined to the sciences. One finds ubiquitous concern among conversationalists with faults of natural language. Faults are seen by members to occur in the prevalence of demonstratives, pronouns, and tenses. Faults are assigned to members to usage by others about whom it is said that they have small vocabularies. Such concerns are accompanied by a prevalent recommendation that terms, utterances, and discourse may be clarified, and other shortcomings that consist in the properties of indexical expressions may be remedied by referring them to "their setting" (i.e., the familiar recommendations about the "decisive relevance of context").

More pointedly, we call particular attention to a conversational practice which has frank methodological intent. One finds conversationalists, in the course of a conversation, and as a recognized feature of that conversation, *formulating* their conversation. Formulating, in conversation, is discussed at length in the following sections.

FORMULATING A CONVERSATION AS A FEATURE
OF THAT CONVERSATION

Among conversationalists it is an immensely commonplace feature of conversations that a conversation exhibits *for its parties* its own familiar features of a "self-explicating colloquy." A member may treat some part of the conversation as an occasion to describe that conversation, to explain it, or characterize it, or explicate, or translate, or summarize, or furnish the gist of it, or take note of its accordance with rules, or remark on its departure from rules. That is to say, a member may use some part of the conversation as an occasion to *formulate* the conversation, as in the following colloquies.

> A: Do you think the federal government can go in and try that man for murder?
> B: No.
> B: It's a matter of state.
> A: [Now let me ask you this.]

> B: You would not be critical at all.
> A: Of Westmoreland.
> B: Of the military—of the—of this recent operation.
> A: Of course I'd be critical.
> B: [Well, you certainly don't show it!]

> JH: Isn't it nice that there's such a crowd of you in the office?
> SM: [You're asking us to leave, not telling us to leave, right?]

> HG: I need some exhibits of persons evading questions. Will you do me a favor and evade some questions for me?
> NW: [Oh, dear, I'm not very good at evading questions.]

> (In fatigued excitement a psychiatric resident pauses in telling a supervising faculty member about his discovery of Harry Stack Sullivan's writings.) Faculty Member: [How long have you been feeling like this?]

> Boston policeman to a motorist: [You asked me where Sparks Street is, didn't you? Well, I just told you.]

These excerpts illustrate the point that along with whatever else may be happening in conversation it may be a feature of the conversation for the conversationalists that they are doing something else; namely, what they are doing is saying-in-so-many-words-what-we-are-doing (or what we are talking about, or who is talking, or who we are, or where we are).

We shall speak of conversationalists' practices of saying-in-so-many-words-what-we-are-doing as formulating. We shall set off a text with brackets instead of hyphens to designate it as a formulation. In the preceding colloquies the formulating that one of the conversationalists is doing appears in brackets.

Two phenomena are of particular interest for us. 1) We offer as observations about practices of formulating that not only are they done, but they are also recognized by conversationalists as constituent features of the conversation in which they are done. We shall speak of this by saying *that* formulating is being done is, for conversationalists, "exhibited *in* the speaking." 2) We offer the further observation that formulating, as a witnessed feature of conversation, is available to conversationalists' report or comment. To have a way of speaking of this we shall say *that* formulating is done is "exhibitable *for* the telling."

Each of the colloquies provides an example of the first phenomenon. An example of the second phenomenon is found in the fact that we report these colloquies and call attention to the work of formulating being done in each. Brackets are used to designate the following features of formulating:

(1) Above all, formulating is an account-able phenomenon. This is to say, a) it is a phenomenon that members perform, and b) it is observable by members. c) In that members can do the phenomenon and observe it, it is reportable.[22] d) The phenomenon is done and reportable by members with texts such as those that are bracketed. (It is done as well with script, utterances, or graphics; that is, with circumstantially particular, notational displays. e) The bracketed text is a phase of an interactional enterprise. Finally, f) the text is meaning differently than the speaker can say in so many words.

(2) All of the foregoing features are practical accomplishments over the exigencies of actual interaction.

(3) The expression, [ ], is prefaced with "doing" in order to emphasize that accountable-conversation-as-a-practical-accomplishment consists only and entirely in and of its work. The prefix "doing" is also used to emphasize that this work of accountable conversation is members' work. That is to say, this work has essential ties to mastery of natural language.

Our illustrations have so far been chosen from laymen's work. The bracketing, and its effects, is relevant as well to the work of social scientists. If we place brackets on topicalized practices in the social sciences with which its practitioners speak of techniques of data collection, of research designs, of descriptive adequacy, of rules of evidence, and the like, we then ask what is the work for which these topics are its accountable texts. For example, linguists speak of "parsing a sentence with the use of phrase markers." By bracketing that text with gloss marks [parsing a sentence with the use of phrase markers], we understand that we are now addressed to the question: What is the work for which "parsing a sentence with the use of phrase markers" is that work's accountable text? The bracketing has similar relevance to the above case as it has to the case where we ask: What is the work for which [playing a game of chess according to the rules of chess] is that work's accountable text?

If we speak of work's accountable text as a proper gloss, we may ask: What is the work for which [speaking without interruption at a cocktail party] is its proper gloss? What is the work for which [the equilibrium size distribution of freely forming groups] is its proper gloss? The following diagram displays these relationships.

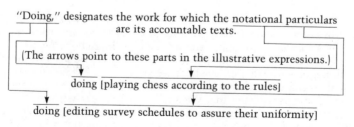

A final remark about brackets: their use reminds us that glossing practices are phases of interactional enterprises. Enterprises of intelligible, particular appearances of organized everyday activities are done unavoidably only and exclusively by competent speakers, who can do them only and entirely through the particulars of notational displays in natural language. Gloss enterprises are practical accomplishments. They are immensely varied phenomena, for they differ in ways dictated by a world of "social fact," albeit a world of social fact that is members' achievements. As practical achievements, gloss enterprises are as immensely varied as are organizational arrangements, for organizational arrangements are such achievements.

According to occasion, doing formulating may be members' undertakings, aims, rules, obligated behaviors, achievements, passing episodes, or standing circumstances. The work is not restricted to special circumstances. On the contrary, it occurs routinely, and on a massive scale. Members are particularly knowledgeable of, sensitive to, and skillful with this work, with doing it, assuring it, remedying it, and the like.

DOING ACCOUNTABLY DEFINITE TALK

We used the analogy of housewives to characterize the prevalence of and insistence by members upon the work of doing formulations as remedies for the properties of indexical expressions. But, as we have noticed, in that formulations consist of glosses, and in that the properties that formulations exhibit as notational displays—properties that are used by speakers to accomplish rational speech—are properties of indexical expressions, the very resources of natural language assure that doing formulating is itself for members a routine source of complaints, faults, troubles, and recommended remedies, *essentially*.

We take the critical phenomenon to consist in this: With ubiquitous prevalence and insistence members do formulations as remedies for problematic features that the properties of indexical expressions present to their attempts to satisfy the aims of distinguishing in actual occasions between objective and indexical expressions, and, in actual occasions, providing objective expressions as substitutes for indexicals. We observe that among members, remedial formulations are overwhelmingly advocated measures to accomplish proper subject matter, proper problems, proper methods, and warranted findings in studying formal structures of practical talk and practical reasoning. We observe that their advocacy of remedial formulations is accompanied by practices with which members are just as overwhelmingly knowledgeable and skilled, practices whereby speakers guarantee and are guaranteed that formulations are *not* the machinery whereby accountably sensible, clear, definite talk is done. Such practices are seen in the following phenomena.

(1) There are innumerable conversational activities in doing which multitudes of names are available for naming them as conversational phenomena. People know the names, can mention the names, summarize with the names, and so on; and yet in the course of the activities the names are not much used. Indeed, a commonplace but little understood phenomenon consists of cases where in doing [saying in so many words what one is doing] the activity is recognizedly incongruous, or boring, or furnishes evidence of incompetence, of devious motivation, and so forth.

(2) There is a tremendous topical coherence in ordinary conversations, and yet conversationalists' formulation of topics is a very special thing. It is rarely done. In any particular case it is not only probably but perhaps irremediably disputable, and though one gets talk that is topical, topical names are not inserted.

(3) It occurs as a commonplace achievement in ordinary conversations—

which for conversationalists furnishes commonplace evidence of conversational competence—that conversationalists title relevant texts, search for, remember, recognize, or offer relevant texts without those texts being topicalized, where success in so doing depends upon vagueness of topic, aim, rule of search, rule of relevance, and the rest, and where the work of storage and retrieval of relevant texts incorporates this vagueness as an essential feature in its design.

(4) Another phenomenon was described in a previous study.[23] Students were asked to write what the parties to an ordinary conversation were overheard to have said, and then to write alongside what the parties actually were talking about. The students, having been set the task of saying in just so many words what the parties were actually talking about, immediately saw that the work of satisfying the task hopelessly elaborated the task's features. Somehow they saw immediately that the very task that had been set—"Tell me as if I don't know, what the parties were literally talking about"—was faulted, not in the sense that the author would not know, or could not or would not understand, or that there was not enough time or paper or stamina or vocabulary in English for a writer to tell it, but that

I had required them to take on the impossible task of "repairing" the essential incompleteness of *any* set instructions no matter how carefully or elaborately written they might be. I had required them to formulate the method that the parties had used in speaking, as rules of procedure to follow in order to say what the parties said, rules that would withstand every exigency of situation, imagination, and development ... [This was the task] that required them to write "more," that they found increasingly difficult and finally impossible, and that became elaborated in its features by the very procedures for doing it.

We take as the critical import of these phenomena that they furnish specifics for the observation that *for the member it is not in the work of doing formulations for conversation that the member is doing* [the fact that our conversational activities are accountably rational]. The two activities are neither identical nor interchangeable.

We notice also that doing formulating is "occasioned." By this we mean that cited times, places, and personnel whereby formulating is done—that concrete, definite, clear, determinate specifications of where? when? who? what? how many?—are unavoidably and without remedy done as accountable phenomena. Also, it is not only that members may use particular rules to provide for the occasioned character of a formulation, but the failure to use particular rules is usable by a member to find what it is that formulating is doing in a conversation, where the fact of formulating does not mean to those doing it that doing it is definitive of its work; but instead doing it can be found to be joking, or being obstinate, and the like.

In short, doing formulating for conversation itself exhibits for conversationalists an orientation to [the fact that our conversational activities are accountably rational]. Doing formulating is not the definitive means whereby the fact is itself done or established. The question of what one who is doing formulating is doing —which is a member's question—is not solved by members by consulting what the formulation proposes, but by engaging in practices that make up the *essentially* contexted character of the action of formulating. Even the briefest consideration of doing formulating in conversation returns us—naïve speaker or accomplished social scientist—to the phenomenon in conversation of doing [the fact that our conversational activities are accountably rational].

What are we proposing when we propose that the question of what one is doing who is doing formulating is solved by members by engaging in practices that make up the *essentially* contexted character of the action of formulating? What kind of work is it for which [the fact that our conversational activities are accountably rational] is its proper gloss?

FORMAL STRUCTURES IN ACCOUNTABLY
RATIONAL DISCOURSE: THE "MACHINERY"

We learn to ask from the work of conversationalists: What kind of "machinery" makes up the practices of doing [accountably rational conversation]? Are there practices for doing and recognizing [the fact that our activities are accountably rational] without, for example, making a formulation of the setting that the practices are "contexted" in? What is the work for which [the fact that our activities are accountably rational] is an accountable text? What is the work for which [definiteness, univocality, disambiguation, and uniqueness of conversational particulars is assured by conversationalists' competence with speech in context] is a proper gloss?

We ask such questions because we learn from the phenomena that are problematic for conversationalists that "time," "place," or "personnel," for example, with which conversationalists say in so many words who, or where, or when, or since when, or how long since, or how much more, or with whom, or what, are contexted phenomena. More accurately, they are *essentially* contexted phenomena.

By "contexted phenomena" we mean that there exist specific practices such that 1) they make up what a member is doing when he does and recognizes [the fact of relevant time, place, or personnel]; 2) they are done with or without formulating *which* now, or where, or with whom, or since when, or how much longer, and the like; 3) they make up members' work for which [practices of objective, clear, consistent, cogent—rational—language] is a proper gloss; and 4) they meet the first three criteria by satisfying the following constraints (to which we refer with the adjective *essential*).

1. They are cause for members' complaints; they are faulted; they are nuisances; troubles; proper grounds for corrective, that is, remedial, action.
2. They are without remedy in the sense that every measure that is taken to achieve a remedy preserves in specifics the features for which the remedy was sought.
3. They are unavoidable; they are inescapable; there is no hiding place from their use, no moratorium, no time out, no room in the world for relief.
4. Programmatic ideals characterized their workings.
5. These ideals are available as "plain spoken rules" to provide accounts of adequate description for all practical purposes, or adequate explanation, adequate identity, adequate characterization, adequate translation, adequate analysis and so forth.
6. Provision is made "in studies by practicing logicians" for each ideal's "poor relatives," as indexical expressions are the poor relatives of scientific knowledge; as natives' practices and natives' knowledge of natives' affairs, practices, and knowledge; as Calvin N. Mooers' descriptors are poor relatives of sets, categories, classes, or collections in formal logic; or, as formal structures in natural language are poor relatives of formal structures in invented languages. For "poor relatives" we understand "embarassing but necessary nuisances," "lesser versions," "nonphenomena," "no causes for celebration," "ugly doubles" that are relied on by members to assure the claims of the relatives that went to college and came back educated. Ideals are not the monopoly of academies, and neither are their poor relatives confined to the streets. Always in each others' company, they are available in immense varieties for they are as common as talk. Being theorized out of existence by members' ironic contrast between common-sense knowledge and scientific knowledge, they are also difficult to locate and report with the use of that contrast.

7. Members are unanimous in their recognition of the foregoing six characteristics of specific practices; they are also unanimous in their use of these characteristics to detect, sense, identify, locate, name— that is, to formulate—one or another "sense" of practical activities as an "invariant structure of appearances."

Speaking practices, insofar as they satisfy such constraints, are inescapably tied to particulars of talk, and thus speaking practices are inexorably exhibited and witnessed as ordered particulars of talk. Insofar as they satisfy such constraints, speaking practices also exhibit the features of "production cohort independence," or "invariant to in and out migrations of system personnel," or "invariant to transformations of context," or "universals." They exhibit features of invariance by providing members' methods with their accountable character as *unavoidably* used methods with which particulars are recovered, produced, identified, and recognized as connected particulars; as particulars in relationships of entailment, relevance, inference, allusion, reference, evidence; which is to say as collections of particulars, or classes, or sets, or families, or groups, or swarms.

Members use these constraints to detect various ways of doing [invariance] in members' practices. Because members do so, we shall use them in the same way, namely, as constraints that speaking practices must satisfy if we are to count those practices as members' resources for doing and recognizing [rational adequacy for practical purposes of natural language]. They provide characteristics of the practices with which members accomplish and recognize rational discourse in its indexical particulars, namely, "practical talk."

What are those practices?[24] We learn some if we ask about a *list* of indexical expressions how long the list might be. To answer this question we need a procedure that will get us a list of indexical terms. Such a procedure is easily available, for we notice that any "one" of the properties of indexical expressions cited [earlier] and any combination of them, may be read as a prescription with which to search an *actual* occasion of discourse, an *actual* utterance, or an *actual* text.

When this is done, we observe the following. Any actual occasion may be searched for indexical terms, and will furnish indexical terms. Whatever is the number of terms in an actual text, that text will furnish members.[25] An actual occasion with *no* text will furnish members. Any member of the list of indexical terms can be used as a prescription to locate replicas. Listing any replica of a member of the list is an adequate procedure for locating another member. Any procedure for finding *a* member is adequate for finding for *all* terms of a language that they are members, which includes "all"—which is to say that in finding for all terms of a language that they are members we are exploring and using the members' use of "all." "A one," "any one," and "all" lists of indexical terms exhibit the same properties as the particular members of "a one," "any one," and "all" lists. Any text without exception that is searched with the use of any one or combination of properties from a list of *properties* of indexical terms will furnish members to the list. Any text without exception that is searched with the use of one or combination of terms from a list of indexical terms will furnish members to the list. Any list of indexical terms can be indefinitely extended, as can any list of properties of indexical terms. Every procedure for finding more members and adding them to the list of properties exhibits the same properties as the members it finds. Every list of properties of indexical expressions can be extended indefinitely. Whatever holds above for "terms" holds equally for "expressions" and "utterances." Finally, the preceding properties remain invariant to such operations as search for, recognition of, collection, counting, forming sentences with, translating, identifying, or performing consistency proofs or computations upon list members.

CONSEQUENCES

We have seen that and how members do [the fact that our activities are account-ably rational]. We have seen that the work is done without having to do for-mulations; that the terms which have to be clarified are not to be replaced by formulations that would not do what they do; that they are organizable as a "machinery" for doing [accountably rational activities]; and that the abstract phenomenon of [accountable rationality] is available to natives, to ethnometh-odologists, and to social scientists since the "machinery," because it is members' "machinery," in the way it is specifically used to do [accountably rational activities] is thereby part of the phenomenon as its production and recognition apparatus. We have given that some structure, and tried to exhibit both the ob-viousness of it, and its enormous interest and pervasiveness for members.

(1) It seems that there is no room in the world definitively to propose for-mulations of activities, identifications, and contexts. Persons cannot be noncon-sequentially, nonmethodically, nonalternatively involved in doing [saying in so many words what we are doing]. They cannot be engaged in nonconsequentially, nonmethodically, nonalternatively saying, for example, "This is after all a group therapy session," or "With respect to managerial roles, the size and complexity of organizations is increasing and hence the requirements necessary for their suc-cessful management also."

The fact that there is no room in the world for formulations as serious so-lutions to the problem of social order has to do with the prevailing recommen-dation in the social sciences that formulations can be done for practical purposes to accomplish empirical description, or to achieve the justification and test of hypotheses, and the rest. Formulations are recommended thereby as resources with which the social sciences may accomplish rigorous analyses of practical actions that are adequate for all practical purposes.

We are *not* saying that it is a specific trouble in the world that one cannot find out what somebody means—what any given person means in any next thing they say or meant in any last thing they said—by using a procedure of requesting a formulation for each piece of talk. But we *are* saying that insofar as formulations are recommended to be definitive of "meaningful talk," something is amiss because "meaningful talk" cannot have that sense. This is to say either that talk is not meaningful unless we construct a language which is subject to such pro-cedures, or that *that* could not be what "meaningful talk" is, or "meaningful actions" either. We *are* saying that we ought not to suppose that in order for persons in the course of their conversations and other ordinary activities to be-have in an orderly fashion, one set of things that has to be involved is that they are always able, say, to formulate their role relationships and systematically in-voke their consequences. For if it is the case that there is no room in the world for that, then either orderly activity is impossible, or *that* requirement for orderly activity is in any actual case relevant, irrelevant, cogent, absurd, wrong, right, etc.—that requirement being formulatable in any actual case as any of these or others, separately or combined, for no more than for all practical purposes.

(2) We took notice initially of the notion that formulating could save the difficulties with indexicals.[26] We saw that formulating could not do that and, furthermore, that indexicals would not need saving from difficulties. We have seen that the allegedly to-be-remedied features of terms are omnipervasive. And so one must entertain the fact that *none* of them needs saving.

(3) Professional sociology's achievement is to have formulated rational ac-countability of social structures of practical activities as precepts of constructive analysis. The social structures of everyday activities, as we remarked before, are understood by the formulations of constructive analysis to consist of such prop-erties as uniformity, social standardization, repetition, reproducibility, typicality,

categorizability, reportability of ordinary conduct, of talk, of territorial distributions, of beliefs about one thing or another that are invariant to changes of production cohorts. The practical technology of constructive analytic theorizing is available, in apotheosis, in the work of Parsons, Lazarsfeld, and RAND techniques of systems analysis. We observe that its practitioners insist that the practices of constructive analysis are *members'* achievements. We learn from practitioners that, and how, adequate application of its precepts to demonstrations of formal structures in actual occasions demands members' competence. We observe, too, that particulars in procedures and results of constructive analysis furnish to members perspicuous exhibits of vaguely known "settings."[27] In every actual occasion of their use, particulars in procedures and particulars in results provide members with the combination of unavoidable, irremediable vagueness with equally unavoidable, irremediable relevance. From practitioners we understand that the combination of essential vagueness and relevance is available to members only, for members' production, evaluation, and recognition. In short, we learn from practitioners of constructive analysis that our findings about formulating are extendable to constructive analysis.

Formulating does not extend to constructive analysis as its gloss, nor is formulating a generalization of the experience of analysis. Least of all is formulating a generalization of the practices of professional sociologists. It is extendable in the ways that doing [constructive analysis] is what *members* do; like [saying specifically in so many words just what we are doing], or [saying what is meant and meaning what is said in a few well-chosen words], or [removing from cell titles the nuisances of indexical expressions], or [mapping the system of real numbers on collections of indexical expressions], or [abstracting methodological paradigms from the work of E.S.R], or [thinking sequentially]. Because doing [constructive analysis] is what members do, what we observe about formulating is observed as well in the practices of professional sociologists doing [constructive analysis]. In that work we see *members* being careful to build context-free descriptions, relevant instructions, perspicuous anecdotes, cogent proverbs, precise definitions of ordinary activities, and context-free formalizations of natural language practices, and using members' competence with natural language practices to assure the doing and recognition of [adequate evidence], [objective description], [definite procedure], [clear, consistent, cogent relevant instructions], [computable conversations], and the rest. In that work we see professional sociologists' insistence on members' competence to assure these glosses as concerted accomplishments.

The machinery of professionals' gloss achievements is described only in barest part by the practices that were described in a preceding section as members' machinery for doing [rational talk for practical purposes]. How such glosses are done has not been elucidated beyond enthnographic remarks furnished by sociological practitioners, both lay and professional. What various kinds of enterprises, such as [objective sociological formulations], [definite instructions], and the like, are as conversational accomplishments is not known.

(4) From an inspection of the work of constructive analysis we learn that rational accountability of everyday activities as practical accomplishments is accounted by members to consist of the practices of constructive analysis. From that work we learn, too, that such accounts are themselves warranted features of that practical accomplishment. From their practices we learn that formal structures in the practices of constructive analysis, which, in the sense described in an earlier section of this paper ("Ethnomethodology's Interest in Formal Structures of Practical Actions") *are formal structures in members' natural language practices,* are *not* available to the methods of constructive analysis. We are not proposing an "impossibility" argument in the sense of a logical proof, nor are we offering an in-principle account of constructive analysis. Nor are we recom-

mending an attitude toward, a position on, or an approach to constructive analysis. Nor are we saying that formal structures are not available to constructive analysis because of trained incapacity, habitual preferences, vested interests, and the like. Most emphatically, we are not offering advice, praise, or criticism.

Instead, we are taking notice of that unavailability as a phenomenon. We offer the observation about that unavailability that it is invariant to the practices of constructive analysis. This is not to say that the phenomenon somehow defies the efforts of constructive analysis. The unavailability of formal structures is assured by the practices of constructive analysis for it *consists of* its practices. The unavailability of formal structures is an invariant feature of every actual occasion of constructive analysis, without exception, without time out, without relief or remedy, no actual occasion being excepted no matter how transient or enduring, the unavailability being reportable, assured, done, and recognized not only unanimously, but with required unanimity by whoever does sociology—or, equivalently, by whoever knows how to talk.

That formal structures in members' natural language practices are not available to the methods of constructive analysis establishes the study of practical sociological reasoning. Ethnomethodological studies have been using that unavailability to locate one or another "piece" of constructive analysis and bring under scrutiny how its achievement is an accountable phenomenon for members. The availability of these studies establishes the *de facto* existence of an alternative to the other prospects and perspectives in this volume, for although formal structures of constructive analysis are not available to constructive analysis, they are not otherwise unavailable; they are available to ethnomethodology. That this is so is less interesting than the question of whether they are available to ethnomethodology uniquely.

NOTES

1. The work for this paper was supported in part by the Air Force Office of Scientific Research, grant Af-AFOSR 757-67. A version of this paper, "On 'Setting' in Conversation," was read at the annual meetings of the American Sociological Association in San Francisco, August 31, 1967, at the session on sociolinguistics, chaired by Dr. Joshua Fishman. Hubert L. Dreyfus, Elliot G. Mishler, Melvin Pollner, Emmanuel Schegloff, Edward A. Tiryakian, E. Lawrence Wieder, and Don H. Zimmerman commented on the paper. Particular thanks are due to David Sudnow and Joan Sacks for their generosity with editorial tasks. An exceptional undergraduate term paper, "Gloss Achievements of Enterprises" by Nancy McArthur, motivated many of the paper's reflections.

2. Emile Durkheim, *The Rules of Sociological Method* (Chicago: University of Chicago Press, 1938).

3. This property is elucidated in Don H. Zimmerman and Melvin Pollner, "The Everyday World as a Phenomenon," in Harold B. Pepinsky, ed., *Studies in Human Information Processing* (in press).

4. Olaf Helmer and Nicholas Rescher, *The Epistemology of the Inexact Sciences* (Santa Monica: RAND Corporation, October 13, 1958).

5. We mean by "infinite task" that the difference and substitutability motivate inquiries whose results are recognized and treated by members as grounds for further inferences and inquiries. It is with respect to the difference and substitutability as aims of inquiry that "infinite task" is understood by members to refer to the "open" character of sociological fact, to the "self-cleansing" body of social scientific knowledge, to the "present state of a problem," to cumulative results, to "progress" and the rest.

6. That is, socially organized in the sense in which this paper is talking of formal structures as accomplishments.

7. Alfred Schutz, *Collected Papers I: The Problem of Social Reality*, 1962; *Collected Papers II: Studies in Social Theory*, 1964; *Collected Papers III: Studies in Phenomenological Philosophy*, 1966 (The Hague: Martinus Nijhoff); *The Phenomenology of the Social World* (Chicago: Northwestern University Press, 1967).

8. I. A. Richards, *Speculative Instruments* (Chicago: University of Chicago Press, 1955), pp. 17–56.

9. We mean that none was called for, and that in other glossing practices something else could be the case.

10. These remarks are adapted from suggestions that we took from Samuel Todes, "Comparative Phenomenology of Perception and Imagination: Part I: Perception," *The Journal of Existentialism*, 6 (Spring, 1966), 257–260.

11. This cannot be emphasized too strongly. Because we used the present perfect tense to report Richards' gloss there is the risk that our description may be read as though we were recommending that Richards' gloss defines *the* way that clear, definite speaking is done. Richards' gloss is only *one* way that clear, definite speaking is done. There are others, which consist of glossing practices different from Richards' gloss. Richards' gloss is used as a perspicuous example, not as a definition.

12. The following excerpt provides two structurally distinct examples. 1) Not only is the speaker making out from what was said, what was meant, by the person whose talk is being quoted by the speaker, but 2) the whole body of talk is introduced by the speaker as showing that its speaker knows what is meant by the talk of a just-prior speaker; that is, it is delivered with "I know what you mean" as its initial part.

T: I know just what you mean. We, we go through this thing every year. My father said, "No gifts." And we tried to analyze what—

B: Does no gifts mean no gifts or does it mean more gifts?

T: No, he, he gave us one reason why "no gifts." And I was questioning the reason. I didn't think it was his, a legitimate reason. I didn't think it was his real reason. He said, "Well, you know how the Christmas, all the stores, uh, well, make such a big killing over Christmas, killing, and Christmas is becoming commercialized, and therefore, I don't wanna be sucked into this thing. I'm not giving gifts this year."

J: "You spend your money and buy something you really want, and I'll spend my money and buy something I really want."

T: But we figured there must be something deeper, because if a guy is aware of, that Christmas is becoming very commercialized, uh, must he submit to this idea and reject it entirely, and end up giving no gifts, or is it because he really doesn't, he's not a person that likes to give anyway?

B: Yeah.

T: And this is just a phony excuse for not giving. And finally, I think we figured out it must be some kind of a, a combination, and he really isn't that stingy.

13. The developmental sense of *becomes* is intended; not its sense of a development in the past that is now finished. To emphasize "process" the sentence might be read as follows: "Instead, his talk itself, in that it is in becoming a part of the selfsame occasion of interaction is in becoming another contingency of that interaction." Similar remarks might be made about "another."

14. William Kneale and Martha Kneale, *The Development of Logic* (London: Oxford University Press, 1962), p. 16.

15. Charles S. Peirce, *Collected Papers, Vol. 2* (Cambridge: Harvard University Press, 1932), paras. 248, 265, 283, 305; Ludwig Wittgenstein, *Philosophical Investigations* (Oxford: Basil Blackwell, 1953).

16. Occasional expressions are discussed in Marvin Farber, *Foundation of Phenomenology* (Cambridge: Harvard University Press, 1943), pp. 237–238; and C. N. Mohanty, *Edmund Husserl's Theory of Meaning* (The Hague: Martinus Nijhoff, 1964), pp. 77–80.

17. Bertrand Russell, *Inquiry into Meaning and Truth* (London: Allen, 1940), Chap. 7, pp. 102–109.

18. Nelson Goodman, *The Structure of Appearance* (Cambridge: Harvard University Press, 1951), pp. 290ff.

19. A review of indexical expressions is found in Yehoshua Bar-Hillel, "Indexical Expressions," *Mind*, 63 ns (1954), pp. 359–379.

20. Hubert L. Dreyfus, "Philosophical Issues in Artificial Intelligence," Publications in the Humanities, No. 80, Department of Humanities, Massachusetts Institute of Technology, Cambridge, Mass., 1967; Hubert L. Dreyfus, *Alchemy and Artificial Intelligence*, P-3244 (Santa Monica: RAND Corporation, December 1965).

21. The reader is asked to read for "all sciences" any inquiries whatsoever that are directed to the detection and assessment of effectiveness of practical activities and to the production of members' accounts of that effectiveness. In addition to the academically taught sciences of the Western world, we include the "ethno" sciences that anthropologists have described, such as ethnomedicine and ethnobotany, as well as the enormous number

of empirical disciplines that have their effectiveness in and as practical activities as their abiding phenomenon: Azande witchcraft, Yaqui shamanism, waterwitching, astrology, alchemy, operations research, and the rest.

22. It is not only because members can *do* formulating and observe it that formulating is reportable. In that members are *doing* and *observing* formulating being done, it is reportable; or in that members do formulating and observe that it *was* done, it is reportable; or in that members when doing it observe it *will have been done,* it is reportable; in that members when doing it observe it *can have been done,* etc. The criterial consideration is not the availability of "tensed" verbs but the temporal structures of such enterprises. Temporal structures of formulating enterprises include of course the availability to members of time references in natural language.

The clumsiness of sentence structure may be something of a benefit if it earmarks the relevance and availability of the extensive, developed, and deep temporal "parameters" of members doing formulations as accountable enterprises. Particular attention is called to the work that David Sudnow is doing on the temporal parameters of accountable glances.

23. Garfinkel, *Studies in Ethnomethodology,* pp. 29–30.

24. Because we are required to learn what these practices are by consulting members, we must require of the methods that we use to locate these practices, and of the practices that such methods locate that they satisfy the same constraints. The arguments to justify this assertion and to show that the method we use is adequate with respect to these requirements are detailed in Harold Garfinkel, "Practices and Structures of Practical Sociological Reasoning and Methods for their Elucidation," in *Contributions to Ethnomethodology.*

25. *Members* of the list has the conventional meaning of *items* of the list.

26. We take notice of how practices of practical sociological reasoning seek to remedy the indexical properties of talk: they seek essentially to do so.

27. We have borrowed from remarks made by Hubert L. Dreyfus about Wittgenstein and Merleau-Ponty during his informal seminar at Harvard University in March 1968.

THE SOCIAL ASCRIPTION OF MOTIVES

ALAN BLUM AND PETER McHUGH

Reprinted from the *American Sociological Review*, 36 (February 1971), 98–109. Used by permission of the authors and the American Sociological Association.

Alan Blum teaches at New York University. Peter McHugh teaches at the City University of New York, Graduate Center.

I. INTRODUCTION

Our intention is to explicate the sociological status of motives. We shall address this issue by describing how ordinary actors employ "motive" as a practical method for organizing their everyday environments. Since motive is used by ordinary societal members to manage their orderly routines, our explication will be a formulation of the ways in which members' practices are grounded in their knowledge. We shall suggest that all sociological conceptions require some version of the common-sense member (of his practical knowledge); and we shall depict motive as one common-sense device for ascribing social membership, since motives are used by members to link particular concrete activities to generally available social rules. Motive, then, is one collective procedure for accomplishing social interaction, and for sorting out the various possibilities for social treatment by linking specific act and social rules in such a way as to generate the constellation of social actions that observers call "persons," "members" and "membership."[1]

II. THE SOCIOLOGICAL POSSIBILITY OF MOTIVE

Social scientists tend to conceive of motives as private and internal characteristics of persons which impinge upon and coerce these persons into various behaviors. In this view, motives are seen simultaneously 1) as "causal" antecedent variables (antecedent to the event of interest), and 2) as characteristic "states" of persons engaging in the behavior. We maintain that these senses of motive are inadequate because they issue from a common misconception of motive, namely that motives are concrete, private and interior "mainsprings" that reside in people, rather than public and observable courses of action.[2]

If sociologists have sought to understand and formulate descriptions of social action, and if the analytic status of social action resides in its character as behavior which is normatively oriented to the very same environment it constitutes, then motive can function as an observer's rule for deciding the normatively ordered character of behavior. That is, motive is a public method for deciding upon the (sociological) existence of action. In this usage, motive is an observer's rule of relevance in that it represents a sociologist's decision (his election) as to how items of concrete behavior are to be reformulated as instance of social action.[3]

The classic roster of terms used by sociologists—social class, community, religion, suicide, bureaucracy, conflict, and the like—all require in their various ways this sort of conception. Motive then, serves as a theorist's election that some rule is relevant for explicating the character of some event as an instance of action. Motive is not in this regard a thing in the world but a way of conceiving social action.

In a more precisely sociological sense, it is observers who introduce a topic into behavior, whether motives or any other. Thus, to say that "social class exists," or that some group is high on need achievement, is for an observer to decide that some collection of persons is oriented to their status as a collective actor and is to be conceived as acting under the auspices of such an orientation. When an observer asserts that the American workers constitute a social class, he is deciding that the collection conceivable as American workers presently show in their behavior their status as a collective actor, the identity of which the observer provides on the basis of their relation to the instruments of production.[4]

The upshot of all this—that motives function as observers' rules of relevance—is that though motives might be described as personal properties or characteristics of persons, they acquire their analytic force as observers' rules for depicting grounds of conduct.[5] Motives are a way for an observer to assign relevance to behavior in order that it may be recognized as another instance of normatively ordered action.

It should now be clear why motives cannot be private and internal; if motives are sociologically depicted in the ascription of rules, the ascription of rules itself requires (presupposes) the use of a language that is public and observable. Even when we speak of "hidden" motives, we are of course engaged in fully intelligible and observable courses of treatment—some public criterion enables us to grasp the topic. The so-called hidden motives, slips, and the like are observable states of affairs which can be discussed in sensible and concerted ways. To treat motives as private is to confuse the state of affairs which motives report with the analytic status of the term, which status is supplied by the public and by generally available rules that make motive reports socially possible and observable modes of social action.[6]

III. GRAMMATICAL AND FACTUAL PERSPECTIVES IN THE FORMULATION OF MOTIVE

We have said that motive is a term regularly employed by actors to accomplish their routine affairs. When practical actors are "doing motives," they are engaged in formulating themselves and their environments, in constructing and treating with their common-sense courses of action. To say "He had the jealous motive to murder her" is to do no more or less than lay out and characterize an environment in such a way as to report on a social state of affairs, to make some behavior possible, to limit the use of other behavioral possibilities, and so forth. The sociological status of the idea rests on whatever must be known in order to produce motive-talk as a recognizable or observable course of action. To provide a motive, then, is to formulate a situation in such a way as to ascribe a motive to an actor as part of his common-sense knowledge, a motive to which he was oriented in producing the action. Thus to give a motive is not to locate a cause of the action, but is for some observer to assert how a behavior is socially intelligible by ascribing a socially available actor's orientation.[7] Questions of orientation do not require factual solutions (they are not either true or false), but rather, grammatical solutions. To talk motives is to talk grammar.

At the same time, however, social psychologists have used motive as a technical term designed to unravel the causal patterning of a sequence of actions (Atkinson, 1958; Cattell, 1957; Lindzey, 1958; Smelser and Smelser, 1963; White, 1963), e.g. need achievement as an antecedent of economic development (Mc-

Clelland, *et al.*, 1953). One problem with such technical usage is that it does not reformulate motive from the perspective of a practical member; i.e., it ignores motive as a social course of action, and so it fails to provide for the relevance of motive as an activity engaged in by practical members.[8]

To treat motive as a cause, as in "What was his motive for suicide?" is to commit one version of the fallacy which Austin (1965) and others have discussed in detail: The fallacy of presuming that suicide is an act which somehow describes some antecedent state of mind which preceded or caused it. On the contrary, to recognize the act of suicide as an intelligible event-of-conduct is to assign to that behavior its identity as social action, in this case by formulating a motive. Thus, motive is a rule which depicts the social character of the act itself. It is not that his suicide reports some antecedent depression, or that murdering his wife reports his jealousy, or that leaving the party reports upon his boredom. Rather, the character of the suicide, the murder, the departure are identified through the clarification of unstated circumstances which make these actions socially recognizable as suicide, murder and departure. To say "I want a motive for the murdered wife" is not to say that I want merely his antecedent state of mind which the wife's murder follows, but is instead to explicate the situation (the context, knowledge, conditions) which makes the event socially possible (a recognizable murder).

The best criticism of the causal account of motive is to be found in Melden's *Free Action* (1961) in which he demonstrates that since any conception of a cause presupposes a description of the very action for which the cause is identified, these accounts violate the necessary assumption of the analytic independence of cause and effect in the Humean model of causality. That is, some thing cannot be cited as a cause of an event if this "something" is involved (presupposed) in the very description of the event; analyses of motive accounts show that whatever is cited as a motive serves to more fully and completely characterize the event for which it is formulated, and cannot then be treated as independent of the event. Melden says: "this explanation does not refer to a present moment, sliced off from what has gone before and what will follow, but to the present action as an incident in the total proceedings" (1961:98–99).[9]

This is why it is elliptical to assert that motive describes only and simply a state of mind, when instead it serves to demand an explication of the circumstances which confer upon this putative state of mind its reasonableness as an account. Because such an explication amounts to a theory or formulation, it would be more correct to say that the quest for a motive (why did he kill her?) is a request for a theory.

IV. MOTIVE AS SURFACE STRUCTURE

We have sought to show that motive acquires its analytic character as a public (methodic) product rather than as a private "state," and that it is to be understood grammatically (as part of the meaning of an action) rather than as a factual report on some contingent, antecedent event. Now, however, we want to show how the analytic sense of motive is not located through a report of usage, but rather by formulating the conditions of knowledge which make such usage possible.

One option to the technical causal idea is thought to be a conception of motives as members' purposes, reasons, justifications and accounts (Gerth and Mills, 1953); Schutz, 1962; Scott and Lyman, 1968; Shwayder, 1966). In this tradition, the actor is used by the observer as a research informant, whose report acquires analytic status because the actor is thought to be a privileged and exclusive source on questions of his motive.

The paradigmatic procedure here is to ask the actor, "Why . . . ?" and expect him to cite a reason, goal, or intention, e.g., "Why did you leave the party?"; "Because I was bored"; "In order to make my appointment"; etc. In some cases we take these reasons and call them symbols and meanings, but that sort of sub-stitution does not really tell us much about the methodical ways in which such statements are generated to begin with—how, for example, the actor is con-strained to cite a reason at all; how it takes the form it does (giving a reason instead of, say, telling a joke); how it comes to be acceptable to the hearer that it *is* an answer. In other words, its status as a common-sense practical device, as opposed to mere idiosyncratic noise or gesture or cue, remains unstated.[10] The methodic social and hence sociological feature of motive lies not in the concrete, substantive reason an actor would give for his behavior, but in the organized and sanctionable conditions that would regularly produce the giving of a reason by a competent member in the first place. The reason given is no more than the surface expression of some underlying rule(s) that the former requires in order to be understood (Chomsky, 1965).

The surface performance which is displayed in the use of motive might be that of offering a reason, goal, or intention, but to provide an account of motive in these terms is to ignore the deep structure which makes the surface display possible at all. As we shall investigate below, motive acquires its analytic status by virtue of the fact that it requires for its use certain deep structures for con-ceiving of "person," "member," "responsibility," "biography," and the like; these deep structures are absolutely necessary for an ordinary member's competent and sensible employ of motive as a device, because they generate the variety of surface reasons he may cite in any particular case. It is through these deep conditions that an analytic conception of the ordinary sociological use of motive is provided.

It should be clear then, that the similarity which typical symbolic interaction accounts appear to achieve with our present formulation—through such phrases as "vocabularies of motives" and the like—is misleading, for they treat concrete speech acts—such as giving reasons or justifications, or citing intentions—as providing an analytic explication of motive, whereas we treat such usage as sur-face phenomena which are made possible by deeper conditions of knowledge. The concrete character of such versions of motive is conveyed in their practice of treating motive as the practical actor's expression of his knowledge, in contrast to the present suggestion that analytic status is supplied through some concep-tion of an observer's method of constructing a practical actor (no matter what he is concretely taken to perform or say).

For example, Gerth and Mills (1953:116) cite Weber as we do but interpret him as using motive as equivalent to "an adequate reason for conduct." On the other hand, we are saying that this usage fails to capture the analytic character of motive as an *observer's decision to treat or reformulate* some behavior as a reason, and that this is an entirely different matter. So too, they see motive as "ascribed through talk" (1953:114) and as a "term" of the talk itself, whereas, in our view, speech is just a medium for the concrete expression of motive, but it is a set of prior and deeper conditions of knowledge which permit an observer to treat talk as intelligibly predicating motive. The symbolic interactionist finds it impossible to formulate a version of motive that is analytically distinct from conventional versions, because he still conceives of motive as a practical actor's concrete report of his state of mind: he only shifts his focus from the state-of-mind to the talk, by treating the talk as some sort of public indicator of the mind. Gerth and Mills show this quite explicitly when they eventually surrender to a concern for questions such as what the differences are between professed motives and "real motives" (1953:119), and with the actor's degree of "awareness" of his motives (1953:125). These are not the questions of those who have grasped the analytic character of motive.[11]

We can now locate the major difficulty which unifies the various conven-tional accounts of motives, i.e., the conception which appears to unify the various sorts of troubles we have been discussing; these accounts pose the problem of motives as a factual rather than a grammatical one, which leads easily to the trap of treating motives as causes, as states-of-persons, and as concrete speech-acts such as reasons, accounts, and justifications. And these accounts treat motives as raising a concrete, factual question of "why?" rather than as attempts to formulate the socially organized conditions under which such a question is sensible to those who raise them. Any strategy which equates the factual surface structure of motive talk with an analytic conception of motive cannot provide any more than a concrete and irrelevant record.[12]

In sum, when we speak of motive, we have in mind neither the technical observer's notion of the causes of an action, nor the actor's report of why an action was done. We do not require either an explanation or reason for the action, but rather some description of the socially organized conditions which produce the practical and ordinary use of motive in the mundane affairs of societal members. To locate motive is thus not to "find" anything but to describe the necessary and analytically prior understandings and conventions which *must* be employed in order for a member even to invoke motive as a method for making a social environment orderly and sensible.

V. THE DEEP STRUCTURE OF MOTIVES

A. Motives Are Observers' Rules

Motives acquire their analytic status as observers' rules. They are not forces or events in the world extraneous to an observer. Motives are sociologically possible only because some practical observer has methods and procedures—i.e., rules—for locating them as events in the world, not because that is where they really are. Because events cannot "exist" sociologically except as courses of treatment, and because courses of treatment are not intelligible except through available social rule, motives cannot be located except by rule. Consequently, motives are accomplished exclusively through the use of such methods and procedures.

When a member says "He had the jealous motive to ———," we expect that the statement can be understood as a description of possible behavior. Of course, there can be disagreement with the surface content of the statement—perhaps he did not have the jealous motive—but it nevertheless remains an intelligible remark because it describes an understandable or socially possible motivated action. Others do not think every such statement literal nonsense. This is again to distinguish between concrete surface phenomena or causal properties (whether the object does or does not have the jealous motive) and the analytic deep structure that makes such phenomena possible (that an observer can talk intelligibly about jealous motive, whatever the factual status of his talk).

The point here is that there must be some rule—of language, interpretation, or culture—by which motive-talk takes life as a description.

Now to say that some rule is available is to remove the sociological habitat of motive from object (the person who had the jealous motive) to discourse about the object (how it is understood that a motive ascription has been made). This is to say, again, that the sociological import of motive resides in its procedural implications for the *treatment* of objects and not in the states of the objects themselves. Motive is a procedure.

This first feature brings motive into the full corpus of sociological ideas: rules must exist for such a procedure as motive to exist. They are socially organized treatments. Motive is not something an actor has—it is not a property of an actor. It is not something the sociologist decides that some person owns, in the sense that it is the "thing" which he owns. Rather, motive is a member's method for deciding what alter owns. Thus, the sociologist does not search for motives in objects of talk and treatment, but in the talk and treatment itself.[13]

One socially organized condition for addressing the topic of motive, therefore, is the assumption of the availability of relevance of a motive ascription rule. The necessary availability of such a rule, or rules, can be seen by noting that motives are a common-sense class of events, in that to do (observe) motives is not to be exclusively doing (observing) something else (writing a play, sleeping). That motives are the topic in any case, as opposed to some other topic or no topic, requires that others understand they are the topic, which in turn requires that the socially available rule for introducing the class "doing motives" be displayed in the behavior of the introducer. As with any form of social behavior, the members themselves conceive the doing of motives to be rule-guided. Thus, one kind of common-sense sociological rule is the motive ascription rule, and the most elemental necessary feature of this deep rule is: there are rules for the ascription of motives.

B. Motivated Objects Are Theorizers

One rule for the ascription of motives therefore is that the observer-user knows there are motive-ascribing rules. A concomitant of this first rule is that the ascriber know (assume, presume) that the *object* knows there are motive-ascribing rules.

In order to be called motivated, the object of an ascription cannot be treated as if he were doing the behavior haphazardly or coincidentally. He is, in other words, treated as if he has the capacity to "know what he's doing." Any object thought to be unable to know what it is doing cannot be treated as motivated, even though that object resembles a human organism, e.g., a brute or an infant. That ascribers know there are rules requires that they impute knowledge to the object that there are rules.[14] Otherwise, the ascriber's knowledge could not be conceived by him to be a practical guide to the object's behavior, since the latter could not be deemed to be oriented.

Alter, as rule-guided, incorporates the fundamental sociological principle that generally available rules are the analytic equivalent of membership (community, group, pair, etc.). Rules make actors' methodicity and concert possible by transforming what would otherwise be nonsense into intelligible social behavior. That alter can be conceived (by observing ego and sociologist) to be rule-guided encompasses the status of motives within general sociology: motive, as with any other sociological classification, refers to certain actions by rule-guided ascribers and objects. The ascriber is rule-guided in his characterization of an object, while the object is (assumed to be) rule-guided in his behavior, and thus assumed to "know what he's doing." Both ego and alter assume of one another that they are, or could be, doing motives. Each is a theorizer, in the sense that both must be looking to rules in order to carry off their activity as doing motives. For motive treatment to occur, as for any kind of membership treatment to occur, ego and alter must necessarily generate for one another their status as members oriented to rules. Here a set of concrete activities is so formulated that those activities become members through the application of a corpus of rules. This is a detailed way of saying they are members of a social relation.[15]

By "rule-guided" we do not mean that actors are automata governed by abstract rules, that rules are clear and unchanging and automatically applied, or that it cannot be difficult, confusing, and vague for members to act like members. We do not mean that actors are rule-governed (Bennet, 1964). On the contrary, it is those who can behave but not act whom we conceive to be rule-governed automata, for they seem only to play out as mechanisms the untransformed universal needs and drives of every man.[16] The distinction between rule-governed and rule-guided is comparable to the one between behavior and action, and it is surely correct that the use of rules by members is an accomplishment in the hardiest sense of the term. We are only asserting that ego and alter must assume, however difficult the application of substantive ascriptions, that *some* corpus of membership rules is being used in behavioral displays before they can be characterized by substantive motive schema. It is necessary that ascriber and object are assumed to be of a certain kind, namely theorizers.

We are not suggesting either that members always neatly agree on what is happening around them, or that the substance of rules is common to all interactants. Whether behavior goes well or badly, whether it "deviates" or "conforms," is not an issue. We do not equate the deep notion of theoreticity with the substance of interaction. Theoreticity is the observed, rule-guided identification of the doing of anything at all, whether well or badly, whether deviant or conforming. (Even to be considered one or the other requires that some imputation of rule be used.)

Take the case of mental illness. If the person is conceived by members to be doing nothing in particular, to be merely a set of either random or universal behaviors, then no question of motive will ever arise (or will arise only once, to be dismissed by the finding of nonmembership). Only when being crazy can be seen as organized or rule-guided—again, as being a display of some membership—does the possibility of motivated mental patients occur.

To be theoretic is thus to be conceivable by some observer as methodically rule-guided, rather than haphazard in behavior. To ascribe a motive, among other ascriptions, is of course to formulate the intelligible character of some behavior. The warrant for motive ascription is that the object be theoretic, that his behavior is capable of being formulated as action, just as it is the warrant for any common-sense facet of membership.

C. Motives Have a Grammar

A third organized condition of motive ascription is a grammar that locates for a potential or would-be ascriber those conditions in the world which give notice that an ascription is to be done. The grammar moves a motive rule into behavior, from availability to ascription. It is a (collection of) rule(s) of use for the doing of an ascription. It depicts for the observer a procedure for actually ascribing available designations to a world populated by members. The grammar links a phenomenon in the world to the available corpus of designations.

This grammar of motives is used whenever an event is to be collected within a biography. We may think of the biography as a collection of "owned experiences," in that actors conceive themselves as having particular pasts which routinely inform an observer about the possibilities for their behavior; and we may think of events as some observer's definition of a situated environment of objects, specific to time and place. Motives are the social characterizations, generally available, the grammar which is used when biography and event are to be linked. The grammar produces for the ascriber a relation between some practical phenomenon and the common sense biography with which that event now comes to be associated through the process of ascription. A common-sense biography is the observer's version of a set of owned experiences (husband), a set which comes into contact with, or is juxtaposed against, particular concrete (and hence socially problematic) phenomena in the world (dead wife). The grammar is the rule (connect the experience—husband—with the event—dead wife) that conjoins the two as an accomplishment of organized and concerted treatment (a jealous motive).

Imagine a hypothetical community where a murder is committed, and the husband of the victim is eventually identified as the killer. Initially, everyone could be suspect, and to "look for the motive" is to address the links between the murder and various collections of owned experience in the community. The ways these experiences are joined with murdered wife methodically generate the motivated (or not) character of any link.

The idea of motive thus serves to formulate for members their interactions, insofar as they conceive interaction as experiences framed in events. Actors are thought by observers to have biographies and to engage the world with them. The grammar produces the link between the two. Motives are resources for connecting an event with a biography, and they generate the event as a member of the class of experiences owned by a body (as depicted in common sense).

Similarly, motives depict for us how the event shows or displays a biography. Insofar as the biography and the event can be seen to be membership, this is done through the ascription of motive. Otherwise—in the absence of such a grammar —observers would be unable to organize the current and flow of socially intelligible events, nor could they observe the products of biography; i.e., they could not see interaction as a course of history. They would be without a temporal method. Events could only be seen to be performed and disembodied, not enacted by some theoretic-nontheoretic incumbent of a situated social world. Motives that characterize biographies enacting events are specific to events and distinctive of biographies. They are a grammar in that they methodically collect these disparate phenomena. And they are social in that they transform what would otherwise be fragmentary series of unconnected immediate events into generally intelligible social courses of behavior. It is through motive as a culturally available designation that the observer recovers alter's membership out of observed temporal phenomena, because motives delineate the biographical auspices of acts in situations.

D. Motives Formulate a Type of Person

The grammar, then, includes some collection of owned experiences which can be allocated to the agent of the act, and some rule(s) for showing the related character of the event and the collection of experiences. Because there are alternative collections (of experience) available, the use of the grammar poses a selectional problem for its user in this sense: it has to include a search procedure for deciding the relevance of one biography (one collection) as compared to other possibilities. The search procedure is essentially the rule for showing the *possible* relevance of the biography for the event. Such a rule amounts to the formulation of a type-of-person.

Thus, when users formulate the biography called "husband," the relevance of which to the event "murdered wife" is decided through a formulation of circumstances and characteristics such as jealousy, they are formulating the biography (husband) as the type of person whose jealousy could produce the event of murdered wife. In this way the grammar is a provision for explicating the link between the biography and the event and this explication is supplied by the formulation of a type of person.

The grammar of motives enables members regularly to address the fact that the relevance of biography to event is formulable through a rule which locates the owner of the biography as the type of person who would do the event.[17] Type of person, then, explicates the circumstances and understandings required to assert the relevance of any biography for the event. The heart of the grammar is thus its rule for formulating a type of person. It is in this sense that any observer's ascription of a motive serves to formulate for some activity, a person.

E. Motives Formulate Actors' Methods

If the application of the grammar is equivalent to the formulation of a type of person, what is required of such a formulation? Note that type of person is an identification of certain characteristics, traits, dispositions, and behaviors which make ownership of the biography relevant to the event. While the items on such a list (characteristics, traits, dispositions, behaviors) all tend to itemize concrete features of the person, they only acquire their analytic sociological interest as descriptions of possible ways of relating to the event, i.e., as potential courses of action. To formulate a type of person is to formulate a course of action on the grounds that no matter what one predicates substantively of persons to make their biographies relevant to the event, such relevance is only assigned on the assumption that the predicates depict a typical, possible course of action. Person, then, depicts a typical possible actor.

To say his motive in murdering his wife was his jealousy is to explicate the circumstances which make him the type of jealous person who would (could) murder his wife—that murdering his wife is one possible method available to him for doing jealousy. In this way, the event is formulated as the agent's possible method for doing whatever the formulation of the motive requires as a course of action.

He killed himself because he was depressed, or he left the party because he was bored—both are observers' ways of saying that killing oneself is a method of doing depression, or that prematurely leaving the party is a way of doing boredom. This understanding is important because members regularly raise the question of motive and address it as a sensible topic only of those classes of events which are recognizable as possible products of actors' methods. Questions such as "What was your motive in spilling the ink?" (Austin, 1966), or "What was your motive in speaking so softly?" come up in ordinary usage when something is fishy, *and* when it is sensible to ascribe to an actor some methodic display of intention or purpose. To assign a motive is then necessarily to assume that the event exhibits possible methodicity.

As we have stated, at the deepest level such methodicity is addressed in the observer's conception of the event as showing the agent's character as a type of person—by the agent's being formulable as a possible method, as it were, to "do" whatever type of person which he is formulated as.[18] The observer assumes, then, that the agent shows in the event (uses the event as) one possible method of identifying himself through his action as a particular type of person: that the murder of his wife identifies him as a jealous type of person, leaving the party as a bored person, and so forth.

When an observer formulates a member in this sense, he is stipulating that whosoever he is formulating has knowledge to act under the auspices of his (the observer's) formulation of a type of person. The formulation of a type of person (of one who has a motive) thus requires the observer to assume that the one so formulated is capable of "showing" the type of person for which the observer's formulation provides. Therefore, when the observer formulates a motive, he is formulating a type of person and is required to assume that the one so formulated is a member in the deep sense of the term, i.e., as one who can generally be expected to know what he's doing in the possible circumstances where he might or could be doing it, circumstances which include those of motive ascription.

No matter what members conceive themselves to be doing when they ascribe motives, we say they are engaged in conceiving others (or self) to be doing whatever activities they do because they "own" a particular collection of experiences which can be used as a normative order for creating sensible events. Those to whom motives are ascribed are thus formulated under the auspices of the following requirements: 1) That they treat such a collection of experiences as possible grounds of action in situations, 2) that other collections of experiences are possible alternative grounds of action, 3) that the activity which is done is the actor's way of showing, to the one who ascribes, the relevance of his own collection of experiences (of showing himself as a type of person), and 4) since every kind of showing as type of person is a method of excluding other possible persons, that the actor as *this* type of person is selectively doing whatever he comes to (since according to his theoretic status in common, he could have come to something else). It is in these ways that regular motive ascriptions are regularly introduced in regular social intercourse; it is in these ways that motives formulate actors' methods.

VI. SUMMARY

In summary, we have attempted to depict the socially organized conditions which members tacitly accredit in their accomplishment of motive as a sensible and observable event. We have tried to demonstrate that motive can be sociological by showing that motive shares with all matters of sociological interest (class, bureaucracy, suicide, etc.) a status as a common-sense formulation. Motive depicts for any observer a course of social action.

Motive is a sociological procedure for describing how organisms show themselves as persons. To gain an identity as a person requires that disparate activities and experience can be collected by actors under some typification, a process which makes the activities graspable for them through the formulation of alter's motivated identity. The condition of membership in common makes it possible for an observer to expect that alter, because he knows what he's doing and hence is responsible, will use common rules as a standard of orientation when he displays his biography in situations, thus knowledgably revealing his type of person.

Given (the observer's imputation of) alter's capacity for knowing what he is revealing, together with his being a differentiable type of person, the observer can also warrantably conceive alter's future, and thus organize not just the current biography and event but future links between the two as well. Motives are a procedure for organizing an historic and regular interactional future.

Most fundamentally, then, whatever a motivated actor does will show his methods for affirming himself as a person. Being responsible and capable of displaying some other collection of owned experiences, the observer is permitted to note that he nevertheless did display the collection he displayed. For any member to ascribe a motive is thus to do no less than to generate a person. It is to formulate from situated performances a responsibly displayed and differentiated collection of experience.

While each of these public and rule-guided conditions must exist for motive ascription to occur sensibly, they can of course be accomplished in a variety of substantive ways which we have not discussed here. For example, that there is a grammar under which a motive ascription rule is invoked suggests that members regularly differentiate between activities which do and do not require the use of that grammar; i.e., there are some activities which needn't be organized according to motive criteria. In the same vein, there are undoubtedly a variety of methods in use by which members identify organisms as possible theoretic actors, e.g., the various ways it is decided that a child is enough of a member to be called a theoretical actor and so a potential object of motive ascription.

More centrally, one pervasive feature of social organization concerns members' methods for tracking and formulating biographies from a universe of possibilities, and the various rules for deciding the relevance of particular biographies as particular types of persons. The bureaucratic method, for instance, is probably very different from the familial one. All these are categorization problems which members regularly resolve, methodically producing the organization of their every day environment. To describe such particular solutions requires other papers, the possibility of which we can now begin to grasp. Being interactional and rule-guided—being a social method (just as bureaucracy, social class, or institutionalization are methods)—confirms that the status of the deep structure of motive is sociological.

NOTES

1. Readers of an earlier draft commented upon the absence of any mention of ethno-methodology as strange. Limitations of space prohibit us from the sort of detailed comparisons which such a topic requires, and there is unfortunately no adequate description of ethnomethodology in the literature; so, for example, Denzin's paper (1969) is hopeless not merely for his misunderstandings, but for his inadequately concrete conception of analysis; e.g., in superficially focusing upon the surface features of the approach—the concern with "meaning," with the "actor's point of view," etc.—he loses sight of the analytic character of ethnomethodology and of analysis in general. Wilson (1970), on the other hand, may understand ethnomethodology but not what to do about it. If ethnomethodology obviates literal description, then suggesting that we be "more explicit and self-concious" (1970:706) is regressive if not vacuous—it is only to ask that we improve on the same literal procedures. As to the contrast between this paper and ethnomethodology, we must first record the great influence of the writings of Garfinkel (1967), though this influence has not worked itself out in our thinking in the ways it has in his students. Ethnomethodology, as it is practiced by these students, not only fails to supply our program with its rationale but denies this rationale at critical analytic points. Ethnomethodology seeks to "rigorously describe" ordinary usage, and despite its significant transformation of standards for conceiving of and describing such usage, it still conducts its inquiries under the auspices of a concrete, positivistic conception of adequacy. Ethnomethodology conceives of such descriptions of usage as analytic "solutions" to their tasks, whereas our interest is in the production of the idea which makes any conception of relevant usage itself possible. Whereas ethno-methodology uses the ordinary world "seriously" (they hope to solve analytic problems by doing naturalistic science on this world), we treat the everyday world as a proximate occasion for initiating inquiry and not as a "fact" to be reproduced. In our respective attitudes toward ordinary language and the everyday world, we have about as much in common with ethnomethodology as Heidegger shares with Austin. Finally, ethnomethodologists would regard our task in this paper as a stipulative exercise in legislating the use of a "concept," while we would treat such an objection as a failure of analytic nerve, as the typical positivist gambit (which goes back at least as far as Protagoras) of refusing to exercise analytic authority, despite the fact that such authority grounds their entire enterprise with its intelligibility. Some of these issues are taken up in detail in work now under way.

2. This misconception leads to the contention that motives are only peripheral to the classic tradition of, say, Marx or Durkheim—that human motivation plays the role of unstated premises and is properly disregarded for analytic purposes (the ecological argument), or requires explication only in order to account for more of the variance (the social psychological argument of Homans, 1964; Inkeles, 1959). We contend instead that motive plays a central role in such traditions, a role we can recognize if we grasp the analytic status of motive rather than its concrete character.

3. For example, the sociological import of economic determinism in Marx is not the impersonal effects of brute facts upon an organism, but rather his formulation of a meaningful environment constructed by and seen from the perspective of a typical actor. To say "economic determinism exists" is to decide to formulate actors as oriented to selected particular features of their socially organized environments in such a way as to enable this orientation (now called "the economy") to produce their routine actions. To describe economic determinism is then to assign a rule of relevance to actors which serves the purpose of explicating social structure by reference to their grounds of action (the economy) as a set of sociologically intelligible events of social structure (economic determinism).

4. This is also the sense in which Weber's Theory of Social and Economic Organization (1947)—particularly the sections in which he depicts types of social relationships—can be read in a fundamental way as a set of methods for conceiving of motives. Each relationship is a different method for formulating actors as acting under the auspices of relevances to which they are methodically and selectively oriented.

5. Thus, conventional notions of motives as concealed premises or as peripherals that increase variance are incorrect in the fundamental sense that it is in the observer's ascription of such rules, and not in the state-of-affairs the ascriptions recommend, that the analytic status of motives resides.

6. There may be a concrete psychological state-of-affairs that corresponds to a motive report. We do not address this and so are not trying to run psychologists out of business. Our purpose, again, is to analytically describe the social organization of motive ascriptions as courses of social action.

7. This is perhaps what some sociologists intend when they invoke phrases like "actor's point of view," "what it means to the actor," and "significant symbol."

8. Technical versions, which causally locate motives in neural circuits, libidinal arrests and the like, reformulate what is essentially a member's device without respect for those relevances and interests of the member which generate the behaviors of interest to the technician. Whatever the efficacy of neural paths, they have no social relevance except as they can be understood to be employed by the members.

This is not a new criticism and has been stated most articulately by the British ordinary language philosophers (Peters, 1958; Austin, 1965).

9. We have not seen successful demonstrations of objections to this position in the philosophical literature, for those who claim that motives *can* be causes, or that motives *do* explain, usually accomplish this by changing the sense of "cause" and by treating "explanation" concretely rather than analytically. Of course, motives *can* be causes if one uses cause in a different sense; our notion is that any different sense makes "cause" a constituent feature of the action (i.e., a presupposed element of the action), and hence, not a "cause" in the ordinary sense at all. But, one is free to do this. Secondly, motives do explain, but by providing a way to see "cause" as an intelligible link, not by citing a cause.

10. We are not making a sampling argument here. Even when an unanalyzed event occurs repeatedly, it remains only a regularity. Lacking analysis, we would still be without an understanding or description of it, regardless of the times and places it had been counted.

11. Though more ingenious than most, Kenneth Burke (1945) is not exempt from these charges, for in his effort to locate the analytic parameters of motive, he confuses analytic and concrete conditions (i.e., the parameters of act, agent, agency, scene, and purpose). However, despite Burke's failure to explicate the grammar of motive, in more than a metaphoric sense, he performs a service by continually keeping before us the notion that the way in which priorities are allocated to these parameters is a function of a theoretic election (that it is observers who formulate motives), though we do not get a description of how such formulations are accomplished.

12. We are not prescribing how motive-talk should be accomplished; rather, we are stating that under any and all occasions of motive-talk in our society, to which we have reference, such talk requires members to make certain assumptions about their environments. Furthermore, their talk shows that they make these assumptions. Again, whether members know these conditions or can report them to us is analytically irrelevant in the same sense that Chomsky's native speakers cannot concretely reproduce his theory even though they do show its correctness and provide for its formulability through their behavior.

13. Note, though, that the concrete talk—the speech act(s), the usage—does not provide the observer with the motive (as some versions of sociology might have one believe), but such analytic status is located in terms of the observer's decision as to what must be known in order to recognize in the talk, the analytic "presence" of motive.

14. We should perhaps remind the reader here that the phrase "knows there are rules" does not imply "knows *the* rules." All kinds of substantive mistakes and arguments over content and application may occur in the course of motive ascription without ever denying that there are rules. What the rules are, and that rules exist, are two quite different ideas, and correspond to our previous distinction between surface and deep structure, respectively. This same distinction carries through to "knowing what he's doing." We can be quite mistaken about what it is we are doing without being treated as if we *couldn't* know, e.g., as in therapy.

15. Take, for example, the brute. There are things which can be said of such an organism, *e.g.*, it is enraged, it is contented, it is sleeping, and so forth. These are characterizations, in that they depict some state of affairs, and rule-guided ascriptions at that. But they are not, and could not be, common-sense ascriptions of motives because the brute's behaviors are not thought to be displays by a rule-guided actor—the brute is thought not to be socially "responsible." He is thought not to be responsible insofar as his activity is, in Weber's terms, behavior rather than action. Nor is the brute thought to be a bona fide member, and for the same reason: he cannot be a member because he cannot be said to know what he's doing through an orientation to member rules.

16. Universals remain constants for the brute, and they govern him in the sense that they are not given the differentiated and variable expression that we think of as motivated social action. Jealousy can be a motive precisely because it is not universal in husbands. Think of thirst as a motive here—what would it be like to enact the thirst drive in such a way as to have it said that "he killed her because he was thirsty?"

324

17. While we separate these features of the grammar for analytic purposes, they are concretely indistinct. As one formulates a biography of owned experiences presumed to be relevant to the event, this presumption can already be informed by an unstated rule which has decided that relevance as the kind of person who would do the event.

18. Perhaps, this is what Aristotle intended in the following: ". . . acts are called just and self-controlled when they are the kinds of acts which a just or self-controlled man would perform, but the just and self-controlled man is not he who performs these acts, but he who also performs them in the way just and self-controlled men do" (1105b 5–9, p. 39).

REFERENCES

Aristotle. *Nicomachean Ethics.* Indianapolis: Bobbs-Merrill, 1962.

Atkinson, J. W., ed. *Motives in Fantasy, Action, and Society.* Princeton: D. Van Nostrand, 1958.

Austin, J. L. *How To Do Things with Words.* New York: Oxford University Press, 1965.

———. "Three Ways of Spilling Ink," in J. H. Gill, ed., *Philosophy Today.* No. 1. New York: Macmillan, 1966.

Bennet, Jonathan. *Rationality: An Essay Towards Analysis.* New York: Humanities Press, 1964.

Burke, K. *The Grammar of Motives.* Englewood Cliffs, N.J.: Prentice-Hall, 1945.

Cattell, R. B. *Personality and Motivation Structure and Measurement.* New York: World Book Co., 1957.

Chomsky, Noam. *Aspects of the Theory of Syntax.* Cambridge, Mass.: M.I.T. Press, 1965.

Denzin, Norman. "Symbolic Interactivism and Ethnomethodology: A Proposed Synthesis," *American Sociological Review,* 34 (December 1969), 922–34.

Garfinkel, Harold. *Studies in Ethnomethodology.* Englewood Cliffs, N.J.: Prentice-Hall, 1967.

Gerth, H., and C. W. Mills. *Character and Social Structure.* New York: Harcourt, Brace, and World, 1953.

Hall, Calvin S., and Gardner Lindzey. *Theories of Personality.* New York: Wiley, 1957.

Homans, George C. "Bringing Men Back In," *American Sociological Review,* 29 (December 1964), 809–18.

Inkeles, Alex. "Personality and Social Structure," in R. Merton, L. Broom, and L. Cottrell, eds., *Sociology Today.* New York: Basic Books, 1959, pp. 249–76.

Lindzey, Gardner. *The Assessment of Human Motives.* New York: Rinehart, 1958, pp. 3–33.

McClelland, D. C., J. W. Atkinson, and R. A. Clark. *The Achievement Motive.* New York: Appleton-Century-Crofts, 1953.

Melden, A. I. *Free Action.* London: Routledge and Kegan Paul, 1961.

Peters, R. S. *The Concept of Motivation.* London: Routledge and Kegan Paul, 1958.

Piaget, J. *The Language and Thought of the Child.* New York: Harcourt, 1926.

Schutz, Alfred. *Collected Papers, Vol. I.* The Hague: Martinus Nijhoff, 1962.

Scott, Marvin B., and Sanford Lyman. "Accounts," *American Sociological Review,* 33 (February 1968), 46–62.

Shwayder, D. S. *The Stratification of Behavior.* New York: Humanities Press, 1966.

Smelser, Neil, and William T. Smelser. "Introduction" to Smelser and Smelser, eds., *Personality and Social Systems.* New York: Wiley, 1963, pp. 1–18.

Weber, Max. *The Theory of Social and Economic Organization.* Translated by Talcott Parsons. Glencoe, Ill.: Free Press, 1947.

White, Robert W. "Ego and Reality in Psychoanalytic Theory," *Psychological Issues,* 3 (1963), 71–141.

Wilson, T. P. "Conceptions of Interaction and Forms of Sociological Explanation," *American Sociological Review,* 35 (August 1970), 697–710.

CHAPTER 8

NEW DIRECTIONS IN SOCIOLOGICAL THEORY

Introduction

The seven theoretical groups dealt with in the preceding chapters clearly do not exhaust all of the theoretical possibilities of sociology. Nor, as we have seen, is there a clearly recognizable orthodox position within the schools. Sociologists, therefore, often resent being labeled with a school. While many dislike being judged as eclectic, they do not necessarily identify with a broad school of thought. Instead, they view their own theoretical position as unique, albeit not always completely formulated. Indeed, in its last stages, graduate training encourages an ideology of individualism—a doctoral dissertation is supposed to be an original piece of work. To a degree, then, the academic setting nurtures idiosyncratic work, and well-socialized sociologists (with a few exceptions, including some radicals who have consciously attempted collective work) usually insist on being their "own person."

Of course, no academic sociologist works in total isolation. Graduate training forces a familiarity with a broad range of sociology, and most sociologists attempt to "keep up with the literature" or at least a specialized part of it. The doctoral dissertation (or master's thesis), however, does force the candidate for a degree to choose a specific topic and treat it to a degree satisfactory to a committee. In practice, this often means satisfying *one* person, the dissertation director. Thus the terminal stages of professional training resemble a master-apprentice relationship. The student, for obvious reasons, chooses a director with whom he or she agrees (or, of course, one who can offer financial support or an easy passage to the dissertation—two other practical considerations). The student becomes in part a disciple, and distinct "mini-schools" often form around the mentor (for example, the "neo-Weberians" who studied with Reinhard Bendix at Berkeley). Part of the young sociologist's identity (or professional credentials) is the degree-granting university (or rather, department); but the answer to the question "Whose student are you?" is clearly important to others (prospective employers, in particular).

There are at least two ways in which new schools evolve. The sociologist can discover similarities in the work of others through the literature of the field and form intellectual alliances. This can involve a felt affinity to sociologists of the past (who are constantly being "rediscovered"). Such like-mindedness can lead to the development of social groupings, special societies, journals, and so on. Alternatively, a "school" can start with social relations involving an influential mentor and followers and can spread by converting outsiders. The emergence of new approaches, sects, specialties, and splinter groups is therefore a common occurrence. (Face-to-face interaction can be overstressed in "school" formation. Often it is the printed word that is more influential. Meeting admired authors in the flesh is often disappointing—they turn out to be human. One whom I respected, and still do for his work, spent an inebriated evening telling Polish jokes.)

Sociologists do not group solely on theoretical grounds. Often, their specialized subject matter is a source of identification, social interaction, and reading of specialized journals and books. Thus, their primary interest may be the sociology of education, science, the military, medicine, deviance, stratification, small groups, and so on. There are also groupings based on the sociologists' personal qualities, such as black, Chicano, and women's caucuses, Jewish and Christian groupings, and so on. Sociologists are also influenced by external political and intellectual influences. Radical sociology is clearly an example of the former, and other disciplines—for example, biology, philosophy, anthropology, and especially psychology—comprise the latter. Several of the schools dealt with in the first seven chapters exhibit such intellectual influences—functionalism, systems theory, exchange theory, and phenomenological sociology had obvious "outside" inputs.

There are numerous candidates for "new" sociologists. Glaser and Strauss (1967) attempted a radically different way to discover what they call "grounded theory." But conventional research and theory testing were largely unaffected (see Brown, 1973), and their concerns have largely been absorbed by ethnomethodology. Gouldner (1970) has called for a "reflexive" sociology that would "*transform* the sociologist, to penetrate deeply into his daily life and work, enriching them with new sensitivities, and to raise the sociologist's self-awareness to a new historical level" (1970:489). It "would be a moral sociology" (p. 491). Radical, humanistic, and phenomenological schools attempt some of these aims but do not yet form anything approaching the full reflexivity that Gouldner advocates. Another promising new sociology has been labeled "dialectical." Schneider (1971) has traced the multiple usage of the term and concludes that dialectical analysis can be useful for contemporary sociology. Friedrichs (1972) goes further, arguing that dialectical sociology might become the dominant paradigm of the immediate future.

The first selection here, by Peter Manning, describes the emergence of what he calls "existential sociology" from various sources, but particularly from ethnomethodology and phenomenology. He traces the changes in post-World War II social theory that have encouraged this emergence. He then outlines the major concepts that distinguish an existential perspective—concepts borrowed in part from existential philosophy—including sentiments, body, self, situation, structure, massification, and leveling. He demonstrates their use in research and suggests their implications for sociology. His article is one of synthesis and describes a plausible unification of several strands of contemporary theory.

The second selection, by van den Berghe, clearly takes into account man's biological being. He draws on animal psychology and biology in formulating a biosocial theory of aggression. Homo sapiens, he claims, is biologically predisposed to territoriality, hierarchy, and aggression. The article has produced heated rebuttals. Fischer (1975) rejects the entire drift of the article because of its alleged assertions; Moberg (1975) finds it a "sordid evolutionary tale" drawn from selective evidence, while Mazur (1975) thinks the comparisons of human societies to primate groups is misleading. Hixson and Scott (1976) are critical of his "evolutionary hypotheses and trait concepts" (p. 1970), Robertson (1976), of his conclusions in general. Van den Berghe (1975, 1976) has given spirited reply to his critics.

The next article, by John Glass, represents the work of a loosely organized "school" of "humanistic sociology" that is difficult to distinguish from some types of radical sociology. Its best-known (and influential) exponent is probably the 1975-1976 president of the American Sociological Association, radical humanist Alfred McClung Lee. The dimensions of the field are sketched by Glass and Staude (1972). While sociology may be seen as having had a humanistic basis throughout its existence (see Berger, 1963; Cuzzort, 1969; and Staude, 1972), to Glass it now in part parallels the humanistic psychology movement which he "discovered" as a graduate student. He argues that the perspective it provides is a useful basis for building a sociology that takes "humanness" into account.

The concluding article, by Stinchcombe, adopts the "structuralism" of French social scientist Claude Levi-Strauss to investigate sociology itself, its myths and rituals. This approach is borrowed from anthropology and is growing in influence. Stinchcombe's subject matter, I trust, will be of some interest to anyone who has the dedication to read this book to its end; for second only to the truly exotic, we are our own favorite subject.

References and Suggested Readings

Berger, Peter L. *Invitation to Sociology: A Humanistic Perspective.* Garden City, N.Y.: Doubleday, 1963.

Brown, George W. "Some Thoughts on Grounded Theory," *Sociology: The Journal of the British Sociological Association,* (January 1973), 1.

Cuzzort, R. P. *Humanity and Modern Sociological Thought.* New York: Holt, Rinehart and Winston, 1969.

Fischer, Claude S. "The Myth of 'Territoriality' in van den Berghe's 'Bringing Beasts Back In,' " *American Sociological Review,* 40 (October 1975), 674–76.

Friedrichs, Robert W. "Dialectical Sociology: An Exemplar for the 1970's," *Social Forces,* 50 (June 1972), 447–55.

Glaser, Barney G., and Anselm L. Strauss. *The Discovery of Grounded Theory: Strategies for Qualitative Research.* Chicago: Aldine, 1967.

Glass, John F., and John R. Staude, eds. *Humanistic Society.* Santa Monica, Calif.: Goodyear, 1972.

Gouldner, Alvin W. *The Coming Crisis of Western Sociology.* New York: Basic Books, 1970.

Hixson, Vivian S., and J. P. Scott. "On van den Berghe's Theory of Aggression," *American Sociological Review*, 41 (February 1976), 169–70.

Mazur, Allan. "Cross-species Comparisons of Aggression," *American Sociological Review*, 40 (October 1975), 677–78.

Moberg, Dennis J. "A Comment on van den Berghe's Biosocial Model of Aggression," *American Sociological Review*, 40 (October 1975), 676–77.

Robertson, Leon S., "A Comment on Biosocial Theories of Aggression," *American Sociological Review*, 41 (February 1976), 169–70.

Schneider, Louis. "Dialectic in Sociology," *American Sociological Review*, 36 (August 1971), 667–78.

Staude, John R. "The Theoretical Foundations of Humanistic Sociology" in Glass and Staude, *op cit.*, pp. 263–69.

van den Berghe, Pierre L. "Reply to Fischer, Moberg and Mazur," *American Sociological Review*, 40 (October 1975), 678–82.

———. "Reply to Hixson and Scott, and Robertson," *American Sociological Review*, 41 (February 1976), 172–73.

EXISTENTIAL SOCIOLOGY[1]

PETER K. MANNING

Reprinted from *The Sociological Quarterly*
14 (Spring 1973), 200–225. Used by permission.

Peter Manning is professor of sociology and psychiatry
at Michigan State University. He is author of *The
Sociology of Mental Health and Illness.*

The early sociologists, most notably Durkheim, argued that social objects must
be approached and studied as one would study natural or physical phenomena.
Their explanatory models were culled from the physical and, to a lesser degree,
from the biological sciences, and their methods were also derived therefrom.
They adopted what has been called an "absolutistic" view of man and society
(Douglas, 1967; 1970b). That is, they assumed that man's behavior was almost
wholly determined by forces external to him and beyond his control. It was
widely assumed that this external, almost changeless and timeless, reality could
be most appropriately studied by means of methods and techniques utilizing scientific categories defined in advance, eschewing the reality of persons in everyday
life, and designed to obtain data that were easily manipulated to produce verifiable and reproducible (i.e., valid and reliable) results independent of the time and
place in which they were gathered. The objectified or absolutistic view of man
and society has not been a canopy subsuming all of sociological effort, but it has,
I argue here, supplied one of the most persuasive and pervasive models of social
theory and research in American sociology in the twentieth century.

The last ten years show signs indicative of the beginnings of a new creative
epoch in sociology. A body of criticism directed toward the absolutistic sociologies has become increasingly focused and sharpened in its critical concerns; it
is accompanied by a substantial corpus of empirical research and now is in the
process of becoming more visible and available to the professional audience in
monographs, edited collections, and journal articles.[2] Although a number of labels have been applied to this developing set of ideas, e.g. , micro-organization,
phenomenological sociology, ethnomethodology, it will be referred to tentatively
in this essay as "existential sociology." It characteristically is concerned with the
position of man in the social world and in social theory; it considers theory and
life to have an intimate and unavoidable connection; it sees the reality of human
social life as situational; and it espouses a methodology that is grounded in the
understandings of everyday life, rather than presupposed *a priori*. Existential sociology thus contains a specific perspective on man which is both implicit and
explicit, a set of methodological presuppositions, and it manifests a view of social
reality which specifically challenges the dominant views of sociology.

The problem of a review essay such as this one is to bring unity and clarity
to a subject without creating the appearance of a false synthesis. Thus, this essay
cannot cover the range of disaffections that churn within sociology, e.g., it systematically avoids a discussion of Marxist or Neo-Marxist theory and eschews

329

detailed examination of the philosophic roots of what has been translated into existential sociology.[3] The review will attempt to clarify: a) the nature of the perceived failings or inadequacies of absolutistic sociologies; b) the characteristics of existential sociology, i.e., its content and central themes; c) six concepts which are ostensively central to the enterprise of existential sociology. The essay is a dramatic exercise which seeks to utilize striking examples. It is a chiaroscuro sketch having no pretentions to theoretic comprehensiveness; it is rather a set of marks toward a theory.

CRITICISM: THE FIRST AND SECOND WAVES

Although by no means has American sociology ever been dominated by a single perspective or methodology—alternative paradigms have always been present— the last ten years contain important criticisms of the conventional sociologies. There are two waves or phases in this intellectual movement. The first phase, beginning in the early sixties, was a breakthrough phase in which previous modes of theorizing were discredited or at least seriously questioned. The second phase, overlapping the first and continuing through the seventies, was a period of establishing and solidifying the dimensions of an alternative, existential perspective.

In the late 1930's Harvard's reputation as a vital center of sociological innovation emerged, and following the war there was a surge of creativity around Parsons.[4] In the late 1950's and early 1960's, the creative energy of Sorokin-Parsons-Merton was seemingly flagging; theorizing was almost reduced to a neo-orthodoxy, a passive exploration of lines of inquiry originally sketched by the triad. A new tone soon began to characterize some sociological analysis, and new premises, assumptions, and problem foci emerged in the work of Coser (1956, 1967), Dahrendorf (1958, 1959, 1968), and Mills (1959). (See also Sprott, 1952; Swanson, 1953; Lockwood, 1956; Wrong, 1961; Black, 1961; Horowitz, 1962; Van den Berghe, 1963; Horton, 1964, 1966; Quinney, 1965.)[5]

These critiques for the most part appeared during the early 1960's, a period of growing strife in American society: the beginning of civil rights activity in the South which later became a national movement; the emergence, following this stimulus, of the harbinger of student activism at Berkeley; the assassination of JFK; the emergence of the conception of the Great Society, perhaps the last flourish of American Liberalism generating unexpectedly powerful demands for change and increased equality; the appearance of the first inklings of the expanded, divisive Vietnam war; the first signs of the inflationary spiral accompanied by the expansion and proliferation of American graduate schools; and the nascent rise of a number of liberation movements which were to capture the headlines of the last years of the sixties. It was a period of great change, of disruption, of new visions and imagination; of new, bright, and rather unrealistic hopes; and of political ferment, especially from the left.

In the years since the late sixties, a new wave of criticism emerged; in some ways it follows the earlier lines of challenge and attack and in others it takes a more philosophical and fundamental character. This second wave of criticism not only contained an explicit and implicit critique of sociological thinking to that time, it made a number of exciting contributions to the intellectual armamentarium of sociology.[6] The most important of these works made significant contributions to sociological *theory* (Tiryakian, 1962, 1965; Berger and Luckman, 1966; Douglas, 1967; Gouldner, 1970; Friedrichs, 1970), to an understanding and appreciation of sociological *concepts* among students (Berger, 1963), to rethinking sociological *methodologies* (Cicourel, 1964; Garfinkel, 1967), and to *deviance* theory (Matza, 1964, 1969). As this new surge of intellectual curiosity escalated, previous work was seen in a new and fresh light. Erving Goffman's work took on new significance in the context of the appearance of additional existential analyses. *The Presentation of Self in Everyday Life* (1959), although a MacIver Award winner, gained new stature (cf. Goffman, 1961a, 1961b, 1963a, 1963b, 1967, 1970, 1971; Berman, 1972). On the west coast of the United States, an indigenous phenomenology flourished.[7] A number of students and colleagues of Harold Garfinkel at UCLA such as Egon Bittner, Edward Rose, Harvey Sacks, Lindsay Churchill, Jack Douglas, and Aaron Cicourel, joined students and associates of Goffman to create a new center of "native" phenomenological sociology which continues to grow.

As if recognizing the growing import of these ideas, the publishing houses, pursuing exuberantly their attempts to meet the apparently insatiable demand for texts and readers in the then exploding colleges and universities, reissued in translation a number of important books (e.g., Schutz, 1962, 1964, 1966, 1967; Mannheim, 1971) and contracted a variety of new original collections—existential in assumptions, method and foci—ranging from careful empirical studies to intemperate attacks upon the conventional sociologies (see Lyman and Scott, 1970; Dreitzel, 1970; Douglas, 1970a, 1970b, and forthcoming; Scott and Douglas, 1972; Sudnow, 1972; Filmer, et al., 1972; Psathas, 1973; Garfinkel and Sacks, forthcoming, and works cited in footnote 2).

The success of this new critical evaluation can best be assessed by detailing the inadequacies which it identified in contemporary theorizing. The differences between the schools of thought in American sociology should not obscure the salient and shared characteristics to which these critiques were directed: *exchange* theories (Homans, Blau), *ecological* theories (Hawley, Duncan), *experimental* sociology ("The Stanford Group"), and *survey research* all share with Parsonian theory a number of assumptions, propositions, and methodological strategies. All are concerned with a social order that is seen as non-problematic, either a construction of the working out of assumed rationality, or of shared values; all assume a high degree of shared meanings which are seen to act as a canopy encompassing and ordering interactions; and all direct attention to the world primarily by means of pre-established categories, axioms, and methods which ignore the reality of everyday life.

To the extent that it deals with *social order* at all, and does not simply assume its existence, conventional theory directs attention to questions suggested by the query, "How is social order possible?" This approach assumes that order is a modal property of societies and that it is maintained as such within some identifiable pattern or sequence. Conventional theory has further assumed that change, as well as order, is *normative*, i.e., that events are to be explained with reference to the normative order, or in response to that order. Aspects of coercive control, non-moral elements such as technological change, and the manipulation of reality that occurs as a result of the differential distribution of the power to define and disseminate mass meanings, are omitted or considered secondarily. Because it does not make social order problematic, this view tends to implicitly support order; a focus upon order-maintenance as a "quasi-automatic" function of a moral order fails to adequately explicate the alternative forms of social order which may emerge in the absence of social control or as a direct consequence of social intervention characteristic of active social control (cf. Lemert, 1967).

Existentialists in particular are committed to viewing social organization as constantly being made apparent, destroyed, repaired, or reconstructed situationally, and to exploring contradictions and conflicts within alternative systems of meaning and the conditions that give rise to and support them. Berger and Luckman (1966) and Goode (1969), for example, call attention to the significance of investigating the degree to which there is a *hegemony* of control over meanings current in a society. How potent and extensive is the influence of a "politics of reality" employed by superordinate groups wielding the power to limit the consideration of a diversity of human behavior and goals?[8] A single conception of reality may be reflected and replicated in institutional orders, maintaining a controlling and legitimating force, excluding or restricting alternative meanings which may be attributed to events by actors.[9] Sociologists have inadequately explicated these taken-for-granted bases of social action; they have behaved like an audience that becomes encapsulated while viewing a movie.

> Since social structures as the intersubjective cadres of social action are latent or covert (in the same sense as is the "ground" in Gestalt psychology), it is for the most part rarely that these "tacit dimensions" of social activity are questioned, that is, that perceptual awareness is directed to them. They are homologous to the "presuppositions" of a scientific theory. In general, sociological observations are hardly different from those of the layman; they focus on what is manifest without seeking to relate it systematically to the latent ground from which they emerge and placing the latter itself under closest scrutiny. By way of analogy, the typical orientation is like that of a spectator at a movie taking as exhaustive of what is there, what is seen on the screen, or even mistaking the contents of the film as a rendition of reality. Not only do we not look back and notice the physical structures which make this reality possible (the projector, the screen), but also—and more important —we do not even think of considering other structures such as the fact that what is acted out is a function of what the director, the producer, and the playwright have wanted to depict on the screen. Who does the staging for institutional life, and with what intentionality, is seldom thought about, since attention is typically addressed only to what is staged. (Tiryakian, 1970:124)

In contrast to a view of society that posits a fairly static set of norms and values governing any given situation (e.g., the Parsonian pattern variables, or any other resource posited as readily available, and circumscribing the range of meanings and action consequences), the existential perspective argues for the need to take into account the *situational and problematic nature of meaning*. Although one can identify analytically a dominant "image" of society and its workings, the actual processes by which people attempt to work out concerted action, and indeed negotiate to establish whether shared meanings are possible, are fragile and almost ephemeral. Consequently, any reality, assumed to operate to insure and defend vested interests, may be called into question, and the problematic nature of meaning may be publicly established. This questioning and symbolization of alternative realities is seen in the activities of guerilla theater, in confrontations, and in the new forms of art and music. Dramatic, artistic, and political events of this sort whirl background assumptions to the foreground, and by forcing people to face them directly, the implicit (but hidden) quality of everyday life is made at times excruciatingly "real." (The 1968 Democratic convention with the shocking nature of the real events was barely upstaged by bizarre Yippie street theater.)

Most sociological theory and methodology assumes a deductive model of social investigation.[10] In many respects, this theoretical position leads to reification of the previously discussed absolutistic conception of society—taking abstractions such as "values," "norms," "roles," and "social classes" as real (see Berger and Pullberg, 1965). Existentialists argue that this form of theorizing has three principal consequences. First, it abstracts everyday life, making man a passive recipient of social pressures, forces, and ideas; men are seen as essentially unaware of their historical and political situations (Wrong, 1961; Quinney, 1965; Zijderveld, 1971). A theory which short-circuits the relationships between men and their actions and minimizes the centrality of human agency tends to insulate men against an awareness of the alternatives available to them for change. Second, sociological explanation that tends to remain at a theoretical and abstract level therefore truncates a link between theory and practice; existentialists assert that human action, based upon the awareness of individual actors, can shape and bend the sociological *deux ex machina* implied by employing as explanatory terms "urbanization," "modernization," "bureaucratization," and "industrialization" (Sallach, 1971). Finally, such a view fundamentally distorts everyday meanings by predefining their nature and limits; it confers meaning on events rather than seeking to discover the uses that meanings are put to by individual persons. Insofar as tacit assumptions and taken-for-granted meanings are the fundamental bases for viewing the world, any approach which fails to take them into account will be engaging in systematic distortion of social reality (Douglas, 1970b). It is this premise that existentialists make foremost and by which the adequacy of alternative methods and approaches are judged.

SOCIOLOGY AND SENTIMENTS

What are the sources of the efflorescence of these alternative modes of explanation? There are two readily identifiable conditions, described by Birnbaum in discussing the crisis in Marxist sociology:

A doctrinal or theoretic crisis in a system of thought occurs when either of two sets of abstract conditions obtains. In one case the possibilities of internal development of a system exhaust themselves; the system's categories become incapable of transformation; the discussion generated by the system becomes scholastic, in the pejorative sense of the term. In the other case the realities apprehended by the system in its original form change, so much so that the categories are inapplicable to new conditions. It is clear that these two sets of conditions often obtain simultaneously; particularly for systems dealing with the historical movement of society, the two sets of conditions of crisis are often quite inseparable. (Birnbaum, 1971:95)

The two conditions he sees as necessary to the precipitation of a crisis in a system of thought appear to be present.[11] There are two facets to this explanation. The first, roughly cast as the argument from science, says that the internal workings of the ideational system are riddled with contradictions, and that it has exhausted its usefulness as an explanatory scheme. This emphasizes the rational, internal dynamics of the ideas or theory which are shown to be inadequate either because of the rise of new paradigms, or because of the breakdown of the explanatory power or proven lack of empirical utility of the ideas. The other argument, the argument from experience, says that theories have an emotional appeal to sociologists. When the realities that the theory must deal with change (or the perception of them changes), sentiment no longer holds and new paradigms are sought.

Parsons' synthesis of European systematic social theory, his contributions to sociological analysis in his essays, and his attempts to bring about a general social science theory represent unequivocally important contributions to American sociology. In providing general frameworks for defining problems, suggesting broad areas for empirical investigation, and in stimulating a number of macro-level historical and comparative studies, Parsons and Parsonians shaped sociological work for a number of years.[12] On the other hand, attempts at careful empirical theory-testing, or even testing of hypotheses derived from the Parsonian framework, have proved to be remarkably unsatisfying.[13] Some tendencies toward a new scholasticism occasionally surface, and a neovitalism or evolutionism now appears to have encapsulated Parsonian theory. To many observers, the ideational system seems exhausted (Bottomore, 1969).

The dominance and decline of this theoretic perspective may be explained also on the grounds that Parsonian theory once but no longer possesses a capacity to resonate the sentiments of sociologists. Collective sentiments, or feelings, surround and embed theories and in part explain their appeal. Accompanying collective sentiments which might characterize a generation are individual sentiments regarding the consistency and appropriateness of theories for depicting the social reality of the sociologist. Within this context it is possible to associate ideas and sentiments. Thus, Parsons reigned as *the* theorist of post-war sociology because his theories reflected the sense of order, stability, middle-class ascendency, and societal consensus for which the post-war generation so yearned. The theory captured a mood in society, a mood of other-direction, conformity, and a belief in corporate growth and profit. His theories "made sense" to members of a generation who had survived the depression and World War II:

Coming out of the war with long-deferred ambitions to live our lives, we settled down, began at once to breed, as if to prove we were still alive, and then proceeded to let our children do our living for us. It was a strange process, gradual, almost imperceptible, as natural as dying. Without quite intending it, we stopped—if we ever really began—making demands on life, perhaps because we thought there was no longer time for such frivolity, that our youth had been used up in the war, and that nothing must interfere with the grimly earnest business of becoming middle-aged. Or it may be that the depression and the war together accustomed us to asking nothing of ourselves, to seeing ourselves with a certain bleak pride as the sacrificial generation, to being grateful simply to have the necessities and utilities of existence. There was also the fact that the war had broken our connections with the past in a peculiarly final way. (Aldridge, 1971:3–4)

On the other hand, one might inquire as to why the Parsonian view appealed less to European emigré scholars and younger American students who were being trained in the early 1960's in colleges and graduate schools of the United States. I suggest it has to do with the failure of social theory to explicate their lives, and its increasing indifference to the existential questions they entertained. The idea system failed to apprehend the realities with which sociologists were faced in the sixties.

As Back and Pettigrew (1971) and others have noted, there is little indication in post-World War II research of an awareness or prescient sensitivity among sociologists to the following, soon to explode, events: a) the emergence of the Black movement, its varied and fascinating permutations; b) the large scale riots of the sixties; c) the growth of the host of liberation movements stimulated by Blacks (Gay, Chicano, Women's, NWRO, etc.); d) the growth and explosion of student activism and its increasing (related) tendencies for isolation, Marxism-anarchism, fragmentation and internal dissension; e) the growth of dissatisfaction and resentment within the middle classes as manifested in tax revolts, school millage defeats, busing antagonism, rallying behind Wallace, Carl McIntyre, and other lesser figures on the local level; f) the country in near self-hypnosis in the wake of the assassinations of 1968.

In sum, we can generalize to say that conventional sociological theory has failed to provide substantial empirical support for its concepts and theories and has inadequately clarified, especially for the younger generation of sociologists who often participated in the events I mentioned above, the jagged and divisive *course of social change* in the United States (cf. Bottomore, 1969). The crisis in the society has, indirectly to be sure, "caused" a profound questioning within sociology of the adequacy of its dominant theories.

CENTRAL CONCEPTS THAT CHARACTERIZE THE EXISTENTIAL PERSPECTIVE

Existentialism is not a coherent and easily summarized philosophic position and can be best characterized as a *reaction against* rationalist philosophies. As Tiryakian observed, "Extentialist thought taken as a whole is replete with paradoxes, internal contradictions, and a general absence of congruity, unity, and systematic order—but these are necessary, and not mere fatuous characteristics of extentialism" (1962:71).

Existentialism developed among a group of European thinkers in the early nineteenth century (namely, Kierkegaard, Dostoevsky, and Nietzsche) who were struck by the overwhelming impact technology and its rational infrastructure were making upon man's situation (see the summaries in Wild, 1955; Barrett, 1958; Reinhardt, 1960; and Tiryakian, 1962). They defined the philosophic tradition to that time as overly rationalistic and excessively committed to a vision of man as a rational animal. Existentialism above all was an attempt to place man at the center of philosophy, man as agent and creator of both meaning and action, a victim of himself, ominously threatened by imprisonment by society. A central theme was the need for a philosophy which would permit man to rise above his external societal existence and to create freedom for himself by acting according to his own self-perceived ("authentic") feelings, thoughts, and meanings. Existentialism is, if it is anything, a philosophy arguing that through his life, man makes decisions and builds up meanings in line with them (if possible), and is in fact forced to act, to accept freedom. Man creates meaning within social relations and his relationship to the world is established by his mode of perceiving his spatial-temporal position in that world. Any system of thought which sees man as only a partial creation, either of his mind, or as a victim of his body, is rejected in favor of a view which restores the wholeness of man: his emotionality, his sentience, his bodily basis for life, his ignorance and error. Weber had established the centrality of man's goal-directed rationality; sociological existentialism sought to establish a framework for understanding the non-rational aspects of human life, especially the situated nature of the emotions. I have chosen six sociologically relevant and empirically utile concepts to discuss here: *sentiments, body, self, situation, leveling,* and *structure.* They may be considered the elements in the determination of human action, or the constraints or limits within which individual choice will operate.

Sentiments

A philosophy that sees all action through the telescope of rationality has the effect of intentionally isolating the man from men. Existentialism, from the first murmurings of Kierkegaard, has asserted the intrinsic and inherent place of emotion in social life (Sartre, 1953; 1962; Warnock, 1965). Man is neither a purely social being embedded in the collective structure (symbols, beliefs, and norms), an externalized symbolic representation, nor is he a wholly internally oriented privatized animal. He is the creature demonstrating both social *and* emotional components. The emotions—lust, greed, fear (especially of death), love, care, trust, despair, and ecstasy—provide the sentimental substructure of society. Being, in the existential sense outlined by Heidegger (1949), is recognized by a standing out, of an appearance in the world in relation to something. *Dasein* is being in the world (literally being there), how man relates to the objects in his world. One fundamental mode of existence is one dominated by *feeling.* The human being is always feeling, i.e., he is always sentient and always experiences *some* mood. This experience sets him apart from the world of objects (although he may invest a feeling in them, as he may invest it in time, in his work, or in other symbolic entities). These feelings, according to existentialists, are as authentic modes of relating to the world as are rational-cognitive modes, and they are a primary and fundamental source of social knowledge (cf. Cooley, 1926, and Roszak, 1969, esp. Chapter 8). Sociologically, of course, there are no "pure emotions," or primordial moods or feelings; they are always channeled by social learning through the filter of culture. What is considered proper and adequate feeling is determined by conventions which are deeply rooted in the prime symbol system of language (cf. Borque and Back, 1971, and the interesting but inchoate, Mary Douglas, 1970).

Nevertheless, the dualistic quality of man presents a constant stress: man is both in the world in body and emotion and outside of it in the symbolic realm that society has collectively established. Man can typically react to an ambiguous situation (defined at many levels of reality) by a search for meaning in the personal or privatistic realm (e.g., suicide, flight, introspective, gnostic activities), or he can become more deeply embedded in collective social life. Societies can turn emotional resources into sentiments to be excluded, set aside, privatized, or forced into secret places and odd cults (hippies, Rosecrucians, Occultists, etc., cf. Tiryakian, 1971). In so doing, they exemplify forces that by advancing rationality create an evermore "abstract society" (Zijderveld, 1971). Or, on the other hand, societies may attempt to accommodate to the demands placed upon them by the rise of movements, proto-political disorders, and new forms of crime and violence: they may thus adopt to new forms of political behavior rather than dismiss them as "irrational," "insane," or "unpatriotic." Existential sociology has a pronounced capacity to richly depict the modes of sentiment underlying social structure . Therefore, it provides an important perspective for the study of social order and/or change.

The Body[14]

In social science literature, the central importance of the self in motivating and organizing social activity in situations is emphasized. However, it is seldom systematically and conceptually linked with the body. In a more general sense, it can be said that the self often seems to float unanchored in space, quite apart from a physical locus.[15] This idealist conception is perhaps a residue of the often reified historic mind-body dichotomy: the body has been given over to the natural and biological sciences (and medicine), while the social sciences have often seized upon the self-conception as an aspect of mind.

Speaking in the most general terms, the body and its associated symbols are important in patterning interaction, in creating social options, as an aspect of the generalized self-image which can be differentially integrated with the body image at given points in time. A person may define himself as disattached from his body, or find his locus of feeling in objects, other people, or in a diffuse anxious non-place and as a location for the reception of stimuli. The self is a source of integration and synthesis of a variety of stimuli interpreted and acted upon by the person and others, and it derives a significant portion of its information from the body.

A key and significant development in the understanding of the body introduced by existentialist thinkers is to turn from generalized and global descriptions of "the body" into discussions of the phenomenologically given fact that there is concrete only a given person's body in the world: *my body* (Schlider, 1950). Being is always being-in-the-body: mine, yours, ours, theirs; never, in any case, purely and simply organism or body as such. The spatial and temporal location of the body is precisely the locus of definitions and meanings. A key concept in this respect is *intentionality*, or the intention or project (plan) of the actor on the basis of which the world becomes meaningful. It follows that holistic social forms such as "bureaucracy," "university," "generation," "politics," will not be perceived nor defined uniformly. Like "society," "body" is fictive and exists initially only in the *concrete*, apparent and real. In this scheme, subject and object are merged in the attitude of natural life (the assumption of everyday life) which is in important ways shaped by the projects and intentions of others. That is, the body exists *intersubjectively* (Sartre, 1953:297–298).

But the body, as my body, is not merely a congeries of stimuli, an aggregate of parts, or discretely activated neurons, it is an *image* as conscious and present (Schlider, 1950; Bruch, 1957). The body image is the organization of action—it is not the body which is seen as moving, but the image of the body. "The part does not act or move because it is a part of the body; as it moves, it becomes a part of the body image" (Schlider, 1950). The body, then, cannot be an object, for it is the means by which objects are constructed. The body is of course, open to the world, and can be conceived as contributing visceral, tactile, and visual information which influences and enters into the activities of the self. The body as present source is mediated by the self as a historical, conscious, collection of past memories and anticipations of the future, and as an intersubjective construction.

Goffman exemplifies one linkage of self and body. In Goffman's paradigm of the body/self constellation, the self is an overall regulator while the body is a domain of self-awareness, a source of self-esteem, and a field for maintenance of appearances. The focus of Goffmanical analysis is continuously with *self* as a ritual object, protected, masked, cloaked, and suffused with symbols. The body, being subsumed under a culturally created network of symbols, is merely (in his scheme) a cultural conveyor of the symbols of self, and a means for extracting deference from others. Goffman claims verbal expression is the most salient channel of communication, ruling the nonverbal codes (the "body language" of posture, gesture, and expression, especially the face), i.e., people attend most to verbal codes in social interaction. On the other hand, most people are aware of the primacy of verbal information and are most capable of controlling this source —this heightens the importance of non-verbal signs and symbols. The information game that is social interaction for Goffman is carried on primarily by means of tokens or *sign-vehicles* that represent ways of conveying messages to others making a claim to identity and self-hood. If the claim is honored by others, a negotiated consensus may be established.

Miscellaneous delicts, slips of the tongue, flooding out (embarrassment), stumbling, or profanation of the body by others are sources of potential violations of the self. Body is the physical frame on which are displayed sign-vehicles (clothes, cosmetics, hair-dos, shoes, hats), a culturally defined object of worth, a channel of communication. Goffman (1963a) elaborated his concern with body in later work on the potentially stigmatizing results of revealed bodily based errors or faults (missing limbs, scars, colostomy, ilostomy, blindness).

The Self

The self in existential analysis, as we have seen, is not easily separated from the body and from intersubjective definitions. We can, however, begin with MacLeod's definitions of the phenomenological method:

By the phenomenological method is meant the systematic attempt to observe and describe in all its essential characteristics the world of phenomena as it is presented to us. It involves the adaptation of what might be called disciplined naivete. It requires the deliberate suspension of all explicit and implicit assumptions e.g., as to the existing stimulus or underlying mechanism, which might bias our observation. The phenomenological question is simply, "What is there?" Without regard to why, whence, or wherefore. (In Tagiuri and Petrillo, 1958:34)

Phenomenological analysis of the self is concerned with the perceived structures of relationships in which the person sees himself as embedded.
The self exists in situations where it is intertwined with sentiments and feelings—the existential self is a sentient self. It is further an intentional self, rooted in interpersonal acts, and having a degree of significance derived from types of relationality to others. The self in a situation is open physically and symbolically to new possibilities; it is a congeries of unfolding, open possibilities.

In our *existential model of the self*, then, there is a supposition that the ontological tendency, the primary movement, is a forward-striving, future-oriented unfolding (remembering that existential being is a becoming). Becoming is not random or due to chance factors solely but the resultant of a) the *self's possibilities* (the "real me" is not tangible but neither is it nonexistent—it is a set of potentialities) and b) *objective environmental circumstances*. The ultimate meaning of the self's becoming, of what a given individual existence signifies, cannot be determined until the self has exhausted all its possibilities. In existential thought this is often taken to be death—death is viewed as the possibility that ends all possibilities since with death no further becoming in this world is possible.(Tiryakian, 1968:79)

Modern social change is perhaps in a very fundamental way revealed by the modes of relating to the world through language and what is defined as authentic and inauthentic communication from the self (Manning and Fabrega, forthcoming). One can in discourse attempt to relate to others through his feelings, and thus use subjectively loaded language; he will communicate to others feelings and moods (Borque and Back, 1971). He may, on the other hand, choose to communicate in the impersonal language of science, or of abstraction. The socialization pattern in western societies creates distinctions between private and public feelings, opinions and behaviors. The growth in societal scale, the bureaucratically organized organizations which dominate it, the impersonal relations so fundamental to commerce (money being the epitome of impersonal or abstracted communication), are conditions contributing to an increase in public language and therefore to increased probability of inauthentic selfhood.

Observers of youthful "counter cultures" suggest that the growing sense of inability to express true feelings, or that age and generational differences impede authentic communication, is a root cause of large numbers of the young's rejection of standard language, their search for new symbols, the flight to new patterns of private communication possible with drugs (Reich, 1970; Roszak, 1969).

If a person invests himself in objects, material objects being the principal temptation in this society, he will be in danger of giving the reality of himself to things outside. Analogously, if he sees himself exclusively through his work, or his role within a bureaucratic structure (for which great pressures exist in this society), he decreases his potential openness to new experiences, to modification and personal change. It is a positive enjoyment and seeking after change, flux, and new experience that Keniston (1971) and Lifton (1970) see as characteristic of student radicals. Personal relationships which broaden human experience, e.g., drugs, happenings, art, music, and drama, are also capable of expanding the possibilities of being. This existential proposition provides Matza (1969), drawing on the earlier work of Becker (1963, 1967), with a basis for a sensitive thematic analysis of the meanings of marijuana use.

The Situation

Although the concept of situation has been widely used in social psychology, it has yet to be given an adequate definition (Cottrell, 1942; Volkart, 1951; Znaniecki, 1952; Lewin, 1951; Stebbins, 1967; Ball, 1972). This concept has been employed in divergent ways.[16] Being in the world, for existentialists following Sartre, involves an awareness of being in that particular place, time, and concrete situation—a situation is always *my* situation, *your* situation, or the situation of *some* person. Insofar as one is aware of being in the world he is aware that others perceive him; awareness of action is identical with awareness of himself as an object for the attention of others. A situation is thus both an awareness of a mode of action and an evaluation of that mode. Phenomenologists influenced by Husserl and Schutz place considerably more emphasis upon the importance of the "natural attitude" of persons in the everyday world. Collectively, people share the *natural attitude:* "Socially-sanctioned-facts-of-life-that-any-bona-fide-member-of-society-knows" (Garfinkel, 1967:76). When taking the natural attitude, one assumes that men take the world as given out there, and that they do not question or critically examine the nature of that world (Schutz, 1962).

In both of these conceptualizations, the notion that the actor's *intentions* and definitions are primary is shared, and in addition, there is an acceptance of the importance of others, and information by which the action possibilities of a situation are defined, or against which it is seen as standing out. A general outline of elements of the situation would thus include *information* recognized from the actor's point of view (e.g., social and physical objects, knowledge of internal states and feelings), an *interpretative framework* (arising from the actor's biography and including knowledge of typical occurrences) and a set of *expectations* or possibilities for the behavior of self and other. The definition of the situation is in some important way the situation itself.

However, the persistent question involves *delineating situations;* marking boundaries in such a way that situations can be distinguished one from another and can be analytically compared. This is the task of setting out the phenomenological boundaries of situations. One approach has been to attempt to identify the entry and exit behavior of persons entering associations, another has been based on the study of disruptions of situations. Sherri Cavan (1966) illustrates the ways in which the structure of bar-based conversations is created and honored. Conversations in bars are often initiated with entrance ceremonies, even though bar patrons are generally defined as being "open" to approach and conversation unless they specifically indicate the contrary. Since all persons are defined as substantially open, one may face difficulty in extracting oneself from conversations. Being sensitive to this implicit rule, patrons may interpret long pauses in conversations as an indication that one of the parties should or will leave the interactional field. However, leaving the situation, or terminating the interaction, is signaled, allowing each participant to save face. This face-saving ritual of leave-taking may be non-verbal, such as merely gathering up belongings (cigarettes, change, matches, etc.), silently turning away, or offering a curt nod. The other will busy himself in other activities thus signaling his agreement to the action. Even a brief leaving will be read as terminating the encounter unless it is openly declared to be an exception. And, "Once the other has returned to the spatial proximity the two share, any further talk between them requires the same ceremonial opening that began the initial conversation" (Cavan, 1966:56). These non-verbal and verbal exchanges are not so much a part of the situation as they can be said to constitute a definition of the situation. The unstated assumptions that govern interaction in the situation are assumed to be known as matters of course—as Cavan points out, only when an exception might be inferred does one have to explicitly counter it ("I'll be right back . . ."). On the other hand, *violations* have been seen by others as the most revealing clue to unstated rules. Goffman (1967) provides exquisite examples of breaches of an unstated situational order in his work on embarrassment, face-work, cooling out the mark, and stigmatization. Situational order is indicated by the reactions of members to the loss of poise of a fellow by say, a slip of the tongue, a drool, a stumble, or spilling food. They attempt to repair the scene by pauses, by downcast eyes, by avoidance of glances, by shifting positions, by accepting apologies. The "moral wholeness" of both the one in error and those on whom the error was committed is thus restored.

Each of the two approaches illustrated above has merit and contains important insights useful in situational analyses. A situational analysis, it would seem, should attend to *boundaries* of situations, *disruptions* of everyday expectations, and the *internal characteristics* or elements of the situation (Watson, 1958).

In a field study, the author and Horacio Fabrega Jr. attempted to delineate analytic dimensions of illness episodes among ladino families in the highlands of Chiapas, Mexico.[17] Interviewers asked respondents who were members of a panel of families from whom base-line health status information had been elicited to describe all illnesses that had been experienced by any member of the family over the previous two-week period. Included in the protocol were the following dimensions of illness episodes a) *content* of the episode (definitions of ego and significant alters of the meaning of the episode) b) *symptoms* (elicited by a standard "systems review") c) *discomfort* (duration, rate of onset, level of discomfort) d) *behavioral changes* (altered function in familial, occupational, or leisure roles) e) types of *help-seeking*, options and costs. An *illness graph* was employed to codify responses; categories or parameters of the dimensions (a–e above) formed rows while each day of the two weeks preceding the day of the interview formed a column. The presence of data in any given parameter, e.g. cough under dimension b, symptoms, was entered in the graph from the day of onset until the termination date. The graph thus provides data on the boundaries of the episode, in both objective terms (days) and in subjective terms (the marking of onset and termination of the episode), and on the analytic dimensions of the episode (a–e above). This approach allows the fine-grained depiction of a situation that is suffused with moods and sentiments, intimately involves bodily states and self-definitions, and the response of social groups to variably defined "crisis events."

Other "crisis" situations can be viewed as alterations of a taken-for-granted world. The drama or artistic experiences, through the pairing of objects in the everyday world with a larger symbol system (based on the signified-signifier relationship) materialize a new and creative experience. The study of the common experiences of a social segment, such as listening to rock music, provides a field for analysis of the situation as the self and body are infused with moods.

The Leveling of Society

A theme present in a number of existentialist writers, and subsequently adopted by sociologists, is the "leveling" or massification argument. Previous ages and times were characterized by a homogenous social structure, bound together by shared meanings, collective representations of those meanings, clearly and unambiguously defined social relations and roles, and an integrated cosmology. In contrast, complex, differentiated societies are governed by distance between groups, growing equality, heterogeneous bases of integration (organic solidarity), fractionated symbolic worlds, ambiguity of roles and relationships marked by anonymity, amorality, and ingenuousity. In contrast to the Durkheimian thesis which sees the growth of individuality through organic solidarity as a positive feature (although riddled with the paradox of the potential for anomie or dérèglement), existentialists from Kierkegaard and Ortega y Gassett, through such modern writers as Schelsky, Luckmann, and Zijderveld, see the leveling process as a source of deindividuation and deracination.

The governing rule of modern society is abstraction; the rule of the public over the person; of the state through the technological mechanism over the group; of the escalation of the egalitarian spirit which by making everyone a member only of the larger mass, makes everyone no one. The increase in size in the society makes closeness to the realms of political decision-making and power more problematic; simultaneously, however, these forces increasingly impinge on the daily life of the person. Institutions, as they ramify in the extensiveness and intensiveness of their involvement in the lives of people (think of the very real escalation in power and force of the police, of the welfare system, and of the schools in the last five to ten years), can no longer command the loyalty of participants. The machinations of large bureaucracies, distant, almost imaginary in their power, nevertheless deeply affect the lives of modern man in pervasive and subtle ways. In fact, the very subtlety of institutional influence, those influences that produce the "organizational man," may explain the degree of insidious control they possess. As institutions grow in power and authority, and become at the same time less resilient and subject to change, the person sees them as looming further in the distance, disconnected from his experiences and needs.

Nowhere is this more clearly illustrated than in politics. As meanings become more diverse, competition to establish meanings ensues, and a degree of disconnectedness becomes almost inevitable. Political phenomenon can be seen as intrinsically absurd or meaningless: very few political acts have clear, immediate, measurable meanings and fewer still have consequences which can be traced to a single causal sequence or event. Distant, complex, diffuse, and continuous events such as wars, elections, the passage of bills through Congress, the meaning of integration, riots, police actions, are ambiguous. They have the property of *expressive action*: they are captured by symbols, the intent of which is to condense and focus interest by means of limited symbols on a few of the possible themes. From these symbols, people may construct meanings relevant to their own concrete existence: political symbols provide a screen in which meanings may be projected, ambivalences dissolved or created, reassurances gained or lost, and a reading taken on the status of a given group in a social-moral hierarchy (cf. Klapp, 1968). Politics in an abstract society involves the process of creating, projecting, and maintaining images; as such it is as much a matter of appearances as it is a matter of accomplishments.

Political groups intent upon the creation and maintenance of power seek to systematically construct those political meanings that will lead, or constrain, a populace to espouse slogans containing a set from among an available group of symbols. In this way, they attempt to create a hegemony of meanings representing consistent, consensual, political values. They may in addition draw upon rituals and myths to solidify the belief that as a political group they represent the dominant ideology. In modern society, political *leaders* evolve rhetorics, or symbolic metaphors, which induce a following: the rhetoric serves to bind together leader and led in a common definition of the political situation. The *audience*, in turn, enters into an implicit dramatic contract with politicians who will represent and symbolize their political position, and to work for its more general acceptance in the society. The politician serves, by adopting a line or rhetoric, by inducing followers to espouse it and by working for its diffusion and legitimation, to shape the political interests in society. Some social themes, e.g., the morality of integration, the immorality of the "hippies," and the "exploitation of women," are thus singled out, isolated, underscored, and dramatized. We can see that in an abstract society with fractionated meanings and competition over the control of the core of moral values, politics can no longer be seen as a reflection of interest groups in society. Rather, politics can more fruitfully be seen as a process which *creates interests* (cf. Edelman, 1963, 1971; Merelman, 1969).

An important implication of this discursus on politics is that it provides evidence for the thesis that the modern world is increasingly ruled by *imagery* and abstraction, social distance, and problematic meanings. Mass images, many of them politically sponsored meanings, tend to dedifferentiate and radically equalize experience (Jerzy Kosinski's books, 1968, 1971, are shocking literary illustrations of the dehumanizing effect of images, especially those created by the mass media). Existentialists recognized the levelling effect of the public language and imagery in the early nineteenth century (Nietzsche, Dostoevsky, Kierkegaard); they now gather adherents as reality grows to meet the most pessimistic of their predictions.

Structural Analysis

There is considerable disagreement among the existential sociologists concerning the most appropriate mode of structural analysis. On the one hand, linguistic analysts among the ethnomethodologists (Garfinkel, Sacks, Turner, Blum) are concerned with *micro-structures* of order: the ethnography of situations and the conditions under which people attribute order or disorder to events. A focus is micro-order as constructed in experimental situations, often coupled with a search for philosophic and linguistic rules, especially "deep rules of structure," accounting for orderly conversations (Cicourel, 1968). Throughout there is a concern with *structure* as apperceived in language use and in situations. In the linguistic segment of ethnomethodology, the concern has been with discovering those evolving rules and patterns of structure that make it possible for people to conduct conversations, to open and close them, to communicate messages, to heal breaches in the conversation and the like.

Another theoretic approach to structural analysis has adopted a Durkheimian posture, drawing on the writings of the *L'Aneé Sociologique* group (Durkheim, Mauss, Hubert, Hertz). Many contemporary anthropologists see the task of structural analysis as linking the perceptual structures of the mind with the symbolic systems of a society or group. In this fashion, they seek to bridge the phenomenological concern with the mode of relating and perceiving the world with traditional sociological and anthropological concern with elucidating patterns of symbols. The extent to which this mode of analysis can be seen as "existential" hinges upon the degree to which one sees the mind as having distinctive or identifiable properties, such as a binary decision making structure which works on the basis of perceived contrasts and polarity as a property conferred on the world by these innate mental operations. In Levi-Strauss, Leach, Beidelman, and Tiryakian, the above-mentioned linkage *is* assumed, and the connection between the existential model of analysis, focusing on the modes of experiencing the world as given, and objectifying the world in that fashion are seen as continuous and consistent. Let us illustrate this mode of analysis, keeping mindful that it is a very controversial approach to anthropological data, rejected by many as a violation of existential assumptions and tenets. The claim is that it reduces the variations in concrete social structures into mere polarities and contradictions rather than specific processes, situations, or sequences of structures.

In Durkheim's work there are a number of explicated and important *dualities: sacred* and *profane; body* and *soul; practice* and *theory; individual* and *society; mechanical* and *organic* solidarity. These poles are seen as being a product of the group-nature of social life; that life is always lived in groups having divisions (clans, phatries, moeities), superordination and subordination. The basis of the logical system of classification in primitive groups is the internal division of group life; its logic supplied the logic for ordering the plant, animal, and transcendent world. The existence of the mediating force of the transcendent world, under which the polarities were subsumed, allowed life to proceed. In the concept *homo duplex*, man as a unique embodied being, as well as a social product owing social existence to the collectivity, there is a tension, a source of social change and growth. Man, as was later developed by Jaspers, is confronted with the *antinomies* of existence, his *rationality* (his socially constructed capacity for rule-governed action and thought) and his *irrationality* or subjectivity.

We may note the tension between society (the collective representation) and body, the contradiction that is mediated by the self. The tension which is felt between these systems of meaning is resolved in one fashion by privatistic blurring of self-other obligations (or body-self-obligations) in the use of marijuana. Marijuana use represents symbolically the shifting of modalities of experience — the alteration of the perception of the locus of control as being "within" to seeing it as being "without." There is a close fit between the symbols, meanings, and experiences associated with the effects of these drugs and the everyday experiences sought by many young persons. In the situation of use, the separation of the "mind" and the "body" are not taken as normal, but a state to be avoided, and a sense of concrete wholeness is sought. It is this sense of wholeness that is the essence of the experience of being high. The experience of smoking casts one's self with others "out there," while the self retains a sense of partial being in the body. It is a form of socially constructed madness. It diffuses the self, but it re-creates it in the context of other trusting selves. When this superordinate self-consciousness appears, there is nothing (as Laing points out) between *it* and *me* or *us* and *them*; there is no is, only being. Being in this submerged moody situation actualizes feelings as the locus of social bonding. As such, the ties of the marijuana user to other users are above all found in the situation of use itself. The prime experience is the experience of use itself, where instead of having meanings and roles ascribed by others in an impersonal fashion, the *doing is being.*

COMMENT

This review is not an attempt at a comprehensive coverage of existential sociology. It is rather a selective review of the challenge that existential sociology represents to the dominant vision of society and man incorporated in absolutistic social theory. The word, "challenge," issuing from the vocabulary of a language of conflict, may be excessive; perhaps, it is better seen as an extension or reformulation of the contribution that existential sociology can make to the modification of conventional models of society and man. A few observations will serve as a concluding comment rather than a summary; a summary would be pretentious and premature.

The contribution an existential approach can make to conventional theory is most importantly epitomized by the nature of its conception of findings, method, and theory. Whereas other theories attempt to discover truth in the world and evaluate their findings by means of *objective standards,* or canons of agreement among men as to the correspondence between a statement and the facts as they appear in the world, existential thinkers locate the truth of a statement in a less abstract and more troublesome locus. It is their contention that truth emerges from a relationship. A person is always *in the world* and relating to it in a given fashion. The world stretches out for him from a given point (his body) in time and space. In the act of seeing, choosing to cast attention on an object, consciousness shifts from one's self to the other, and thus one chooses a new mode of relating to the world. Tiryakian succinctly summarizes the subject-object (knowing and the known) problem of existential thought and explains how it departs from the rational model in which other social theory is cast:

> The subject-object cleavage, essential to traditional rationalism, is incompatible with an existential approach: existence literally refers to a state of standing out, or emerging . . . and applied to man, human existence suggests a coming-out, a presentation of the individual to the world and the world to man. An implication of this perspective is that if the thinking process rests fundamentally upon the existence of the thinker, then no matter how "objective" the philosopher may think he is, no matter how personally detached he seeks to be from the objects of his knowledge, there will always be an existential nexus between the self and its objects. . . . Insofar as the image of man is not subordinated to one single factor, such as man's rationality, it means that other facets hitherto not stressed in the mainstream of the philosophical tradition will have to be taken into account in dealing with existence. (1962:75–76)

Although the criteria of rational theory may be applied to existential theories, at least one implication of this characteristic of existential theories is that *they must reflect in a meaningful sense the perspective of a significant segment of the social world.* Theory and the everyday life of the person, as he views it, must come into a new relationship in which they are bound together by a sense of verisimilitude and correspondence of experience and abstraction. The strength of the existential approach is that it attempts to be "reflexive": It should reflect in its working and in its assumptions a deepened self-understanding on the part of the theorist as well as those to whom he wishes to communicate or understand, and should launch its attempt at understanding from a position that is self-informed and self-aware (cf. Habermas, 1970).

NOTES

1. I appreciate the pointed and helpful critiques of the paper made by friends and colleagues, especially Jack Douglas, Horacio Fabrega Jr., and David Sallach. I would also like to thank those who helped me to see that all of life's situations are not mere data, nor are they necessarily enhanced as a result of being viewed through sociological prisms.

2. The focus has grown from a set of review articles e.g., Tiryakian (1962, 1965, 1968), Psathas (1968), Douglas (1970b) and by Denzin, Wilson, and Wieder and Zimmerman in Douglas, (1970b), and Sallach, 1971. The empirical research has been gathered in such collections of original work as Douglas, 1970a, 1970b, and forthcoming; Lyman and Scott, 1970; Sudnow, 1972, Scott and Douglas, 1972; and Psathas, 1973. The availability of materials is attested to by the above listing of articles, books, and collections. In addition, the ASA since at least 1967 has had at least one ethnomethodology section; seminars and sections have appeared at regional meetings as well.

3. European Neo-Marxists (Lukacs, Marcuse, Lichtheim, Althusser, Lefebvre, Habermas and Gramsci) and Third World Marxists (Debray, Fanon, Mao, Che Guevara) continue to influence American sociology. It has been suggested (David Sallach, personal communication) that the similarities between the pattern of development and spread of Marxism and existentialism are striking. The involvement and interconnections between Marxism, phenomenology, and existentialism cannot be traced here. There are shared sources of influence, e.g., Kierkegaard, Dostoevsky, Heidegger, Husserl, and modern thinkers such as Merleau-Ponty and Sartre are, or have been, Marxists. See Hughes, 1958 and 1969; Laing and Cooper, 1964; Desan, 1966; Thody, 1960; Sallach, 1972. There have been additional influences on existential sociology from linguists and ordinary language philosophers such as Wittgenstein, Austin, and Chomsky; from literary critics such as Kenneth Burke and from within sociology it has drawn on Mannheim, Simmel, Weber, and to a lesser degree on Vierkant, Gurvitch, Mauss, Durkheim, and W. I. Thomas.

4. See the fascinating intellectual autobiography of Talcott Parsons (1970) for a discussion of this post-war ferment at Harvard.

5. The principal weaknesses of the Parsonian model (as representative of a general style and type of theorizing) were identified as 1) its tendency to opt for an *equilibrium* or homeostatic model of society which implicitly supported the *status quo*; 2) its corollary inability to account for radical, disruptive, or total system changes; 3) its *"oversocialized"* *conception of man,* who in the strongest terms of criticism was seen as a submissive puppet who had internalized the dominant value system, was in passive agreement with the authority structure of society, and lacked personal autonomy; 4) its assumption that society was an *integrated* moral unit; 5) its almost exclusive emphasis on *moral rules* and values as the basis for social order which overlooked the importance of compromise, corruption, conflict, and situational negotiation and power employed for purposes of control; 6) its misuse of the biological metaphor.

6. Several works written by philosophers, psychiatrists, and anthropologists began to attract attention and were discussed by sociologists in articles and reviews. The psychiatric work interested sociologists, students of mental illness (Scheff, Goffman, Lemert), and there is evidence of an appreciation of sociological work in psychiatrist R. D. Laing's writing (1960, 1965, 1970); Foucault's *Madness and Civilization* (1967) and the work of Binswanger, (1967), May, Angell, and Ellenberger starkly and dramatically challenged the traditional, i.e., psychoanalytic and biologistic, framework for the study of mental illness. Also indicative of new intellectual ferment in psychiatry was the gathering of a group of insightful and talented men around Erik Erikson at Harvard. The "psychohistory group," including David Riesman, Robert J. Lifton, Kenneth Keniston, and Robert Coles, contributed a number of articles and monographs, most notably Keniston's (1966, 1968) and Erikson's work on the young which became the paradigm for a series of continuing studies by sociologists, psychiatrists, and psychologists. New attention was also turned toward anthropology as a result of the sheer brilliance of Levi-Strauss in *Structural Anthropology* (1963), *The Elementary Structures of Kinship* (1969), *The Raw and the Cooked* (1969), *Tristes Tropiques* (1963), and *The Savage Mind* (1966). A continuing influence was philosopher Thomas Kuhn's *The Structure of Scientific Revolutions* (1962).

7. Jack Douglas (personal communication) supports this view of the emergence of phenomenology as a kind of native movement—his coming to the position he articulated in *The Social Meanings of Suicide* came prior to reading extensively in Schutz or Husserl, and he suggests this was true also of others. It is unlikely that many of those presently identified with existential or phenomenological sociology were in fact "converted" in the dramatic fashion portrayed by Heeren and Poss's caricature (1971); it was, as in my case, more a "drift" which later became intellectualized and formalized through reading and conversations. Friendships and informal contacts with convivial people at meetings and the like may account for more modification in ideas than the published works.

8. Jack Douglas (1970:43) argues that there is no single version of reality in American

society which confronts people i.e., ". . . this society is still so pluralistic that there cannot be the degree of "objectivation" of common sense demanded by their theory." Clearly, there is a dominant and conventional version of reality; all Douglas indicates here is the growing number of *alternatives* to the dominant canopy of meaning.

9. More than a philosophic point, the view one takes of reality has very real implications for research. For example, if one adopts the dominant meaning system (and in addition assumes that the law reflects it in a very direct fashion), then one will investigate phenomena defined by the law as illegal, e.g., drug use (or adopt the public's term, "drug abuse") and ask why it is that people come to violate the known, normative structures of dominant society. For convenience or for this previous assumption, the researcher might in turn adopt the record-keeping systems and statistics used by control agencies to maintain the dominant symbolic world. (The argument concerning the inadequacy of official statistics is well developed and articulated in the following: Douglas (1967, 1970, 1971), and Cicourel (1968). In addition, Nanette Davis is now engaged in research which demonstrates the alternative modes of obtaining a service, only one form of which is officially sanctioned, thus showing the "sample" nature of all official statistics.) The official research strategy, as Lindesmith (1965) and Goode (1970) have so clearly established by their own careful evaluation of drug research, leads the investigator to very different conclusions than if he assumes that drug use represents an *alternative reality* which competes with the conventional control system's meanings and interpretations of events. This alternative strategy begins from presuppositions at variance from the conventional meanings and represents in many ways an oppositional ideological framework. From a broader perspective, it can be said that science itself provides a *means of control* in a technocratic society (Gouldner, 1966). The information generated by scientific research, unintended or intended, may be used to make "adjustments" in the control system to enable continued dominance of the "welfare state." Nothing demonstrates more dramatically this control adjustment property of science that the recent series of reports by the Warren Commission, Coroner Commission, the President's Crime Commission (see Douglas, 1971) and the Violence Commission (Skolnick, 1970). When connected with the assumptions of conventional theory that the state is synonymous with the people, the people with the dominant value system, and the dominant value system with the greatest good for the greatest number, the control functions of science are rather starkly apparent to any observer.

10. I have developed this agreement in a forthcoming paper (with H. Fabrega Jr.), "Analytic Induction as a Sociological Methodology."

11. I am sharply truncating the arguments of Gouldner (1970). Interested readers should read *Crisis*, especially Part IV. It is entirely possible that some of the persons discussed as representatives of existential thinking in sociology were affected by either or both of these "forces." It is an empirical question which might be addressed along the lines of Reynolds and Vaughn's studies of symbolic interactionism. I appreciate Jack Douglas's pointing out to me the limits of an entirely "subjectivistic" interpretation of alterations in dominant idea systems.

12. The most significant contributions of Parsonian theory are the comparative and historical works of Levy, (1949, 1952, 1966), Bellah (1957), Eisenstadt (1956,1963) Apter (1965), Merton (1966), and Parsons (with collaborators) (1937, 1951, 1954, 1955, 1956, 1961, 1966, 1969a, 1969b). Although Parsons' own essays could be described as "middle-range theory" following Merton's suggestion, little codification of empirical practices has issued from Parsons, his students, or advocates.

13. Parsons' influence on students and associates is unquestionable, and he has encouraged collaborators and associates to test and expand his ideas. However, his own research, i.e., on the role of the physician, the classroom as an educational system, and the higher educational system, led to empirically grounded essays rather than "theory-testing" or "hypothesis-testing" work in which model the research and writing is cast. (cf. Parsons, 1970). General usage of the scheme, as in Lipset's *The First New Nation* or in references cited in footnote 12, is metaphorical or is used as a compendium of sensitizing concepts. Specific attempts to test have been few and the results equivocal, e.g., Lois Dean, "The Pattern-Variables: Some Empirical Operations," *American Sociological Review*, 26 (1961), 80–90, and Peter M. Blau, "Operationalizing a Conceptual Scheme: The Universalism-Particularism Pattern-Variable Scheme," *American Sociological Review*, 27 (1962), 159–69.

14. Some of this material is summarized from a series of papers addressed to the variable connections between self and body: Manning and Fabrega, 1972a.

15. Traditional features of the self need to be systematically related to the perceptions

that actors have of the conditions of their bodies. Conceptual links must be established between the person's self-concept, which can be described as a socio-psychological entity, to his body conceived of as a physical entity. Some important developments in the conceptualization of the body are found in anthropological literature (cf. Mary Douglas, 1970, the work of Birdwhistell, Hertz, and Turner); however, this work in the Durkheimian tradition sees the body almost entirely as a collectively symbolized entity, or solely as the locus of feelings and the source of one's individuality. Psychological studies that include conceptualizations of the body (i.e., body image, body boundary perception, etc.) typically do not connect this material analytically with interactional processes. On the other hand, social psychological and psychiatric literature which deals with interaction seldom incorporates the body as an integral feature. (Exceptions are the existential analysts such as Binswanger in May, Angell and Ellenberger, and Goffman, discussed below). The latter generalization applies specifically to G. H. Mead, for although he spoke of the integration of mind and body, he failed to explicate and introduce this into the analysis of social conduct. In Watsonian behaviorism, Mead seemed intent upon establishing the dominance and importance of mind in social interaction. It is this attempt that has given subsequent social psychology a disembodied quality (cf. Manning and Fabrega, 1972a).

16. A number of anthropologists have made exciting use of situational analyses, cf. Frake, 1964; Barth, 1965; Hughes, 1968; Epstein, 1967; and Bailey, 1968.

17. This research was supported by NIMH grant MH 21430-01, 1 Roe MSM; a Biomedical Research Fund Grant from Michigan State University and a grant from the Office of International Programs, Michigan State University. The data are reported in part in Manning and Fabrega, forthcoming.

REFERENCES

Aldridge, John W. *In the Country of the Young*. New York: Harper & Row, 1971.

Apter, David. *The Politics of Modernization*. Chicago: University of Chicago Press, 1965.

Back, Kurt W., and Thomas Pettigrew. "Sociology in the Desegregation Process: Its Use and Disuse," in Thomas Pettigrew, ed., *Racially Separate or Equal?* New York: McGraw-Hill, 1971.

Bailey, Frederick G. *Strategems and Spoils*. New York: Shocken, 1968.

Ball, D. W. "The 'Definition of the Situation': Some Theoretical and Methodological Consequences of Taking W. I. Thomas Seriously," *Journal for the Theory of Social Behavior*, 2 (1972), 61–82.

Barrett, William. *Irrational Man*. New York: Doubleday, 1958.

Barth, Frederick. *Political Leadership Among the Swat Pathans*. London: Athlone, 1965.

Becker, Howard S. "Becoming a Marijuana User," in Howard S. Becker, *Outsiders*. New York: Free Press, 1963.

————. "History, Culture and Subjective Experience: An Exploration of the Social Bases of Drug Induced Experiences," *Journal of Health and Social Behavior*, 8 (September 1967), 163–76.

Bellah, Robert. *Tokugawa Religion*. Glencoe, Ill.: Free Press, 1957.

Berger, Peter. *Invitation to Sociology*. New York: Doubleday, 1963.

Berger, Peter, and Thomas Luckman. *The Social Construction of Reality*. Garden City, N.Y.: Doubleday, 1966.

Berger, Peter, and Stanley Pullberg. "Reification and the Sociological Critiques of Consciousness," *History and Theory*, 4 (1965), 196–211.

Berman, Marshall. "Weird but Brilliant Light on the Way We Live Now," (review of Erving Goffman, *Relations in Public*), *New York Times Book Review*, 77 (27 February 1972), 1–2, 10, 12, 14, 16, 18.

Binswanger, Ludwig. *Being in the World*. New York: Harper Torchbooks, 1967.

Birnbaum, Norman. *Toward a Critical Sociology*. New York: Oxford University Press, 1971.

Black, Max, ed. *The Social Theory of Talcott Parsons*. Englewood Cliffs, N.J.: Prentice-Hall, 1961.

Borque, L., and K. W. Back. "Language, Society and Subjective Experience," *Sociometry*, 34 (March 1971), 1–21.

Bottomore, Thomas B. "Out of This World," (review of the work of Talcott Parsons), *New York Review of Books*, 13 (6 November 1969), 34–39.

Bruch, Hilda. *The Importance of Overweight*. New York: Norton, 1957.

Cavan, Sherri. *Liquor License*. Chicago: Aldine, 1966.
Cicourel, Aaron. *Method and Measurement in Sociology*. New York: Free Press, 1964.
———. *The Social Organization of Juvenile Justice*. New York: Wiley, 1968.
Cooley, C. H. "The Roots of Social Knowledge," *American Journal of Sociology*, 32 (July 1926), 59–79.
Coser, Lewis. *The Functions of Social Conflict*. Glencoe, Ill.: Free Press, 1956.
Coser, Lewis, ed. *Continuities in the Study of Social Conflict*. New York: Free Press, 1967.
Cottrell, L. S., Jr. "The Analysis of Situational Fields in Social Psychology," *American Sociological Review*, 7 (June 1942), 370–82.
Dahrendorf, Ralf. "Out of Utopia: Toward a Reorientation of Sociological Analysis," *American Journal of Sociology*, 64 (September 1958), 115–27.
———. *Class and Class Conflict in Industrial Society*. Stanford: Stanford University Press, 1959.
———. *Essays in the Theory of Society*. Stanford: Stanford University Press, 1968.
Desan, Wilfred. *The Marxism of Jean-Paul Sartre*. Garden City, N.Y.: Doubleday, 1966.
Douglas, Jack D. *The Social Meanings of Suicide*. Princeton: Princeton University Press, 1967.
———. "Deviance and Order in a Pluralistic Society," in John McKinney and Edward Tiryakian, eds., *Theoretical Sociology: Perspectives and Developments*. New York: Appleton-Century-Crofts, 1970, pp. 367–401.
Douglas, Jack D., ed. *Deviance and Respectability*. New York: Basic Books, 1970. (a)
———. *Understanding Everyday Life*. Chicago: Aldine, 1970. (b)
———. *Crime and Justice in American Society*. Indianapolis: Bobbs-Merrill, 1971.
———. *Existential Sociology*. Forthcoming.
Douglas, Mary. *Natural Symbols*. New York: Pantheon, 1970.
Dreitzel, H. Peter, ed. *Recent Sociology, No. 2*. New York: Macmillan, 1970.
Edelman, Murray. *The Symbolic Uses of Politics*. Urbana: University of Illinois Press, 1963.
———. *Politics as Symbolic Action*. Chicago: Markham, 1971.
Eisenstadt, S. N. *From Generation to Generation*. New York: Free Press, 1956.
———. *The Political Systems of Empires*. New York: Free Press, 1963.
Epstein, A. L. ed. *The Craft of Sociology*. London: Tavistock, 1967.
Filmer, Paul, Michael Phillipson, David Silverman, and David Walsh. *New Directions in Sociological Theory*. 1972.
Foucault, Michel. *Madness and Civilization*. New York: Pantheon, 1967.
Frake, Charles. "A Structural Description of Subanum 'Religious Behavior,' " in W. Goodenough, ed., *Explorations in Cultural Anthropology*. New York: McGraw-Hill, 1964, pp. 111–29.
Friedrichs, Robert. *A Sociology of Sociology*. New York: Free Press, 1970.
Garfinkel, Harold. *Studies in Ethnomethodology*. Englewood Cliffs, N.J.: Prentice-Hall, 1967.
Garfinkel, Harold, and Harvey Sacks, eds. *Contributions in Ethnomethodology*. Bloomington: University of Indiana Press, forthcoming.
Goffman, Erving. *The Presentation of Self in Everyday Life*. Garden City, N.Y.: Doubleday, 1959.
———. *Asylums*. Garden City, N.Y.: Doubleday, 1961. (a)
———. *Encounters*. Indianapolis: Bobbs-Merrill, 1961. (b)
———. *Stigma*. Englewood Cliffs, N.J.: Prentice-Hall, 1963. (a)
———. *Behavior in Public Places*. New York: Free Press, 1963. (b)
———. *Interaction Ritual*. Chicago: Aldine, 1967.
———. *Strategic Interaction*. Philadelphia: University of Pennsylvania Press, 1970.
———. *Relations in Public*. New York: Basic Books, 1971.
Goode, E. "Marijuana and Politics of Reality," *Journal of Health and Social Behavior*, 10 (June 1969), 83–94.
———. *The Marijuana Smokers*. New York: Basic Books, 1970.
Gouldner, Alvin W. "The Sociologist as Partisan: Sociology and the Welfare State," *American Sociologist*, 3 (May 1966), 103–16.
———. *The Coming Crisis in Western Sociology*. New York: Basic Books, 1970.
Habermas, Jurgen. *Toward a Rational Society*. Boston: Beacon Press, 1970.
Heeren, J., and B. Poss. "'Becoming a Reality Constructionist: An Unexplored Area of the Sociology of Sociology," *American Sociologist*, 6 (May 1971), 158–60.
Heidegger, Martin. *Existence and Being*. New York: Regnery, 1949.

Horowitz, I. L. "Consensus, Conflict, Co-operation: A Sociological Inventory," *Social Forces*, 41 (December 1962), 177–88.

Horton, John. "The Dehumanization of Anomie and Alienation," *British Journal of Sociology*, 15 (December 1964), 283–300.

———. "Order and Conflict Theories of Social Problems as Competing Ideologies," *American Journal of Sociology*, 71 (May 1966), 701–13.

Hughes, Charles. "Structure, Field, and Process in Siberian Eskimo Political Behavior," in M. J. Swartz, ed., *Local-Level Politics*. Chicago: Aldine, 1968, pp. 163–89.

Hughes, H. Stuart. *Consciousness and Society*. New York: Vintage, 1958.

———. *The Obstructed Path: French Social Thought in the Years of Desperation*. New York: Harper Torchbooks, 1969.

Keniston, Kenneth. *The Uncommitted*. New York: Harcourt Brace Jovanovich, 1966.

———. *Young Radicals*. New York: Harcourt Brace Jovanovich, 1968.

———. *Youth and Dissent: The Rise of a New Opposition*. New York: Harcourt Brace Jovanovich, 1971.

Klapp, Orrin. *Symbolic Leaders: Public Dramas and Public Men*. Chicago: Aldine, 1968.

Kosinski, Jerzy. *Steps*. New York: Bantam, 1968.

———. *Being There*. New York: Harcourt Brace Jovanovich, 1971.

Kuhn, Thomas. *The Structure of Scientific Revolutions*. Chicago: University of Chicago Press, 1962.

Laing, R. D. *The Self and Others*. London: Tavistock, 1960.

———. *The Divided Self*. London: Penguin, 1965.

———. *The Politics of Experience*. New York: Ballantine, 1970.

Laing, R. D., and David Cooper. *Reason and Violence: A Decade of Sartre's Philosophy*. New York: Vintage, 1964.

Laing, R. D., David Cooper, and Aaron Esterson. *Sanity, Madness and the Family*. London: Tavistock, 1964.

Lemert, Edwin. *Human Deviance, Social Problems, and Social Control*. Englewood Cliffs, N.J.: Prentice-Hall, 1967.

Levi-Strauss, Claude. *Structural Anthropology*. Translated by C. Jacobson and B. G. Schoepf. New York: Basic Books, 1963. (a)

———. *Tristes Tropiques*. Translated and abridged by J. Russell. New York: Atheneum, 1963. (b)

———. *The Savage Mind*. Chicago: University of Chicago Press, 1966.

———. *The Elementary Structures of Kinship*. Translated by J. H. Bell and J. von Sturmer. Edited by Rodney Needham. Boston: Beacon Press, 1969. (a)

———. *The Raw and the Cooked*. Vol. 1. New York: Harper & Row, 1969. (b)

Levy, Marion J., Jr. *The Family Revolution in Modern China*. Cambridge, Mass.: Harvard University Press, 1949.

———. *The Structure of Society*. Princeton: Princeton University Press, 1952.

———. *Modernization and the Structure of Societies*. 2 vols. Princeton: Princeton University Press, 1966.

Lewin, Kurt. *A Field Theory of Social Science*. New York: Harper & Row, 1951.

Lifton, Robert J. *History and Human Survival*. New York: Random House, 1970.

Lindesmith, Alfred. *The Addict and the Law*. Bloomington: Indiana University Press, 1965.

Lockwood, David. "Some Remarks on 'The Social System,' " *British Journal of Sociology*, 7 (June 1956), 134–46.

Lyman Stan, and Marvin Scott. *A Sociology of the Absurd*. New York: Appleton-Century-Crofts, 1970.

Mannheim, Karl. *From Karl Mannheim*. Collected letters edited by Kurt Wolff. New York: Oxford University Press, 1971.

Manning, Peter K. "Analytic Induction," in Robert B. Smith, ed., *Social Science Methods: An Introduction*. New York: Free Press, forthcoming.

Manning, Peter K. and Horacio Fabrega Jr. "Analytic Induction as a Sociological Methodology." Unpublished paper. East Lansing: Michigan State University, 1972. (a)

———. "Self and Body." Unpublished paper presented to Social Science in Medicine Conference, August 1972, Elsinore, Denmark. (b)

———. "The Phenomenology of Change: The Experience of Self and Body in the Chiapas Highlands," in G. Psathas, ed., *Phenomenology and Sociology*. New York: Wiley, 1973.

Matza, David. *Delinquency and Drift*. New York: Wiley, 1964.

———. *Becoming Deviant.* Englewood, Cliffs, N.J.: Prentice-Hall, 1969.

Merelman, R. "The Dramaturgy of Politics," *Sociological Quarterly,* 10 (Spring 1969), 216–41.

Merton, Robert K. *Social Theory and Social Structure.* Rev. ed. New York: Free Press, 1966.

Mills, C. Wright. *The Sociological Imagination.* New York: Oxford University Press, 1959.

Parsons, Talcott. *The Structure of Social Action.* New York: McGraw-Hill, 1937.

———. *The Social System.* Glencoe, Ill.: Free Press, 1951.

———. *Essays in Sociological Theory.* Rev. ed. Glencoe: Free Press, 1954.

———. *Societies: Evolutionary and Comparative Perspectives.* Englewood Cliffs, N.J.: Prentice-Hall, 1966.

———. *Politics and Social Structure.* New York: Free Press, 1969. (a)

———. *Sociological Theory and Modern Society.* New York: Free Press, 1969. (b)

———. "On Building Social System Theory: A Personal History," *Daedalus,* 99 (Fall 1970), 826–81.

Parsons, Talcott, Edward A. Shils, and Robert Bales. *Working Papers in the General Theory of Action.* New York: Free Press, 1951.

Parsons, Talcott, and Robert Bales. *Family: Socialization and Interaction Processes.* Glencoe: Free Press, 1955.

Parsons, Talcott, and Neil J. Smelser. *Economy and Society.* Glencoe, Ill.: Free Press, 1956.

Parsons, Talcott, Edward A. Shils, Kaspar Naegle, and Jesse Pitts, eds. *Theories of Society.* 2 vols. New York: Free Press, 1961.

Psathas, George. "Ethnomethods and Ethnoscience," *Social Research,* 35 (September 1968), 500–520.

Psathas, George, ed. *Phenomenology and Sociology.* New York: Wiley, 1973.

Quinney, Richard. "A Conception of Man and Society for Criminology," *Sociological Quarterly,* 6 (Spring 1965), 119–27.

Reich, Charles. *The Greening of America.* New York: Random House, 1970.

Reinhardt, Karl F. *The Existential Revolt.* 2d ed. New York: Frederick Ungar, 1960.

Roszak, Theodore. *The Making of the Counter Culture.* Garden City, N.Y.: Doubleday Anchor, 1969.

Sallach, David. "Critical Theory and Critical Sociology: A Second Synthesis." Unpublished paper presented to the Society for the Study of Social Problems, Denver, 1971.

———. "Class Consciousness and the Everyday World of the Worker of Marx and Schutz." Unpublished paper presented at the annual meeting of the American Sociological Association, New Orleans, 1972.

Sartre, Jean-Paul. *Being and Nothingness.* Translated by H. Barnes. New York: Washington Square, 1953.

———. *Sketch for a Theory of the Emotions.* Translated by P. Mairet. London: Methuen, 1962.

Schlider, Paul. *The Image and Appearance of the Human Body.* New York: International Universities Press, 1950.

Schutz, Alfred. *Collected Papers. Vol. I.* Edited by M. Natanson. The Hague: Martinus Nijhoff, 1962.

———. *Collected Papers, Vol. II.* Edited by A. Broderson. The Hague: Martinus Nijhoff, 1964.

———. *Collected Papers, Vol. III.* Edited by I. Schutz. The Hague: Martinus Nijhoff, 1966.

———. *The Phenomenology of the Social World.* Translated by G. Walsh and F. Lehnert. Evanston, Ill.: Northwestern University Press, 1967.

Scott, Robert, and Jack D. Douglas, eds. *Theoretical Perspectives on Deviance.* New York: Basic Books, 1972.

Skolnick, Jerome. "Violence Commission Violence," *Transaction,* 7 (October 1970), 32–38.

Sprott, W. J. H. "Principia Sociologica," *British Journal of Sociology,* 3 (September 1952), 203–21.

Stebbins, R. "A Theory of the Definition of the Situation," *Canadian Review of Sociology and Anthropology,* 4 (August 1967), 148–64.

Sudnow, David, ed. *Studies in Social Interaction.* New York: Free Press, 1972.

Swanson, G. E. "The Approach to a General Theory of Action by Parsons and Shils," (review of Talcott Parsons and E. A. Shils, eds., *Toward a General Theory of Action), American Sociological Review,* 18 (April 1953), 125–34.

Tagiuri, Renato, and Luigi Petrillo, eds. *Person Perception and Interpersonal Behavior.* Stanford: Stanford University Press, 1958.

Thody, Phillip. *Jean-Paul Sartre: A Literary and Political Study.* London: Macmillan, 1960.

Tiryakian, Edward. *Existentialism and Sociologism.* Englewood Cliffs, N.J.: Prentice-Hall, 1962.

———. "Existential Phenomenology and Sociology," *American Sociological Review,* 30 (October 1965), 647–88.

———. "The Existential Self and the Person," in K. J. Gergen and C. Gordon, eds., *The Self in Social Interaction.* New York: Wiley, 1968, pp. 75–86.

———. "Structural Sociology," in John McKinney and Edward Tiryakian, eds., *Theoretical Sociology: Perspectives and Developments.* New York: Appleton-Century-Crofts, 1970, pp. 111–35.

———. "Sociology in the Age of Aquarius." Unpublished paper presented at the annual meeting of the American Sociological Association, Denver, 1971.

van den Berghe, Pierre L. "Dialectic and Functionalism: Toward a Theoretical Synthesis," *American Sociological Review,* 28 (October 1963), 695–705.

Vaughan, T., and L. T. Reynolds. "The Sociology of Symbolic Interactionism," *American Sociologist,* 3 (August 1968), 8–14.

Volkart, Edmund, ed. *Social Behavior and Personality: Contributions of W. I. Thomas to Theory and Social Research.* New York: Social Science Research Council, 1951.

Warnock, Mary. *The Philosophy of Sartre.* London: Hutchinson and Co., 1965.

———. *Existentialism.* London: Oxford University Press, 1970.

Warnock, Mary, ed. *Sartre: A Collection of Critical Essays.* Garden City, N.Y.: Doubleday Anchor, 1971.

Watson, J. "A Formal Analysis of Sociable Interaction," *Sociometry,* 21 (December 1958), 269–80.

Wild, John. *The Challenge of Existentialism.* Bloomington: University of Indiana Press, 1955.

Wrong, D. "The Oversocialized Conception of Man in Modern Sociology," *American Sociological Review,* 26 (April 1961), 183–93.

Zijderveld, Anton C. *The Abstract Society.* Garden City, N.J.: Doubleday, 1971.

Znaniecki, Florian. *The Cultural Sciences.* Urbana: University of Illinois Press, 1952.

BRINGING BEASTS BACK IN: TOWARD A BIOSOCIAL THEORY OF AGGRESSION[1]

PIERRE L. VAN DEN BERGHE

Reprinted from the *American Sociological Review*, 39 (December 1974), 777–788. Used by permission of the author and the American Sociological Association.

Pierre L. van den Berghe is professor of sociology at the University of Washington.

In the last few years, an increasing number of anthropologists, zoologists, ethologists, and primatologists have been suggesting that we look at humans as one biological species among many (Alexander, 1971; Campbell, 1972; Crook, 1970; Eisenberg and Dillon, 1970; Morris, 1967b, 1969; Simpson, 1972; Tiger and Fox, 1966, 1971, 1973). By now, most sociologists fully accept the necessity of a cross-cultural approach to define the range of human behavior. They continue, however, for the most part, to resist cross-specific comparisons (Mazur, 1973; Tiger and Fox, 1973) for largely dogmatic reasons. They have postulated a sharp discontinuity between human and non-human behavior, and thus refuse to accept the relevance of the latter to the former. Yet, how else are we to know what is specifically *human* behavior?

At the risk of belaboring the obvious, let me summarize what I think we may safely accept as established facts concerning comparative animal behavior, with special reference to mammals, and even more especially to our close relatives the higher primates (monkeys and apes).

1. The behavioral repertory of every species is determined in part by a set of biological predispositions which are at least to some extent species-specific.
2. Animal behavior is modifiable through learning in response to environmental conditions, and the degree to which behavior is modifiable is a function of the organism's complexity and its intelligence.
3. Many forms of behavior (known as "imprinting" or "critical period" behavior) are the product of a necessary interplay between biological predispositions and environment, which points to the artificiality of opposing these two sets of behavioral determinants.
4. The above propositions hold for both human and non-human behavior, most certainly for mammalian behavior; and the "uniqueness" of human behavior has been misunderstood. Human behavior is indeed unique in the sense that the behavioral repertory of every species is unique in some respects, but human behavior is not radically discontinuous from that of other species. Man is *not* unique in transmitting socially learned behavior, and there is no reason to assume that our biological make-up does not affect our behavior when it so clearly affects that of other species. Indeed, it makes no sense to divorce behavior from biology, since the behavior of any species is so directly linked with its biological evolution.

The implication of these propositions is that we should conceptualize human behavior much as we do that of other mammals, namely as the product of a complex interplay of bio-genetical and environmental factors. That is, the human body is not simply a bundle of drives (hunger, sex, etc.) and a set of capabilities (opposable thumbs, a large convoluted brain, vocal cords, upright stature), a mere carnal vector, as it were, for an infinitely malleable culture. For all the plasticity and diversity of behavior on which we pride ourselves, our behavioral repertoire, though probably greater than that of any other animal known to us, is far from infinite. There *is* such a thing as human nature, just as there is a chimp nature, or an elephant nature.

Our basic question is: why is man so aggressive compared to other primate species? My argument, derived in large part from the work of zoologists, primatologists, and ethologists (Collias, 1944; Kummer, 1968, 1970, 1971; Scott, 1958, 1962, Stokes, n.d.; Washburn and Hamburg, 1968; Wynne-Edwards, 1965), runs as follows: the root cause of aggression is competition for resources. There are two basic ways of regulating that competition: territoriality, which establishes monopoly rights over resources within a portion of usable space, and hierarchy, which creates an order of precedence in access to, and distribution of, resources. The relationship between territoriality and hierarchy on the one hand and aggression on the other is twofold. So long as hierarchy and boundaries are accepted, aggression is inhibited; but it is in the nature of both boundaries and hierarchies that they are not suffered gladly. Both are violently challenged and no less violently defended. Keen resource competition leads to the development of either territoriality, or hierarchy, or both, to prevent a constant war of all against all; but, at the same time, the more hierarchy and territoriality there are, the more numerous the occasions for the aggressive challenge and defense of monopoly and privilege. Thus, species tend to be aggressive to the degree that they are hierarchical and/or territorial. Population pressure is obviously related to resource competition. Holding resources constant, increased density will lead to increased aggression through increased pressure on material resources. In addition to population pressure on material resources, resource competition, and thus aggression, in Homo sapiens are also greatly exacerbated by socially created demands for both material and psychic resources (see Schema 1).

Schema 1. A causal model of the relationship between population pressure, aggression, territoriality, and hierarchy.

Homo sapiens scores higher on territoriality, hierarchy, aggressivity, and population pressure than most mammals, and nearly all of our nearest relatives, the higher primates.[2] This is so because he competes more fiercely and constantly over a wider range of both material and social resources than any other species, so wide a range, in fact, that his needs have become insatiable. Human needs are insatiable because they are in such great part social and artifactual rather than simply material.

Human aggression has, in the first instance, a biological basis in territoriality and hierarchy; but since the "Neolithic Revolution" (the development of agriculture a few thousand years ago), the cultural elaboration on our biological propensities toward territoriality, hierarchy, and aggression has caused a quantum jump in these phenomena which must now be understood in *both* biogenic and sociogenic terms.

Before returning to the main argument, however, I must attempt to do briefly three things:

1. Define my basic terms, since considerable controversy surrounds their use.
2. Establish that Homo sapiens does indeed score highly on these variables compared to other primates.
3. Since my argument will be in good part cross-specific, establish that three of these traits, aggressiveness, hierarchy, and territoriality, are built into our in-born behavioral repertoire, though obviously also elaborated on culturally, and greatly modifiable through learning and environmental conditions.

If I seem to stress especially biological factors, it is not because I deem them overwhelmingly determinant of behavior, but rather because they have been so overwhelmingly ignored in social science. What seems no longer tenable at this juncture is any theory of human behavior which ignores biology and relies exclusively on socio-cultural learning as an explanation, as does, for instance, Bandura (1973) in his theory of aggression. Learning theorists, social behaviorists, and cultural determinists are not wrong in stressing the importance of adaptive learning in response to environmental conditions. Indeed, man, not-withstanding his greater virtuosity, is far from being alone in his capacity to learn and adjust. Rather, most social scientists have been wrong in their dogmatic rejection and blissful ignorance of the biological parameters of our behavior. A systematic re-examination by social scientists of the biological basis of behavior is long overdue.

By *aggression*, I mean physical assault or the threat thereof directed at a co-specific (i.e., a member of the same biological species). Predation (i.e., killing other species for food) is clearly not aggression. Thus, the "killer-ape" theory of human aggression (namely that we are aggressive because we became predatory for a few million years of our primate evolution) does not make much sense (Ardrey, 1961). It may explain why so many of us find killing such good fun, but not why we so often kill our fellow men in anger. Leopards do a lot of killing, but are not very aggressive animals. Baboons are relatively aggressive primates, but do little killing. Humans kill a lot of other animals for fun and profit, and of fellow humans in anger or in self-defense. While both forms of behavior are probably in-born, they are very different nonetheless.

Territoriality means the defense of a relatively fixed space against occupation and/or use by co-specifics. It is to be distinguished from the concept of "social space" which is an imaginary space that *moves* with ego. Thus when I keep my physical distance from other people, wherever I happen to be, I am not engaging in territorial behavior. Neither am I being territorial when I try to keep blue jays out of my garden. I am, however, territorial when I endeavor to keep my neighbor's children out of my house or garden. Species, such as baboons or macaques, that forage in areas that may subsequently be used without challenge by other bands of the same species, and that do have a social space around the group which may not be invaded with impunity are said to have "home-ranges," but are not territorial, as defined here.[3]

Finally, by hierarchy I shall mean a relatively stable rank order between co-specifics which determines preferential access to desirable resources, including the labor and sexual favors of co-specifics. Hierarchy is expressed through *dominance-submission* behavior, which is typically highly ritualized in many primate species, and which often assumes a pseudo-sexual form, such as presenting the genitalia, displaying the penis, mounting, and the like. (In North American culture, we speak of getting "screwed," "shafted," or "fucked" to mean being on the losing side of a relationship.)[4]

Next, I have to show that Homo sapiens, compared to most other mammals, and particularly primates, is highly aggressive, densely settled, hierarchical, and territorial. About the first three, there is, I believe, little argument to the contrary. No mammal species comes even close to our rate of aggressiveness, and especially of lethal aggressiveness. Many other species display aggression and even engage in stylized combat, but almost never to the point of killing each other. In nearly all mammals except man, the first signal of submission on the part of the losing animal automatically inhibits aggressiveness in the victor. Thereafter, the loser is typically ignored by the winner. Humans can surrender in combat; but, as we well know, prisoners are almost never ignored and allowed to trot off peaceably: they are killed, tortured, mutilated, raped, incarcerated, eaten, enslaved, or if they are lucky, exchanged or ransomed. The old Roman saying, *homo homini lupus*, is clearly slanderous to wolves. It if were true, we should be far better off.

That we are overcrowded hopelessly beyond the hunting and gathering mode of existence for which our hominid evolution prepared us is likewise evident. Our overcrowding has grown steadily for many thousands of years, and the rate at which it grows is itself geometric.

As for hierarchy, it is equally obvious that no mammal is as stratified as we are.[5] Many other species, to be sure, have a "pecking" or precedence order, often based on strength, which allows the observer to rank order the individuals of a group. A few highly hierarchized primates such as baboons and macaques even have ruling oligarchies of adult males, and there is some evidence of infant monkeys "inheriting" socially the status of their mothers, thus suggesting the incipient existence of social classes among some subhuman primates. Many primate species, however, especially the arboreal ones such as gibbons, lemurs, and others, have almost no dominance order. No mammal species comes close to Homo sapiens in the elaborateness, and multiplicity of invidious distinctions.

This leaves territoriality, a concept with which sociologists are not accustomed to work, and thus a phenomenon which many are not prepared to recognize in humans. Man is not only highly territorial, but he is territorial at practically every level of social organization: the family has its home, the juvenile gang its "turf," the ethnic group its ghetto, the state its national territory. Even monastic orders and "counter-culture" communes dedicated to ideals of equality and propertylessness post no-trespassing signs against outsiders, and establish pecking orders between their members. Few higher primates are highly territorial (the gibbon being an exception), and many are scarcely territorial at all (e.g., chimpanzees, and most terrestrial primates such as baboons). Even highly territorial animals are almost invariably territorial at one level only, that of the individual or the reproductive "family" unit (mother and offspring, or mates).[6]

There remains the most controversial task of arguing that aggression, hierarchy, and territoriality are, despite a wide range of cultural elaboration, part of our biological heritage. Our run-away demography is, of course, largely a cultural achievement, being the result of vast improvements in productive and medical technology. Here, we cannot adduce any firm proof, but simply present presumptive evidence. Perhaps the best presumption that a behavior pattern is at least in part biogenetically determined is its universality within a species. This is especially true of Homo sapiens with his wide range of cultural adaptations to his widely different habitats. The near ubiquity of man on our planet is an adaptive feat shared by very few species, and then mostly by species that are symbiotic with, or parasitic on, man, such as fleas, dogs and rats. The probability of the same basic behavioral syndrome being arrived at in all or nearly all cultures in the absence of any biological predisposition is very slender indeed. My argument here is that, although the *detailed* cultural manifestations of human aggression, hierarchy, and territoriality vary greatly, the *basic* species-wide aspects of these phenomena are too similar to enable one to reject the hypothesis of *at least partial* biogenic determination.

Homicidal aggression exists in all or practically all cultures, and some forms of it are condoned practically everywhere. A few cultures are said not to engage in warfare, but they are characterized either by extremely low population densities (e.g., the Eskimos) or by extreme weakness in relation to their neighbors (e.g., the Pygmies in relation to neighboring Bantu groups). In the first case, competition for resources is minimized; and, in the latter, avoidance of war is the result not of a peace-loving nature, but of a realistic fear of being wiped out. There is hardly a culture which is not riddled with interpersonal or inter-group conflict, although some cultures are somewhat more successful than others in suppressing some of the outward violence characteristic of human aggression. Both hierarchy and territoriality as we shall see later are simultaneously means of suppressing aggression (when people "know their place," a locution that interestingly expresses pecking order in territorial terms), and a source of aggression. Additional evidence for the biological basis of aggression is the degree to which it is hormonally controlled through testosterone both in humans and in other mammals. Differences in hormonal levels explain why males are consistently more aggressive than females, not only among humans, but in most other mammalian species as well.

As for hierarchy, it is true that many societies are classless according to the usual definitions of class. However, all human societies are clearly hierarchized *at least* by age and sex (adult males being dominant over adult females, adults of either sex being dominant over children, and older children being dominant over younger children), and almost invariably by at least a loose kind of prestige hierarchy among adult males as well. That is, the *least* hierarchical of human societies are approximately as stratified as the *most* hierarchical of the non-human primate societies, like the various baboon and macaque species. Most human societies are, of course, much more elaborately hierarchical than this. Beyond the sheer fact that Homo is always *hierarchicus* (Dumont, 1970), there are rather striking cross-cultural similarities in the specific behavioral repertoire of dominance and submission. Thus, in most cultures, dominance is expressed through a posture of standing taller or higher, while submission is manifested through bowing or crouching. Without knowing anything about a foreign culture, the stranger can gain through superficial observation a fairly accurate picture of its hierarchy. This would hardly be possible if the "grammar" of hierarchy were purely or even primarily cultural, as the grammar of speech was long thought to be.[7]

At first glance, it would appear that the expressions of territoriality are quite diverse in Homo sapiens. Some cultures are nomadic, others sedentary. Some stress individual land tenure, while others are more communal. Some specify international boundaries to the last meter, while others happily tolerate vast stretches of no man's land or every man's land. This cultural diversity, however, hides profound similarities. First, the universality of territoriality in the species is striking. In no society that I know of, can a stranger simply enter someone else's home without some ritual of warning and harmless intent. In all or nearly all human societies, the family unit (nuclear or extended) has some territorial space (if only an alcove in a "long-house"), even where the stress is on com-

munalism. Even monks and nuns have individual cells. If it were not for territoriality, why would not each monk go and sleep where the fancy struck him?
Similarly, nearly all societies specify international boundaries (though not always
precise ones). These boundaries can be crossed by strangers, as indeed can the
boundaries of family territory, but subject to special conditions that do not apply
to the owners or natives. Moreover, these conditions are strikingly similar
throughout the species: basically, the stranger must give warning of his presence
(e.g., through some kind of noise) and must go through a ritual of harmless intent.
Above all, he cannot show any aggressiveness, but must assume a meek, sub-
servient posture, unless he is prepared to face aggressive territorial defense
behavior.

As for the "bio-grammar" of hierarchy, the "bio-grammar" of territorial behavior is sufficiently universal in Homo sapiens for any total stranger to behave
in such a way as to avoid being killed for territorial invasion.[8] The roles of guest
and host are astonishingly universal (about as universal, for example, as the bio-
grammar of sexual attraction which is also highly transferable cross culturally, but
not at all cross-specifically); and violations of these rules unleash violent conflict.
The sheer fact that thousands of explorers, travelers, missionaries and the like
have lived to tell the tale of friendly contacts with total strangers is powerful
evidence for the existence of a species-specific bio-grammar of territorial behavior. The negative cases of those who got killed are generally traceable to universally recognizable transgressions of territorial behavior (such as carrying weapons,
and behaving arrogantly and aggressively).

Let us return to the main aim of this paper, which is to suggest a hypothesis
accounting for the remarkably high level of human aggression.

There are at least three main theories of human aggression recently advanced
by ethologists, paleontologists, and others concerned with human evolution.
None of them is very convincing. The most widespread one, popularized, for example, by Ardrey (1961, 1966), is that man is highly aggressive because he developed as a "killer ape." The outstanding weakness of that theory is that it confuses two very different types of behavior: predation, which is inter-specific, and
aggression, which is intra-specific. It is true that Homo sapiens, in his extensive
propensity for cannibalism and other forms of exploitation of his co-specifics, has
tended to blur somewhat the dividing line between predation and aggression; but,
even so, killing other animals for fun and profit and killing other humans in anger
are clearly distinguishable activities. The leap necessary to explain aggression in
terms of predation is not warranted by the cross-specific evidence. There seems
to be little if any relationship between the two phenomena, and thus little ground
to accept such a relationship in humans.

A second theory of aggression, advanced by Konrad Lorenz (1966), is that
aggression is common to a great many species, but that basically species fall into
broad categories: either their biological endowment to kill is meager, like that
of chickens or pigeons, and a lot of bickering goes on, but without serious consequences; or the animals have lethal natural weapons (such as wolves and other
predators), but inhibitory mechanisms signifying defeat block aggression in the
victor, and thereby prevent fatal injuries. Applied to humans, the Lorenz theory
suggests that man is so lethal to his fellows precisely because he is biologically
so poorly adapted to killing, and as such, has not developed effective in-born aggressive inhibition. Man kills with culturally and recently developed weapons,
and has not yet had time to develop biological blocking mechanisms. Our technology of destruction has far outstripped in effect, our biological restraints. While
Lorenz goes some way in explaining why human aggression is so commonly homicidal, it does little to account for the relatively high level of human aggression
itself.

Finally, a third theory, advanced by Louis Leakey, suggests that it was the humanization of man and especially the development of speech in the last quarter million years or so of human evolution that turned man against man. The characteristically human aspect of aggression, says Leakey, is that it is organized and premeditated. This takes abstract speech. Here, I think that Leakey unwisely restricts the definition of aggression. Of course, it takes speech to plan military campaigns and execute them; but the scope of human aggression is far wider and the origin far more ancient than the more complexly organized forms of it such as warfare. Surely, mute hominids were perfectly capable of bashing each other over the head, and most probably did.

In somewhat the same vein as Leakey's theory of human aggression is Bigelow's (1969). Cooperation and aggression, argues Bigelow, are but two sides of the same coin. Humans cooperate for conflict, and the two qualities evolved side by side as hominids became increasingly intelligent. The more intelligent humans learned to cooperate in order to better wipe out other groups. In-group cooperation and inter-group conflict are characteristic of man. The difficulties with Bigelow's thesis are several. First, Bigelow's theory does not explain why humans should have such a powerful urge to destroy each other in the first place. Second, it does not account for intra-group aggression or inter-group cooperation, both of which occur with some frequency. Thirdly, the theory postulates the uniqueness of Homo sapiens and thus lacks generality. It may take brains to be cooperatively nasty, but the theory does not explain plain dumb nastiness.

Besides these biological and evolutionary theories of aggresssion, there have, of course, been many attempts to account for aggression in terms of learning (Bandura, 1973), or in terms of psychic mechanisms such as the frustration-aggression theory (Dollard, et al., 1939). The frustration-aggression theory has been the object of a vast critical literature (Allport, 1954), and its scientific status can best be described as shaky. As for social behaviorists they have indeed established that aggression, like other forms of behavior, is subject to experimental manipulation; but to say that aggression, like all behavior, is a matter of conditioning, is scarcely explanatory of aggression as a form of behavior different from, say, salivating or copulating.

So, let us try to formulate a theory of aggression which is both generally applicable to Homo sapiens as well as to other species, and which differentiates aggression from other forms of behavior.

Cross-specifically, aggressive behavior serves the basic function of gaining access to or defending scarce resources for which other members of the same species compete. (Violence between species, which is not aggression, takes the entirely different form of seeking to eat, or to avoid being eaten.) There are two common ways of regulating competition for resources: territoriality and hierarchy. In the first case, a species spreads on the ground, dividing space into mutually exclusive territories to be exploited by small numbers of non-competitive individuals: lone adults, mothers and offspring, or mates. Hierarchy regulates competition by establishing an order of access to, or a scale of distribution of, resources between the members of a group.

The common element to the two solutions of territoriality and hierarchy is that, while they regulate competition and thus aggression, they also require a great deal of aggression, both to maintain and to change. Boundaries and pecking orders are constantly tested, i.e., they are both challenged and defended. Aggression, then, is a mechanism making for both stability and change, the two ubiquitous sides of social organization.

To simplify the problem, let us restrict our cross-specific comparison to the primates. We find an interesting inverse correlation in primate species between territory and hierarchy: the territorial species are typically minimally hierarchical (even to the extent of sex equality and minimal sexual dimorphism); conversely, the hierarchical species tend not to be territorial. It is also noteworthy that the territorial species (such as gibbons and many lower primates) tend to be the most aboreal, while the hierarchical species (baboons, macaques) are more terrestrial.

Chimpanzees, which are partly aboreal and partly terrestrial, seem to have the best of both worlds: abundant food minimizes competition, and they are neither territorial nor strongly hierarchical. As might be expected, they show little aggression, although Jane Goodall has shown, in a striking simian confirmation of Marx's notion of primitive accumulation of capital, that artificial feeding increases both aggression and dominance behavior. Placing large bunches of bananas in a restricted space immediately increased resource competition even though it merely added a surfeit to the already abundant food supply of the chimpanzees' rain forest habitat. This clearly suggests that for humans and non-humans alike resource competition is not primarily a product of mere scarcity to sustain basic biological needs, but that surplus accumulation of resources is likely to lead to an escalation of secondary needs and to an intensification of resource competition, aggression, and hierarchy. Perhaps the relation between resource scarcity (in relation to basic food needs) and resource competition is curvilinear. We might expect acute competition under conditions of starvation, least competition under conditions of satiation without surplus, and again more competition under conditions of superabundance. Gibbons, who live in territorial nuclear families, defend their territories through loud but bloodless screaming. Baboon aggression takes mostly the form of defending or challenging the existing hierarchy within a given troop.

By now it should be clear where this argument leads us: Homo sapiens is unique among primates in being both highly hierarchical and highly territorial. Therefore, he can be expected to be doubly aggressive: externally, he fights wars of territorial defense and aggression (between states, between gangs); internally, he fights struggles for supremacy (class struggles, generational and sex conflicts, military coups, and so on).

The next question is why Homo sapiens is both highly territorial and highly hierarchical. Here we get on much more speculative ground, because the answer to the problem is to be sought in hominid evolution. The living primates can give us hunches about human evolution, but they are not humans stopped dead in their evolutionary tracks. They are different species that evolved along separate tracks. We still know very little about hominid evolution. Earlier, I suggested that hierarchy was a way of regulating resource competition, but, for terrestrial primates, it is much more than that: it is a sine qua non of survival. Without the protection of trees, and lacking the fleetness of herbivores, a lone primate on the open savanna is a vulnerable morsel for the great cats, and even for pack-hunting canines. Therefore, all terrestrial primates had to seek the protection of organized numbers. That, in turn, meant a coalition of adult males to defend each other and the females and infants against large predators.

Early hominids were not only terrestrial primates, but terrestrial primates turned predators, or, better, turned scavengers and predators. Their social organization was probably broadly similar to that of contemporary baboons with the major difference that there was no need for females and infants to accompany the males on hunting-and-scavenging trips (as female and infant baboons do in foraging trips). The adult-male-dominated hierarchy of early hominids served both defensive and offensive functions, for they were both predators and potential prey. As predators, they were biologically implausible. Until the relatively late development of efficient throwing weapons (spear, bow and arrow), man's ability to tackle big mammals was relatively limited. It seems more probable that his best bet, besides preying on reptiles, birds, and small mammals, was to become a scavenger (like his natural symbiotic species, the dog) by stealing carcasses from the large felines. To scare large cats away, of course, took several men banding together. Early hominids opted for hierarchy and tyranny, because the egalitarian, anarchical solution of spreading out on the ground into mutually exclusive territories was not a viable option for a terrestrial primate.

Why and how, then, did we become territorial as well as hierarchical? We do not know, of course, but it is at least tempting to speculate that the crucial intervening factor was population pressure. As hunters, gatherers, and scavengers, hominids had definite population limits, both in the size of the band (probably around fifty, to judge by contemporary hunters and gatherers, although the latter are far more efficient than early hominids), and in terms of absolute numbers that a given area could support. Yet, intelligence gave hominids the ability to fill these limits to capacity very rapidly, and thus to create strong population pressures that could be solved more quickly by homicidal aggression than by starvation. Population pressure, of course, was not a uniquely human predicament, but war seems to be a uniquely human solution to it. Survival thus meant not only banding together against biologically more adept carnivores, but banding together against competing predatory hominids, including very possibly hominids of closely related but biologically distinct species. The "killer ape" thus became not only simultaneously predator and prey to other species, but also to his own species. Through organized cannibalist warfare, man is the only mammal to blur the otherwise sharp dividing line between *intra*-specific aggression and *inter*-specific predation.

Since endemic warfare between human bands has probably been universal or nearly so for hundreds of thousands if not millions of years, it is quite possible, indeed plausible, that territoriality at the band level developed as a means of regulating inter-band aggression. War was a quick and effective way to reduce population pressures; but, unfortunately, it had its dangerous and unpleasant sides. Territoriality became a way to avoid continuous warfare, with perhaps infanticide as a safer (to the dominant adult males) alternative for reducing population pressure. "International relations," to the extent that they developed beyond the stage of bashing one another over the head and running off with captured females, probably took the form of territorial agreements: "This is my turf, and this is yours. Let us each keep on our side." Inter-band ties may then have been further consolidated by matrimonial exchanges and incest taboos so dear to anthropologists, but it seems probable that these niceties followed rather than preceded the development of territoriality.

So far, we have considered human evolution through the hunting, scavenging, and gathering stages for which he evolved biologically into a highly competitive, and hence territorial, hierarchical and aggressive primate. Then came the greatest revolution in human history, the food growing one. Man suddenly found himself playing an entirely new ball game. Material resources increased dramatically; but resource competition, far from decreasing, was exacerbated by the technological breakthrough. Population exploded, but even if population pressure on the band's food resources was temporarily relieved, the new technology suddenly meant the vast expansion of the scope of social resources, especially labor and the artifacts it could produce.

Unlike natural resources, social resources and their artifactual byproducts are relatively unlimited; and unlike basic biological needs which are quickly sated, social needs are intrinsically insatiable. Surplus material production vastly increased the scope for resource competition, and the biological predispositions toward territoriality and hierarchy were culturally elaborated on far beyond the limits of the primate hunting band. As we know, surplus material production meant the rise of classes of rulers, priests, peasants and slaves, of centralized states, of organized means of violence and coercion, of a technology of destruction which immensely increased the lethality of human aggression, of alienation of land and of the product of labor from the producers, of population density and concern for *Lebensraum*. In short, with the enormous cultural jump that agriculture represented for humanity, Homo sapiens intensified and elaborated culturally on his biological predispositions toward territoriality and hierarchy.

Let us now return to the problem of aggression. Ethologists have long known that population density, or better, population pressure, in many species is directly related to aggression. With some species, there even seems to be a fairly definite threshold beyond which any increase in crowding unleashes a veritable orgy of aggression in an otherwise relatively unaggressive animal. For man, there does not appear to be such an absolute threshold, but the evidence linking aggression and population pressure is strong. If criminologists, for example, spent more time correlating violent crime rates (and violent police behavior and other forms of counter-aggression) with population pressure, they might change their perspective considerably. The negative correlation, for instance, between violent crime rate and social class might well be a spurious one, with population pressure as the intervening variable: crowded urban proletarians appear to have high rates of violent crimes, but not, it seems, uncrowded peasants.[9]

We are now in a position to specify somewhat better the parameters of a six-variable model of human aggression. *Resource competition* within the species (including competition for human resources, notably control of labor and sex), leads to *aggression*. *Population pressure* is one of the main factors aggravating resource competition, and thus aggressiveness. Equally important in recent human history (last six to eight thousand years), are the *socially created needs*, which, being intrinsically insatiable, maintain a high level of resource competition even after basic biological needs are sated. Aggression in turn is managed or suppressed through the main mechanisms of *territoriality* and *hierarchy*. The former defines monopolistic rights of resource exploitation within a given space. The latter establish a rank-order of access to, and/or a scale of distribution of, both material and social resources. However, territoriality and hierarchy not only manage and suppress aggression; they also provoke it. Aggression is only suppressed so long as territoriality and hierarchy are tolerated by all parties concerned. Both territoriality and hierarchy, however, evoke challenge, as do other forms of privilege; and the challenge in turn evokes counter-aggression. The fundamental contradiction in territoriality and hierarchy is that, while they appear to regulate aggression, and, therefore, to provide a solution to it, they also contain within them a dialectic of conflict: territorial rights and hierarchical privileges are both aggressively defended and challenged. Homo sapiens, being the most hierarchical, territorial, and for his size, densely settled, mammal, it should not surprise anyone that he is also the most lethally aggressive to his own species and devastatingly predatory on other species. Territoriality and hierarchy are the dual answer to the Hobbesian problem of order that so long obsessed sociologists. But they are not a very good answer because they simultaneously cause and suppress aggression. They prevent our being constantly at each other's throats, but they also insure that the social order based on force which they create will be violently challenged and no less violently defended.

Surely, there must be a better way to manage our affairs. The point of view presented here is not one of biological determinism pure and simple. Rather, I suggest that, for both humans and "lower" animals, behavior is the product of a complex interaction of biological predispositions and environmental conditions. To say that we must be prepared to entertain seriously the hypothesis that we are by nature aggressive, territorial, and hierarchical does not mean that we are slaves to our glands. As I have stressed, the extent to which our capacity or propensity for aggression is exercised is a function of many environmental variables, both physical and man-made, which make for varying levels and types of resources competition.

The development of culture in man (also present in other primate species, but in much more rudimentary form) does make for *some* discontinuity. However, a holistic view of human behavior makes it imperative that we also look at the important continuities between ourselves and other species, instead of only singing the praise of our discontinuities. Our cultural capability has allowed us to transform our environment so profoundly as to make our biological adaptations obsolete, or, worse, maladaptive. In Desmond Morris' (1969) ironic simile, we have caged ourselves in zoos of our own creation; and like caged animals, we have developed pathological forms of behavior: our concern for status has become obsessive; our territorial imperative has become rapaciously acquisitive beyond any need for survival; and our weaponry has increased a million-fold the destructiveness of our aggressiveness.

The obvious need now is to develop our capacity for controlled biosocial change. This we can only do if we first realize that the problem exists. If we are to have any chance of success in controlling the nefarious effects of our acquisitive territoriality, our status striving, our aggressiveness and our run-away fertility, we must understand better the biological parameters of the social behavior of our species. The recognition that our behavior is in part biologically determined is by no means a counsel of despair. Biology is no more destiny than history is. The assumption that biological evolution moves at a desperately slow pace is made patently obsolete by our biological technology. Animal breeders have long known how rapidly controlled biological selection can modify a species. The spectre of eugenics conjures staggering ethical problems, of course; but sticking our social scientific heads into the biological sand (a slander on the ostrich, by the way) is hardly a solution either.

NOTES

1. This paper has benefited from a critical reading by Robert Burgess, Pamela Kennedy, Pepper Schwartz, David Spain, and Lionel Tiger. To my mentor, George Homans, I owe, among many other things, an apology for my irreverent pastiche, on the tenth anniversary of the publication of his "Bringing Men Back In."

2. The literature on primate behavior has grown enormous in the last decade, and much of it is of excellent quality; this has not saved it from being largely ignored by sociologists except in incidental footnotes in introductory tests. Among the best summaries of that literature are Kummer (1971), and Morris (1967a).

3. The term *territoriality* covers a rather wide range of behavior which varies greatly from species to species. Some species defend territory primarily by marking with scent (e.g., dogs); others by aggressive threat displays or vocalizations (e.g., gibbons). Some animals defend territory primarily for breeding purposes, others mostly for exclusive exploitation of resources. The significant fact is not so much the diversity of forms of territoriality between species but the relative fixity of it within a species. For example, man defends his territory both by marking and by aggression; he has both breeding territories (the home), and territories for monopolistic resource exploitation (farms, mines, fishing territories, international boundaries). Indeed, man has even gone to the extent of reshaping the territorial behavior of another species, namely the dog, to defend his own. Man tries (rather unsuccessfully) to curb the marking behavior of his domesticated dog, and rechannels (rather successfully) the aggressiveness of the dog to defend his territory against other humans. The man-dog relationship is one of the great success stories of symbiosis. Two hunting and scavenging species drew on their complementary skills to become more efficient killers than either could have been by itself. In addition, the dog became man's first (and cheapest) early warning system. The ability of the dog to adopt his master's prejudices in the way he defends human territory is nothing short of extraordinary. It has been widely observed, for example, that in racist societies, dogs, too, become racist, often without conscious training of their masters. In South Africa, for example, dogs of white owners tend to reserve their most ferocious barking for blacks.

4. This pseudo-sexual character of dominance-submission behavior suggests that gender inequality, which is present in most primates, and markedly so in terrestrial primates, has become a generalized model for other forms of inequality as well. Besides gender, the other fundamentally biological inequality in primates is, of course, age; and it is interesting

to note that the subordinate partner in a sexual relationship is almost invariably the younger one. In humans, this is true both of heterosexual and homosexual relationships. I have dealt with age and sex inequality at length elsewhere (van den Berghe, 1973).

5. A classic ploy of sociologists in rejecting the validity of cross-specific comparisons is to deny that the same categories of behavior apply to humans and other animals. In the case at hand, for instance, it is claimed that stratification in human societies differs fundamentally from a dominance order among other animals. The truth of the matter is that both individual and collective forms of hierarchy are found in both human and non-human societies. Age segregated juveniles or ruling oligarchies so common among savanna baboons, for example, are every bit as much social classes as their counterparts in human societies. Human social class can be far more elaborate, of course; but there is no reason for refusing to use the same conceptual categories of behavior across species, provided one bewares of anthropomorphism. The same anti-comparative argument has been used in relation to aggression. Organized human aggression as in war, it has been argued, is radically different from individual violence found in other animals. Here too, both human and non-humans engage in both individual and collective violence. Ruling oligarchies of baboons, for instance, often gang up in a quite organized manner against challengers. If the fear of anthropomorphism were to stifle any attempt at cross-specific comparisons of behavior, then the fear of ethnocentrism should have killed off anthropology long ago.

6. Here I disagree with Mazur (1973) who concludes that human territoriality is not, at least in part, biologically determined. His entire argument is phylogenetic. He attempts to show that the more closely related species are phylogenetically, the more likely they are to share behavioral traits in common. Conversely, he argues that if behavioral traits can be shown to be shared by closely related species, then they can be presumed to be biologically determined. Up to a point, the argument is cogent; but the reciprocal does not follow. When two closely related species exhibit different patterns of behavior, it does not follow that, therefore, these patterns are *not* biogenic. For instance, the Hamadryas baboon has a social organization and a mating pattern quite different from those of closely related species of savannah baboons (Kummer, 1968, 1971; Washburn and DeVore, 1961). In a famous incident when zoo conditions interfered with the natural sex ratio in a colony of Hamadryas baboons, a deadly pandemonium broke loose, with several monkeys killed. Hamadryas baboons behave much the same whether in zoos or in the wild, and so do other baboons, thus indicating considerable inborn predisposition of behavior. Yet, those morphologically nearly identical species behave quite differently from each other. The fallacy in Mazur's argument is the assumption that biological evolution is necessarily very slow and is not easily reversible. There is no reason to assume that such biological adaptations to environment as sexual dimorphism for example, cannot be appreciably modified in a few scores of generations (a few thousand years, on the human time scale). This is a much shorter span of evolution than that which separates even fairly closely related species, and certainly man from any other primate. As regards territoriality, the various species of gibbons (who are apes and thus close relatives of Homo sapiens) share with man a high degree of territoriality. So do many lower primates, though it is true that chimpanzees, gorillas and most terrestrial Old World monkeys are not highly territorial. Human territoriality, much like that of gibbons and of many lower primates, shows too much uniformity and universality within the species, however, to enable one to discount the biogenic hypothesis.

7. As regards speech, too, there is increasing speculation among linguists, that there might be an underlying, innate "generative grammar" common to all forms of human speech (Chomsky, 1968). Certainly, the way in which speech is acquired is amazingly similar in all cultures, and occurs at the same age (in the second year of life) thereby suggesting a similarity with phenomena of imprinting and "critical period" learning. Gender identification, acquired nearly universally and irreversibly by human young, roughly at the same time as speech, probably falls in the same category of imprinting phenomena, necessitating a complex interplay of genetic and environmental factors at a crucial and limited time during the individual's maturation period.

8. The concept of bio-grammar was developed by Lionel Tiger and Robin Fox (1971). It refers, by analogy to the grammar of a language, to the rules of behavior which are species-specific and determined by genetic factors.

9. No doubt, the relationship between crime and population density is not a simple one. Some highly crowded areas such as Tokyo seem to have much lower rates for crimes of violence than relatively less crowded areas such as Detroit, thus indicating a wide range of cultural variability. However, within a society (i.e. controlling for culture), the relation-

ship between violent crime and population density seems to hold. Even then, it is far from perfect; but even if density were to account for, say, no more than 20 or 30 percent of the variance within a culture, it would still be a significant finding. After all, population density is only a crude indicator of population pressure. Spatial resources are only one of a whole range of resources, competition for which produces aggression.

REFERENCES

Alexander, R.D. "The Search for an Evolutionary Philosophy of Man," *Proceedings of the Royal Society of Victoria*, 84 (1971), 99–102.

Allport, Gordon W. *The Nature of Prejudice*. Cambridge, Mass.: Addison-Wesley, 1954.

Ardrey, Robert. *African Genesis*. New York: Atheneum, 1961.

———. *The Territorial Imperative*. New York: Atheneum, 1966.

Bandura, Albert. *Aggression: A Social Learning Analysis*. Englewood Cliffs, N.J.: Prentice-Hall, 1973.

Bigelow, Robert. *The Dawn Warriors*. Boston: Little, Brown, 1969.

Campbell, Bernard, ed. *Sexual Selection and the Descent of Man, 1871–1971*. Chicago: Aldine, 1972.

Chomsky, Noam. *Language and Mind*. New York: Harcourt, Brace, and World, 1968.

Collias, N. E. "Aggressive Behavior Among Vertebrate Animals," *Physiological Zoology*, 17 (1944), 83–123.

Crook, John Hurrell, ed. *Social Behavior in Birds and Mammals*. London: Academic Press, 1970.

Dollard, John, et al. *Frustration and Aggression*. New Haven, Conn.: Yale University Press, 1939.

Dumont, Louis. *Homo Hierarchicus*. London: Weidenfeld and Nicolson, 1970.

Eisenberg, J., and W. Dillon, eds. *Man and Beast*. Washington, D.C.: Smithsonian Institution Press, 1970.

Kummer, Hans. *Social Organization of Hamadryas Baboons*. Chicago: University of Chicago Press, 1968.

———. "Spacing Mechanisms in Social Behavior," in J. Eisenberg and W. Dillon, eds., *Man and Beast*. Washington, D.C.: Smithsonian Institution Press, 1970.

———. *Primate Societies*. Chicago: Aldine, 1971.

Lorenz, Konrad. *On Aggression*. New York: Harcourt, Brace, and World, 1966.

Mazur, Allan. "A Cross-Species Comparison of Status in Small Established Groups," *American Sociological Review*, 38 (October 1973), 513–30.

Morris, Desmond. *Primate Ethology*. London: Weidenfeld and Nicolson, 1967. (a)

———. *The Naked Ape*. London: Jonathan Cape, 1967. (b)

———. *The Human Zoo*. New York: McGraw-Hill, 1969.

Scott, J. P. *Aggression*. Chicago: University of Chicago Press, 1958.

———. "Hostility and Aggression in Animals," in E. L. Bliss, ed., *Roots of Behavior*. New York: Harper & Row, 1962.

Simpson, George Gaylord. "The Evolutionary Concept of Man," in Bernard Campbell, ed., *Sexual Selection and the Descent of Man, 1871–1971*. Chicago: Aldine, 1972.

Stokes, Allen W. *Aggressive Man and Aggressive Beast*. Logan, Utah: Utah State University, n.d.

Tiger, Lionel, and Robin Fox. "The Zoological Perspective in Social Science," *Man*, 1 (March 1966), 75–81.

———. *The Imperial Animal*. New York: Holt, Rinehart and Winston, 1971.

———. "Animal, Venerable, Imperial," *The Columbia Forum*, 2 (Fall 1973), 26–81.

van den Berghe, Pierre L. *Age and Sex in Human Societies: A Biosocial Perspective*. Belmont, Calif.: Wadsworth, 1973.

Washburn, S. L., and I. De Vore. "The Social Life of Baboons," in C. H. Southwick, ed., *Primate Social Behavior*. Princeton: Van Nostrand, 1962.

Washburn, S. L., and D. A. Hamburg. "Aggressive Behavior in Old World Monkeys and Apes," in Phyllis C. Jay, ed., *Primates: Studies in Adaptation and Variability*. New York: Holt, Rinehart and Winston, 1968.

Wynne-Edwards, V. C. "Self-regulating Systems in Populations of Animals," *Science*, 147 (1965), 1543–48.

THE HUMANISTIC CHALLENGE TO SOCIOLOGY[1]

JOHN F. GLASS

Reprinted from the *Journal of Humanistic Psychology* 11 (Fall 1971), 170–183. Used by permission.

John Glass is a faculty member and Culture and Society Series Coordinator at the California School of Professional Psychology, Los Angeles. He is co-editor of *Humanistic Society: Today's Challenge to Sociology.*

When I began graduate study in sociology at UCLA in 1962, I discovered the then emerging humanistic psychology movement, became involved with the Sensitivity Training program at UCLA, and read two books which had just been published, Abraham Maslow's *Toward a Psychology of Being,* and Carl Rogers' *On Becoming a Person.* While my career as a sociologist was profoundly altered from that time on, I quickly discovered that almost no sociologists were aware of this movement or the manifestations of it (Maslow called it the Unnoticed Revolution) because it is still almost completely overlooked by much of the intellectual community. I did find it flourishing at UCLA among a small group of professors in the business school. The Human Relations Research Group, later becoming the Division of Behavioral Science at UCLA's Graduate School of Business Administration, did some of the early groundwork in T-group theory and organizational development and influenced a considerable number of behavioral scientists who came in contact with them, including Abraham Maslow (see his book *Eupsychian Management,* 1965), Carl Rogers, and J. F. T. Bugental (Bugental, 1967). While I pursued the requirements for a Ph.D. in sociology, I moonlighted in the business school and was greatly enriched both personally and professionally.

In the last several years there have been a number of developments that I see as related to humanistic psychology. The rapid increase in popularity of T-groups (encounter groups, sensitivity training, etc.) and the emergence of more than a hundred growth centers and other manifestations of what is known as the human potential movement have been nothing short of phenomenal. The development of a counterculture (Roszak, 1969) and New Left Movement among youth on a scale never before witnessed, the appearance of radical caucuses in sociology, political science, and economics, Woman's Liberation, and more, are all signs of social change with humanistic aspects.

In psychology, this movement has gone the farthest. Maslow (1968) wrote in the introduction to the second edition of *Toward a Psychology of Being* that humanistic psychology is now quite solidly established as:

a viable third alternative to objectivistic, behavioristic (mechanomorphic) psychology and to orthodox Freudianism. It is beginning to be *used* especially in education, industry, religion, organization and management, therapy, and self-improvement. . . .

I must confess that I have come to think of this humanist trend in psychology as a revolution in the truest, oldest sense of the word, the sense in which Galileo, Darwin,

Einstein, Freud, and Marx made revolutions, i.e., new ways of perceiving and thinking, new images of man and of society, new conceptions of ethics and of values, new directions in which to move. . . .

This psychology is *not* purely descriptive or academic, it suggests action and implies consequences. It helps to generate a way of life not only for the person himself within his own private psyche, but also for the same person as a social being, a member of society. (p. iii)

What does this revolution mean for sociology? In this article I would like to give an account of where sociology is *at*, and where it converges with some of the developments mentioned above.

A CRITIQUE OF FUNCTIONALISM

The dominant approach in sociology today, that of functionalism—best personified by the work of Talcott Parsons—is being attacked from many sides. Basically, the functionalist views society as a set of institutions serving its functional needs, ignores historical perspective, and sees change and conflict as deviations rather than as inherent social processes. The dominant concern of functionalism is with order in society—an order based on man's conformity to shared values, and one in which joy, freedom, self-fulfillment, and other aspects of man stressed by the humanistic psychologist usually don't appear. The model of man, often not explicit in such theories, frequently resembles McGregor's Theory X and the behaviorist-psychoanalytic models for which humanistic psychology is providing an alternative. Although it is acknowledged that social order is a function of shared values, the values themselves are seldom considered and are thought of not so much as man-*made*, man-*transmitted*, or man-*received*.

Analogous to those psychologies which emphasize the body-mind dualism, functionalism hardly acknowledges that men have bodies:

Modern Sociological Functionalism focuses on "social systems" that are seen primarily as systems of symbolic interaction, not between embodied men but between disembodied "role players"; between psychic "selves" who communicate-from-a-distance but who never seem to touch, to hold, to feed, to strike, to caress. (Gouldner, 1970: 431)

Criticisms of the structural-functional school and mainstream sociology are not new (Lynd, 1939; Sorokin, 1956; Mills, 1959; Black, 1961; Stein & Vidich, 1963; Horowitz, 1964; Reynolds & Reynolds, 1970), but have steadily increased and culminated in Alvin Gouldner's critique, *The Coming Crisis of Western Sociology* (1970).

The critique of functionalism is not so much that it does not allow for a humanistic model of man, but that it is, both implicitly and explicitly, conservative and justifies the status quo:

A theory is conservative to the extent that it: treats . . . institutions as given and unchangeable in essentials; proposes remedies for them so that they may work better, rather than devising alternatives to them; foresees no future that can be essentially better than the present, the conditions that already exist; and, explicitly or implicitly, counsels acceptance of or resignation to what exists, rather than struggling against it. (Gouldner, 1970: 332).

The model of man that sociology uses too often reflects the same despairing view of other social sciences:

The premise that man acts so as to satisfy needs presupposes a negative conception of the good as amelioration or the correction of an undesirable state. According to this view, man acts to relieve tension; good is the removal of evil and welfare the correction of ills; satisfaction is the meeting of a need . . . peace is the resolution of conflict; fear of the supernatural or of adverse public opinion is the incentive to good conduct . . . (Lee, 1948: 392)

Social science today focuses on man's adjustment to society, on conformity and adaptation, on man as a controlled product of society and culture rather than as a determiner of his own fate. Sociology's view of man is reflected in the subfield known as "deviant behavior" which deals exclusively with pathological deviations: poverty, crime, delinquency, mental illness, alcoholism, etc. What about deviance in the other (healthy) direction? There are almost no studies of creativity, joy, self-fulfillment, or of social institutions and organizations that facilitate these!

Can we not learn as much about human nature and behavior by looking at alternatives, at the positive side of man, as we can by repeated documentation of our ills, a path which has had unintended consequences—that of making the pathological appear inevitable or "normal"?

Shortly before his death, Maslow became increasingly irritated at this subculture of despair. Many sociologists deserve his characterization of despairing debunkers who deny the possibility of improving human nature and society, or of discovering intrinsic human values, or of being life-loving in general (Maslow, 1970: x).

SOME ALTERNATIVES TO FUNCTIONALISM

A number of newer sociological theories are prominent today, in addition to functionalism: the interactionist perspective—best known through the work of Erving Goffman (1959, 1967), the exchange theories of Peter Blau (1964) and George Homans (1961) and the ethnomethodology of Harold Garfinkel (1967). Goffman's dramaturgical approach deals with appearances—how people manage situations and impressions in everyday interpersonal relationships. Garfinkel's ethnomethodology, while similar in its focus on everyday interactions, is more interested theoretically in the tacit understandings and assumptions that underlie social life. Exchange theories come closest to behavioristic psychology.

What all these theories have in common is an active view of men as builders and users of social structure, not simply as receivers or transmitters (Gouldner, 1970: 378ff). Their focus is on social interaction; they are ahistorical and social-psychological in nature.

What is interesting is that the view of man implicit in these newer theories is not much different from the functionalist view. Goffman deals almost exclusively with deception, deceit, stigma, and the effects of repressive institutions on the individual. His work, as well as that of Garfinkel, is full of the embarrassments, discomforts, intrigues, and other "deviant" behavior that persons carry on in their encounters with each other and in making out with the institutions of their society. Coercion, despair, and pessimism abound in Goffman's books, and part of his popularity probably comes from the fact that he makes a sort of hero out of the underdog.

There is much of value in the work of these theorists; they are masters at direct, qualitative observation, but they do not deal with the healthy side of man and society any more than the functionalists do.

The Radicalization of Sociology

A radical movement has emerged in sociology and several other social sciences (see "The New Sociology," Time, 5 January 1970, for a journalistic overview). Many of the younger sociologists active in this movement were graduate students in the sixties, the period when functionalism came under increasing attack, and they experienced the reemergence of social concern which had been dormant in the fifties.

Gouldner sees the failure of functionalism as a theory closely tied to the failure of our welfare state to deal with some of our most urgent social, political, and economic problems. He predicts the growth of a "radical sociology," which, while it will not become the dominant perspective of academic sociology, will grow in influence, particularly among the younger generation.

Deutsch and Howard's *Where It's At* (1970), and Deutsch (1970) give comprehensive introductions to the radical perspective in sociology. Radical critiques principally revolve around the enormous dependence of sociology and sociologists on government sponsored research, and more generally, on the whole nature of the sociological enterprise as supporting and being supported by the establishment. Sociological research is seen as serving corporate needs; the value focus is on stability and the maintenance of the system, and the socialization of its members into the system as it is, rather than as it might be. Radicals see the proper role of sociology as providing a structural analysis of society exposing repression, alienation, racism, inequality, and war as resulting from established value systems and power structures. Manipulation, oppression, control, and dehumanization of man are not proper functions of sociological research according to this viewpoint.

Closely allied in some respects to the radical movement in sociology is an increasing interest in a "sociology of sociology," or a reflexive sociology, as Gouldner calls it. A reflexive sociology transcends sociology as it now exists. It is also a radical sociology, in Gouldner's opinion:

Radical, because it would recognize that knowledge of this world cannot be advanced apart from the sociologist's knowledge of himself and his position in the social world, or apart from his efforts to change these. Radical, because it seeks to transform as well as to know the alien world outside the sociologist as well as the alien world inside of him. Radical, because it would accept the fact that the roots of sociology pass through the sociologist as a total man, and that the question he must confront, therefore, is not merely how to *work* but how to *live*. (1970: 489)

TOWARD A HUMANISTIC SOCIOLOGY

Basically, I see the criticisms of sociology today and the possibilities for a humanistic sociology in a broader context than the radical critiques that have recently come from within sociology. Nor should a liberal-radical debate among humanists divide us.[2] Rather, I see humanistic sociology as a perspective, not an ideology or prescription for social change, that has relevance for many areas of sociology, especially methodology, applied sociology, and the very nature of the sociological enterprise itself.

New Directions in Methodology

A growing number of sociologists (Cicourel, 1964; Bruyn, 1966; Strauss and Glaser, 1967; Blumer, 1969; Filstead, 1970; Staude, 1971) are concerned with developing a methodology for sociology that is more appropriate for the study of human behavior than the positivistic methods which were borrowed from the natural sciences via the assumption that the social sciences should be approached with the same methods and objectives. Under various names—existential or phenomenological sociology, ethnomethodology, symbolic interactionism, participant observation—a number of sociologists are taking as their point of departure the world as the individual or group studied sees it and constructs it, rather than how the researchers themselves predefine or categorize it. They recognize that man is a thinking, feeling, experiencing, intentional being, and that he should not be studied as an object, thing, or subject detached from the researcher who gathers "information" about him. Rather, the proper study of human behavior requires an intuition, an empathy, an awareness of the other as a person who places meanings on his behavior and who cannot really be understood without an awareness of the relationship between the researcher and the subject and self-awareness on the part of the researcher (Argyris, 1968; Glass & Frankiel, 1968).

Humanistic sociology allows and even welcomes speculation, predictions, and theorizing about the future and unrealized possibilities for man and society. This prediction is very different from the predictions currently dominant, which are mainly extrapolations. Nettl emphasizes this clearly:

Prediction in modern sociology no longer has anything to do with the counterposing of alternatives which might be attained by conscious action, but consists merely of extrapolating existing trends on the assumption that the future is simply more of the present. American sociology is thus exceedingly supportive of the here and now which it characterizes as modernity. (1968: 303).

Sociologists preoccupied with realism and scientism are reluctant to delve into areas where empirical verification is impossible. Yet, as Lynd (1958: 219) has pointed out so well: "Realism that excludes the longer, enduring purposes of men and men's unrealized dreams is less than full realism . . . the utopianism of one era has repeatedly become the basic norm of decency for the next." If we assume that man has some control over his environment and that change is not a predetermined or mechanical process, then biased theories (Bierstedt, 1960) and speculation about the future are worthy activities for social scientists.

The humanistic social scientist's highest commitment is not a worship of science but a concern for man. What is argued for is an enlarged view of science, beyond the narrow goals of control and prediction, of studying only what is quantifiable or measurable, away from the behavioristic, positivistic, and technicist ethos borrowed from the hard sciences. In an interview, Michael Polanyi, chemist, philosopher, and one of the great sociological thinkers of our time said: "Sociologists set aside the motive of belief in freedom because it is intangible. They claim that they can explain all human activities in society without being concerned with right or wrong. They want to consider only things that can be handled by what they think are the methods of physics."[3]

Objectivity is to be sought, not through studied indifference to meanings, but through heightened awareness of the assumptions used and values involved, making them clear and open to examination (Lynd, 1958: 114). This can be achieved, according to Maslow, by enlarging our conception of objectivity to include not only "spectator-knowledge" (laissez-faire, uninvolved knowledge, knowledge about, knowledge from the outside), but also experiential knowledge and what he calls love-knowledge or Taoistic knowledge. Just as love can be so complete and accepting that it becomes non-interfering, liking someone just as he is with no impulse or need to change him, Maslow holds that we can love truth the same way. It takes great love to let something alone, to let it be and become:

. . . it is possible to love the truth yet to come, to trust it, to be happy and to marvel as its nature reveals itself. One can believe that the uncontaminated, unmanipulated, unforced, undemanded truth will be more beautiful, more pure, more *truly* true than that same truth would have been had we forced it to conform to a priori expectations or hopes or plans or current political needs (Maslow, 1970: xxxv).

Applied Sociology

A humanistic approach to science does not necessarily mean that the scientist seeks to change or alter what he studies. I feel strongly, however, that applied social science has a central and rightful place in any social science that seeks to be humanistic.

Maslow (1970) also believes that normative zeal (to do good, to help mankind, to better the world) is quite compatible with scientific objectivity and makes conceivable a better science with a far wider jurisdiction than it now has when it tries to be value neutral (leaving values to be arbitrarily affirmed by nonscientists on nonfactual grounds).

Applied social science and "action" research (Sanford, 1970) are misunderstood by many and are often in disfavor with those on the far left as well as with traditional academics. The radicals point to the fact that most money for social science research comes from the government and thus inextricably involves the researcher with the Establishment; traditionalists often question the appropriateness of applied research in a "pure" academic discipline. I agree with Warren Bennis, who stated in a recent book review: "It may be that applied social sciences may revitalize their parent disciplines and that the line between 'pure' and 'applied' social science is illusory. The harsh confrontation between theory and practice may bring about newer models, not only capable of solving problems, but of substantially augmenting social theory."[4]

Sociologists and psychologists, even many humanistically oriented ones, have been astonishingly unaware of the literature and developments in what Maslow calls normative social psychology—more commonly known as applied behavioral science, human relations, or organizational development.[5] In the field of applied behavioral science, men such as Chris Argyris, Warren Bennis, and Robert Tannenbaum can be characterized as liberal humanists—liberal because they seek change within the system, and humanists because their underlying values, methods, and assumptions about human nature (McGregor's Theory Y) are very similar to those of the humanistic psychologists. Indeed, there is some overlap in membership between the two groups.

Much of applied behavioral science is more applied sociology than applied psychology especially where change is sought in social institutions, systems, and organizations, but sociologists have largely given up by default their influence in such efforts.

POSSIBILITIES FOR A HUMANISTIC SOCIOLOGY

Sociology needs an alternative to the "despairing debunkers" who focus exclusively on the dark side of man and the repressive nature of society, and who ignore human possibilities and potentials in their preoccupation with pathology, cynicism, and hopelessness. And sociology, I contend, is essential to an understanding of man from a holistic and humanistic perspective.

Psychologists must remember that man is inescapably a *social* being; he becomes human only through interaction with others and the world he finds himself in. This is the flaw of "pure" existentialism and of *intrapersonal* psychology, which considers man in a vacuum, the individual apart from the society he lives in. To believe that the individual can achieve fulfillment as an isolated person is sheer folly, but some humanistic psychologists appear to take this view. Creation of the self is a process, something that is developed through interaction and contact with society, and this is a life-long process. Symbolic interactionists (e.g., Blumer, 1969) are quite clear on this.

Yet there is indecision in sociological theory over the relationship between the individual and society. Functional theories tend to define the nature of man by his cultural and social world. The fulfillment of the self is seen as no more than the satisfactory internalization of that culture, which needs only adequate opportunities to express its possibilities. Winter poses the question squarely:

The problem is essentially whether society determines the content of the self or furnishes the cultural and social milieu in which the self actualizes its freedom and fulfillment. If society provides the substance of the self, then freedom is basically found through conformity to the possibilities made available by society. If the self is more than an expression of social process, then freedom is the pre-supposition of culture, even as culture is the actualization and enrichment of human freedom and sociality. (1966: 32)

This problem is not an academic one—it was raised recently by John Holt in a letter to *Commentary* (August 1970: 6): "Most people define education as sculpture, making children what we want them to be. I and others . . . define it as gardening, helping children to grow and to find what they want to be."

Maslow and most humanistic psychologists hold the "gardening" theory and Maslow has carried the issue a step farther by his study of healthy individuals:

Practically every serious description of the "authentic" person extant implies that such a person, by virtue of what he has become, assumes a new relation to his society, and indeed to society in general. He not only transcends himself in various ways; he also transcends his culture. He resists enculturation. He becomes a little more a member of his species and a little less a member of his local group. My feeling is that most sociologists and anthropologists will take this hard. I therefore confidently expect controversy in this area. (Maslow, 1968: 11)[6]

A central task of humanistic sociology, then, would be to ask which institutions and social arrangements, supported by which values and norms, promote the capacity and ability of groups and individuals to make free and responsible choices in light of their needs to grow, to explore new possibilities, and to do more than simply survive. Man is more than a player of preexisting roles, he is a meaning maker and value chooser. He chooses his existence within a social and cultural context. This is not solely a psychological or interpersonal phenomenon but one that is greatly influenced by the interaction of the individual with society, interaction that has consequences both for society and the individual.

Humanistically inclined sociologists might ask what the social correlates of trust, interdependency, autonomy, and other individual characteristics are in terms of groups, associations, and other social structures—from the family to the giant corporation.

A study of the values and ideologies by which men and societies live is as fundamental an issue in sociological analysis of a humanistic nature as it is to the humanistic psychologist concerned with individual behavior.[7] A humanistic sociology would study the degree to which specific values, and institutions based on those values, facilitate or hinder the "good" society. We need to study the social and personal consequences of the values held in our society, not only as preached, but as practiced.

CONCLUSION

I am somewhat troubled by the nagging thought that perhaps the most important issues to which we need to address ourselves have not received the emphasis they should. The debates over applied vs. pure research, the similarities and differences between humanistic psychology and sociology seem to be overshadowed by the following:

(1) The crisis our society seems headed for—an impending clash between two cultures. These are not the two cultures of C. P. Snow, but the new and the old, the emerging counterculture based on the joy and the fulfillment of human needs and potentialities and the established culture with its scarcity psychology and blind subservience to technology. The pressures for change and the possibilities for repressive reaction seem enormous. Slater (1970) provides a brilliant analysis of this crisis.

(2) The traditional faith of humanists in science and technology to solve all our problems must be tempered with the reality that the desired outcome is by no means certain, without furthering the mistaken notion that humanistic social scientists are antiintellectual and antiscience.

(3) There is a deeply felt ambivalence over the individualism vs. social commitment issue. There is a danger that some of our emphasis on existentialism and the subjective side of man will lead us to a further separation from nature, history, and community—a danger well captured by Paul Shepard:

The proponents of this fanatic individualism retreat from a hostile and absurd world to an inner life where the only values are personal and subjective. By valuing only the unique and the individual, they rightly oppose mass man and the treatment of human beings as replaceable machines—at the price of ecological nihilism. (as quoted in Means, 1969: 258)

Slater (1970) also poses the dilemma accurately:

On the one hand there is increasing experimentation with communes and communal arrangements, and a serious awareness of the Nuremburg Trials and their proclamation of man's personal responsibility to all men. On the other hand, there is a great fascination with the concept of anarchy—with the attempt to eliminate coercion and commitment in any form from human life. (p. 148)

Wrestling with these issues may yet provide humanists from all the sciences with their greatest challenges and opportunities.

NOTES

1. This is a revision of a paper presented at the 8th Annual Meeting, Association for Humanistic Psychology, Miami Beach, Florida, September 1970. I wish to thank Judith Glass, Steven Deutsch, James Elden, and Charles Hampden-Turner for their helpful comments on the earlier versions of this paper.

2. I do not wish to use the terms "humanist" and "radical" interchangeably even though there is overlap between the two. Humanists can be radical, liberal, or conservative, the sociologist Peter Berger being an outstanding example of the latter. *See* his chapter "On Conservative Humanism" in Berger and Neuhaus (1970), and also Berger (1963).

3. As quoted in *Psychology Today*, May 1968, p. 20.

4. As quoted in *American Journal of Sociology*, January 1969, p. 430.

5. This growing movement largely originated from the work of Kurt Lewin and the founding of the National Training Laboratories (now NTL Institute for Applied Behavioral Science) over 20 years ago (see Tannenbaum, Weschler, and Massarik, 1961; Maslow, 1965; Bennis, Benne, and Chin, 1969; Schmidt, 1970).

6. The new "fourth force" in psychology, Transpersonal, might be matched by a Transcultural sociology dealing with values, social structures, and social behavior that seems to be universal, culture free, and transcendental from a sociological perspective.

7. Richard Means' excellent work, *The Ethical Imperative* (1969), makes a persuasive case for the need to make the study of values and their consequences a central focus in sociology.

REFERENCES

Argyris, C. "Some Unintended Consequences of Rigorous Research," *Psychological Bulletin*, 70 (1968), 185–197.

Bennis, W., K. Benne and R. Chin, eds. *The Planning Change.* 2d ed. New York: Holt, Rinehart and Winston, 1969.

Berger, P. L. *Invitation to Sociology.* Garden City, N.Y.: Doubleday Anchor, 1963.

Berger, P. L., and R. Neuhaus. *Movement and Revolution.* Garden City, N.Y.: Doubleday Anchor, 1970.

Bierstedt, R. "Sociology and Humane Learning," *American Sociological Review*, 25 (1960), 3–9.

Black, M., ed. *The Social Theories of Talcott Parsons.* Englewood Cliffs, N.J.: Prentice-Hall; 1961.

Blau, P. *Exchange and Power in Social Life.* New York: Wiley, 1964.

Blumer, H. *Symbolic Interactionism: Perspective and Method.* Englewood Cliffs, N.J.: Prentice-Hall, 1969.

Bruyn, S. T. *The Human Perspective in Sociology: The Methodology of Participant Observation.* Englewood Cliffs, N.J.: Prentice-Hall, 1966.

Bugental, J. F. T. *Challenges of Humanistic Psychology.* New York: McGraw-Hill, 1967.

Cicourel, A. V. *Method and Measurement in Sociology.* New York: Free Press, 1964.

Deutsch, S. E. "The Radical Perspective in Sociology," *Sociological Inquiry*, 40 (1970), 85–93.

Deutsch, S. E., and J. Howard. *Where It's At: Radical Perspectives in Sociology.* New York: Harper & Row, 1970.

Filstead, W., ed. *Qualitative Methodology.* Chicago: Markham, 1970.

Friedrichs, R. W. *A Sociology of Sociology.* New York: Free Press, 1970.

Garfinkel, H. *Studies in Ethnomethodology.* Englewood Cliffs, N.J.: Prentice-Hall, 1967.

Glass, J. "Toward a Humanistic Sociology," *Association for Humanistic Psychology Newsletter,* 6 (April 1970), 1–2.

———. "The Presentation of Self and the Encounter Culture: Notes on the Sociology of T-Groups," *Comparative Group Studies,* 3 (November 1972).

Glass, J., and H. Frankiel. "The Influence of Subjects on the Researcher: A Problem in Observing Social Interaction," *Pacific Sociological Review,* 11 (1968), 75–80.

Goffman, E. *Presentation of Self in Everyday Life.* Garden City, N.Y.: Doubleday Anchor, 1959.

———. *Interaction Ritual.* Garden City, N.Y.: Doubleday Anchor, 1967.

Gouldner, A. W. *The Coming Crisis of Western Sociology.* New York: Basic Books, 1970.

Hampden-Turner, C. *Radical Man: The Process of Psycho-social Development.* Garden City, N.Y.: Doubleday Anchor, 1971.

Homans, G. *Social Behavior: Its Elementary Forms.* New York: Harcourt Brace Jovanovich, 1961.

Horowitz, I. L., ed. *The New Sociology.* New York: Oxford University Press, 1964.

Lee, D., "Are Basic Needs Ultimate?" *Journal of Abnormal and Social Psychology,* 43 (1948), 391–395.

Lynd, H. M. *On Shame and the Search for Identity,* New York: Science Edition, 1958.

Lynd, R. S. *Knowledge for What?* Princeton, N.J.: Princeton University Press, 1939.

Maslow, A. H. *Eupsychian Management.* Homewood, Ill.: Richard D. Irwin, 1965.

———. *Toward a Psychology of Being.* 2d ed. New York: Van Nostrand, 1968.

———. *Motivation and Personality.* 2d ed. New York: Harper & Row, 1970.

Means, R. L. *The Ethical Imperative: The Crisis in American Values.* Garden City, N.Y.: Doubleday, 1969.

Mills, C. W. *The Sociological Imagination.* New York: Oxford University Press, 1959.

Nettl, J. P. "Are Intellectuals Obsolete?" *Nation,* 4 (March 1968), 300–305.

Reynolds, L. T., and J. M. Reynolds, eds. *The Sociology of Sociology.* New York: McKay, 1970.

Rogers, C. R. *On Becoming a Person.* Boston: Houghton Mifflin, 1961.

Roszak, T. *The Making of a Counter Culture.* Garden City, N.Y.: Doubleday Anchor, 1969.

Sanford, N. "Whatever Happened to Action Research?" *Journal of Social Issues,* 26 (1970), 3–23.

Schmidt, W. H. *Organizational Frontiers and Human Values.* Belmont, Calif.: Wadsworth, 1970.

Slater, P. E. *The Pursuit of Loneliness: American Culture at the Breaking Point.* Boston: Beacon Press, 1970.

Sorokin, P. *Fads and Foibles in Modern Sociology.* Chicago: Regnery, 1956.

Staude, J. R. "Theoretical Foundations for a Humanistic Sociology." Paper presented at the American Sociological Association Annual Meetings, September 1971 at Denver, Colorado.

Stein, M., and A. Vidich, *Sociology on Trial.* Englewood Cliffs, N.J.: Prentice-Hall, 1963.

Strauss, A. L., and B. G. Glaser. *The Discovery of Grounded Theory: Strategies for Qualitative Research.* Chicago: Aldine, 1967.

Tannenbaum, R., I. Weschler, and F. Massarik. *Leadership and Organization.* New York: McGraw-Hill, 1961.

Winter, G. *Elements for a Social Ethic: Scientific and Ethical Perspectives on Social Process.* New York: Macmillan, 1966.

A STRUCTURAL ANALYSIS OF SOCIOLOGY

ARTHUR L. STINCHCOMBE

Reprinted from *The American Sociologist*, 10 (May 1975), 57–64. Used by permission of the author and the American Sociological Association.

Arthur Stinchcombe teaches at the University of California, Berkeley.

The fundamental observation of structural analysis in Levi-Strauss[1] is that institutionalized systems of exchange (of women, material goods, symbols) rest on a double system of distinctions. On the one hand, those who can or must exchange according to the norms of the system must be distinguished from those who cannot—for instance, a kinship system must define the boundaries of endogamy within which the system is institutionalized (e.g., the tribe). On the other hand, the units which can or must exchange must be distinguished from each other, at least so that one can be defined as lacking something that the other can furnish—for example, in kinship systems the exogamous unit that needs a wife must be distinguished from the unit eligible to supply a wife. It is this peculiar irony of the central forms of solidarity being defined by a system of differentiation that has captured Levi-Strauss' imagination.

The second part of Levi-Strauss' argument is that in order to talk about society and solidarity, the mythical system must have symbolic distinctions in it corresponding to the distinctions between subgroups that need each other in the system of exchange. Moieties or sections or lineages that are exogamous need to be contrasted symbolically with the moieties or sections or lineages with which they exchange. But these contrasts must be "mediated" by other contrasts that distinguish the exchanging partners from the rest of the world.

In particular, Levi-Strauss is interested in the system of mythical distinctions that contrasts objects in the natural world from those that can enter into a specific exchange system as cultural objects with an agreed cultural definition. Material goods in the form of food, for example, occur in the form "raw" in nature. By being cooked *by a social unit of the exchange system*, they become food that can be used in ritual exchanges in the system. Thus the mythical symbols having to do with the raw/cooked distinction can be used to discuss the transformation of socially insignificant objects into socially significant objects in an exchange system.

Likewise, women when they come into the world are merely children born to a certain mother. By a mythological as well as a social process, they become women descended from a certain social group, such that they can be exchanged in marriage, and that marriage can be distinguished from incest, rape, or seduction. The social meaning of exchanges of women between kin groups is discussed mythologically in terms of myths of descent, of "blood," and the like.

Finally a symbolic object is created by rituals, by social work performed to lend meaning to the symbol, a meaning in terms of the exchanges to take place.

The bread and wine become symbols of the body and blood, to be exchanged by the Church for symbols of subjection (e.g., kneeling) by the rituals of the communion service.

THE STRUCTURE OF SCIENTIFIC EXCHANGE SYSTEMS

Clearly the discipline of sociology (especially within a country) is a system of exchange, in which students correspond to women as being people of low status and power who must be "placed" in other departments, job offers correspond to material goods which are exchanged partly to show mutual respect, partly to improve each other's material positions, and scientific papers are symbols exchanged. The units corresponding to exogamous groups in kinship systems are departments, which therefore must be normatively defined as being incompetent in some respect or other, and consequently in need of exchange.

A student must be socially defined as a student of a certain descent, or as we say "specialization," by an apprenticeship and sponsorship system involving dissertation committees and the like. Raw creativity in a wide variety of fields does not produce a social object which can "fill a slot" in the normatively defined needs of other departments. The discomfort of students who find they have to be *either* a theorist *or* a sociologist of education *or* a social psychologist *or* a methodologist is a reflection of this need for them to be related to the normative definition of the needs of other exogamous groups.

The ritual method of producing a student is called "training" or "education," and its purpose in the exchange system is to establish lines of descent, "lineages," which can then have something to offer other lineages that is distinct from what they already have. The mythology of "specialization" and "training" then is the fundamental form in which a raw brain becomes an exchangeable student. The personnel committee is the core of the departmental ritual system which defines needs of the exogamous group, by declaring the department to be incompetent in the following x fields (by ideologies of "balance" or "coverage"), and consequently in need of students from other descent lines.

The exchange of job offers is closely related to the exchange of students, except that people are hardly ever in fact exchanged. At least the ratio of offers to acceptances is very high as compared to the situation in student exchange. Instead the production of a job offer is like cooking a ritual meal, in which reciprocation is expected to be in the long run rather than immediately, especially by a reciprocal job offer when the time comes. The core of the meaning of the system is that it represents a way for a department to reaffirm the value of other departments, to recognize what kind of lineage they are, and to express a normatively valid need for the lineage to which the offer is made. The required immediate ritual exchange is that the person to whom the offer is made must show "seriousness," i.e., that he would find it worthwhile also to be in the other lineage.

The ritual process by which a scientific paper is produced is, of course, the refereeing process. This is a certification that an intellectual product may be put on a vita as a serious symbol of the worth of the person and of his lineage. It can then be exchanged as scientific knowledge, and its previous exchange as a mimeographed paper is ritually validated. This ritual system is discussed in terms of distinctions of "competence" or "talent" and is especially crucial for defining the boundaries around the discipline, in contrast to anthropologists or political scientists or statisticians, from whom we learn but with whom we do not exchange.

Thus the crucial managers of the exchange system are: dissertation committees, which produce students of a certain lineage, and personnel committees which produce needs for them; senior faculties, which produce job offers to members of other senior faculties and the people who show seriousness in response to such a show of respect; and referees of scientific journals or of book publishers, who produce certified symbols of science for the vita.

The central structural fact about the system of exchange overall is that it is rather strongly bounded, in all three exchanges, by disciplinary boundaries, and moderately strongly bounded by national labor markets. If I were to name the ten most interesting students of social structure in the world, maybe two or three would be officially sociologists, and maybe four or five North Americans. The list is of course personal to me, and I would not be so ritually gauche as to provide the list, but the experience is probably common. But the historians, economists, psychologists, anthropologists, and political scientists are not in the same exchange system, nor are most of the non-North-Americans. That is, we do not exchange students, do not exchange job offers (when I was young and naive, I used to propose to hire whomever I thought was the best person for a given set of intellectual tasks, regardless of discipline or nationality; I learned better), and do not referee each others' papers.

THE STRUCTURE OF THE SOCIOLOGICAL MYTH

The core ritual for asserting the boundaries around the discipline as a whole is the annual convention. It is based on two basic mythical postulates: that we are interested in what each other has to say, and that we are competent judges of each other's work. There is attached to this ritual a formal representation of both the system for exchange of students (a placement service) and of exchanging certification of scientific papers (the sessions). There is also formal representation of the two sorts of lineages, namely specialties and departments. The governing bodies of the exchange ritual are carefully balanced by specialty and by what is euphemistically called regional representation, but is actually departmental. Subsystems of exchange of scientific papers ("sessions") are set up along the lines of specialties, and the lineages have "Chicago breakfasts," "Hopkins parties," "Berkeley dinners" and so on. The exchange of job offers is partly set up at the convention as well, as people who meet in the powerful committees politely inquire of each other whether they might be willing to move.

But overlaid on this are some master rituals of disciplinary solidarity, the Presidential address (which is ritually non-specialized), the open cocktail party, the "business" meeting at which there is no business, and so on. Further we notice various informal rituals of lineage heads (who structurally conflict for the allocation of positions for students, job offers, and space in the journals) meeting for drinks and carrying out rituals of mutual respect. Further there will be participation of the integrating figures of the discipline—almost always former chairmen of leading departments and experienced in "balance"—visiting to participate in specialty meetings and showing up to grace lineage parties of other departments.

The central myth then is that for all the internal distinctions, we are engaged in a common intellectual enterprise whose collective purpose is different from that of anthropology, political science, economics, or history. There is therefore an attempt to create the sense of a distinctive competence, a "sociological theory," as the common (and foolish) criticism of theoretical papers as being "too psychological" or "just economics" shows. This is backed by a set of myths about having acted in common—through some famous fathers of the discipline—to do a set of things no one else can do.

The converse of this process takes place in university bargaining over faculty posts. That is, it might offhand seem more rational to hire a distinguished social historian like E. J. Hobsbawm or Alfred Chandler, who are better sociologists than most of us, to fill sociological needs by a person in the history department. But the history department has to agree to be incompetent in sociology—whatever the facts, and so avoid wasting their posts to further the sociological enterprise—in order to claim that sociology is incompetent in history—whatever the facts. Thus the definition of the boundaries is an agreement to exchange students, job offers, and papers within the boundaries, and to agree to be incompetent across the boundaries to preserve the integrity of disciplinary exchange systems.

The central role of figures of historical origin of disciplines in this mythical system is illustrated by the comment of a history professor at Johns Hopkins shortly after a sociology department was established there. "We have been reading Weber in the History Department since the 1920's. I don't see why now we need a whole department to read Weber." The first barb in this is the use of the verb "to read" in place of "to do research like." The implicit argument is that sociology's relation to Weber is mythical, that one is more likely to learn to do comparative history in a history department. (The correctness of this attribution of the mythical character of our commitment to comparative history may be shown by the fact that, of the three sociologists I can think of who do Weber's kind of research, Reinhard Bendix, Barrington Moore, and S. N. Eisenstadt, one has divorced the discipline, one has been divorced by the discipline, and the third has his satrapy on the periphery.) The second barb is the denial of monopoly over the mythical figure, and hence implicitly over the competences supposedly distinguishing the discipline.

But once the distinction between sociology and the scholarly world at large is established mythically by discussions of the "sociological approach," and consequently the distinction of sociological student exchange, job-offer exchange, and refereeing processes is justified, then the exogamous subunits must be mythically defined. As in kinship systems, this has two aspects: locality and descent. Each exogamous unit at a certain locality is supposed to have ties and alliances with others in the system ("affinal relations"), by representing the other lineages in the locality group. The central device by which this is supposed to be achieved is the exchange of students. In order for the system to work, each department must be willing to define itself as in need of students from another lineage.

There are two overlapping systems for doing this, a primitive one of "specialties" and a sophisticated one of "approaches." When one is explaining "needs" to an administration, one uses the language of specialties. We need someone in African studies, or juvenile delinquency, or organizational sociology. Some people inside departments actually take that rhetoric seriously, I suppose on the Lewis Carroll principle that what I say three times is true, and I am forced to say it to the administration. But the sophisticated version is that one will look for someone in an approach or academic tradition that is making another department famous. One wants the best student of Robert K. Merton or Otis Dudley Duncan or Talcott Parsons, rather than a sociology of science student or a quantitative stratification student or a theorist at the *most* general level. Or one wants to represent the ethnomethodological approach or the structural approach or the mathematical models approach. (The verb "represent" is actually often used.)

This tension has to do with the different character of the exchange system of the university (which I am mainly ignoring here) and that of the discipline. The university exchanges control over recruitment (making disciplines possible) for the predictable performance of some set of teaching tasks in courses that have names and, more important, numbers. The Registrar depends on Sociology 107 always being the sociology of deviance, substitutable from year to year and never something a person might take six times. Of course, a university knows substantively that it's a pretty poor department in which that is literally true, and that particularly, over the course of 20 years, it is a failure if it is the same course at all. Further they do not really care whether the person who teaches it is primarily famous for contributions to the symbolic interactional sublineage, or to the quantitative sociology sublineage, or to the Marxist sublineage in which the criminals are the oppressed. Thus every appointment has to be clothed in two rhetorics, one about "needs" for "specialties" for the university and one about "representation" of "approaches" for "diversity" in the departmental faculty.

Both of these distinctions are largely mythical. For instance, one of the more interesting papers in the symbolic interactionist tradition is James S. Coleman's (1957) much ignored paper on multidimensional scaling about 20 years ago. By formalizing mathematically the symbolic interactionist postulate that an attitude was an action tendency toward a socially defined object, he derived an interesting series of consequences about how attitude items might be related statistically. Now such an achievement ought to make him a candidate for a job where a department "needs" a symbolic interactionist. Of course it does not, because in the mythical system symbolic interactionism and mathematical sociology (especially scale construction) are different lineages, and a bastard child is not of much use in the exchange system until he or she has been ritually accepted as descended from the lineage. In this case, most of the official mathematical lineage from which Coleman ritually descended did not understand G. H. Mead, and the symbolic interactionist lineage did not understand the statistics, so the paper was aborted (this very often happens to bastards). The point is that the paper was fighting the solidly entrenched mythology that symbolic interactionism and mathematical sociology were different "approaches," and it has the same mythical difficulty as would be shown by having a mythical elephant as clever and deceptive as the mythical deermouse. How would you know whom to hire if symbolic interactionists could be the same thing as mathematical sociologists?

Thus the mythical system has to have cross-cutting distinctions between "specialties" and "approaches" on the one hand, and "departments" on the other. Departments have to be locality groups, and consequently a delicate balanced network representing the system as a whole; they must also be lineages, and consequently dominated by one "approach" rather than another.

From the point of view of the individual, one is confronted with having to agree with one's department that one is incompetent in enough fields and approaches so that the department as a collectivity has "needs." Considering yourself (and your students, by a kind of feudal generosity) to be competent at everything in the discipline is the same sort of crime as incest, for it is a normative betrayal of the exchange system

Suppose that we tried in fact to hire the smartest people, regardless of "specialty" or "approach." Since there is nothing very difficult about sociology, such a group of people could satisfy the university by teaching everything. They could presumably replace themselves, by "training" people to be flexible about "approaches" and "specialties." But then like a kinship group with no incest taboo and no exogamy, they would have no ground for exchange, no necessity to be members of a "discipline." And that means they would have few grounds to urge *their* students on other departments. There would be a unidimensional prestige ranking instead of a partial ordering by "specialties" and "approaches," more like the Oxford-Cambridge axis in England than like the system in the U.S., with the consequent relative weakening of "disciplines" as opposed to "colleges" as the guiding integrative institutions. That is, the master rituals would be elite rituals rather than specialty rituals, and the central mythical distinctions would be to distinguish the elite from the mass, rather than lineages from each other. But you can only get away with such a claim if you are actually as good as Oxford and Cambridge, far better than the rest of the universities. No university in the U.S. is that much better than another five or six, so unilateral exchange with the elite giving their students to the mass is not a structural possibility.[2]

Thus we get the multiplication of fake controversies over "approaches," usually formulated in lineage terms, organized around the founder of the lineage.

The question is whether one is in the true descent of G. H. Mead or Karl Marx or Paul Lazarsfeld or Max Weber, not whether what one has to say makes sense. The tiny philosophical differences between Mead and Parsons have to be blown up into contrasting approaches; when you add a simple notion like unconscious norms, similar to grammatical norms, to the symbolic interactionist tradition, you get a full blown sect of ethnomethodology. A convenience in presenting quantitative results has to be blown up into a full blown revolution, in path analysis and dependence coefficients, so as to create a Duncan and Boudon lineage.

I am not arguing of course that path analysis is not a substantial convenience, nor that the place of unconscious norms in social interaction was not greatly underplayed before Garfinkel. These are both real advances. What I am arguing instead is that there is a tremendous rush to create new "approaches" which can only be explained by the necessity to create new needs. Otherwise we would just learn path analysis and about unconscious norms and go on about our business. A person who likes Karl Marx would not be expected to agree to be incompetent in the work of Howard Becker or James S. Coleman.

Besides these distinctions based on needs, we must have a mythical set of devices for justifying the national closure of labor markets. The most amusing difficulty with this is the Canadian system, which is required to try to hire Canadians from United States graduate departments. Their recruitment letters are models of the universalisms particularism dilemma. But we all want to go abroad, and to have somebody else pay for it because it is a public service. There are only two ways for it to be a public service—either we are incompetent and have to learn, or they are incompetent and we have to teach. Now obviously the decent thing to do from the point of view of international scientific solidarity is to assert both at once, i.e. to treat national scholarly traditions as lineages.

But if one asserts international differences in competences, why are we not exchanging students and job offers and refereeing articles across the boundaries? I would argue that most of the international differences are about as mythical as most of the differences between departments and approaches within a given nation. That is, there are some minor intellectual differences. I would judge that on the average it would take a competent English sociologist about six months to become a competent North American sociologist; a little less for Israel, Scandinavia, and Japan; more for West Germany and the communist countries. The reverse process is about the same order of magnitude. That is, it would take about six months for a competent North American sociologist to become a competent English sociologist, a little less for Israel, Scandinavia, and Japan, a little more for West Germany and the communist countries. I would say this is about the distance between specialties and approaches in the United States. It takes about six months to become an ethnomethodologist or a path analysis expert or a specialist in race relations or deviant behavior.

But that is like saying it would only take six months to learn the norms and rituals of the Clan of the Elk. It is true enough, and if all we were really up to were honoring the Elk and advancing the science respectively, that would be enough. But as Levi-Strauss has pointed out, the purpose of having totems is to make people who are all basically the same into fundamentally different *kinds* of people, so there is some excuse for passing women, gifts, and ritual performances among them. The triviality of learning to be of the Clan of the Elk has nothing to do with the matter. The point is that an Elk is a different beast than a Cougar, and is competent to produce women that a Cougar can marry, feasts to which a Cougar can be invited, and ritual symbols that a Cougar is not in a sufficiently sacred position to produce.

In particular what we have to establish internationally is that these are a different breed of people with whom it is useful to exchange visits, but not students, job offers, and scientific papers. This is a very uncomfortable business in academic life, and goes far to explain why visiting fellows from abroad are so systematically, if selectively, ignored. Having been on both sides of this process, in Chile, England, and the Netherlands as a visitor and here as a host, I have some experience of the dilemma. A foreigner may possibly get taken seriously *until* some serious decision has to be made. But a foreigner does not normatively prevent my student from being hired, my United States peers from getting job offers, and my papers from being published. Fellows from abroad are interesting enough men and women, but after all these are serious matters. This non-seriousness of the way foreigners are treated is of course difficult to justify on universalistic grounds.

THE MYTHOLOGY OF BECOMING IN SOCIOLOGY

On the basis of the structural requirements of the system of exchange, Levi-Strauss argues that there must be a mythology about the transformation of the world of nature into the world of culture, which turns innocent people, food, and natural objects into clan members, ritual feasts, and sacred symbols. Thus every mythological system must have a system of distinctions which distinguishes the natural world according to its potentiality in terms of the social world. A child as a natural object has to be distinguished according to his or her potentiality to become a member of a certain lineage; a raw piece of meat has to be distinguished as appropriate for Thanksgiving or Easter, or for a feast of the Clan of the Elk; places (or a wafer and wine) have to be distinguished as potential churches (or potential body and blood of Christ).

Furthermore on top of this detailed definition of nature in terms of its cultural potentialities, there must be a mythology of becoming, in terms of which children become wives, the raw becomes cooked, the bread and wine become a sacrament.

Thus there is a double mapping mythologically of the natural world on the social world. In the first place, distinctions in the natural world have to correspond in a rough way with the distinctions needed for the society, though they are arbitrary from the point of view of a scientific description of nature (Levi-Strauss goes to great length to show that the "unscientific" descriptions of nature by primitive people do not indicate lack of powers of observation, but rather the uses to which the description is to be put culturally). In the second place, there has to be a system of mapping of distinctions of the transformative processes, so that one knows when a natural child becomes a marriageable woman, a piece of meat becomes a feast, a piece of bread becomes the body of Christ. That is, there is a mythical representation of the productive process by which natural objects become social objects. This interest in production and its ideological representation is what allows Levi-Strauss to talk in pseudo-Marxist terms about what he is doing, for the central symbol that represents French national intellectual solidarity is that the most diverse sorts of people should claim to be Marxists.

The associated mythology in sociology is that which describes what turns a bright person into a competent person, a young person of promise into a senior faculty member and lineage head, and a research result into a scientific paper. These involve on the one hand distinctions among events in nature. Some undergraduates are bright and some are not. Some young scholars have promise and some do not. Some research results are original and solid and some are not. But in each case there is also an overlaid distinction about the cultural process. Some bright people are educated or trained to be sociologists and some are not. Some young people of promise have not "done anything since" and some have. Some research results have been responsibly interpreted for the discipline and some have not. In short, some of nature is edible and some is not, but overlaid on that, some is cooked and some is not. (And even when natural foods are not cooked, when we eat raw ground beef or crisp fruits and vegetables, they have to be seasoned and served in special dishes or cut into elegant strips or taken together with very highly cultured cheese; eating apples picked in an orchard is not "having a meal." Raw creativity likewise has to be cultured, or at least taken along with a good dose of cultured learning.)

The mythology of turning a bright person into a competent person is a combined one of testing the distinction in nature—was he really bright—and transforming the nature into a cultured product. The transformation process is "training," and involves demanding that the person be ready to participate in the exchange system of his "specialties." This involves especially being ready to reproduce, for the locality group, the network of lineages of ideas that constitutes the exchange system as a whole. You cannot be a certified competent stratification person unless you can acknowledge (knowledgeably) the contributions of the lineage of Marx and that of O. D. Duncan. That is, you must be cultured so that the mythology that we are all interested in each other's work is a viable myth. You need not be required to reproduce the lineage of thought on stratification of, say, Clifford Gertz, because that is protected behind the two barriers of his being an anthropologist and his being a specialist in religion. The crucial part of Ph.D. specialty examinations is that they certify that you are allowed to be incompetent for the rest of your life in areas not covered on the examination, because they are not in your specialty.

The "training" part of the mythology, which involves establishing that somebody needs you, is organized around research apprenticeship and the dissertation. This is the process by which, although solidly standardized as a specialist, a competent person is established as distinctive, as a woman some particular other exogamous unit ought to want to have in marriage. The neuroses of the disssertation are essentially similar to the neuroses of coquetry, in which the person needs to establish that he or she is uniquely desirable, though also a good solid person by the standards of general eligibility.

The process by which a young person of promise is turned into a lineage head (a "senior professor") has the same mixture of components of testing nature and "maturation." But there is the additional problem that appointing a new lineage head changes the character of the locality group. There are some strong patrilocal patrilineal systems in academia in which the exchange of young people of promise is the only respect that is paid to other lineages, and those few young people of promise actually promoted are those that reinforce the distinctiveness of the lineage. Such irresponsibility to the exchange system is called "inbreeding" in polite conversation, "incestuous" policy in private. But usually there is a compromise between local rule and respect for the exchange system, and distinguished outside members of the profession are consulted about the promotion to prevent "inbreeding." And in fact it is a pretty doubtful transformation process if it is not validated by a job offer from the outside. The transformation of the Clan of the Elk into the Clan of the Cougar by transforming foreign elements into lineage heads is what makes gossip about departments one of the core elements of the mythical system of sociology.

That is, part of the myth has to do with the production of a senior professor from a young person of promise, with tenure corresponding to initiation into a lineage. But the second part of the mythology has no exact counterpart in lineage systems, for the new professor transforms the character of the lineage. Rather than generational succession of essentially the same kind of men, the women (students exchanged) become men (professors), making the lineage itself a product of the exchange system, just as the true genetic, as opposed to social, lineage system is in marriage systems. This makes the question of what is happening to a particular department an interesting subject of gossip.

MYTH AND REALITY

Levi-Strauss does not, of course, maintain that there is no substantive distinction between raw and cooked food. Likewise it would be foolish to equate a competent sociological paper to the raw creativity of a sophomore bull session. The sociological competence of historians, anthropologists, or political scientists is indistinguishable in general from that of sociologists, but like the cooking of women of the wrong lineage, it can be hard work, and can be well or badly done.

Whatever its other social functions, a myth gets some of its vigor from its relation to reality. As the practical household units of a primitive tribe change, by ecological changes or by warfare or by the failure of descent lines to reproduce, the mythical system of kinship either loses its vigor or changes to correspond to the new reality.

The sect-forming tendency in sociology is likewise grounded in the reality that no one can do everything (though perhaps some can do anything), just as exogamous clans linked in exchange rings are grounded in the reality that it would be exhausting, if perhaps fun, to marry everybody. The petty chauvinism of sociological sects results in destructive feuding just as overweening clan loyalty does; it is not only a betrayal of the exchange system but also a Bad Thing. The social supports of the universalism of scientific standards, the dominance of competence over sect loyalty in the scientific status system, are derived from the exchange system.

The tendency for the Oxford-Cambridge axis to award status for Common Room wit and for the entertainment value of scholarly findings may seem a pleasant contrast to the deadly dullness of the average refereed paper, but jokes are, after all, often mistaken observations about the world. In particular the jokes of an incestuous elite ingroup also form a mythical system, shaped by the social requirement *not* to exchange on the basis of equality. Mythical inequality is as likely to produce distortions of reality as the mythical substitutability of Sociology 107 from year to year. The incest of the Pharoahs was grounded in a distinction among superior and inferior lineages every bit as mythical as that between Cougars and Elk, and considerably less amusing in its consequences. But the mythology of inequality is a topic not relevant to many of Levi-Strauss' societies, and not well developed by him.

If sociology's relation to Weber is as mythical as the relation of the Church to Christ, we must take what comfort we can from the fact that at least both chose first class myths.

NOTES

1. The following account of what Levi-Strauss was up to is mainly based on his early work on kinship (Levi-Strauss, 1963, 1969a), modified in the light of the argument about symbols in his discussion of primitive cognitive psychology (Levi-Strauss, 1966). I have borrowed a few things from his analysis of mythology (Levi-Strauss, 1969b), but have been able to use very little of it because I do not understand it.

2. In England it is very precarious in sociology; at least three universities compete seriously with the big two (the big two are not very good in sociology) and a system much more like the American disciplinary one is developing, a system unlike the unilateral system in the humanities and some of the sciences.

REFERENCES

Coleman, J. S. "Multidimensional Scale Analysis," *American Journal of Sociology*, 63 (November 1957), 253–63.

Levi-Strauss, Claude. *Totemism.* Translated by R. Needham. Boston: Beacon Press, 1963.

———. *The Savage Mind.* Chicago: University of Chicago Press, 1966.

———. *Elementary Structures of Kinship.* Translated and edited by J. H. Bell, J. R. Sturmer, and R. Needham. Boston: Beacon Press, 1969. (a)

———. *The Raw and the Cooked.* Translated by J. Weightman and D. Weightman. New York: Harper & Row, 1969. (b)